GÖTTINGER ORIENTFORSCHUNGEN

IV. REIHE ÄGYPTEN 38

Herausgegeben von Friedrich Junge

Classification and Categorization in Ancient Egypt
Vol. 7

2010

Harrassowitz Verlag · Wiesbaden

Arlette David

The Legal Register of Ramesside Private Law Instruments

2010

Harrassowitz Verlag · Wiesbaden

Recherche effectuée dans le cadre du projet „Classifiers and Categorisation in Ancient Egypt“, dirigé par O. Goldwasser, Université Hébraïque de Jérusalem, F. Junge et F. Kammerzell, Université de Göttingen, sous les auspices du Niedersächsisches Ministerium für Wissenschaft und Kunst, Hannover et de la fondation „Niedersächsisches Vorab der Volkswagenstiftung“

Bibliografische Information Der Deutschen Bibliothek:
Die Deutsche Bibliothek verzeichnet diese Publikation in der Deutschen Nationalbibliografie; detaillierte bibliografische Daten sind im Internet über http://dnb.ddb.de abrufbar.

Bibliographic information published by Die Deutsche Bibliothek:
Die Deutsche Bibliothek lists this publication in the Deutsche Nationalbibliografie; detailed bibliographic data is available in the internet at http://dnb.ddb.de.e-mail: cip@dbf.ddb.de

For further information about our publishing program have a look at our website http://www.harrassowitz.de/verlag

Printed on permanent/durable paper.
Printing and binding: Hubert & Co., Göttingen
Printed in Germany

ISSN 0340-6342
ISBN 3-447-06143-8

A mon père,
Juste parmi les Justes,
Michel David ז״ל

Contents

Foreword

The present research was made possible by an Intramural Research Fund Career Development Award of the Hebrew University (2004-2006).

I am deeply grateful to Dr. Ben Haring who did not baulk at the arduous task of reading this manuscript, making apposite suggestions, and for sharing his insights and vast knowledge of Deir el-Medina, its inhabitants, and their textual productions; to Dr. Deborah Sweeney and Dr. Raphael Ventura, who are not only eminent specialists in Deir el-Medina, devoted teachers at Tel-Aviv University, but also true friends, never forgetting the warm word that makes all the difference; to Prof. Orly Goldwasser for being my teacher and the one who saw the potential of my legal formation. I especially thank David Warburton who went to the immense trouble of correcting the entire manuscript; I owe much to his expertise and criticism, provided with humor and generosity.

My warmest thanks to Prof. Ogden Goelet, Prof. Christopher J. Eyre, Prof. Brenda Danet, Dr. Sebastian T. Richter, Dr. Edward Bleiberg, curator of Egyptian, Classical, Ancient Middle Eastern Art at the Brooklyn Museum and his assistant Ms. Kathy Zurek-Doule, and Dr. Helen Whitehouse at the Ashmolean Museum (Oxford), for answering my questions and/or providing useful material; to the Griffith Institute and Prof. Jaromir Malek for authorizing the use of numerous pages of Černý's Notebooks to complete the corpus of ostraca presented in this study, as well as to Mr. Nicola Harrington for providing excellent scans of the material.

Once more, I am deeply grateful to Prof. Friedrich Junge for his renewed confidence, and to Dr. Barbara Krauss and Harrassowitz for graciously accepting for the third time a manuscript in the GOF collection.

Love, support, and patience were amply supplied along the way by my mother Rosa, David, Lou, and Julian; when I count my blessings, I always count you all twice.

« C'est un bon testament, un testament, morbleu,
Bien fait, bien cimenté, qui doit vous tenir lieu
De tendresse, d'amour, de désir, de ménage,
De femme, de contrats, d'enfants, de mariage. »

Jean-François Regnard, Le légataire universel, acte I, scène 7.

Introduction

This work is the logical sequel to my earlier *Syntactic and Lexico-Semantic Aspects of the Legal Register in Ramesside Royal Decrees* (David 2006) that dealt with the language of the normative genre of public law in the Ramesside Period. Pursuing the analysis of the legal registers of the Ramesside Period, the obvious next step was to investigate the language of documents pertaining to the private sphere, in order to establish the linguistic features of that specific genre, and to compare them with the dialect used in public sphere normative instruments. The corpus of the Ramesside private law instruments was the basis of a *genre-oriented* grammar of a definite period in the context of a specific *état de langue*. The purpose of this series (which should be completed by a further volume devoted to the *contentious* genre) is to survey the various written legal registers of an epoch (synchronous approach) and compare them with parallel registers during previous and sometimes later periods (diachronic approach) in order to assess patterns and changes.

The typological qualification of the genre under examination may be approached in several ways[1]. Danet (1980: 459) used Searle's taxonomy of speech acts where the philosopher of language[2] qualified the utterances involved in contracts and wills as *commissive speech acts* that 'commit the speaker to do something in the future.' As a basis for the qualification of the genre of private law instruments, the *commissive legal genre*, this definition poses some problems. First of all, wills, gifts and contracts are complex documents involving many kinds of provisions, and thus many other categories of speech acts; some of their provisions display for instance, assertive (e.g. general statement), directive (e.g. imposition of specific conditions to the other party)[3], even expressive aspects (e.g. praise of the legatee's positive behavior). Furthermore, a typical public law genre, the statute may also involve commissive speech acts (for instance when a state such as Belgium commits itself in a law to remedy an environmental issue in the context of international cooperation).

My typological approach is based on the general legal concept of the freedom of private individuals to take decisions concerning their property[4], as expressed in private law instruments covering bilateral acts (involving the consenting wills of two parties at least, e.g. contracts[5]) as well as unilateral expressions of *will* such as wills and gifts[6]. Of course this

1 Of course, the qualification of the legal genre under discussion was neither conceived of, nor expressed by the ancient Egyptians in this fashion.
2 Searle (1976); Searle & Vanderveken (1985).
3 Concerning directive and commissive acts in contracts, see Trosborg (1997: 59-62).
4 French: *autonomie de la volonté des particuliers, libre disposition des biens.*
5 In the broad sense of agreements between parties having legal consequences; we do not take into consideration here the notion of unilateral contracts and will not broach the issue of agreement versus promise(s).

involves the notion of commitment (commissive acts), but does not exclude other types of speech acts. As in modern legal systems, the principle of individual freedom in the domains of contracts or gratuities does not mean that all matters are left to the discretion of the disposing party (or parties), but that the willingness to contract or to make a will/gift, the determination of the content of the deed within the limits imposed by the legal system, and the source of undertakings are decisions of the disposing party or parties only. As a matter of fact, this autonomy concept was formulated in a Ramesside document as a principle enunciated by the king: *ḫr ḏd [Pr]-ꜥꜣ ꜥ.w.s. imi iry s nb ꜣbwtw.f m ꜣḫttw.f* 'And Pharaoh L.P.H. said: "Let every man do what he wants with his assets."' (*pTurin* 2021, line II.11).

Private law deeds therefore belong to a specific *consentient legal genre* associated with a specific language, subject, style and communicative purpose, and determined by the private interests of individuals. As for the purpose of the genre, it may be *archival*, as described by Jackson (1995: 112): 'to put certain information (…) "on the record" as having been agreed, in case it should ever need to be retrieved and used in the future.' The communicative purpose of the Ramesside written law deed is to record an expression of will having legal consequences, related to an immediate or postponed transfer of assets or to the rendering of services. And as we shall see, one of the major issues of our Egyptian material concerns the legal force attached to the record as opposed to the verbal commitment.

Evidently, only the written legal register has been analyzed, the *legalese* associated with provisions concerning the regulation of relationships between people and the fate of goods and property. Characteristic situational parameters of this Ramesside register are the following[7]:

- participants: mainly single private addressor (testator, donor, contracting party), one or more private addressees (legatees, donees, cocontracting party[8]), with or without audience (witnesses, court);
- relations addressor/addressee(s): addressor of same or higher status (owner of assets, elder, sometimes office holder), shared personal knowledge (of persons, assets, general context); extensive interactiveness (contracts), slight interactiveness (e.g., a will recorded in court with a cross-examination procedure), or none (unilateral deeds); usually personal relationship of kin or contractual type;
- setting: private (domestic place) or public (court, workplace), generally familiar to participants, usually in immediate time-space (at least for the verbal transmission of the contents, although epistolary transactions do exist and the instrument may constitute an after-the-fact record), the specific place and time of communication either known (dated record) or unknown;

---

6 Although consensus is obviously a matter of multiple parties, consent may be used 'Par ext[ension], [concernant] la volonté de l'auteur d'un acte unilatéral (consentement de la partie qui s'oblige)' (Cornu 2003: 210).
Both Common Law and Roman Law (Civil Law or Continental) systems have been taken in consideration in an attempt to throw light on the legal mechanisms in the corpus; sometimes one of these systems seemed better suited to highlight the material, sometimes the other. In any case, modern terminology and concepts are inadequate to render the precise meaning of institutions that are still largely an enigma to us, but they represent one of the comparative tools used to explain to ourselves and to communicate to the readers legal mechanisms, since one can only relate to such a material by using a teminology meaningful to both the writer and the reader. Concerning the inadequacy of using 'classical' terminology and institutions when dealing with ancient Egypt material, see Mrsich (1975: 1235-7).

7 Based on Biber's model framework (1994: 40-1).

8 Each party to a bilateral contract should be considered as being both addressor and addressee.

- channel: mixed mode (spoken/written), handwritten medium, usually not embedded in a text associated with a different register (although a letter may include contractual or testamentary provisions);
- relation of participants to the text: usually edited speech of addressor (production), comprehension of the addressee remaining unknown (except in cases of recorded cross-examination procedures), probably perceived as important by addressor/addressee (personal attitude of the addressor perceived in grounding/oath/curse provisions, personal attitude of the addressee perceived in answer during a cross-examination procedure);
- purpose: deeds purported to be based on facts, recording an expression of will related to the transfer of rights/assets and/or the creation of obligations;
- topic: specialized level of discussion, on specific legal subjects (inheritance, gift, partition, contractual relationship).

One of the main challenges encountered during the research was establishing the corpus, as the nature of documents potentially relating to private law is not always clear. The authors of the texts were generally not explicit, many texts are fragmentary, and the specificities of the Egyptian pharaonic legal system and social organization are often quite elusive, making it a laborious task to evaluate whether documents may be qualified as a) wills, gifts or contracts; and b) as an autonomous legally binding act, self-sufficient to produce full legal effects[9].

Concerning the first issue, the existence of wills in ancient Egypt is still denied for instance by Mrsich (2005: 157-8) because he feels that the idea of *Letztwilligkeit* contradicts the Egyptian belief in life after death; but it seems unreasonable to take such a narrow view of Egyptian pragmatism, as the texts collected in our corpus show[10]. Written contracts, on the other hand, as we shall see, are not attested for the Ramesside Period. The qualification of borderline cases as wills, gifts. or contracts is a problem of legal categorization common to all legal systems, be they ancient or modern. I decided to include an analysis of some borderline cases as well as partitions, which are clearly not consentient legal genre documents, as they add important information concerning wills. All dubious cases and texts not belonging to this genre were explicitly signaled as such.

The second issue (autonomy of legally binding acts) relates to the nature of the legal system in ancient Egypt until the end of the Ramesside Period: was it predominantly oral or written? What was the value of the written act in the Ramesside cultural context? Ramesside Egypt's paucity of written *contracts*, *wills*, and even *laws* is not only due to a severe case of archaeological bad luck, but must be explained by the slow maturation of the oral legal practice to a written one and by the perception of the legal act *per se*. The primary vehicle for

9 *Actes fondateurs, source de droit.*

10 Another issue still subject to debate is the existence of private immovable property in ancient Egypt (see e.g. Eyre 1994; Jasnow 2003: 120-1, 2003b: 276-7, 2003c: 328-31, 2003d : 801; Manning 2003 : 838 ; Menu 2004: 195-6, 275 'la propriété privée ne porte que sur de très petits terrains à condition qu'ils servent à la construction (tombeaux, maisons)' and 'le propriétaire d'une maison n'est pas propriétaire du terrain sur lequel la maison est construite'; Mrsich 2005: 165-75). But the conclusion seems inescapable that such ownership did in fact exist in Ramesside society in which there was a transmission of assets, both movable and immovable, not limited in scope by the transmitter (see *infra*). See also McDowell (1992: 197).

expressing one's will remained oral, the *source de droits et d'obligations*[11] being the constitutive or *dispositive*, legally binding verbal act, of which the written document represented an *a posteriori* record, not an authoritative text[12]. In certain cases however, this record of a primary oral expression of will seems to have acquired a legal force demanding attention in our research.

Multiple dilemmas had thus to be faced:

1. *Textual genre*: **consentient legal *vs.* other genre**
   Some fragmentary texts could be part of epistolary or narrative constructions, although they are classified as 'non literary' on the basis of their script and general layout[13]. Other documents may be personal notations and memos, 'book-keeping' records, transaction accounts and quittances, entries in an administrative journal, or even apprenticeship exercises[14]. Litigation or arbitration proceedings, thus belonging to the *contentious* genre, may not always be excluded, even if not expressly referred to. Janssen (1982: 256) contends that the 'majority of the non-literary ostraca do not consist of official documents, but *aide-mémoire*'; nevertheless, there is still room for doubt in assigning communicative purposes to many documents. Moreover, the same document may mix two genres, such as the epistolary and *consentient* legal genres.
   The issue is linked, although not limited, to uncertainty concerning the *origin and use of the instrument*: **private *vs.* public sphere** (administrative, court) **instrument**.
   An administrative brief record of a private deed could occur if the transaction had a bearing on tax imposition for instance, the text belonging to a bureaucratic recording genre. Summaries of private law instruments or excerpts thereof could be embedded in the minutes of a trial, produced as evidence of one party's legal right, thus belonging to the judicial *contentious* genre. Nevertheless, both *authentic* (written by a public official or body acting as a notary) and *olographic* (handwritten by the testator) or *quasi-olographic* (written by a professional scribe for an illiterate testator) wills do belong to the *consentient legal genre*.
2. *Value of the instrument*: **original *vs.* copy, draft, excerpt, summary.**[15]

11 'tout élément générateur de droit subjectif ou d'engagement (...), vertu créatrice propre des actes et des faits juridiques ou de l'autorité seule de la loi' (Cornu 2003 : 846). In modern systems based on Roman Law, the expression of will, source of rights and obligations, may be effected orally, in writing or even tacitly.

12 It is worth recalling Černý's remark concerning the will of *Naunakhte* (1945: 42): '[It] follows the pattern of all Egyptian legal documents; like them it consists of an oral deposition made by the party before the court or witnesses and written down by a professional scribe. Thus it was not the written word alone, but the spoken word subsequently recorded as an actual event on a papyrus or ostracon that conferred upon the document its legal validity.'

13 A problematic issue with epistolary texts, for instance, see Gasse (1992: 52).

14 In spite of the fact that many 'non literary' ostraca are written in a very cursive, rapid and professional script, deprived of usual *class exercises* errors, see Černý (1931: 213). See also McDowell (2000) concerning the features of students' exercises and her remark (p. 223) that they may 'go unrecognized unless they are signed, dated, or furnished with verse points'. The sole recognized exercises concerning bureaucratic language and style are to be found in the Miscellany-type corpus (mostly letters), quite different from the texts forming the present corpus.

15 Concerning draft and duplication issues, see *inter alii* Allam (1968) and Donker van Heel & Haring (2003: 1-38), but also Janssen (1961: 4-5) concerning the relationship between the businesslike hand and the original value of *pLeiden* I 350 v° (ship's log).

Some documents belonging to our corpus are not readily understandable to the contemporary reader, partly because they do not represent original deeds, but are only handy summaries or excerpts of their contents, details obvious to the writer and/or addressees being omitted[16], or because the document was not yet understood as an autonomous legally binding act. In the case of a title deed brought by a party to prove his right, for example, only relevant excerpts and/or a paraphrastic summary are provided and recorded[17]. Modern legal instruments may roughly belong to the following instrumental categories: original deed; duplicate (second original); exact copy; extract; most of which can be official or unofficial products. The issue of the official document's value is quite difficult to assess in our material, and again one may question the relevance of modern qualifications in the ancient Egyptian case (at least for the period from the Old to the New Kingdom). Indeed, the issue of a legal original document as such does not often arise in Ramesside sources[18]; the 'original deed' is in fact a verbal act, whereas the various records ('copies') are official or private renditions of it[19]. Notions such as *original document* serving as the basis for the *best-evidence rule* are utterly foreign to to this legal system; but the falsification of legal records is a well-known means of establishing a legal right (see e.g. *Mes*). Even the notion of a *draft* of a legal document seems to be absent from the Egyptian lexicon, although drafts may exist in practice. The issue of the autonomy of legally binding acts should thus be questioned with these remarks in mind. And even if the document represents only an excerpt or copy of a legal instrument, many features of the complete text must have been preserved (as is obviously the case when the same features appear repeatedly in documents of the same kind), and may be used, albeit with caution, for our linguistic purpose.

As we have already noted, a general **verbal *vs.* written** issue in the legal system must be addressed, as it appears that most expressions of will were still verbal during the New Kingdom[20]. For instance, in *pCairo* JE 65739, the buyer tells the judges about the verbal contract she agreed to: 'he [the seller] said to me: "Buy this girl, and give me a price for her." So he said to me. And I purchased the girl and gave him a [price] for her'[21]. But at the

16 Malinine (1947: 96) for extracts on ostraca; Théodoridès (1965: 107).

17 Concerning reference to important documents during Old Kingdom legal procedures but the necessity of an actual quotation during the Middle Kingdom, see Der Manuelian (1986: 16).

18 One such case is evidently *pTurin* 2021, as lines IV.2-3 record the vizier's order to record the verbal proceedings and the execution of a copy of this record for the High Court of Thebes.

19 Donker van Heel & Haring (2003: 95-6).

20 Malinine (1947: 94); Théodoridès (1993: 95): the 'mode de confection d'un testament (exactement comme pour une donation), il est simple: le disposant fait une déclaration orale devant l'autorité compétente qui l'authentifie par la sanction et l'enregistrement'. Although Menu (1988: 166, 168) notes an increase in written contracts from the 18th dynasty onwards, yet she attests the persistence of the verbal conclusion of contracts in Deir el-Medina (1998: 303). See also Haring (2003b: 256-67) on written record and oral practice in Deir el-Medina; Eyre & Baines (1989: 109-14) about textual features that must be related to oral performance as well as to reading process constraints; for Old/Middle Kingdom signs of orality in *wḏt-mdw* dispositions, see Mrsich (2005: 195) and for references to verbal wills, see the *Balat tablet* 5955 and the *Cairo letter to the dead* JE 25975; Vernus (2005: 126) notes also the 'primauté théorique de l'oral à travers les relations complexes qu'il entretient avec l'écrit dans le domaine juridique'. Concerning the value of the legal deeds from Kahun, see the pertinent analysis of Ganley (2003a and 2003b) and especially his conclusions (2003b: 40-4) about the value of the written deed during the Middle Kingdom; see also Goedicke (1986: 79ff.).

21 Gardiner (1935: 142).

same time, proceedings before the court resulting from a conflict arising from this transaction were recorded in a meticulous way; should we then think in terms of an *orality of agreement and literacy of conflict* in Ramesside Egypt?

The general issue of *literacy vs. orality* cannot to be expressed as a simple dichotomy: there is a whole gamut of coexistential models in various cultures and periods[22], and even modern literate societies hold fast to deeply rooted oral practices and thought processes in legal contexts. This coexistence of written and oral expression and thought in the legal field is certainly evident in Ramesside Egypt. Our corpus is constituted mostly of documents from Deir el-Medina. This was a closed and possibly atypical, relatively literate, high status community. In any case, it is our main source, and it has bequeathed to us a large repertoire of written documents but – as we shall see – no true written contracts. A rather interesting evolutionary parallel may be observed in other cultures, such as the well-documented ancient Anglo-Saxon society, although the comparison has its limits. The work of Danet & Bogoch (1992, 1992b, 1994) concerning ancient Anglo-Saxon wills is especially informative[23], having been done in the context of a society in which the written act did not yet have a fully autonomous legal force, a stage of literacy that may be akin to the situation in Ramesside Egypt. Both authors note (1994: 101) that in Anglo-Saxon England of the 5th to the 11th centuries A.D. 'members of the feudal aristocracy, as well as high-ranking personages in the Catholic Church such as bishops and archbishops made wills in oral ceremonies.' They add (p. 105) that 'the legal act of bequeathing was conducted orally, documents were after-the-fact records of the binding event that already had taken place.'

If this is also the case with the Egyptian material, most of the documents in our possession were indeed composed *a posteriori*, perhaps for evidence[24] and certainly for memorization[25], but did not themselves constitute the contract or the will by themselves; the binding, dispositive act instrument of legal change remained the preceding verbal speech. Concerning orality and literacy in Deir el-Medina in general, Haring (2006: 110) refers to 'an oral village culture' in which 'Actions that required more formality, such as jurisdiction and important transactions, would have been effected with appropriate oral expressions, significant gestures, and witnesses present'[26]. He concedes that in the course of time, the recording practice increased with the villagers' growing literacy, but

22 For an overview of legal orality and literacy in several cultures and periods, see Tiersma (2007). For ancient Greece, see for instance Robb (1994), Thomas (1996), and Gagarin (2008); for early Anglo-Saxon society, see *infra* Danet and Bogoch (1992, 1992b, 1994).

23 Bearing in mind that 'technical sublanguages can be more similar cross-linguistically than disparate sublanguages within the same language' (Biber 1995: 22).

24 See Jasnow (2003c: 311-3) for the use of documents as evidence during the New Kingdom.

25 In modern law systems, the record of legal instruments may be submitted to formal requirements such as the use of templates, authentication by a notary, signatures of the parties, witnesses, official seals, etc. The functions of written formal requirements extend far beyond memorization and evidence: 'Thanks to these requirements, it is also possible to identify the type of legal act in question. At the same time, formal requirements can guarantee the publicity of the act, and enable conservation of the information concerning the act. Besides, these requirements promote mature reflection by the parties (…) lend dignity to the act, and contribute to the personal involvement of the parties to it.' (Mattila 2006: 32). In the case of ancient Egyptian notarial wills, these functions are evidently met: documents such as *Naunakhte*, *pAdoptions* and *pTurin* 2021 were obviously not recorded merely to remember the name of the witnesses to the verbal legal act.

26 *Contra*: Théodoridès (1966: 47).

functioned only as an *aide-mémoire*. Documents were not sufficiently decontextualized to be understood without extra-textual knowledge[27]. Although the extensive use of oaths and procedural witnesses[28], and the absence of literal reference to a normative text in legal procedures may remain proof that in Egyptian society the spoken word was a primary mode of legal transaction, other elements testify to the fact that certain documents became mandatory sources of legal obligations[29]. And when Haring[30] sees the use of a narrative style in Deir el-Medina legal documents as proof of an oral culture, one must note that narratives are never completely absent in modern forensic genres either; a legal case is also a *story,* and depositions remain verbal presentations recorded by the competent authority.
Thus an important point must be considered: apart from the general state of orality/literacy in Ramesside Egypt[31], the issue of oral practices in the legal sphere must be taken into account[32]. Even in the modern Western world where the printed text is omnipresent, orality still pervades the legal practice: court sessions are *hearings* at which oaths, witnesses depositions, cross-examinations are delivered or performed orally[33], as is the court's pronouncement of the sentence. Some contracts remain oral, although certain types of agreements require a written form; but intrinsically, the *instrumentum* (the written act), although legally binding, confirms the previously agreed *negotium* (the legal act, transaction)[34]. Even in the case of a notarial will, the procedure usually recommends reading the provisions aloud. The interrogation of a suspect/witness during preliminary investigation of a criminal case is usually recorded *verbatim*, but the deposition is read

27 Haring (2003b: 265-6).

28 Witnesses to the act (attesting witnesses, *témoins instrumentaires*), not eyewitnesses to an event (*res gestae* witnesses, *témoins judiciaires*); for the importance of witnesses attesting to the legality of a procedure and the absence of eyewitnesses in disputes in Greek society of the 7th – 6th centuries B.C., a society of restricted literacy, see Robb (1994: 104-20) who brings other examples of the same situation in *societies in transition* from early German codes, the Roman Law of the Twelve Tables, and early Anglo-Saxon law (pp. 116-9). Robb demonstrates that written records of a legal transaction did not constitute proper evidence of the transaction, only the testimony of witnesses to an oral transaction, summoned in advance, did. Of course in Ramesside Egypt, eyewitnesses to an event did exist (see e.g. *Tomb Robberies*) alongside witnesses to an oath or a will, as in modern legal systems; the relation of witness testimony and written evidence is complex in Ramesside Egypt (see e.g. the *Mes* affair; see also Ganley 2002: 77-8).

29 See for instance the Ramesside royal decrees exemplifying the situation of a partially literate society in which only some specific normative rules are written, along with major oral legal sources (David 2006). Compare this with the evolution from evidentiary to dispositive documents in Mesopotamia towards the end of the Old Babylonian Period (Goddeeris 2002: 15) or with the evolution of ancient Anglo-Saxon wills (Danet & Bogoch 1994). See also the situation in Greece during the 7th-6th centuries B.C. with the first written laws from Crete and the tension between written and oral law during a phase of 'slowly spreading literacy' (Robb 1994: 84-120).

30 *ibid.*, 259-60.

31 See Baines & Eyre (1983).

32 For survival of 'the spoken word in legal procedure' of 13th century England, see Clanchy (1993: 272-8): 'The forms which had been suited to a purely oral procedure were preserved and ossified when documents were introduced.'

33 Although the French principle of *oralité des débats* has been minimized by the exchange of written *conclusions* before or during the hearing. Certainly a distinction must be made between civil and criminal proceedings, as in modern Anglo-American legal systems in which all pleadings in civil actions are made in writing. And of course our modern legal systems are increasingly hostile to any kind of oral evidence, producing rules against oral wills, oral conveyances of landed property, earwitnesses, and hearsay, etc. (see Hibbitts 1992: 896).

34 Cornu (2003: 480) for the continental legal system and Garner (2004: 341) for the Anglo-American one in which the written contract is merely 'a memorial of the agreement'.

aloud for confirmation before signature. The interaction between lawyer and client is mostly verbal. Since any kind of legal transaction is ultimately interpersonal, a direct verbal exchange must be part of the process, even in a society in which literacy has been completely interiorized. The predominance of *jus scriptum* in many modern systems has not abolished verbal practice[35].

Then what may be considered to be signs of the intrinsinc legal value of the written act, the 'text-as-object' as Danet (1997: 30) calls it? Danet & Bogoch[36] have provided a list of criteria concerning the value of ancient Anglo-Saxon written wills and they are relevant to our own study. Signs of the value of the text as *legal object* are the following;

- when meta-comments about writing as an operation not taken for granted are lacking or reduced to the mere mention of the recording scribe in the colophon;
- lesser use of delocutive[37] narrative forms, significant use of locutive and performative forms;
- curses strengthening the will's performativity;
- ordered structure, cohesion marks;
- standardization;
- linguistic stylization devices;
- decontextualization and objectification of the document.

Many of these criteria are encountered in our material.

On the other hand, Ong (1982: 36 ff.) has established a series of 'characteristics of orally based thought and expression' that are present in our material: additive (paratactic or coordinative), aggregative (use of formulae and clichés), redundant, traditionalist, close to the human life world, highly polarized, not distanced, present-based and situational features[38]. But some of these are recognized trademarks of legal registers; and other aspects of the Ramesside legal documents demonstrate a complexity and sophistication that are associated by Ong with the literate mind. For instance, the extremely complex Egyptian system of categorization of abstract legal concepts is a deeply rooted writing-based system

35 Cornu (1990: 250-1): 'c'est par *référence à la parole* que le droit nomme tous les actes-clé de sa création et de sa réalisation. (…) Le législateur *parle* ; il *édicte* ; de lui viennent les *interdits* ; on relève son *silence*. Le juge *dit* le droit (il fait acte de *juridiction*) ; il *prononce* sa sentence. La force de la convention est fondée sur le respect de la *parole donnée* (…). Chaque député est une *voix* dans l'assemblée (…). La coutume s'énonce en *dicton* ou en *proverbe*. A l'audience, le juge *entend* les avocats ou *écoute* le réquisitoire ; dans l'*auditoire* ou ailleurs, il provoque l'*audition* des parties. Plusieurs voies de droit ou de recours (…) tirent leur nom de prestations vocales : *appel, contredit, plainte, complainte*, action de *jactance*, *clameur* de haro… Dans la saisie immobilière, les observations sont des *dires*. Le procès lui-même est *contradiction*. La *personne* même, sujet de droit, est pour l'étymologie, dans sa capacité de faire sonner sa voix à travers son masque (*per sonare*), et l'*infans* (*in, fari*) est au niveau profond de l'incapacité parce qu'il est incapable de parler. Tout se passe comme si la bouche était l'organe du droit, et la parole le droit en action.' These are all metaphors based on mouth-related activities; see *infra* the category represented by the  classifier. For examples of the complementarity of writing and verbal practices in the elaboration of legal documents, see Cornu, *ibid*., pp. 256-9.

36 Danet & Bogoch (1994: 107-27); Danet (1997).

37 For the linguistic terminology and its definition, see *infra Structuralist syntactic analysis*.

38 Baines (1983: 588) has already noted that 'sharp distinctions between oral (formulaic) and written (free, non-repetitive) are not visible in ancient Near Eastern material. Formulae, which are the basis of the Parry-Lord hypothesis of oral composition (…), are nearly as characteristic of written texts as of improvised poetry; in both they ease the process of composition and often the comprehension of the message, especially in letters and documents.'

of a type unknown to mainly oral cultures[39]. Furthermore, the notarial function of the court proves that oral procedure was not always perceived as a sufficient means of protecting dispositions, although the recourse to witnesses and oaths was a common procedure. One may also ask why so many oaths were indeed recorded. The falsification of records as a means of simulating a legal right is indeed evidence of the intrinsic value of the written document[40]. We cannot entirely dismiss the possibility of autonomous written acts obligatory for the parties on certain occasions[41].

Hibbitts (1992) recommends that we be more precise and instead referring to *oral culture*, we should perhaps talk about *performance culture*, as non-written vehicles comprise a five sense experience including not only verbal material but also mainly image and motion-based experiences. The usual combination of channels of communication in the legal practices of moderately literate societies may be viewed as a total experience in which 'Law is not so much said, sung, gestured, or felt as it is holistically performed'[42]. One is struck by the relative lack of information obtained for ancient Egyptian visual, gestual, tactile, and savory legal texture: no reference is made to special sounds, use of symbolic objects, motions, contact, ceremonies involving eating and drinking in the course of a legal procedure or agreement such as those evoked by Hibbitts.

In view of these remarks, the oral-literate dynamics must be assessed not as an opposition between two cultural ways, but as an interplay involving a whole gamut of forms and relationships; although we are obviously not dealing with a fully literate culture, some aspects of the Egyptian literate experience were already deeply assimilated during the Ramesside Period[43].

Another issue related to the value of the instrument is the respective value and use of **ostracon *vs.* papyrus**.

Janssen[44] notes that 'ostraca did possess some value as legal documents' and that there was 'no distinction in this respect between papyri and ostraca,' adding that nevertheless, the ostraca do not represent 'actual legal deeds' as there is no mention of witnesses. He has demonstrated[45] that papyrus was not exorbitantly expensive; it could be used for semi-official purposes, such as the 'rough draft of an official report'[46].

The choice of ostraca as a medium is the subject of constant debate[47]; evidently the administration used ostraca in its day-to-day activity and kept them, at least temporarily, as

---

39 Ong (1982: 55).

40 Of course the written legal text had not yet achieved a 'sacrosanct' value demanding exact copies and precise referencing (concerning a similar issue related to statute wording in 15th century England, see Tiersma 2007: 18-9).

41 See for instance Théodoridès (1970: 176-8, 214-5) concerning the necessity of establishing a written *imyt-pr*.

42 Hibbitts (1992: 945).

43 One more point to consider is the status of the scribe, which is indeed higher than the status of a commoner during the Ramesside Period, but not necessarily as high as that of the scribe in a society of restricted literacy such as in 6th century B.C. Greece (see the example of the highly privileged scribe in the Cretan Afrati inscription, Robb 1994: 87-9).

44 Janssen (1975: 511, 513).

45 *Ibid.*, pp. 447-8.

46 Janssen (1966: 94).

47 For summaries of the question, see McDowell (1990: 5-7); Donker van Heel & Haring (2003: 2-5).

they are sometimes accompanied by dockets which prove some sort of filing[48]. Some of the ostraca were kept for an extended period[49]. Nevertheless, Janssen[50] doubts that ostraca were kept in large official archives. Menu[51] suggests that ostraca were used in Deir el-Medina as negotiable instruments and accordingly as autonomous legally binding documents; they could also represent only the evidence of a debt. In any case, the villagers (and the scribes working at the site) used ostraca for their notes and epistolary local exchanges as this material was readily available *in situ* and was already the preferred medium for sketches and exercices.

As for our corpus, one must note the relatively high proportion of papyri for the main wills and gifts group (4 papyri against 5 ostraca) and the partitions (6 papyri against 5 ostraca), whereas ostraca are almost exclusively involved in the *(social) gifts or else?* and *contract-related provisions* groups (see these chapters *infra*). The three wills recorded on papyrus (*Naunakhte*, *pAdoptions*, *pTurin* 2021) share many common features, not all of which are present in wills on ostraca: they are *authentic* long documents recorded in court, obviously in the presence of family members, presented neatly, written in a script with calligraphic tendencies, with corrections, using both locutive and delocutive modes, and including the most complete provisions and clauses, named witnesses and officials, *recital* (see *infra*), elaborated colophons, and performative provisions.

3. *Nature of the instrument*: ***ỉmyt-pr vs.*** **other kinds of legal instrument (*ʿwty h3rwyt, sḫ3, sš, ḫtmt,* etc.)**.

   In the great majority of cases, their redactors did not bother to define the deeds during the New Kingdom. The pre-material of many documents mentions a verbal statement (*ḏd*(*t*), *sḏm r3*), the instrumental record of which is not qualified. In the few cases in which internal characterizations are provided, the interpretation of the terminology[52] used is also subject to debate due to the Egyptians' lack of 'consistency' and the limitations of our own comprehension of the legal lexicon.

4. *Legal issue definition*: **will *vs.* gift**; **inheritance *vs.* 'break-up' *property settlement*; sale *vs.* loan, lease/hire, credit**.

   The legal issue is never internally qualified in our corpus, as it appears that legal transactions do not usually have a specific name in the ancient Egyptian legal system. In any case, headings alone do not suffice to determine the kinds of legal issues we are dealing with, as 'true uniformity was never reached because alternative document headings remained current at the same time'[53]. No special lexeme such as 'to bequeath' was used to imply a testamentary *disposition*; any transmission of property or temporary transfer of limited rights on assets was formulated with the help of the ubiquitous *rdi* 'to give'. Eyre (1992: 210) contends that 'it is typical of Egyptian documents that a 'will' is virtually

48 For example *oGardiner/Ashmolean* 36; for a list, see Donker van Heel & Haring (2003: 12-3).
49 Allam (1968: 124-7).
50 Janssen (1975b: 295).
51 Menu (2004: 257).
52 See Donker van Heel & Haring (2003: 85-123): 'Egyptian text denominatives'.
53 Donker van Heel & Haring (2003: 180).

indistinguishable from any other class of property transfer' as it is a 'merely witnessed procès verbal'[54]. So what makes a will a will in cultures, either ancient or modern?

Modern legal definitions and categories are based on associated criteria (essential elements), the combination of which is required for a notion to be qualified as such[55]. For instance, the minimal conditions or associated criteria for a modern will are: a unilateral expression of will, revocable, to the effect of patrimonial transmission of property *mortis causa*, for the benefit of legatee(s). Thus an *olographic* will is valid as long as it contains certain minimal requirements[56], but one may write it down in the least conventional way and its format may not be a clear indication of the legal issue it deals with. Although the combination of these criteria in our Ramesside documents is essential for us to qualify the issues at hand, it is not always obvious.

The main objection to the unilateral character of the will stems from the fact that the legatees are sometimes asked to participate in a cross-examination procedure before the court authenticating the will (*pTurin* 2021), and even associated with the testator in the title of the document (*oPetrie* 18, *pAdoptions*). This objection may be dismissed as family members appear for the sole purpose of testifying that they have no objections to the will in order to prevent litigation[57]; furthermore, persons other than the testator are only nominally associated in the pre-material of the will as attendants to the record of the testator's statement.

Concerning the ancient Egyptian autonomy of decision with respect to testamentary dispositions, it is rash to make a statement like 'the concept of the last will and testament, central to Anglo-American legal traditions, is inappropriate; a man's ability freely to bequeath his property was so limited by custom that the concept of the will is largely irrelevant' (Eyre 2007: 233). Even in some modern legal systems, the law can protect the inheritance rights of children by instituting an obligatory hereditary portion (*réserve héréditaire*)[58] for their rightful beneficiaries, reducing the portion of assets that the testator can bequeath to whomever he wants (*quotité disponible*) to a small fraction of the entire legacy. For instance, the French Code Civil, articles 913 and 921, states that in case a person has three children, he can only bequeath a fourth of his assets by will, which certainly limits his ability to freely bequeath his assets but does not render the concept of the will irrelevant.

As for the contemplation of the testator's death, it seems that the distinction between *donatio inter vivos* and *testamentum mortis causa* was not of prime importance to the Egyptians. The New Kingdom wills that have survived do not contain a specific *mortis*

54 See Černý (1945: 42): the will 'follows the pattern of all Egyptian legal documents; like them it consists of an oral deposition made by the party before the court or witnesses and written down by a professional scribe'; see also Pestman (1982b: 174). For similar conclusions regarding Demotic documents, see Clarysse (1995: 95-8).

55 Cornu (2003: 268).

56 For example in some continental systems, the will must be written entirely by the hand of the testator, dated and signed by him.

57 Théodoridès (1966: 55-60, 66-70).

58 *Legitime, legal portion*: 'The part of a testator's property that his or her children (and occasionally other heirs) are legally entitled to regardless of the will's terms' (Garner 2004: 920).

causa mention[59] as is sometimes the case during the Old Kingdom[60] and after the New Kingdom[61]. In some cases, immediate gift and testamentary provisions to be enforced after the event may coexist in the same document (*oGardiner/Ashmolean* 272, *pTurin* 2021). On the linguistic level, the use of the future *iw.f r sḏm* in the *descent and distribution rule* (the legal rule by which a descendent's property is passed on) may be an indication of a will, but in the case of the omission of the preposition *r*, there is always room for doubt; furthermore, the document may record the donor's intention to make a gift in the near future, expressed in the same form. We are also faced with a general problem of categorization of legal concepts, ancient or modern, concerning what we may call 'borderline cases'. Modern legal systems' *partage d'ascendant* and *donatio mortis causa* blurr the edges of will (*mortis causa*) and gift (*inter vivos*) categories. Generally speaking, this *blurring of legal categories* pervades modern legal categorization. For instance, wills may include the acknowledgement of a child. In French modern Law, the *institution contractuelle* is a hybrid instrument, part contract and part will, whereby the instituing person irrevocably confers the right to inherit all or part of his assets at the time of his death to a specific beneficiary[62]; in practice, this agreement is restricted to marriage contracts in favor of one of the spouses or by a third party in favor of one of them before or during their union.

Patrimonial partitions also exemplify the complexity of the matter: some ancient Egyptian divisions of assets were due to the separation of a couple which was not the consequence of the death of one spouse [63], but the cause of the apportionment cannot always be established in lacunary documents. In the ancient Egyptian mind, wills, gifts and 'break-up' partitions may have belonged to the same legal category of apportionments.

Concerning the precise nature of contracts, our subtle categories are not always transposable to Egyptian legal institutions as they belong to another culture, and the lack of details in most of the records often do not permit an assessment of their essence;

5. *Legal step involved*: **expression of will creating rights and obligations *vs.* authentication, execution, notification, litigation**.

   The lack of context and clear enunciation of the nature of the procedure makes it extremely difficult to decide in certain cases which legal step is covered by the documents.

   For instance, patrimonial transmissions were sometimes recorded in writing before a court or witnesses[64]. In this case, the court acted as notary, authenticating the will for publicity and evidence, and sometimes even questioning some members of the family to assess facts and rights, as well as their intelligence of the provisions and attitude to them (see *pTurin* 2021). After the testator's death, the will had to be executed and the assets divided according to its provisions. A written record of the partition was probably a normal

59 Although in *pAdoptions*, *Nbnfr*'s mention of an eventual contestation of his siblings 'on my death on the morrow after tomorrow' can be taken as an allusion to the *mortis causa* specificity of the transmission.

60 *Nkꜥnḫ* tomb inscription, *Urk.* I, 162 line 12: *ink ir iwꜥw r hrw ḫpy(.i) im r imntt wdft* 'I am the one who made an heir for the day when (I) shall depart to the West, be it tardily.'

61 For instance *Nḫtfmwti*'s *statue Cairo* CG 42208 (22nd dynasty); repeated several times in *pMoscow* 123, lines 2-4 (70 B.C.).

62 Cornu (2003: 478): 'institution d'héritier par contrat'.

63 See *oGardiner/Ashmolean* 157.

64 The presence of titled, official witnesses cannot always be qualified as a court session, see McDowell (1990: 145, 155); Janssen (2005: 105-6).

procedure designed to prove and keep track of the various assets attributions. But an unsatisfied creditor or disinherited party could object to the will in court by suing the legatees, a procedure recorded by an official scribe. What legal step did the document record?

The dilemma may thus concern the often ambiguous **notarial *vs.* decisional function of the court**: in the case of lacunary documents, it is not always possible to determine if the court is acting as judge of a legal dispute, in which case the document is a mere litigation protocol, or performing its notarial duty[65]. Furthermore, since both litigation protocols and private instruments notarized in court can be introduced by more or less extensive quotations or summaries of *title deeds* (wills, gift deeds, *ỉmyt-pr*, court proceedings, etc.) expressing the right of a party, the overall qualification of the legal step involved may constitute quite a brain teaser.

In each instance, our decision to include a document in the corpus of private law instruments and our qualification of the text's value and nature, the legal step and overall legal issue involved have been based on textual and documentary features as well as contextual criteria. By *textual* features we understand linguistic (lexical, syntactical, prosodic, textemic), semantic (related to the classifiers of the hieroglyphic/hieratic scripts), graphical, and content-related criteria; *documentary* features relate to the material and state of the document as an object; *contextual* features concern the integration of the document in an environment that enriches its meaning (provenance locus, reference to textual and legal context). The following parameters have been used:

a. **state** of the document: fragmentary or complete, leaving or not leaving room for doubt
b. **material** used:
   - ostracon, papyrus (perhaps implying a more official, definitive instrument, and its archiving, although some ostraca have been found with a docket), but also lapidary medium (stela, tomb wall)
   - height of the papyrus indicative of genre[66]
   - fiber orientation of papyrus[67]
c. **script**:
   - cursive hieratic *de la pratique,* the tachygraphic business hand for private and bureaucratic usage; *chancery script*, a more sacralized version of the cursive hieratic; the *uncial* traditional book hand hieratic with a calligraphic tendency[68]; and their evolution from the 19th to the 20th dynasty[69]
   - changes of hand implying a multi-part procedure, the addition of documents to constitute a file

65 See Théodoridès (1966: 47); McDowell (1990: 155).
66 See Černý (1945: 30 n.5): about 42 cm not uncommon for legal and business matters and mostly 21 cm for literary pieces and letters. Valbelle (1985: 31) adds that some private documents 'sont rédigés sur des feuilles simples ou de petits fragments de papyrus coupés à cet effet dès l'antiquité'.
67 Černý (1939: xvii-xx and 1945: 30 n.5); Gardiner (1940: 23) about the practice of writing short legal texts on the recto across the fibers and on the verso along them, as with letters.
68 Vernus (1990: 44-5).
69 For instance, 'extravagant ligatures and cursive strokes' of the business hand by the end of the 20th dynasty for Černý & Peet (1927: 31).

- corrections[70] implying either a revised school exercise, mainly in epistolary texts, an important document that has undergone a second lecture, the update of a record
- abbreviations[71]
- conventional marks (*ditto,* margin diacritical marks) implying a business or accounting tachygraphic practice
- two-color usage (bichromy) to highlight/distinguish[72]
- verse points: may be scribal 'check marks' that sometimes appear in 'real accounts papyri and comparable documentary materials', not only in poetic compositions, to ensure that 'all the relevant entries on the master document had been correctly transferred over to the copy' (Goelet 2007: 113). But no verse points appear in our corpus, even in the double partition list of *Naunakhte*'s file
- direction of script across the papyrus (see *supra*)

d. **location** of the find indicating a private (in dwelling or tomb) or official archive[73] (in temple, palace, administrative bureau or worksite) or another strategic position for business. Numerous Ramesside administrative notes concerning work were discarded in bulk in the areas where the Gang worked in the Valleys of the Kings and Queens[74]. Specific dump locations in Deir el-Medina in the vicinity of the *Grand Puits*, the presumed site of lost administrative premises, may constitute discarded archives
e. **external reference** in another text to the same protagonists or situation, providing contextual insight
f. **internal characterization** of the legal **instrument** (material document) involved, legal **procedural step**, and/or abstract legal **issue** in pre-material, body, colophon of the text or docket
g. internal elements pointing to a **record deprived of legal value**: layout and textemes specific to other genres, only brief or passing mention of a legal instrument or transaction, absence of essential clauses
h. internal elements indicating an ***authentic*** **deed**: recorded in an official forum for authentication, often on papyrus, neat presentation[75], formulaic and cohesive structure, standardization, delocutive/locutive textemes, archaisms and degree 1 or 2 Neo-Egyptian features (see *infra*), inclusion of title deed excerpt/summary; complete pre-material with

70 Černý (1931b: 212-3) has suggested that corrections were more frequent on ostraca than on papyrus, and on 'literary' exercises ostraca than on 'non literary' ones written by expert scribes in a rapid cursive hand (see also Goelet 2007: 122-3 concerning typical students' errors).

71 For instance, Dawson (1925: 247) says of *pBM* EA 10335 that its 'general style of handwriting is a cursive legal script, full of abbreviation-strokes.' But abbreviation strokes are also present in school exercises.

72 Posener (1951: 77): 'Les rédacteurs des écrits juridiques et administratifs, qui ont été parmi les premiers à mettre au point l'usage de la bichromie, l'abandonnent avant les copistes des textes religieux et littéraires'.

73 Concerning the notion of *archives*, see the recent Milan Congress (9.2008) where the notion of public archives, to be understood as true consultation archives or as places of deposition, and even as a symbols of administrative power with limited functional aims (Eyre), has been the subject of debate, especially following the communications of Trapani, Allam and Eyre.

74 Eyre (1987: 26).

75 Valbelle (1985: 31): 'On classe habituellement, parmi les documents officiels, ceux qui comportent le nom du roi régnant dans le libellé de la date et les expressions développées pour désigner l'institution de la Tombe tout en offrant une présentation soignée.'

full dating[76], including the titulary of the reigning king and archaic anaphora, legal step, named parties and beneficiaries, forum, object, internal characterization of the instrument; locutive *recital* with statutory, precedent, or equity ground; operative part using typical clauses; authentication procedure; elaborate colophon naming witnesses and scribe; docket implying archiving and filing with documents connected to the case

i. internal elements indicating an **administrative record**[77] **of bureaucratic interest**: recorded for administrative purpose, such as work log or taxation, sometimes on reused literary papyri[78], generally brief, factual delocutive excerpt of main administrative interest, pre-material with full[79] or abbreviated dating, use of archaic anaphora, names of main parties and agents; absence of locutive *recital*; formulaic style, margin diacritical marks and abbreviations used in bookkeeping[80];

j. internal elements indicating a **private memo or communication of personal interest**: recorded by the interested individual or by a scribe at his demand for private purpose, relating to private concerns or relationships between individuals, using locutive/allocutive modes or impersonally brief, requiring reliance on extra-textual knowledge (names often omitted, absence of date or brief dating), idiosyncratic/idiolectical tendencies, abnormal structure and absence of fixed pattern of multiple textemes, non formulaic, degree 2 or 3 Neo-Egyptian features, various textual genres recorded on the same document in private archives[81]

k. internal elements indicating a **will**: transmission of an entire patrimony or a significant part of it, absence of *consideration* (payment given in exchange), unilateral deed; preceding title deed justifying the testator's ownership rights; delocutive pre-material with full dating and archaic anaphora in the case of an *authentic*[82] instrument, date of the record different from the *traditio*/partition date (when known), legal step, name of the testator and heirs, object, forum, internal characterization of the instrument as *imyt-pr*; locutive *recital* with old age/*mortis causa* mention, retributive principle, statutory ground; operative part using future *descent and distribution* rules, *rdi*/*pš*, performative provision of bequests, type/origin of shares/assets, list of heirs, *no-contest/terrorem* clause, *exemption from hotchpot* (see *infra*), *advancement*, exclusions relating to specific items, designation of an executor, notification; authentication procedure; colophon concerning the recording scribe, record order, copy, witnesses; file additions concerning particular bequests, partition, family members' oaths and statements/*traditio*/forfeiture; docket implying archiving of the will

l. internal elements indicating a **gift**: transmission of assets constituting only a fraction of the donor's patrimony, absence of *consideration*, unilateral deed; preceding title deed justifying the donor's ownership rights; delocutive pre-material with full dating and archaic anaphora in the case of an *authentic* instrument, coincidence between the document's date and the *traditio*, legal step, names of donor/donees, forum, object, *rdi*; locutive *recital* with

76 Valbelle (1985: 61 n.4) notes that most *documentary* papyri and ostraca are dated, but as Eyre (1987: 27) remarks, 'Full datings are not common at any period.'

77 See Sweeney (2001: 18) for a partial list of common features in administrative texts (she includes *ir ink* and *rdyt* 'what was given').

78 Valbelle (2003: 159).

79 Generally at the beginning of the book.

80 See Megally (1977).

81 Valbelle (2003: 160).

82 In the legal sense.

statutory ground; operative part using performative provision, absence of future, notification, list of shares/assets, *exemption from hotchpot*, repayment of estate's debt; colophon; addition of partition

m. internal elements indicating a **partition of private assets** not resulting from contractual relationships, nor from a public sanction nor a couple's separation, but being the **execution of will/gift** provisions (preliminary *allotment* or material execution of the partition): mainly delocutive mode, absence of title deed; brief delocutive pre-material usually dated, internal characterization of the instrument, name of the owner of the divided assets, mention of beneficiaries, object, legal issue/step, executors' names; absence of *recital*; main texteme with partition list, notification, use of *rdỉ/ỉṯỉ/pš/dnỉ/ỉwꜥt/nty n/ny-sw*, list of similar assets/shares, mention of quantities of items, deficit/excess of share, repayment of estate's debt, accounting features, use of future/present (preliminary *allotment*) or past (after-the-fact record of material execution); colophon; addition of specific arrangements between coheirs such as renunciation in favor of a sibling

n. internal elements indicating a **contract**: delocutive pre-material with date, mention of all parties, internal characterization of the instrument, object; operative part mentioning the *essentialia* and all major points of agreement such as *mutual assent* of the parties, the *consideration* and its valuation, terms and conditions (e.g. credit, delivery, restitution), warranty, and including performative form and relevant lexemes such as *rdỉ, ỉnỉ, ỉṯꜣ, šsp, ỉrỉ, r-ḏbꜣ*, etc.; colophon.

Of course, one may argue with these choices. There is always room for discussion in such a perplexing matter where so much is left to the personal logic of the observer. But at least the criteria used are presented for the reader's scrutiny.

The texts are presented in chronological order in each category, dated, with a reference to their hieroglyphic version (generally from *KRI*), and tentative definitions of the instrument, the legal step and the legal issue based on the criteria developed *supra*. Following the literal transliteration[83] and translation of each texteme is a discussion of its dialectal features; the categorization of lexemes related to a legal concept appearing in the texts conclude their analysis.

The framework; terminology

The framework is basically the same as that adopted for the analysis of the Ramesside royal decrees (David 2006) with some additions. For convenience, the definitions and general directives in this previous work are repeated below.

a. Structuralist syntactic analysis

The structuralist, textual-analytic approach has been favored at the Hebrew University since H. J. Polotsky taught linguistics there (the Polotskyan Jerusalem School), and it is the reference framework adopted here (see Shisha-Halevy 1998: 10-12). As for the terminology used, some

83 The transliteration principle for Neo-Egyptian spelling and Semitic lexemes adopted here is based on a **what you see is what you get** *parti pris*, mainly in order to allow morphological and orthographical comparisons to be made.

central concepts related to (socio-) linguistics have too often been misunderstood, and it is of crucial importance to define them properly. The definitions of key words used to describe syntactic forms and constructions are mostly to be found in Shisha-Halevy (1988 and 1998) and in his numerous books and articles on Egyptian, Coptic, and other languages. For the sake of clarity, a basic glossary follows:

- *actor*: 'noun or pronoun expressing the carrier-out of an active action, the undergoer of a passive action, or the one who is in a state ("grammatical subject")', e.g. The postman always rings twice;
- *adjunct/expansion/modifier/satellite*: optional or secondary structural element, extending or qualifying another (adnominal; adverbal; adnexal; ad-pattern), e.g. It's always fair weather;
- *adnexal*: 'verb form attaching a rhematic element to a clause or phrase', e.g. Some like it hot;
- *adnominal*: expansion or modifier of a nominal element, e.g. The man who knew too much;
- *aorist*: conjugation form expressing general, natural, or habitual atemporal action, e.g. Gentlemen prefer blondes;
- *articloid*: mainly phoric (referential) determinator, i.e. *pꜣ, tꜣ, nꜣ* in the Ramesside legal registers, as opposed to an automatic, grammaticalized article (Löfstedt 1981);
- *augens*: reinforcer modifying a nominal form and containing a pronominal element referring (mostly back) to this nominal form, e.g. I myself;
- *binomials*: fixed collocations composed of two or more lexemes syntactically, semantically, and prosodically related, e.g. Signed, sealed, delivered (Malkiel 1959);
- *converb*: verb form of adverbial status and function, e.g. Some came running;
- *deictic*: pointing out, indicating, e.g. This property is condemned;
- *delocutive*: pertaining to the 3rd person, e.g. She couldn't take it;
- *determinator*: 'marker of a noun with respect to specificity and definiteness', e.g. All the Vermeers in New York;
- *focus*: 'center or highlight of the communication stretch' (macrosyntactic information), e.g. It was only to see you that he came by;
- *interlocutive*: pertaining to the 1st - 2nd persons, e.g. You can't cheat an honest man;
- *locutive*: pertaining to the 1st persons, e.g. I hate actors;
- *marker*: formal characteristic, e.g. in Egyptian, the plural grapheme 𓏥 for number;
- *marked:* 'term of an opposition that is positive with regard to the presence of a specific linguistic feature', e.g. un chien et une chienne, for gender;
- *nexus*: 'the special interdependence and link of theme and rheme' (microsyntactic, nominal, adverbial, verbal), e.g. My name is nobody;
- *nucleus*: grammatical center of a phrase that defines its paradigm, e.g. Lost angel;
- *quantifier*: marker of quantity or number in a noun phrase, e.g. Another 48 hours;
- *relational*: expansion of a nominal element (sometimes with the help of a *relator*) with which it has a specific relationship (appurtenance, association, kinship, etc.), e.g. The father of the bride;
- *rheme*: structural constituent conveying information about the theme (microsyntactic information), e.g. Where were you when the lights went out?;

- *story/commentary*: a most valuable distinction of fundamental textual categories and the associated tempus systems based on the speaker's attitude (Weinrich 1973: 22ff.; Prince 1987: 14, 91). The story (*Erzählung – récit*) is marked by the speaker's detachment relative to the speech situation, and is an 'objective' discourse about another situation, e.g. a novel. The 'subjective' commentary (*Besprechung – commentaire*), on the other hand, implies the involvement of both the speaker and the addressee in the speech situation; Weinrich (*ibid.*, 33) gives the following examples of commentary: 'dialogue dramatique, mémorandum politique, éditorial, testament, rapport scientifique, essai philosophique, commentaire juridique, et toutes les formes du discours rituel, codifié et performatif.' Thus the various textual genres may be viewed in this larger context, and the textemic analysis must take into account the specific features of the two textual categories. Weinrich's dichotomy was already acknowledged by Hintze (1950-52) when he distinguished the objective story (*Erzählung*) and the subjective commentary (*Rede*) in the *Late Egyptian Stories*;
- *texteme*: subtextual signaled and bounded unit presenting a distinctive system of grammar such as dialogue, narrative, exposition, report;
- *theme*: structural constituent containing given or presupposed information (microsyntactic information), 'what is being discussed', e.g. Where were <u>you</u> when <u>the lights</u> went out?;
- *topic*: (con)textual information discussed (macrosyntactic, extraclausal information) that signals, maintains, and affirms textual thematic continuity and cohesion, and relates to the entire theme + rheme nexus, e.g. <u>A good movie</u>, that's entertainment.

One may usefully add to this lexicon a few terms borrowed from narratologic studies (Prince 1987):

- *alethic modality:* qualification of a statement by a possibility, impossibility, or necessity modal operator, e.g. You <u>can't</u> win them all;
- *deontic modality:* qualification of a statement by a permission, prohibition or obligation modal operator, e.g. You <u>may</u> sleep on the sofa, if you want;
- *isotopy:* 'The repetition of semiotic features that institutes the coherence of a text. (...) In its more restricted acceptation, (...) the repetition of semantic units in a text (...). In its broadest sense, (...) the repetition of units at any and all textual levels (phonetic, stylistic, rhetorical, syntactic, prosodic, etc.).' (Prince 1987: 47), e.g. <u>Signed, sealed, delivered</u>, I am yours;
- *tag clause:* 'A clause (...) accompanying a character's discourse (...) and specifying the act of the speaker or thinker, identifying him or her, and (sometimes) indicating various aspects of the act, the character, the setting in which they appear, etc.' (Prince 1987: 95), e.g. <u>He said</u> that he was on the verge of a significant breakthrough;
- *tagged direct discourse:* 'A direct discourse accompanied by a tag clause.' (Prince 1987: 96), e.g. – <u>Are you coming tonight? she asked</u> full of hope.

b. Sociolinguistic analysis of registers, genres, and dialects

Concerning sociolinguistic aspects of language and literature, the basic definitions used in the present study are to be found in Even-Zohar (1990), Hasan (1973: 253-292), Bakhtin (1981),

Gregory (1967: 177-198) and, for Egyptologic studies, Goldwasser (1990 and 1999). Again, for the sake of clarity, the definitions of the main terms used are provided below:

- *dialect*: variety of language, idiom;
- *diglossia*: 'use of two varieties of a language in the same speech community', one of them being regarded as superior to the other by the speakers (prestige associated with abundant written literature and higher education) (Ferguson 1964: 429);
- *genre:* recurrent textual form associated with a specific language, subject, style, communicative purpose (for example, the consentient legal genre). See Hodge & Kress (1988: 7); Bhatia (1993: 13-16) ('each genre is an instance of a successful achievement of a specific communicative purpose using conventionalized knowledge of linguistic and discoursal resources'); Ferguson (1994: 17, 21-3); Jackson (1995: 90-92);
- *heteroglossia:* 'internal stratification of any single national language into social dialects, characteristic group behavior, professional jargons, generic languages, languages of generations and age groups, tendentious languages, languages of the authorities, of various circles and of passing fashions, languages that serve the specific sociopolitical purpose of the day, even of the hour', differentiated by various social pressures and contexts (Bakhtin 1981: 262-263);
- *idiolect:* variety of language, idiom associated with a specific individual, 'the individual who speaks and writes (...). The individual is, so to speak, the smallest dialect unit: each speaker has his own IDIOLECT.' (Halliday, McIntosh & Strevens 1964: 94-95);
- *register:* 'variety of language distinguished according to use (...). The crucial criteria of any given register are found in its grammar and lexis.' (Halliday, McIntosh & Strevens 1964: 87-88; Halliday 1989: 44 'functional variation'). For the factors correlating with a register (subject-matter, situation type/setting, participant roles, mode and medium of discourse, purpose), see Hasan (1973: 271-272), Biber (1994: esp. 40-4). 'Written legal language may be considered a particular register of the "grapholect"' (Jackson 1995: 111). As Biber (1994: 34) explains, 'registers can range from extremely high-level varieties' (formal/informal, spoken/written, low/high), 'varieties at several intermediate level' (associated with specific textual genres), 'extremely low-level varieties' or subregisters (that we have associated with specific *textemes*); but note that Biber[84] uses *register* 'as the general cover term associated with all aspects of variation in use'.

  Biber (1995) uses the notion of *dimensions of register variation* in his comparative approach using linguistic parameters (dimensions) in order to establish similarities and differences among registers. 'Dimensions are defined by distinct groupings of linguistic features that co-occur frequently in texts'[85], 'interpreted in terms of the communicative functions shared by the co-occuring features'[86]. He has, for instance, identified six basic dimensions of variation in English[87]: involved *vs.* informational production, narrative *vs.* non-narrative discourse, situation-dependent *vs.* elaborated reference, overt expression of argumentation *vs.* not overtly argumentative, abstract *vs.* non-abstract style, on-line informational elaboration marking stance *vs.* edited or not informational;

84 Biber (1995: 9).
85 For lists of linguistic features of English and other languages, see Biber (1995: 94-103).
86 *Ibid.*, p. 19.
87 *Ibid.*, pp. 141-68.

- *repertoire:* 'aggregate of laws and elements (either single, bound, or total models) that govern the production of texts' (Even-Zohar 1990: 17); 'a combination of "grammar" and "lexicon" of a given "language"' formed of individual elements (morphemes, lexemes), syntagms and models ('combination of elements + rules + the syntagmatic ("temporal") relations imposable' on the text[88];
- *sociolect:* variety of language or idiom associated with a particular social class or status group (Hasan 1973: 255-258 'social dialect');
- *technical dialect:* variety of language or idiom associated with a particular profession or occupation;
- *temporal dialect:* variety of language or idiom isolated in terms of time (Gregory 1967: 180-182);
- *topolect:* variety of language or idiom associated with a specific geographical unit;
- *vernacular:* colloquial language (*low dialect*, see Hodge & Kress 1988: 87, 108; Goldwasser 1999), sometimes *educated* vernacular and even *standard or normative* vernacular (that underwent a process of canonization or legitimization by the dominant circles);
- *written as if spoken* (Hasan 1973: 280): 'texts that might be defined as those "attempted to be written as if spoken" could be the closest parallel to the term "spoken language" of modern linguistics' (Goldwasser 1990: 203-204, on the basis of Gregory 1967: 191 'the speaking of what is written to be spoken as if not written').

Note that the definition of *legal* language, varieties, genres, registers, and discourse have been addressed in many different ways by linguists (for a summary of various positions, see Kurzon 1997).

c. Legal discourse analysis

Legal texts are the object of interdisciplinary research in philosophy (Austin's 1962 and his followers' Speech Act theory), forensic rhetoric, social sciences, anthropology, and linguistics (pragmatics, sociolinguistics, psycholinguistics, legal semiotics, text linguistics – texts typological research – and discourse/genre analysis, the study of the legal discourse in a lexical, syntactic, rhetorical, prosodic, and functional perspective); see Danet (1980: 453-470) and Goodrich (1994: 2085) for a summary of the various approaches.

Various studies of legal discourse, as practiced first by Mellinkoff (1963), then by Bhatia (1993, 1994), Charrow *et alii* (1982), Crystal & Davy (1969), Danet (1980, 1984, 1985, 1990), Gunnarsson (1984), Gustafsson (1984), Jackson (1995), Kurzon (1984, 1986), Maley (1994) *inter alii*, were of prime importance in establishing whether there are constants in legal registers of various cultures and a transcendent legal repertoire in terms of geography and time.

See also David (2004, 2006) for an analysis of the legal register of Ramesside royal decrees[89].

88 Even-Zohar (1990: 39, 41).

89 Richter (2002) adopts a similar approach concerning Coptic legal documents.

d. Neo-Egyptian[90] registers

The classification of Neo-Egyptian texts as 'literary' or 'administrative' used by Černý and Groll (*LEG*)[91] and based on the syntactic forms from which the language they represent is built, was not followed in this study, as it presents numerous conceptual difficulties. First of all, each text may contain several segments representing different registers; secondly, the terminology used confuses genre and dialects, as a text written in a 'literary' language is not always a 'literary' piece (see most royal decrees), and the 'administrative' language is not always used in administrative documents (see the *Wenamun* controversy[92]). Moreover, most texts are composed of elements belonging to both languages, but in various dosages or stages of development. Although the concepts of literary and non-literary texts have not been unanimously adopted, Groll's (1975) seminal article distinguishing the Neo-Egyptian verbal formations (*pure Middle Egyptian*, *specific literary Late Egyptian*, and *non-literary*) has paved the way for analysis by various scholars of Neo-Egyptian diglossia.

Following Vernus (1982), Winand (1992) has proposed a model of three *registres d'expression* (*néo-égyptien partiel*, *mixte*, and *complet*), based on morphologic and orthographic signifiers, on an axis between the *égyptien de tradition* (an artificial language based on Middle Egyptian) and the *néo-égyptien* (the 'written as if spoken' language)[93]. This model constitutes the basis of our attempt to find an instrument of analysis applicable to any text written between the 18th and the 20th dynasties, whatever its genre, registers, purpose, medium, or script. We have adapted this model and it has been divided into four degrees of basic changes *vis-à-vis* the 'classical' language of Middle Egyptian (degree 0) represented by its two central prototypes, the tale of *Sinuhe* and the *Coffin Texts* (note that the same dialect is represented by central members belonging to different genres). Each degree is associated with syntactic, lexicographic, morphologic, and/or orthographic criteria[94]; the model may be further refined by dividing each degree into sub-degrees corresponding to more specific precisions. Within a limited time/genre corpus, the model must be applied to each register and even every texteme in the texts (each register and texteme within a text may represent a different degree of Neo-Egyptian, which means that any given text may include several degrees of Neo-Egyptian).

Our Neo-Egyptian text analysis model for distinguishing dialectal features is:

a. **degree 0**: syntactic, lexicographic, morphologic, and orthographic forms present in Middle Egyptian 'classical dialect' (reference: *Sinuhe, CT*) [conservatism];
b. **degree 1**: lexicographic, morphologic, and orthographic variance from the degree 0 introduced during the New Kingdom [adaptation];

90 Refering to the language of the New Kingdom (see French *néo-égyptien* and German *Neuägyptisch*).

91 See Goldwasser (1990) on this issue.

92 See *inter al.* Scheepers (1992), Satzinger (1997), Goldwasser (1999: 17-8), Baines (1999), and Schipper (2005).

93 This model is also followed by Junge (2005: 23).

94 This explains the choice of a 'complete transliteration' of our texts, including e.g. semi-vowels usually left out by modern transliterations. Of course, this choice neither reflects a particular statement concerning the original pronounciation of Neo-Egyptian, nor a specific attitude towards the work that has been done concerning 'syllabic' or group writing, but only the desire to highlight spelling and morphologic uses since a hieratic or hieroglyphic version of the texts is not provided here.

c. **degree 2**: degree 0 forms + degree 1 adaptations + some new (sometimes rare or ephemeral[95]) syntactic forms [innovation];
d. **degree 3**: very few degree 0 forms (with degree 1 adaptations) + maximum new, finalized syntactic forms comprising a different system, perhaps closest to the vernacular of the period during which the text under consideration was composed (reference: 21st dynasty *Wenamun*[96]) [autonomy].

For each texteme, a list of *Neo-Egyptian characteristics* (degree 1, 2, or 3 features) and of *'Classical' degree 0 forms used* (Middle Egyptian forms) has been established, and a further *General dialectal features* rubric added in order to summarize the results of the two preceding rubrics, assigning a degree of Neo-Egyptian to the entire texteme. The method used consists of (a) classifying the forms encountered in a texteme in the *'Classical' degree* 0 or *Neo-Egyptian* categories, (b) determining the general dialectal features of the texteme on a scale between absolute conservatism (degree 0) and a new system *vis-à-vis* Middle Egyptian (degree 3). This second step is achieved by considering the global nature of the Middle Egyptian *cum* Neo-Egyptian blend, not the number of forms in each category: degree 1 for a classical base with lexical, morphologic, or orthographic adaptations, degree 2 for a classical base with adaptations and new forms, degree 3 for a different *état de langue*. For example, in the case of a texteme constituted by some Middle Egyptian constructions, morphologic New Kingdom adaptations of Middle Egyptian forms, and a few new Neo-Egyptian forms, the texteme would be qualified as degree 2 Neo-Egyptian in the *General dialectal features* rubric. On the other hand, the absence of new syntactic forms would induce a degree 1 Neo-Egyptian[97].

Note that the progression from degree 0 to 3 is not simply a matter of chronology, but of genre and register also. The use of specific forms belonging to a particular degree is conditioned by the purpose of the texts and corresponds to a deliberate strategy[98]. The language of any Neo-Egyptian text is the result of a skilful blend of ancient and new, prestigious and expressive, conservative and dynamic modes of expression.

e. Semiotics, cognitive linguistics, and categorization

The theoretical framework of the study of script classifiers (the old-fashioned terminology 'determinatives' does not reflect their classificatory function) is provided by Rosch (1978), her school (Lakoff 1986; Taylor 1989), and Goldwasser's (1995, 1999b, 2002) pioneering studies of the categorization system of Egyptian script. It may not be superfluous to reiterate the theoretical context of this research, already delineated in a previous study of the [INFERIORITY-PERTURBATION] category (David 2000: 31-33). Classifiers in the

95 Forms that will ultimately disappear from Neo-Egyptian written texts and be replaced by other forms; e.g. conjunctive *ḥnʿ ntf sḏm*.

96 Although probably a late 21st dynasty composition (Sass 2002; Schipper 2005), it is usually viewed as representing the final stage of Neo-Egyptian. See Junge (2005: 17-20) concerning the definition of what I call Neo-Egyptian ('Late Egyptian').

97 Note that this is often the case in the pre-material of the Ramesside documents, as it is a nominal construct with a conventional communicative perspective.

98 See Goldwasser (1990, 1991, 1999); Jansen-Winkeln (1995).

hieroglyphic system represent iconic elements having no phonetic value, but assigning lexemes to semantic classes (the hieroglyphic script has other pictograms associated with other values and reading strategies: phonograms or paronomasia devices, logograms or word-signs, and repeaters[99] constituting pictorial tautologies). Classifiers may stand in a taxonomic relation with the lexeme (hierarchical set-inclusion in a superordinate – basic level – subordinate type of system), a schematic (metonymic, contiguity) relation (of the part/whole; stuff/object; container/contained type) or metaphoric (mapping of a conceptual domain in terms of another conceptual domain)[100]. Thus hieroglyphic classifiers reflect a system of knowledge organization and their icons provide the 'politically correct' (reflecting dominant class ideology), conventional *prototype elect* mental images for the category they represent (Goldwasser 2002). In Rosch's cognitive linguistics theory[101], a system of categorization is conceived to provide 'maximum information with least cognitive effort' (principle of cognitive economy) so that 'the perceived world comes as a structured information' (principle of anthropocentricality) in a precise space/time context. In each category, members show various degrees of membership, certain members representing prototypes (best members/examples and cognitive reference points), usually not unique. Most abstract domain superordinate categories have no clear-cut boundaries and their members may entertain several types of relations with the classifier that represents them (see for instance the 'bad bird', David 2000). A semantically complex lexeme usually belongs concomitantly to several categories (double or even quadruple classification). In a previous study (David 2006), the corpus of some fifty Ramesside royal decrees dating from 1300 to 1100 B.C. provided a representative and coherent sample of Ramesside Period official legal terminology and forensic categorization system. The results of the analysis of classifiers made it possible to affirm that lexemes used to designate legal operations or facts, a lexicon not exclusive to the legal register but consistently used in this environment, are categorized by a limited number of classifiers, principally: for [ABSTRACT], for [BINDING], for [COERCION], for [MOTION], for [LEG], for [UNION/DIVISION] and for [INFERIORITY/PERTURBATION]. Each category represents a tentative classification of abstract concepts that is similar to modern legal categorization. The in-depth analysis of the [MOTION] and [LEG] categories classifiers in the legal context (David 2007) revealed some of the metaphorical processes at work (as studied by Lakoff & Johnson 1980) in the conception and representation of ancient Egyptian legal categories, and demonstrated the similarity between ancient Egyptian and modern legal categorization systems[102]. See the table *Occurences of classifiers in the Ramesside private law instruments infra.*

f. Glossary of legal terms used in the book

- *acquets*: 'marital acquisition that is presumed to be community property (…). Property acquired by either spouse during the marriage.' (Garner 2004: 24)

99 Goldwasser (2006: 21-2).
100 Goldwasser (2002: 10-35).
101 Rosch (1978: 28).
102 For modern legal metaphors, see e.g. Winter (1989, 2001) and bibliography in David (2007).

- *adscriptus*: 'added, annexed, or bound by or in writing; enrolled or registered' (Garner 2004: 56); used here for an addition in another hand
- *advancement*: 'payment or gift to an heir (esp. a child) during one's lifetime as an advance share of one's estate, with the intention of reducing or extinguishing or diminishing the heir's claim to the estate under intestacy laws' (Garner 2004: 57); antonym: *exemption from hotchpot*
- *allotment*: 'share or portion of something, such as property previously held in common' (Garner 2004: 83)
- *assertory oath*: 'oath by which one attests to some factual matter' (Garner 2004: 1101)
- *authentic instrument*: writing received 'before a notary public or other public officer' (Garner 2004: 142)
- *authenticate*: 'to render authoritative or authentic, as by attestation or other legal formality'; *authentication*: 'broadly, the act of proving that something (as a document) is true or genuine, esp. so that it may be admitted as evidence' (Garner 2004: 142)
- *bilateral contract*: 'affecting or obligating both parties' (Garner 2004: 172)
- *consensual*: 'created or existing by mutual consent without formalities such as a written document or ceremony' (Garner 2004: 323)
- *consideration*: 'something (such as an act, a forbearance, or a return promise) bargained for and received by a promisor from a promise; that which motivates a person to do something, esp. to engage in a legal act.' (Garner 2004: 324); Roman law: 'Cause d'un contrat, contrepartie' (Dahl 2001: 420)
- *datio in solutum*: 'discharging of an obligation by the giving and acceptance of something other than the thing due' (Garner 2004: 423)
- *deed*: written legal act made between private persons and effecting the transfer of an interest, right or property, or creating an obligation binding on some person(s) (broad sense); concerning the various meanings and uses of *deed*, see Garner (2004: 444-6)
- *descent and distribution rules*: 'the rules by which a decedent's property is passed, whether by intestate succession or by will' (Garner 2004: 477)
- *devolution*: 'the act or an instance of transferring one's rights, duties, or powers to another; the passing of such rights, duties, or powers by transfer or succession' (Garner 2004: 484)
- *disclaimer*: 'renunciation of one's legal right or claim' (Garner 2004: 496)
- *disposition*: 'act of transferring something to another's care or possession, esp. by deed or will' (Garner 2004: 505)
- *donatio inter vivos* (gift): 'voluntary transfer of property to another without compensation' (Garner 2004: 709)
- *donatio mortis causa*: 'gift made in contemplation of the donor's imminent death' 'burdened with a condition imposed by the donor' (Garner 2004: 710, 526)
- *donation-partage*: 'modalité de partage d'ascendant dans laquelle l'ascendant fait donation de ses biens présents et les partage par anticipation entre ses descendants, héritiers présomptifs' (Cornu 2003: 320)
- *essentialia*: 'terms or qualities essential to the existence of a particular right or contract' (Garner 2004: 585)

- *eviction guarantee*: in the continental legal system, 'obligation pour le vendeur de défendre l'acquéreur contre le trouble apporté par autrui à sa possession (...)' (Cornu 2003: 418)
- *external manifestation of will*, in the sense of French *manifestation de volonté*: 'action d'exprimer sa volonté (par écrit, oralement ou même tacitement) en vue d'un effet de droit (...) Ex. le testament, manifestation unilatérale de volonté' (Cornu 2003: 551)
- *fiat*: 'Latin "let it be done"' (Garner 2004: 657)
- *fiduciary bequest (fideicommissary substitution)*: the testator's 'designation of a person to succeed another as beneficiary of an estate' involving the substitution of legatee or heir (Garner 2004: 1471); see also *fideicommissum* (*ibid.*, 657-8). In fact, we are dealing with an *estate in fee tail*, 'An estate that is heritable only by specified descendants of the original grantee' (Garner 2004: 650)
- *general warranty*: 'warranty against the claims of all persons' (Garner 2004: 1618)
- *gift with exemption from hotchpot* (*gift with praecipuum*): the hotchpot is 'the blending of items of property to secure equality of division, esp. (...) in cases in which advancements of an intestate's property must be made up to the estate by a contribution or by an accounting' (Garner 2004: 755); thus a *gift with exemption from hotchpot* is not subject to rules of division. French *donation préciputaire, dispense de rapport*
- *instrument* (*instrumentum*): 'written legal document that defines rights, duties, entitlements, or liabilities' (Garner 2004: 813)
- *manual gift*: 'gift of movable, tangible property, made by delivery without any formalities' (Garner 2004: 710)
- *mass(-asset)*: 'intangible asset (...) that is made up of several components but that is considered a single entity' (Garner 2004: 126)
- *mutual assent*: 'agreement by both parties to a contract, usu. in the form of offer and acceptance' (Garner 2004: 124)
- *negotium*: legal matter, transaction
- *no-contest (in terrorem) clause*: 'provision designed to threaten one into action or inaction; esp., a testamentary provision that threatens to dispossess any beneficiary who challenges the terms of the will' Garner (2004: 1073)
- *notification*: 'formal announcement of a legally relevant fact, action, or intent' (Garner 2004: 1093)
- *operative part*: 'part of a legal instrument that gives effect to the transaction involved' (Garner 2004: 1124)
- *partage d'ascendant*: 'transaction by which an ascendant himself distributes [part of all of] his estate among his descendants, determining the shares of each. It can be done in the form of an *inter vivos* donation, or by will.' (Dahl 2001: 241)
- *partition*: 'act of dividing; esp., the division of real property held jointly or in common by two or more persons into individually owned interests' (Garner 2004: 1151)
- *promissory oath*: 'binds the party to observe a specified course of conduct in the future' (Garner 2004: 1101)
- *property settlement*: 'judgment in a divorce case' or 'contract' that 'divides up the assets of divorcing spouses' (Garner 2004: 1255)
- *quittance*: 'release or discharge from a debt or obligation' (Garner 2004: 1283)

- *real contract*: 'a contract requiring something more than mere consent, such as the lending of money or handing over a thing', (Garner 2004: 347)
- *recital*: 'preliminary statement in a contract or deed explaining the reasons for entering into it or the background of the transaction, or showing the existence of particular facts'; it is 'dealing with matters such as how the buyer and the seller came together' in sales contracts (Garner 2004 : 1298)
- *synallagmatic*: 'contract in which the parties obligate themselves reciprocally, so that the obligation of each party is correlative to the obligation of the other' (Garner 2004: 349)
- *title deed*: 'deed that evidences a person's legal ownership of property' (Garner 2004: 446)
- *tradition* (*traditio*): 'delivery of an item or an estate' (Garner 2004: 1534)
- *ususfruct*: 'right to use and enjoy the fruits of another's property for a period without damaging or diminishing it' (Garner 2004: 1580)
- *waiver*: 'voluntary relinquishment or abandonment – expressed or implied – of a legal right or advantage' (Garner 2004: 1611)

Part One: Wills, gifts, and partitions

I. The corpus

a. Wills and gifts

1. ***oDeM* 108** (19th dynasty, Seti I)
2. ***oGardiner/Ashmolean* 90** (19th dynasty, Ramesses II)
3. ***oGardiner/Ashmolean* 55** (19th-20th dynasty, Ramesses II-III)
4. ***oGardiner/Ashmolean* 272** (20th dynasty, Ramesses III)
5. ***pAshmolean Museum* 1945.97 & 1945.95, *pDeM* 23 & 25** (*Naunakhte*) (20th dynasty, Ramesses V)
6. ***pBoulaq* 10 = *pCairo* CG 58092** (20th dynasty, Ramesses VI)
7. ***oPetrie* 18** (20th dynasty, Ramesses VII)
8. ***pAshmolean Museum* 1945.96** (*pAdoptions*) (20th dynasty, Ramesses XI)
9. ***pTurin* 2021 r° & *pGeneva* D 409** (20th dynasty, Ramesses XI)
10. Elliptic records of movable assets: (social) gifts or else?

In an attempt to be exhaustive, we must add various texts dealing with private transmissions of movable assets (mainly consumables) within the scope of Janssen's work on gifts (1982, 1997: 55-86), with the additions made by Grandet (2003). Generally simple, brief notes called *memoranda* by Grandet, they are to be understood in a larger context of reciprocal gift exchanges for Janssen, whereby 'these were no free manifestation of frienship and love, they were socially obligatory'[103]. If we agree with his view (exchange with postponed *consideration*), we should not be concerned with these texts in this part of our work, as one of the essential elements of *donatio* is the absence of consideration, its gratuitous quality. Furthermore, most of them are *a posteriori* brief records, not legal deeds, and as such do not belong to the *consentient genre*. As we shall see, these documents are often fragmentary or especially elliptic, their context and nature are unclear in the absence of extra-textual information, and they might represent payments of undisclosed services or goods, regular maintenance allowances, administrative supplies, or even true gifts without *consideration* (the use of the omnipresent verb *rdi* to express any kind of transmission does nothing to help unravel the mystery). The picture of the *gifts* category would be incomplete should these texts escape reassessment; thus, these documents, following the non-exhaustive list suggested by Janssen and Grandet, are treated separately.

Related documents:

- ***oGardiner/Ashmolean* 63** (20th dynasty, Ramesses IX), **178** (20th dynasty, Ramesses IV?)
- ***oBerlin* P 10631** (20th dynasty), **12406 & *oGlasgow* D 1925.71** (20th dynasty, Ramesses III-VI), **14328** (20th dynasty, Ramesses IV)
- *oCairo* CG 25583, **25624 & 25365** (20th dynasty, Ramesses III), **25650** (20th dynasty, Ramesses IV), **25660 & JE 37649** (20th dynasty, Ramesses IV)

---

103 Janssen (1997: 256).

- ***oDeM* 134** (20th dynasty, Ramesses III-IV), **222** (20th dynasty, Ramesses III), **282** (20th dynasty, Ramesses IV), **643** (20th dynasty, Ramesses III-IV), **666** (20th dynasty, Ramesses III), **934-948** (19-20th dynasties), **952** (?)
- ***oFaulkner* 1** (20th dynasty, Ramesses IV?)
- ***oGlasgow* D 1925.66** (19th-20th dynasties), **1925.76 & *oGardiner/Ashmolean* 52** (20th dynasty, Ramesses III)
- ***oLouvre* E 3262b,f,g** (20th dynasty, Ramesses III)
- ***oMichaelides* 48 r°** (19th dynasty, Ramesses II?)
- ***oOIC* 17005** (19th dynasty)
- ***oPetrie* 31** (20th dynasty, Ramesses III-IV)
- ***oPrague* H 24** (20th dynasty?)
- ***oQueen's College Oxford* 1115** (20th dynasty, Ramesses IV)
- ***oTurin* 57010** (20th dynasty, Ramesses III)
- ***pDeM* 11** (20th dynasty, Ramesses V).

b. Partitions

Partitions of assets may result from several types of situation:
- a donor/testator may assign ownership rights to beneficiaries by distributing distinct assets in a *partage d'ascendant* (see *supra* for this notion; e.g. *oDeM* 108);
- if the partition is not automatic, heirs can request the division of the joint property consisting of inherited assets in order to take possession of their share in severalty (although such a demand does not appear explicitly in Ramesside documents, some partitions may have been the result of such a procedure, e.g. *oGardiner/Ashmolean* 223, probably a petition for partition before the oracle; for the Ptolemaic period, see *pMattha*, col. VIII);
- a couple's separation (by death or '*consensual*') results in the partition of the community property (see e.g. the *recital* of *pTurin* 2021 r° & *pGeneva* D 409), possibly in conformity with a legal provision or custom that defines the proportion of assets attributed to both of them.

These are situations leading to settlements with regard to partitions of rights, in which a decision is made concerning attributions of shares. The execution of such settlements by distributing material *allotments* of property among the entitled beneficiaries, sometimes after an inventory of the assets of the deceased (e.g. *oGardiner/Ashmolean* 36) is also called a partition; in the sources, one must try to distinguish between the decisions attributing or confirming rights and the physical transfer of the assets. Of course, documents recording the material execution of partitions in the context of succession[104] are not by themselves private law deeds, they do not belong to the *consentient genre*, but are included in our analysis in order to complete the picture presented by the wills/gifts corpus. We may assume that some of the documents listed below constitute attachments to lost wills. Also belonging to this list are *pDeM* 23 & 25 (*Naunakhte*) and the last part of *pBoulaq* 10 (see *supra*).

1. ***oGardiner/Ashmolean* 89** (19th dynasty, Ramesses II)
2. ***oLouvre* E 13156** (*oLouvre* E 2425, *oAnastasi*) (19th dynasty, Ramesses II)

104 Partitions resulting from a couple's separation have not been taken into consideration as it is not clear if the patrimonial division was a product of one of the parties' unilateral decision, of a mutual agreement or public settlement, or of the application of legal dispositions or customs.

3. ***oDeM* 112 & 964** (20th dynasty, Ramesses III-IV)
4. ***oBerlin* P 12636 v°** (20th dynasty, Ramesses III)
5. ***oDeM* 586** (20th dynasty, Ramesses III-IV)
6. ***pDeM* 30** (20th dynasty, Ramesses III-IV)
7. ***pTurin* 2070** (20th dynasty, Ramesses VI-IX)
8. ***pTurin* 1885 v°** (20th dynasty, Ramesses VI-VII)

Some texts have been excluded from the corpus as they were probably not concerned with wills, gifts, and the ensuing private divisions of assets (e.g. *oDeM* 231 and 434, *pTurin* 1880 v° 5,2-6,5, although they include the lexeme *pš*)[105]; other documents, too fragmentary for study, were impossible to analyze with pertinent results (e.g. *oGardiner/Ashmolean* 254, albeit using the lexeme *pš*; the lower inscription in *S3mwt*'s tomb, a private endowment for the domain of a goddess, but the readable and relevant fragments are mentioned in our text).

II. Wills, gifts, and partitions in other periods

In order to examine our corpus in a diachronic perspective, a list of texts from the preceding periods belonging to the consentient legal genre has been established, even though some of them are embedded in other genres belonging to the general textual program of tombs. To the autobiography of the tomb's owner may be added, for instance, royal epistolary decrees addressed to the owner, precisions concerning the origin of the man's wealth, testamentary provisions and gifts *inter vivos* made by him, as well as funerary foundation acts/contracts organizing the assets and personnel assigned to the man's cult. Private funerary foundation acts represent both unilateral *dispositions mortis causa* (although not tranferring the ownership of assets to heirs) and contractual agreements with priests for the cultic service; they can be viewed as trusts. During the Old Kingdom, most were established established by an *wḏt-mdt m r3.f* (verbal decree) of the tomb's owner in a fashion and format similar to a royal decree, a unilateral expression of will before witnesses; an *ỉmyt-pr* may also be mentioned (see *infra*). Although legal heirs may be chosen as *k3*-priests of the funerary cult or supervisors of the trust,

105 The case of *oGardiner/Ashmolean* 157 has also been omitted as it consists of an inventory of the 'amount of assets of (the) workman *Nḫtmini* that are in his house after he repudia[ted] *Wʿbti*, his former woman', thus resulting in the couple's separation and partition of assets, with incidental remarks about a few items that he gave to at least two men, probably his sons.
oDeM 764 has also been excluded from our corpus as it consists of brief division guidelines (by a court, oracle, private person or authority?) probably in the context of a couple's separation, following the division key 2/3 – 1/3 for the man and the woman with assets given at the time of the separation to the children as in *pTurin* 2021 and *oGardiner/Ashmolean* 157. The brief text reads: (1) *ỉr wn n3 ʿḏ3w* (2) *šriw ỉr n3 ḫt m* 3 *dnỉt wʿt* (3) *n n3 ʿḏ3w wʿt n p3 ʿḥ3wty wʿt* (4) [*n*] *t3 st-ḥmt ḫr ỉr wn ỉw.f r ỉrt* (5) *ḫrt n n3 ʿḏ3w ỉm n.f p3 rwy* (6) *3ḫt nb ỉw p3 r*-3 *n t3 st-* (7) *ḥmt* 'Should the children be infants, make (= divide) the assets into 3 shares: one for the children, one for the man, one [for] the woman; and if he will look after the children, give him the 2/3 of all assets, while the 1/3 is for the woman'. For Grandet (2000: 6-7), it is the draft of a will; the problem of qualifying it as a will is of course the very general and laconic redaction and the use of the imperative (no other example of the imperative appears in our corpus), and also the fact that in case of a will, the beneficiaries cannot be the testator, his companion and their children. Grandet believes that the man and the woman mentioned are elder children of the testator, but then the formulation is rather strange and without parallel; furthermore his contention that 'l'homme était contraint de s'occuper des enfants sous peine de perdre non seulement l'usufruit de leur part mais encore sa propre part d'héritage' whereas the woman's share remained 'inaliénable' cannot be confirmed by any other Ramesside document. See Toivari-Viitala (2003: 96); Eyre (2007: 230) : 'it is unclear whether it represents some general statement of law and custom at the dissolution of a marriage, or the specific resolution of an individual case.'

and testamentary provisions in favor of heirs and contracts with priests may be added in the same textual environment, the distinction between these categories is often blurred in a rather intricate way. Thus the same texts may be involved both in the chapter on wills, gifts and partitions and in the chapter on contracts *infra*.

Wills or gifts briefly mentioned in documents belonging to other genres were not taken in consideration (e.g. *Mṯn*'s autobiography; *Bbi*'s *stela Leiden* V 88; *pBrooklyn* 35.1446 v° Text B, the transcript of an official inquiry concerning testamentary provisions[106]). *S3b3stt*'s *stelaphorous statue Louvre* E 11673 (18th dynasty) inscribed with a testamentary disposition for Théodoridès (1965: 123 ff.) is unfortunately too damaged to decide if it should be included. This list may not be exhaustive, and if this meager collection is all that has survived, it may only constitute an indication for these periods:

a. Old Kingdom
- *Nk3wrᶜ tomb* (4th dynasty)
- *Nkᶜnḫ tomb* (5th dynasty)
- *Wpmnfrt tomb* (5th dynasty)
- *Ṯnti tomb* (6th dynasty)
- *Ꞽdw tomb* (6th dynasty)
- *Balat tablet* 5955 (6th dynasty)
- *Balat tablet* 3689-7, 8 & 11 (6th dynasty)

b. Middle Kingdom
- *pKahun* VII.1 = *pUC* 32037 (12th dynasty)
- *pKahun* I.1 = *pUC* 32058 (12th dynasty)

c. New Kingdom
- *Snims stela Cairo* CG 34016 (18th dynasty)

Concerning later periods, relevant comparisons with *abnormal hieratic* and Demotic material are discussed in our text. Demotic testamentary dispositions are conveyed by donation deeds, clauses of marriage contracts, divisions of property, and documents of sale[107]; Demotic partition records are well documented[108].

106 Théodoridès (1960: esp. 105-7).

107 See Martin (1995: 59-60); Clarysse (1995: 96-8); Manning (2003: 835); Malinine (1967) considers *pMoscow* 123 as a true testament, but in Clarysse's opinion it is in the form of a donation that will be valid after the death of the disponor.

108 See Depauw (1994: 43-5) for general remarks concerning Demotic donations, wills, and divisions.

III. Textual analysis

A. Wills and gifts

1. *oDeM* 108

Date: 19th dynasty, Seti I
Hieroglyphic version: *KRI* I, 409 n.8
Instrument:

* **state** – damaged

* **value – excerpt**[109]**?**: limestone ostracon, brief essential information, incomplete (absence of title deed and *recital*, minimalistic colophon, unnamed forum/witnesses/scribe, absence of warranty against claims, or submission and sealing by the vizier or other official procedure related to the *imyt-pr*).

* **nature – main provisions of an *imyt-pr*** (internal characterization), concerns legal rights to assets. In our corpus – aside from *pBN* 237, carton 1 (transverse line 21)[110] – it is the sole case of an *imyt-pr* instrument; the 18th dynasty royal guidelines to the vizier *Rekhmire* state that such a document had to be submitted to and sealed by the vizier (*Urk*. IV, 1111, 6 *inn.t(w) n.f imyt-pr nb ntf ḫtm st*)[111].

* **genre – consentient legal**: formulaic style, ordered layout; business hand, minor errors, absence of corrections or business practice diacritical marks; concerns private interests; found together with various 'administrative'[112] ostraca of the same period in courtyards 1214-1215, the location of the *Trou Schiaparelli*, close to the northern votive chapels, 'provenant probablement d'un magasin de la nécropole situé en ce lieu ou dans ses parages'[113]; delocutive textemes (and locutive reference), degree 1 Neo-Egyptian features, fully dated and with archaic anaphora, named testator/beneficiaries.

Donker van Heel & Haring (2003: 89, 121) suggest that the ostracon may have belonged to *P3šd* personally, 'a reminder of his decision' (but we must note that it cannot be a simple memo scribbled by the testator to remind himself of the dispositions he made, due to the formalism of the text) or 'the actual *imyt-pr*' (but it is too incomplete to be taken as such).

Legal step: **external manifestation of will** (with performative) concerning movable assets transmission (*rdit ḫt*) before witnesses (probably the court for Allam 1973b: 43; in this case the court acted as notary producing an authenticated document).

Legal issue: **will**: absence of *consideration*, unilateral deed, presence of *descent and distribution* rules expressed in the future and using the lexeme *psš*, concerning the

109 For Seidl (1957: 23 'Entwurf zu einer Hausurkunde'), Kitchen (*RITANC* I, 300), and Bierbrier (1975: 25), it may be a *draft will* by *P3šd*. Nevertheless, it is highly improbable that an *imyt-pr* was drafted by the testator himself.

110 The papyrus is part of a necropolis journal, of unknown provenance, damaged, and probably a palimpsest, dating to the 20th dynasty reign of Ramesses VI. The transverse line that seems unrelated to the distribution of grain rations and a visit to a god mentioned in the rest of the papyrus is the following: [*ʿwtyw*] *imy-prw ir.n ni-swt* [...] *n 3ḫttw.f nb nt*[...] '[deeds] of transfer that did the royal [...] of all his assets tha[t...].' Helck (2002: 448) reconstructs the line as 'Akte des Testaments, das der kgl. [...] gemacht hat über alle seine Sachen, die [ihm] König *Nb*[*-m3ʿt-*]*Rʿ*[*-mrj-Jmn* gegeben hatte?]'. Following Černý (1952: 29, n. 154), the Leiden Deir el-Medina database and Donker van Heel & Haring (2003: 89, 121) propose viewing it as a docket concerning an oracle of *Imnḥtp* I approving a will.

111 See Théodoridès (1962: 87); Donker van Heel & Haring (2003: 88).

112 Haring (2006: 109, n.25).

113 Bruyère (1930: 27-30).

transmission of the entire patrimony[114] of the testator (*ḫt{t} nb*), the beneficiaries being the testator's children, including a list of specific bequests using performative forms. Théodoridès (1970: 178) notes that the *ỉmyt-pr* functions as a *partage d'ascendant* (see *supra* for this notion).

Textemic features:

1. Pre-material

The pre-material texteme[115] is identificative and as such provides essential information concerning the date of the procedure, object, testator (name and mention of his occupation), instrument, and beneficiaries, thus presenting the macrosyntactic topic of the document[116].

The focus of this exposition texteme[117] is informational[118] (high noun frequency, careful integration of information using infinitives, prepositional phrases for packing information), without involvement on a personal level (delocutive exposition); it is not narrative, involves no nexus, no finite forms, not marked in terms of tense and aspect; it favors maximal detachment of context (situation-independent)[119] and elaborate, explicit reference (full dating, anaphoric cohesive reference to the date, proper names); the texteme is non argumentative, but authoritative (maximum of *high dialect* forms with archaic texture, classical binomials) and formulaic; it results in a careful, official production.

Date: (1) [*rnpt-sp ? ꜣbd*] 2 [… *sw*] 10 [*ẖ*]*r ḥm n ni-swt bity Mn*[*mꜣꜥt*]*rꜥ* [*ꜥ.w.s*…]
[Year ?, month] 2 [of … season, day] 10, [un]der (the) majesty of (the) King of Upper and Lower Egypt *Mn*[*mꜣꜥt*]*rꜥ* [L.P.H…]

archaic anaphora: (2) […*m*?] *hrw pn*	[…on?] this day
Title:	
object: *n rdỉt ḫt.f*	of transmitting his assets
testator: *ỉn wꜥw*[120] *n ỉst Pꜣ*[*š*]*dw*	by (the) member of (the) Gang *Pꜣ*[*š*]*dw*
instrument: (3) [… *ḥr*] *ỉrt n.f ỉmyt*[121]*-pr*	[… by] making on his behalf an *ỉmyt-pr*
beneficiaries: (*n*) *nꜣ.f ẖrdw*	(for the benefit of) his children.

114 For Allam (1983: 22, 32), the document also organizes the transfer of an abstract right (the apportioning of the grain allowance).

115 For the pre-material of the Ramesside royal decrees, see David (2006: 18-9).

116 Similarily, in ancient Anglo-Saxon wills, the three-part structure of the will is headed by the *notificatio* that 'introduces the testator, states his/her purpose or the function of the document itself, and very often cites the authority backing the will.' (Danet & Bogoch 1994: 116).

117 Concerning the exposition as the introduction of a narrative, see Weinrich (1973: 114-5); Prince (1987: 28) and his references; in our case the exposition texteme is also followed by a narrative, the *recital*.

118 Concerning dimensions of register variation, see Biber (1995). Textemic variation may be assessed in a similar way, the smaller textual units (textemes or *subregisters* in Biber's terminology) presenting distinctive systems of grammar with specific combinations of linguistic features (lexical, syntactical, etc.) functionally and conventionally associated with the situational parameters established in our Introduction *supra*. For an example of co-occurrence patterns of linguistic features reflecting shared function, thus underlying dimensions of register variation in English, see Biber (1995: 141-69).

119 The pre-material is self-sufficient and does not necessitate personal knowledge of the specific conditions of reception of the text for its comprehension.

120 Literally 'soldier of the gang' (Černý 2001: 112) as crews are named and organized on the model of army/navy gangs.

121 For the presence of the feminine marker, see Wimmer (1995: 80).

* Neo-Egyptian characteristics:
- (*n*) *nꜣ.f ẖrdw*: preposition omission, a characteristic of Neo-Egyptian registers (it may be a case of haplography);
- use of the Neo-Egyptian possessive determinator for kinship (*nꜣ.f ẖrdw*), see the references in David (2006: 60);

* 'Classical' degree 0 forms used:
- date full format, but presenting only part of the royal titulary # year + month + day + *ḫr ḥm n ni-swt bity* + PN (prepositional phrase, adnominal expansion of the date) #. It is the most complete date on an ostracon in our corpus of wills and gifts. Compare with *Naunakhte* for an example of full dating with longer titulary on papyrus.
  For an analysis of the composite classical date format using 'serial numbers' (albeit in ptolemaic sacerdotal decrees), see Simpson (1996: 83-5);
- presence of relator *n*: *ḥm n ni-swt bity* (subject relation); *wꜥw n ist* (part/whole relation); *hrw pn n rdit* (explicit temporal relation). For discussion of the inexistence of a **pnn* form, see David (2006: 224-5);
- proximal archaic anaphora *hrw pn* (+ relational expansion *n rdit ḫt.f*), *pn* being used at this linguistic stage with limited lexemic constituency. We observe two constructions in our corpus: # *hrw pn sḏm* # as in *pAdoptions*, or with the relator # *hrw pn n sḏm* # as in *oDeM* 108 and *Naunakhte*; the form following *hrw pn* (*n*) is thus the infinitive, and the heading formula is Classical Middle Egyptian, as are most headings[122]. The use of *hrw pn* (*n*) implies the nominalization of the verb following it and the actor in the transmission is introduced by the preposition *in*; the anaphora thus contributes to the process that leads to an abstract and compact mode of expression on top of referential cohesion. Note that in our corpus, temporal reference is far more pervasive than spatial reference to the forum before which the procedure is performed.
  For a similar use of archaic anaphora in the Ramesside royal decrees, see David (2006: 19, 34). As for the general use of *hrw pn* following the date in legal documents, Megally (1977: 64-5) notes that it becomes frequent after the 18th dynasty, attributable to the fact that 'la date est enregistrée plus ou moins *in extenso*, ce qui l'isole dans un sens de la suite des données et nécessite qu'elle soit reprise par cette expression elliptique.' For the combination of # date + *hrw pn* # in headings of various Deir el-Medina documents, see Donker van Heel & Haring (2003: 124-78). For the formula # *hrw/hꜣ pn ḏd* # in the pre-material of abnormal hieratic contractual provisions of the 25th-26th dynasties, see Malinine (1953: 8-9).
  In our corpus of wills, the archaic anaphora always follows the date, but is absent after the date in *oGardiner/Ashmolean* 272 (gift), and most partition records (except for *pTurin* 1885). Janssen (2005: 108) contends that the presence or absence of the archaic anaphora is not significant in the corpus of Deir el-Medina ostraca dealing with donkeys. Haring (2003b: 253) notes globally that 'uniformity [of headings] generally developed at a later date in the recording of private and judicial matters than in collective administration' in Deir el-Medina, but this may be due to the relative scarcity of 19th dynasty documents of this type found in the site. He also acknowledges[123] that the degree of uniformity of the headings is somewhat lower than suggested by his tables.
  The date is an important feature of modern wills, essentially because they are revocable deeds, which also seems to have been the case in ancient Egypt (see for instance the

122 See Haring (2003b: 253) for Deir el-Medina practice.
123 *Ibid.*, pp. 254-5.

revocation of an *imyt-pr* by another *imyt-pr* specifically mentioned in *pKahun* VII.1). It is important to note that archaic reference devices are also used in modern wills[124] as they are in other legal genres (David 2006: 34). A precise date, a reference highlighting the importance of this date, and archaism are all formulaic devices adding to the authority of the procedure, and also to the document recording this legal action. Thus the archaic anaphora should not be taken as a 'neutral' element, even in the case of short notes regarding donkey transactions, as its presence or absence in combination with other factors may imply different textual genres (see our suggestions *infra*, in the *Contract-related records* chapter).

Concerning the format of the pre-material of the *imyt-pr* outside the Ramesside period, one may note differences in the pre-material, and especially the title, of the *imyt-pr* on the *Stèle juridique de Karnak* JE 52453 (17th dynasty), line 4: # date + *imyt-pr irt.n* N PN *n* N PN #. Of course, the *Stèle* is the lapidary and ornate version of a legal file and not only of the *imyt-pr* that represents, in this case, an onerous transfer with an operative part rather different from the provisions of a will. The *imyt-pr* of *Snims*' *Stela Cairo* CG 34016 (18th dynasty) is introduced by the following formula: # date + *ḥr ḥm n* + royal titulary + *imyt-pr* [*irt.n*] N PN *n ḥmt.f* [*ẖrdw.f imy*] *rnw.f iry* + list of relatives' names #; unfortunately, what follows is badly damaged and it is not clear if it constitutes a *recital* or the operative part of the *imyt-pr*[125]. Here the archaic anaphora is used in the colophon (*Urk*. IV, 1070 l. 9): [*ḫtm*/*irw*?] *in ḫ3 n ṯ3t* [*m*] *hrw pn m-b3ḥ* (...).

As in earlier periods, the only text designated as an *imyt-pr* during the Old Kingdom is *Nbk3wḥr*'s (*imyt-pr tn*); it is headed by # PN *ir.f wḏt-mdt* #[126], concerns the funerary foundation, but does not contain testamentary dispositions in favor of the heirs. In terms of linguistic comparison, it is thus of no relevance to our *oDeM* 108;

- gender marked infinitive *irt*;
- *irt n.f:* the preposition *n* with suffix is co-referential with the agent (Hintze 1950: 81-91, although his use of '*dativus*' – *ethicus* or *reflexivus* – is inappropriate for a language that ignores *casi*);

* General dialectal features: degree 1.

* Legal formula: year + month of season + day + *ḥr ḥm n* + royal titulary (date) + *hrw pn* + *n* + infinitive (object) + *in* (testator: occupation and PN) + [*ḥr*] *irt n.f* + instrument + beneficiaries.

2. Operative part

These are the legal provisions, 'the part of a legal instrument that gives effect to the transaction involved.'[127]. The main provisions of the document concern the general mode of distribution of the assets (*descent and distribution*) and the attribution of specific assets to named legatees (French *partage d'ascendant*). Note the absence of a *recital* before the operative part, and of a report form introducing the main provisions of the will as a binding speech act. Nevertheless, the specific bequests are expressed with locutive reference after an impersonal and general rule of distribution.

---

124 Kurzon (1986: 53-4).

125 See also Théodoridès (1970: 148 ff.) who believes that there are two deeds involved in this section of the stela.

126 Concerning the relation between an *imyt-pr* and a *wḏt-mdt*, see Goedicke (1970: 199), Théodoridès (1971) and Mrsich (2005: 236).

127 Garner (2004: 1124).

This texteme again reflects an informational focus (impersonal/unspecified referent of *iw.w psš* of agentless passive value, informative monologue with locutive reference, high frequency of nouns in a topicalized structure signaling a new texteme and for clarity), minimal personal involvement (locutive possessive suffixes), structured format; non-narrative discourse using future and performative forms; rather referentially explicit (phrasal and clause initial coordination, proper names, relative clause); non argumentative; abstract style (agentless passive, prominence of the inanimate object of the bequests); authoritative (maximum of high dialect forms), non spontaneous, isotopic, and formulaic.

***Descent and distribution* rule**: *iry ḫt{t} nb iw.w psš.w* (4) [*m-m m*]*sw nb*
As for all assets, they will divide them [among] all [desc]endants.
***Disposition* of specific bequests**:
iry nꜣy.i ḫꜣrw nꜣy.i ḏꜣnḏꜣr msti (5) [*iw.w*] *n Ỉmn*(*ms*)
As for my copper tools, my woodwork baskets, [they belong] to *Ỉmn*(*ms*);
ḫr iry šꜣmḫꜣbwy m-mitt nꜣ n šꜣmw n ḏꜣrt (6) *iw.w n Nfrmsnwt*
And as for (the) *šꜣmḫꜣbwy*-vessel as well as the wooden *šꜣmw*, they belong to *Nfrmsnwt*;
ḫr ir pꜣ wpy n tꜣ Ḥnwt iw.f (7) (*n*) *Nwbtmšꜣs*
And as for the festival portion of the Mistress[128], it belongs (to) *Nwbtmšꜣs*;
ḫr ir pꜣ di ir n.i ꜣst ḥsb (8) *n Mḫꜣib*
And as for the grain allowance that *ꜣst* made for me, (the) balance belongs to *Mḫꜣib*;
(Verso 1) *ḫ*[*r*] *mni* 2 *n Ḥḥnḫ*
An[d] (the) 2 mooring posts belong to *Ḥḥnḫ*;
[*ḫ*]*r* (v. 2) *ꜥnḫ rhdt* 1 *ḥnw* (v. 3) *nb n wꜣḏw iw.w* (v. 4) *n ꜣst*
[A]nd (the) mirror, 1 frying-pan[129], all items of green stone, they belong to *ꜣst*.

* Neo-Egyptian characteristics:
- spelling (*iry, ḫtt, mni*);
- absence of concord of *nb* (*ḫt{t} nb; [m]sw nb; ḥnw nb*);
- preposition omission (*iw.w psš.w; iw.f* (*n*) *Nwbtmšꜣs* may be a case of haplography);
- use of the Neo-Egyptian possessive determinator for material ownership (*nꜣy.i ḫꜣrw*, etc.);
- Neo-Egyptian lexemes (*ḫꜣrw, msti, šꜣmḫꜣbwy, šꜣmw;* for *ḏꜣnḏꜣr*, see Hoch 1994: 389-91 'may be related to the Semitic root *zll*');
- Neo-Egyptian delocutive plural suffix (*iw.w, psš.w*);
- cataphoric articloid (*pꜣ wpy, pꜣ di*). Concerning *articloids*, see *supra* the basic glossary of syntactic terms and David (2006: 35-6);
- *šꜣmḫꜣbwy m-mitt nꜣ n šꜣmw n ḏꜣrt*: coordinator *m-mitt* between topicalized nouns, the first one not determined, the second determined. This placement of the coordinating *m-mitt* is mostly attested during the New Kingdom; in predated examples, the coordinator follows both nouns (*Hatnub graffiti* 23, line 7 and 24, line 11). For an extensive repetition of the coordinator in the operative part of a will, see *Naunakhte*;
- exophoric articloid (extratextual deixis, context-dependent) for a specific goddess in the Deir el-Medina community (*tꜣ Ḥnwt*);

* 'Classical' degree 0 forms used:

128 See *RITANC* I, 300 for possible identifications of the goddess.
129 Janssen (1975: 425).

- relator *n* with plural articloid (*n3 n*); in 'religious dedication' relation[130] (*p3 wpy n t3 Ḥnwt*); in material relation (*š3mw n ḏʿrt; ḥnw nb n w3ḏw*);
- *descent and distribution* rule constructed with # *iry* (topicalizer) + N (topicalized assets[131]) + *iw.w psš.w* (future, object with plural reference to a collective feminine *ḫt nb*) #.
  Of course the future is conjectural as the preposition has been omitted (Neo-Egyptian feature), but it is used in the provision that establishes the division mode since the partition is meant to take effect upon the testator's death (see *Naunakhte*, lines III.8 and IV 2 *iw.st r h3y ḥr pšt* and *bn iw.w r ʿḳ r pšt*). As there is usually no mention of this event, the use of the future is the sole indication of a *mortis causa* act[132]. The preposition is also omitted in the *descent and distribution* rule of *pAdoptions* v.8.
  Although the same formula (topicalization + future) is used in other documents, the lexemic component is not always identical: *psš* and *sw3ḏ*[133] in *pAdoptions*; *ʿḳ r psšt* and *di in Naunakhte*. Preserved wills from earlier periods do not record a future *descent and distribution* rule (e.g. *pKahun* VII.1 and I.1 are concerned with a unique legatee, so that a future partition need not be taken into account).
  The use of the characteristic casuistic-logic formula with general scope is familiar in legal documents (for Ramesside royal decrees, see David 2006: 57-9); the construction consisting of # topicalization of assets + future # emphasizes the centrality of the inanimate object of the disposition in the legal text, the future implying a necessary distribution but in an indeterminate future. Topicalization marks the beginning of the new texteme of the operative part and also clearly itemizes the entries of the list and specifies them. Note that the formula # topicalized heirs + positive/negative future # is used in the consentient genre to express a retributive principle[134] or a disinheritance rule[135];
- specific bequests list constructed with topicalized objects of the bequest followed by an adverbial attribution of ownership right: # *ir(y)* (topicalizer) + N (items) + *iw.w*/N *n* PN #. Note the absence of topicalization in the case of *ḫ[r] mni* 2 *n Ḥḥnḫ*, and the absence of *iw.f* (N *n* PN) in lines 7-8 and verso 1.
  The adverbial nexus expresses a constitutive act, the attribution of ownership rights in specific (and general[136]) bequests when in the dispositive texteme of a will. It represents an implicit performative in this context[137], although *iw.f n* N is generally interpreted as a future form[138]. For Shisha-Halevy[139], it is a predicative possession that

130 Simpson (1996: 69), concerning Ptolemaic sacerdotal decrees.

131 Universalities (*ḫt{t} nb, ḥnw nb n w3ḏw*) or items specified by their marking as topic.

132 But see *Snims stela Cairo* CG 34016 concerning a will in the form of an *imyt-pr*: the testator mentions in a rather damaged section *ḥnʿ p3.i hrw* [*n ʿnḫ*] 'with my day (= time) [of life]', and concerning his companion *m p3.s hrw n ʿnḫ* 'in her day (= time) of life' in contrast with the dispositions concerning the situation after her death.

133 This lexeme is used in a general bequest, not in a *descent and distribution* rule.

134 *Naunakhte* Doc. I, lines II.6-7, *infra*.

135 *Naunakhte* Doc. I, lines IV. 7-12, *infra*.

136 See *oPetrie* 18 *infra*.

137 See *infra oGardiner/Ashmolean*55 and *Naunakhte*'s Doc. IV, line 3 for the use of the same construction, albeit in other textemes, in the context of a recognition of rights, not their attribution, thus not expressing performativity.

138 For instance by Satzinger (1976: 198-9) 'Der Adverbialsatz des Futurums' 'In testamentartigen Verfügungen', but he translates *iw.f n.f* as 'es soll ihm gehören', a deontic modality; see also Winand (1996: 128ff.) 'constructions analogiques du futur III'.

139 (1978: 60-1, n.35). See also Shisha-Halevy (2007b: 248).

is excluded from his discussion of the nature of the extraposed noun followed by *ỉw.f* + adverb. The use of an adverbial nexus with prepositional rheme as performative is certainly not an isolated case in Egyptian: see *infra ỉw.f ẖry* 100 *n sẖ* (penalty apodosis in oaths); *ỉw.f m-s3* PN in curses (see royal decrees).

Performative speech acts (Austin 1962) are about statement and performance, as uttering a performative is *doing things with words* (as opposed to true or false *constative* speech acts). Obvious are *explicit* performatives of the type 'I promise,' 'I do,' 'I swear,' 'I bet,' or 'I hereby bequeath,' ritual words formally required, but there are also *implicit* performatives that do not have the same form[140]. It has been contended that any utterance eventually has a 'performative flavor'[141]; the question is certainly one of context and of performativity gradation (concerning these questions and relevant bibliography, see David 2006: 39-40; for explicit performatives in our corpus, see *infra pAdoptions* and *pTurin* 2021, both belonging to late 20th dynasty).

'Wills by definition are performative documents' but they 'are peculiar in that their performative nature involves a delay of the performance' (Finegan 1982: 119); a will 'does not perform the act of bequeathing', it is a 'reversible performative' or 'a declaration of intention or wish' as the bequest 'takes place only when the testator can no longer reverse the will', its post-condition of felicity being the testator's death[142] and the presence of assets at that time. In modern legal systems, the right of the heir is acquired only at the time of the testator's death; see e.g. the Belgian Civil Code, article 1014: 'Tout legs pur et simple donnera au légataire, *du jour du décès du testateur*, un droit à la chose léguée'. The testator may always change his mind and his will. The heir has a *vocation successorale*, meaning a 'droit éventuel' 'qui existe dès avant [l'ouverture de la succession] à l'état de virtualité, d'éventualité'[143].

In ancient Egypt, the inheritance right of heirs remained conditioned by the testator's decision not to invalidate his will and the performance of his right in the event of the testator's death, even though the testator utters *ỉw.w n* PN. The performative statement does not automatically imply that in the Egyptian view, the right of the heir concerning the specific bequest is an immediately enforceable one[144]. But Pestman (1969: 60) contends that 'Even though the actual moment at which the children receive the inheritance may be, as a rule, that moment at which their father or mother dies, this does not alter the fact that they already, that is before the *de cuius* dies and before the inheritance falls due, have certain rights to this inheritance'[145]. Pestman bases his opinion on the fact that in some instances the children are present during the recording of the will and are asked if they agree to its contents (as in *pTurin* 2021); but as we shall discuss later, what is expected from the children, at least up to the end of the New Kingdom, is perhaps confirmation that they will not contest the will in the future. The question remains open, although the attribution of assets to the heir, to be later enforced, is constituted by the testator's performative speech[146].

140 Kurzon (1986: 7).

141 Jori (1994: 2092).

142 Kurzon (1986: 42, 47); Danet & Bogoch (1994: 134 n.7).

143 Cornu (2003 : 934).

144 Théodoridès (1960: 98): 'Un testament est pratiquement, en droit égyptien, un engagement pris pour un transfert de propriété différé *post mortem*. Etant donné la révocabilité du testament, ce transfert ne peut certainement pas avoir lieu avant la mort du disposant.'

145 See also Pirenne (1934: 303) and Théodoridès (1964: 62).

146 For Pirenne (1934: 303), the public record of a verbal declaration during the Old Kingdom explains the assimilation of wills to gifts, as 'Le testament apparaît, en effet, comme une donation faite du vivant du

The performative speech attributing a bequest has a double time-frame appurtenance: a here-and-now constitutive statement, and a postponed execution in an indeterminate future, as is the case with curses. As a matter of fact, the same adverbial nexus *ỉw.f n* PN is used in other performative contexts, such as in the curses of the operative part of some protection Ramesside decrees (e.g. *Kanais decree*, line 15). Evidently, a curse is performative speech (both blessings and curses are viewed as *behabitive* performatives by Austin, reactions to the behavior of the addressee)[147]; saying a curse accomplishes it, you cannot be un-cursed. Cursing is partly warning, partly punishment, even when the execution of the threat is to be performed in another world, after the criminal's death, and by supernatural actors, see David (2006: 124). In both wills and curses the construction deals with the present and the future; performativity and futurity are always linked[148].

The form *ỉw.f n* N is already used in testamentary provisions from *Ṯnti*'s tomb (6th dynasty[149], spelled  *n* PN), in 6th dynasty *Balat tablet* 5955, in Middle Kingdom *pKahun* VII.1 (*ir p3y.i pr* (…) *ỉw.f n n3y.i n ẖrdw*)[150], and *pKahun* I.1 (N *n* PN). Other forms of performatives are common in ancient prescriptions organizing the mortuary foundation, already during the Old Kingdom: *n rdi.n(.i) sẖm* N 'I do not allow the empowering of', an explicit performative (e.g. in *K3mnfrt?Cairo block* CG 1432 of the 5th dynasty), and *di.n(.i)* 'I give' used in the tomb provisions of *Nk3wrᶜ* (4th dynasty) and *Wpmnfrt* (5th dynasty). Most of the Old Kingdom foundation acts, regulations, and testamentary provisions are presented as authoritative verbal declarations of the tomb's owner, using either the qualification of *wḏt-mdt* (*m r3.f*) 'a verbal order (of his mouth)'[151] or a simple *ḏd*.

As for the locutive possessive suffix used in *oDeM* 108 specific bequests, it is to be understood not only as an indirect transcription of the testator's verbal manifestation of will[152], a legitimizing tool (only the owner may transfer the property), but also as a feature deemed to enhance his actual ownership up to his death. The general format of the will remains delocutive as the record represents a reconstruction of an oral enactment. A delicate balance between delocutive and locutive textemes is characteristic of the structure of the wills, and it is already perceptible in the testamentary provisions of *Nk3wrᶜ tomb* (4th dynasty): delocutive pre-material, but locutive *dispositions* (*di.n(.i)*). The delocutive mode represents the objective, impersonal hand of the authority registering facts and decisions; it uses a very formal language and layout and gives to the document its detached and informational texture.

---

donateur, créant, en cas d'enregistrement, un droit acquis pour les légataires, mais ne recevant son exécution qu'après la mort du testateur.'

147 Austin (1962: 159).

148 Muñoz (2006).

149 See Strudwick (2005: 202).

150 Note the pertinent remark made by Ganley (2003a: 19) concerning the dispositions of *pKahun* VII.1: 'It is not clear if this deed is a record of an enforceable oral *disposition* made before witnesses, or if it was the actual making of the written deed before witnesses with knowledge of its contents that gives it effect.' Ganley prefers the first option, on the basis of 6th dynasty *pBerlin* P 9010 and of the use of vernacular *p3y.i* in *pKahun* implying the record of a spoken discourse. Goedicke (1970: 195) assumes that 'Der eigentliche rechtsschöpferische Akt liegt in der mündlichen Deklarationen', the record being a *Beweisstück*.

151 Compare with ancient Anglo-Saxon wills before the thirteenth century: 'the will was an essentially oral act, even when it was recorded in writing. The persons present witnessed the testator making his bequests 'with his own mouth'; they 'saw, were present, and heard' the transaction.' (Clanchy 1993: 254).

152 See Théodoridès (1964: 62): 'En Egypte, et vraisemblablement depuis l'Ancien Empire, le testament se fait sous forme d'une déclaration publique, qui est actée et enregistrée.'

The locutive texteme, on the other hand, represents the intimate resolution of the testator and as such uses a 'more' Neo-Egyptian mode of expression in Ramesside documents. Interestingly, Danet & Bogoch (1994: 112) note concerning ancient Anglo-Saxon wills that 'the trend towards first-person renderings indicates that testators and scribes were attempting to invest the written document with performative power.' Danet[153] adds that the use of the locutive mode instead of the delocutive report is an essential feature of a constitutive instrument to which performativity has been transferred. These observations are consistent with Finegan's (1982: 115) concerning the language of modern wills: a will is 'a proclamation rather than an address' (...) it has a title (...) and a self-identified speaker (...). It also has witnesses and an audience, but it lacks an addressee because there is no way to know who will survive the testator' which explains the 'absence of second person pronouns' and imperatives from wills.

As for the *descent and distribution* rule, the marking of the material assets as the topic in each specific bequest illustrates their centrality in the legal text and contributes to effect an objective style without mention of the agent of their distribution; the performative forms that follow them instead of the future in the previous provision also convey certainty as to the principle of attribution, but a postponed execution to an undeterminate future. It seems that topicalized nominal segments followed by modal, performative, future or adverbial forms are major patterns in legal registers from the Old to the New Kingdom (see again their centrality in royal decrees, David 2006: esp. 57-9);

- proclitic coordinator *ẖr* + topicalizer *ỉry*: consistently, the coordinator fronts each bequest added to the first item in the list (but the topicalizer has been omitted on the verso of the ostracon).

  The same use of the coordinator *ẖr* in front of the topicalizer *ỉr* as a cohesive device[154] was observed in the Ramesside royal decrees (David 2006: 67).

  Note that the hieratic text is ordered in such a way that almost every line begins with the adverbial nexus attributing ownership, an important visual feature translating the internal planning of the instrument, stylistic visual features similar to modern textual organization of legal provisions for cohesive purposes. The isotopic structure of the bequests may betray a careful edition of the original verbal speech, although repetition is a well-known tool used to confer an ordered and controlled structure to verbal productions[155]; in our document, isotopy increases the solemnity and hence the authority of the performative attribution of movables. Note that topicalization of the objects of the inheritance is used in both the *descent and distribution* rule and the specific bequests, revealing a more general isotopy in the operative part. Isotopy is also a primary tool used in the *descent and distribution* rule of *pAdoptions*, v° lines 7-9[156]; interestingly, it is also a powerful feature in the operative part of a much later Aramaic deed of bequest from Elephantine, *pKraeling* 9[157], acting prosodically to reinforce the authority of the text and reassure the beneficiary of the bequest.

- *p3 di ỉr n.ỉ 3st*: perfect relative form (*ỉr* PN);

---

153 Danet (1997: 26).

154 For *ẖr* as coordinator and particle that 'découpe le message en paragraphes', see Neveu (1988: 105). See also cohesive devices in ancient Anglo-Saxon wills (Danet & Bogoch 1994: 118).

155 Ong (1982: 39-41).

156 For the use of isotopy in other legal genres and cultures, see e.g. Elephantine Aramic conveyances built on the model of priestly literature (Porten 1993).

157 Porten & Szubin (1987).

* General dialectal features: degree 1.
* Legal formulae:
- *descent and distribution* rule: *ỉry* N (object) + *ỉw.f psš* [*m-m m*]*sw nb* (partition mode)
- *disposition* of specific bequests: *ỉr*(*y*) N (object) + *ỉw.f n* PN (ownership right)

3. Colophon

Concerning the nature of the colophon texteme, see David (2006: 110). The brief technical-legal texteme puts an informational focus on the procedural context of the deed; it is highly detached, integrated (here limited to a prepositional phrase). The colophon[158] is rather vague in this case as witnesses are not named; it constitutes a simple mention of the general circumstances in which the procedure was carried out (compare with *Naunakhte*'s will colophon as well as its *adscriptus*). Haring (2003b: 264) notes that the use of colophons as authenticating devices remained rare in Deir el-Medina and belong exclusively to the 20th dynasty.

Witnesses: *m-bꜣḥ mtrw*	Before witnesses.

* General dialectal features: degree 0.
* Legal formula: unspecified witnesses: *m-bꜣ ḥ mtrw*.

Categorization of terms of special relevance in the legal register:

- *rdi ḫt*𓏛: to give, transmit assets/material property. The papyrus roll, a metonymic/metaphoric classifier of the superordinate [ABSTRACT] category, is typically used to classify diverse types of material assets conceptualized as an abstract global entity usually accounted in an inscribed document (metonymy '*SUBSTRATUM FOR CONTENTS*' or '*INSTRUMENT FOR ACTIVITY*'), their accounting also representing an abstract mental activity. Old Kingdom (*ỉ*)*ḫt* is already classified with the 𓏛 classifier when it has a generic meaning of the type *res*. See David (2006: 27, 47-8) and (2007).
- *ỉri ỉmyt-pr*: to make a (written) deed of transfer (with or without *consideration*).
  When classified, the *ỉmyt-pr* deed adopts during the Old Kingdom (e.g. *Kꜣmnfrt*? *Cairo block* CG 1432) as well as during the New Kingdom the 𓏛 classifier of the [ABSTRACT] category (the main choice during the 18th dynasty, e.g. *Snims stela Cairo* CG 34016) or the 𓍘 classifier of the [BINDING] category (the choice of the Ramesside Period, e.g. *Kanais decree*, see David 2006: 129).
  Note that the absence of a classifier does not mean that the *ỉmyt-pr* was not written[159], the written lexeme simply does not convey in this case any visual categorization information.

158 Ancient Anglo-Saxon wills also had their colophon, the *sanctio*, a closing section that may include a curse and a blessing, 'the location of copies of the documents, (…) lists of witnesses who were present at the oral ceremony, or who heard the written version read aloud and confirm its provisions' (Danet & Bogoch 1994: 116); note that sometimes witnesses were not named in ancient Anglo-Saxon non-autonomous wills (*ibid.*, 122).

159 *Contra*: Donker van Heel & Haring (2003: 87-8).

Furthermore, the papyrus roll represents a larger semantic field than the script domain: it also represents abstract concepts, such as  (David 2006: 27).

As for the nature of the *ỉmyt-pr* mentioned from the Old Kingdom to the Late Period, various interpretations have been proposed, among which are the following:

* for Mrsich (1968), during the Old Kingdom, this *Hausurkunde* organizes the **funerary foundation**, but it is not a testamentory provision. Mrsich distinguishes several meanings of the lexeme *pr* and stresses the '"fundus" (Grund samt Gebäuden) und "familia" (Familie, Vermögen und Menschen)' components of the expression, 'ein herrschaftsrechtlicher Grundbegriff' (pp. 25-31, esp. 31). In the case of later periods, it may not be so: in Ramesside *oDeM* 108, the *ỉmyt-pr* is evidently not related to a mortuary foundation;
* for Pestman (1969: 62), the Middle and New Kingdoms *ỉmyt-pr* is 'a written document in which a **fictitious lawsuit** is recorded' to 'transfer property rights.' This is apparently not the case here;
* for Théodoridès (1970: 177-8; 1993: esp. 101-5), although it is not limited to inheritance, in this context an *ỉmyt-pr*, a unilateral deed, is necessary when the patrimonial transmission **derogates to the legal *devolution*** mode, so that it expresses the individual's intention. It is an 'acte de disposition, de volonté individuelle, qui n'affecte pas, ne modifie pas, les autres actes en eux-mêmes, mais bien les droits de propriété mis en jeu par eux, ou en dehors d'eux.'[160]. This is also the position of Donker van Heel & Haring (2003: 87-90). Note that Théodoridès's contention (1977: 59) that the intestate succession organized the division of the assets in equal parts among the children is not absolutely proven, as we only know about norms stipulating 'Let every man do what he wants with his assets' (*pTurin* 2021 r° & *pGeneva* D 409), 'It is to the one who buries/has buried that the assets should be given' (*pBoulaq* 10), and about the various solutions adopted in testamentary provisions;
* for Menu (1971: 157, n.3) 'l'*ỉmyt-per* sert, la plupart du temps, à sanctionner le transfert d'une **universalité** de fait, en garantissant son intégralité permanente' (p. 156, n.2 : 'indivisible et indissociable du but pour lequel elle a été constituée'). Although it does concern the transfer of a universality of assets, we can see in *oDeM* 108 that some movable assets are personally attributed (Menu admits p. 157, n.3 that 'les anciens Egyptiens eux-mêmes ont pu perdre de vue cette fonction principale de l'*imyt-per*, ne retenant que son effet secondaire, translatif');
* for Gödecken (1980: 141) the *ỉmyt-pr* represents a 'bestimmten Form der Bezitsübertragung' in which the transmitted assets stay under the **control of their owner** but the right to use them is transferred to the beneficiary of the act. This is true of only part of these documents, as some of them effect a complete transfer of ownership, although they are not contracts (see Mrsich 2005: 179);
* for Logan (2000: 70), it is a 'transfer-document' of 'permanent legal right not only to own the property but also **to bequeath property'**. But we know that the Egyptians could limit in an *imyt-pr* the right of the beneficiary to bequeath the assets by a *fiduciary bequest* (fideicommissary substitution) imposing an obligation upon the legatee (e.g. in *pKahun* I.1), or limit the right of the beneficiary to the *usufruct* of assets until death, the assets being then transmitted to the testator's heirs (e.g. *Snims' stela Cairo* CG 34016);

160 (1993: 101).

All types of assets may be transmitted by *imyt-pr*, even bread and beer (e.g. *Nkʿnḫ*'s 5th dynasty tomb) and functions[161]. In general, assets transmitted by *imyt-pr* do not leave the **family** cell *sensu largo* (*imyt-pr* 'what is in the house,' with house as a metonymy for family estate/dominion). They are transmitted to a son by his mother (*Mṯn tomb* inscription, 4th dynasty), to a woman by her companion (*pKahun* I.1, 12th dynasty), to a daughter by her father (*Nḫtfmwti statue Cairo* CG 42208, 22nd dynasty), to his foundation by the king (*Kanais* decree, 19th dynasty). The Old Kingdom funerary foundation inscriptions specifically ensured that the trustees would not be able to transmit the trust's assets to *anyone* by *imyt-pr* (*K3mnfrt*? *Cairo block* CG 1432: 'I do not allow the empowering of any mortuary priest relative to the transmission of land, people, [any assets that I have constitued for their use for the mortuary offerings on my behalf] therewith, in payment to anyone (or) by giving an *imyt-pr* to anyone'). In wisdom literature, the *Instruction of Ptahhotep* (*pPrisse,* 314) emphasizes the need for the good man to transmit his assets by the means of an *imyt-pr*, perhaps to ensure continuity of the patrimony. But an *imyt-pr* may also be used in the context of a transmission of a public charge to a party who has no kinship relation with the alienor (see *pKahun* II, 1).
The value of the *imyt-pr* has not yet been finally assessed.

- *psš* ×: to divide (assets). The spelling is classical: for Old Kingdom spellings *psš/pšs*, see e.g. *Snnwʿnḫ tomb*, 5th dynasty and *Balat tablet* 3689-7, 8 & 11[162], 6th dynasty; *pš* represents the Neo-Egyptian orthography (see *infra*); for Demotic *pš* and Coptic **πωϣ**, see Richter (2002: 247-8). For Janssen (1975: 531-3) the verb refers to a situation of joint property resulting 'from inheritance, from joint work (...) or from joint purchase.'
  During the Old Kingdom, the lexeme is usually not classified, but when it is, it adopts the classifier of the [ABSTRACT] category; see e.g. *Snḏmib tomb*, 5th dynasty (*Urk*. I, 65 line 5). Middle Kingdom scribes use either or × to classify *psš,* and also both of them, e.g. Newberry (1893: pl. 26, lines 22-3) in *Ḫnmḥtp* II Beni Hasan tomb. The double classification of the lexeme implies its appurtenance to both superordinate [UNION/DIVISION] and [ABSTRACT] categories. On the one hand, division is represented by the metaphoric crossed objects classifier, the *crux decussata*, conceptualizing division by a schematization process in terms of geometrical relationships and spatial organization (see David 2006: 78-80; 2007). In fact, the × classifier is not unlike our own schematic representation of mathematical division ÷ (separation of two minimalist abstract objects/fields by a line drawn between them). On the other hand, since division of property is a legal activity dealing with physical as well as abstract operations of apportioning, the papyrus roll classifier is added to the crossed objects classifier; furthermore, since many partition records belong to our corpus, we may infer that it led to a written procedure. Another classifier used with *psš,* mainly in Ramesside papyri, is the superordinate [COERCION] category classifiers and (see *Naunakhte infra*), probably because joint property and any resulting division request are imposed on the heirs and imply a certain use of constraint (for a discussion of the classifier and the semantic category it represents, see David 2006: 27-8). It is worth noting that the Demotic *Hermopolis Code* dating from the Ptolemaic Period mentions the case of a man who dies

161 van den Boorn (1988: 181-3); Théodoridès (1993: 81 n.10, 89): 'patrimonalisées'.

162 Lines 2-3: *r psš pr ḫt nb nt* N PN *n ḫ[rdw.f]* 'in order to divide the house and all the assets of the N PN for [his] ch[ildren]'.

without having written a *sẖ n dni*, a deed of apportionment (col VIII, l. 30),[163] in which case the eldest son takes control of the assets and the other children may ask for the partition.

- *iw.f* /N *n* PN: to be for PN, to belong to.
- *ḥsb* [?]: account, balance. See Megally (1977: 53-5) 'la balance (…) regroupe l'essentiel de l'ensemble de la comptabilité d'une situation donnée ou de transactions, confrontant les deux éléments comptables opposés de cette situation.'

From the Middle Kingdom the classifier × is often represented by under the influence of hieratic; it refers to the semantic category of [UNION/DIVISION], but it is also an ancient phonetic pictogram of the lexeme *ḥsb* 'to break, to count' (David 2003: 572-7). Bookkeeping essentially deals with visual organization of numbers and substantives, opposing results, highlighting graphically the balance, and with mental mathematical operations. Thus key-operations of abstraction, division, opposition are represented in the categorization system by a metaphorical process expressed by the geometrical relations exhibited in the × classifier.

- *m-bꜣḥ* *mtrw*: in presence/before witnesses (see McDowell 1990: 21-2); for Demotic *mtr*(*e*) and Coptic ⲙⲛⲧⲣⲉ, see Richter (2002: 219-21).

As frontality is not only associated with general body posture but also with male corporal identity and the exposure of male genitals (*bꜣḥ*, 'phallus', attested since Middle Kingdom, but probably used before), the Egyptians categorized the situational *m-bꜣḥ* from Middle Kingdom times with the [ABSTRACT] category classifier to distinguish the spatial expression from anatomical issues through a metaphorical process. During the Old Kingdom, *m-bꜣḥ* is not classified, but *ḏr-bꜣḥ* takes the classifier (e.g. *Ḥrḫwf* tomb in *Urk*. I, 127 line 11). As for the lexeme *mtrw*, it is classified by both the [MALE-HUMAN] classifier and the schematic version of the two fingers of the [CONTROLLED ACTIVITIES?] category which may have a phonetic relation to the lexeme (see David 2006: 241).

163 Donker van Heel (1990: 93); see also Pestman (1987: 67) for *pꜣ sẖ pš* in the archive of the Theban Horos family; Depauw (1997: 144) *sẖ dnit pš*; Manning (2003: 840). Depauw (1997: 145) adds that wills 'as specific type of document are virtually non-existent in Demotic', although testamentary dispositions are recorded in marriage settlements, (fictitious) sales, and *sẖ dnit pš* division documents in the form of unilateral declarations of the heirs after division (see *supra*).

2. *oGardiner/Ashmolean* 90

Date: 19th dynasty, Ramesses II
Hieroglyphic version: *KRI* III, 683 n.7
Instrument:

* **state –** slightly damaged

* **value – original/copy/draft?**: limestone ostracon, brief but sufficient information, seemingly complete although lacking closing formula, date,[164] and address. Bakir (1970: 32) notes that letters written on ostraca 'always lack an address' (visible on the outside of the letter in the case of papyrus), as 'the introductory formula is exposed to view and serves as an address' and (p. 56-7) that model and real letters (of the early 19th dynasty) using the *ḏd* formula or sent to inferiors do not bear greetings. Letters on ostraca generally lack a closing formula 'probably due to lack of space, and to the fact that they are brief notes delivered locally'[165].

* **nature – private letter with legal consequences**: absence of internal characterization; concerns legal rights about assets. Nevertheless, note the absence of mention on papyrus 'And you shall keep my letter so that it may serve as a testimony in your favor' as e.g. in *pBerlin* P 8523, *pMallet* IV, *pBN* 198 III, *pBN* 199 I, *pBM* EA 10100, *pAnastasi* V 14, 6, *pBM* EA 10373.

* **genre – epistolary**: brief introductory epistolary formula with the names of both sender and addressee, brief greetings, contents without any type of epistolary style phrases common to school models, absence of specific layout except for the list; business hand, scribal errors, and possibly one correction; concerns private interests; from unknown provenance; delocutive/allocutive textemes, degree 1 Neo-Egyptian features.

Bakir (1970: 2) notes that letters on ostraca are 'doubtful cases' 'which may be models of (i.e. writing exercises), or drafts for, real letters.' In his list of epistolary ostraca[166], he does not include our text, but when dealing with his examples of letters on ostraca, he highlights their use 'for local communication'[167]. The document is thus probably not a model letter (presence of brief greetings and absence of formulaic message that usually constitutes a worthy school exercise), neither a summary copy (presence of greetings), but a private authentic letter locally sent (in spite of scribal errors such as *mwt{t}*, *ʿnḫ-n-niwt* , the hypothesis of a correction suggested by *KRI* III, 683 for *m ḳ{t}b[w]* and the degree 1 Neo-Egyptian features of this early 19th dynasty document).

Legal step: **external manifestation of will** (with performative) concerning the transmission of assets, and **notification** (*rdit rḫ.kwi*) of information

Legal issue: **isolated testamentary bequest or gift**[168]: absence of *consideration*, unilateral manifestation of will, use of the *psš* lexeme, performative attribution of ownership, retributive principle for grounding, reference to the origin of the assets transmitted, the absence of *descent and distribution* rule and of future form being due to the fact that the *disposition* concerns a specific fraction of the sender's assets (days of servants' service) transmitted to a unique beneficiary who is one of the testator's sons[169]. The usual lack of

164 Sweeney (2001: 18): 'Letters in Ancient Egypt are seldom dated.'
165 Bakir (1970: 69).
166 *Ibid.*, p. 13; the ostracon does not appear either in Sweeney (2001).
167 Bakir (1970: 23, 69).
168 For Théodoridès (1968: 95).
169 See Davies (1999: chart 13).

reference to the time of distribution of the assets (immediate or upon the 'testator's' death) does not allow us to state categorically that this is a gift or a testamentary disposition.

External reference is provided by *oGlasgow D* 1925.83/*oColin Campbell* 17, a parallel already made by McDowell (1993: 22-5) for whom the letter of *oGlasgow* 'concerns the execution of the inheritance which was arranged in [*oGardiner/Ashmolean* 90]' (p. 24); a similar group of servants is referred to in *oGardiner/Ashmolean* 90 and *oGlasgow*, but the names of the addressee and of the brother of the sender of this last letter do not seem to belong to the family referred to in *oGardiner/Ashmolean* 90.

It is clear that *oGardiner/Ashmolean* 90 is an isolated example in our corpus of an epistolary document expressing *quasi-olographic* testamentary or gift dispositions as opposed to the provisions recorded in the context of a public procedure before witnesses or a court acting as notary.

Textemic features:

1. Pre-material

Minimalistic but typical epistolary introductive texteme, with informational focus (high noun frequency, careful integration of information using prepositional phrases, delocutive exposition), and formulaic socio-linguistic indicator (brief complimentary preamble). Again the pre-material is not narrative, does not involve a nexus, and is not marked in terms of tense and aspect; situation-independent; not argumentative; authoritative (maximum of high dialect forms).

Title	
object: Recto (1) *ḏd*	Communication
sender: *n ṯ3y mḏ3t Ḳn*	of (the) sculptor *Ḳn*
addressee: *n s3.f Pndw3ww*	to his son *Pndw3ww*:
Greetings: (2) *m ꜥ.w.s.*	In L.P.H.!

* 'Classical' degree 0 forms used:

- # *ḏd n* + occupation + PN #: although *ḏd n* is often seen as a *sḏm.n*.N Middle Egyptian form, 'to express an action simultaneously spoken of and performed', a 'deliberate archaism', or 'a true perfect because the sender is looking forward to the time when the letter is received'[170], it is more probably an infinitive + relator like most title textemes. The introduction consists of two delocutive formulae characteristic of the *epistolary* genre: the introductory formula # *ḏd n* sender *n* addressee # and the complimentary preamble # *m ꜥnḫ wḏ3 snb* #[171] conform to the much simplified layout of letters on ostraca; this brief complimentary preamble is used between equals or from superior to inferior[172]. Bakir notes that formulae using the lexeme *ḏd* and devoid of elaborate greetings suit 'official or business matters' and that the *ḏd* formula, rare on papyrus, is widely used on ostraca until the late 20th dynasty[173]. For a similar use of the introductory and greetings formulae on ostraca, see e.g. *oDeM* 116.

* General dialectal features: degree 1.

* Legal formula: -

---

170 Bakir (1970: 49).
171 *Ibid.*, pp. 49 and 55.
172 Sweeney (2001: 234).
173 Bakir (1970: 47-8).

2. Contents

The provisions are expressed first in a delocutive mode with locutive reference (the performative attribution of ownership) already observed in the *consentient legal* genre operative part, and although the following part is devoid of formulae specific to the epistolary genre, it uses an allocutive mode characteristic of this last genre. Although no true *recital* is embedded in the letter, the retributive principle grounding the *disposition* is briefly mentioned.

This texteme again reflects an informational focus (impersonal/passive and agentless form of the notification formulae belonging to an official abstract style, high frequency of nouns in topicalized structure and relational expansions, integrated information with prepositional phrases), but with minimal personal involvement (allocutive forms, one locutive modal form but with no personal focus or stance/affect expressed, presentative *ptri*), in a careful and structured format; non-narrative discourse using performative forms; rather referentially explicit (phrasal coordination, proper names) but with some context-dependent expressions (*nty m niwt nty m ḳbw*; *psšw* 2; *wꜥt ḥr Ḳn*); minimally argumentative/persuasive (necessity modal, cleft sentence); authoritative (maximum of high dialect forms), non spontaneous and formulaic.

Grounded legal *disposition* of specific bequest:

ỉr hrw nb n bꜣkw n ꜥnḫ-n-niwt (3) *Mꜣꜥtnfrt tꜣy.i mwt{t} nty m niwt nty m ḳbw* (4) *ỉw.w n Pndwꜣ*[*ww*] *pꜣy.i šri di.i rḫ.k* (5) *rn.sn*

As for every (work)day of (the) servants[174] of *ꜥnḫ-n-niwt* [175] *Mꜣꜥtnfrt*, my mother, who are in town (or) who are outside[176], they belong to *Pndwꜣ*[*ww*], my son; I must inform you of their name:

1- (I.6) [*ḥm*] *ꜥn*[*ḥtp*]*w*	[the servant] *ꜥn*[*ḥtp*]*w*
2 – (7) [*ḥm*] *Nfrs*[*ḫrw*]	[the servant] *Nfrs*[*ḫrw*]
3 – (8) *ḥm* [*Ḥsyḥrimntt*]	the servant [*Ḥsyḥrimntt*]
4- (9) *ḥm Ỉr*[*y.f*]	the servant *Ỉr*[*y.f*]
5 – (II.1) *ḥm Pꜣrhny*	the servant *Pꜣrhny*
6 – (2) *ḥm Nꜣḫy*	the servant *Nꜣḫy*
7 – (3) *ḥmt Nḏmtḥms* [*ḥnꜥ*][177]	the servant *Nḏmtḥms* [with]
8 – (4) 3 *ẖrd*[*w.st*?]	[her?] 3 childr[en]

Verso (1) [*ỉw nꜣy*?]*.sn šri* *šri* [*nb*?] (2) [*n*?] *ṯꜣy* (*mḏꜣt*) *Pndwꜣww pꜣ*[*y.ỉ*] (3) [*šri*] *nty nfrw n.ỉ*

[All their] son(s) (and) daughter(s) [belong to?] (the) sculptor *Pndwꜣww*, m[y son], who has been good to me[178] (**retribution**).

174 Hofmann (2006: 115) : personnel. Concerning slavery, see among others Loprieno (1997) and Jasnow (2003c : 319), the latter summarizing the issue of slavery during the New Kingdom in the following statement: 'As in the Old and Middle Kingdoms, it is often difficult to determine the degree of servile status of subordinate persons'.

175 *ꜥnḫ-n-niwt* . The expression has lost its feminine concord markers and is followed by classifiers of the [MALE-HUMAN] and [FEMALE] categories. Concerning the meaning of the expression *ꜥnḫ-n-niwt*, see Janssen (1999) who dismisses the usual *citizeness* as 'In the language of these people [of Deir el-Medina] *niwt* is Thebes, but it was not there that these *ꜥnḫw-nw-niwt* lived' (p. 185), and believes it is neither a mark of status nor of age, and suggests translating it as *Mrs*. See also Toivari-Viitala (2001: 38-48), and Junge (2005: 157) who concludes that it designated 'married women above the social level of service personnel'.

176 Allam (1973: 168), Hofmann (2006: 114); for McDowell (1993: 23) 'which are double'; *RITA* III, 460: 'or who are inside (the Village)'.

177 As in *oGlasgow D* 1925.83 r°, line 6.

Notifications concerning personnel and shares:
(4) [*r*] *rdit rḫ.kwi n3 n b3kw nty m ḳ{t}b*[*w*] (5) *ptri p3 tp-rd n* [?](6) *wnn n.i psšw* 2 *iw wꜥt n3y*[*.i*...]
[To] inform you of the servants who are outsid[e]: see the instructions of [?]. It is to me that (the) 2 shares belong, one being m[y...].
[*r*] (7) *rdit rḫ.kwi t3y.i psšwt wꜥt* [*ḥr mwt.i*?] (Edge) *wꜥt ḥr Ḳn*
[To] inform you of my shares: one [on account of my mother?], one on account of *Ḳn*.[179]

* Neo-Egyptian characteristics:
- absence of concord of the relator (*b3kw n ꜥnḫ-n-niwt M3ꜥtnfrt*);
- use of the Neo-Egyptian possessive determinator for kinship (*t3y.i mwt; p3y.i šri*) and ownership (*t3y.i psšwt*);
- Neo-Egyptian spelling: *šri* and *ꜥnḫ-n-niwt* (without feminine nucleus); *m ḳbw*; *psšw* 2;
- binomial *šri* *šri* : for binomials in general, see Malkiel (1959); in modern legalese, see Gustafsson (1984); in Ramesside royal decrees, see David (2006: 26-7 with further bibliography). This binomial and other closely related doublets always present the male gender before the female; its reference is masculine singular (e.g. *Naunakhte*, Doc. IV line 3). Note the absence of a disjuncter between both gender binomials, as well as the spelling of feminine *šri* . Another binomial, related to filiation, is to be found in the funerary foundation inscription of *Snnwꜥnḫ*'s *tomb* (5th dynasty), in the form *msw* *nw msw* , each generic lexeme being classified in both the male and female categories, the male icon again preceding the female.
  Our doublet is not to be confused with the legal male inheritance clause *m s3 n s3* (*iwꜥ n iwꜥ*), used to guarantee male transmission of assets and their indivisibility (*Stèle juridique de Karnak* JE 52453, lines 7-9; *Amarah stela*)[180].
  Binomials in general are frequent in ancient Anglo-Saxon wills[181] as well as in modern testamentary provisions, the most famous being today the ubiquitous and redundant title *Last Will and Testament*, usually followed by a multi-binomials provision of the type 'I Arnold Johnson a resident of Mesa Arizona of Maricopa County, State of Arizona, being of sound and disposing mind and memory, do make, publish and declare this my last WILL AND TESTAMENT, hereby revoking and making null and void any and all other last Wills and Testaments heretofore by me made'[182] (our underlining)[183]. Similar are triplets of the type 'I give, devise and bequeath all of said rest, residue and remainder of my property to...'. This parallelism feature of legal texts may be considered 'a form of oral residue, left over from oral ritual communication, where mnemonic devices facilitate performance', but they emphasized the fact that 'the poetic features of language are mobilized to 'thicken' or give body to the document, to

178 Kitchen translates (*RITA* III, 460) '[They shall not take] them, (be it) either son or daughter [of mine...]; (but only) Pendua my son who has been good to me, (shall) take (them).'
179 The sender is probably not referring to himself; the other *Ḳn* of the family is the father of his 2nd companion (Davies 1999: chart 13). Does it mean that the sender got some share through his father-in-law?
180 Théodoridès (1964: 53-4).
181 Danet & Bogosh (1992: 105-6).
182 Tiersma (1999: 101).
183 See also in French legal genres, e.g. the binomials *je donne et lègue*, *choisis et appelés*, *comprendre et reconnaître*, or *en la présence réelle, simultanée et non interrompue*.

enhance its performative capacity'[184]; the function of (prosodic) isotopy in oral expression is not only mnemonic but also ritualizing[185].
Of course, binomials are also present in other ancient Egyptian registers; nevertheless, some doublets are especially employed in legal jargon (see e.g. *ẖwi mki*, David 2006: 26-7). For the extensive use of binomials in Coptic legal documents, see recently Richter (2002: 109-23);

- plural delocutive suffix *w* (but the classical *sn* is also used: *rn.sn*) and masculine allocutive suffix (*rḫ.kwi*);
- *ptri pꜣ tp-rd n* [?]: # Neo-Egyptian presentative *ptri* + cataphoric articloid + N + relator + [?] # in a segment designed to refer the addressee to relevant information. The presentative is constructed with a nominal object, as is *m.k* in Middle Egyptian (David 2000b);
- cataphoric articloid (*pꜣ tp-rd; nꜣ n bꜣkw* – with relator);

* 'Classical' degree 0 forms used:

- *ir hrw nb… iw.w n* PN: topicalized nominal object of bequest followed by an implicit performative attribution of ownership (see *supra*). Topicalization again marks the beginning of a new texteme;
- relator *n* in nature (*hrw nb n bꜣkw*), in ownership (*bꜣkw n ꜥnḫ-n-niwt*), and unclear kind of relation in frozen expression (*ꜥnḫ-n-niwt*);
- *di.i rḫ.k*: independent prospective (deontic modality) followed by its prospective object[186], an allocutive, modal form of the notification formula *r rdit rḫ.tw* (see *infra*). The form *di(.i) rḫ.k* already appears in the introduction of epistolary documents from Kahun dating from the Middle Kingom[187];
- PN *pꜣ[y.i šri] nty nfrw n.i*: relative clause with converb (stative) and determined antecedent. The statement represents the grounding of the disposition and employs a well-known formula with the locution *nfr n* appearing in the *recital* of *oPetrie* 18, lines 6-7, *pAdoptions*, line 19, and *pTurin* 2021, line II.3, based on a retributive principle, here not in its contrasted form (see *infra*). The main rationale for ancient Egyptian testamentary and gift *dispositions* is the proper fulfilling of moral and economical responsibilities towards a parent;
- [*r*] *rdit rḫ.kwi*: # preposition + infinitive + prospective object of the infinitive #, 'for your information' lit. 'to let you know', an allocutive form (as in *oGlasgow* D 1925.66) of the notification formula (see *supra*) associated with the epistolary genre; for the impersonal form of notification, see *infra*.
  Note the use since the Middle Kingdoms of *r rdit rḫ.k*, e.g. *pBerlin* P 10470, line I.2; *pBrooklyn* 35.1446, insertions B line 6 and C line 4[188];
- *nꜣ n bꜣkw nty m ḳ{t}b[w]*: anaphoric/cataphoric plural articloid;
- *wnn n.i psšw* 2: topic-initial cleft sentence with marked thematic imperfect that-form *wnn*.N and adverbial focus (ownership statement); the form *wnn.f* acts as a

---

184 Danet & Bogoch (1992: 106).
185 Lord (1987: 57-62).
186 Winand (1992: 213) notes that the Neo-Egyptian 'autonomous' prospective is always spelled *di*, never *rdi*.
187 See e.g. *pUC* 32109E, line 1: [… *ḏ*]*d di rḫ.k ḥr rdit* [...] '[… speak] so (I) might let you know about letting […]'. Luft (1984) sees in *di.i* a 'non-initial prospektiven *sḏm.f*', and the formula as a 'Vorläufer des coniunctivi futuri'. One should also note the formula *di(.i) rḫ*.N in the epistolary *Balat tablet* 3689-7, 8 & 11 (6th dynasty) dealing with a partition of assets.
188 Hayes (1955: pl. 5 and 6).

'convertisseur déprédicatisant aux temps duratifs'[189]. The function of the cleft sentence is of a polemic/grounding nature as it highlights the ownership of the testator.
For a discussion of cleft sentences with thematic *wnn.f* in Ramesside royal decrees as well as the relevant bibliography, see David (2006: esp. 52);

* General dialectal features: degree 1.

* Legal formula: *disposition* of specific bequest: *ỉr* N (object) + *ỉw.f n* PN (ownership attribution)

Categorization of terms of special relevance in the legal register:

- *hrw n b3kw*: workday, day of service (lit. 'day of servants'). See *hrw m ḥm* in *pBerlin* P 9784, *pGurob* II,1-2 (Théodoridès 1968) and in the *Bryce tablet,* also from the 18th dynasty; see David (2006: 66) for *b3kw* workdays/service yield in Ramesside royal decrees.
  Here both [MALE-HUMAN] and [FEMALE] categories classifiers are used ([BOTH SEXES] category), and indeed we can see from the list of servants that both sexes are represented.
- *ỉw.f n* PN: to belong to.
- *psš(t)*: share. See *supra psš* (to divide assets).
- *(r) rdỉt rḫ.k*: to let know, to inform (see *infra r rdỉt rḫ.tw*).
  The superordinate [ABSTRACT] category classifier refers to a mental cognitive process, although it may be that at a very early stage the classifier referred only to the [WRITTEN THINGS] category. The basic ontological metaphor '*IDEAS ARE OBJECTS*'[190] may explain the use of the papyrus scroll classifier to represent the superordinate [ABSTRACT] category (reification); the metaphorical process complements the metonymies '*INSTRUMENT FOR ACTIVITY*' and '*SUBSTRATUM FOR CONTENTS*' using the papyrus scroll for the written provisions (David 2006: 27; 2007: 11). Furthermore, in ancient Egyptian culture, knowledge is archetypically embodied in the written word.

189 Shisha-Halevy (1978: n.43).
190 Lakoff & Johnson (1980: 10).

3. *oGardiner/Ashmolean* 55

Date: 19th-20th dynasties, Ramesses II-III[191]
Hieroglyphic version: Černý & Peet (1927: 38-9)
Instrument:

* **state** – fragmentary
* **value – probably excerpt**: limestone ostracon, important information missing (absence of pre-material with date and names, colophon, etc.), but with a probably connected list of assets on the recto. It may be the *recital* of a legal document.
* **nature – legal instrument**: absence of internal characterization, concerns legal rights about assets.
* **genre – consentient or contentious?**: unspecific layout; business hand, absence of errors and of business practice diacritical marks; concerns private interests; of unknown provenance; delocutive texteme and locutive reference, degree 2 Neo-Egyptian features; use of the lexeme *th3mw* and reference to probable opponents ('their mother'); context-dependent.

It is difficult to assess the genre of the document; it could be part of a settlement in court, although no reference is made to the forum, witnesses, or oaths, only a personal account of the situation, the use of *th3mw* and a possible adverse party referred to laconically. It may also be part of the *recital* of a court-authenticated will in which the testator reveals the background to his decision and his motivation. Of course one cannot completely dismiss the possibility of it being a private *memorandum*.

Legal step: **explicit recognition of rights** regarding assets, not a manifestation of will.
Legal issue: **property rights of the members of a couple**: no mention of a unilateral deed by the writer, absence of many typical will clauses, but statement of ownership, universalities of assets, grounding, use of *rdi* and *pš* lexemes, family relationships.

Although some elements may be interpreted as belonging to testamentary provisions[192], a major problem with such a qualification, besides the absence of other clauses related to wills, is the fact that the only statement that appears to be in the form of a *bequest* (*ẖr ỉr 3ẖt nb… ỉw.w n t3y.(ỉ) ḥmt*) concerns assets that are *not* the property of the disponor, as he confirms that the woman brought them to his house, probably as her share in the community of assets. This acknowledgement on the part of the man and the ensuing list may recall the Demotic 'things of a woman' brought into the couple's household[193].

In spite of these important reservations, we have chosen to include the document with the testamentary instruments, since it may represent part of the *recital* of a will.

Textemic features:

1. *Recital*?[194]

A commentary texteme dealing with the ownership of assets, probably not assigning rights, only recognizing them. The text is highly context-dependent (information crucial for our understanding is missing). Although informational (monologue based on topicalized nouns,

191 See the spelling of *m-n-ḏr*.
192 Černý (1937-38: 46) and Allam (1973: 161). For Pestman (1961: 127), it may be a case of divorce; for Toivari-Viitala (2001: 94), it is a 'statement of a settlement of property', but the precise nature of this settlement cannot be assessed.
193 Concerning Demotic law, see Manning (2003: 842).
194 See *infra Naunakhte*'s *recital* for a typical example of a Ramesside *recital* in the context of a will.

using attributive expansions), it contains strong elements of narrator involvement (locutive pronouns, unspecified referent, use of intensifier, present tense, generalized content words, cleft sentences, discourse particle, converted sentences); it does not contain specific narrative forms but it depicts past events in a concise manner (anteriority of relative form and participles, temporalis); it is not overtly persuasive.

Recognition of property rights:
Verso (1) *ỉw ỉr nꜣ ḥnw ỉ.dỉw.f* [*n.ỉ*] (2) *pꜣ rwy dỉdyt n.ỉ m-n-ḏr pš.f* [*st*] (3) *ỉrm tꜣy.w mwt ỉw tꜣy.st pš* (4) *m-dỉt.st ḥꜥw.st*
ḫr ỉr ꜣḫt nb sp sn nty m (5) *pꜣy(.ỉ) pr ỉw.w n tꜣy.(ỉ) ḥmt ḥnꜥ nꜣy.st* (6) *ẖrdw yꜣ mntst r.ỉntw st* (7) [...] *ỉw ỉ.ỉr.ỉ ỉr.f r* (8) [...] *r thꜣmw* [...]
But as for the items that he (= my father?)[195] transmitted [to me], (they constitute) the 2/3 (of the community property) given to me after he divided [it] with their[196] mother, while her share (= 1/3) is in her own possession.
And as for all assets, all of them, that are in my house, they belong to my woman[197] and her children. Indeed, it was she who brought them [...], whereas it is in order to summon? [them?...] for/against [...] that I did it.

* Neo-Egyptian characteristics:
- *ỉw ỉr nꜣ ḥnw... pꜣ rwy*: positive nominal statement identifying a category of assets, constructed as # contrastive coordinator *ỉw* + topicalizer *ỉr* + determined and expanded noun (theme) + determined and expanded numeral (rheme) #.
  For a contrastive topicalization expressed by *ỉw swt ỉr* in the Ramesside royal *Nauri decree*, see David (2006: 104). The fact that the statement opens with *ỉw* indicates that it may not be the beginning of the text. *ỉw* indicates contrast, but it is not the converter, rather a 'freies *ỉw* ohne die Bedeutung des Zustandssatzes'[198] (but apparently not in a parenthetical context).
  As for the Neo-Egyptian nominal nexus # topicalizer + nominal theme + nominal rheme #, it has been perceived as a neutralized topicalization[199], the topicalizer's function being reduced to the signalization of the theme when the theme is not followed by a nexus but only by a (determined) noun, the rheme. But in our case, it does not

195 Černý (1937-38: 46) and Théodoridès (1964: 67; 1969: 158). A different view was previously taken by Černý & Peet (1927: 39) who suggested that it is the father of the first woman of the writer who is meant here, and that the father gave assets to his daughter on the occasion of the union, but claimed them back after the separation. The problem with this thesis is the fact that the 2/3 is brought into the community property by the man, certainly not by the father of the 'bride', and we cannot see how it would be her father who 'divided [it] with their mother' after the couple's separation, the division being certainly a matter for the couple or at least the 'husband'.

196 Siblings or more probably half-brothers of the narrator, against whose claims the text was prepared.

197 The lexeme *ḥmt* is translated *woman* and not *wife*, although it is often translated as the latter in Egyptological literature (see for instance Toivari-Viitala 2001: 18-28 on the subject). It seems to connote specifically sexual maturity (written with the hieroglyph, reminiscent of the *tota mulier in utero* adage...), and when used in the expression *ỉri m ḥmt* it does not indicate *married status* as often suggested, but sexual union. Any so-called evidence (*pDelM* 27, *pBM* EA 10416, etc.) offered to prove the existence of a formal marital union prior to the Late Period is, in our view, inconclusive (Allam 1975; *contra*: Toivari-Viitala 1998, Gee 2001). Egyptian partnerships were formed chiefly with the intention of founding a family, marked by cohabitation, the union was expressed sexually and in caring for the couple's children.

198 Satzinger (1976: 227-31).

199 Satzinger (1976: 16) sees the overall construction as a 'neutralisierte segmentation'; see also Shisha-Halevy (1978: 66 Obs.12) for the 'fonction thématique' of *ỉr*.

seem that we can dismiss the topicalizing function of *ir*, since the topicalized pattern is a major feature of ancient Egyptian legal discourses (see also the following sentence). I prefer to see this as a case of deletion of the pronominal theme resumptive to the topicalized noun # topicalized noun + ø pronominal theme + nominal rheme # and consecutive function of the topicalized noun as theme of the nexus (see *LEG*, Ex. 1486 from *pMayer* A 3, 23, belonging to the *contentious* legal genre). Again the construction 'objectifies' the statement – focused as it is on a category of assets –, the transmission by the father being brought as its adnominal expansion;

- cataphoric articloid (*nꜣ ḥnw i.diw.f; pꜣ rwy didyt*);
- *nꜣ ḥnw i.diw.f*: perfect relative form with prothetic *yod*;
- *pꜣ rwy didyt*: geminating participle without prothetic *yod* (anteriority). The non-significant, neutralized feminine mark is established with the dual masculine referent *pꜣ rwy*; the final *y* is sometimes appended in Neo-Egyptian to participles of *rdi*[200]. As for the germination of a perfect form, we already observed it in Ramesside royal decrees with perfect passive participles or stative forms (David 2006: 62, 128);
- *m-n-ḏr pš.f*: temporalis constructed with # compound preposition + that-form *sḏm.f* without prothetic *yod* #.
  The spelling of the compound preposition indicates the Ramesses II-III period[201]; the *n* is dropped after Ramesses III's reign, thus making it a blatant transitional degree 2 form.
  The *sḏm.f* is a that-form relatively future (viewed in terms of the initial state of affairs)[202];
- Neo-Egyptian spelling (*pš, ꜣḫt, thꜣmw*);
- Neo-Egyptian prepositions (*irm; m-dit.st,* its spelling being a compromise between *m-di* and *m-ḏrt*) and omission of a preposition such as (*n* or *r*) *ḥꜥw.st*;
- Neo-Egyptian possessive determinator for kinship (*tꜣy.w mwt, tꜣy.(i) ḥmt; nꜣy.st ẖrdw*) and ownership (*tꜣy.st pš, pꜣy(.i) pr*);
- Neo-Egyptian delocutive suffix pronoun *w* (plural) and *st* (feminine);
- *ḫr ir ꜣḫt nb… iw.w n tꜣy ḥmt*: topicalized noun followed by an adverbial recognition of ownership: # coordinator (with opposition nuance, see *infra*) *ḫr* + topicalizer *ir* + determined noun expanded (assets) + adverbial nexus *iw.w n* N #. The construction marks a change of topic.
  Although *iw.w n* N resembles the performative used in the operative parts of wills, it cannot be a performative attribution of ownership since 'her third' belongs to the woman and may not be disposed of by the narrator. Thus the very same form can be a performative in one context and a simple recognition of right in another; similarly, one may utter a performative 'I swear' after being asked to tell the truth in a courtroom, but the same form is a non-performative utterance in a non-legal context, such as 'It was unbelievable, I swear I've never seen that before'. Jori (1994: 2092) notes that 'it is often difficult to say whether an utterance expresses a performative or not, and the same utterance, taken by itself, can be interpreted both in a constative and in a performative

---

200 Winand (1992: 353-4).

201 Winand (1992: 248 & 249, n.116).

202 Polotsky (1944: 85 for *ḏr sḏm.f*); Frandsen (1974: 166). Winand (1992: 245, 256, 265 ff.) considers it to be a prospective on the basis of 'copte et les graphies des *3ae inf.* (-y), des *2ae gem.* et du verbe *iy/iw*', and distinguished from the (*i.*)*sḏm.f* prospective that-form. Junge (2005: 89, 143, 226-8) sees it as a 'subjunctive-prospective' implying 'an unspecified past time'. A circumstantial form is suggested by *LEG*, 410 in view of a unique case of *m-ḏr sḏm.n.f*.

sense.' It is thus a matter of 'contexts and situations'. Legal recognition is a 'formal admission that a person, entity, or thing has a particular status'[203], thus a *constative* for the Austinian school;

- absence of concord (*ȝḫt nb... nty*);
- *yȝ mntst r.intw st*: cleft sentence, a participial statement constructed with # assertive discourse particle *yȝ* + rhematic delocutive pronoun (focus) + perfect participle with prothetic *r* (theme) + dependent pronoun (object) #. Because the one who brings assets to the house is their owner, the focus is on *mntst*.

  For Borghouts (1972: 272, ex. 9, although he also accepts the participial statement option) and Winand (1992: 268 and n. 18), the form *i.in.t.s* is a prospective that-form more consistent with the context and the presence of the prospective mark *t*. But the context seems to require a past form (the woman brought the assets to the house at the beginning of the cohabitation), and the particle *yȝ* highlights this fact. The participial statement has an explicative value; it is the grounding of *iw.w n tȝy.(i) ḥmt ḥnˁ nȝy.st ẖrdw*.

  The prothetic *yod* for the verb *ini* is noted by Winand[204] only during the 20th dynasty, its *r* form being attested during the entire New Kingdom.

  The absence of gender/number distinction of the Neo-Egyptian participle has been emphasized[205]; furthermore, the participle in a classical participial statement construction is also immutable[206]. The mark *tw* of our participle parallels examples with *t(/)w* without significant reference[207].

  Concerning *yȝ*, Winand (2004: 109) underlines that it 'introduit un propos présenté comme correspondant à la vérité des choses, un propos qui n'appelle pas de discussion';
- *iw i.ir.i ir.f... r thȝmw*: converted topic-initial cleft sentence constructed with # converter *iw* + analytic that-form[208] (thema) + adverbial focus (rhema) #. Since the text is incomplete, the point made is lost, but it may refer to the cause of a litigation process. Other types of cleft sentences may be converted by *iw*; for participial statements, see Groll (1967: 57).

* 'Classical' degree 0 forms used:

- *ȝḫt nb sp sn*: isotopy (classical intensity iteration) to emphasize the fact that all the movables in the house are owned by the woman (the house itself belongs to the narrator). Concerning the intensity iteration, note that 'Reduplication applied to adjective indicates intensification or increase', an application of the metaphor *'MORE OF FORM IS MORE OF CONTENT'*[209].
- classical conversion of present adverbial nexus (*iw tȝy.st pš m-dit.st*) although with Neo-Egyptian possessive, preposition, and suffixes.

* General dialectal features: degree 2 (some forms have a prothetic *yod*, others do not; there are transitory forms in the texteme).

* Legal formulae: - identification of a category of assets: *ir* N (assets) + *pȝ rwy* (fraction in community property)

---

203 Garner (2004: 1299).

204 Winand (1992: 364).

205 *LEG*, 466 and Winand (1992: 353-5).

206 *EG* § 373.

207 Groll (1967: 54-6, esp. Ex. 196 from *Horus and Seth* 7, 11-2: *mntk i.wp.tw tw ḏs.k* 'It is you who judged yourself by yourself').

208 Frandsen (1974: 280) notes the use of the rare *i.ir.i ir.f* form instead of *i.ir.i i.ir.f*.

209 Lakoff & Johnson (1980: 127-8).

- recognition of ownership: *ir* (object) + *ỉw.w n* N

2. List of movable and immovable assets

Recto (1) […] *ʿt ḳd* 2	built hut/workplace[210]: 2
(2) *ḥibyt* 1	naos-shrine: 1
(3) […]	[…]
(4) […]	[…]
(5) *bꜣn*[*w*…]*ỉ*[…]	millston[e…]
(6) […]	[…]
(7) *ṯꜣ*[*bw*?…]	*ṯꜣ*[*bw*-vessel?…]
(8) […]	[…]
(9) […]	[…]
(10) *mn*[*y*?…]	jewel?[…]
(11) *ḫt hꜣdmw rd*[*wy*] 1	wooden fo[ot]stool: 1
(12) *sbỉw* 5	doors: 5

* Neo-Egyptian characteristics:
  - Neo-Egyptian lexemes (*ḥibyt*);
  - Neo-Egyptian spelling (*hꜣdmw, sbiw*).

* 'Classical' degree 0 forms used: *ḳd* (participle without prothetic *yod*)

* General dialectal features: degree 1.

* Legal formula: -

Categorization of terms of special relevance in the legal register:

- *rdỉ*: to give, transmit, bequeath.
- *rwy*: 2/3. The part of the community property of the couple brought by the man. See, *inter alii*, Černý (1937-38; 1945: 49); Théodoridès (1964: 66-72; 1966: 40, 53-7; 1968b); Allam (1975: 1172;1981: 119).
  The evidence for such key of partition seems limited to the New Kingdom, although Vernus (1986: 84-5) believes that an earlier text, the *Edfu stela Cairo* JE 52456 of the 17th dynasty, alludes to the same 1/3 (for the woman) – 2/3 (for the man). A similar key of partition of the community property is used in early Demotic *pTsenhor*[211].
- *pš*: to divide, a share. See *supra*.
- *m-dỉt.f*: in his possession.
  For the Egyptian distinction between ownership and possession, see Glanville (1928: 306), Hayes (1955: 118), Théodoridès (1970b), Vernus (1986: 82-3) and David (2006: 61).
- *ꜣḫt*: assets, material property. Neo-Egyptian lexeme classified as the classical *ḫt* (see *supra*).
- *ỉw.f n* N: to be for, belong to.
- *ỉnỉ*: to bring (into the community property).
- *thꜣmw*: to claim, summon? Probably Neo-Egyptian spelling of the lexeme *thm* attested since the Second Intermediate Period (*Kamose stela Luxor* J 43 in Helck 1975b: 94 line 21), with the meaning 'to interfere, penetrate, drive, knock, bring' (*Wb* V, 321-2).

210 Demarée (2006: 57-66): the *ʿt* is a workplace outside the village of Deir el-Medina.
211 Pestman (1994: 25).

The lexeme *thm* is usually either classified by the 𓂾 [LEG] category classifier or by the double 𓂾𓂻 [LEGS MOTION] category classifiers (see David 2006: 27-8 and 2007: 10), as motion is implied by the semantics of penetration, drive, perforation (the substantive *thm* 'perforation' is attested in medical papyri since the Middle Kingdom with the 𓂾 [LEG] category classifier). The abstract notion of interference (*thm*) as a behavior condemned by criminal law decrees (e.g. *Nauri decree*, line 26) is also classified by 𓂾𓂻, probably reflecting the metaphor '*CRIME IS MOTION*' at the basis of the notion of transgression, or by the couplet 𓂾𓂡, adding the nuance conveyed by the semantical field of the [COERCION] category.
Here *thm* is classified with the basic level [MOUTH LINKED ACTIVITIES] category classifier. Černý (1976: 204) indicates the Egyptian *thm*𓂾 as the etymology of the lexeme **ⲧⲱϩⲙ̄** 'knock (on door), summon, invite'. The classifier 𓀁 probably indicates that the lexeme has the same connotation of summoning as in Coptic. It certainly refers to the oral aspect of the legal procedure, the voicing of the claim in court or the verbal summons to appear in court. Modern legal notions such as *claim*, *appeal*, or *citation* are also based on [MOUTH LINKED ACTIVITIES]; although claims, appeals, and citations are issued in writing today, their etymology corresponds with verbal utterances (Latin *clamare* 'to cry out', *appellare* 'to address someone, accuse' and *citare* 'to summon, proclaim').

4. *oGardiner/Ashmolean* 272

Date: 20th dynasty, Ramesses III
Hieroglyphic version: *KRI* VII, 283-4 n.268 A 356
Instrument:

* **state –** damaged
* **value – original/draft/copy?:** limestone ostracon, brief essential information with abreviated date without archaic anaphora, absence of title deed, *recital* or colophon, but probably complete instrument of this type (simple declaration before witnesses concerning a specific legal point, in order to serve later, with the donor/donee/witnesses named, as well as the significant addressee)
* **nature – legal instrument, perhaps to serve as a title deed** (absence of internal characterization), concerns legal rights to assets
* **genre – consentient legal**: formulaic style, ordered layout; business hand, accounting practice abbreviation, one addition above the line; concerns private interests; of unknown provenance; delocutive/locutive textemes, degree 2 Neo-Egyptian.

Legal step: communication (*ḏd*)[212] in public (but not in court) of an **external manifestation of will** concerning movable assets status (*twnw*) and division (*pš*).

Legal issue: **gift with *exemption from hotchpot*[213] (relating to future inheritance)**: absence of *consideration*, unilateral deed, *exemption from hotchpot*, and general mention of a division (*twnw… m-ḥꜥw, pš*) between siblings but no future *descent and distribution* rule (this is not the man's testament); it concerns the transmission of specific items of the testator, the beneficiary being doubtless one of the testator's children, and includes a short list of specific valuated movables.

A similar issue is treated in the context of the will of *Naunakhte* (lines III.3-4), not as a separate declaration, but as a remark of the testatrix concerning one of the heirs.

Textemic features:

1. Pre-material

Date: (1) *rnpt-sp* 14 *ꜣbd* 1 *ꜣḫt sw* 2	Year 14, month 1 of inundation season, day 2
Title:	
legal step: *ḏdt.n*	What said
disponor: *ꜥꜣ n ist* [*Nḫwmmwt*]	(the) foreman [*Nḫwmmwt*]
addressee: [*n*] (2) *ḥmt.f Wbḫt*	[to] his woman *Wbḫt*
forum: *m-bꜣḥ mtrw idnw Ḥsyswnbf* […]	before witnesses: deputy *Ḥsyswnbf*, […]

* Neo-Egyptian characteristics: -
* 'Classical' degree 0 forms used:
  - *ḏdt.n* N: classical relative neutrum *sḏmt.n*.N, an archaism already recognized in the legal registers by Gardiner (1935: 141). It replaces the construction seen *supra*: # date + archaic anaphora + infinitive #. Compare with Doc. IV in *Naunakhte*'s file (lines 1-2), also constructed without the archaic anaphora: *ḏd n* N PN *m-bꜣḥ* (list of witnesses);
  - relator *n* used in dominion relation (*ꜥꜣ n ist*);
* General dialectal features: degree 0.

212 Donker van Heel & Haring (2003: 171): 'deposition'.
213 Donker van Heel & Haring (2003: 171): 'decision taken (…) about an extra share in his inheritance for one of his sons.'

* Legal formula: date + *ḏdt.n* N PN (communication) + *n* (addressee) + *m-bꜣḥ mtrw* N PN (forum)

2. Operative part

purpose marker: (3) *r-nty*	to wit:
statement quotation: *exemption from hotchpot*[214]	
m.k twnw ỉmnḫꜥw [pꜣy šrỉ] (4) ỉnk m-ḥꜣw n nꜣy.f snw r-ḏrw.w	
See that (the) bonus of *ỉmnḫꜥw*, [this son] of mine, is in excess of (the) ensemble of his siblings:	
(5) *ḥsmn ỉꜥ* 1 *ỉr n dbn* 11	bronze washing bowl: 1, worth 11 *dbn*
(6) *ḥsmn wp* 1 *ỉr n dbn* 8	bronze knife: 1, worth 8 *dbn*
dmḏ 1[9]	total: 1[9] (*dbn*),
(7) *mtw.f ꜥḳ r pšw*[215] *ỉ[rm.w]*	and he will enter the division w[ith them].

* Neo-Egyptian characteristics:
- purpose marker *r-nty*, introducing the content of the statement (*ḏdt*). A possible etymology of *r-nty* is *r rdit rḫ.k* (*r*) *ntt,* a notification formula[216]. Compare with *Sꜣmwt*'s tomb (lower inscription) from the reign of Ramesses II, the text concerning the gift opening with # full date + *hrw pn ḏd n* N PN (…) *r-nty* # 'this day of (the) statement of N PN (…) to wit:'. Also *pAdoptions*, lines 13-6: the pre-material of the will of the testatrix is constructed with # full date + *hrw pn ḏdt n* N PN (…) *r-nty* (*recital*) #;
- *m.k twnw… m-ḥꜣw n nꜣy.f snw r-ḏrw.w*: # classical presentative *m.k* (involvement feature in oral speech) + expanded N (theme) + adverbial rheme *m-ḥꜣw n* + determined, specific N and trailing position augens #.
  Although the presentative is followed by a noun, it does not seem to be the classical construction # *m.k* + nominal object + adverbial adjunct # (David 2000b), the grammaticalized presentative (without actual reference to the feminine addressee) being followed by an adverbial nexus expressing the status of the items (probably an implicit performative), itself protatic to the following conjunctive.
  Although the text does not include a *recital*, the presentative *m.k* is used to involve directly the addressee, his companion, in the definition of the status of some items given to a son, either because the addressee will be the executor of the will or because she will be one of the legatees of her mate. Other features of involvement such as deictics are used in the operative part of some of our texts.
  The first part of Doc. IV in *Naunakhte*'s file (lines 1-2) is similarly constructed, but without *r-nty*: *ḏd n* N PN *m-bꜣḥ* (list of witnesses) + *ptri* (Neo-Egyptian form of the presentative) + *i.diw.i pꜣ[y] ỉꜥ iw.f ḥr ir[t] ḥmti dbn* 13.
  As for the adverbial rheme, compare with *Naunakhte* Doc. I, lines III.3-4: *diw.i n.f ḥsmn ỉꜥ m twnw m-ḥꜣw nꜣy.f irw*;
- *ỉmnḫꜥw* [*pꜣy šrỉ*] *ỉnk*: kinship relation and high specificity expressed by # PN + Neo-Egyptian deictic *pꜣy* + N + *ỉnk* locutive independent pronoun possessor # (as in *pAdoptions,* lines 6 and verso 4). Compare with *pꜣy* 4 *ẖrdw ỉnk* (*Naunakhte* line IV.7).

214 The beneficiary receives an exemption of restoring the *advancement* made.

215 Although the spelling seems to indicate *pš.w*, *pšw* also refers to 'division' and 'shares' (see e.g. *oLouvre* E 13156).

216 David (2006: 223-4) for *r-nty* in epistolary royal decrees.

Hyperdetermination[217] is a known characteristic of modern legal registers;

- Neo-Egyptian possessive determinator for kinship (*nꜣy.f snw*);
- Neo-Egyptian plural delocutive suffix *w;*
- *mtw.f ꜥḳ*: full-fledged conjunctive as apodosis of *m.k twnw Ỉmnḫꜥw* [*pꜣy šri*] *ink m-ḥꜣw n nꜣy.f snw r-ḏrw.w*. It is the conjunctive that introduces the matter of the division (the main issue is always introduced by the conjuctive), probably concerning the partition of the speaker's assets after his death, although the formulation is ambiguous. There are no 'embryo-conjunctive' forms in the corpus (compare with the royal decrees, David 2006: 62-3);
- *ỉ*[*rm.w*]: Neo-Egyptian preposition;

* 'Classical' degree 0 forms used:

- *m-ḥꜣw n*: with relator, see *Wb* III, 17.11-12 and an early example in *pPrisse* 7,10;
- *ỉr n dbn* + quantifier: although the construction representing the valuation of an item on the basis of a weight of metal unit (*dbn*) is ubiquitous, its analysis is problematic: for *EG* § 422.3 a passive *sḏm.f* ''amounting to', lit. 'it is made for''; for Janssen (1975: 9, n.20) an unspecified *ỉri.n*; for Junge (2005: 158) a 'passive *sḏm.w*'.

  It probably consists of # passive perfect participle *ỉr* + relator *n* + unit + quantifier #; the participle does not seem to be an imperfect form (absence of gemination even in early examples). Note that the list of items is not introduced by the notification formula;

* General dialectal features: degree 2.

* Legal formula: *r-nty* (object of statement) + *hotchpot* exemption: *m.k twnw* PN *m-ḥꜣw n nꜣy.f snw* (bonus) + list (detail of items) + *mtw.f ꜥḳ r pš.w ỉ*[*rm.w*] (partition)

Categorization of terms of special relevance in the legal register:

- *ḏd:* to say, state, declare.
- *m-bꜣḥ* *mtrw*: before witnesses.
- *twnw*: bonus, advantage (*m-ḥꜣw* *n*: in excess of). See Gardiner (1956: 17) for *twnw* in *pTurin* 1882, 3(9) 'reward'; Allam (1973: 270-1, n. 10); *oGardiner/Ashmolean* 103 and 272; *Naunakhte* Doc. I, (*m*)*twnw*; *dwn* in *pTurin* 2021, 2, 5 classified by the superordinate category of [MOTION] classifier . The icon that sometimes precedes the classifier is in fact a phonetic classifier, an icon summarizing a lexeme's phonetic value already established by phonograms[218].

  The lexeme *twnw* 'difference' with the classifier is attested from the Second Intermediate Period in mathematical *papyrus Rhind*. As for the superordinate [MOUTH LINKED ACTIVITIES] category classifier , see *infra Naunakhte*.
- *ꜥḳ* *r pšw* : to enter into a share/division, to inherit a share. See *infra Naunakhte*.

217 Danet (1980: 477): '*Over-precision* characterizes the specification' in legal English.

218 See *Wb* V, 359-60 for a list of similarily classified lexemes; David (2006: 25 n.25).

5. *pAshmolean Museum* 1945.97 & 1945.95 and *pDeM* 23 & 25 (*Naunakhte*)

Date: 20th dynasty, Ramesses V
Hieroglyphic version: *KRI* VI, 236-43 n.20
Instruments:

* **state –** complete, well preserved
* **value – (exact?)**[219] **copy or original**: several papyri apparently relating to the same case, complete information with date (Docs. I & IV), all parties and officials named, name of the forum, *recital*, lists of people and movables, oaths, witnesses, elaborated colophons.
* **nature – notary** *ꜥwty hꜣrwyt* ***declaratory deed*** **and related documents** (internal characterization) written before a court and witnesses. Only instrument labelled this way in our corpus.
* **genre – consentient legal** (the main document): formulaic style, ordered layout, full dating, archaic anaphora; Doc. I is a not uncommon format for legal material (43 cm high); the file concerns private interests; delocutive/locutive textemes, degree 2 Neo-Egyptian.

The file, reconstructed in modern times, is the work of six hands: the two hands of Doc. I are neat and ordered, a 'belle écriture bien claire'[220] ; that of Doc. II is 'large, thick and clumsy' with ligatures; that of Doc. III is a 'smaller and neater' business hand with more isolated signs[221]; Doc. IV is the work of two business hands, the first 'bold writing with good forms and orthography', the careless second hand 'abounds in mistakes of all kinds'[222]. Use is made of administrative practice abreviations, there are errors, corrections (probably after re-reading), and one major error in Doc. I, line IV.8.

Concerning the provenance of the documents, *pAshmolean Museum* 1945.97 and 1945.95 were acquired on the market but seem to originate from Deir el-Medina like *pDeM* 23 & 25 that were found among various fragments of letters, business documents, medical-magic, religious and literary pieces, from 'the trapezoid space south of P 1165' 'among the ruins of the tombs and chapels to the north of the village'[223]. These documents were perhaps a private archive[224] and our file would be a rare case of a docket (label with summary mention on the rolled papyrus) in a private context; but in fact there is no proof that all the papyri came from the same archive and only Doc. I is labelled with a docket[225].

Legal step: Doc. I is an **external manifestation of will** concerning the transmission of assets with **notification** of specific information concerning the heirs and disinherited children (*r rdit rḫ.tw*) recorded in court. On the same papyrus follow the records of the representation (*wḥm sprw*) in court of the husband and children (*adscriptus*). The execution of the **partition** (*pšt n ꜣḫt*) is recorded on Docs. II and III; two public statements (*ḏd*) of the

---

219 For Théodoridès (1969: 111), Doc. I is not a 'copie conforme du procès-verbal de la séance' but an 'expédition délivrée à l'intéressée' (1966: 43, 54-5) as there is a scribal correction in Doc. I and the title deeds justifying the ownership of the testatrix are not mentioned.

220 Théodoridès (1966: 32) who adds 'ce papyrus est magnifique'.

221 Černý (1945: 37); Donker van Heel & Haring (2003: 21, 158 n.139) 'both with well-practised hands'.

222 Černý (1945: 40).

223 Donker van Heel & Haring (2003: 102 n.101); Černý (1945: 36).

224 The file was 'kept at home by the interested party (the heirs)' for Donker van Heel & Haring (2003: 11-3 and 102), but is thought to be an *Originalprotokoll* 'ins Gerichtsarchiv' by Allam (1973: 273-4).

225 The other papyri found in the same area, such as *pChester Beatty* I-XIX and *pDeM* 1-17 (Pestman 1982: 155) are not labelled, and it is strange that only Doc. I would have been docketed in the archive; either Doc. I was not found there or it was found there but came from a public archive where it was classified by a docket written in an official register.

husband (with the oath of one of his sons) concerning the ***tradition*** of an item are recorded in Doc. IV.

Legal issue: **will and related procedure**: absence of *consideration*, unilateral deed concerning the transmission of the entire patrimony to the children of the testator; use of *rdi, pš, swꜣḏ*; typical clauses (future *descent and distribution* rules, implicit performative for attribution of right, mention of old age and retributive principle in the *recital*, *exemption from hotchpot*, *advancement*, exclusion relating to specific items, lists of heirs and disinherited children); *tradition* of movable assets, partition of lots of similar value.

Textemic features:

A. Document I (*pAshmolean Museum* 1945.97)

1. Pre-material

Date: (I.1) *rnpt-sp* 3 *ꜣbd* 4 *ꜣḫt sw* 5 (2) *ḫr ḥm n ni-swt bity nb tꜣwy Wsrmꜣꜥtrꜥ Sḫprnrꜥ ꜥ.w.s.* (3) *sꜣ Rꜥ nb ḫꜥyw mi Tm Rꜥmss Ỉmnḥrḫpšf Mrỉmn ꜥ.w.s. di ꜥnḫ ḏt nḥḥ*
Year 3, month 4 of inundation, day 5, under (the) majesty of (the) King of Upper (and) Lower Egypt, lord of (the) two lands, *Wsrmꜣꜥtrꜥ Sḫprnrꜥ* L.P.H., son of Re, lord of crowns like Atum, *Rꜥmss Ỉmnḥrḫpšf Mrỉmn* L.P.H., given life forever (and) ever.

archaic anaphora: (4) *h[r]w pn*	This d[a]y
Title:	
object & instrument: *irt hꜣrwy n ꜣḫt{tw}.st*	of making a declaration record of her assets
testator: (5) *ỉ[n ꜥ]nḫ-n-niwt Niwtnḫtti*	b[y the ꜥ]*nḫ-n-niwt Niwtnḫtti*
forum: *m-bꜣḥ ḳnbt [t]n*	before [t]his court[226]:
(6) *ꜥꜣ n ist Nḫtmmwt*	foreman *Nḫtmmwt*
(7) *ꜥꜣ n ist Ỉnḥrḫꜥw*	foreman *Ỉnḥrḫꜥw*
(8) *sš Ỉmnnḫtw n pꜣ ḫr*	scribe of the Necropolis *Ỉmnnḫtw*
(9) *sš Ḥršriw*	scribe *Ḥršriw*
(10) *sš ḳdw Ỉmnḥtpw*	draughtsman *Ỉmnḥtpw*
(11) *rmṯ ist Tinrmntiw*	workman *Tinrmntiw*
(12) *rmṯ ist Tꜣ*	workman *Tꜣ*
(13) *sš ḳdw Pntꜣwrt*	draughtsman *Pntꜣwrt*
(14) *rmṯ ist Wsrḥꜣt*	workman *Wsrḥꜣt*
(15) *rmṯ ist Nbnfr*	workman *Nbnfr*
(16) *rmṯ ist Ỉmnpꜣḥꜥpy*	workman *Ỉmnpꜣḥꜥpy*
(17) *ꜣṯw Ỉmnnḫt*	*ꜣṯw*-officer[227] *Ỉmnnḫt*
(18) *ꜣṯw Rꜥms*	*ꜣṯw*-officer *Rꜥms*
(19) *rmṯ ist Nbnfr sꜣ Ḫnsw*	workman *Nbnfr*, son of *Ḫnsw*.

* Neo-Egyptian characteristics:
- Neo-Egyptian spelling of *hꜣrwy, ꜣḫt{tw}*;
- delocutive feminine singular suffix *st*;

226 Deir el-Medina's court consisted mainly of local members of the gang of workers as well as outside officials such as the *ꜣṯw*-officers and the scribes of the vizier.

227 *wꜥrtw* for Černý (1945: 43) and Théodoridès (1966: 36). See McDowell (1990: 55-9); Frandsen (1990: 170) 'proctors'; Janssen (2005: 15).

- exophoric articloid (extratextual deixis, context-dependent) for specific administrative unit of the Theban area (*pꜣ ḫr*);
- absence of feminine mark of [ꜥ]*nḫ-n-niwt* (usually written in the file with added plural marker, as in *oGardiner/Ashmolean* 90);

* 'Classical' degree 0 forms used:

- relator *n* in dominion (*ꜥꜣ n ist*), subject (*ḥm n ni-swt bity*), contents (*hꜣrwy n ꜣḫt{tw}.st*)[228], unclear kind of relation in frozen expression ([ꜥ]*nḫ-n-niwt*), and administrative department dependance relations (*sš* PN *n pꜣ ḫr*);
- *di ꜥnḫ*: traditional blessing formula, see *EG* § 378;
- traditional binomials *ni-swt bity*, *ḏt nḥḥ*, and trinomial *ꜥnḫ wḏꜣ snb*. The classical binomial *ḏt nḥḥ* is used instead of its degree 1 counterpart *r nḥḥ ḥnꜥ ḏt* (see David 2006: 128);
- *hrw pn irt hꜣrwy*: infinitive as relational expansion of the archaic anaphora, as seen in *oDeM* 108, but here without relator;
- archaic cataphoric proximal demonstrative *ḳnbt tn* + members list: since the archaic demonstrative has an extremely restricted use in Neo-Egyptian, limited to a few lexemes (see *LEG*, 40-1 list of examples with *hrw, pr, st*; the list is incomplete), it is significant that the pre-material of our document contains two examples of archaic demonstrative used with a different type of referentiality and different lexemes. A similar use of archaic demonstrative pervades modern legal registers (David 2006: 34). For other cataphoric uses of the archaic proximal demonstrative in Ramesside royal decrees, see David (2006: 116, 123, 169).
  The list is ordered hierarchically in descending order of rank (diminishing progression)[229], but interestingly the two *ꜣṯw*-officers appear among the workmen towards the end of the list, and two workmen precede the second draughtsman, after the scribes and foremen.

* General dialectal features: degree 1.

* Legal formula: date (year, month of season, day + *ḥr ḥm n* + royal titulary) + *hrw pn* + infinitive (object) + *in* (testator) + *m-bꜣḥ ḳnbt* [*t*]*n* (forum with list).

2. *Recital*

Brief narrative preamble concerning facts followed by a justificatory comment of the author of the speech. The preamble is an aetiologic information texteme essential in most legal documents as it provides their legal and factual justification; it is nowadays a fixture of most instruments of normative, contentious, and consentient genres in an attempt to prevent interpretational dissension, and was always present in important Ramesside royal decrees concerning criminal law (David 2006: 19, 30).

In the consentient legal genre, the preamble takes the form of a *recital*; it may be viewed as the causal chain of events that has determined, in the opinion of its author, his course of action and the redaction of the document, with a commentary on his part concerning the grounds of the deed[230].

---

228 Note that for Théodoridès (1966: 36, n. 21), it is a case of *n* instead of *m* preposition.

229 See Fischer (1973) and for hierarchical lists in Ramesside royal decrees, David (2006: *esp*. 33).

230 Many narrative structures comprise both a dynamic chain of events and a static commentary on those events, the author's intrusion, where 'the narrator explains the meaning or significance of a narrative

A funerary provision of the 6th dynasty (in *Ỉdw*'s *tomb*) protecting a gift after the donor's death is already grounded by the following locutive statement: [*iw swt ir.n*(*.i*)] *nn n* PN *tn n wr n im3ḫ.s m ḫt*(*.i*) *n ḏd.s ṯs šnꜥ ib*(*.i*) *n iw.s r tr m* [*ꜥnḫ.i*] '[But I have done] this because of the greatness of her state of *im3ḫ* in (my) family, because she did not say a word that (my) heart rejected, because she did not do an evil thing at the time of [my life]'[231].

The Ramesside *recital* is a written narrative presented as a genuine verbal and public monologue but consisting of stereotypical expressions and a conventional, strictly limited storyline with a predictable structure: here the socio-economic condition of *nmḥy* of the testatrix, her view of the facts essentially proving that she fulfilled her maternal duties. Thus, although it is a locutive speech introduced by a delocutive tag clause (perfect report) as a quoted discourse, using features of personal involvement such as *ir ink* (indicating personal focus, a conventional register marker) and *gr ink*, a dynamic verbal style, markers of direct interaction with the court (allocutive pronouns, *ptri*, humility formula, deictics), impersonal generalization, isotopy (*ḫr ptri*), contrast, and unspecified referents, it also has informational features such as topicalization of nominal syntagms expressing a customary contrasted retributive principle, and an extremely synthetic style adapted to the written format. The narrative discourse mainly uses past tense (perfect report and sequential) to describe interpersonal relationships, introduced by a *verbum dicendi.* The narrative is followed by a segment in which the testatrix comments on the facts in a contrastive structure: her present diminished circumstances due to her age and the fact that her children are not all taking care of her, adding the reciprocity principle on which all wills are apparently based. The *recital* is highly context-dependent (deictics, pronouns, no proper names) and argumentative (the markers of interaction also have a suasive effect, as does the contrastive reciprocity principle), and uses a moderately low register of expression (degree 2 Neo-Egyptian with fewer classical forms).

tag clause: (II.1) *ḏdw.st* She said:

statement quotation: *ir ink* *ink* *nmḥy n p3 t3 n Pr-ꜥ3 ꜥ.w.s.* (2) *irwy.i sḫpr.w p3y* 8 *b3kiw tn-myw* (3) *iw.i ḥr dit n.sn grg-pr m 3ḫt nb nty tw.tw ḥr ir.f* (4) *n n3 nty mi ḳd.w ḫr ptri tw.i i3wt.ki* (5) *ḫr ptri bn st ḥr irt ḫrt.i gr ink*

As for me, I am *nmḥy* of the land of Pharaoh L.P.H. I brought them up, these 8 servants of yours. And I gave them an establishment (consisting) of all assets that one constitutes for those who are in their position.

And see me, I am old (now). But see that it is not (as if) they are taking care of me, yes me.

retributive principle:

(6) *ir p3 w3ḥ nb drt.f ḥr drt.i im.w iw.i r di n.f 3ḫt.i*

(7) *ir p3 nty bwpw.f dit n.i bn iw*[*.i*] *r di n.f m 3ḫt.i*

As for each one who laid his hand on my hand among them, I shall give him my assets.

As for the one who did not lend (a hand) to me, I shall not give him (any) of my assets.

* Neo-Egyptian characteristics:
- tag clause *ḏdw.st*: Neo-Egyptian perfect form of the *verbum dicendi* signaling the transition between the pre-material and the monologue of the *recital*, an editorial

element, makes value judgments, refers to worlds transcending the characters' world, and/or comments on his or her own narration.' (Prince 1987: 14); Shisha-Halevy (2007).

231 For Strudwick (2005: 189): 'while she was alive'.

formula associated with an oral formula (*ỉr ỉnk*)[232]; see also *oPetrie* 18. The addition of an intrusive *w* to the stem is elsewhere attested for the perfect (e.g. *pAbbott* 7, 8: *ḏdw pꜣy ḥꜣty-ꜥ*).

The main mode of the will is locutive, but the quoted words are certainly far from representing the actual original spoken ones; the record consitutes a shorter version of the verbal speech, retaining only essential elements; it is an official record translating the general idea of the speech of the testatrix, a constructed quotation[233]. As a delocutive report form of this type is used at the head of the will of the testatrix, we may assume that the recorded speech-act before a power invested assembly was a fully performative, constitutive, binding act. But the combination of the oral speech and the standardized authenticated record may both be important for the will to be binding (see our remarks concerning the text-as-object *supra*). The use of a typical and standardized *storyline* by the scribe implies that the written version of the will is more abstract than the personal oral speech of the testator, the written deed being concerned with the main principle justifying the dispositions. The fact that it is not a *verbatim* transcript of the oral speech and that it does not mention specific oral practices besides its orality (the tag clause) indicates that the record has an intrinsic legal value. Note that the 6th dynasty *Balat tablet* 5955, the record by an official of the verbal will of a testator, uses *ỉw ḏd.n.f*, an Old Egyptian perfect report form, as a tag clause introducing his locutive declaration. See also the case of the Ramesside royal decrees and their autonomy in David (2006: 36). For modern constitutive rituals with record, see Danet (1997: 26); concerning contemporary fact-construction within the courtroom, see Jackson (1988: 61 ff.);

- Neo-Egyptian spelling (*nmḥy, ptrỉ, bꜣkỉw, ꜣḫt*);
- delocutive feminine singular *.st* and plural suffix*.w* (*sḫpr.w, ḳd.w, ỉm.w*);
- *ỉr ỉnk* *ỉnk* *nmḥy*: formulaic opening of the reconstructed direct speech conceived as # topicalizer *ỉr* + locutive independent pronoun (with the [HUMAN-MALE] classifier) + classical nominal nexus with independent pronoun theme (with the [FEMALE] classifier) and nominal rheme #. See similar pattern in Coptic of interlocutive topicalized theme[234].

The formula # *ỉr ỉnk* # signals a speech act related to the speaker's motivation (prominent topic) based on the exposition of factual ground, as in *oPetrie* 18; a 'statutory' ground is of course introduced by other means (see *pTurin* 2021). Its essential function is to introduce a personal statement of the speaker, based on his view of the events or situation and personal motives[235]. Once again topicalization is a central feature not only as the opening of the *recital* but also in legal genres.

As for # *ỉnk nmḥy* #, it represents the self-presentation of the testatrix as a simple 'citizen', not in a dependent status and entitled to possess private assets (see *infra* for

232 Haring (2003: 148), in depositions.

233 Note a slight internal contradiction on the subject in Théodoridès (1966: 47): 'Le scribe note les déclarations qui lui sont faites dans le langage de la personne qui parle', but 'est-ce le scribe qui, après coup, a donné une "forme" – car il y en a une, incontestablement – à sa déclaration'.

234 Shisha-Halevy (1984: 176; 1988: 17-8).

235 For Haring (2003: 148-9), the use of *ỉr ỉnk* seems reserved for oral depositions concerning wrongful acts, and is not used in case of a decision of the author concerning his assets, for instance in a will; this is obviously disproved. See also Sweeney (2001: 18) 'typical opening words of litigants' speeches in court'.

the notion of *nmḥy*). In *ir ink, ink* 𓀀 is gender-indifferent[236] (the self) as opposed to *ink* in *ink*𓁐 *nmḥy* (female identity).

Since *ir ink* quite frequently marks the beginning of *recital*s, it may be a formal marker of the *written* texteme, perhaps part of a true recorded speech but certainly a formal, standardized feature of the written text;

- cataphoric articloid (*pꜣ tꜣ*) ;
- *irwy.i sḫpr.w*: perfect locutive report, analytic form, with characteristic double *yod* of the auxiliary, see Winand (1992: 194 & 197-8). The causative infinitive *sḫpr.w* with Neo-Egyptian suffixed plural delocutive object is viewed by Černý (1945: 33) as a non-suffixed infinitive with plural strokes; but if one considers that the following *pꜣy* 8 *bꜣkiw tn-myw* stands in apposition (*epexegesis*[237]) to the object *w*, the deictic effect of this last segment is reinforced, as well as the opposition *ink* (me) – *w*/*pꜣy* (them/these).

  Having drawn attention to herself and identified her status, the speaker reports her relevant behavior, as in most autobiographic Egyptian records (see e.g. the classical autobiography constructed on the model # titles + name + *ḏd(.f)* + *ink sꜣ s* (...) + *iw ir.n.i* (*mꜣꜥt*...) #. The perfect *irwy.i sḫpr.w* refers to a general past behavior of the speaker;
- *pꜣy* 8 *bꜣkiw tn-myw*: # singular deictic determinator + quantifier + plural N + Neo-Egyptian form of allocutive possessive (Middle Egyptian *n.ṯn-imy*, *EG* § 113.3 'A more emphatic equivalent of the English possessive adjective') #. In this type of syntagm, the deictic determinator is always singular with a quantifier superior to 2, but the substantive is plural (see also *pAdoptions*), as in Middle Egyptian[238]. Note the compatibility of deixis marker (high specificity), quantifier and possessive ('fuzzy specificity'[239]).

  The syntagm refers to the object of *sḫpr.w* in a direct address from inferior to superior, the lexemic choice of *bꜣkiw* expressing by contrast the highest status attributed to the court members by the speaker[240]; it is of course metaphorical and not to be taken literally as Eyre (1992: 211) does. A humility formula was already used in the epistolary genre during the Old Kingdom, as in *Balat tablet* 3689-7, 8 & 11 and *pBoulaq* 8 (6th dynasty), with the expression *bꜣk im* 'the servant there'[241], meaning the writer of the letter[242].

  For a similar use of the allocutive possessive in Ramesside epistolary royal decrees (direct address from the superior body to an inferior one), see David (2006: 225-6, 232-3) *pꜣy sš tiwy* 'this scribe of yours' and *wꜥ šmsy tiw* 'one attendant of yours';
- sequential locutive preterit *iw.i ḥr dit* (narrative form) opposed to the preceding report perfect (*irwy.i sḫpr.w*)[243].

---

236 Satzinger (1976: 11) notes that the gender indifference of *ir ink* 𓀀 'unterstreicht den formelhaften Charakter' of the expression.

237 Clarifying or specifying addition like the English *i.e.* In Neo-Egyptian stories, the *epexegesis* may be introduced by *m* (Hintze 1950: 131) in the narrative; in *Rede*, by *in*/*nꜣ*/*n* (Hintze 1952: 290).

238 *EG* § 261.

239 Shisha-Halevy (2007b: 228-9, 249).

240 See Théodoridès (1966: 37, n.24): 'formule de déférence'.

241 Eichler (1991: 26) with references; Shisha-Halevy (2007b: 238): 'pragmatically specific', *im* 'marking deprecating deixis'.

242 Omnipresent in the Middle Kingdom epistolary archives of Lahun, see e.g. *pUC* 32109B.

243 See Frandsen (1974: 8-9) for the use of the sequential after a report form in legal registers.

The preterit fits the causal chain of events that forms the *recital*, its additive structure intended to reinforce the legitimacy of the provisions. In the modern Anglo-American legal system it is customary to use the expression *narrative recital* for the *whereas clause*[244] of the preamble of a contract/deed, since behind each case there is a story and a narrative of persuasion[245] (cf. legal *narratio*[246]). The *recital* basically combines features of the commentary (*Besprechung – commentaire*, subjective quality marked by the locutive report and *ir ink*) and the story (factual narrative using sequential preterit). Furthermore, this narrative is meant to be verbally expressed, and one of the characteristics of orality is that oral expression is additive, whereas written expression is subordinative[247]; the chain of sequential preterites is especially appropriate for the verbal narration of the *recital*.

Concerning narratives in Coptic child gift deeds, see Richter (2005) who also notes the stereotyped quality of the *narratio* in this corpus, a story combining actual as well as fictive elements;

- absence of concord of the adjective (*ꜣḫt nb*);
- N *nb nty tw.tw ḥr ir.f*: relative durative generic present, with impersonal Neo-Egyptian thematic pronoun, Neo-Egyptian form of the infinitive instead of classical *irt*, and masculine resumptive object *.f* referring ultimately to *grg-pr*.
  The entire statement is marked by a high degree of generalization through the use of the impersonal, the non-actual present and the generic *ꜣḫt nb*. See Groll (1970: 47) for a similar construction in *pSalt* 124 v° I.3 (*nꜣ ḫt nty tw.tw ḥr dit.w*)[248];
- *nꜣ nty mi ḳd.w*: substantivized relative sentence with # cataphoric articloid + relative adjective + adverbial rheme #, expressing generality;
- *ḫr ptri tw.i iꜣwt.ki*: # proclitic coordinator + Neo-Egyptian presentative *ptri* + Neo-Egyptian locutive thematic pronoun + stative (actual present) #. The present circumstances of the testatrix are contrasted with her past activity; *ḫr ptri* twice introduces the arguments of the testatrix concerning her decision to disinherit some of the children (*ḫr* has in this case a contrastive value[249], it functions as coordination and demarcation[250]). Thus the cohesive *ḫr* with *ptri* introduce a climax in the *recital*, ending the sequential chain of the narrative *sensu stricto* with a segment of a commentary nature expounding the main arguments motivating her decisions; the same device is used in the *recital* of *pAdoptions*, line 22, and in *pTurin* 2021, line 8.
  The function of *ptri* is to involve the audience[251] and put the focus on the present diminished state of the testatrix. This orality device aims to reduce the distance between the speaker and the audience; other markers of involvement with the addressees of the

244 'A preamble often consists of a series of clauses introduced by the conjunction *whereas*' (Garner 2004: 1214).

245 For narratives in law and law as literature, see Gewirtz (1996); for a study of narratives in Common Law trial process, see Jackson (1988); for the use of *stock stories* or a storyline with adaptations of details but constant central plot in modern criminal trials, see Morison & Leith (1992: 184-9).

246 *Narratio* in legal terminology designates 'Hist. A declaration, complaint, or petition in which the plaintiff sets out the facts of a case; an oral narrative by the plaintiff of the facts and legal arguments on which the claim is based. The term has also been called the "conte" or "tale"' (Garner 2004: 1049).

247 Ong (1982: 37-8).

248 See David (2006: 91-2) for an example of relative present expressing habit in a Ramesside royal decree, with references.

249 Hintze (1950: 64 and 1952: 208, 210), both in narrative and Rede textemes.

250 Neveu (1988: 104); ; David (2006: 67).

251 For a discussion of involvement features in oral speech, see Chafe (1982) and Biber (1995: 141-51).

speech are the allocutive mode and stress markers such as *gr ỉnk,* as well as humility towards superiors with *bꜣkỉw tn-myw*.

As *ptrỉ* may be considered a 'substitute of Middle Egyptian *mk*'[252], the construction with *ptrỉ* could be compared to classical # *m.k* + nominal form + adverbial adjunct # (David 2000b). But Neo-Egyptian also has patterns in which the classical presentative *m.k* is directly followed by an adverbial form without a dependent pronoun[253], and of course the same is true for *ptr*. Thus we may have here # *ḫr ptrỉ* + *tw.ỉ ỉꜣwt.kỉ* (adverbial present nexus) #, like its negative counterpart *ḫr ptrỉ bn st ḥr ỉrt*. Note that *m.k* is never used in the *recital* of our Ramesside wills, as it belongs to a higher register of expression.

The *old age argument* can already be found in the gift of *pKahun* VII, 1: *ḫft ntt wỉ tn.kwỉ* 'because I am old now'. In the *Amarah stela* (*Stela Brooklyn* 38.544) of late 20th dynasty[254], we find a similar idea motivating a woman's *dispositions*: *tꜣy šriw mnts ỉr n.ỉ ỉꜣw* 'this daughter (of mine), she is the one who acted on my behalf when I became old'. A similar formulation is also used in an Aramaic deed of bequest from Elephantine, *pKraeling* 9, dated to 404 B.C.: 'I, Anani have given it [a house] to Jehoishma, my daughter upon my death in affection because she supported me when I was old of days.'[255]

Although *Naunakhte* mentions her old age, she adds nothing about her health by the time she states her will (the *sound health* clause, similar to modern 'sound in body and mind' and referring to the capacity of the disponor) as can be seen in some Old Kingdom tomb provisions such as *Nkꜣwrꜥ*'s *tomb*, 4th dynasty (*ꜥnḫ ḥr rdwy.f ny mn.f ỉḫt* 'living (= standing) on his (own) two feet, while not suffering any thing'), or the *Kꜣmnfrt*? *Cairo block* CG 1432, 5th dynasty ([*sk*] *sw ꜥnḫ ḥr rdwy.f*);

- *ḫr ptrỉ bn st ḥr ỉrt*: # proclitic coordinator *ḫr* + presentative *ptrỉ* + Neo-Egyptian negator *bn* + dependent pronoun + converb (negative present) #[256].
  It is the main ground for claim of the testatrix[257], and *ḫr* has a strong contrastive value;
- Neo-Egyptian delocutive plural dependent pronoun *st*;
- *ẖrt.ỉ gr ỉnk*: # N + locutive possessive suffix + clause final stress particle *gr* + independent locutive pronoun reinforcing the possessor #[258].
  The call for the attention of the audience was openend by *ḫr ptrỉ tw.ỉ,* relayed by the closing *gr ỉnk*;

252 Junge (2005: 333).

253 Goldwasser (2001: 125-8).

254 Picture in Fairman (1938: pl. XI); better pictures were kindly sent to me by Dr. Bleiberg, curator of Egyptian, Classical and Ancient Middle Eastern Art at the Brooklyn Museum and his assistant Ms. Zurek-Doule; I am extremely grateful to both of them for their kind help.
The complete sandstone stela found in the temple of Amarah West is the hieroglyphic record of two brief verbal statements (*rꜣ, ḏd*) on a lapidary monument decorated with a religious scene, undated. Obviously the stela is not a will, but concerns an inheritance and either a renunciation or a gift on the part of the owner of the stela in favor of his sister (?) and a renunciation or a testamentary disposition of a mother (?) in favor of the same woman, perhaps after court proceedings (Théodoridès 1964). The first statement uses the construction # *ỉr ḫt nb* (…) *ns-sw* N PN # which in this context may not be an implicit performative but a constative (see *infra*), whereas the second declaration uses # *ỉr* N (…) *dỉ.t.s n* PN #, a construction that does not appear in the operative part of Ramesside wills.

255 Porten & Szubin (1987: 182).

256 See *LEG* § 20.2.4.

257 For Sweeney (2001: 205), it is a 'statement rather than a complaint'.

258 See *LEG*, 2.1.6; Černý (1945: 33.h); Hintze (1952: 290-1) 'pronominale Hervorhebung' in *Rede* textemes; Junge (2005: 165). Of course both *ỉr ỉnk* and *gr ỉnk* are also to be found in stories (e.g. in *Wenamun* 2, 12).

- *ir p3 w3ḥ nb… iw.i r di*: topicalized category of heirs constructed with # topicalizor *ir* + *p3* substantivizer articloid + perfect participle + distributive *nb* (with singular anaphoric *n.f*) #, in parallel with the topicalized category of disinherited children # *ir* + *p3* + *nty bwpw.f dit* (negative perfect relative clause) #, both followed by the locutive future (*bn*) *iw.i r di* (with Neo-Egyptian form of the infinitives instead of classical *dit*, but with the preposition retained)[259]. The categories are thus expressed either by a synthetic form (participle) or by an analytic relative sentence with negative perfect, always fronted by topicalization (as category marker).
  The topicalized nominal category refers to a past behavior of the heir that conditions his inheritance rights, hence the use of the perfect in the topicalized category and the future in the second part of the statement. The future is the tense of the will *par excellence*; the formulation expresses *causality*, the stated future consequence of a past behavior.
  The *recital* in ancient Egyptian wills usually culminates with a contrastive retributive Justice principle, what Seidl (1957b) calls the *Prinzip der notwendigen Entgeltlichkeit*, a reciprocal principle of good for good, bad for bad. In ancient Egyptian belief the same principle governs personal fate, recalling some legal theories of retributivism in the realm of criminal law. The mention of retribution is highly conventional in our texteme. The first examples of the contrasted retributive principle belong to the Old Kingdom (e.g. *PT* Spell 485; *Urk*. I, 122 lines 10-6). In the realm of the family, moral 'mutual responsibilities of family members' consist of 'support of elderly parents, their proper burial by the eldest son, and the maintenance of the mortuary'[260], and support in old-age is still the main motivation of the bequest of a father to his daughter in an Aramaic papyrus from Elephantine dated to 404 B.C., *pKraeling* 9[261]. The negative-positive polarity is common in the legal frame such as the negative and positive intent in the preamble *sensu stricto* of Ramesside royal decrees (David 2004: 37 and 2006: 30, 41 ff., 50 ff.), or curses followed by blessings for positive behavior (*ibid*. 117, n. 22 with references), as well as in other contexts (e.g. religious genres).
  The hands metaphor for the positive behavior of the children renders the mutual benefit idea otherwise expressed by 'I've been good to them, they've been good to me (*nfr n.i/iri n.i nfr*)' used in the *recital* of other wills. Note that a similar metaphor is used in the *Teaching of Amenemhat*: *rdi.n.i n.f ʿwy.i* 'he whom I had given my hands (used it to plot)'.
  Finally, one must note the opposition *iw.i r di n.f 3ḫt.i* (positive – immediate object of *di*) versus *bn iw*[*.i*] *r di n.f m 3ḫt.i* (negative – mediate object with preposition *m*). It may be an additional means of rendering the fact that a positive attitude entitles one to the entire assets, whereas a negative one forbids even a partial bequest (*m* – from);

* 'Classical' degree 0 forms used:
  - relator *n* used in 'citizenship'/residence and dominion relations (*nmḥy n p3 t3 n Pr-ʿ3*);
  - perfect participle without prothetic *yod* (*w3ḥ*);
  - use of the suffix possessor with *drt.i/f* (body part) and *3ḫt.i* (ownership);
* General dialectal features: degree 2.
* Legal formula: *recital* = *ḏdw.st* (tag clause) + *ir ink* (prominent topic) + *ink* N (identity) + *irwy.i* (positive behavior) + *ḫr ptri tw.i i3wt.ki ḫr ptri bn st ḥr irt ḫrt.i* (commentary - main ground: old age but negative behavior of some children) + retributive principle: *ḫr ir* (category of legatees) + (*bn*) *iw.i r di*.

259 A progressive tense for Satzinger (1976: 195-6).
260 Jasnow (2003: 118-9).
261 Porten & Szubin (1987: esp. 189-91).

3. Operative part

A complex ensemble divided into two categories in the form of nominal lists of heirs and disinherited children; in each category, the testatrix deals with specific issues related to certain children. The texteme mixes short delocutive frame-like headings using a notification formula and locutive quotes from the monologue of the testatrix, as again the provisions were expressed by her orally before the court. The sequence of the lists follows the sequence of the positive and negative attitudes of the preceding contrastive retributive principle. Note the absence of a general *descent and distribution* rule concerning all the children, explained by the variety of situations of inheritance (with or without restrictions) and disinheritance.

Informational focus and detachment mark the notification formula and ordered list of proper names (high noun frequency). The quoted speech is marked by features of involvement (locutive, pronoun without specified referent in the oral speech, reference depending on the delocutive cotext and situation, deictics, performative), but also by informational features (it is brief, uses phrasal and clause-initial coordination for integration, nominal topicalization structure), and presents some classical forms, although the register is of a degree 2 Neo-Egyptian. No narrative is involved in the speech of the testatrix (only one form of report as a commentary), the texteme is not overtly argumentative nor abstract in style.

Notification of list of heirs and specific issues:
(III.1) *r rdit rḫ.tw n3 rmṯ ist ḥmwt rdi.s n.w*
For information (relative to) the workmen and the women to whom she gave (a share):

(2) *rmṯ ist M33nnḫtwf*	the workman *M33nnḫtwf;*
(3) *rmṯ ist Ḳnḥrḫpšf*	the workman *Ḳnḥrḫpšf* -

gift with *exemption from hotchpot*:
ḏdw.st diw.i n.f (4) *ḥsmn iꜥ m twnw m-ḥ3w n3y.f irw bdt ḫ3r* 10
she said: I gave him a bronze washing bowl as a bonus over and above his fellows[262] (worth) 10 sacks of emmer;

(5) *rmṯ ist Ἰmnnḫt*	workman *Ἰmnnḫt*;
(6) *ꜥnḫ-n-niwt W3stnḫti*	*ꜥnḫ-n-niwt W3stnḫti*;
(7) *ꜥnḫ-n-niwt Mnꜥtnḫtti*	*ꜥnḫ-n-niwt Mnꜥtnḫtti* -

***descent and distribution* rule and exclusion relative to specific items:**
ir ꜥnḫ-n-niwt Mnꜥ[t]nḫtti (8) *ḏdw.st r.s iw.st r h3y ḥr pšt m 3ḫt.i nbt* (9) *ḥry-ḥr t3 ipt bdt rdiw n.i p3y.i* 3 (10) *ḫrdw ꜥḥ3wty m-mitt ꜥnḫ-n-niwt W3stnḫti* (11) *m-mitt p3y.i hnw n sḳnn i.di.w n.i m p3y sḫr*
Concerning *ꜥnḫ-n-niwt Mnꜥ[t]nḫtti*, she said relating to her: 'She will come to a share from all my assets, except for the *oipe* of emmer that my 3 male children gave to me as well as *ꜥnḫ-n-niwt W3stnḫti*, likewise (excepting) my jar of fat that they gave to me in this fashion.'

Notification of list of disinherited children and specific issues:
(IV.1) *r rdit rḫ.tw n3y.st ḫrdw i.ḏdw.st*
For information (relative to) her children of whom she said:
exclusion concerning the community property:
(2) *bn iw.w r ꜥḳ r pšt m p3y.i r-3* (3) *i.ir.w ꜥḳ r p3 rwy n p3y.w it*
They will not enter into a share in my 1/3 (of the community property), (but) it is the 2/3 of their father[263] that they shall enter:

(4) *rmṯ ist Nfrḥtpw*	workman *Nfrḥtpw*

262 Théodoridès (1966: 38, n. 34) notes a similar use of *iry* in Demotic (*iry n pš*: coheir).
263 Her second companion.

(5) *ꜥnḫ-n-niwt Mnꜥtnḫtti*[264] *ꜥnḫ-n-niwt Mnꜥtnḫtti*
(6) *ꜥnḫ-n-niwt Ḥnwtšnw* *ꜥnḫ-n-niwt Ḥnwtšnw*
(7) *ꜥnḫ-n-niwt Ḫꜥtꜣnbw* *ꜥnḫ-n-niwt Ḫꜥtꜣnbw*

exclusion concerning her private assets:

ir pꜣ[*y*] 4 *ḫrdw* (8) *ink* <*bn*> *iw.w r ꜥḳ r pšt m ꜣḫt*{*tw*}*.i nbt* (9) *ḫr ir ꜣḫt nb n sš Ḳnḥrḫpšf pꜣy.i hi* (10) *m-mitt nꜣy.f swt*{*t*} *ḥnꜥ pꜣy wḏꜣ n pꜣy.i it* (11) *m-mitt tꜣy ipt bdt r.nwy.i* (12) *m-mitt pꜣy.i hi bn iw.w r pšt.w*

As for thes[e] 4 children of mine, they will <not> enter (the) division of all my assets. And as for all assets of (the) scribe *Ḳnḥrḫpšf* my (first) man, as well as his immovable property ('places')[265] together with this storehouse of my father[266], as well as this *oipe* of emmer that I collected with my man, they will not share them.

descent and distribution **rule concerning her companion's private assets**:

(V.1) *ḫr ir pꜣy* 8 *ḫrdw ink iw.w r ꜥḳ r pšt* (2) *ꜣḫt n pꜣy.w it m pšt wꜥ*

And as for these 8 children of mine, they will enter (the) division of assets of their father as one share[267].

advancement[268] **relative to specific items**:

(3) *ḫr ir pꜣy.i ḳꜣḥꜣnꜣ i.diw.i n.f r in n.f ꜥḳw* (4) *m-mitt pꜣ ḫꜣ n dbn* 7 (5) *m-mitt pꜣ irwrw n dbn* 7 (6) *m-mitt tꜣ ꜥnt*{*n*} *n* 6 *dbnw ir n dbn* 40 *iw.w n.f r pšt* (7) *bn iw.f r ꜥḳ r ḥmti nbt gr iw.w n nꜣy.f snw*

And as for my *ḳꜣḥꜣnꜣ* vessel (caldron?) that I gave to him (unnamed)[269] to buy himself food, as well as the spike of 7 *dbn*, and also the *irwrw* vase of 7 *dbn*, and the adze of 6 *dbnw*, (total) worth 40 *dbn*, they belong to him for a share. He will not inherit any further copper (items), they belong to his brothers.

* Neo-Egyptian characteristics:
- Neo-Egyptian delocutive plural *.w* (*n.w*) and feminine suffix (*.st*);
- cataphoric articloid (*nꜣ rmṯ ist ḥmwt; tꜣ ipt bdt; pꜣ rwy; pꜣ ḫꜣ; pꜣ irwrw; tꜣ ꜥnt*{*n*});
- Neo-Egyptian lexemes: *twnw* (*mtwnw* for Černý 1945: 33-4 on the basis of Doc. IV, line 8); *irwrw*; *ḫꜣ* (for Janssen 1975: 312-7 connected to Akkadian root *ḫll*; Hoch 1994: 243-4);

264 The name appears both in the list of the heirs and of the disinherited children, as well as in the lists of Docs. II and III. The legatee is to be excluded from the partition of grain and fat given by other children to their mother.

265 She obviously inherited from her first companion; inherited assets (from her companion and her father) are of course her personal property, independent of the community property of her present partnership.

266 As Allam (1973: 272-3) notes, 'Es wird dabei deutlich, daβ der Nachlaβ in verschiedene Massen aufgeteilt wird, so daβ die Erblasserin über jede Masse anders verfügen kann.'

267 McDowell (1999: 40) translates *m pšt wꜥ* as 'on equal terms', but the meaning is rather *together* (joint property) than an issue of partition of their father's inheritance that she could not ensure in her own will. Théodoridès (1966: 43, n.49) translates it as 'au moyen d'une division unique' and adds in a note that the children will inherit on equal terms in accordance with the legal mode of *devolution* if their father dies intestate.

268 Théodoridès (1964: 59; 1969: 114) 'désignation de part', 'conversion de prêt en avance d'hoirie'.

269 A blatant example of context-dependency, although not sufficient by itself to contest the autonomy of the deed as self-sufficient to produce legal effects. As Théodoridès (1966: 31) recognizes, 'Bien des précisions manquent dans l'acte, car elles étaient de notoriété publique au moment de sa rédaction', but it does not automatically imply that a prior, separate oral ceremony represented the 'real' will as in ancient Anglo-Saxon society (Danet & Bogoch 1994; Théodoridès 1966: 47). On the contrary, the purpose of the court session is to record and authenticate the will as an expression of the intimate intention of the testatrix, the precise aim of a modern notarial will.

- Neo-Egyptian possessive determinator for kinship (*nꜣy.f ỉrw; pꜣy.ỉ* 3 *ẖrdw; nꜣy.st ẖrdw; pꜣy.w ỉt; pꜣy.ỉ hỉ; pꜣy.ỉ ỉt; nꜣy.f snw*) and ownership (*pꜣy.ỉ hnw, pꜣy.ỉ r*-3; *nꜣy.f swt{t}; pꜣy.ỉ ḳꜣḥꜣnꜣ*). But note the use of the suffix possessor with *ꜣḫt.ỉ* (ownership);
- Neo-Egyptian spelling (*ꜣḫt, pš*);
- tag clause *ḏdw.st*: see *supra*. It twice introduces quoted direct speeches, comments of the testatrix concerning some of the heirs, and once a whole segment of quoted speech concerning the disinherited children;
- *dỉw.ỉ*: perfect locutive report in a direct speech commentary concerning one of the legatees (note the presence of intrusive *w* as in perfect *ḏdw.st supra*).

  Although Théodoridès (1966: 50-3) recognizes that the form is a perfect, he prefers to use the future to translate it (as does McDowell 1999: 39), since the testatrix 'proclame en substance, maintenant, qu'elle n'en [the washing bowl] exige pas le rapport, ce qui signifie qu'elle convertit les prêts qu'elle lui avait consentis en avance d'hoirie' and he assumes that the scribe that wrote the text after the verbal declaration of the testatrix made a mistake in using the perfect after using the relative form *rdi.s n.w*. Nevertheless, she may simply be mentioning the fact that the *tradition* of the item has been done in the past with the intention that it should be considered a bonus in the future inheritance.

  Note in *Sꜣmwt*'s tomb (lower inscription) from the reign of Ramesses II, the text concerning the gift opens with full date, followed by *hrw pn ḏd n* N PN (...) *r-nty + dỉw.ỉ ḫt.ỉ nb ḥnꜥ* [...] *Mwt* 'this day of (the) statement of N PN to wit: "I gave all my assets with [... to] *Mwt*"', *dỉw.ỉ* being the same report form.

  Although presented in a locutive mode, the transcription of the oral speech must have been of a summarizing, formatted nature adapted to the written notarization;
- relative perfect forms with prothetic *yod*: *ỉ.dỉ.w, ỉ.dỉ.ỉ* and *r.nwy.ỉ* with prothetic *r* in reported locutive speech and *ỉ.ḏdw.st* in the delocutive frame-like heading; thus the presence of the prothetic *yod* is not used here as an exclusively low register mark.

  For Černý (1945: 33.k), *rdi.s* and *rdi.w* are also Neo-Egyptian forms of the relative with the prothetic *yod* written as *r*; but Winand (1992: 376) notes about the prothetic *r* that 'cette graphie est extrêmement rare (15 cas sur 594 formes avec préfixe, soit 2,5 %)'. Examples of prothetic *r* forms are to be found from early 19th to at least mid-20th dynasty;
- Neo-Egyptian cataphoric demonstrative (*pꜣy wḏꜣ, tꜣy ỉpt*);
- *bn ỉw.w/f r ꜥḳ/ pšt.w*: future negated by Neo-Egyptian negator. Note that although this form belongs to the quoted as if spoken segment, the preposition has not been omitted.

  The future is used to convey the *descent and distribution* rule, exheredation is expressed by the same negated form;
- *m-mitt*: repeated use (7 times in this texteme) of the phrasal coordinator between determined nouns (mostly assets); a similar use, although less repetitive, is to be found in *oDeM* 108 and *oPetrie* 18;
- *ỉ.ỉr.w ꜥḳ r pꜣ rwy*: topic-initial cleft sentence expressing contrast with analytic that-form. The focus is on the assets that will be shared by the disinherited children, as opposed to the category of assets they will not share;
- *ỉr pꜣ*[*y*] 4 *ẖrdw ỉnk* <*bn*> *ỉw.w r ꜥḳ*: topicalized category of disinherited children # *ỉr* + *pꜣy* singular deictic determinator + quantifier + plural noun + *ỉnk* locutive independent pronoun possessor (kinship relation) + negated future *ỉw.ỉ r ꜥḳ* #. See also *ḫr ỉr pꜣy* 8 *ẖrdw ỉnk ỉw.w r ꜥḳ*. Topicalization is used to categorize as well as to mark a change of topic.

The locutive possessor is appended to a highly specified noun[270] (see *supra p3y* 8 *b3kiw tn-myw*).

The absence of the negator in this provision of exclusion concerning the private assets of the testatrix constitutes a serious error, and must clearly be viewed as such. The purpose of the *adscriptus* may have been to close an argument relative to this mistake (see *infra*);

- *ḫr ir 3ḫt nb* (…) *bn iw.w r pšt.w*: coordinated topicalized category of assets followed by future negative statement in the exclusion concerning *Naunakhte*'s private assets;
- *ḫr ir p3y.i ḳ3ḥ3n3 i.diw.i… iw.w n.f*: the *advancement* provision uses the formula # coordinator + topicalized nominal segment + performative attribution of ownership of specific items #.

  Interesting are the relationships between the future and the performative in our testamentary provisions, quite well illustrated by the *recital* and the operative part: the retribution principle, the *descent and distribution* rule and the exheredation/exclusion formula are constructed with the future since they deal with the principle of a future partition, whereas the attribution of specific items, including *advancement*, or a general bequest to a unique legatee is expressed by the implicit performative *iw.w n.f*;
- Neo-Egyptian spelling (*3ḫt{tw}.i*; for *ḳ3ḥ3n3*, see *ḳḥn* in Janssen 1975: 415-8);
- absence of concord of the adjective (*3ḫt nb*) following an example of marked concord with the same lexeme (*3ḫt{tw}.i nbt*);
- Neo-Egyptian form of the infinitives (*iw.i r di; r in*; *iw.w r pšt.w*);

* 'Classical' degree 0 forms used:

- *r rdit rḫ.tw*: lists of heirs and disinherited children are both introduced by the well-known classical Egyptian formula # *r* preposition + infinitive (purpose) + dependent impersonal/passive prospective object of *rdit* #, followed by determined and expanded nouns (*n3 rmṯ ist ḥmwt rdi.s n.w* and *n3y.st ẖrdw i.ḏdw.st*).

  The formula acts as categorial divider, as would modern devices such as paragraphing. Since the literal translation of *r rdit rḫ.tw* is 'to cause that be known', obviously announcing that the purpose is to communicate the following matter to an unspecified party, what is called in modern legal jargon a *notification*. The conventional translation 'list' alone does not convey this sense[271], so we should prefer 'for information'[272] or *notification* (of list).

  The formula can be found in letters (in allocutive form: e.g. *oGardiner/Ashmolean* 90, *oGlasgow* D 1925.66), in authenticated instruments dealing with private matters (e.g. *Naunakhte*, *pBoulaq* 10), in documents dealing with private matters brought to the attention of some undefined public (e.g. *oDeM* 941, *oBerlin* P 12406 & *oGlasgow* D 1925.71, *oBerlin* P 14328, *oBerlin* P 10637, *oCairo* CG 25612), in petitions to the oracle (e.g. *oPetrie* 16), in administrative journals (e.g. *pTurin* 2070), in court proceedings (e.g. *oGardiner/Ashmolean* 36), as well as in collective necropolis matters (e.g. deliveries, tomb inspection, etc.)[273]. Here, as in the epistolary

---

270 *LEG* § 2.2.2. But Junge (2005: 165) describes the use of the independent pronoun in extraposition as an 'appositional modification of unspecified nouns or those which cannot otherwise be specified' or as first member of a nominal nexus.

271 For Grandet (2000: 7), documents headed with the impersonal *r rdit rḫ.tw* are *mémoires*, by which he probably indicates that they have no legal value as instruments, but this is obviously not the case here.

272 See Sweeney (2001: 18) 'for your information'; Haring (2003: 143) 'Pour que l'on soit informé'.

273 See Donker van Heel & Haring (2003: 147 n.110).

oGardiner/Ashmolean 90 and in *pBoulaq* 10 in our corpus, the formula appears in the operative part.

The most extensive study of the formula in the context of Deir el-Medina is provided by Haring (2003: 153) who suggests considering the impersonal form as an evolution of the personal one, although he adds that the impersonal form, representing the king, is used as early as the Old Kingdom in official letters (e.g. in *Ḥrḫwf tomb* in *Urk.* I, 128 line 7). He also contends[274] that the formula became very popular in Deir el-Medina in private business material 'because it enabled scribes to develop new formulas in the vernacular' during the 20th dynasty since the 'first half of the Twentieth Dynasty appears to have been the *floruit'* of this formula, 'reserved for accounts of transfers, payments, debts and property-divisions'.

The impersonal/passive diathesis is a common feature of legal registers, both ancient (see for instance in Ramesside royal decrees, David 2006: 21) and modern[275]. The formula is reminiscent of some ancient Anglo-Saxon wills' *notificatio* such as 'Here in this document it is made known to whom [X] grants his possessions'[276].

Note that the preamble *sensu stricto* (negative intents list) formula of Ramesside royal decrees uses a similar construction: *r tm (r)dit* + impersonal/passive prospective, acting as divider between categories of crimes (David 2006: 44-5);

- perfect relative forms (*rdi.s, rdiw pꜣy.i* 3 *ẖrdw*); we already noted that these are viewed as cases of relatives with prothetic *r* by Černý (1945: 33.k, 34.q);
- *iw.st r hꜣy, iw.w r ʿḳ*: delocutive future (with Neo-Egyptian form of the suffixed actor) used in the quoted direct speech to express the *descent and distribution* rule to be enforced at the time of her death;
- concord of the adjective (*ꜣḫt.i nbt ; ḥmti nbt*);
- relator used for container/contents (*hnw n sḳnn*), ownership (*rwy n pꜣy.w it; ꜣḫt nb n sš; pꜣy wḏꜣ n pꜣy.i it; ꜣḫt n pꜣy.w it*), and weight/value relations (*pꜣ ḫꜣ n dbn* 7; *pꜣ irwrw n dbn* 7; *tꜣ ʿnt{n} n* 6 *dbnw*);
- *bdt ḫꜣr* 10: # generic noun + *Badal* apposition (non-specific noun + quantifier) #[277];
- *ḫr* used as proclitic coordinator before topicalizer *ir*;
- *ir n dbn* 40: total of items evaluated expressed with the construction # passive perfect participle *ir* + relator *n* + unit + quantifier #;

* General dialectal features: degree 2.

* Legal formulae:
  - lists of children: *r rdit rḫ.tw* (notification) + determined N
  - gift with *exemption from hotchpot*: *diw.i n.f* + item + *m twnw m-ḥꜣw nꜣy.f irw*
  - *descent and distribution* rule and exclusion relative to specific items: *iw.st r hꜣy ḥr pšt m ꜣḫt.i nbt* + *ḥry-ḥr* (exception)
  - exclusion from a category of assets: *bn iw.w r ʿḳ r pšt m* + assets
  - *advancement* relative to specific items: *ḫr ir* (object) + *iw.w n.f r pšt*

4. Colophon

Specific, technical meta-comment about the writing reduced to the mere mention of the recording scribe. The document itself is referred to as the object of the commentary ('done').

274 Haring (2003b: 253); Donker van Heel & Haring (2003: 147, 162).

275 Finegan (1982: 118-9).

276 Danet & Bogoch (1994: 117).

277 Edel (1955-64: vol. I, 129-30): 'partitiven Apposition' that corrects the preceding noun.

Informational focus, specificity (proper noun, title), detachment and integration (passive participle + prepositional phrase, absence of nexus). See the closure of modern wills of the type 'Par devant Maître (PN), notaire à Paris.'

Recording:
(8) *ỉrw ỉn sš Ỉmnnḫtw n pꜣ ḫr ḫnỉ*
Done by (the) scribe of the Forbidden Tomb *Ỉmnnḫtw*.

- * Neo-Egyptian characteristics:
  - exophoric articloid (extratextual deixis) for specific administrative unit of the Theban area (*pꜣ ḫr ḫnỉ*). The necropolis scribe is 'the highest administrative authority within the village'[278];
- * 'Classical' degree 0 forms used:
  - *ỉrw*: perfect passive participle without prothetic *yod* used with agent;
  - relational expansion (*sš n pꜣ ḫr ḫnỉ*) with administrative department dependance relation ;
- * General dialectal features: degree 1.
- * Legal formula: redactor identification: *ỉrw ỉn sš* + PN + department

Adscriptus (in another hand)

One year later, the second companion of the testatrix appears in court with his children in a procedure related to *Naunakhte*'s will. Like Théodoridès (1964: 59), Pestman (1982b: 174-5) contends that one of the children, *Nfrḥtpw,* has obviously contested the will earlier, as he swears not to contest it again, and the father acts 'as some kind of executor' of the will. As far we can see, the father's appearance in court with his children is concerned first with the acknowledgement of the conformity of the testamentary documents, then with a statement concerning the disinherited *Nfrḥtpw*. Since the will was authenticated by the court, it should not have been a problem to reject any claim of a disinherited child... as long as the testamentary document was not ambiguous. We saw that a very important error had been made by the scribe who forgot the negator in the sentence *ỉr pꜣ*[*y*] 4 *ḫrdw ỉnk* <*bn*> *ỉw.w r ꜥḳ r pšt m ꜣḫt*{*tw*}*.ỉ nbt* 'As for thes[e] 4 children of mine (including *Nfrḥtpw* and three sisters of his), they will <not> enter (the) division of all my assets.' This negation was 'the most essential word of the whole text'[279]. If the will in our possession is a faithful copy of the original notary act, perhaps the same mistake was made in the original instrument? And if *Nfrḥtpw* noticed the error, did he believe that he had a case for contesting the partition that excluded him? This would mean an issue related to the interpretation of the will and the determination after her death of the original intention of the testatrix as expressed orally in court. Théodoridès (1964: 59 and 1966: 56) believed that in the case of a *vice de forme*, the matter should have been within the court's competence; this is probable, but the court could have used the testimony of a next of kin concerning the interpretation of the true intention of the testatrix and an eventual correction of the original act. More importantly, we have here proof of the legal importance of the written document almost as an autonomous legally binding deed, like a modern written will

278 Donker van Heel & Haring (2003: 102).
279 Pestman (1961: 68 n.7).

interpreted, in case it is unclear, following the intention of the deceased[280] as she expressed it verbally or by any other means.

Of course, this short addendum (four lines in column V and six short lines in column VI) or document attached to the file is not part of the will of the testatrix, only of the same case. It belongs to the *contentious genre* and not to the consentient genre since it closes a contestation of the will; but as a valuable procedural item that seems salient for the evaluation of the autonomy of the written testamentary document, we chose to include it in our analysis of *Naunakhte*'s last will and testament.

1. Pre-material

The textemic features of a contentious genre document's pre-material are similar to those of a consentient genre act.

As in modern filing systems, the documents connected with a certain case are filed chronologically with it. It is probably for this reason that the date has been abbreviated (no mention of the reigning king), as the *adscriptus* does not consist of the original record of the court proceedings but of its mention added on the same sheet of papyrus as the will itself.

Date:	
(9) *rnpt-sp* 4 *ȝbd* 3 *ȝḫt sw* 17	Year 4, month 3 of inundation, day 17
archaic anaphora: *hrw pn*	This day
Title:	
object (legal step): *wḥm sprw*	of (the) representation
forum: *r ḳnbt*	to court
parties: *ỉn rmṯ ỉst Ḫꜥmnwn* (10) *ḥnꜥ nȝy.f ẖrdw*	by (the) workman *Ḫꜥmnwn* with his children,

* Neo-Egyptian characteristics:
  - Neo-Egyptian possessive determinator for kinship (*nȝy.f ẖrdw*);

* 'Classical' degree 0 forms used:
  - archaic anaphora *hrw pn* + infinitives (*wḥm* and *sprw* with Neo-Egyptian intrusive *w*) in a classical Middle Egyptian heading (see *supra);*

* General dialectal features: degree 1.

* Legal formula: date + *hrw pn* + infinitive (object) + *r* (forum) + *ỉn* (party)

2. Operative part

The testimony and the oath are reconstructed, edited, written quotations of speeches made by the parties, briefly introduced by delocutive tag clauses. As we will see concerning the oath, only a formulaic and rather restricted part of the depositions is presented in the record. Clearly, the direct speech does not represent the actual vernacular used during this period but a stereotypical phraseology belonging to the legal register.

The texteme's focus is both informational (delocutive introductions, nominal topicalization, prepositional phrases, attributive expansions, use of proper nouns, edited formulaic style, monologue) and involved in a stereotypical way (locutive, intensifiers, contractions/deletions,

280 We already know of a court case of the end of the Old Kingdom involving the issue of the existence and authenticity of a written will (*pBerlin* P 9010) on which the plaintiff bases his claim.

pronominal unspecified referent meaning contextual dependency, not interactive); the frame is narrative (report form, delocutive use for human participants, tag clauses using *verbum dicendi*), but the quotations are non-narrative (present, future) and not inserted in the dialogue that the court procedure implies. Contrary to the *recital* of the will, the general topic is not the author of the statement (absence of *ir ink*), but *Naunakhte*'s will (*ir nꜣ sšw i.irt ꜥnḫ-n-niwt Niwtnḫtti ḥr ꜣḫt.st*).

Testimony concerning instrumental conformity:
tag clause: *m-ḏd* saying:
deposition quotation: *ir nꜣ sšw i.irt ꜥnḫ-n-niwt Niwtnḫtti* (11) *ḥr ꜣḫt.st iw.w m-mitt ꜥḳꜣ sp sn bn iw rmṯ ist Nfrḥtpw pš im.w*
As for the documents that made *ꜥnḫ-n-niwt Niwtnḫtti* concerning her assets, they are very exactly conform; (the) workman *Nfrḥtpw* will not inherit thereof.
***Promissory* oath of *Nfrḥtpw*[281] (warranty with penalty)**:
irwy.f (12) *ꜥnḫ nb ꜥ.w.s. m-ḏd mtw.i pn<ꜥ>* (*rꜣ.i*) *r mdwt m-im ꜥn iw.f ẖry* 100 *n sẖ šwy m ꜣḫt{tw}*
He took an oath of (the) Lord L.P.H. saying: 'Should I rever<se> (my undertaking) in order to contest (the will) again, he is liable to 100 blows (and) deprived of assets.'

* Neo-Egyptian characteristics:
- *ir nꜣ sšw i.irt ꜥnḫ-n-niwt* PN... *iw.w m-mitt*: topicalization of *Naunakhte*'s will (specificity) followed by an adverbial nexus (present), the conformity formula;
- cataphoric articloid (*nꜣ sšw*);
- *i.irt*.N: perfect relative form with prothetic *yod* and *t* that does not represent concord, attributive expansion of *nꜣ sšw*;
- negative future *bn iw*.N *pš* (omission of preposition) in a *descent and distribution* rule assertion, with *iw* in front of a nominal actor[282]. Thus the same construction is used in the *consentient* and the *contentious* genres to assert disinheritance;
- Neo-Egyptian spelling (*ꜣḫt, pš*);
- use of Neo-Egyptian delocutive plural suffix *.w* (*im.w*) and feminine suffix pronoun *.st* (*ꜣḫt.st*);
- *irwy.f*: perfect delocutive report expressing legal formality, with final *wy*[283], the usual form to introduce an oath;
- *mtw.i pn<ꜥ> r mdwt... iw.f ẖry* 100 *n sẖ*: atemporal locutive conjunctive (*mtw.i pn<ꜥ>*) followed by a delocutive adverbial nexus (*iw.f ẖry* 100 *n sẖ*). The oath's standardized formula is not recorded *in extenso*; it is precisely because it is stereotyped that it may be abbreviated, deprived in record of its introductory address[284].

  It is a *promissory* oath expressing the renunciation by a legatee to contest the will (*waiver of suit*)[285], under the guarantee of a penalty for perjury or non-compliance. Here the person taking the oath appears to establish in the oath itself the penalty in case of perjury, although the penalty is expressed in a delocutive mode. Furthermore, as *ꜥn* is used, the issue here is the withdrawal or refrainment from an action already committed

---

281 *irwy.f* is to be understood as the father's oath for Seidl (1957b: 276).
282 See Satzinger (1976: 208-9).
283 *LEG* § 4.2.2-4; Frandsen (1974: 9); Winand (1992: 193-6).
284 Bedell (1973: 127).
285 See Wilson (1948: 143-49, esp. ex. n.105): 'promissory oath in a juridical setting'; Menu (1998: 27): 'garantie de l'inviolabilité d'une promesse ou d'un engagement'.

in the past, assuming that the *promissory* oath concludes a disagreement with the will; compare with Demotic *sẖ n wy* agreed withdrawal after trial[286].
Two main issues arise in relation to this type of oath.
First, the discrepancy between the locutive *mtw.i pn*<ꜥ> and the delocutive *ỉw.f ẖry* 100 *n sẖ*. It is usually viewed as an error to be corrected, 'a strange confusion of *oratio recta* and *oratio obliqua*'[287], the result of the fact that the oath was formulated in indirect speech[288], 'a scribal quirk in the recording of oaths'[289]. Of course, as it is a frequent phenomenon, it should not be treated as a mere 'error': it appears e.g. in the oaths of *pBoulaq* 10; *pTurin* 2070 v°, col. II; *pBM* 10052, 5, 5; 14, 4-5 and 23-4; 15, 17; *pBM* EA 10403, 2, 5; *pBerlin* P 10496 v. 2-6, 12 ff.; *pSalt* 124 v° 1, 6; *oDeM* 133; *oOIC* 12073. Non-compliance with the self-pledged commitment[290] is usually expressed in a locutive mode as a personal failure ('if I don't' – the oath is a statement of the potential offender), whereas its consequences may be presented as the locutive continuation of the direct speech, the full endorsement of the consequences ('I am punished'), or by the delocutive mode, as a public matter expressed by the enforcement authority ('he is liable, deprived'). We cannot be sure that the [locutive + delocutive] cases are instances of an oath forced upon the person who takes it (is this the case in the *Naunakhte* oath?), and that in the [locutive + locutive] cases, the oath is more of a voluntary nature[291]. An oath is primarily a verbal speech, but in fact we do not know precisely how the procedure was constructed: was the person taking the oath always repeating the formula after someone (as e.g. in *pCairo* JE 65739) or enunciating the oath *proprio motu* and deciding the nature of the penalty? Does the written formulation reflect a variation in the verbal procedure? Consider parallel formulations such as *oIFAO* 424 + *oPetrie* 9 and *oAshmolean* 1933.810, two versions of the same dispute[292]: the first version, *oIFAO* 424 + *oPetrie* 9 v° 1-2, reads [*mtw.ỉ tmt*] *ỉw.f ẖr* 100 *n sẖ* [*šd* 10 *n dbn n*] *ḥmt* ***m-dỉ.f*** '[Should I not], he is liable to 100 blows [(and) confiscation of 10 *dbn* of] copper in **his** possession', while *oAshmolean* 1933.810 r° 5-6 reads *mtw.ỉ tmt ỉw.f ẖr* 100 *n sẖ šd* 10 *n dbn n ḥmt* ***m-dỉ.ỉ***.
A similar issue of locutive/delocutive variation in ancient Anglo-Saxon wills has been noted by Danet & Bogoch (1994: 110-2) and explained variously: 'a product of lack of care in the organisation of the document, or of the scribe's confusion as to what stance he is supposed to take *vis-à-vis* the substance of the document. Is he supposed to be primarily a transcriber of the own words or stance of the testatrix, or is his mandate to provide a third-person summary of what the testatrix said? Or is he, as we would argue, experimenting with the transfer of performativity to writing, but perhaps uncertain as to how to do so?'. These remarks are obviously relevant to our material, since *ỉw.f ẖry* 100 *n sẖ* represents an implicit performative form (see *infra*).
The second issue concerns the existence of a so-called protatic conjunctive. Shisha-Halevy (1995: 309-10 and 1989: 44-6) suggests viewing the oath as an inversion of the usual apodotic conjunctive placement resulting from the 'contiguity of the "events" in the two clauses', the protatic circumstantial nexus in this case following the conjunctive

286 See Allam (1994: esp. 25); Depauw (1997: 143); Manning (2003: 831-2).
287 Černý (1945: 36.jj); Wilson (1948: 138, n. 59); Allam (1973: 271, n.33).
288 Junge (2005: 220, 291).
289 Bedell (1973: 128).
290 The oath may be viewed as a promise to oneself delivered in public.
291 Kaplony (1975: 1191): 'Die Gerichtsprotokolle lassen nicht erkennen, wann freiwillig, wann auf Befehl geschworen wird'.
292 Donker van Heel & Haring (2003: 27-9, 160).

apodosis. Although this hypothesis is seductive, the fact remains that nothing proves the adverbial nexus to be circumstantial in our case[293]. Shisha-Halevy himself admits that 'L'hypothèse d'une forme-modèle indépendante *iw.f* + adverbe en néo-égyptien ne peut être écartée'[294].

A list of constructions forming the apodoses of oaths established by Frandsen (1974: 130-40) encompasses non-converted forms: *iw.i/f ẖr* + quantifier (*n*) N; *iw.f m* + infinitive; *iw.f r.i*/N; *iw.i* + stative; that-form *i.iri.f sḏm/i.sḏm.f* in cleft sentence; *sḏm.tw*.N passive prospective; the only dubious case is represented by *pBM* 10052, 2, 16, with *iw irw*.N, a converted perfect passive for Frandsen. Spiegelberg (1892: 80) adds *tw.f sḏm* and the imperative to the list. These are cases of independent adverbial nexuses, mostly inherited from Middle Egyptian; it should not surprise us to find many extant cases of non-converted *iw*-sentences in Neo-Egyptian, especially in genres, registers, and textemes heavily reliant on formalism and prone to a conservative tone. Diachronically, in Demotic, the second segment of the royal oath may be fulfilled by the non-converted *iw.i m-sꜣ.k*: e.g. *pBM* EA 10425, line16 *iw.i tm dbꜣ.w n.k iw.k m-sꜣ.i* 'Wenn ich sie Dir nicht zahle, dann sollst Du hinter mir sein'[295]. Furthermore, the contiguity of the crime and its sanction is never expressed by a protatic conjunctive in other function-logic textemes which are criminal law provisions or curses (David 2006: 56-65, 100-3). In the case of curses, we have seen that the curse already performs part of the penalty; the penalty is not entirely postponed to actual crime performance, it precedes it. Of course, *iw.i/f ẖry* 100 *n sẖ* is another case of performative adverbial nexus (pronouncing the oath is in itself an early sanction), the locutive form highlighting its status. It belongs to the same paradigma as *iw.f n* N (implicit performative attribution of ownership); *contra*: Winand (1996: 134-6) 'constructions analogiques au futur III'.

The solution may be, as Baer[296] suggested, to see the conjunctive as apodotic to the sometimes elliptical/abbreviated protasis *wꜣḥ*.PN, a protasis-apodosis system expressing the 'crime', itself macrosyntactically the protasis of the penalty:

$$\{[\textit{wꜣḥ}.\mathrm{PN}]_{\text{protasis}} + [\textit{mtw.i pnꜥ r.i}]_{\text{apodosis}}\}_{\textbf{crime protasis}} + \{\textit{iw.i/f ẖry}\ 100\ \textit{n sẖ}\}_{\textbf{penalty apodosis}}$$

i.e. 'May Amun be clement, may the Ruler L.P.H. be clement, should I commit perjury,' (crime protasis) 'I am/he is liable to 100 blows' (penalty apodosis).

The conjunctive raises the main issue in the protasis, consistent with the use in Ramesside royal decrees of the conjunctive in the enunciation of the crime and sometimes of a performative in the penalty expressed as a curse (David 2006: 102-3, 124). The crime protasis opens with a modal form, followed by a conjunctive representing the *functional core*[297] of the protasis, having no modal value[298]. The fact that the *iw.i/f ẖry* 100 *n sẖ* penalty is translated by 'shall' by all the authors does not mean that the adverbial nexus in the penalty represents a future form. On the contrary, it is a performative present. The penalty clause of the *promissory* oath resembles a self-

293 See the hesitancy in Junge (2005: 290) 'independent sentence', although on p. 235 'old *iw*-sentence or Present Circumstantial (in NIMS-function)' which means (p. 210) 'formally it is a Present Circumstantial, but functionally it is sententially independent.'

294 Shisha-Halevy (1978: 60, n.31).

295 Pestman (1968: 102-3).

296 Bear (1965: 137 n. 3); see also Frandsen (1974: 128) and Junge (2005: 235, 291).

297 High-level rhematicity of the conjunctive (Shisha-Halevy 1995: 306).

298 Shisha-Halevy (1995: 311-2).

imposed curse guaranteed by the god/king, usually expressed by an adverbial nexus (with again the double time-frame appurtenance).

As for the use of the verb *pnˁ* in the formulation of our oath, it has numerous parallels: *oBM* 5625 v° 10 (*[mt]w.i pnˁˁ.i r mdt*)[299]; *oDeM* 133 (*mtw.i pnˁ r mdwt ˁn*); *pBM* EA 10335 v° 16-7 (*mtw.i pnˁ r3.i ˁn*); *pBM* EA 10053 v° 2, 18 (*mtw.i pnˁ r3.i ˁn*); *pBoulaq* 10, v° 15 (*mtw.n pnˁˁ.n r mdt*); *oBodleian Library* 253 (*mtw.i pnˁ r n3t3 t3 šrit*). Thus the oath represents a 'serment judiciaire (…) déféré par l'autorité pour clore une contestation, une plainte ou une déposition faite en justice'[300]. The formula *pnˁ* (*r3.i*) *r mdwt m-im* 'reverse (my undertaking) in order to contest' is used by the grantor to warrant the grantee against his own behavior; another formula, *bn mdw.i*/N *im.f* 'without my/N's contestation about it; I/N will not contest' is used by the grantor to warrant the grantee against his own or a third party's contestation (e.g. *Naunakhte*'s Doc. IV line 3; *oTurin* 57173); a third formula, *bn ˁḥˁ* N *ḥr pḥwy.f* 'nobody shall stand on its back', is used only to warrant against a third party's contestation (e.g. *oDeM* 62; close is *pAdoptions* line 6 formula *m n3y snw r ink ˁḥˁ r ḳw n.st*);

- *m-im*: Neo-Egyptian form of the classical adverbial modifier *im*[301];

* 'Classical' degree 0 forms used:

- (PN) *m-ḏd*: tagged speech marker opening the quotations of the deposition and the *promissory* oath instead of the perfect report form of the *verbum dicendi* encountered earlier in the will. See also *pTurin* 2070 v°, col. II *infra* for its use to introduce an oath. For other examples of the use of the converb in legal registers, see David (2006: 36);
- use of the relator *n* in an unclear kind of relation in a frozen expression (*ˁnḫ-n-niwt*) and between quantifier and noun (100 *n sḫ*);
- non converted adverbial nexus *iw.f ḫry* 100 *n sḫ* (implicit performative);
- *šwy*: delocutive stative with final *y*[302]. The stative is an adnexal expansion of *iw.f ḫry* 100 *n sḫ*;
- *iw.w m-mitt ˁḳ3 sp sn*: # thematic *iw.w* (pronominal reference of the Neo-Egyptian plural suffix: topicalized *n3 sšw*) + adverb + intensifiers *ˁḳ3* (intensity expression) and *sp sn* (intensity iteration) # constituting a non converted adverbial nexus. The present is used in the deposition to formulate a general legal assertion, the confirmation of the document's conformity, and the document itself is marked as topic in an 'objective' style;

* General dialectal features: degree 2.

* Legal formulae:
- instrumental conformity: *ir* + N (documents) + *iw.w m-mitt ˁḳ3 sp sn*
- *descent and distribution* rule: *bn iw*.N *pš im.w* (disinheritance)
- *promissory* oath: *irwy.f ˁnḫ nb ˁ.w.s.* (report) + *m-ḏd* (tag clause) + *mtw.i pn*<ˁ> (*r3.i*) *r mdwt m-im ˁn* (perjury) + *iw.f ḫry* 100 *n sḫ šwy m 3ḫt*{*tw*} (penalty)

299 Blackman (1926: pl 36).

300 Théodoridès (1967: 120).

301 *LEG*, 130.

302 Winand (1992: 114) notes this ending of the delocutive masculine singular stative during the 20th dynasty for the *3ae inf.* verbs.

3. Colophon

Contrary to the colophon of *oDeM* 108, this texteme is highly informational and specific (proper nouns and nominals expressing administrative functions, constituting a prepositional phrase).

Witnesses:
(VI.1) *m-bȝḥ ʿȝ n ist Ḫʿw* (2) *ʿȝ n ist Nḫwmmwt* (3) *sš Ḥrišri n pȝ ḫr* (4) *ȝṯw Rʿms ȝṯw* (5) *Pntȝwrt sȝ Nḫtmin*
In the presence of foreman *Ḫʿw*, foreman *Nḫwmmwt*, scribe of the Necropolis *Ḥrišri*, *ȝṯw*-officer *Rʿms*, *ȝṯw*-officer *Pntȝwrt* son of *Nḫtmin*.

* Neo-Egyptian characteristics:
  - exophoric articloid (extratextual deixis) for the specific administrative unit of the Theban area (*pȝ ḫr*);

* 'Classical' degree 0 forms used:
  - relator *n* in dominion (*ʿȝ n ist*) and administrative department dependance relations (*sš* PN *n pȝ ḫr*);
  - hierarchically ordered list (diminishing progression).

* General dialectal features: degree 1.

* Legal formula: specified witnesses: *m-bȝḥ* + function + PN

Label on the verso

Brief external mention of the nature of the instrument, its author, and its object. The focus is of course informational (nominal segment with attributive expansion, proper noun) although the unspecified referent of *ȝḫt{tw}.w* is counter-productive for that purpose.

The docket was written after the death of the testatrix as it mentions the assets being the heirs' property[303]. It should have been labelled in order to be easily retrieved among other documents in an archive, but we have seen that no other document along with which it may have been found bears a label. No seal is mentioned.

The only other document close to our corpus and bearing a docket is *oGardiner/Ashmolean* 36 (*wpwtw m tȝ ḳnbt*); few documents bear a docket in Deir el-Medina and most of them 'derive from a judicial environment'[304].

ʿwty hȝrwyt i.[irw ʿnḫ-n-niwt Niwtn]ḫti n ȝḫt{tw}.w
Declaratory deed/roll that [*ʿnḫ-n-niwt Niwtn*]*ḫti* [made] of their assets.

* Neo-Egyptian characteristics:
  - Neo-Egyptian lexeme (*ʿwty*) and spelling (*hȝrwyt; ȝḫt{tw}.w*);
  - *i.*[*irw*.N]: probably relative form with prothetic *yod*;
  - Neo-Egyptian delocutive plural suffix pronoun *.w* (*ȝḫt{tw}*);

* 'Classical' degree 0 forms used:
  - relator *n* for contents/object relation (*ʿwty hȝrwyt n ȝḫt{tw}.w*)[305];

303 Pestman (1982b: 179 n. 10); *contra*: Černý (1945: 32) and Théodoridès (1966: 35) who believe it is a scribal error.
304 Donker van Heel & Haring (2003: 12-3).

* General dialectal features: degree 2? (depending on *i.*[*irw*.N])
* Legal formula: *ʿwty h3rwyt* (instrument) + *i.*[*irw*.N] PN (author) + *n 3ḫt*{*tw*}.*w* (object)

B. Documents II (*pDeM* 23) and III (*pDeM* 25)

Both Docs. II and III were found in the necropolis of Deir el-Medina and they are complete papyri, palimpsests, each written in a different hand (see *supra*), probably concerned by the actual partition of the movable assets between *Naunakhte*'s children (concerning the division of her real property, *Ḳnḥrḫpšf*'s immovables and the storehouse of her father mentioned in her will, we do not have specific indications and they may have remained undivided).

For Černý (1945: 51), Doc. II could be the preliminary draft of Doc. III, the carefully written final record; Donker van Heel & Haring (2003: 21) suggest that either one might have been used as a draft for the other or that 'both could have been written using a draft [mother copy] now lost', adding a pertinent remark 'Why the draft P. DeM 23 was also kept along with the final list is then a mystery' (p. 23). There are some differences between the two lists: spelling issues; different number of divisions; one occasion of a different sequence of names; Doc. II graphically divides the list into groups of 5 bequests using horizontal strokes, whereas the division is realized in Doc. III by means of the lexemic divider *wḥm ky pšt*; change in names (*Nbnḫti* is substituted in Doc. II for *Wsrnḫti* in Doc. III; but neither of them is mentioned in the will and *W3stnḫti,* one of the legatees in the will, does not appear in the lists[306]).

Since a partition represents 'l'opération matérielle de répartition des biens en lots distincts (formation et attribution des lots)'[307], and equal *allotments* are formed by constituting 'autant de lots égaux qu'il y a d'héritiers copartageants (…) en déterminant concrètement les biens qui composent chacun', one may ask if the lists represent the preliminary scriptural constitution of the *allotments* as a function of each heir's share[308] or the record of the actual division of the items in the house of the testatrix following and executing concretely the constitution of the *allotments*[309]. Perhaps each list represents a different phase, one being the preliminary *allotment*, the other one the consecutive physical repartition of the items (as in *oDeM* 112 and 964?), although both use # *rdyt* (*n*) PN # that seems to imply an after-the-fact record of an actual distribution.

In spite of the fact that the testator could personally attribute specific items in his will by *partage d'ascendant* (e.g. *oDeM* 108 and 586, *Naunakhte* Doc. I), partition lists executing the will do not belong to the testamentary provisions or to the *consentient genre*. They are part of the procedural execution of the will. Again, they are so intimately related to the case that we are presenting them below (see also *infra* the chapter on partitions).

The documents consist of a unique texteme, its focus being informational (notification formula, high noun and proper noun frequency, relational expansions, agentless passives, delocutive mode, absence of nexus, prepositional phrases, quantifiers, listing layout denoting structural elaboration with lexemic/graphic dividers) but not situation-independent as there is a

305 For Théodoridès (1966: 35), *n* instead of *m* preposition.

306 For Černý (1945: 51), *Nbnḫti* is *W3stnḫti*'s husband, and he seems to consider *Wsrnḫti* and *W3stnḫti* to be one and the same person, although *W3stnḫti* is a woman and *Wsrnḫti* is always classified by the male classifier.

307 Cornu (2003: 634 and 538).

308 For Valbelle (1985: 80) they are 'deux listes de biens préparant leur répartition'.

309 As Černý (1945: 51) and Grandet (2003: 8) believe it, 'the five heirs paying six visits to their mother's house, and on each occasion dividing up a set of objects of approximately equal value'.

case of an unspecified allocutive referent and precise contextual information such as date, locus, and circumstances is lacking; it is non narrative; actualized lexically but grammatically of a high, authoritative register. The main structural features of the lists are their graphic organization and isotopy; redundancy and order imply permanence and legitimacy, the two most prized values of administrative and accounting genres.

Document II (*pDeM* 23)

Notification of partition list:

(1) *r rdit rḫ.tw pꜣ pšt n ꜣḫt n* (2) *tꜣy.tn{n} mwt*

For information (relative to) the division of assets of your[310] mother:

rdyt Ỉmnnḫtw bꜣnw (3) 1	what was given (to) *Ỉmnnḫtw*: 1 millstone
rdyt Wsrnḫti bꜣnw 1	what was given (to) *Wsrnḫti*: 1 millstone
(4) *rdyt Mnꜥnḫtti iḳꜣ(y)r* 1	what was given (to) *Mnꜥnḫtti*: 1 *iḳꜣ(y)r*
(5) *rdyt Ḳnḫrḫpšf iḳꜣyr* 1	what was given (to) *Ḳnḫrḫpšf*: 1 *iḳꜣyr*
(6) *rdyt Mꜣꜣnnḫtwf hꜣrwti* 1	what was given (to) *Mꜣꜣnnḫtwf*: 1 box
(7) *rdyt Mnꜥnḫtti mḏꜣt* 1	what was given (to) *Mnꜥnḫtti*: 1 mortar
(8) *rdyt Ỉmnnḫt mḏꜣt* 1	what was given (to) *Ỉmnnḫt*: 1 mortar
(9) *rdyt Ḳnḫpšf mḏꜣt* 1	what was given (to) *Ḳnḫpšf*: 1 mortar
(10) *rdyt Nbnḫti mḏꜣt* 1	what was given (to) *Nbnḫt*: 1 mortar
(11) *rdyt Mꜣꜣnnḫtwf ḫt gꜣtyr* 1	what was given (to) *Mꜣꜣnnḫtwf*: 1 *ḫt gꜣtyr* box
(12) *rdyt n Ỉmnnḫt tbw* 1	what was given to *Ỉmnnḫt*: 1 *tbw* (= *dbwt*)
(13) *rdy(t) n Mnꜥnḫtti tpw* 1	what was given to *Mnꜥnḫtti*: 1 *tpw*
(V° 1) *rdyt Ḳnḫpšf rdwy mꜣsty* (2) 1	what was given (to) *Ḳnḫpšf*: 1 pair of *mꜣsty* legs
rdyt Mꜣꜣnnḫtwf kꜣyrti 1	what was given (to) *Mꜣꜣnnḫtwf*: 1 *kꜣyrti*
(3) *rdy(t) Wsrnḫti dbw* 1	what was given (to) *Wsrnḫti*: 1 *dbw*
(4) *rdy(t) Mnꜥtnḫtti ipt* 1	what was given (to) *Mnꜥtnḫtti*: 1 corn-measure
(5) *rdy(t) n Ỉmnnḫti ipt* 1	what was given to *Ỉmnnḫt*: 1 corn-measure
(6) *rdy(t) n Wsrnḫti ipt* 1	what was given to *Wsrnḫti*: 1 corn-measure
(7) *rdyt Ḳnḫpšf wnšw* 1	what was given (to) *Ḳnḫpšf*: 1 sledge
(8) *rdy(t) Mꜣꜣnnḫtwf wnšw* 1	what was given (to) *Mꜣꜣnnḫtwf*: 1 sledge
(9) *rdyt Ḳnḫpšf ꜥbw mꜣ(s)ty* 1	what was given (to) *Ḳnḫpšf*: 1 *ꜥbw mꜣ(s)ty*
(10) *rdy(t) Ỉmnnḫti ḫt ḥtpw* 1	what was given (to) *Ỉmnnḫt*: 1 wooden offering table
(11) *rdy(t) Nbnḫt ḥtp* 1 *mḏꜣt* 1	what was given (to) *Nbnḫt*: 1 offering table, 1 mortar
(12) *rdyt Mnꜥtnḫtti ḫꜣdy* 1	what was given (to) *Mnꜥtnḫtti*: 1 *ḫꜣdy*
(13) *rdyt Mꜣꜣnnḫtwf inr? gꜣt[y?]*[311] 1	what was given (to) *Mꜣꜣnnḫtwf*: 1 bo[x?]

Document III (*pDeM* 25)

Notification of partition list:

310 Locutive for Černý (1945: 38).

311 The online Leiden Deir el-Medina database suggests the reading *inr gꜣf* 'griddle-stone' (Janssen 1975: 327-8).

(1) *r rdit rḫ.tw pꜣ pšt n ꜣḫt* (2) *tꜣy.tn mwt*	
For information (relative to) the division of assets of your mother:	
(3) *rdyt n Ỉmnnḫtw bꜣnw* 1	what was given to *Ỉmnnḫtw*: 1 millstone
(4) *rdyt n Wsrnḫti bꜣnw* 1	what was given to *Wsrnḫti*: 1 millstone
(5) *rdyt n Mnʿtnḫt iḳꜣyr* 1	what was given to *Mnʿtnḫty*: 1 *iḳꜣyr*
(6) *rdyt n Ḳnḫpšf iḳꜣyr* 1	what was given to *Ḳnḫpšf*: 1 *iḳꜣyr*
(7) *rdyt n Mꜣꜣnnḫtwf hꜣrw* 1	what was given to *Mꜣꜣnnḫtwf*: 1 box
(8) *wḥmw ky pšt*	Again another division
(9) *rdyt n Mnʿtnḫtti mḏꜣt* 1	what was given to *Mnʿtnḫtti*: 1 mortar
(10) *rdyt n Ỉmnnḫt mḏꜣt* 1	what was given to *Ỉmnnḫt*: 1 mortar
(11) *rdyt n Ḳnḫpšf mḏꜣt* 1	what was given to *Ḳnrḫpšf*: 1 mortar
(12) *rdyt n Mꜣꜣnnḫtwf gꜣwtyr* 1	what was given to *Mꜣꜣnnḫtwf*: 1 *gꜣwtyr* box
(13) *rdyt n Wsrnḫti mḏꜣt* 1	what was given to *Wsrnḫti*: 1 mortar
(14) *wḥm ky pšt*	Again another division
(15) *rdyt n Ỉmnnḫt dbwt* 1	what was given to *Ỉmnnḫt*: 1 *dbwt*
(16) *rdyt n Mnʿtnḫtti tpw* 1	what was given to *Mnʿtnḫtti*: 1 *tpw*
(17) *rdyt n Ḳnḫpšf rdwy n mꜣsty* 1	what was given to *Ḳnḫpšf*: 1 pair of legs of *mꜣsty*
(18) *rdyt n Mꜣꜣnnḫtwf kꜣyrti* 1	what was given to *Mꜣꜣnnḫtwf*: 1 *kꜣyrti*
(19) *rdy(t) Wsrnḫti dbwt* 1	what was given (to) *Wsrnḫti*: 1 *dbwt*
(20) *wḥm ky pšt*	Again another division
(V° 1) *rdyt n Mnʿtnḫtti ipt* 1	what was given to *Mnʿtnḫtti* : 1 corn-measure
(2) *rdyt n Ỉmnnḫt ipt* 1	what was given to *Ỉmnnḫt*: 1 corn-measure
(3) *rdyt n Wsrnḫti ipt* 1	what was given to *Wsrnḫti*: 1 corn-measure
(4) *rdyt n Ḳnḫpšf wnš* 1	what was given to *Ḳnḫpšf*: 1 sledge
(5) *rdyt n Mꜣꜣnnḫtwf wnšw* 1	what was given to *Mꜣꜣnnḫtwf*: 1 sledge
(6) *wḥm ky n pšt*	Again another division
(7) *rdyt n Ḳnḫpšf ʿbw mꜣsty* 1	what was given to *Ḳnḫpšf*: 1 *ʿbw mꜣsty*
(8) *rdyt n Ỉmnnḫt ḥtpw rd* 1	what was given to *Ỉmnnḫt*: 1 legged? offering table
(9) *rdyt n Wsrnḫti ḥtpw* 1 *mḏꜣt* 1	what was given to *Wsrnḫti*: 1 offering table/basket, 1 mortar
(10) *rdyt n Mnʿtnḫtti ḫꜣdy* 1	what was given to *Mnʿtnḫtti*: 1 *ḫꜣdy*
(11) *rdyt n Mꜣꜣnnḫtwf gꜣwtyrt* 1	what was given to *Mꜣꜣnnḫtwf*: 1 box
(12) *wḥm ky pšt*	Again another division
(13) *rdyt n Ỉmnnḫt šꜣḳꜣyr* 1	what was given to *Ỉmnnḫt*: 1 *šꜣḳꜣyr*
(14) *rdyt n Ḳnḫpš{t}f hꜣry rdwyt* 1	what was given to *Ḳnḫpšf*: 1 foot-rest?
(15) *rdyt n Mꜣꜣnnḫtwf hꜣry rdwyt* 1	what was given to *Mꜣꜣnnḫtwf*: 1 foot-rest?
(16) *rdyt n Mnʿtnḫtti hꜣry rdwyt* 1	what was given to *Mnʿtnḫtti*: 1 foot-rest?
(17) *rdyt n Wsrnḫti hꜣry rdwyt* 1	what was given to *Wsrnḫti*: 1 foot-rest?

* Neo-Egyptian characteristics:

- cataphoric articloid (*pꜣ pšt*);
- Neo-Egyptian possessive determinator for kinship (*tꜣy.tn mwt*);
- Neo-Egyptian lexemes: *iḳꜣ(y)r, hꜣry/hꜣrw(ti), gꜣ(w)tyr(t)* (Janssen 1975: 198-9), *tbw/dbw(t)* (*ibid.*, 203-4), *tpw, mꜣsty, kꜣyrti* (Hoch 1994: 331-2, 335 'probably related to the Egyptian [*ḳrḥt*] (a vessel), which entered Hebrew as a loan קלחת "cauldron; large (cooking) pot"'), *ḫꜣdy, šꜣḳꜣyr* (Janssen 1975: 200-3);
- Neo-Egyptian spelling (*ꜣḫt, bꜣnw*);
- preposition omission: *rdyt* (*n*) PN;

* 'Classical' degree 0 forms used:
- partition lists introduced by the impersonal notification formula: # *r* preposition + infinitive (purpose) + dependent impersonal/passive prospective object of *rdit* #, followed by determined and expanded noun (*p3 pšt n 3ḫt* (*n*) *t3y.tn mwt*) #. The formula used to introduce the lists is typical of headings of division accounts of private property[312]. A different formulation of the same idea is used in *pTurin* 2070 partition list: *r rdit rḫ.tw swt n* PN [*nty i*]*w.w pš.w*. Interestingly, the earliest mention of a partition, dating to the 6th dynasty, is made in a letter using an early version of the notification formula: the *Balat tablet* 3689-7, 8 & 11 uses # *di(.i) rḫ*.N # after the introductory epistolary formula. The official charged with executing the first step of the partition (apparently the constitution of a list of shares and their beneficiaries) informs the member of the *ḏ3ḏ3t* that ordered it that it has been done; the second step (probably the actual transmission of the shares)[313] will be effected by another agent;
- relator *n* for object (*pšt n 3ḫt*), ownership (*3ḫt n t3y.tn mwt*), type (*ky n pšt* only once), part/whole (*rdwy n m3sty*) relations;
- partition lists form: # *rdyt* (+ preposition *n*) + PN + object item (without articloid) + quantifier (number of units) # (agentless attribution). The form *rdyt* is a classical (archaic) perfect passive participle, lit. '(what was) given', used without article[314], implying an *a posteriori* record of the partition.

  Note that this formulation is similar to the one used in records of transmissions of movable assets interpreted by Janssen as social gift exchanges and in the so-called contracts (see *infra*). The formula # *rdyt* (*n*) PN N quantifier # is used in other partitions, e.g. *oDeM* 112, *pTurin* 1885 (see *infra*);
- *wḥm(w) ky* (*n*) *pšt*: nominal syntagm introducing the divisions of assets five times in Doc. III (instead of a graphic delimitation in Doc. II). It is constructed with # participle *wḥm(w)* + quantifier *ky* (+ relator) + N (relational expansion) #, acting both as section divider and coordinator.

  For the use of *wḥm* 'adverb' 'de nouveau, dito' in New Kingdom legal and accounting documents, see Megally (1977: 66-9);

* General dialectal features: degree 1.

* Formula: - notification of partition list: *r rdit rḫ.tw p3 pšt n 3ḫt* (*n*) + possessor
  - partition list: *rdyt* (*n*) PN (recipient) + object + quantifier

D. Document IV (*pAshmolean Museum* 1945.95)

This document purchased by Gardiner involves *Naunakhte*'s companion and some of their children; it represents two public statements from the man concerning the transmission of a metal bowl to one of the children and the subsequent *promissory* oath of his son. As Černý (1945: 52) notes, the 'connecting link' between this text and *Naunakhte*'s will is the bowl transmitted by *Naunakhte* to her son (Doc. I, lines III.3-4) and apparently used by the father.

The issue is interesting because it involves the restitution of an item given by the testatrix as a *gift with praecipuum* (*gift with exemption from hotchpot*) to one of her legatees, mentioned as such in her will ('I gave him a bronze washing bowl as a bonus over and above his fellows') but in the possession of a third party.

---

312 Donker van Heel & Haring (2003: 158) and *supra*.

313 For another interpretation of the function of the second official, see Philip-Stéphan (2008: 45).

314 See Winand (1992: 368 'tournures figées, appartenant à la langue administrative ou judiciaire', 370-1).

The document is divided into two parts, each written in a different hand, probably those of *Ỉmnnḫt* and *Mꜣꜣnnḫtwf* who are named in the second part in relation to recording fees. What is the relation between the two parts? The witnesses are similar, except for *Ḥrỉnfr* and *Mꜣꜣnnḫtwf* who appear in the first part instead of *Nbnḫt* (and *Ḫꜥmnwn* himself listed as a witness) in the second. The first part is not dated and consists of a direct address to the witnesses by the father, stating the value of the vessel, probably as a basis for compensation, and grounding the right of the heir. The second part, longer and with more errors, is briefly dated[315] and consists of the agreement between the father and the son, stating also the absolute right of the son but without grounding, adding a compensation for the father and a *promissory* oath of the son to guarantee it, as well as details of the recording fees of the agreement probably paid by both interested parties. The first part is the record of the unilateral verbal statement on which the second part, the agreement linking the transmission of the vessel and its compensation, is based (and they must relate to a procedure concluded the same day).

But why should the owner of the item pay in compensation a regular stipend to his father upon receipt of an item that was his by inheritance? Pestman (1982b: 176 and 180 n.15) contends that in exchange for the bonus and after having made her will, the testatrix stipulated a compensation for the father (the bowl still being in the couple's possession) consisting of an income in grain. He notes that 'the words "10 khar of emmer" have been inserted on a later occasion, at the end of the line that deals with the washing-bowl'; but then again, this is conjectural. We may in fact be faced with a compromise ending a dispute that arose after the death of the testatrix between the father and the son; an agreement is reached not only on the basis of the legal right of the son but also with regard to his moral duty towards his father. Nowhere is it indicated that the procedure was conducted before a court, but the statements concluding the negotiations were made in public (compare with *adscriptus* of Doc. I).

A. First part: unilateral recognition of a right of ownership

This statement confirms the right of the second party; it may be made separately before the main agreement as a basis for the document establishing the end of a contentious situation, as some kind of evidence. It consists of a brief statement before seven witnesses.

1. Pre-material

Highly informational focus of the texteme (no nexus, noun with relational expansion, prepositional phrase, proper nouns), situation-independent, integrated, but undated.

Title:	
legal step: (1) *ḏd*	Statement
party: *n rmṯ ỉst Ḫꜥmnwn*	of (the) workman *Ḫꜥmnwn*
forum: *m-bꜣḥ*	before
rmṯ ỉst ꜣnynḫt	workman *ꜣnynḫt*
rmṯ ỉst Ḳdꜣḫttwf	workman *Ḳdꜣḫttwf*
rmṯ ỉs[*t*] *Ḥrỉnfr*	workma[n] *Ḥrỉnfr*
(2) *rmṯ ỉst Nfrḥtpw*	workman *Nfrḥtpw*
[*r*]*mṯ ỉs*[*t*] *Ỉmnnḫt*	[w]orkma[n] *Ỉmnnḫt*
rmṯ ỉst Mꜣꜣnnḫt[*wf*]	workman *Mꜣꜣnnḫt*[*wf*]

315 For Donker van Heel & Haring (2003: 175 n.188), it could precede *Niwtnḫtti*'s will or date of another reign.

rmṯ ist Ḫnsw	workman *Ḫnsw*:

* 'Classical' degree 0 forms used:
- *ḏd n rmṯ ist*: # infinitive + relator *n* + N (actor relation) #. Concerning the use of the heading in Deir el-Medina documents, see Donker van Heel & Haring (2003: 170-1) 'Depositions' that the authors believe use the relative form *ḏd*(*t*).*n*.N;

* General dialectal features: degree 0.

* Legal formula: infinitive (legal step) + *n* (actor) + *m-bꜣḥ* (forum)

2. Operative part

Short texteme with an involvement dimension (presentative, allocutive, demonstrative, present tense), but also making an informational general statement (agentless passive, binomial); non-narrative; it must be an edited summary of the declaration and it does not use a tag clause as the heading is constructed with the *verbum dicendi*.

Tradition:
ptri i.diw.i pꜣ[*y*] *iꜥ iw.f* (3) *ḥr ir*[*t*] *ḥmti dbn* 13
See that I give thi[s] washing bowl wort[h] 13 copper *dbn*.
Grounded and warranted confirmation of ownership right:
iw.f n Ḳnḥrḫpšf bn md[*t*] *šriw šriwt im.f b*[*n*] *sḏm* [*rꜣ*].*f iw bn sw* (*m*) *pšt nb*
It belongs to *Ḳnḥrḫpšf* without a son's (or) daughter's contestation about it; his [statement] should not be heard, because it is not a(ny) share.

* Neo-Egyptian characteristics:
- *ptri i.diw.i*: # Neo-Egyptian spelling of the presentative *ptri* + that-form (object of *ptri*) with prothetic *yod* (simultaneity) # in a direct address to the assembly of witnesses; the use of the presentative, the deictic *pꜣ*[*y*] and the actual present in the next sentence point to the relative present tense of *i.diw.i*[316].
  The procedure consists of a public handing over of an item to its rightful owner accompanied by a verbal declaration, neither a promise of a future restitution[317] nor a promise by 'elliptic' oath[318];
- Neo-Egyptian deictic *pꜣ*[*y*];
- *bn md*[*t*] N (…) *b*[*n*] *sḏm* [*rꜣ*].*f*: the first segment consists of a circumstantial non-existence # *bn* + N/infinitive + relational expansion #, without *iw* converter; concerning the evolution of the classical # *nn* N # construction, see David (2006: 127, 231).
  Černý (1945: 40) views *bn md*[*t*] *šriw* and *b*[*n*] *sḏm* [*rꜣ*].*f* as two prospective *bn sḏm*.N, probably because he sees the entire statement as a promise, but the statement of ownership is better completed by a segment that underlines the unconditionality of *Ḳnḥrḫpšf*'s ownership right; see the same construction in Ramesside royal decrees for the exclusion of some kind of nuisance (*ḫw mkw nn ḫꜥmtw* 'retained and preserved without being threatened;' *n rdit ḏꜣ.tw tꜣ* 'while not allowing that be interfered;' *st ḏsrt n wšr* 'a holy place without deprivation' in David 2006: 126-7, 145, 168-9). In *LEG*, 336, the form *bn md*[*t*] N is viewed as a locutive prospective *bn sḏm.i* 'I shall not hear

316 Winand (1992: 274-7) admits that the 'prospective' value of *i.sḏm.f* is challenged by certain examples.
317 As Černý (1945: 40, 52) and Pestman (1982b: 175) viewed it.
318 Donker van Heel and Haring (2003: 175).

of it in the future', a modal form, but as the suffix is not written and in the following segment there is only a point in the hieratic text (probably instead of 𓂋), this solution is conjectural. Clearly, *b*[*n*] *sḏm* [*r3*].*f* may be analyzed in the same # *bn* + N/infinitive + relational expansion # way, but in view of other examples of the warranty (see *infra*), it seems always to involve a modality that corresponds with the prospective.
We may view the provision as a warranty against claims of coheirs[319]. As for *b*[*n*] *sḏm* [*r3*].*f*, the masculine suffixed pronoun may refer to 'a son (or) daughter' or to *Ḳnḥrḫpšf*. The first option prohibits hearing the claim (*inadmissibility*; *irrecevabilité des oppositions*), whereas the second excludes the necessity of a statement by *Ḳnḥrḫpšf* (defendant) in order to activate the warranty. Following the structure of other texts providing similar guarantees, the first alternative should be preferred, even if the construction or lexemic usage are not identical (although note *infra* the *eviction clause* of 25th dynasty *pLouvre* E 3228e)[320]. Here are some examples of *warranty clauses*[321]:

- 5th dynasty *Wpmnfrt tomb*, lines 13-4: *n ꜥy sn nb r.s ḥmt nb msw nb r.s ḫ3w s3(.i)* 'without any brother's title deed/right against it, any woman, any children against it, except my son';
- Second Intermediate Period *Stèle juridique de Karnak* JE 52453, lines 6-10, in an *imyt-pr* recording the onerous transfer of a function: *wnn.s n p3 s (…) nn rdit ḏ3.tw (r.)s in rmṯ nbt ḥr-ntt rdi.n.f n.i swnt.s ir nty nb r iit r spr n* N *r-ḏd iw n(.i) t3 i3t m rdi* ***sḏm****.tw n.f ḥr-ntt (…) ir iw s3 nb s3t nbt sn nb snt nbt s nb n h3w r-ḏd iw n(.i) t3 i3t m rdi* ***sḏm****.ṯw n.sn* 'It is without allowing any objection to it by anyone that it (the office) is for this man (…), since he paid me its price. Should anyone come to N claiming: "the office belongs to (me)", don't let (any)one heed him since (…); should any son (or) any daughter, any brother (or) any sister, (or) any kinsman come to say: "the office belongs to (me)," don't let (any)one heed them';
- 18th dynasty *Snims Cairo stela* CG 34016 (*Urk*. IV, 1070 lines 16-7): *ir iw s3 nb s3t nbt snw nb snwt nbt s nb n h*[*3*]*w.i r* ***mdt*** [*m t3 i*]*myt-pr ir.n.i n p3.i msw* 4 *m rdi* ***sḏm****.tw n.sn* ' Should any son (or) any daughter, any brothers (or) any sisters, (or) any kinsman of mine come to contest [this *i*]*myt-pr* that I did for my 4 children, don't let (any)one heed them';
- 18th dynasty *Nfrprt*'s *stelaphorous statue Cairo* CG 42121, lines 20-1, recording a royal decision: *ir iw.ty.f(y) nb r* ***mdt*** *m rdi* [***sḏ***]***m****.tw n.sn m ḫ3 nb n ni-swt* 'Should anyone come to contest (it), don't let (any)one [h]eed them (him) in any office of the king';
- 25th dynasty *pLouvre* E 3228e, lines 8-9, an abnormal hieratic sale contract[322]: *ir p3 nty iw.f* ***mdi bn sḏm.ti r3.f*** *m ḫ3i nb n sḫw* 'As for the one who shall contest (it), his statement should not be heard in any hall of records';

- *iw bn sw (m) pšt nb*: converted negative adverbial nexus expressing the ground of the warranty (*exemption from hotchpot*). In Middle Egyptian, *iw* and *nn* are mutually exclusive, but it is well-attested in Neo-Egyptian[323]. Note the use of distributive *nb* (quantifier) in negative context;
- absence of concord of *nb* (*pšt nb*);

319 Allam (1967: 17) 'Verzichtsklausel', 'Nichtanfechtungserklärung' and (1977: 95-6) 'clause de renonciation'.
320 See Černý (1945: 41e).
321 See also Pestman (1961: 132).
322 Malinine (1953: 36-7, 41 n.18).
323 Gilula (1970: 210); David (2006: 51-2) in Ramesside royal decrees.

  - spelling of both genders binomial *šriw* *šriw* as in *pAdoptions* (compare with *oGardiner/Ashmolean* 90);
- * 'Classical' degree 0 forms used:
  - converted adverbial nexus *iw.f ḥr ir*[*t*];
  - *iw.f n* PN: adverbial nexus, recognition of ownership. Perhaps not strictly speaking an implicit performative, as the author of the utterance only confirms the ownership of his son, but in a way he attributes it again by recognizing it;
- * General dialectal features: degree 2.
- * Legal formula: *iw.f n* N (recognition of ownership right) + *bn md*[*t*] *šriw* *šriw* *im.f* (warranty) + *b*[*n*] *sḏm* [*r*ꜣ].*f* (inadmissibility of claim) + *iw bn sw* (*m*) *pšt nb* (ground)

B. Second part: agreement between the two parties

1. Pre-material

Date: (4) *rnpt-sp* 3 ꜣ*bd* 3 ꜣ*ḫt sw* 10	Year 3, month 3 of inundation, day 10
archaic anaphora: *hrw* {*n*} *pn*	This day
Title:	
legal step: *n ḏd*	of (the) statement
first party: *n rmṯ ist Ḫ*ꜥ*mnwn*	of (the) workman *Ḫ*ꜥ*mnwn*:

- * 'Classical' degree 0 forms used:
  - *hrw* {*n*} *pn*: archaic anaphora;
  - relator *n* in temporal (*hrw pn n ḏd*) and actor relation (*ḏd n rmṯ ist*);
- * General dialectal features: degree 0.
- * Legal formula: date + *hrw* {*n*} *pn* + *n ḏd* (object) + *n rmṯ ist* PN (party)

2. Operative part

The texteme has a complex structure, presenting first the locutive declaration of the father, probably accompanying the *tradition* of the bowl, the pre-material *hrw pn n ḏd* acting as tag clause, then a delocutive report introducing the direct speech constituting the promise and the oath of the son. The last locutive segment – regarding the recording fees – probably belongs to the speech of the son. Clearly there is some confusion in the record concerning pronominal reference (*Ḳnḫpšf p*ꜣ*y.f šri*), but this time it is not in the oath; context-dependency is also noticeable in the last part of the document (*p*ꜣ*y.w it* referring to *Ỉmnnḫt* and *M*ꜣꜣ*nnḫtwf*, their family ties being known to us by virtue of Doc. I).

Informational detachment is perceptible in the texteme (noun topicalization with relative expansion, high noun frequency, agentless passive, binomials, prepositional phrases, list with proper nouns, monologues), as well as in the involvement dimension (locutive, present tense, unspecified referent, possibility modals, contraction/delition, deictic *p*ꜣ). It has a narrative structure (report and sequential forms, delocutive frame with human participants, tag clauses using *verbum dicendi*) presenting two monologues, not a dialogue between the two parties. Again it is highly formulaic and is not a complete record of the original statements of the parties.

Warranted confirmation by first party of ownership right: *ir pꜣ iʿ i.di.i rmṯ ist Ḳnḫpšf pꜣy.f* (5) *šri iw.f n.f bn mdt šri šri tꜣ ḥmt Ḳn m-im.f bn sḏm rꜣ.f m dwꜣt*

As for the washing bowl that I give (to the) workman *Ḳnḫpšf* his (= my) son, it belongs to him without contestation of a son, a daughter, (or) *Ḳn*'s woman about it; his statement should not be heard in (the) future.

***Tradition* by first party**: *swꜣḏ hrw {n b}<p>n m-bꜣḥ*

Handing over this day in presence of:

rmṯ ist ꜣnynḫt	workman *ꜣnynḫt*
(6) *rmṯ ist Ḳdꜣḫtf*	workman *Ḳdꜣḫtf*
rmṯ ist Nbnḫt	workman *Nbnḫt*
rmṯ ist Ḫnsw	workman *Ḫnsw*
rmṯ ist Nfrḥtpw	workman *Nfrḥtpw*
rmṯ ist ꞽmnnḫtw	workman *ꞽmnnḫtw*
rmṯ ist Ḫʿmnwn (7) *ḥʿt.f*	workman *Ḫʿmnwn* himself,

Promise[324] of compensation by second party:

iw ḏd rmṯ ist Ḳnḫpšf iw.i r dit n.f ḫꜣr 2 ¾

while (the) workman *Ḳnḫpšf* said: I shall give him 2 ¾ *ḫꜣr*.

***Promissory* oath by second party (warranty with penalty)**:

iw iw.f irt ʿnḫ n nb ʿ.w.s. r-ḏd wꜣḥ ꞽmn wꜣḥ pꜣ ḥḳꜣ ʿ.w.s. (8) *mtw.i nḥm pꜣy di n pꜣy.i it* (*iw.w*) *r irt nḥm pꜣ mtwn ink*

And he took an oath of (the) Lord L.P.H. saying: 'May Amun be clement, may the Ruler L.P.H. be clement should I seize this grain allowance[325] of my father, (they) shall make a seizure of this bonus of mine';

Recording fees:

iw.i ḥr <dit> tiwbty ʿ 1 *n rmṯ ist* (9) *ꞽmnnḫt iw.f ḥr dit ʿfd* 1 (*n*) *rmṯ ist Mꜣꜣnnḫtwf* (*r-*) *ḏbꜣw nꜣ sšw i.ir.w ḥr rꜣ pꜣy.w it*

And I <gave> 1 pair of sandals to (the) workman *ꞽmnnḫt* and he (= the other party) gave 1 wooden chest (to the) workman *Mꜣꜣnnḫtwf* (in) payment of the records[326] that they made concerning (the) statement of their father.

* Neo-Egyptian characteristics:

- *ir pꜣ iʿ i.di.i rmṯ ist... iw.f n* PN: topicalization of expanded noun and statement of ownership *iw.f n* PN;
- cataphoric articloid (*pꜣ iʿ; tꜣ ḥmt; nꜣ sšw*);
- *i.di.i*: imperfect relative form with prothetic *yod*. Although it is again a locutive texteme, we do not find the same markers of public direct address as in the first part of the papyrus, but as the physical handing over of the item is noted, the statement must be almost simultaneous with the handing over (*contra*: Allam 1973: 56 and Pestman 1982b: 176 who understand that *Ḫʿmnwn* states 'that he has handed over the washing-bowl (…) in conformity with his promise', although the mention of the *tradition swꜣḏ hrw* {*n b*}<*p*>*n* follows *i.di.i*);
- preposition omission (*i.di.i* (*n*) *rmṯ ist; dit ʿfd* (*n*) *rmṯ;* (*r-*) *ḏbꜣw*);

324 Although the promise is an 'engagement unilatéral', it may be included in an agreement 'comme clause d'un contrat' (Cornu 2003: 701).

325 A regular stipend supplied by the children to their ageing parents (McDowell 1998: esp. 210-2).

326 For Baines & Eyre (1983: 74-5) and Donker van Heel & Haring (2003: 112), the statements were recorded by two brothers of *Ḳnḫrḫpšf*, whose services had to be remunerated, instead of paying for the service of a professional scribe.

- Neo-Egyptian possessive determinator for kinship (*p3y.f šri; p3y.i it; p3y.w it*);
- *bn mdt* N… *bn sḏm r3.f*;
- *m-im.f*: Neo-Egyptian form of the classical modifier *im.f* ;
- *m dw3*: abbreviation of binomial *m dw3 r-s3 dw3*[327];
- *iw ḏd*.N: tag clause, delocutive converted perfect report[328] indicating the simultaneity between the *traditio* and the promise, thus underlining their interdependence (agreement by compromise);
- *iw iw.f irt*: although puzzling[329], it seems that we have here another instance of the use of *iw* as a coordinator (see *supra oGardiner/Ashmolean* 55: *iw ir n3 ḥnw… p3 rwy*) followed by a sequential *iw.f ḥr sḏm* (the preposition is omitted);
- exophoric articloid (extratextual deixis) referring to the reigning king (*p3 ḥk3*);
- *promissory* oath constructed as $\{[$*w3ḥ*.PN$]_{\text{protasis}}$ + $[$*mtw.i nḥm*$]_{\text{apodosis}}\}_{\textbf{crime protasis}}$ + $\{$(*iw.w*) *r irt nḥm*$\}_{\textbf{penalty apodosis}}$. The protasis-apodosis system expressing the 'crime' (with a modal prospective delocutive protasis and a locutive atemporal conjunctive apodosis) is itself the protasis of the penalty apodosis (see *supra*), expressed by an elliptic future.
  For Černý (1945: 41, j(8)), the idea of an analytic future (*iw.w*) *r irt nḥm* is irrelevant as 'auxiliaries were never used in the infinitive'; he suggests viewing *nḥm* as a participle or *r irt* as the that-form *r.irtw*, 'though a future use of *iir.f sḏm* without a stressed adverbial predicate (…) can hardly be paralleled.' Frandsen (1974: 212-3) adopts this last option and finds the focus in the following 'converted present' clause: 'it is together with my giving one pair of sandals to B and one box to C (…) that one shall take away my reward'. The main problem with this option is the fact that it makes the recording fees part of the penalty although the payment is shared by the father and the son (see *infra*). We prefer to give an entirely nominal status to *nḥm* and translate *irt nḥm* as 'to make a seizure' instead of taking *nḥm* as an auxiliated verb.
  The oath guarantees the execution of the promise, the penalty being the divestiture of the bonus attributed to the legatee, a compromise concluding a disagreement.
  The solemn *w3ḥ Imn w3ḥ p3 ḥk3* is a binomial with prosodic weight on the second member, the sequence of the two members being always the same. In abnormal hieratic contractual provisions of the 25-26th dynasties a similar binomial is used[330]: *w3ḥ/ꜥnḫ Imn ꜥnḫ Pr-ꜥ3*. Note that binomials are an important feature of ancient Anglo-Saxon oaths of fealty[331]: 'By the lord, before whom this relic is holy, I will be to N. faithful and true, and love all that he loves, and shun all that he shuns, according to God's law, and according to the world's principles, and never, by will nor by force, by word nor by work, do aught of what is loathful to him.';
- Neo-Egyptian anaphoric demonstrative *p3y* (*p3y di*);
- *p3 mtwn ink*: locutive independent pronoun possessor of a noun already specified by the demonstrative/articloid (see *supra p3*[y] 4 *ḫrdw ink*);

---

327 Allam (1967: 18, n.25); Janssen (2005: 80).

328 Frandsen (1974: 194-9); Junge (2005: 153, 156-7).

329 Černý (1945: 41). For Allam (1973: 257, n.8) it may be an erroneous repetition of *iw*; for Wente (1961: 122) it is an instance of *iwiw.f r ir*, a converted future form (as for McDowell 1998: 211), with actor 'confusion', the segment being translated as 'for I will swear an oath by the Lord'; for Théodoridès (1977: 74) it is a converted past form 'concomittante dans l'antériorité'; for Winand (1992: 491) 'Je lui donnerai… quand il prêtera un serment' but it does not make sense that the father should take an oath that obviously guarantees the promise of his son.

330 Malinine (1953: 13).

331 Hibbitts (1992: 902).

- Neo-Egyptian lexeme (*mtwnw*) and spelling (*šri*; *ḥꜥt.f*; *ꜥfd;swꜣḏ*);
- *iw.i ḥr <dit>* (…) *iw.f ḥr dit*: locutive and delocutive sequential forms used by one of the parties, the parallelism of the construction and the lexemic usage again emphasizing the bilateral nature of the agreement.
  This segment does not belong to the oath as often previously thought[332], as it adds information concerning the personal contribution of the two parties to the expenses. It may be the sequel of *iw iw.f irt* after the tag clause using a converted perfect report form *iw ḏd rmṯ ist Ḳnḥpšf*.
  At the end of the title deed of *pBoulaq* 10, line 14 there is a similar parallelism of two sequentials with the lexeme *di*: *iw.f dit n.st pꜣy.f wt iw.tw dit n.f tꜣy.st pš* 'And he gave her his coffin, and one gave him her share'. Sequentials are also used at the end of documents concerning partitions in order to add further developments, e.g. in *oLouvre* E 13156, although here the sequential does not follow any nexus, only a long nominal segment;
- *i.ir.w*: perfect relative form with prothetic *yod*;
- Neo-Egyptian suffixed delocutive plural (*w*).

* 'Classical' degree 0 forms used:
  - *iw.f n* PN: statement of ownership *iw.f n* PN;
  - both genders binomial *šri* *šri* (although the feminine member has lost its feminine mark);
  - use of the relator for temporal (*hrw {n b}<p>n*), address (*ꜥnḫ n nb*) and kinship (*pꜣy di n pꜣy.i it*) relations;
  - archaic anaphora (*hrw {n b}<p>n*);
  - future *iw.i r dit* (with preposition);
  - *r-ḏd*: tagged speech marker opening the oath after sequential *iw.f* (*ḥr*) *sḏm*, although *m-ḏd* has been used in line V.12;
  - *wꜣḥ*.PN/*pꜣ* N: modal prospective, optative in the complete oath protasis;

* General dialectal features: degree 2.

* Legal formulae:
  - *ir* N (object) *iw.f n* N (recognition of ownership right) + *bn md*[*t*] *šri* *šri* N *m-im.f* (warranty) + *bn sḏm rꜣ.f m dwꜣt* (inadmissibility of claim)
  - tradition: *swꜣḏ* + *hrw pn* + *m-bꜣḥ* (witnesses)
  - *promissory* oath: *iw iw.f irt ꜥnḫ nb ꜥ.w.s. r-ḏd* (tag clause) + *wꜣḥ Ỉmn wꜣḥ pꜣ ḥḳꜣ ꜥ.w.s.* (optative) + *mtw.i nḥm* (forfeiture) + (*iw.w*) *r irt nḥm* (penalty)
  - payment of recording fees by both parties: *iw.i ḥr <dit>* (price) + *n* (beneficiary) + *iw.f ḥr dit* (price) + (*n*) (beneficiary) + (*r-*)*ḏbꜣw* (*consideration*)

Categorization of terms of special relevance in the legal register:

- *iri hꜣrwy*: to make a dated record of a legal matter, perhaps an entry in a court's session journal (see Kruchten 1981: 154-5). For *hꜣrwy*, see Černý (1945: 32), Redford (1986: 97-126), Donker van Heel & Haring (2003: 101-4 with reference to two other documents using the lexeme and related to the necropolis administration).

332 With the exception of Pestman (1982b: 180 n.12). See Černý's uncertainty (1945: 40) as to the delocutive form, since he understands this segment as part of the oath, which does not make sense.

The 18th dynasty spelling of *hꜣrwy* (with the same classifier) is *hrwyt*[333], but the lexeme goes back to the 12th dynasty at least, probably with the same classifier[334]. The classifier of the basic level [BINDING] category is used with lexemes implying a rolled document ready to be archived (David 2006: 23-4). As the purpose of the public session is the record of a will in court, a notarial will is a type of *hꜣrwy* and it is to be archived (see its docket) and should also be mentioned in the court log (*pDeM* 26 may be such a journal).

- *ꜥwty* *hꜣrwyt* : dated record of a legal matter, 'acte authentique' (Théodoridès 1966: 34), 'pièce enregistrée' (Théodoridès 1970: 147). Černý (1945: 32) translates *ꜥwty* as 'roll'; it may be related to the ancient *ꜥ* (document, with the classifier), although it is linked to *ꜥrt* 'roll' by Théodoridès (1970: 147) and Donker van Heel & Haring (2003: 101).

  Following the *Wb* I, 208-9.17-1, *ꜥrt* is usually classified by during the Old Kingdom (e.g. *Giza coffin Cairo* 1787, 4th dynasty, in *Urk*. I, 22), during the Middle Kingdom, and since the 18th dynasty (see *pTurin* 2021 IV.3 *ꜥrw nt ḏmꜥ*).
  Here too the classifier used for both lexemes is the one of the [BINDING] category, the suggestion of archiving being perfectly suited to the fact that this characterization of the instrument appears on a docket, meaning the papyrus was rolled, attached with a string and labelled with a docket before being archived.
- *ꜣḫt* : assets.
- *nmḥy* : the voiceless, a simple female 'citizen'.
  Černý (1945: 31) and Gardiner (1940: 24) 'free woman'; Théodoridès (1965: 109-28; 1966: 36-7, n.23; 1969: 111-2 n. 31; 1977: 72-3) 'particulière ayant des biens privés'; Cruz-Uribe (1982: 49-52, 63) 'derives from the word for "orphan"' 'Being an orphan suggests that the individual is not attached in any sort of (beneficial) relationship as one would experience when dependent upon one's parents', 'unencumbered'; Eyre (1994: 128) 'a person responsible socially and economically for his own household'; Jasnow (2003c: 316-7).
  As many scholars have observed[335], the lexeme underwent a semantic evolution, from a negative concept (orphan, deprived of) in the Middle Kingdom to what seems a positive term in our *pAdoptions* and many other New Kingdom examples (although the first meaning was never abandoned). The term is still used in Demotic and Coptic[336]. We cannot say that during the New Kingdom *nmḥw* became an entirely positive concept, it is only indicated in several texts that the simple 'citizen' has some rights over immovable assets and that he may pay taxes (e.g. in *pValençay* I v°, lines 2-3); not being in a state of economic dependency does not mean having the status of a *sr* with all the privileges attached to high status in the politico-administrative hierarchy.
  The lexeme *nmḥ* 'orphan' was apparently not classified during the Old Kingdom (*PT* 1285b, Spell 535); during the Middle Kingdom, the same lexeme uses the classifiers , or or a combination of them, and *nmḥyt* as a designation of women is either not classified or classified by (e.g. in *pKahun* I.3 = *pUC* 32163, lines 3-7). Although not to be taken in the sense of orphan here, the lexeme *nmḥy* is still classified by the

333 *Wb* II, 500.26; Faulkner (1962: 159).
334 Černý (1945: 32-3), *pBerlin* 10012.
335 e.g. Gauthier (1936: 66-7).
336 Malinine (1953: 54-5); Richter (2002: 252-3) for ⲣⲙϩⲉ 'frei sein' in Coptic, from *rmṯ-nmḥ*.

classifier of the superordinate [CHILDHOOD] category to which the [FEMALE] classifier has been added. The first classifier may have been retained from the basic 'orphan' semantics and be of no significance, but it may also denote a status acquired by birth or some kind of incapacity; in the last case, the semantic field of the [CHILDHOOD] category has been extended to encompass other forms of dependency, 'states like the state of a young child.' The child icon would thus be associated with an abstract status, the status being personified ('*IDEAS ARE PEOPLE*'[337]). Furthermore, the process relies on the idea that '*SIGNIFICANT IS BIG*'[338], since being a young child means to be socially unsignificant in ancient Egyptian society. The child's sitting position on the absent maternal lap is opposed to the adult standing to exert a claim (see *ʿḥʿ infra* and David 2007: 8), reflecting the orientational metaphor '*LOW STATUS IS DOWN*'[339].

Young children are represented in Egyptian iconography and hieroglyphic script as prototypical male children[340] pointing to their mouth or sucking one finger (usually the right hand index[341]). Textual sources such as *PT* 664 describe the infant (*nḫn*) as having a finger in his mouth. Apart from the 'oral stage' issue, the helplessness of the young child may be indicated by the fact that he is, like the Roman toddler, *in-fans* 'one who does not talk yet,' and as such dependent on care and understanding of his needs, as opposed to the other icon of an adult man pointing to his mouth 𓀁 and referring to the [MOUTH LINKED ACTIVITIES] category but not to a state of dependency.

Indeed, the *in-fans* idea is expressed in *pAnastasi* II vº 4-5 in connection with good wishes: *bn nmḥw.k mi ʿḏd* 'May you not be voiceless as a youngster'. This hypothesis may help us to understand some negative uses of *nmḥw* related to a *voiceless* category of individuals in society, not specifically poor, not enslaved, but uninfluential and in need of a representative; the antonym of the voiceless is *wsr* or *sr,* and Kruchten (1981: 32 n.41) notes that 's'appliquant à tout individu habitant en Egypte, le terme [*nmḥ*] désigne celui-ci dans ses rapports avec la puissance royale, représentée par les *srw*'. 'Voiceless' means being unable to express oneself, to *voice* one's opinion, to have *voice* in the matter (think of 'a voice' as representing today the first attribute of citizenship in a democracy). The *nmḥw n pꜣ tꜣ n Pr-ʿꜣ* is 'the *in-fans* of the land of Pharaoh,' the simple Egyptian 'citizen' of whom the king takes care, represented by the high officials' voice (thus concurring with the conclusion of Kruchten, but for other semantic reasons). A rather good example of voiceless 'citizen' is ironically the ever *Eloquent Peasant*, since his rather articulated speech is not heard by Pharaoh without the high steward's recommendation; being eloquent does not help the voiceless without adequate intercession by a mandated authority.

And indeed, in *oBorchardt*, Amun, 'Vizir du pauvre' for Théodoridès (1965: 114) and 'Juge du pauvre' for Posener (1971), intercedes in favor of the *nmḥ*, he is *Ỉmn-Rʿ pꜣ ʿn wšbw n nmḥ* '*Ỉmn-Rʿ*, the one who answers for the voiceless'; the god intercedes so that 'the court would as one voice answer on behalf of the voiceless' (*dỉ.f wn tꜣ ḳnbt m rꜣ wʿ wšb.sn ḥr nmḥ*). The *nmḥ*'s 'inaudible voice' is only heard by the god (*stela Berlin* 23077[342]): 'Amen-Rê (…) who hears prayer; Who comes at the voice of the distressed

337 Lakoff & Johnson (1980: 47).
338 *Ibid*., p. 50.
339 *Ibid*., p. 16.
340 Goldwasser (2005: 100).
341 Feucht (1980: 424, 426-7); Wilkinson (1992: 20-1).
342 Gunn (1916: 83).

humble one'. A metonymic-metaphoric expression of the same idea is represented in the round by the votive ears and ear-stelae dedicated to gods[343].

- *grg* 𓏛-*pr*: establishment, equipment (lit. house establishment). Polotsky (1930: 198-9); Černý (1945: 44) 'to found (*grg*) homes (*pr*)'; Théodoridès (1966: 37, n. 26) 'fonder un foyer'; Clère (1968: 174-5); Allam (1973: 270, n. 7) for further references; Toivari-Viitala (2001: 68-9, 75-6) 'Founding a house(hold)' that she relates in our case to dowry. The idea is attested since the Old Kingdom (without classifier), also in the context of an inheritance, in the *Cairo letter to the dead* JE 25975, line 12, but as the duty of a son towards his father: *grg s3.k pr.k mi grg.k pr it.k* 'May your son equip your house as you equipped the house of your father'. In the Middle Kingdom, the expression *grg-pr* is classified with the papyrus scroll in *pPrisse* 10, 8-10. The association of *grg* and *nmḥ* is also to be found in Demotic land leases: *grg n rmṯ nmḥ* 'equipment of a *nmḥ*-person'[344].
  Apart from a house and a few movable assets, the patrimonial establishment probably involved several more abstract operations, records and transfers of rights; it is the superordinate [ABSTRACT] category classifier that is used here to represent the ensemble of these operations as well as the moral principle behind an institution based on kinship duty.
- *iri ḫrt*: to look after (an elderly parent). See the references in Černý (1945: 33.g) and Théodoridès (1966:63-4).
- *di* (*m*) *3ḫt* 𓏛: to give, transmit assets. See supra *rdi ḫt* 𓏛.
- *r rdit rḫ.tw*𓏛: to let be known, for information (relative to). See *supra* for the discussion of the notification.
- (*m*)*twnw*𓀁: bonus, advantage. As for the superordinate [MOUTH LINKED ACTIVITIES] category classifier 𓀁, it implies a metaphorical process that links the semantic fields of alimentation and economic advantage (for another use of the 𓀁 classifier based on the simile '*allocating economic resources to a temple is like feeding an organism*' and an alimentary metaphor in the context of Ramesside royal decrees, see David 2006: 24-5). What links our lexeme to the [MOUTH LINKED ACTIVITIES] category is another instance of the complex metaphor '*IDEAS ARE OBJECTS*' (the abstract notion of economic advantage is mapped to the semantic field of concrete objects that may physically sustain an organism). An economic abstract concept is understood in terms of a human basic activity, using the metaphor '*IDEAS ARE FOOD*'[345]. We use a similar metaphor when we assess that 'increased savings will *eat into expenditure* on vacation travel'.
  The fact that we have here apparently the only instance of categorization of (*m*)*twnw* with the help of the 𓀁 classifier is another case of the classification versatility of some abstract concepts already observed in the study of the categorization of legal lexemes in Ramesside decrees (David 2006).
- *h3y* 𓂻 *ḥr pšt* 𓏛𓀜 and *ʿḳ* 𓂻 *r pšt* ×𓀜: to inherit a share, lit. to come down to/enter into a share.

The lexeme *h3y* is classified with the 𓂻 classifier from the Old Kingdom period (representing the instrument and its dynamics for the action), *ʿḳ* being during the same

343 See e.g. Andreu (2002: 258-60).
344 Eyre (1994: 128) and his references.
345 Lakoff & Johnson (1980: 46-7).

period mostly devoided of classifier, although the [MOTION] classifier is also attested (e.g. *Ḥrḫwf tomb* in *Urk.* I, 122 line 14). Verbs of motion are often used to indicate an abstract movement, a legal operation (e.g. 'to enter into possession of'); clearly what is meant here is the transmission of the right (the still undivided share) that precedes the physical *tradition* of the items, so that it is an abstract motion categorized by the classifier. The categorization process is based on a metaphorical process, the abstract 'enter into a share' being a metaphorical projection of a bodily experience. The walking legs classifier thus categorizes legal concepts in the [MOTION] category using precisely the same metaphoric strategy to conceptualize them as we do, here an orientational UP-DOWN metaphor for the lexeme *hꜣy* as English 'befall' and French 'échoir' (from Latin *excidere*, 'to fall from'), as the inevitable consequence of the force of gravity (although the downwards motion may be used as a negative metaphor, here the concept is positive as what is down may be grasped[346]). For an extensive analysis of the classifier and some of its uses in the legal field, see David (2007); see also *ḫnw pr/ꜣḫt* in *oPetrie* 18 *infra*.

- *pš* ×: to share, divide.
- *pšt* × / / : share, division.
- *r*-3: third (the woman's share in the community property).
- *rwy*: two-thirds (the man's share in the community property).
- *st* : immovable property ('place').
  For Helck (1961-70: 337-49) and Demarée (2006: 57), *swt* in Deir el-Medina sources represents a group of buildings assigned to the workmen as official property, encompassing the notions of *pr* (house in the village), *ʿt* (hut/workplace outside the village), *ʿḥʿt* (tomb) and *ḫnw*. Although McDowell (1990: 123) assumes that the *swt* are inalienable properties, our texts prove that some of the buildings at least are bequeathed.
  The superordinate taxonomic [HABITAT] category classifier consists of the somewhat schematic top-view representation of a building. Whereas the fundamental legal distinction between 'movables' and 'immovables' is based in modern Anglo-American and Romano-Germanic systems of law on a motion criterion, in ancient Egypt, movable and immovable assets are not classified in the [MOTION] category[347], *st* belonging to the [HABITAT] and the generic *ḫt* to the [ABSTRACT] category. They are not really opposed in our text in lines IV.9-10 (*ḫr ỉr ꜣḫt nb n sš* PN (...) *m-mỉtt nꜣy.f swt{t}*) as *swt* is covered by *ꜣḫt nb*.
- *ỉni*: to bring, acquire. For *ini* 'to buy,'see Gardiner (1906: 34.22); Peet (1932); Allam (1973: 269 and n. 25);
- *ỉw.f n* N: to be for, to belong to.
- *wḥm* *sprw* *r ḳnbt* : representation to the court (McDowell 1990: 15).
  The verb *wḥm* 'to repeat' is classified by the superordinate [ABSTRACT] category classifier, customary since the Middle Kingdom, although the classifiers and are also to be found during the New Kingdom; the verb of motion *sprw* by the superordinate [MOTION] category classifier since the Middle Kingdom[348]), and mainly

346 See Lakoff & Johnson (1980: 20-21) for mixed metaphors based on differend kinds of experiences.
347 But compare with *mnmnt* 'taxable moving property' (Goldwasser 2002: 72-8 and David 2006: 75).
348 McDowell (1990: 15), *spr* 'to approach'.

not classified or classified with the boat during the Old Kingdom; the *ḳnbt* court is classified by its [MALE-HUMAN] composant since the First Intermediate Period, the classifier being in a metonymic relation to the lexeme (a member for the whole body).

- *m-mitt* *ꜥḳ3* : exactly conform.
  Conformity or likeness is obviously an [ABSTRACT] category member as a general result of a mental process that compares two situations or objects. In *pTurin* 2021, conformity is expressed by *iri mitt* *m* (to conform to, to act in conformity). See David (2006: 111, 174-5) for other conformity formulae.
  As for *ꜥḳ3* and its double classification since the Middle Kingdom (during the First Intermediate Period only the classifier appears[349]). I proposed elsewhere (David 2006: 241 and 257) considering the two fingers as the classifiers of the basic level category of [CONTROLLED ACTIVITIES], where 'precise measurement is made by taking into account fine measure units, the fingers (digit, finger breadth)', the prototypical unit being of course a body part ('natural kinds of experience' being primarily based on our bodies[350]). In the case of actual measurements, the fingers represent the metonymy '*INSTRUMENT FOR ACTIVITY*,' and two fingers a reinforcing isotopy (compare with the French metaphor 'être à *deux* doigts du but' meaning very close), what Lakoff & Johnson (1980: 127) termed an example of iteration based on the metaphor '*MORE OF FORM IS MORE OF CONTENT*' (see also the added *sp sn*). Precision being prototypically a quality attached to measurement, it is classified by two fingers; being an abstract notion, the [ABSTRACT] category classifier completes the picture.
- *iri ꜥnḫ n nb* ()[351] *ꜥ.w.s.*: to take an oath of (the) Lord L.P.H (see McDowell 1990: 36).
  The lexeme *ꜥnḫ* 'to swear' is attested since the Old Kingdom although not classified at that time, and *ꜥnḫ* 'oath' is attested since the Middle Kingdom unclassified or with the classifier; it is not classified in our text; when classified, it is usually categorized by the classifier in the [MOUTH LINKED ACTIVITIES] category as it is always a verbal statement. The numerous oath documents that we possess (see *infra*) are after-the-fact records of a public oral declaration.
- *pn(ꜥ)* (*r3*) *r mdwt* : to reverse (an undertaking) in order to contest. See Malinine (1947: 104-5) and McDowell (1990: 20-1) concerning *mdw m*; Théodoridès (1965: 94) for *mdw ḏw m* in the *PT* and (1967) for *pnꜥ r mdt*; Rabinowitz (1958: 146) concerning *mdt* and Semitic דבר.
  The verb *mdw* (unclassified) is already attested during the Old Kingdom in the sense of 'to complain about' with the preposition *ḥr* (block from a *Lisht tomb* of the 5th dynasty[352]); in the Middle Kingdom, it is already classified with the classifier. As for *mdwt*, the [MOUTH LINKED ACTIVITIES] category covers both orality and emotion-related semantic fields.
  The lexeme *pnꜥ* 'to turn upside down' is attested during the Old Kingdom with the upturned boat ; it is classified in the [MOTION] category since the New Kingdom, when it also acquires the meaning found in legal texts as here. The classifier of *pn(ꜥ)*

349 e.g. in Griffith (1889: table 15, line 4).
350 Lakoff & Johnson (1980: 117).
351 For the [DIVINE] category classifiers, see Shalomi-Hen (2000; 2006).
352 Goedicke (1970: 116-7).

is opposed to in terms of direction of motion pertaining to the source-path-goal schema, the generic forward motion being classified by , so that the opposite direction represents a subcategory of the general [MOTION] category. Again, this is a case of abstract motion, '*going back* on a statement' being a picturesque way to *re*consider it (French '*revenir* sur ses déclarations'), a product of the metaphors '*ACTION IS MOTION*' and '*AN ARGUMENT IS A JOURNEY*'[353]. Note that in *pBM* EA 10335 v° 16-7, *pnꜥ* is classified by [354], the inverted metonymic boat classifier of the [CROSSING] category and the [COERCION] category classifier; in *pBoulaq* 10, only the upsidedown boat is used. The boat icon also underwent a change of direction, like the legs in motion (that may also take the upsidedown form). Motion by boat is another prototypical motion in the Nilotic environment and as such, the boat metaphor is often used in textual and pictorial discourses (in Ramesside royal decrees, see David 2006: 55-6).

- *ẖry* *sẖ* ×: liable to a beating.
  For the classification of *ẖry* 'to be under,' see David (2006: 153). The lexeme *sẖi* 'to beat, blow,' a physical penalty, undergoes here a double classification with the [UNION/DIVISION] × classifier (conflict expressed in geometrical relationships, see David 2003; 2007: 11-2) and the [COERCION] classifier representing here physical violence. The verb *sẖi* is already attested during the Old Kingdom, with the hand or the fist as classifier, while the substantive *sẖt* may appear with the classifier [355]. During the Middle Kingdom, the classifiers appear, and in the New Kingdom it is the turn of the [UNION/DIVISION] × classifier.
- *šw* × *m* (*ꜣḫt*): deprived of (assets), disinherited.
  The superordinate [UNION/DIVISION] category × classifier (separation expressed in geometric terms, see David 2003; 2007: 11-2) and the superordinate [INFERIORITY-PERTURBATION] category classifier (David 2000: esp. 42-3 for the first examples of classification of *šw* with the 'bad bird', expressing an inferiority characterized by deprivation; 2007: 11) both complete the complex and tend to numerous metaphorical associations abstract concepts of deprivation, destitution and disinheritance.
- *rdyt* ( ): 'what was given'. See *rdi ḫt supra*.
  For formulae constructed with this form, see Donker van Heel & Haring (2003: 150-2, 155-6, 158). Although *rdi* is usually not classified, the classification in the superordinate [ABSTRACT] category of *rdyt* since the Middle Kingdom[356] probably signifies that it has gained substantival status (abstract 'transmission, bequest').
- *ḏd*: statement, declaration. See McDowell (1990: 18).
- *mdt* : contestation. See *supra*.
- *sḏm* ( ) *rꜣ*: a hearing of/to hear a deposition/statement. See *infra sḏm rꜣ n* PN in *oGardiner/Ashmolean* 36, the document bearing a docket that mentions *wpwtw m tꜣ ḳnbt*, thus produced during a court session. For *rꜣ* 'deposition, statement' and *sḏm rꜣ* 'hear a deposition', see McDowell (1990: 18-20); Donker van Heel & Haring (2003:

353 Lakoff & Johnson (1980: 90); for the study of the Egyptian [MOTION] category, see David (2007).
354 Dawson (1925: pl. XXXVIII).
355 *ÄW* I, 1192.
356 *Wb* II, 465.6.

168-9) and Haring (2003: 148). Formula of deposition since the first half of the 20th dynasty (the shorter *rꜣ n* PN being older).

The use of the lexeme *sḏm* is particularily well attested in the Egyptian legal field: the judge is a 'hearer', a court session is a 'hearing', and a judge may not remain *sḫ-ḥr* 'face-deaf' (refusing to take cognizance) as mentioned in the *Nauri decree* (David 2006: 105-6). The divine is also conceived as a listening instance (see *supra nmḥy*). The emphasis on the virtue of listening is a leitmotif of the *sapientia* genre, referring to *mꜣꜥt* (e.g. the *Instruction of Ptahhotep,* in Lichtheim 1973: 73-75). Actual and metaphorical aurality is also of prime importance in the Anglo-American legal field, especially in criminal procedures: 'the accused is due a "hearing": lawyers for the defense and for the prosecution call orally sworn witnesses who, under oral questioning, offer oral testimony. Jurors are required to listen to to that testimony, to oral arguments, and to the eventual instructions from the judge. In a few jurisdictions, jurors are not even permitted to take notes of what they hear. After deliberation, they return to declare their verdict orally. The court, after hearing further oral submissions, literally "pronounces" sentence.'[357]

The lexeme *sḏm* is classified in the [ABSTRACT] and [MOUTH LINKED ACTIVITIES] categories since the 19th dynasty (the two classifiers  are alternative classifications of the lexeme since the Middle Kingdom); double classification is an important feature of legal categorization during the Ramesside Period. Thus hearing (aurality) is classified by its counterpart (verbality) represented by the man pointing to his mouth .

- *swꜣḏ*: to hand over, *tradition* – a material, physical transfer, but also an abstract transfer of rights. Eyre (1992: 213) notes that it is normally understood in the abstract sense and also has a symbolic aspect when used as a physical transmission (compare *infra* with *pAdoptions*).

  Examples from all periods concern abstract transmission: e.g. transfer of function in *Bbi Leiden stela* V 88 (Middle Kingdom)[358]; transfer of land in *pBerlin* P 8523, line 10 (21st dynasty); transfer of an inheritance in *Urk*. IV, 807, line 2 (18th dynasty, inscription of Thutmes III in the temple of Wadi Halfa); transfer of immovable property in 20th dynasty *oFlorence* 2620, although it may be accompanied by a symbolic act before witnesses.

  Most examples of physical handing come from New Kingdom sources: e.g. handing down of tools in *oFlorence* 2625 (20th dynasty); of a donkey in *oDeM* 133 v° 2 (20th dynasty); of people in *pAbbott* 7, 15 (20th dynasty).

  The lexeme *swꜣḏ* does not indicate which type of legal transmission is effected (sale, loan, etc.). Note that *rdi* may also cover the transfer of a right on an item or the material transmission of an object[359], and that *rdi* and *swḏ* are even attested together in the *Stèle juridique de Karnak* JE 52453, line 17: *rdi.n.i… m swḏt* [360]. Janssen (2005: 77) notes that *swḏ/swꜣḏ* seems to 'put some stress on what actually happened', something that *rdi* does not.

357 Hibbitts (1992: 895).

358 See Mrsich (1975: 1252 n.32).

359 Pestman (1982b: 179 n.6).

360 Théodoridès (1957: 41-2 and 1958: 66 n.6): 'confier', 'prêter', 'donner (remettre) en faisant en sorte qu'il y ait (re)transmission'.

The lexeme is not classified here; under its classical spelling *swḏ*, it is already classified in the 9th (?) dynasty *Dmḏibtȝwy Coptos R* criminal law decree, line 27, by the papyrus scroll 𓏛 classifier, its usual classifier[361]. Thus *swḏ* 𓏛 belongs to the [ABSTRACT] category, although exceptionally in 12th dynasty *Stela BM* 101, lines 2-3, it is linked to the [MOUTH LINKED ACTIVITIES] category (*swḏ* 𓀁*.ṯn iȝwt.ṯn n ẖrdw.ṯn* 'May you transmit your offices to your children').

- (*r*-) *ḏbȝw*𓏛𓀜: in payment, exchange, compensation. Implies the presence of a *consideration* in contractual relationships.
  The lexeme *ḏbȝ* is not classified or classified by the papyrus scroll already during the Old Kingdom, and the same may be said about the Middle Kingdom Period. The double classification in the [ABSTRACT] and [COERCION] categories is thus a New Kingdom feature and may express the binding character of the contractual obligation, here the payment of a service.
- *sšw* 𓍼: written provisions, records (the instruments and the texts); see Donker van Heel & Haring (2003: 110-2).
  The [BINDING] category classifier has replaced the previous papyrus scroll classifier 𓏛 as observed *supra*.

361 See Spiegelberg (1896: 9, 33).

6. *pBoulaq* 10 (*pCairo*CG 58092)

Date: 20th dynasty, Ramesses III or VI 'in view of persons mentioned' in the Leiden Deir el-Medina database (Demarée 2006: 59 'mid dyn. 20')[362]

Hieroglyphic text: *KRI* V, 449-51 n.A.13

Instrument:

* **state –** slightly damaged

* **value – incomplete copy or original?**[363]: papyrus with essential information such as preceding excerpt or summary of an undated title deed, act *sensu stricto* with abbreviated date, named settlor and beneficiaries, but without mention of the forum, scribe, witnesses, *recital*, colophon, docket.

* **nature – legal instrument**: no internal characterization, concerns legal rights about assets.

* **genre – consentient legal:** formulaic style, ordered layout; 21 cm high papyrus with fiber orientation typical of legal texts; concerns private interests; dated, with archaic anaphora; delocutive and locutive textemes, degree 2 Neo-Egyptian features; title deed mentioning a legal norm, a precedent (see *oPetrie* 16), an oracle, an oath, and a court.

The text is the work of two business hands, neatly divided between a title deed – the recto – written in a 'far bolder hand'[364] and the verso (deed and material partition) in a different business hand, thus the result of a two-step redaction in a file; there are scribal errors and a correction above one line, but no business practice diacritical marks. It was found among debris in the Theban necropolis of Assassif.

Legal step: public hearing (*sḏm r3*) of a **notification** list of inherited immovable assets for their transmission (*r rdit*), and material **partition** (*pšw.w*) during the same day, followed by the **oath** of the donees.

Legal issue: ***donation-partage***: absence of *consideration*, unilateral deed (a warranty of the donees follows the material partition); use of *rdi* and *pš*; absence of specific clauses except the repayment of the estate's debt; concerns part of the father's patrimony (the immovables inherited from his father), for his chidren; list of shares of the same type with dimensions of the immovables; coincidence between the date of the declaration and the date of the *tradition*; no mention of old age or death, of future *descent and distribution* rule, and of clear performative form (contrary to *oDeM* 108 which is a *partage d'ascendant* in the form of a testament, including future *descent and distribution* rule and specific bequests with performative attribution). It thus represents a *partage d'ascendant* in the form of a gift[365].

---

362 As for the main case expounded in the title deed, it is dated by Janssen & Pestman (1968: 143) to the end of the 19th dynasty or beginning of the 20th dynasty; they also date the precedent referred to in the title deed and recorded in *oPetrie* 16 to the beginning of the 20th dynasty (*ibid*., p. 155). In view of this element and of the recent dating of *pBoulaq* 10 to the reign of Ramesses VI, we may conclude that the sequence [*oPetrie* 16 – the litigation between *Ḥwy* and his brothers – *pBoulaq* 10] belongs in its entirety to the 20th dynasty.

363 But draft for Seidl (1957: 27).

364 Janssen & Pestman (1968: 139).

365 See Théodoridès (1966: 60). But it is a will for Janssen & Pestman (1968: 138, 151; p. 141 K they contend that the entire text reflects an oracular procedure in which court members are 'involved') and *KRI* V, 449. For Allam (1973.II: 28, 38, 42, 52 *et passim*; 1985: 5) it is a 'Klageerwiderungsschrift' (counterclaim, *demande reconventionnelle*) on the recto but a 'Schenkung auf den Todesfall' with 'Realteilung' on the verso and it is interpreted as a 'Niederschrift über einen Erbstreit' by Helck (2002: 226). Donker van Heel & Haring (2003: 168-9) suggest that instead of the text of *Ḥ3y*'s original 'deposition' (*r3*), we have the dated account of the property division specifying the individual shares introduced by the formula *r rdit rḫ.tw*; but in our view, the document should not be relegated to a mere partition account as it is preceded by an

Textemic features:

A. Preamble: title deed (excerpt of proceedings or summary of a dispute before a court[366])

The title deed consists of the donor's submissions before a court (*m-bꜣḥ nꜣ srw*). Missing are at least the pre-material with the date, the forum, and the technical colophon, but these may not always be present in title deeds recorded before wills or gifts as they represent summaries or excerpts of the original[367]. It also lacks the verdict of the court and probably the outcome of the case (see *infra* the remark concerning lines 14-5).

Ḥꜣy intends to prove his right over the assets he wants to transfer to his children. It seems that *Tꜣgmyt* and *Ḥwynfr* were *Ḥwy*'s parents, and that *Ḥwy*'s (half) brothers contested his rights; *Pꜣṯꜣwmdiỉmn* may be the father of *Tꜣgmyt*[368].

Recital

Interestingly, the *recital* of the title deed comprises distinct parts that are not always present in the *recital* of the main will or gift. The *recitals* of wills and gifts in our corpus consist mainly of the quotation of a locutive statement made by the testator or donor and introduced by a tag-clause, directly following the pre-material (see *Naunakhte*, lines II.1-7; *oPetrie* 18, lines 3-8; *pAdoptions*, lines 16-26[369]). The *recital* in the context of the contentious genre in our title deed is introduced by the notification of a list in delocutive mode as an objective, substantial presentation of the facts, a *recital* being mainly an aetiologic information texteme; the list replaces the narrative that is usually the first part of the *recital*. The notification of the list of expenses recounted by *Ḥꜣy*'s father is followed by a locutive segment, the monologue of *Ḥꜣy* that has many common features with the other *recitals* in our corpus, such as features of involvement, stress markers, contrasted retributive principle, etc. But the main interest of the *recital* resides in the various means and arguments *de jure* used by *Ḥꜣy* to establish the legitimacy of his right: a 'statutory' ground, the equity principle[370] and a precedent are all brought up in order to convince the judges. Thus the *recital* in contentious proceedings may not only be about establishing facts and using the retributive principle, as is the case in private deeds, but it may also use additional specific legal arguments.

---

elaborated title deed, there are two lists of the same assets, the first introduced by the notification formula and the second by a report form, and the partition is closed by a warranty promise.

366 For Donker van Heel & Haring (2003: 176), the entire donor's submission is an elaborated question to the oracle consisting of 'a deposition presenting a certain state of affairs that is considered unjust by the petitioner, and about which the deity is asked to express his decision', introduced by the formula *r rdit rḫ.tw*. But as the addressee is an omniscient god, such a precise report should be unnecessary and questions addressed to the oracle are generally very short (except for a few texts such as *oBerlin* P 10629, *oBM* EA 5637, *oPetrie* 16) and they do not include statutory or precedent grounding which are irrelevant to the god. The oracle is consulted within the context of a judicial procedure before a court.

367 The title deed in *pAdoptions* is a summary of a will but the pre-material and the colophon are recorded. Another probable case of litigation involved in a title deed is to be found in Middle Kingdom *pBrooklyn* 35.1446 verso text B dealing with a liberality of a man to his children and mate; the title deed was apparently dated but the text is too damaged to reach definite conclusions regarding its layout.

368 Suggested by Théodoridès (1967b: 114).

369 Concerning the *recital* of *pTurin* 2021, the first part is missing, but the fragments of text in our possession appear to belong to a long *recital* from I (x+2) to II.11, including the statutory ground (see *infra*).

370 Théodoridès (1969: 152).

Notification of expenses' list:
Recto (1) *r rdit rḫ.tw ꜣḫt* [*i.diw rmṯ ist Ḥwy n tꜣy.f mwt*?][371]
For information (relative to the) assets [that the workman *Ḥwy* gave to his mother?]:

- (2) *rdy(t).n.f n ꜥnḫ-n-niw{w}t Tꜣ*[*gm*]*yt tꜣy.f mwt st ḳrs* 1 (3) *iw di.f pꜣy.st wt* 1 *n Pꜣ*[*tꜣwm*]*diimn ir n dbn* 40[372]
  what he gave to (the) *ꜥnḫ-n-niwt Tꜣ*[*gm*]*yt*, his mother: 1 place of burial, after he had given her 1 coffin for *Pꜣ*[*tꜣwm*]*diimn*, worth 40 *dbn;*
- (4) *wḥm sp rdyt.n.f n.s wt* 1 *r ḳrs.st iw irwy.f st ḳrs* (5) *n Ḥwynfr pꜣy.f it*
  again, what he gave to her: 1 coffin for her burial, after he had made a place of burial for *Ḥwynfr,* his father.

Statement quotation: *ḫr ptri pnꜥ st nꜣ ḫrd*[*w*] (6) *n ꜥnḫ-n-niw{w}t Tꜣgmyt r wḫꜣ ꜣḫt.st m pꜣ hrw* (7) *ḫr iw mbwpwy.st ḳrs pꜣy.st it ḫr mbwpwy nꜣy.st ḫrdw* (8) *ḳrs(.st) gr mntyst ꜣḫt.st pꜣ nty st ḫr wḫꜣ.f m* (9) {*m*} *pꜣ hrw ḫr iw mbwpwyw.w ḳrs ir{n}m pꜣy.i* (10) *it m-di ḳrs.f pꜣy.f it ḥnꜥ tꜣy.f mwt*
But see that the childr[en] of (the) *ꜥnḫ-n-niwt Tꜣgmyt* have contested it in order to claim her assets today, although she did not bury her father. And her children did not bury her either. It is her assets that they are claiming today, although they did not (participate in the) burial with my[373] father when he buried his father and his mother.
'Statutory' ground[374]: *ḫr i.di.tw ꜣḫt* (11) *n ḳrs ḫr(.f m) pꜣ hp n Pr-ꜥꜣ ꜥ.w.s.*
But it is to the one who buries that one should give (the?)[375] assets according to the norm of Pharaoh l.p.h.
Equity argument (plea for justice to the oracle): *pꜣy.i nb ꜥ.w.s. nfr ꜥ.w.s.* (12) *ptri tw.i m-bꜣḥ nꜣ srw imi irwy.w pꜣ nfrw*
My good l.p.h. lord l.p.h., see, I am before these officials: let them do the Good (= let Justice be done!)
Precedent (analogy principle): (13) *ḫr ptri di.tw*[376] *tꜣ st n Tꜣnḥsy n Sꜣwꜣḏyt m-di ḳrs.st*[377] (14) *iw.f dit n.st pꜣy.f wt iw.tw dit n.f tꜣy.st pš m-bꜣḥ nꜣ srw* (15) *ḫr iw m* (= *in*) *ni-swt Ỉmnḥtpw ꜥ.w.s. rdit st n.f m tꜣ ḳnbt*
But see, it is to *Sꜣwꜣḏyt* that the immovable property ('place') of *Tꜣnḥsy* was given because of her burial; and he[378] gave her his coffin, and her share[379] was given to him before these officials, since it was the king *Ỉmnḥtpw* l.p.h. who granted it to him in this court.

---

371 Allam (1973: plate p.89) proposes the following reconstruction: *r rdit rḫ.tw ꜣḫt* [*nb n rmṯ ist Ḥwy*], although it is not a matter in the title deed of all the assets of *Ḥwy* but of what he gave for the burial of his mother and the extent of his subsequent right in her inheritance; Spiegelberg (1892: 16) had earlier proposed *r rdit rḫ.tw ꜣḫt* [*n ḳrs n Ḥꜣy sꜣ Ḥwy*], but again the text does not deal with *Ḥꜣy*'s burial. No reconstruction is proposed in *KRI* V, 449; Donker van Heel & Haring (2003: 176) propose '*iḫt* [*nb n* NN]'. The formula of our reconstruction is based on *oBerlin* P 12636 v° of the same period (*r* [*r*]*dit rḫ.tw ꜣḫt i.diw rmṯ Ỉpwy n Nbwiry*).

372 See *oBrussels* E 6311, perhaps a reference to the same transaction occurring during the reign of Amenmesse (end of the 19th dynasty).

373 *Ḥꜣy* is speaking.

374 *Argument de texte.*

375 All or some of them? See Théodoridès (1969: 147): 'des biens' and subsequent discussion.

376 Added above line but misplaced.

377 The case summarized in the precedent's reference has been preserved in *oPetrie* 16; in fact, this ostracon records the plea of *Sꜣwꜣḏyt* to the oracle, and the issue of the dispute is given by *pBoulaq* 10.

378 The use of delocutive suffixes leaves the identity of the parties unclear; it is difficult to establish if this is the conclusion of the main litigation of the title deed between *Ḥwy* and his brothers, or of the precedent involving *Sꜣwꜣḏyt* and *Tꜣnḥsy,* this last option usually being adopted, see e.g. Théodoridès (1967b: 117), Allam (1973: 290). If it is the conclusion of the precedent, then the title deed does not give the outcome of the *Ḥwy*'s case, only his pleading, which is rather strange…

* Neo-Egyptian characteristics:
  - Neo-Egyptian possessive determinator for kinship (*tꜣy.f mwt, pꜣy.st/f it, nꜣy.st ḫrdw*), divine address (*pꜣy.i nb nfr*) and ownership relations (*pꜣy.f/st wt*), although one must note *ꜣḫt.st*;
  - simultaneous use of Neo-Egyptian possessive determinator and quantifier (*pꜣy.st wt* 1);
  - *iw di.f, iw irwy.f*: # converter *iw* + perfect[380] *di.f/irwy.f* #, converted[381] delocutive commentary forms following the list of expenses using relative forms (*rdy(t).n.f*);
  - *ḫr ptri pnʿ st nꜣ ḫrd*[*w*]: # contrastive proclitic coordinator *ḫr* + presentative *ptri* (involvement feature in oral speech) + *sḏm*.N perfect that-form object of *ptri* (without *prothetic* yod) + dependent pronoun (object) #.
    Note the absence of a tag clause in front of the statement. The cohesive contrastive *ḫr* (polemic) with *ptri* introduces a climax in the *recital* in the commentary mode (*Naunakhte*, lines 4-5; *pAdoptions*, line 22; *pTurin* 2021, line 8). Here *ptri* is constructed with a nominal form like the classical *m.k* (see *supra*);
  - cataphoric articloid *pꜣ* (*nꜣ ḫrdw* PN; *pꜣ hp n Pr-ʿꜣ*; *tꜣ st n* PN);
  - feminine or plural delocutive suffix *st* and plural *w*;
    Junge (2005: 159) is unsure whether to translate *st* as feminine or plural, as the delocutive plural is also expressed by *w* (*mbwpwyw.w, irwy.w*). But feminine *st* is consistently written  (*wḫꜣ ꜣḫt.st, mbwpwy.st ḳrs pꜣy.st it, nꜣy.st ḫrdw, ꜣḫt.st pꜣ nty*), whereas plural *st* appears as 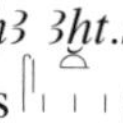 (*pnʿ st, pꜣ nty st ḥr wḫꜣ.f*);
  - deictic articloid (*m pꜣ hrw, nꜣ srw*);
  - *ḫr iw mbwpwy.st/w ḳrs*: # contrastive proclitic coordinator *ḫr* + converter *iw* + negated perfect *mbwpwy.f sḏm* #, twice with the same lexemic constituency; these are concessive clauses[382] based on a contrasted principle of retribution (the one who did not contribute financially to the burial cannot recover the expenses from the succession). The perfect is a commentary tense. Compare with the formulation in *oPetrie* 16 verso line 2: *iw bwpwyw nꜣy.f snw i.iry irm.f.*
    The negator's morphology is attested during the reigns of Ramesses III and IV[383]; if *pBoulaq* 10 is indeed to be dated to Ramesses VI's reign, this would constitute a late example of the form;
  - *ḫr mbwpwy nꜣy.st ḫrdw ḳrs(.st) gr mntyst*: # contrastive proclitic coordinator *ḫr* + negated perfect *mbwpwy.f sḏm* + clause final stress particle *gr*[384] + Neo-Egyptian spelling of the delocutive independent pronoun reinforcing the object of *ḳrs* #. See *Naunakhte*, line II.5 (*ḫr.i gr ink*) in the same texteme;
  - *ꜣḫt.st pꜣ nty st ḥr wḫꜣ.f*: focus-initial cleft sentence[385] constructed with # *ꜣḫt.st* (nominal rheme marked as focus, extraposed object of *wḫꜣ*) + *pꜣ nty st ḥr wḫꜣ.f* (substantivized

379 For Théodoridès (1969: 153-60), the woman's share (1/3) in the community property she had with her husband.

380 For the morphology of the perfect with 'double *yod* en finale', see Winand (1992: 193-5).

381 For the converted perfect, see *LEG* § 63.2.8 'it indicates pluperfect tense', Frandsen (1974: 194-9) 'relative past time' and Junge (2005: 153, 156-7).

382 Frandsen (1974: 202-3); Groll (1973: 69).

383 Winand (1992: 204-5), although his example from *KRI* VI, 251.4 (*oGardiner/Ashmolean* 137) may date from Ramesses V's reign.

384 See Shisha-Halevy (2000: 97).

385 Junge (2005: 159) views the construction as 'a Late Egyptian nominal sentence, type Pseudo-Cleft Sentence: noun phrase + nominalized relative clause: "her property is what they claim"'; in *LEG* § 2.6.2, ex. 79, the sentence is translated as a cleft sentence 'It is her possessions that they are seeking today.'

relative clause theme with adverbial nexus (actual present with *m p3 hrw*) and resumptive masculine singular suffix *.f* for the feminine collective *3ḫt.st*) #.
Note the parallelism used for contrast in order to illustrate the fundamental opposition of right and wrong behavior: *r* ***wḫ3 3ḫt.st m p3 hrw*** (A) ***ḫr iw mbwpwy****.st* ***ḳrs*** (B) (…) ***3ḫt.st*** *p3 nty st ḥr* ***wḫ3.f m*** *{m}* ***p3 hrw*** (A) ***ḫr iw mbwpwyw****.w* ***ḳrs*** (B). Balanced patterns are features of oral expression (Ong 1982: 34-5);

- *m {m} p3 hrw*: preposition redundancy;
- Neo-Egyptian preposition *ir{n}m;*
- *m-di ḳrs.f*: temporalis *m-ḏr sḏm.f* following a negated perfect, the spelling of the compound preposition being characteristic of the reigns of Ramesses III-V[386]. In this construction, the *sḏm.f* is a that-form (see *supra oGardiner/Ashmolean* 55 *m-n-ḏr pš.f*); the time indication of the temporalis is always past[387];
- *ḫr i.di.tw 3ḫt n ḳrs ḫr(.f m) p3 hp n Pr-ʿ3*: topic-initial cleft sentence with # contrastive proclitic coordinator *ḫr* + impersonal that-form with prothetic *yod* (thema) + object + beneficiary (adverbial focus) #, a quotation marked by the use of the abbreviated  (*p3 hp n Pr-ʿ3*). Either this last form represents the Middle Egyptian present trailing tag clause, in which case the nominal actor should be preceded by *m*[388], which is consistent with the two signs following *ḫr* (*ḫr.f m p3 hp*)[389], or it is the preposition *ḫr* + N[390], but then the addition of the two signs remains unexplained.
As we have previously noted (David 2006: 161, 259, 261), *normative* Ramesside royal decrees (protection/criminal law decrees), contrary to epistolary decrees, do not use prothetic *yod* forms, thus it may not be the precise quotation of a written decree; furthermore, the quotation concerns a general legal principle. See also the different formulations of the 'statutory' reference in *pTurin* 2021, lines II.11 and III.4-5;
- *p3y.i nb ʿ.w.s. nfr ʿ.w.s.*: either this syntagm is linked to the preceding 'statutory' ground and is apposed to *ḫr(.f m) p3 hp n Pr-ʿ3 ʿ.w.s.*[391], or it belongs to the following direct address to the oracle of *Imnḥtp* I, the deified king of the 18th dynasty, patron of the Theban necropolis workers[392]. First, *hp n Pr-ʿ3* is a very general expression, not attached to a specific king, as when we say 'the law states that', 'according to the law'; it is meant as the positive law that applies to our social system or as the *principe de droit*[393]. Secondly, *p3y.i nb ʿ.w.s. nfr ʿ.w.s.* is directly followed by the imperative address *ptri*, and the addressee is not the *srw* counsel mentioned by the deictic *n3*. Allam contends that 'the phrase *ʿnḫ wḏ3 snb* always refers to Pharaoh and cannot be taken to be addressed to a god, if any', but as we can see in *oIFAO* 556, *oDeM* 576 and *oGardiner/Ashmolean* 51[394], all of them are questions addressed to the oracle and beginning with the formula *p3y.i nb nfr ʿ. w. s.*; we may dispute this contention and affirm that the segment belongs to the plea for justice to the oracle of *Imnḥtp* I (the fact is also confirmed by the use of the abridged formula l.p.h. after the name of *Imnḥtp* I in line 15).

386 Winand (1992: 248).
387 *LEG*, 410.
388 *LEG*, 157.
389 Théodoridès (1969: 147).
390 Junge (2005: 159).
391 Helck (1961-70: 347); Théodoridès (1967b: 116 and 1969: 147); Allam (1973: 290-3 and 1992: 383); *LEG* ex. 246, but in Groll (1993: 134) it belongs to the next sentence; Junge (2005: 159).
392 Janssen & Pestman (1968: 140-1); McDowell (1990: 119); Donker van Heel & Haring (2003: 176).
393 Théodoridès (1969: 161).
394 See also Donker van Heel & Haring (2003: 176 n.193).

Concerning the interaction of secular and oracular justice in *pBoulaq* 10, see Jin (2001);

- *ptri tw.i m-b3ḥ n3 srw*: # Neo-Egyptian spelling of the presentative *ptri* (involvement feature in oral speech) + Neo-Egyptian thematic pronoun *tw.i* + adverbial rheme (present) #; see *Naunakhte*, Doc. I, line II.4 (*ḫr ptri tw.i i3wt.ki*);
- *imm irwy.w p3 nfrw*: # 3rd person causative imperative + delocutive prospective + object#.

The address to the god is thus a strong, general plea for justice. The god must inspire or impose justice on the *srw*, although such a general plea is never formulated in other oracular texts that have survived; at best, *oBM* EA 5637, dated to Ramesses III's reign, stipulates (v° 5-6) *ir p3y.i nb r dit n.i p3 thi nbt* [...] 'May my Lord act in order to give me this transgressor (?)'. But *oMichaelides* 47 (19th dynasty), the protocol of a lawsuit before the *ḳnbt*, opens with the following exhortation after the full, solemn date: *imi iry.tw t3 ḳnbt m p3 ḫr m-s3 hpw n m3ˁt* 'Let the court of the Tomb be made following the norms of Justice.'[395] This concept of *p3 nfrw* or Maat may represent our multifaceted concept of equity, a fundamental notion both in Romano-Germanic and Anglo-American juridic systems. In the Anglo-American system of law, '*equity* is a CHAMELEON-HUED WORD; (...) (1) what is fair and just; (2) natural law (...); (3) a system of law that corrects failures of justice in the main body of the law; (4) a theory of justice in which the operation of legal precepts is adjusted to the exigencies of special circumstances; (5) a body of law that was administered in the English Court of Chancery (...); (6) (in civil law) a method of interpretation of Code provisions in accordance with the spirit and general purpose of the statute; and (7) (in Anglo-American law) a body of legal precepts that introduces into law, in suits for specific relief, criteria of justice that are based on higher ethical values than those ordinarily required in actions for damages.'[396]

- *p3 nfrw*: non-phoric articloid with notion name (abstraction, referring to the concept of 'Justice', *m3ˁt/nfrw* being the antithesis of *isft/bin*).

Note the masculine singular articloid (*n3* is already normally used in the Amarna period[397]) with the abstract *nfrw*;

- *ḫr ptri di.tw.*N *n S3w3ḏyt*: # contrastive proclitic coordinator *ḫr* + Neo-Egyptian presentative *ptri* + cleft sentence object of *ptri* [classical impersonal/passive perfect that-form *sḏm.tw.*N[398] (thema) + adverbial rheme and focus (*n S3w3ḏyt*)][399] #. The focus may be on the winning party in the precedent, as he was the one who defrayed the funerary expenses (*Ḥwy* identifies himself to him) or on the motive of the attribution of the property (*m-di ḳrs.st*);
- *m-di ḳrs.st*: for Junge (2005: 159), as *ḳrs.st* cannot be an active form (the woman has been buried) and the temporalis has an active diathesis, the form may not be a temporal *m-ḏr sḏm.f*, but a 'preposition before noun, "because of something"';

---

395 Compare with Ptolemaic sacerdotal decrees: *ti ir.w p3 hp n rmṯ nb/n n3 rmṯw* 'causing that Justice be done for everyone/for the people' (Simpson 1996: 41).

396 Garner (1987: 220).

397 *Wb* II, 259.2.

398 Concerning the passive perfect that-form, see Winand (1992: 310-4), who considers that this form always has a suffix pronoun as actor in passive diathesis and that for the verb *di*, the form *di.tw* is limited to the times of Ramesses II, otherwise being *didi.tw*.

399 For a construction similar to the one analyzed here, see e.g. *pSallier* I 9, 3: *ḫr ptri iṯ3y.tw.w m-di.i didi.tw.w n imy-r pr* PN 'But see that it is from me that they were taken, (and) that it is to the steward PN that they were given'.

- *iw.f dit n.st* and *iw.tw dit n.f*: brief conclusion with two sequential past narrative forms (prepositions omitted), the parallel construction expressing the mutual dependence of the events;
- *ḫr iw m* (for *in*) N PN *rdit st*: # contrastive proclitic coordinator *ḫr* + converter *iw* + participial statement[400] with focus marker[401] + N PN (rheme focus) + perfect participle[402] (theme) #. The construction highlights the authority who gave right to one of the parties, also emphasizing the analogy with the case at hand, conducted before both the judges and the deified king;

* 'Classical' degree 0 forms used:
- *r rdit rḫ.tw*.N: notification formula expressed by # *r* + infinitive *rdit* + prospective passive, object of *rdit* # ;
- relative neutrum *rdy*(*t*)*.n.f*: once written without *t*[403]; this excludes the possibility of a that-form suggested by Groll (1993: 128). The notification of partition lists in Doc. II and III of *Naunakhte* use the isotopic *rdyt* (*n* PN), thus also relative forms, as items of the lists after the notification formula;
  Note the use of *wḥm sp* to coordinate the two items of the list (*rdy*(*t*)*.n.f*);
- use of the relator: *ḫrd*[*w*] *n ꜥnḫ-n-niw*{*w*}*t* (kinship relation); *ꜥnḫ-n-niw*{*w*}*t* (unclear kind of relation in frozen expression); *pꜣ hp n Pr-ꜥꜣ* (authorship relation); *ir n dbn* 40 (value relation)*; tꜣ st n Tꜣnḥsy* (ownership relation);
- use of *ḥnꜥ* as coordinator between two determined nouns (*pꜣy.f it ḥnꜥ tꜣy.f mwt*)*;*
- *ḳrs* (line 11): (im)perfect participle (without *prothetic* yod);

* General dialectal features: degree 2.

* Legal formulae: *recital*
  - notification of expenses' list: *r rdit rḫ.tw*.N [...] + *rdy*(*t*)*.n.f n* (beneficiary)
  - statement quotation: *ḫr ptri* (commentary based on the retributive principle)+ *ḫr i.di.tw ꜣḫt n ḳrs ḫr*(*.f m*) *pꜣ hp n Pr-ꜥꜣ ꜥ.w.s.* ('statutory' ground) + *pꜣy.i nb ꜥ.w.s. nfr ꜥ.w.s. ptri tw.i m-bꜣḥ nꜣ srw imi irwy.w pꜣ nfrw* (plea for justice to the god); *ḫr ptri* + cleft sentence (precedent).

B. Act *sensu stricto*

Note the absence of *recital.*

1. Pre-material

Date: Verso (1) *rnpt-sp* 8 *ꜣbd* 3 *prt sw* 25	Year 8, month 3 of winter, day 25,
archaic anaphora: *h*{*ꜣ*}*rw pn*	this day
Title:	
legal step: *sḏm rꜣ*	of hearing (the) declaration

400 Frandsen (1974: 224) '*iw* + cleft sentence'.

401 For the same confusion between *in* and *m* in Ramesside royal decrees participial statements, see David (2006: 121, 146).

402 The participle may be conceived as a prothetic *yod* form (*r.di.t*) as *LEG*, 464 (Ex. 1288) and Junge (2005: 159) view it; note the intrusive *t*. Winand (1992: 348, 355) notes that the perfect participle of *rdi* is usually spelled *dit* or *i.dit* and that the prothetic *yod* is in the majority of cases affixed to *rdi* from Ramesses III to VIII.

403 For Junge (2005: 157) because *ꜣḫt* is often masculine, but both relative forms are used in the same way, as entries of the list after the notification formula which most probably included a relative form as an expansion of *ꜣḫt*.

donor: *n Ḥ3y s3 Ḥwy*	of *Ḥ3y* son of *Ḥwy*
object: *ḥr n3y.f* (2) *swt n p3y.f it r dit.w*	concerning his immovables of (= inherited from) his father in order to give them
beneficiaries: *n n3y.f ẖrdw m* (*p3*) *hrw*	to his children today.

* Neo-Egyptian characteristics:
- Neo-Egyptian possessive determinator for kinship (*p3y.f it; p3y.f ẖrdw*) and ownership relations (*n3y.f swt*);
- Neo-Egyptian plural delocutive suffix *w*;

* 'Classical' degree 0 forms used:
- archaic anaphora *h{3}rw pn* (opposed to following deictic *m* (*p3*) *hrw*);
- use of relator *n* for authorship (*r3 n Ḥ3y*) and original ownership relation (*swt n p3y.f it*);
- *h{3}rw pn sḏm r3 n Ḥ3y*: compare with *oGardiner/Ashmolean* 36 (*sḏm r3 n Sẖti*), also a nominal segment # *hrw pn sḏm* # as in *Naunakhte*, lines I.4 and IV.9, and *pAdoptions*, lines 2 and 14-5 (the heading formula is Classical Middle Egyptian, as are most headings);
- *r dit.w*: purpose. The form may also be viewed as a participle *rditw* or *r.ditw*, since the actual partition is reported under the same date following the notification of the list of immovable assets;

* General dialectal features: degree 1.

* Legal formula: abbreviated date + *hrw pn* + *sḏm r3* (object) + *n* (donor) + *ḥr* (object) + *n* (beneficiaries)

2. Operative part

Note that the notification of the bequests and the actual partition are written by the same hand on the same date but that there are some differences in the two lists. The operative part does not comprise a performative form, it is more a list of shares than an attributive statement.

Notification of shares:
r rdit rḫ.tw.w For information (relative to) them[404]:
(3) *t3 ḥbt nty r-gs t3 isbt* [*n*] *Ḳ3ḥ3* 1 *n mḥ* 7 *wsḫt* 3 *šsp* 4
the shrine[405] that is beside the shelter [for] *Ḳ3ḥ3*: 1 (share[406]) of 7 (length x) 3 cubits, 4 palms width;
(4) *t3 ʿt nty r-gs p3 ḫnw n Ḥwy* (*n*) *Grg Mr*[407] 2 *3wt* 13 *wsḫt* 8 *šsp* 3 *mḥ* 7 ½ 8 *šsp* 4
the hut/workplace[408] that is beside the chapel[409] of *Ḥwy* (for) *Grg* (and) *Mr*: 2 (shares of)
13 length (x) 8 (cubits,) 3 palms width;
(and) 7 ½ (length x) 8 (cubits,) 4 palms (width);
(5) *p3 iwtn nty t3y.f št3yt m-im.f* (*n Bp3s3*) 1 *n mḥ* 6 *wsḫt* 6
the site[410] where is his cave/cellar (for *Bp3s3*): 1 (share) of 6 (length x) 6 cubits width;

404 The assets for each child.
405 Janssen & Pestman (1968: 158-9).
406 See line 9 *m dnit*.
407 = *Mntiwp3ḥʿpy*, see *pBoulaq* v° 9 (Janssen & Pestman 1968: 148, n. g); other authors do not see these as abbreviations of two proper names, but as *grg* 'Stockwerke' (Helck 1961-70: 339) or 'Stück Land' (Allam 1973: 291 n.19).
408 Demarée (2006).
409 Janssen & Pestman (1968: 161-2).

(6) *tꜣ ꜥt n ꜥꜣnḫtw* (*n Pnniwt*) 3 (= 2) *n mḥ* 7 *wsḫt* 7 *šsp* 3   8 *wsḫt* 3 the hut/workplace of *ꜥꜣnḫtw* (for *Pnniwt*): 3 (= 2 shares) of 7 (length x) 7 cubits, 3 palms width (and) 8 (length x) 3 (cubits) width; (7) *pꜣ mr n sš Rꜥms* (*n*) *Ḳꜣḥꜣ* 1   9 *wsḫt* 3 the pyramid of (the) scribe *Rꜥms* (for) *Ḳꜣḥꜣ*: 1 (share) of 9 (length x) 3 (cubits) width;

* Neo-Egyptian characteristics:
- plural delocutive suffix *w*;
- cataphoric articloid (*tꜣ ḥbt, tꜣ ꜥt, pꜣ ḫnw, pꜣ iwtn, pꜣ mr*). Note that in *tꜣ isbt* [*n*] *Ḳꜣḥꜣ*, the articloid seems exophoric;
- absence of concord of the relative adjective (*tꜣ ḥbt nty, tꜣ ꜥt nty*);
- Neo-Egyptian possessive determinator for ownership (*tꜣy.f štꜣyt*);
- *m-im.f*: Neo-Egyptian form of the classical modifier *im.f* (preposition redundancy);
- *n* preposition omission before some of the beneficiaries;

* 'Classical' degree 0 forms used:
- *r rdit rḫ.tw.w*: notification formula # *r* + infinitive *rdit* + prospective passive, object of *rdit* (+ Neo-Egyptian plural object suffix) #;
- list of shares with dimensions of immovables: # determined N (immovable) + expansion + (*n*) PN (donee) + quantifier (number of shares) [(+ *n*) *mḥ* (unit) + *ꜣwt* + quantifier (length) + *wsḫt* + quantifier + *šsp* (small unit) + quantifier (width)] #.
  The construction differs from the list with implicit performative # *ir* Ṇ *iw.f n* PN # seen e.g. in *oDeM* 108 with movables (and not preceded by the notification formula); it has no direct parallel in our corpus. It does not seem to constitute a nexus (*n* PN should apparently not be taken as a rheme), and although each entry represents a specific bequest to a child, the formulation does not formally convey the expression of an attribution of right in the operative part;
- use of relator *n* for measurement (1 *n mḥ*)[411] and ownership relations (*pꜣ ḫnw n Ḥwy; tꜣ ꜥt n ꜥꜣnḫtw; pꜣ mr n sš Rꜥms*);

* General dialectal features: degree 1.

* Legal formula: notification: *r rdit rḫ.tw.w* + list: immovable + *nty* (location)/*n* (ownership) + *n* PN (donee) + number of shares + *n* (dimensions)

C. Addition

Material partition report followed by the oath of the beneficiaries; of course this segment does not belong to the consentient genre, as it represents the execution of the decision of the donor. A dispute may have arisen during the material partition among its beneficiaries, justifying the taking of the oath, as we shall see that not every material partition is followed by an oath of the beneficiaries; compare e.g. with the partitions of immovables of *pTurin* 2070 v°, col. II (with oath) and of *oDeM* 112 and 964 (without oath).

Material partition:	
(8) *pšw.w n.sn m rnpt sp* 8 *ꜣbd* 3 *prt sw* 25	2
They were divided for them in year 8, month 3 of winter, day 25 -	2[412]:

410 Demarée (2006: 59); McDowell (1990: 124): 'plot of ground'.

411 The expansion is viewed as attributive by Shisha-Halevy (2007b: 240).

(9) *tꜣ ꜥt nt r-gs pꜣ ḫnw n Mntiwpꜣḥꜥpy ḥnꜥ ꜥnḫ-n-niw{w}t Grg m dnit* 2 (10) *ḥnꜥ tꜣy.st štꜣyt n mḥ* 13 *wsḫt n mḥ* 8 *šsp* 3 *tꜣ ꜥt n mḥ* 7 ½ *wsḫt* 8 *šsp* 4
the hut/workplace that is beside the chapel to *Mntiwpꜣḥꜥpy* and (the) *ꜥnḫ-n-niwt Grg* as 2 shares, with its cave/cellar of 13 (length x) 8 cubits, 3 palms width; the hut/workplace of 7 ½ (length x) 8 cubits, 4 palms width;
(11) *tꜣ ḥbt ḥnꜥ pꜣ mr n Rꜥms n Ḳꜣḥꜣ*[413]
the shrine and the pyramid of *Rꜥms* to *Ḳꜣḥꜣ*;
(12) *pꜣ iḥꜣy n ꜥꜣnḫtw ḥnꜥ pꜣy.f mḫr n Pnniwt*[414]
the stall of *ꜥꜣnḫtw* and his/its granary to *Pnniwt*;
(13) *pꜣ iwtn nt r-gs pr ḥꜣty-ꜥ n niwt n Bpꜣsꜣ n mḥ* 6 *wsḫt* 6 *tꜣy.f štꜣt im.f* (14) *nty n.f r-ḏbꜣ wttyw [sšw m ḳdwt?]*[415] 2 *nty m pꜣ ḫnw diwyw* (*n*) (15) *Tꜣgmyt tꜣ ḥmt Ḥw[ynfr]* (**repayment of the estate's debt**)
the site that is beside (the) house of (the) mayor to *Bpꜣsꜣ* (*Bs*) of 6 (length x) 6 cubits width, (and) his cave/cellar in it which[416] was for him[417] in payment of 2 [painted?] coffins that are in the cellar/chapel (and) that were given (to) *Tꜣgmyt*, the woman of *Ḥw[ynfr]*
***Promissory* oath of the donees (warranty with penalty)**
[…] *ḏd mtw.n pnꜥꜥ.n r mdt iw.w ḫr* (16) 100 *n sḫt [šꜣbt*[418]*] šw.n m tꜣy.n pš*
[…] saying: 'Should we reverse our undertaking to contest (it), they are liable to 100 blows [of the rod] (and) deprived of our share.'

* Neo-Egyptian characteristics:
- *pšw.w*: delocutive passive perfect report, a form found exclusively in a legal context[419]; the agentless passive is the mark of an informative discourse. The statement is followed by the list, but without notification formula;
- delocutive suffix *.w* (plural) and *.st* (feminine);
- cataphoric articloid (*tꜣ ḥbt, tꜣ ꜥt, pꜣ ḫnw, pꜣ iwtn, pꜣ mr, pꜣ iḥꜣy, tꜣ ḥmt*);
- absence of concord of the relative adjective (*tꜣ ḥbt nty, tꜣ ꜥt nty, tꜣy.f štꜣt im.f nty, wttyw* […] 2 *nty*);
- exophoric articloid (*pꜣ ḫnw n Mntiwpꜣḥꜥpy*);
- anaphoric articloid (*tꜣ ꜥt n mḥ*);
- Neo-Egyptian possessive determinator for ownership (*tꜣy.f štꜣyt; tꜣy.n pš*), inclusion of construction (*tꜣy.st štꜣyt, pꜣy.f mḫr*);
- *nty n.f r-ḏbꜣ* N: relative phrase, not in concord with the antecedent *tꜣy.f štꜣt*;
- […]-*ḏd*: tagged speech marker introducing the *promissory* oath, instead of the perfect formula *irwy.f ꜥnḫ nb ꜥ.w.s. m-ḏd* (but compare with *iw iw.f irt ꜥnḫ n nb ꜥ.w.s. r-ḏd* in *Naunakhte,* Doc. IV);
- *mtw.n pnꜥꜥ.n r mdt iw.w ḫr* 100 *n sḫt [šꜣbt?] šw.n m tꜣy.n pš*: *promissory* oath formula, a warranty with penalty after the partition. Note the locutive conjunctive (transgression) and delocutive performative adverbial nexus (penalty), but also the redundant locutive

412 Does this mean 'second part of the same date procedure'?
413 Note the absence of dimensions and number of shares, and the grouping of shares for the same donee.
414 Compare with line 6 *supra*, '3' shares comprising a hut. Again, no dimensions or number of shares here.
415 As in *oPetrie* 16, line 2.
416 Regarded as an independent sentence by Janseen & Pestman (1968: 148-9), although they do not exclude the construction we opted for.
417 *Ḥwy*, see the title deed.
418 As in *oPetrie* 18 v° 7 and *pTurin* 2070 v°2, 9, although Allam (1973: 191, n.36), following Spiegelberg, suggests restoring *mtw.n*.
419 See Frandsen (1974: § 17) and David (2006: 20-1) in Ramesside royal decrees.

suffix of *pnꜥꜥ.n* and *šw.n* (again locutive!) usually absent in this formula; also absent is the adverbial *m-im* after *r mdt*. See *supra*;

* 'Classical' degree 0 forms used:
- list of shares with dimensions of immovables (not in each case): # determined N (immovable) + expansion + *n* PN (donee) (+ quantifier (number of shares)) [+ *n mḥ* (unit) + quantifier (length) + *wsẖt* + quantifier + *šsp* (small unit) + quantifier (width)] #.
- perfect passive participle without prothetic *yod* (*diwyw*);
- use of relator *n* for measurement (N *n mḥ*), ownership (*pꜣ ẖnw n* PN*; tꜣ ḥbt ḥnꜥ pꜣ mr n Rꜥms; pꜣ ỉhꜣy n ꜥꜣnḫtw*), in unclear kind of relation in frozen expression (*ꜥnḫ-n-niwt*), dominion relation (*ḥꜣty-ꜥ n niwt*) and between quantifier and noun (100 *n sḫt*);
- use of the coordinator *ḥnꜥ*: # PN *ḥnꜥ* N PN # (*Mntiwpꜣḥꜥpy ḥnꜥ ꜥnḫ-n-niw{w}t Grg*); # *pꜣ* N *ḥnꜥ pꜣy.f*/*pꜣ* N # (*tꜣ ꜥt… ḥnꜥ tꜣy.st štꜣyt; tꜣ ḥbt ḥnꜥ pꜣ mr; pꜣ ỉhꜣy n ꜥꜣnḫtw ḥnꜥ pꜣy.f mḫr*);

* General dialectal features: degree 2.

* Legal formulae:
- partition: *pšw.w n.sn m* (date) + list: immovable + *nty* (location)/*n* (ownership) + *n* PN (donee) (+ *m dnit* (number of shares) + *n* (dimensions))
- repayment of the estate's debt: object + *nty n.f* (recipient) *r-ḏbꜣ* + object
- *promissory* oath: [...] *ḏd* (tag clause) + *mtw.n pnꜥꜥ.n r mdt* (perjury) + *ỉw.w ẖr* 100 *n sḫt* [*šꜣbt*] *šw.n m tꜣy.n pš* (penalty)

Categorization of terms of special relevance in the legal register:

- *r rdit rḫ.tw*: to let be known, for information (relative to).
- *ꜣḫt*: assets.
- *(r)di* ( ) : to give, donate.
- *pnꜥ (rꜣ) r mdwt*: to reverse (an undertaking) in order to contest.
- *wḫꜣ*: to claim.
  Classified with the superordinate [MOTION] category classifier since the Middle Kingdom (see David 2007: 7) as an abstract member of the category (to seek or claim is to <u>go after</u> something). Motion is associated in many forensic metaphors with legal action (conceptual metaphor '*ACTION IS MOTION*').
- *hp*: legal norm, rule. It represents the abstract juridic norm; see David (2006: 65-6).
- *srw*: officials (members of the *ḳnbt*).
- *nfrw*: Good, Right, Justice; for *Mꜣꜥt*.
  Abstract concept, classified with the papyrus roll of the superordinate [ABSTRACT] category. On the notions of *mꜣꜥt*/*nfrw* and *isft*/*bin* and their classification, see David (2000: 53-4).
- *st* : immovable asset.
- *pš*: share, to divide.
- *ḳnbt*: court.
  Note the added superordinate [COERCION] category classifier, implying the power of the court (metaphor of 'the long arm' of the personified legal institution).
- *sḏm rꜣ*: hearing of a deposition/statement.

- *dnit*: share. For Théodoridès (1970: 193 n.296), 'part qui revient théoriquement à', while *pš* expresses 'le résultat de l'opération effective de partage'. Both *p*(*s*)*š* and *dni*(*t*) mean 'division, share', '*p*(*s*)*š* is typical of hieratic texts, with *dni*(*t*) more typical in the formulae of Demotic documents, but there is considerable overlap and no technical distinction.'[420] The *Wb* V, 464 indicates that the basic root of *dni*-lexemes was a *ḏni* root classified by a hoe-like[421] classifier (*PT* 716); *dni* 'austeilen, zuteilen' is already mentioned in *PT* 1284b and 1965a without classifier (*ÄW* I,1478). For Demotic and Coptic, see Richter (2002: 275-6).
  As for the visected cartouche, it is a literal representation of a cut-off object (there is of course an icon representing the complete cartouche). Nevertheless, there is no clear indication of the reason for this iconic choice of a cartouche as a cut object. The sign is used here as a logogram[422]. The [ABSTRACT] category classifier may complete the picture, the apportionment being the result of a mental process implying computation, recorded in a deed of apportionment, and dealing with abstract rights and ensembles of assets.
  The × classifier of the [UNION/DIVISION] category appears to be used sparingly to classify *dni* (e.g. *pMayer* B, line 1: *dni* 'portions').
- *r-ḏb3*: in exchange for, compensation, payment.
- *ḫr* *sḫt*[ ]: liable to blows. Note the probable absence of the [UNION/DIVISION] category classifier for *sḫt*.
- *šw* × *m pš* ×: deprived of a share.

420 Eyre (1994: 124, n.74).
421 *EG*, 523.
422 See also *oDeM* 586.

7. *oPetrie* 18

Date: 20th dynasty, Ramesses VII
Hieroglyphic version: *KRI* VI, 430 n.A8
Instrument:

* **state** – damaged

* **value – excerpt?**: limestone ostracon, incomplete (dated but without royal name, unnamed forum[423]/witnesses/scribe, rather brief operative part, absence of title deed and colophon).

* **nature – legal instrument**: absence of internal characterization, concerns legal rights about assets.

* **genre – probably consentient legal**: formulaic style; business hand, few errors, no corrections, no business practice diacritical mark but abbreviation of the season in the date, and unique use of bichromy in our testamentary corpus (black ink with part of the date in red ink); concerns private interests; unknown provenance; delocutive and locutive textemes, degree 2 Neo-Egyptian features; abbreviated date with archaic anaphora, *recital*.

Due to the presence of 'two parties' in the pre-material (*ḥnꜥ* often unites two contending parties) and of two closing oaths, it is described by many scholars[424] as legal proceedings between a man and his wife. The concept of 'two parties' mentioned in the pre-material collides with our conception of a will as a unilateral deed. But there are other examples of documents concerned with testamentary provisions mentioning two parties: *pAdoptions* r° line 15, where the testatrix is mentioned as attendant in the pre-material; in *pTurin* 2021 r° line II.2, the testator also mentions the presence of the beneficiary in the *recital* (the pre-material is missing). Furthermore, partitions may also be headed by the mention of two parties: *oGardiner/Ashmolean* 36 (*sḏm r3 n* PN (…) *ḥn*[ꜥ…]); *pTurin* 1885 v° (*pš 3ḫt* (…) *in* N PN *ḥnꜥ ꜥnḫ-n-niwt* PN). The solution may be that there is only one testator, but he comes to court or before witnesses with the main beneficiary of his statement as attendant; the manifestation of will is still unilateral on the part of the testator, although the public procedure requires or admits the presence of the beneficiary (note that in the case of *Naunakhte*'s will, the children are also present during the court's session as the use of deictic *p3y* 8 *b3kiw* in line II.2 makes clear)[425].

But a *contentious* legal genre cannot be totally excluded because of the oaths following the operative part; the second oath represents a promise probably ending a contestation, either during a lawsuit or as a preventive measure added to the will.

Legal step: **external manifestation of will** (with performative) concerning the transmission of a universality of assets, including immovables; unfortunately, the crucial part that defines the legal step in the pre-material is lost.

Legal issue: **perhaps a will**: absence of *consideration*, *disposition* of general bequest using performative form (no future distribution rule, because the will concerns a universal legacy to a unique legatee), transmission of the entire patrimony of the testator (*3ḫt nb*), kinship

423 Donker van Heel & Haring (2003: 167) suggest that this indication could have been written on the rubbed top of the reverse side.

424 Pestman (1961: 151 n.6, 153, n.12); *KRI* VI, 430; Toivari-Viitala (2001: 44, 81-3, 92-3, 103 n.52): 'an inheritance settlement or a divorce settlement'; McDowell (1990: 144, 155): 'a man cuts out of his will a woman who neglected him during his illness'.

425 Following Seidl, Allam (1977: 94) assumes that a 'déclaration d'adhésion' or an 'adhésion tacite' of close family members is necessary for the will to be valid. But it may only be a way of ascertaining that they will not contest the will after the testator's death.

relation between the testator and the beneficiary not being excluded, *recital* expressing retributive principle and disinheritance, mention of type/origin of assets.

A man would not need to authenticate his will in court if he chose to make a general bequest to his (grand-)son, his legal heir, unless he is disinheriting other children, which is perhaps the case here with a daughter. But then curiously, a woman (his daughter?) mentions in her oath that one of her penalties in case of perjury should be to be deprived of all her father's assets; moreover, the purpose of the woman's oath is obviously to restrict her from approaching the testator's house, but why?

Of course a will was not necessary to exclude one's companion (who seems to have no legal inheritance rights), or sister (automatically excluded by offsprings) from an inheritance; one major problem is the absence of extra-textual information and the fragmentary state of the document, and thus the difficulty of confirming the identity of *Tintpꜣip*, the 'sister,' and the person who took the second oath.

Textemic features:

1. Pre-material

Date: (1) [*rnpt-sp*] 7 *ꜣbd* 4 *š(mw) sw* 11	[Year] 7, month 4 of s(ummer), day 11
archaic anaphora: *hrw pn*	This day
Title:	
legal step: (2) [*sḏm rꜣ? n ḏdt?*][426]	[(of the hearing) of the statement?]
testator: *ir.n rmṯ ist Ỉmnpꜣḥʿpy*	that made (the) workman *Ỉmnpꜣḥʿpy*
attendant: *ḥnʿ ʿnḫ-niwt Tintpꜣi[p]*[427]	with *ʿnḫ-niwt Tintpꜣi[p]*.

* Neo-Egyptian characteristics:
- absence of relator of *ʿnḫ-niwt*;

* 'Classical' degree 0 forms used:
- archaic anaphora *hrw pn*;
- *ir.n rmṯ ist*: *sḏm.n*.N perfect relative form (without prothetic *yod*);

* General dialectal features: degree 1.

* Legal formula: date + *hrw pn* + [object] + *ir.n rmṯ ist* PN (demanding party) + *ḥnʿ ʿnḫ-niwt* PN (attendant)

2. *Recital*

tag clause: (3) [*ḏd*].*f*	He [said:]
statement quotation: *ir ink pꜣ mr iw n.i* […] *iw.i ḥr ḏd n tꜣy.i snt ir* […] (4) […] *n ꜣḫt ink iw.st šmt n.s r Sḫt iw.i irt ꜣbd{t}*1 *iw.i ḥms.k(wi) iw.i* (5) *wʿ šsp sw pꜣ dꜣiw i.di n.i pꜣ Pr-ʿꜣ ʿ.w.s. iw.st itꜣ.f i.irw.s* […][428] (6) […] *iw.i ḥms.k(wi) bn st ink bwpwy.sw irt n.i nfr rmṯ ist Ỉmnwʿ* (7) [*pꜣy.i šriw iw*].*f ḥr irt n.i nfr iw.i gꜣbw.kwi pꜣy.f šriw pꜣy* (8) [*Nḫmmwt m-rʿ?*]	

426 Allam (1973: 234 n.1) 'Kommen' 'Streit (*ḏd*)' and Toivari-Viitala (2001: 81) suggest restoring 'the disputing'.

427 See Černý (2001: 357) for the name.

428 *KRI* proposes, with many question marks [*wnmt irmw*].

As for me, the sickness entered me […] and I said to my sister (= beloved?)[429]: 'Do […][430] for (the) assets of mine.' And she went for it (or herself) to (the) Field (= Valley of the Kings)/country side[431], while I spent one month sitting[432] alone. She is (the) one who took the garment that the Pharaoh L.P.H. gave to me. And she seized it. It is […] that she did [it?...][433], when I was sitting without what is mine[434]. She was not good to me, (but the) workman *Ỉmnwꜥ*, [my son,] he was good to me when I was feeble; his son, this [*Nḫmmwt* too?][435] (**retributive principle**).

* Neo-Egyptian characteristics:

- tag clause [*ḏd*].*f*: Neo-Egyptian delocutive perfect report, as before *Naunakhte*'s *recital*;
- *ỉr ỉnk pꜣ mr ỉw*: opening of the direct speech # topicalizer *ỉr* + locutive independent pronoun + non-converted adverbial nexus with stative rheme #. Satzinger (1976: 134, 156) notes that after *ỉr* N, verbs of motion do not appear in a perfect (report form), but in a present constructed with stative, the expression of an inchoative 'Tatsache, nicht Beschreibung eines Vorgangs oder einer Situation'.
  As we have seen in *Naunakhte*'s will, the motives are expressed in a locutive mode following the delocutive tag clause and introduced by the prominent topic, the testator himself. Here, the ultimate reason in the causality chain that brought him to act as he did was his illness, the progression being the following: sickness – vulnerability – exploitation by the woman – assistance by the son. Thus the *recital* is not based here on an anterior and permanent positive behavior of the testator as is the case with *Naunakhte* and *pAdoptions*, for instance;
- exophoric articloids (extratextual deixis) referring to the sickness that affected the locutor (*pꜣ mr*) and to the reigning king (*pꜣ Pr-ꜥꜣ*);
- *ỉw.ỉ ḥr ḏd* is the first of a series of narrative sequential past forms (the preposition is omitted in most consecutive forms). The factual ground is based on a chain of past events that decided the testator to act as he does. The sequential is not immediately preceded by the report form as in *Naunakhte* line II.2 and *pAdoptions* line 16, but by the adverbial nexus with stative;
- Neo-Egyptian possessive determinator for kinship (*tꜣy.ỉ snt*, *pꜣy.f šrỉw*);
- Neo-Egyptian spelling (*ꜣḫt* and *gꜣbw*);
- *n ꜣḫt ỉnk* : possession expressed by the locutive independent pronoun in the form N *ỉnk*. Note that the noun does not have to be otherwise determined (*LEG* § 2.2.2.1);
- Neo-Egyptian delocutive singular feminine suffix *st*/*sw* and dependent pronoun *sw*. Note that the classic feminine delocutive suffix *s* is also used in the same texteme;
- cataphoric articloid (*pꜣ dꜣỉw*);
- *ỉ.dỉ*.N: perfect relative form with prothetic *yod*;
- *ỉ.ỉrw.s*: that-form with prothetic *yod* (anteriority) probably followed by an adverbial focus in lacuna;

429 Kinship or mates, opinions vary (Toivari-Viitala 2001: 82, n.489); nothing proves that *Tintpꜣỉp* is the speaker's *snt*.

430 Toivari-Viitala (2001: 81) proposes 'Do [good for me and you will get some] of my property'.

431 Černý (2001: 91); Toivari-Viitala (2001: 81, n.488) suggests 'an expression used for the woman leaving the existing relationship'.

432 Clère (1968): *ḥmsỉ* means living in this context; see also Pestman (1961: 54 n.4).

433 Helck (2002: 404) restores 'und verbrauchte es zusammen mit […].'

434 Toivari-Viitala (2001: 82): 'I was living (alone) when she was [eating together with…]. She is not mine.'

435 Helck (2002: 404) restores 'Sein Sohn (ist) mein [Erbe].'

- *bn st ink*: circumstantial and negated possession with # Neo-Egyptian negator + neutral/feminine delocutive dependent pronoun + locutive independent pronoun expressing possession # (constructed as a thetic statement)[436]. The pattern recalls Middle Egyptian # *nn* N.*f* # expressing a non-appurtenance relation (e.g. *Sinuhe* B 212, *nḥḥ nn ḏrw.f ḏt nn ḫnty.s*); the independent possessive pronoun is used instead of the classical suffix. On the circumstantial nature of the # *bn* N # construction, see *supra Naunakhte,* Doc. IV, line 3;
- *bwpwy.sw irt n.i nfr*: negative perfect in a summarizing commentary relative to the woman's attitude towards the author. The perfect of the subjective commentary is here opposed to the detached story's sequential (for the tense opposition of story *vs.* commentary, between 'monde raconté et monde commenté', see Weinrich 1973).
  Note that the negative attitude of the woman is contrasted with the positive behavior of the son (*bwpwy.sw irt n.i nfr* in parallel with *rmṯ ist Imnwᶜ* [*p3y.i šriw iw*].*f ḥr irt n.i nfr*); for the affirmation of the good behavior of the heir, and especially the contrasted retributive principle in the *recital* of *Naunakhte*, *supra*;
- Neo-Egyptian anaphoric demonstrative (*p3y*);

* 'Classical' degree 0 forms used:
- statives used to describe the weakened condition of the speaker in contrast with the dynamic, aggressive action of the woman: *iw* (in non-converted adverbial nexus *p3 mr iw*), *ḥms.k, wᶜ* and *g3bw.kwi* (in converted adverbial nexuses *iw.i ḥms.k*(*wi*) *iw.i wᶜ* and *iw.i g3bw.kwi*). For the morphology of the statives, see Groll (1970: 227-8) and Winand (1992: 131);
- *ir*: imperative (?) without prothetic *yod*[437];
- *šsp sw p3* N: nominal nexus constructed with # rheme (participle) + dependent pronoun theme + determined relational expansion of the rheme (object) #[438] designating the one responsible in an accusatory mode;

* General dialectal features: degree 2.

* Legal formula: *recital* = [*ḏd*].*f* (tag clause) + *ir ink* (testator) + *p3 mr iw* + sequential past (causality chain) + *bwpwy.sw irt n.i nfr* PN [*iw*].*f ḥr irt n.i nfr* (contrasted behavior of main protagonists)

3. Operative part

***Disposition* of general bequest**: *ir 3ḫt nb ink ḥnᶜ t3 st ḳrs m-mitt st nb n p3y.i* (9) [*it*…] *m-mitt* [*p3 pr*?] *ink iw.w n Nḫmmwt p3y.i* (10) [...]
As for all assets of mine, with the burial place, as well as any immovable of my [father…] as well as [this house?] of mine, they belong to *Nḫmmwt*, my [son's son?][439]

* Neo-Egyptian characteristics:
- Neo-Egyptian spelling (*3ḫt*);
- *3ḫt nb ink*: possession expressed by the locutive independent pronoun with collective noun expanded by the totalizing *nb*. Note that the list is constructed with # topicalizer + hyperonym (all-inclusive) + included/detailed hyponyms coordinated by *ḥnᶜ* or *m-mitt*

436 For Groll (1967: 112 n. 329), it is an adjectival nexus (without adjective), the 'negation of the '*ink sw*' pattern', although all her other examples are of the type # *bn ink sw*/*p3* N #.

437 For the distribution of *i.ir* and *ir* imperatives in Neo-Egyptian, see Winand (1992: 177).

438 Groll (1967: 34-8): 'adjectival *nfr sw*'.

439 Helck (2002: 404) suggests restoring 'Enkel.'

(specific *t3 st ḳrs*, [*p3 pr*?] *ink* and singular *st nb n p3y.i* […]). Compare the construction of the list to the lists encountered in the royal decrees (David 2006: esp. 33) where the hyperonym was always placed at the end of the list;
- cataphoric articloid (*t3 st ḳrs*);
- absence of concord of *nb* (*3ḫt nb; st nb*);
- Neo-Egyptian possessive determinator for kinship (*p3y.i* [*it*]);
- Neo-Egyptian delocutive plural *.w* suffix;

* 'Classical' degree 0 forms used:
- *ir 3ḫt nb ink… iw.w n* PN: general bequest (universal legacy to a unique legatee) on the model of previous *dispositions* of specific bequests (topicalized assets + performative). Note the absence of specific mention of the *descent and distribution* rules with future construction, since there is a unique legatee;
- relator *n* for kinship relation (*st nb n p3y.i* [*it*]);

* General dialectal features: degree 1.

* Legal formula: *disposition* of general bequest: *ir 3ḫt nb ink* (all-inclusive object) + *ḥnʿ* N and *m-mitt* N (specific objects) + *iw.w n* PN (ownership right)

4. Addition

Due to the damaged state of the ostracon, the context of the oaths is far from clear (who is taking them, who is *ỉmnḥtp*?). If *oPetrie* 18 does indeed constitute a will, oaths of others than the testator are not really parts of it – given the presumably unilateral nature of such documents. Yet additions on the verso representing guarantees of acceptance – probably ending a dispute – are written in the same hand as the testamentary provisions in the present case. The genre would thus be contentious, as the *adscriptus* following *Naunakhte*'s will, or the oath should be taken as a preventive measure added to the will.

All the features associated with the oath are of course present in this brief texteme.

Oath of a man (*Nḫmmwt* ?)
(verso 1-4) *irwy.f* [*ʿnḫ n nb ʿ.w.s. r-ḏd*?…] *rmṯ* [*ist*...]
He (*Nḫmmwt* ?) took [an oath of (the) Lord L.P.H. saying?: '… (the) work]man […]'
***Promissory* oath of *Tintp3ip*/the *snt*? (warranty with penalty)**
irwy.st ʿnḫ n nb ʿ.w.[*s.*] (5) *r-ḏd bn i*[*w*]*.i r ḫnw p3 pr mitt 3ḫt* [*nb rmṯ ist*?] (6) *ỉmnp3ḥʿpy mtw.i r ḫnw n* [*p3 pr mitt 3ḫt nb p3y.i*…] (7) *iw*[*.i*] *ḫr*[*y*] 100 *n sḫt š3b*(*d*/*t*) [*šw*]*.k*(*wi*) *m 3*[*ḫ*]*t nb* [*n*] *p3y*[*.i*] *it iw.f r dit* (8) *ir.st ʿnḫ n nb ʿ.w.s. r-ḏd bn iw.i r ḫnw n sš-ḳdw ỉmnḥtp m r3-ʿ*
She took an oath of (the) Lord L.P.[H.] saying: 'I shall not approach the house nor [any] asset [of (the) workman?] *ỉmnp3ḥʿpy*; should I approach [the house or any asset of my …, I] am liabl[e] to 100 blows of (the) rod, [deprive]ed of all a[ss]ets [of my] father', (and) he shall cause that she would take an oath of (the) Lord L.P.H. saying: 'I shall not approach (the house) of (the) draughtsman *ỉmnḥtp* either'.

* Neo-Egyptian characteristics:
- Neo-Egyptian delocutive feminine*.st* suffix;
- perfect delocutive report *irwy.f*/*irwy.st*, the usual form introducing the quotation of an oath;
- *bn iw.i r ḫnw*: the first part of the oath ('May Amun be clement…') has been omitted. The negative future expresses the promise, a renunciation of a certain action, seemingly

a *disclaimer*; if indeed 'approach' means 'claim', it represents a self-imposed restraining order.

On the basis of the spelling of *ẖnw*, the construction appears to be a Neo-Egyptian independent # *iw.f* + adverb #[440]. But Wente (1967: 63-4) proposes that in this particular case,  may be the infinitive  'to approach' with the wrong classifier, as in following *mtw.i r ẖnw*; in fact, there are other cases of this misspelling, e.g. in the formula *ẖnw n/m ni-swt tkn n/m bity*[441].

Could it be an heir's renunciation of an inheritance? The lacunae are here unfortunately irreparable.

For examples of renunciation ('Abstandsschrift') by a party of the right to contest a situation after losing in court or in a contractual context, especially in Ramesside and Demotic documents, see Allam (1985; 1994); for the agreement not to approach a disputed land during the Middle Demotic period, see Manning (2003: 852);

- cataphoric articloid (*p3 pr…* [*rmṯ ist*?] *Imnp3ḥꜥpy*);
- *p3 pr mitt 3ḫt* [*nb*]: *mitt* used as coordinator between nouns (omission of preposition *m*);
- *mtw.i r ẖnw* (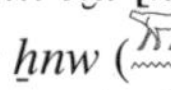): apodotic conjunctive to an elliptic protasis *w3ḥ* PN (see *supra*). Note that this time, the preposition *n* is used before the object.

  The conjunctive may in rare cases be constructed with the preposition *r* as # *mtw.f r* + infinitive #. We may point to the same confusion between  and 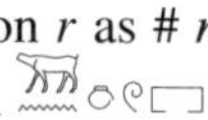 as in *bn iw.i r ẖnw supra*[442];
- *š3b(d/t)*: Neo-Egyptian lexeme from Semitic origin; see Hoch (1994: 276-8) 'identified with the Semitic root *šbt*' and Hebrew שבט. Note also the spelling of *sẖt* compared to *sẖ* in *Naunakhte*;
- Neo-Egyptian modifier *m r3-ꜥ* in trailing position[443], referring to previous oath relative to the assets of *Imnp3ḥꜥpy* (two negative promises);

* 'Classical' degree 0 forms used:

- relator *n* for kinship (*st nb n p3y.i* [*it*]; *3*[*ḫ*]*t nb* [*n*] *p3y*[*.i*] *it*), address (*ꜥnḫ n nb*), and ownership relations (*ẖnw* (*p3 pr*) *n sš ḳdw*) as well as between quantifier and noun (100 *n sẖt*);
- *r-ḏd*: tag clause introducing the oath (as in *pAshmolean Museum* 1945.95, line 7) after the perfect report;
- *iw*[*.i*] *ḥr*[*y*] 100 *n sẖt*: non converted locutive (on the basis of following [*šw*]*.k*) present adverbial nexus, an implicit performative (see *supra*);
- [*šw*]*.k*(*wi*): locutive stative, adnexal expansion of *iw*[*.i*] *ḥr*[*y*] 100 *n sẖt* (compare with *šwy*, delocutive stative with final –*y* in *Naunakhte*, line V.12);
- *ir.st*: prospective, object of *rdi*. Note again the delocutive form, although it must be part of the penalty expressed in the locutive mode (see *supra*);

---

440 See Satzinger (1976: 198-201); Shisha-Halevy (1978: 60) 'signification *future*'; Winand (1992: 510-17) 'constructions analogiques du futur III' 'une des conséquences de la disparition de la préposition *r* et de la réinterprétation de la particule *iw* comme assumant seule le sens futur'.

441 See *Das digitalisierte Zettelarchiv des Wörterbuches der ägyptischen Sprache*, documents DZA 28.220.450, *statue Cairo* CG 1134 of the 19th dynasty; DZA 28.220.490, TT 23 of *Ṯ3y* of the 19th dynasty; DZA 28.220.370, *statue Cairo* Wb 45 of the 22nd dynasty.

442 Černý (1949: 27) suggests understanding the form as the equivalent of *mtw.f i.sḏm*; Winand (1992: 471-2) sees in the few instances of *mtw.f r sḏm* a 'surcodage dû à une analogie avec le future III', and in our particular case 'un exemple susceptible de s'interpréter comme un cas où le prédicat est un complément circonstanciel' i.e. *r-ẖnw-n* (*ibid.*, 470 §736); Junge (2005: 104) believes it is a case of 'hypercorrection'.

443 Hintze (1952: 303-4); *LEG* § 8.9.4; Junge (2005: 87).

* General dialectal features: degree 2.
* Legal formula: *promissory* oath: *ỉrwy.f ꜥnẖ nb ꜥ.w.s.* (report) + *r-ḏd* (tag clause) + *bn ỉw.ỉ r ẖnw* (negative promise) + *mtw.ỉ r ẖnw* (forfeiture) + *ỉw*[*.ỉ*] *ẖr*[*y*] 100 *n sẖt,* [*šw*]*.k*(*wỉ*) *m ꜣ*[*ẖ*]*t nb* (penalty)

Categorization of terms of special relevance in the legal register:

- *ꜣẖt*: assets.
- *st*: immovable property ('place').
- *ỉw.f n* PN: to belong to PN.
- *ỉri ꜥnẖ n nb ꜥ.w.s.*: to take an oath of the Lord L.P.H.
- *ẖnw* (*n*) *pr*/*ꜣẖt*: to approach (a house/assets). If the expression is to be taken literally, then the oath is to be understood as a self-imposed restraining order[444]; but the meaning could be metaphorical, the verb of motion meaning a claim on the possession of assets. As for the use of the [HABITAT] category classifier, we have seen that it might be an 'error' for the [MOTION] classifier (*ẖn* 'to approach', attested since the Middle Kingdom) by a 'homophonic contamination' process that assigns the same classifier to homophonic but not synonymic lexemes (David 2007), connected to the presence of the preceding *r* preposition that usually forms the compound *r-ẖnw*[445].
  Motion is associated with claiming, an aggressive behavior, since '*ACTION IS MOTION*', a conceptual metaphor: 'Litigation is a judicial "proceeding"; (...) the parties cite supporting "grounds" for their "motions"; alternatively, parties may decide to "forgo" their procedural rights'[446].
- *ỉw.f ẖry* (*sẖt*): liable to (blows).
- [*šw*] *m* (*ꜣẖt*): deprived of (assets).

444 *De facto* a divorce settlement for Toivari-Viitala (2001: 82).
445 See also Wente (1967: 64) 'phonetic association' or semantic association between approaching and entering.
446 Winter (1989: 2232); see David (2007).

8. *pAshmolean Museum* 1945.96 (*pAdoptions*)

Date: 20th dynasty, Ramesses XI
Hieroglyphic version: *KRI* VI, 735-8 n.19
Instrument:

* **state** – complete

* **value – partial copy?**[447]: papyrus, comprising essential information, such as full dating including royal titulary, all parties and witnesses named, title deed, *recital* and elaborated colophons, but missing the mention of forum and scribe, the curse in the title deed (although the original may have been conceived in the same incomplete way).

* **nature – legal instrument** (no internal characterization) concerning personal status and legal rights about assets.

* **genre – consentient legal:** fiber orientation characteristic of short legal documents (text running across fibers on the recto, along them on the verso)[448]; palimpsest (at least the recto); formulaic style, ordered layout, full dating, archaic anaphora; the ordered script is the work of 'an accomplished hand'[449] but with errors, corrections 'both in and above the line' probably due to a second lecture, abridged provision of line 7, joint statement of year 18 abruptly followed by a locutive texteme representing the *recital* of the testatrix, absence of business practice diacritical marks; concerns private interests; locutive/delocutive textemes, degree 2 Neo-Egyptian.

The papyrus was acquired, but probably originated from *Sprwmry*, from a family archive[450] perhaps left in a tomb.

Legal step: record (*sš*) of declaration (*ḏdt*) being an **external manifestation of will** (with explicit performative) concerning the status of a brother and the transmission of assets (*ẖt nb*), before witnesses (probably a court; in this case the court acted as notary producing an authenticated document).

Legal issues: **will and related adoption**: absence of *consideration*, unilateral deed concerning the transmission of the entire patrimony to the 'children' of the testator; use of *pš, dni, swꜣḏ*; typical clauses (future *descent and distribution* rule, retributive principle in the *recital*, mention of types of assets, *terrorem* clause, designation of executor, title deed justifying the ownership rights of the testatrix, family member present as special witness). No specific bequests are recorded and the principle of division seems to be of equal shares for each of the heirs. Note that a mention of the death of the testator is made in the excerpt of the will of the companion of the testatrix (title deed). An explicit performative is used for the adoption of the brother.

There remains the issue of the main purpose of the document: was the document recorded in order to free slaves (see the *terrorem* clause[451] where the crucial segment is

447 For Seidl (1957b: 277-8), it is a 'Kopie' used by the legatees as title deed; for Théodoridès (1965: 107) an 'expédition de l'acte'.

448 Gardiner (1940: 23).

449 Gardiner (1940: 23).

450 For Eyre (1992: 207-8), it belongs to the category of 'private documents, kept in family archives, and not official court records', consisting of an 'abbreviated and partial procès verbal of [*Nꜣnfr*'s] statement', where the 'holder of the document had a record of the occasion, and of the normal declarations by which the business had been solemnized and publicized before witnesses'.

451 *No-contest* clause; especially adequate to render the use of a curse threatening those who challenge the will (see *infra*).

missing)[452], to adopt a brother so that he may inherit the assets of the testatrix (see the explicit performative at the head of the operative part)[453] or to organize the succession of the testatrix (the adoption of the brother and the declaration about the status of the children being made in order to enable them to inherit)?[454] We believe it is this last option[455], mainly because the title deed is produced by the testatrix to prove her rights over the assets she is willing to bequeath and because the clarification of the status of the beneficiaries is a necessary step in order to enable them to inherit the assets of the testatrix. Thus the performative utterance concerns the adoption of the brother (legal fiction in order to inherit) which is followed by a *terrorem* clause affirming the proper status of the slave's children in order to inherit the assets and by the *descent and distribution* rule dividing the assets between them.

Textemic features:

A. Preamble: title deed

Excerpts of the will of the companion of the testatrix, embedded in a summarizing narrative by the testatrix[456], but respecting the sequence of testamentary provisions.

We are dealing with a will[457], a unilateral deed, which of course may contain provisions concerned with matrimonial property. Modern wills may also go further than strict inheritance provisions; a testator may have a broader picture in view, organizing the future of his family by adding conditions to the bequests in his will. Modern legal categorization acknowledges many borderline cases, such as, for instance, postnuptial agreements that may 'define each spouse's property rights in the event of death'[458] (of course these are mutual understandings between two parties, not unilateral wills).

The title deed does not constitute a 'marriage contract,' as there is no evidence of such contracts during the Ramesside Period and the document represents a unilateral[459] expression of will, without mention of a *consideration*. It is not a *property settlement* since the testatrix later refers in her will to having become a widow (excluding a separation of the couple). It is not a 'non-divorce settlement' from his first 'spouse' by a man contemplating a second 'marriage': since their union is not subject to formal declarations on the part of the members of a couple, it may be reasonable to assume that a 'non-divorce' should not be either. A man did not need to 'marry' the slave-surrogate mother and we have no indication that he provided for her or their children; the slave remained a slave, and *N3nfr*'s status did not change. No

---

452 For Rabinowitz (1958: 146) we are dealing with a 'manumission document' by way of adoption, as in ancient Babylonia.

453 For *KRI* VI, 735, our document is an 'Act of Adoption'.

454 For Seidl (1957b: 277), it is an 'Adoptionstestament', as for Théodoridès (1965: 84). For the use of the mechanism of adoption in order to transfer assets to a person who is not a legal heir in early Mesopotamian law, see VerSteeg (2000: 106), and in ancient Greece, see Robb (1994: 108).

455 *Contra*: Eyre (1992: 210) for whom it is 'a non-divorce settlement', 'a cross between a marriage settlement, a property settlement, and a will, or rather a mixture of all three', 'a sort of trust' (*ibid.*, 213). See the discussion *infra*.

456 Théodoridès (1965: 80): 'Synthèse de son [the deed's] contenu avec extraits'.

457 *Contra*: Eyre (1992: 209) for whom it is either a gift, although the death of the testator is expressly foreseen (*m p3y.i mt n dw3w r-s(3) dw3w*), a fact that Eyre acknowledges, or 'a marriage settlement and a will, although the device is that of adoption'.

458 Garner (2004: 1206).

459 Late marriage settlements (Pestman 1961: 21-4) mention both parties in the pre-material but the deeds are constructed in the locutive/allocutive mode, the man voicing the agreement that concerns the rights and obligations of both sides.

settlement was needed since he treated his first companion 'as a daughter' and not as an enemy. He is providing for his companion in the period after his death because they have no children to take care of her; a widow has no legal rights of inheritance concerning the assets of her companion, and there are legal heirs (his siblings).

As for the adoption, the issue will be discussed *infra*.

For another example of the summary[460] of a will used as title deed to a will, see *pKahun* I.1 (*pUC* 32058). Documentary evidence of wills seems to have been used as early as the Old Kingdom, see e.g. 5th dynasty *Wpmnfrt tomb*, with pictorial description of the heir facing the testator and holding a document in his hand, probably the record of the testamentary provisions, and lines 13-4: *di.n(.i) n.f* (list) *n ꜥy* ⇐ *sn nb r.s* 'I give him (list of assets) without any brother's title deed (or right of claim[461]) against it'.

1. Pre-material

Complete date with temporal precisions relating to the accession of the king. Eyre remarks (1992: 209) that the act was formalized 'during celebrations for the accession of Ramesses XI, an occasion that would give them the maximum of publicity.' Thus the notary document has a formal weight designed to increase its authority beyond the fact that the will is received and recorded in the presence of numerous witnesses, probably in the forum of a court. The emphasis on temporal deixis with its elaborate reference to the textual context demonstrates both the informational focus of the pre-material and the careful production of an official document. On the other hand, the absence of spatial reference (forum), as is often the case, is puzzling.

Date: (1) *rnpt-sp* 1 *ꜣbd* 3 *šmw sw* 20 *ḫr ḥm ni-swt bity Rꜥmss Ḫꜥwmwꜣst ꜥ.w.s. Mryimn ḥkꜣ nṯr* (2) *Ꞽwnw ꜥ.w.s. di ꜥnḫ ḏt r nḥḥ*
Year 1, month 3 of summer, day 20, under (the) majesty of (the) King of Upper (and) Lower Egypt, *Rꜥmss Ḫꜥwmwꜣst* L.P.H. *Mryimn*, divine ruler of Heliopolis L.P.H., given life for ever (and) ever.
archaic anaphora: *hrw pn* This day
temporal precisions: *s(p)rt ḫꜥw n nṯr pn špss n Ꞽmn iw.f ꜥḥꜥ ḫꜥw* (3) *wdnw n Ꞽmn*
of proclamation of (the) accession ('appearance in glory') of this noble God (King Ramesses XI) to Amun, rising, shining, making offerings to Amun.

* Neo-Egyptian characteristics:
- Neo-Egyptian form of the infinitives (*s(p)rt*; *ḫꜥw n nṯr, wdnw*);

* 'Classical' degree 0 forms used:
- traditional official texts binomials *ni-swt bity, ḏt r nḥḥ* (compare with *ḏt nḥḥ* in *Naunakhte*), and trinomials *ꜥnḫ wḏꜣ snb*. Prosodic effects are also to be noted in *ꜥḥꜥ ḫꜥw wdnw*;
- *di ꜥnḫ*: see *EG* § 378;
- archaic anaphora *hrw pn* (+ infinitive *s(p)rt*, a classical Middle Egyptian heading) and *nṯr pn;*
- relator *n* for subject relation (*ḫꜥw n nṯr pn*);
- *iw.f ꜥḥꜥ ḫꜥw wdnw*: converted adverbial nexus (concomitance).

460 Ganley (2003a: 21).
461 For *ꜥy* 'beanspruchen', 'ein Rechtsdokument besitzen', see *ÄW* I, 253.

The two first rhemes consist of univalent verbs that could be converbs (*ḥr*) *sḏm* or statives[462]; the third one, *wdnw*, bivalent, is an infinitive in (*r*) *sḏm* purpose[463] or (*ḥr*) *sḏm* converb;

* General dialectal features: degree 1.
* Legal formula: date (year, month of season, day + *ḫr ḥm* + royal titulary) + *hrw pn* + infinitive (temporal precisions)

2. *Recital*

This narrative texteme constituting a *recital* related to the title deed is different from the *recital* of the main record: it does not represent the words of the testator himself but is a paraphrasing of the background of his decision in the form of a story told by his heir. Consequently, the linguistic strategy is completely different. Although the texteme begins with a delocutive narrative form and uses the proper name of its actor, the personal stance of the narrator is expressed by the omnipresent locutive pronouns and the closing *r-ḥrw-r ỉnk*. The depictive discourse uses past narrative tenses and leads to a tag clause introducing a quotation of the operative part of the will. In short, this *recital* does not represent the original *recital* of the will of *Nbnfr*, although the pre-material seemed to refer to the genuine document and a direct reference to 'writings' was made by the testator in this respect. Another important example of this type of 'contraction' between time-frames of events and records is to be found in the act *senso strictu*.

Summarized grounded facts:
ꜥḥꜥ.n ỉryw Nbnfr pꜣy.ỉ hꜣy sšw n.ỉ šmꜥyt (4) *n Stẖy Nꜣnfr ỉw.f ỉrt(.ỉ) n.f n* (= *m*) *šriw ỉw.f sšw n.ỉ n* (= *m*) *pꜣ sꜣwt nb ỉw bn n.f šriw* (5) *šriw r-ḥrw-r ỉnk*
Nbnfr, my man, made writings for me, a singer of Seth, *Nꜣnfr*. And he made/treated (me) for himself as a daughter; and he wrote down on my behalf all his (assets)[464], because there is not a son or daughter to him except myself,

* Neo-Egyptian characteristics:
  - possessive for couple relationships (*pꜣy.ỉ hꜣy*);
  - Neo-Egyptian spelling (*ỉryw*.N, *hꜣy, šriw*);
  - *ỉw.f ỉrt, ỉw.f sšw*: sequential past, preposition omitted; note the form of infinitive *sšw*. The sequential *ỉw.f sšw n.ỉ n pꜣ sꜣwt nb* represents the narrative equivalent of a general

462 For the dynamic/static constructions of position verbs, see Satzinger (1976: 149-50). Thus the opposition between (*ḥr*) *ꜥḥꜥ*/stative could be translated as 'rising/standing'; the opposition between (*ḥr*) *ḫꜥi*/stative is more difficult to assess.

463 Satzinger (1976: 246) views the construction as *ỉw.f* (*ḥr*) *ꜥḥꜥ* (*ḥr*) *ḫꜥi* (*r*) *wdn* 'indem er sich erhebt und erscheint, um (…) zu opfern', which means two converbs (*ḥr*) *sḏm* and one purpose of which the preposition has also been omitted. For Groll (1984: 47-8), it is a 'circumstantial first present' constructed with three (*ḥr*) *sḏm* converbs expressing 'past continuous tense'.

464 *pꜣ sꜣwt nb* 'all his'; but the excerpt of the operative part of the title deed concerns *mꜥḏꜣ nb* 'all the *acquets*', including the slave that has been bought by the couple and common assets. Those who might contest the will are presented as claiming *dniw* 'the shares' of their brother. Théodoridès (1965: 82 n.15, 104) suggested that the scribe who recorded the deed only reproduced the dispositions (of the operative part) directly relating to the slave, thus the *acquets*; Théodoridès (1961: 42) previously suggested viewing it as a distinction made by the testator himself between two categories of assets on the basis of their origin, the capital and the *acquets*.

bequest in the performative mode: e.g. *ỉr ꜣḫt nb ỉnk* (+ categories of assets) *ỉw.w n* PN in *oPetrie* 18, lines 8-9.

The first *ỉw.f ỉrt(.ỉ) n.f n (= m) šriw* has been viewed by some authors[465] as an official adoption of the woman by her companion in order to make her the universal legatee of his assets; others[466] suggested interpreting the sentence as a figure of speech, since a man bequeathing all his assets to a woman behaves towards her as he would towards a child, his legal heir (see *infra*).

More importantly, for our purpose, is the reference to written documents as a source of rights is a formal proof of the function of the text as legal object, the legally binding *instrumentum* detached from the *negotium*;

- prepositions *n*/*m* confusion (*ỉrt n šriw*; *sšw n pꜣ sꜣwt nb*). For *sš m* (object), see *Wb* III, 476;
- *pꜣ sꜣwt nb*: Neo-Egyptian spelling and use of the independent pronoun *sꜣwt*[467] in the syntagm # substantivizer articloid *pꜣ* + delocutive masculine possessor *sꜣwt* + totalizing *nb* #; compare with *oPetrie* 18 r°, line 8 *ꜣḫt nb ỉnk*. We have already observed the propensity of legal texts to use archaisms, revisiting old forms and even creating pseudo-archaisms (*supra* and David 2006: *esp*. 98-9);
- *ỉw bn* N: converted non-existence expressing the ground of the decision with # converter + Neo-Egyptian negator + noun #;
- both genders filiation binomial *šriw šriw*;
- *r-ḥrw-r ỉnk*: # compound preposition (with preposition *r* redundance) + independent locutive pronoun # instead of classical *ḥrw-r.ỉ*. The pronoun *ỉnk* is for *LEG* § 2.2.2 (f) a possessive independent pronoun 'equivalent of a suffix'; but its use here and in line 6 indicates a marked pattern in its opposition to the suffixed one;

* 'Classical' degree 0 forms used:

- *ꜥḥꜥ.n ỉryw* PN[468]: narrative past compound # *ꜥḥꜥ.n* (auxiliary nominal theme) + *ỉryw*.PN (adverbial *sḏm.f* rheme) #, for detached informative account in evolution mode. It is followed by the Neo-Egyptian sequential past. For the actor-related opposition *ꜥḥꜥ.n sḏm*.PN - *ꜥḥꜥ.n sḏm.n.f* in Neo-Egyptian, see Groll (1973: 69), Winand (1992: 181); e.g. *oNash* 1, lines 6 and 9. both archaic forms belong to the legal and story registers[469], perhaps as markers of the high dialect in the written legal genre and a reminder that legal deeds are personal stories. Groll (1984: 55-6) sees in the construction an 'emphatic formation' expressing past tense with *ꜥḥꜥ.n* 'nominalizer of an initial main clause, namely the perfect' *ỉryw*.N, the focus being on the sentence's final '*m-bꜣḥ* extensions,' a specific feature of the 'Spermeru dialect' of which the text is for her representative. Apart from the problematic assertion of a topolect in Neo-Egyptian as in other previous stages of Egyptian, this analysis does not take into consideration the

465 e.g. Gardiner (1940: 25).

466 Théodoridès (1962b: 25-6) who compares this case with *pTurin* 2021 where a woman inherits from her companion without being adopted by him, see *infra*.

467 *LEG* § 2.2.1-4; *EG* § 62 for the Old Egyptian origin of the form and its 'archaic' texture already in Middle Egyptian.

468 Although *ꜥḥꜥ.n sḏm.f* exists in Middle Egyptian, it is considered here by Satzinger (1976: 243) and Junge (2005: 276) as a Neo-Egyptian adaptation of *ꜥḥꜥ.n sḏm.n.f*; but as both forms subsist in the actor-related opposition *ꜥḥꜥ.n sḏm*.PN - *ꜥḥꜥ.n sḏm.n.f* in Neo-Egyptian, they are presented as Middle Egyptian forms. Of course the opposition of the two forms is not a classical one.

469 Hintze (1950: 31-6); Satzinger (1976: 243-6).

textemic division of legal texts, i.e. pre-material, preamble/*recital*, operative part, and end colophon naming the witnesses to the act.
The segment represents a *recital* by the woman of the circumstances of her companion's will. It is not a transcription of the original will of her companion joined to the act *sensu stricto*, but an elaborated summary in a narrative form (with delocutive and locutive references) introducing short quotations. It is different from the title deed in *pBoulaq* 10, a summary of a dispute before a court and not a narrative texteme, and thus unique in our corpus. Nevertheless, a similar construction appears in the testamentary *Snims stela Cairo* CG 34016 of the 18th dynasty, in a segment that seems to represent a *recital*[470], although the document is badly damaged.
For other examples of the use of this narrative construction in other legal registers, see e.g. *Nbḫprwrʿ Ỉntf* 17th dynasty royal decree (Petrie 1896: pl. VIII); Gardiner (1906) and *pMunich* ÄS 809 for 18th dynasty documents; Spalinger (1984: 634 n.9); *pAbbott* r° 7, line 6;
- relator in religious dedication relation (*šmʿyt n Stḫy*);

* General dialectal features: degree 2.
* Legal formula: *ʿḥʿ.n iryw* PN… *iw.f sḏm* (object) + *iw bn* filiation binomial *r-ḥrw-r ink* (ground)

3. Operative part

Quotation of an excerpt of the testator's will.

tag clause: *m(-ḏd?)*[471] (say)ing:
***disposition* of general bequest:** (*ir*) *mʿḏ3 nb i.irw.i irm.st iw.i sw3ḏ.w* (6) (*n*) *N3nfr t3y.i ḥmt*
(As) for all *acquets* that I made with her, I shall transmit them (to) *N3nfr* my woman.
***no-contest* (*terrorem*) clause:** *m* (= *ir*)[472] *n3y snw r ink ʿḥʿ rḳw n.st m p3y.i mt n* (= *m*) *dw3w* (7) *r-s(3) dw3w mtw.f ḏd imi tw dniw n p3y.i sn*
As for these brothers of mine standing and confronting her on my death on (the) morrow after tomorrow, and saying: 'Give (the) shares of my brother' (*omitted testator's curse*?).

* Neo-Egyptian characteristics:
- confusion of prepositions: *n* for *m* (*n dw3*) and *m* for *ir* topicalizer (*m n3y snw*);
- omission of prepositions: (*ir*) *mʿḏ3; iw.i swḏ.w;* (*n*) *N3nfr* (haplography);
- Neo-Egyptian lexeme (*mʿḏ3*);
- *i.irw.i*: perfect relative form with prothetic *yod*, attributive expansion of *mʿḏ3 nb*;
- Neo-Egyptian preposition (*irm*);
- delocutive singular feminine *st* and plural *w* suffixes;
- Neo-Egyptian spelling of lexeme *sw3ḏ*;
- possessive for couple relationships (*t3y.i ḥmt*) and physical state (*p3y.i mt*);

470 See the use of *m.k* (*Urk.* IV, 1069 line 16).
471 Groll (1984: 45). Théodoridès (1963: 92 n.6) and Allam (1973: 260 n.6 'Hervorhebung eines Substantives am Anfang des Satzes') suggest reading *in* instead of *m* (focalization), a solution that recalls the confusion between *ir* topicalizer and *in* focus marker in the *Nauri* decree (David 2006: 56 n.85). Furthermore, *m-ḏd* would be consistent with a quotation of the text (*sš*), detached from the oral speech of the testator that would probably be introduced by *ḏdw.f* or *r-nty*; this is consistent with the use of the *instrumentum* (*sš*) as source of legal rights.
472 Théodoridès (1964: 50) suggests restoring '*ir wʿ* (?)' or '(*ir p3* ?) *m n3y snw*' (1965: 83).

- *m nꜣy snw r ỉnk*: topicalized category of legal heirs, the kinship relation being expressed by # Neo-Egyptian deictic determinator + N + *r* + locutive independent pronoun (possessor) #, to be compared with verso line 4 and *oGardiner/Ashmolean* 272, lines 3-4.
  For *LEG* § 2.2.2.I (f), the possessive independent pronoun 'acts as the equivalent of a suffix', the only examples coming from *pAdoptions* (this case and *r-ḥrw-r ỉnk supra* line 5). As there are in our text two cases of use of the independent pronoun after a preposition, it cannot be taken as an error, but the presence of the preposition is disturbing in this syntagm;
- *m nꜣy snw r ỉnk ꜥḥꜥ rḳw… mtw.f ḏd*: topicalization of contestant # *m* (= *ỉr*) topicalizer + determined N + *ꜥḥꜥ rḳw* (participles without prothetic *yod*, attributive expansion)[473] + *mtw.f ḏd* (conjunctive tag clause) + direct speech #; either the nexus expressing how to deal with the contestant or a threat is missing.
  We have here a case of *no-contest clause* with topicalization of a category of legal heirs not respecting the provisions of the will, an illustrative direct speech summarizing their pretention, the second part of the testator's statement being missing, probably a threat in order to guarantee the legatee against a legal heir's contestation of the will (see *infra* the similar provision of the testatrix)[474]. The participles constituting the binomial *ꜥḥꜥ rḳw* have an atemporal value, although the contestation must be posterior to the testator's speech. For the use of a participle other than *sḏm.ty.fy* in the protasis of a threat, see examples in Morschauser (1991: 9-10). As for *mtw.f ḏd*, it is a full-fledged conjunctive, tag clause opening an illustrative direct speech, apodotic to *ꜥḥꜥ rḳw*. The 'crime' (a brother's claim of a share of the assets) is expressed by the conjunctive, as is the case in royal decrees dealing with criminal law, in the casuistic texteme describing the crimes (David 2006: 67-8).
  Théodoridès (1965: 83 n.21, 107) and other scholars have suggested that a simple equivalent to 'qu'on le déboute' is missing, a 'clause de style.' Allam (1967: 18) equated this provision with *pAshmolean Museum* 1945.95 line 5 warranty against claims of coheirs: *ỉw.f n.f bn mdt šrỉ šrỉ tꜣ ḥmt Ḳn m-ỉm.f bn sḏm rꜣ.f m dwꜣt* 'it belongs to him, without contestation of a son (or) a daughter (or) *Ḳn*'s woman concerning it, without a hearing of his deposition in the future'; but this warranty is not part of the will. Furthermore, the use of *m* as topicalizer preceding the category of family members excludes constructions such as the one exemplified by *pAhsmolean Museum* 1945.95. A better solution may be found in 18th dynasty *Nfrprt*'s *stelaphorous statue Cairo* CG 42121, lines 20-1, recording a royal decision: *ỉr ỉw.ty.f(y) nb r mdt m rdỉ [sḏ]m.tw n.sn m hꜣ nb n nỉ-swt* 'As for anyone who will come in order to contest (it), don't let one [h]ear them (him) in any office of the king', but again this is not a Ramesside will. Thus we suggest that the missing 'penalty' consists, on the model of the provisions of the testatrix, of a curse of the type *nk sw ꜥꜣwt nk ꜥꜣwt ḥmt.f*, since the Ramesside Period abounds in such threats (see *infra*). The construction # *m* (=*ỉr*) *nꜣy snw r ỉnk ꜥḥꜥ rḳw n.st* (…) + curse # has a parallel in the *Amarah stela* (*Stela Brooklyn* 38.544) of the late 20th dynasty: *ỉr pꜣ nty ỉw.f mdt ỉm.f ỉrỉ Ỉmn-Rꜥ nỉ-swt nṯrw m-sꜣ.f r sꜣsꜣ.f Mwt m-sꜣ ḥmt.f Ḫnsw m-sꜣ ḫrd.f ḥḳr.f* 'As for the one who will contest it, Amun-Re, King of the Gods, is after him in order to repel him, Mut is after his wife, Khonsu is after his child so that he will starve'[475] (with performatives);

473 Groll (1984: 52) sees *m nꜣy snw r ỉnk (ḥr) ꜥḥꜥ* as a 'first present pattern'.
474 See also *Ỉdw tomb* (6th dynasty), for the protection of a gift after the donor's death.
475 Théodoridès (1964: 65).

- *mortis causa* binomial (*m*) *dwꜣw r-s*(*ꜣ*) *dwꜣw*[476]. Interestingly, *pꜣy.i mt n dwꜣw r-s*(*ꜣ*) *dwꜣw* is one of the rare mentions of the testator's death in wills from the Old to the New Kingdom, a direct indicator of the main criteria of the testamentary category[477]. The reluctance to relate to one's inexorable fate in texts relating to the disposal of material assets is equally illustrated by the absence of the reference and by the binomial's reference to a far and indefinite time space.
  The first instance of the binomial is noted in another legal document of the 18th dynasty, *pBerlin* P 9785, line 16: *m dwꜣ* (*ḥr-*)*sꜣ dwꜣ*[478]. The formula is also frequently used in oaths warrantying against claims by the person taking the oath or a third party during the Ramesside Period (see *infra*); it is also the case later, e.g. in abnormal hieratic *pLouvre* E 3228e (25th dynasty), concerning the vendor's oath guarantee after payment in full of a slave: 'Je n'ai pas de : fils, fille, frère, sœur, personne au monde entier susceptible de faire une contestation à son sujet [*mdw n-im.f*], dorénavant [*dwꜣ ḥr-sꜣ dwꜣ*]' (Malinine 1953: 37 lines 7-8, 41 n.17);

* 'Classical' degree 0 forms used:

- (*ir*) *mꜥḏꜣ nb i.irw.i … iw.i swꜣḏ.w*: # topicalized determined noun + relative perfect expansion (category of assets) + future (preposition omission, plural resumptive suffix)#, an embedded locutive quotation of a significant excerpt of the will in the narrative.
  The testator does not use the implicit performative attribution of ownership *iw.f n* N/PN in the *disposition* of a general bequest, but apparently a locutive future *iw.i* (*r*) *sḏm*. This formulation is not used elsewhere in our corpus; a delocutive/impersonal future is used to formulate the *descent and distribution* rule, e.g. in *oDeM* 108 (*iry ḫt*{*t*} *nb iw.w psš.w*), but *iw.i swꜣḏ.w* is not concerned with a general rule of division of the inheritance since there is apparently only one legatee. We would have expected an explicit performative such as the one used in the operative part of the act *sensu stricto* for the adoption (*tw.i i.iri*), with marker of performativity *m pꜣ hrw*. Interestingly, in a cleft sentence in the colophon of the title deed, the testator recalls the bequest to *Rnnfr* by using the lexeme *swꜣḏ* and the marker of performativity (*ptr i.irw.i swꜣḏ n Rnnfr* (…) *m pꜣ hrw*). Since we are dealing with a summary of the will, reformulation may account for the discrepancy;
- relator *n* in possessor relations (*dni n pꜣy.i sn*);
- *imm tw*: # imperative + dependent allocutive pronoun *tw* # followed by the object *dniw n pꜣy.i sn*.
  The use of the dependent allocutive pronoun after the imperative is common in Middle Egyptian and survives in Neo-Egyptian[479].

---

476 Concerning this formula, see Gardiner (1940: 24); Malinine (1947: 105); Rabinowitz (1958: 145) on Semitic influence, as a similar binomial appears in the cuneiform Alalakh Tablets in penalty clauses; Janssen (2005: 80).

477 See also *Nkꜥnḫ tomb*, 5th dynasty (*skw ḥp.k r imnt nfr*[*t*] *m nb imꜣḫ*); *Ꞽdw tomb*, 6th dynasty (*ink ꜣḫ* [*ikr*] *mnḫ*).

478 Théodoridès (1965: 93 n.57).

479 See *EG* § 337.1 for *tw* as 'reinforcer' of the imperative; Winand (1992: 167-9): 'quand l'élément de renforcement est présent, il y a toujours un COD [direct object] exprimé'.
Nevertheless, Erman (1933: § 357) understood *imi tw* as an abbreviated form of the impersonal causative *imi di.tw*, followed by Groll (1984: 49), but criticized by Frandsen (1974: 264), as *imi tw* can, for instance, be followed by a suffixed pronoun (*imi tw.f*); in *LEG* § 24.5.2, it is said to be an abbreviated form of *imi didi.tw* 'cause one to give', a 'more polite and less abrupt means of saying 'give'', on the basis of Ex. 980, *oDeM* 235, 5 (spelled *imi didi.ti*!).

The segment of direct speech *imi tw dniw n pꜣy.i sn* represents a pseudo-quotation designed to illustrate the claim of a legal heir in a more vivid and concrete way; it probably does not constitute a true 'spoken vernacular' since it uses the Middle Egyptian allocutive reinforcer of imperative and the relator (but see the use of the Neo-Egyptian possessive in kinship relationships). The same expressive strategy is used in the *imyt-pr* of the Second Intermediate Period *Stèle juridique de Karnak* JE 52453, lines 7-10, in a warranty against claims: *ir nty nb r iit r spr n* N *r-ḏd iw n(.i) tꜣ iꜣt m rdi sḏm.tw n.f ḥr-ntt* (…) *ir iw sꜣ nb sꜣt nbt sn nb snt nbt s nb n hꜣw r-ḏd iw n(.i) tꜣ iꜣt m rdi sḏm.ṯw n.sn* 'As for anyone who will come to N to make a claim saying: "the function comes to me", do not let (any)one listen to him because (…); if any son, any daughter, any brother, any sister (or) any relative should come to say: "This office belongs to (me)," do not let (any)one listen to them'. We have observed the same tendency to illustrate the criminal provisions of royal decrees with a fictional direct speech, as well as the recent trend of recommending the incorporation of practical illustrative cases in statutory provisions in order to enhance their clarity (David 2006: 68);

* General dialectal features: degree 2.

* Legal formulae:
- *disposition* of general bequest: *m* (*ḏd*? *ir*) *mꜥḏꜣ nb i.irw.i irm.st* (*acquets*) + *iw.i swꜣḏ.w* + (*n*) PN (beneficiary)
- *no-contest* clause: *m* (= *ir*) N (legal heirs) + *ꜥḥꜥ r ḳw n.st* (action against the legatee) + *m pꜣy.i mt n dwꜣw r-s(ꜣ) dwꜣw* (time frame) + *mtw.f ḏd* (tag clause) + *imi tw dniw* (claim) (+ curse?)

4. Colophon

Witnesses: *m-bꜣḥ mtryw ḳnw* (8) *ꜥšꜣt* In the presence of very numerous witnesses:
ḥry iḥ Ryr ḥry iḥ Kꜣirywsw ḥry iḥ Bniryrdwꜣnfr (9) *m-bꜣḥ ḥry iḥ Nbnfr sꜣ ꜥnrkꜣiꜣ m-bꜣḥ šꜣyrdnnꜣ Pꜣkꜣmn* (10) *m-bꜣḥ šꜣyrdnnꜣ Sꜣtꜣmniw ḥmttw.f ꜥḏdwꜥꜣ*
stable-master *Ryr*, stable-master *Kꜣirywsw*, stable-master *Bniryrdwꜣnfr*[480]; in the presence of stable-master *Nbnfr*, son of *ꜥnrkꜣiꜣ*; in presence of (the) *šꜣyrdnnꜣ Pꜣkꜣmn*; in the presence of (the) *šꜣyrdnnꜣ Sꜣtꜣmniw*, (and) his woman *ꜥḏdwꜥꜣ*.
Special witness: *ptr i.irw.i* (11) *swꜣḏ n Rnnfr tꜣy.i ḥmt m pꜣ hrw m-bꜣḥ Ḫwirywmw tꜣy.i* (12) *sn*
See that it is in the presence of *Ḫwirywmw,* my sister, that I have entrusted today *Rnnfr*[481], my woman.

* Neo-Egyptian characteristics:
- Neo-Egyptian spelling (*swꜣḏ; ḥmttw.f; sn*; *ꜥšꜣt*) and lexeme (*šꜣyrdnnꜣ,* see Albright 1934: 51.13 and 57.11; Gardiner 1940: 24-5);
- *ptr i.irw.i swꜣḏ… m-bꜣḥ* PN: the Neo-Egyptian presentative *ptr,* a marker of involvement with the addressees, is followed by its cleft sentence-object: # analytic that-form *i.irw.i swꜣḏ* (theme) + focus on the adverbial rheme (*m-bꜣḥ Ḫwirywmw*) #. The fact that the colophon relating to the attesting witnesses seems to be quoted in its

480 Allam (1990: 191): *Bniry sꜣ Dwꜣnfr*.

481 = *Nꜣnfr*; on the spelling modification, see Eyre (1992: 208, n.5) who suggests that this first part 'was copied from an earlier text written in a different hand'; but this does not explain the fact that it is only in the last sentence of the title deed that the proper name is spelled as in the main document. See also the change from *Pndiw* to *Pꜣdiw infra*.

entirety is indicative of the importance of this part of the deed: the testator is addressing the witnesses publicly and orally and emphasizing the presence of a legal heir as witness to the act. The direct style (allocutive, locutive modes) with the presentative is indeed part of the formulation of notarial wills (see *supra*), essentially in their *recital*, but it is unusual in our colophons; this focalization pattern must be distinguished from the explicit performative *tw.i ỉ.ỉrỉ.f/ỉrt* (*infra*). As for the use of focalization patterns in colophons, see David (2006: 110-1). Note that contrary to the opinions of Théodoridès (1965: 84 n.23), Allam (1967: 18)[482] and Eyre (1992: 211), it is not said that the sister accepts the transmission of property, but the emphatic remark about her presence signifies that she cannot ignore the testator's expression of will;

- Neo-Egyptian possessive determinator for kinship (*tꜣy.i sn*) and couple relationships (*tꜣy.i ḥmt*);
- deictic articloid (*pꜣ hrw* opposed to archaic, pre-material formulaic *hrw pn*).

* 'Classical' degree 0 forms used:
- hierarchically ordered list (diminishing progression).

* General dialectal features: degree 2.

* Legal formulae: - witnesses: *m-bꜣḥ mtryw ḳnw ꜥšꜣt* + function + PN
- special witness: *ptr* (direct address) + *ỉ.ỉrw.i swꜣḏ n* PN *m pꜣ hrw* + *m-bꜣḥ* PN (witnessing by a legal heir)

B. Act *sensu stricto*

The new complete date introduces a joint declaration by the couple (locutive plural mode) concerning the common acquisition of a slave, or at least a statement of the man attended by the testatrix. But then we encounter the *recital* of a will and related matters expressed in a singular locutive mode, obviously representing the voice of the testatrix. On the basis of the pre-material, the entire piece seems to be presented as the man's will, the joint acquisition being recorded as part of the *recital*[483]. But this is not consistent with the rest of the document presented exclusively as the record of the will of the testatrix in the singular locutive mode. It is clear that the will has been recorded after the companion of the testatrix died (see v°11: *ỉw.i m ḫꜣrt ỉw pꜣy.i hꜣy mttw*). The tentative reconstruction of the document by Cruze-Uribe (1988) as resulting from the couple's initiative to care for the children and emancipate them (while the husband was still alive) is unconvincing on a syntactic-textemic and contextual base: major use of female locutive forms except in excerpts of the man's will; grounding retributive principle of the verso relating to the past, not to the future, and to the widow only; nature of the will as a 'one voice act' and presence of preceding title deed.

The only possible way of understanding this part of the document is as a compressed presentation[484] of two separate events, the statement of the man[485] with the attendance[486] of *Rnnfr* concerning the joint acquisition of the slave, introduced as another title deed posterior to the man's will, and *Rnnfr*'s notarial will, with only one dated pre-material[487]. These two events

482 But Allam (1977: 94) admits that the agreement is not a verbal one, but represents a 'consentement tacite'.

483 On the controversy, see Gardiner (1940: 28-9) and Allam's summary (1990).

484 Compare with the missing curse in the record of the title deed.

485 Eyre (1992: 208, n.8) sees the joint declaration of purchase as 'an undated internal quotation (perhaps 'quoted' from undated oral memory rather than a written text).'

486 Concerning the attendency of beneficiaries or family members, see *supra*.

487 The date of the pre-material must be the one of the will of the testatrix, but the designation of the stating party and the attendant belong to the record of the joint acquisition of the slave.

are recorded as a unique deed representing the will of the testatrix. As it is conceived, the beginning of the document looks more like a 'matrimonial' community act under the man's name than as the woman's will; fortunately, we have already seen that a woman could dispose of her assets in her own name, without a man's assistance. Since the *recital* begins with the joint acquisition of the couple expressed in a plural locutive, a careless scribe may have thought it to be the man's initiative when copying the document[488].

1. Pre-material

Date: (13) *rnpt-sp* 18 *3bd* 1 *3ḫt sw* 10 *ḫr ḥm ni-swt bity nb t3wy Mnm3ʿtrʿ Stpnptḥ ʿ.w.s. s3 Rʿ nb ḫʿw* (14) *Rʿmss Ḫʿwmw3st Mryimn ḥk3 nṯr Ἰwnw di ʿnḫ ḏt r nḥḥ*
Year 18, month 1 of inundation, day 10, under (the) majesty of (the) King of Upper (and) Lower Egypt, Lord of (the) Two Lands, *Mnm3ʿtrʿ Stpnptḥ* L.P.H., son of Ra, Lord of (the) crowns, *Rʿmss Ḫʿwmw3st Mryimn,* divine ruler of Heliopolis, given life for ever (and) ever.

archaic anaphora: *hrw* (15) *pn*	This day
Title:	
legal step: *ḏdt*	of (the) statement
acting party: *n ḥry iḥ Nbnfr*	of (the) stable-master *Nbnfr*
attendant: *ḥnʿ ḥmt.f šmʿy n Stḫy Sprwmry Rnnfr*	with his woman, chantress of Seth of *Sprwmry, Rnnfr,*

* Neo-Egyptian characteristics: -
* 'Classical' degree 0 forms used:
  - traditional official texts binomials *ni-swt bity, ḏt r nḥḥ*, and trinomial *ʿnḫ wḏ3 snb*;
  - *di ʿnḫ*: see *EG* § 378;
  - archaic anaphora *hrw pn* + nominal form, neither an infinitive nor a relative neutrum *ḏdt.n.*N[489], but a verbal noun. The fact that *ḏdt* is used here instead of *ḏd* implies a clear process of abstractization, a feature well known in modern legal and bureaucratic dialects and by which concrete acts are made 'into static abstract concepts'[490]. Compare with earlier *S3mwt* tomb (lower inscription) dating from the reign of Ramesses II, where the text concerning the gift opens with # full date + *hrw pn ḏd n* N PN (...) *r-nty* #. The second part of *pAshmolean* 1945.95 opens with # short date + *hrw* {*n*} *pn n ḏd n* N PN # ;
  - relator for subject (*ḏdt n ḥry iḥ*) and religious dedication (*šmʿy n Stḫy*) relations;
* General dialectal features: degree 0.
* Legal formula: date (year, month of season, day + *ḫr ḥm* + royal titulary) + *hrw pn* + *ḏdt* (object) + *n* (acting party) + *ḥnʿ* N PN (attendant)

2. *Recital*

purpose marker: (16) *r-nty*	to wit:
grounded statement quotation:	

488 Gardiner (1940: 28-9) 'inaccuracies', 'carelessness or muddleheadedness'; Théodoridès (1965: 106-7): 'bévue (...) d'un scribe ultérieur', 'Il en résulte que nous n'avons pas devant nous le document original, mais une expédition de l'acte'.

489 *Contra*: Théodoridès (1965: 84).

490 Charrow, Crandall & Charrow (1982: 183).

in.nn ḥm Diwniḥwttiry r swnw iw.st ms pꜣy (17) 3 *ẖrdw wꜥ ꜥḥꜣ st-ḥmwt* 2 *dmḏ* 3 *iw.i iṯꜣy.w iw.i* (18) *sꜥnḫ.w iw.i dit iry.w pꜣ ꜥꜣ.w iw.i pḥ pꜣ hrw irm.w iw.w* (19) *tmt irt bin ḫr.i iw.w irt n.i nfr iw mn šriw šriw()* (20) *inn mntw iw ḥry iḥ Pndiw ꜥḳw r pꜣy.i pr iw.f irt Tꜣimnniwt* (21) *tꜣy.w sn(t) ꜥꜣ(t) m ḥm{w}t iw ink sw iw*[491] *pꜣy.i sn šriw <sw> iw.i šsptw.f* (22) *n.st sw m-di.st m pꜣ hrw ḫr ptri iry(.i) st m {m} rmṯ nmḥw n* (23) *pꜣ tꜣ n Pr-ꜥꜣ ꜥ.w.s. inn iw.st ms bn šriw bn šriw iw.w m rmṯ* (24) *nmḥw n pꜣ tꜣ n Pr-ꜥꜣ ꜥ.w.s. mitt ꜥḳꜣ sp sn iw.w irm ḥry iḥ Pndiw* (25) *pꜣy sn šriw ink iw nꜣ šriw irm tꜣy.w sn ꜥꜣt m pꜣ* (26) *pr n Pꜣdiw pꜣy ḥry iḥ pꜣy sn šriw ink*
We acquired (the) servant *Diwniḥwttiry* for a price; and she gave birth to these 3 children, one male, 2 females, total 3; and I took them, and I sustained them, and I enabled their growth. And I have reached this day with them, and they were not bad to me, (but rather,) they were good to me since there was no son (or) daughter besides them (**retributive principle**). And (the) stable-master *Pndiw* entered my house[492], and he made *Tꜣimnniwt,* their eldest sister, a woman[493], because mine he is, since <he is> my younger brother; and I accepted him for her. He is with her today.
And see, it is to the status of *nmḥw* person of the land of Pharaoh L.P.H that (I) have elevated her. Should she bear either a son or a daughter, they (will) have the status of *nmḥw* people of the land of Pharaoh L.P.H., indeed in exactly (the) same (manner), while they (= the brothers of *Tꜣimnniwt*) are with (the) stable-master *Pndiw*, this younger brother of mine, because these children are together with their elder sister in the house of *Pꜣdiw*, this stable-master, this younger brother of mine.

* Neo-Egyptian characteristics:

- purpose marker *r-nty*, introducing the content of the statement (*ḏdt*) direct speech and having a purpose meaning 'to let know that', 'to wit'. See *supra oGardiner/Ashmolean* 272, line 3: *ḏdt.n* N… *r-nty* (+ operative part);
- *in.nn*: perfect report form followed by a series of sequential past narratives[494], as we have already encountered in the *recital* of *Naunakhte*.
  It could theoretically be a that-form *in.n* without prothetic *yod*[495], nominal theme of the focalized adverbial rheme *r swnwt*, the cleft sentence highlighting the fact that the slave was in fact acquired with community property; but the legal *recital* is a narrative texteme that often uses the report + *iw.f ḥr sḏm* forms.
  The beginning of this *recital* is in strong contrast with the usual *ir ink…*;
- Neo-Egyptian spelling (*ḥm*, *šriw*, *sn*; *ptri*);
- delocutive singular feminine *st* and plural *w* suffixes;

491 Absent in *KRI*, but clearly present in hieratic and Gardiner's hieroglyphic version.

492 Gardiner (1935: 143) considered *ꜥḳ r pr* to be 'the technical term for entry upon marriage' as well as 'less regular sexual enterprises'; Pestman (1961: 10) and Toivari-Viitala (2001: 74 n.446) propose various meanings for the expression *ꜥḳ r pr*, and Toivari-Viitala suggests 'to propose or negotiate a marriage' in our text. The expression is obviously rather general, although it may mean cohabitation as in *pTurin* 2021-*pGeneva* D 409.

493 *Iri m ḥmt*: see *supra* the note concerning cohabitation and 'marriage' during pharaonic times.

494 Frandsen (1974: 87) and Groll (1984: 44); *LEG* §14.9.1 and for the suffix spelling 2.4.1.

495 For Winand (1992: 260), the perfect that-form *sḏm.n.f* disappeared after the reign of Ramesses II, was replaced by the perfect *sḏm.f,* and was already extremely rare during the 20th dynasty; but see *infra iry.i* and the use of classical that-forms in Ramesside royal decrees (David 2006: 181,185, 240, 246).

- Neo-Egyptian form of the infinitives (*ms*, *tmt*, *ꜥḳw*, *iṯꜣy*); for Groll (1984: 43), the infinitive *šsptw.f* is followed by the 'new dependent pronoun' *tw.f*, but it is more probably a Neo-Egyptian form of the infinitive with suffix object[496];
- replacement of the feminine  classifier by  (*iw.i dit iry.w, st-ḥmt, iw.i šsptw.f, tꜣy.w sn*(*t*));
- sequential narrative past forms in locutive and delocutive mode (omitted preposition) expressing the causal chain of events leading the testatrix to her decision (*iw.st ms, iw.i iṯꜣy.w, iw.i sꜥnḫ.w, iw.i dit, iw.i pḥ, iw.w tmt irt, iw.w irt, iw.*N *ꜥḳw, iw.f irt, iw.i šsptw.f*);
- Neo-Egyptian deictic determinator *pꜣy* used in nominal syntagms either with quantifier (# singular *pꜣy* + quantifier + plural N #: *pꜣy* 3 *ẖrdw*) or with already specific noun (# PN + (*pꜣy* N +) *pꜣy* N + attributive expansion + locutive independent pronoun #: *Pꜣdiw pꜣy ḥry iḥ pꜣy sn šriw ink*). Compare with *Naunakhte* (*pꜣy* 8 *bꜣkiw tn-myw; pꜣy* 8 *ẖrdw ink*);
- 3 *ẖrdw wꜥ ꜥḥꜣ st-ḥmwt* 2 *dmḏ* 3: determined noun representing a group followed by the list of its elements in the form # [lexical quantifier *wꜥ* + attributive expansion]♂ + [N + graphic quantifier]♀ + Total: graphic quantifier #. The list represents a repartition by gender with numerically increasing progression and male preeminence;
- *iry.w pꜣ ꜥꜣ.w*: Groll (1984: 57-8) states that *pꜣ* and the suffixed pronoun are incompatible, and thus she takes *pꜣ* to be 'the demonstrative which expresses belonging', a construction that 'does not exist in the Theban dialect';
- deictic articloid (*pꜣ hrw*) in the *recital* is opposed to archaic, formulaic *hrw pn* in the pre-material; furthermore it opposes the past purchase of the slave and the time of the locutive statement of the testatrix.
  Concerning the expression of the present situation of the testatrix, note that in *Naunakhte* II.4, the testatrix uses the stative in her *recital* (*ẖr ptri tw.i iꜣwt.ki* – with a verb of quality), while in *pAdoptions*, the dynamic sequential *iw.i pḥ* with deictic *pꜣ hrw* introduces a new event expressed by a verb of motion;
- Neo-Egyptian prepositions (*irm, m-di.st*). Note that when used with objects, *m-di.f* relates to possession; with people, it means close accompaniment[497], but not necessary guardianship;
- *iw.w tmt irt bin*: negative sequential past[498], with infinitive as 'negatival complement' following *tmt*.
  The link between the present (diminished) condition of the testator and the behavior of the heirs is made in *Naunakhte*, *oPetrie* 18 and *pAdoptions*, but with a different construction in the three instances. In *Naunakhte*, lines 4-5 (*ẖr ptri tw.i iꜣwt.ki ẖr ptri bn st ḥr irt ẖrt.i gr ink*), the bad treatment of the testatrix by some heirs is not an extension of the preceding sentence concerning the present elderly status of the testatrix, but is constructed on the same syntactic level, a parallel construction

496 See Winand (1992: 98-100) for a summary of the question; David (2006: 22-3).

497 Théodoridès (1958: 104-5).

498 For Groll (1984: 58-60), it is 'the negative equivalent of the circumstantial first present' (another of the characteristics of the 'Spermeru dialect' in her opinion) not a sequential past, since it refers 'to the same time span' as *iw.i pḥ pꜣ hrw*, so that *iw.w tmt irt bin* 'does not express a further step in the narration' but 'a necessary extension of the preceeding verbal formation'. But she does not see the preceding *iw.i iṯꜣy.w iw.i sꜥnḫ.w iw.i dit iry.w pꜣ ꜥꜣ.w* as a similar case, although both last *iw.i sḏm* forms appear to represent simultaneous actions. In *LEG* § 39.3.1 Ex. 1175, the same *iw.w tmt irt bin* is described as a negative sequential. Frandsen (1974: 87 Ex. 6) and Satzinger (1976: 240) view the form as a negative sequential past, the form of the negative converted present being *iw bn sw ḥr sḏm* (Frandsen 1974: 208). See also Winand (1992: 444).

introduced by the climax marker *ḫr ptri*, so that two 'simultaneous' elements of the narrative are expressed in the same form. In *oPetrie* 18, lines 6-7 (*bwpwy.sw irt n.i nfr rmṯ ist ꞽImnwꜥ* [*p꜃y.i šriw iw*]*.f ḥr irt n.i nfr iw.i g꜃bw.kwi*), the sequence has been inverted and the past diminished state of the testator expressed by a converted adverbial nexus with stative rheme adnexal to the bad/good behavior of the family. In *pAdoptions*, *iw.i pḥ p꜃ hrw irm.w iw.w tmt irt bin ḥr.i iw.w irt n.i nfr*, the not bad/good behavior of the heirs is on the same level as the arrival at the present situation, both expressed by sequential past forms. Note again the contrastive retributive principle with opposition of the negative element # *iw.w tmt irt bin* # preceding the positive one # *iw.w irt nfr* #. Thus, although the same relationship is established in the *recital* between the weak state of the testator and the assistance of the heir[499], it is not expressed in a uniform way by a fixed formula;

- *iw mn šriw šriw*(): converted non-existence of undetermined both genders filiation binomial. The converter is followed by *mn*, 'the negative counterpart of *wn*'[500], a contraction of *nn wn*.N[501].

  In preceding title deed, lines 4-5, we had *iw bn n.f šriw šriw*, with expression of the possessor[502]. In *oBM* EA 5624, we are told of a man *iw mn di.f šriw ꜥḥ꜃w* 'having no male child with him', with *di.f* for the possessor (see *LEG* § 29.5.1);
- *inn mntw*: # Neo-Egyptian exclusion particle *inn*[503] + delocutive independent pronoun #.
  Note the fact that *inn mntw* belongs to the same paradigm as preceding *r-ḥrw-r ink* in the *recital* of the title deed, line 5, and as *wpwt* PN in following oath, verso line 4;
- Neo-Egyptian possessive determinator for kinship (*t꜃y.w sn, p꜃y.i sn*) and ownership (*p꜃y.i pr*);
- *iw ink sw iw p꜃y.i sn šriw* <sw>: two converted nominal nexuses.
  The first expresses possession # *iw* converter + locutive independent pronoun (rheme, possessor) + delocutive dependent pronoun (theme, possessed) #. Although the rhematic possession construction is classical Middle Egyptian, its conversion is not[504].
  The second is identificative with # *iw* converter + determined nominal (theme) and missing dependent pronoun[505] (rheme) #.
- *ḫr ptri iry(.i) st m* {*m*} *rmṯ nmḥw*: # *ḫr* proclitic coordinator + Neo-Egyptian presentative *ptri* + topic-initial cleft sentence [*iry(.i)* perfect that-form[506] (without prothetic *yod*) theme + adverbial rheme *m nmḥw* (focus)] #. The cleft sentence

499 An idea similar to the image of 'staff of old age', the son (heir) who must support and care for his father.

500 Frandsen (1974: 171).

501 Polotsky (1960: 410, Obs. 1); Frandsen (1974: 283); Junge (2005: 172).

502 For Groll (1970: 23), the difference between the two patterns is that *iw bn n.f šriw* implies biological children, whereas *iw mn šriw* refers to adopted ones.

503 Gardiner (1940: 25 (e)); Černý (1941: 110-112) proposed the etymology '**in-nn-wn*', *contra*: Osing (1974) 'eine weitere Schreibvariante der neuägyptischen Partikel ; Green (1980: 22): 'non-initial, non-conditional and essentially prepositional', from Neo-Egyptian *m-bi꜃t*. Green's new reading of *inn mntw* in *pAdoptions* as two independent pronouns is rather dubious, and his last example from a 20th dynasty graffito (*ibid.*, 25) confirms the paradigm (*y꜃ mn m-di.i wꜥ inn mnt*{*i*}'Indeed, I have no one but you').

504 See Junge (2005: 170-1).

505 Théodoridès (1965: 86) completes *iw(.f m) p꜃y.i sn šri* instead of the proposed reconstruction with the dependent pronoun.

506 Groll (1984: 44): a form with 'pluperfect' tense value.

highlights the status conferred by the testatrix on the servant. The form of the feminine dependent pronoun object of *iry(.i)* is an archaism at this linguistic stage.
The climax of the *recital* is introduced by the cohesive *ḫr* and the marker of involvement *ptri*, as in *Naunakhte*'s *recital*, lines II.4-5, and consists here of the new status attained by the girl due to the testatrix. Again this construction ends the chain of sequentials and the narrative *sensu stricto*, and opens the commentary part of the *recital*, exposing the main grounds for her decisions in the operative part;

- *m {m} rmṯ nmḥw*: preposition redundancy[507], a Neo-Egyptian feature usually observed with the proposition *r*. The use of the « *m* of predication » for the focus of the cleft sentence is consistent with the fact that the *nmḥw* status of the servant is acquired, not intrinsic;
- cataphoric articloid (*pꜣ tꜣ n pr-ꜥꜣ; pꜣ pr n Pꜣdiw*);
- *inn iw.st ms bn šriw bn šriw iw.w m rmṯ nmḥw*: condition protasis # Neo-Egyptian *inn* conditional[508] + *iw.f (r) sḏm* (future)[509] # and adverbial nexus apodosis # *iw.w m* N #. The condition expresses the legal repercussions of the measure taken by the testatrix in favor of her brother's wife on the status of children to come. Due to the action of the testatrix, in the event that children are born, they will automatically acquire their mother's new status. The birth of children is the essential conditioning event, the unknown element of the equation[510], but the consequence of the birth is straightforward for the testatrix, the acquisition of the *nmḥw* status is presented as a present generic statement[511] (the adverbial apodosis is a further case of a non-converted *iw*-sentence inherited from Middle Egyptian in legal context[512]). The attitude of the testatrix towards the reality of the condition is neutral, unmarked[513];

507 For preposition redundancy in Ramesside royal decrees, see David (2006: 98-9, 225-6).

508 The *inn*-condition is 'auf die nichtliterarischen Texte beschränkt' (Satzinger 1976: 108).

509 Satzinger (1976: 106) notes that *inn*-protases may be constructed with *iw.f r/ḥr sḏm inter alia*, and when the protasis is constructed with the present, the apodosis has a future meaning (illustrated by an example showing the same apodosis as ours: *LRL* 68, 2 = *pBN* 198 II, line 12 *ḥr inn tw.k ḏd ꜥrw nꜣ iw.i m nmḥw* 'And if you say "Out from here!," I shall be a *nmḥw*' (Černý 1941: 108 ex. 14). For *LEG* § 17.10.1, 'there apparently exists neither a **inn iw bn sw (ḥr) stp.f* formation nor a **inn iw.f (ḥr) tm stp.f* formation, but a *inn bn iw.f (r) stp.f* formation does exist'.
For Shisha-Halevy (1978: 58), it is a case of thematization of the conditional protasis in a cleft sentence, the focus being on the adverbial apodosis.

510 For Frandsen (1974: 49) and Green (1980), the construction is a realis condition. For Satzinger (1976: 108) the future protasis expresses 'weniger ausgeprägt' potential condition compared to other examples. For Groll (1984: 45), the future protasis expresses a 'distant and hypothetical' future. Concerning the criterium of classification of conditional sentences adopted here, see note *infra*.

511 Junge (2005: 126) contends that the apodosis is a '*iw*-sentence expressing future time' (see also Winand 1996: 137 'construction analogique du future III'), but as in the case of *iw.f n* N, the adverbial nexus is NOT a future statement.

512 See Satzinger (1976: 106) for the independent constructions in the apodosis of *inn*-condition sentences. For Groll (1984: 58), it is a 'main clause', *iw* functioning both as 'a base of a non-initial main clause' and as exponent of future (as in *iw.f (ḥr) tm sḏm* of the 'Theban dialect'). It is another characteristic of the 'Spermeru dialect' for her, as usually only the *iw* converter may be followed by adverbial phrases. But we have already noted other Middle Egyptian non-converted adverbial nexuses, probably explained by legal conservatism and the desire to convey a high register feel rather than by topolect (see e.g. *iw.f n* PN and *iw.f ḥry* 100 *n sḫ supra* in examples from the Theban area). Frandsen (1974: 50) notes that 'It has been maintained that the apodosis of conditional sentences should be *iw.f ḥr sḏm* (…), but our material as well as De. evidence shows this to be incorrect.'

513 See Funk (1985) concerning the typology of conditional sentences and the criterium of the speaker's attitude towards the reality of the condition.

- *bn šriw bn šriw*: Neo-Egyptian positive disjuncter *bn* placed before each of the two objects of *iw.st ms* (same lexeme, different gender). Note that in the motives of the title deed, no disjuncter is used with gender filiation binomial (*iw bn n.f šriw šriw*).
  Gardiner (1940: 25 (*h*)) suggests that *bn… bn* is to be regarded as the interrogative *n*(*ꜣ*)…*n*(*ꜣ*), 'unknown elsewhere';
- *iw.w m nmḥw mitt ꜥkꜣ sp sn*: # adverbial nexus + adverbial expansion (*m-*)*mitt* (Neo-Egyptian omission of preposition) + intensifiers *ꜥkꜣ* (intensity expression) and *sp sn* (intensity iteration) # (see *infra mi-ḳdw ꜥkꜣ sp sn*). Compare with *Naunakhte*'s documents conformity (*iw.w m-mitt ꜥkꜣ sp sn*);
- *iw.w irm ḥry iḥ Pndiw*: converted actual present adverbial nexus, the rheme consisting of the Neo-Egyptian preposition *irm* followed by an expanded noun;
- anaphoric articloid (*nꜣ šriw*);

* 'Classical' degree 0 forms used:
- relator *n* used in 'citizenship'/residence and dominion (*nmḥw n pꜣ tꜣ n Pr-ꜥꜣ*), and ownership relations (*pr n Pꜣdiw*);
- *iry.w*: modal prospective object of *rdi*, with final *-y* as *3ae inf.* verbs in Middle Egyptian[514].
  Groll (1984: 57) regards it as a passive form, the equivalent of 'Theban dialect' *iri.tw*, but it seems that we must regard *iri pꜣ ꜥꜣ.w* as an active expression in which *.w* is the plural delocutive actor, lit. 'they may do their growth';
- *sw m-di.st m pꜣ hrw*: non-converted actual present adverbial nexus (albeit with Neo-Egyptian preposition, delocutive suffix, and temporal deictic *m pꜣ hrw*). This is a statement constating a situation, not a performative speech act;
- *iw nꜣ šriw irm tꜣy.w sn*: converted adverbial nexus (the basic construction is classical, but with several Neo-Egyptian elements, see *supra*);

* General dialectal features: degree 2.

* Legal formula: *recital* = *r-nty* + *ir.nn* (report) + *iw.f/i sḏm* (narrative of positive behavior of the testator) + *iw.w tmt irt bin ḥr.i iw.w irt n.i nfr* (positive behavior of the legatees) + *iw mn šriw šriw*() (absence of other legal heirs) + *ḫr ptri* (commentary: main ground)

3. Operative part

Since the main ground of the deed is that the eldest sister has become a *nmḥw*, and thus her children will have the same status, the first provision in the operative part is the 'adoption' of the brother of the testatrix in order that he may inherit. The sequence is perfectly logical. The next step is to protect the status of the children, and finally to deal with the partition of the assets of the testatrix, the testamentary disposition *sensu stricto*. Note the absence of a tag clause preceding the adoption provision, as though this performative utterance still belonged to the *recital* in spite of the syntactic form used (explicit performative); *ḏd.st* precedes the *terrorem* clause.

Adoption:
tw.i i.iri.f n.i (v. 1) *m šriw m pꜣ hrw mi-ḳdw ꜥkꜣ sp sn*
I make him (= *Pndiw*) for me as a son today very precisely in every respect.
***Terrorem* clause**:

514 Polotsky (1976: 23-4); for Neo-Egyptian: Winand (1992: 222).

ḏd.st wꜣḥ Ỉmn wꜣḥ pꜣ (2) *ḥḳꜣ ꜥ.w.s. tw.ỉ ỉrt nꜣ rmṯ* [*m šrỉw.ỉ/ỉwꜥ.ỉ/nmḥw*?][515] *ỉ.ỉrw.ỉ spẖr.w*[516] *m rmṯ nmḥw* (3) *n pꜣ tꜣ n Pr-ꜥꜣ ꜥ.w.s. mtw šrỉw šrỉwt sn snt n tꜣy.w mwt* (4) *pꜣy.w ỉt mdwt ỉm.w wpwt Pndỉw pꜣ(y) šrỉw ỉnk ỉw* (5) *bn st m-dỉ.f m bꜣkỉw m rꜣ-ꜥ ỉwnꜣ ỉw.w m-dỉ.f m snw šrỉw* (6) *ỉw.w m rmṯ nmḥw n pꜣ tꜣ nk sw ꜥꜣwt nk ꜥꜣwt ḥmt.f pꜣ nty ỉw.f* (7) *ḏd bꜣkỉ r wꜥ ỉm.w*

She said: May Amun be clement, may the ruler L.P.H. be clement, I make these people (= the two brothers of *Tꜣỉmnnỉwt*) [as my children/my heirs/*nmḥw*?]. It is as *nmḥw* people of the land of Pharaoh L.P.H. that I register them; and should a son, a daughter, a brother, a sister of their mother (or of) their father contest it, except *Pndỉw* this son of mine, since they are not with him as personnel anymore, being with him as young siblings (and) having (the) status of *nmḥw* people of this land, may the donkey copulate[517] with him, may the donkey copulate with his woman, whomever shall call servant[518] one of them.

***Descent and distribution* rule**:

ỉnn wnw m-dỉw.ỉ ꜣḥwt m sḫt ỉnn (8) *wnw m-dỉw.ỉ ḫt nb n (=m) pꜣ tꜣ ỉnn wnw m-dỉw.ỉ šꜣwꜣtyw ỉw.w pš.w n* (9) *pꜣy.ỉ 4 ẖrdw ỉw Pꜣdỉw m wꜥ ỉm.w*

If there should be in my possession fields in (the) country, if there should be in my possession any assets in this land, if there should be in my possession *šꜣwꜣtyw*[519], they will divide them for my 4 children, *Pꜣdỉw* being as one of them.

Grounded designation of executor:

ỉr nꜣ mdwt ỉ.ḏd.ỉ (10) *r-ḏr.w sp sn st swꜣḏ n Pꜣdỉw pꜣy šrỉw ỉnk ỉrt n.ỉ nfr* (11) *ỉw.ỉ m ẖꜣrt ỉw pꜣy.ỉ hꜣy mttw*

As for the full and complete statement[520] that I made, it is entrusted to *Pꜣdỉw*, this child of mine who has been good to me since I became a widow for my man is dead (**retribution**).

* Neo-Egyptian characteristics:

- *tw.ỉ ỉ.ỉrỉ.f*: locutive present, preposition omitted, with a prothetic *yod* Neo-Egyptian infinitive[521] followed by its object delocutive suffix[522]. Another present form in line v.2 (*tw.ỉ ỉrt*) is regulary constructed, although also without preposition. The value of the form is indubitably here an explicit performative[523], with *m pꜣ hrw* acting as a marker of performativity (proximal deixis). Vernus (1985) has underlined the fact that Egyptian performative statements are carried by various patterns (*sḏm.n.ỉ*, *ỉw.ỉ ḥr sḏm* in Old and Middle Egyptian[524]; *tw.ỉ (ḥr) sḏm* in Neo-Egyptian); to these we can add the

515 The crucial segment is lost.

516 Théodoridès (1965: 88 n.42 'métathèse') and Allam (1967: 18) correct *sphr* in *spẖr* (to bring up) as in *oVarille* 30.

517 See Janssen (1988b) for New Kingdom pejorative sense of an otherwise Old/Middle Kingdom neutral verb.

518 In this particular case, we cannot agree with Hofmann (2006: 115) who regards *bꜣk* during the Ramesside Period as a collective expression to be translated as 'personnel.'

519 Théodoridès (1958: 104-5): merchants; Cruz-Uribe (1988: 223, n.6): merchandises.

520 Théodoridès (1965: 135): 'toutes les affaires'. He understands the sentence as designating the adopted brother as a *gérant d'affaire*, since he does not regard this document as the will of *Nꜣnfr* (*ibid*., n. 222), but 'une expédition de l'acte d'adoption délivrée à Pédiou' (*ibid*., 84 'déclaration d'adoption').

521 Winand (1992: 86).

522 *LEG* § 11.2.3.

523 Gunn (1924: 69-74), Stricker (1938: 83-4), Frandsen (1974: 53), Satzinger (1976: 124-5): 'synchronous present', the authors sometimes adding intuitively 'hereby' to their translation of the sentence; Heckel (1957: 23-5, 46) concerning the Old Perfective 'im Koinzidenzfall' quotes *Psalm* 33, 9 'So er spricht, so geschiehts', a neat definition of the performative; *LEG* § 19.4.1: 'present continuous'. For the value of 'hereby' in the performative environment, see Kurzon (1986: 6-7).

524 Vernus (1985: 315 n. 15) mentions the use of the performative *dỉ.n.ỉ* in testamentary dispositions of the Old Kingdom (*Nkꜣwrꜥ tomb*, 4th dynasty and *Wpmnfrt tomb*, 5th dynasty). Performative present is attested in 12th

implicit performative *iw.f n*.N as well as the pattern found in oaths (*iw.f ẖry* 100 *n sẖ*). Of course not all instances of *tw.i* (*ḥr*) *sḏm* are performative; it depends on the desire of the speaker to create the legal effect and the context of the utterance, its 'felicity conditions'. But in the dispositive of a will, with the marker of performativity *m pꜣ hrw*, these conditions are met; in a scalar perspective, *tw.i* (*ḥr*) *sḏm m pꜣ hrw* represents a true performative utterance, and it is used first to effect the legal fiction of adoption.
As for the contents, the testatrix acts in conformity with the counsel given in *oBerlin* P 10627, a 20th dynasty letter to a scribe, the second and last Ramesside document relating to adoption; a man writes the following to the addressee (lines 9-13): *ir pꜣ nty iw mn* {*ir*} *m-di.f ꜥḏdw ḫr in.f n.f ky nmḥw sḫprw.f mntf dit mw r ḏ(rw)t.f* {*tw.k*} *m šriw ꜥꜣ n ḥꜥt.f* 'As for the one who has no children, he should acquire for himself another one, a *nmḥw* (orphan; voiceless), so that he may bring him up. It is him who will put water on his hands as eldest son of his flesh';

- deictic articloid (*m pꜣ hrw*), marker of performativity;
- tag clause *ḏd.st*: see *supra*. The perfect report introduces a quoted direct speech of the testatrix (*terrorem* clause);
- Neo-Egyptian delocutive singular feminine *st* and plural *w* suffixes, and delocutive plural dependent pronoun *st*;
- exophoric articloid (extratextual deixis) referring to the reigning king (*pꜣ ḥkꜣ*) and Egypt (*pꜣ tꜣ* in line 6);
- *tw.i irt nꜣ rmṯ* [*m šriw.i*?]: second locutive performative (Vernus 1985: 310), this time included in the threatening oath;
- anaphoric articloid (*nꜣ rmṯ*);
- *i.irw.i spḫrw m rmṯ nmḥw*: relatively present analytic that-form with prothetic *yod*, theme of a cleft sentence with adverbial rheme-focus including prominent lexeme *nmḥw*;
- cataphoric articloid (*pꜣ tꜣ n pr-ꜥꜣ*);
- *mtw*.N *mdt*: atemporal conjunctive in the delocutive apodosis (the 'crime', see *supra*) of the threatening oath.

The threatening/damnation oath represents a third form of oath alongside the *promissory* and *assertory* ones, although it is generally not recognized as such in Egyptological studies: Wilson (1948: 148) classifies this oath in his 'promissory oath in a juridical setting' category, for Théodoridès (1965: 87 n.40, 112), it is not an oath but 'une simple imprécation d'origine populaire', and Nordh (1996: 3) notes that a curse is aimed at a recipient 'who must be somebody else than the sender, otherwise it is an oath'. But our *terrorem* clause uses the formulary protasis (*wꜣḥ Ỉmn wꜣḥ pꜣ ḥkꜣ ꜥ.w.s*) and the apodosis (*mtw*.N *mdwt im.w*) of an oath, so that formally it must be associated with it, although this 'oath' is not introduced by the usual *irwy.st ꜥnḫ nb ꜥ.w.s. m-ḏd*, but by *ḏd.st,* and the threatening element is central here. The main qualification issue is due to the fact that the threatening oath (*wꜣḥ Ỉmn wꜣḥ pꜣ ḥkꜣ ꜥ.w.s.* (…) *mtw šriw šriw sn sn n tꜣy.w mwt pꜣy.w it mdwt im.w* (…) *nk sw ꜥꜣwt nk ꜥꜣwt ḥmt.f pꜣ nty iw.f ḏd bꜣki r wꜥ im.w*) is cut first by a performative related to the children's status (*tw.i irt nꜣ rmṯ* [*m šriw.i/iwꜥ.i/nmḥw*?] *i.irw.i spḫr.w m rmṯ nmḥw n pꜣ tꜣ n Pr-ꜥꜣ ꜥ.w.s.*) and then by a long comment concerning the brother of the testatrix and the children (*wpwt Pndiw pꜣ(y) šriw ink iw bn st m-di.f m bꜣkiw m rꜣ-ꜥ iwnꜣ iw.w m-di.f m snw šriw iw.w m rmṯ nmḥw n*

dynasty dispositions from *pKahun* VII.1 (*iw.i ḥr rdit pꜣy.i mty n sꜣ n* N, concerning an onerous gift) and *pKahun* I.1 (*iw.i ḥr irt imyt-pr n ḥmt.i; iw.i ḥr rdit n.s*), both without marker of performativity.

pꜣ tꜣ), in a way that is reminiscent of modern legalese structure: 'extreme precision' combined with 'misplaced phrases, injected in middle of clauses' (*hyperbaton*) and 'subordinate clause embeddings'[525], 'long sentences and complex sentence structure' and 'statement of exceptions within the rule'[526].

Wilson (1948: 148) suggests that the curse may be used 'because the customary law of Egypt was inadequate to protect her desires'. But this may not be the only reason to record a curse in the written text. It may be interesting (albeit audacious), to compare the Egyptian case with the situation of another oral culture in transition to literacy, since this transition implies at a certain point the mobilization of resources in order to confer on the newborn text the authority that only the spoken word had until then. The rather distant example of curses in ancient Anglo-Saxon wills presented below may suggest some reflections concerning the use of threats in Ramesside testamentary provisions; of course, the comparison has its limits.

By the end of the first millennium A.D., at a time of the transition to literacy in medieval Europe, 'Anglo-Saxons felt it prudent to end the will with a curse on anyone who meddled with its terms.'[527] As in ancient Egypt Late Period donation stelae where there is an increased use of curses of the type we meet here, donations of property to the Church in Anglo-Saxon documents made an abundant use of curses, and sometimes a sacralized version of the documents was publicized as in the ancient Egyptian context. The Anglo-Saxon curses had a highly formulaic structure very similar to that of Egyptian curses ('If anyone does X, may he suffer Y'). Danet & Bogoch (1992, 1992b, 1994), in an extensive research on the subject showed that the curses were not mere residues of a performative oral ceremony that preceded the record of the will, but 'second-order performatives' 'mobilised to strengthen the performative potential of the *document*'[528] at a time when the written act itself began to be invested with some authority. The function of the curses was not merely to protect the document as an object against physical damage but also its provisions, thus treating the text of documents as potentially performative, since the text created legally binding situations requiring long-term preservation. There was quite a high degree of 'stylization' in Anglo-Saxon curses: assonance, symmetrical structure and complex parallelisms, use of binomials, end-weight principle, verbal repetition, pairing with a blessing were all used to give weight to the written word and play the 'magic flute' that reinforces the sense of control over uncontrollable elements (compare with *wꜣḥ Ỉmn wꜣḥ pꜣ ḥḳꜣ ; šrỉw šrỉw sn sn n tꜣy.w mwt pꜣy.w ỉt ; nk sw ꜥꜣwt nk ꜥꜣwt ḥmt.f*). These curses invoked pagan beliefs and the views of the Church about sin and afterlife:

> 'And he who shall detract from my will which I have now declared in the witness of God (…) may he be delivered into the abyss of hell to Satan the devil and all his accursed companions and there suffer with God's adversaries, without end, and never trouble my heirs.'[529]

This invoking of Satan and hell is reminiscent of the function of the Egyptian curses as 'verbalized rituals, as execration rituals' 'aimed at generating Maat by annihilating the

525 Charrow, Crandall & Charrow (1982: 176-7).

526 *ibid.*, p. 184.

527 Tiersma (1999: 11). Of course, in the case of *pAdoptions*, the curse does not specifically reinforce the testamentary dispositions except the one concerning the children's status; but it is used in a testamentary context.

528 Danet & Bogoch (1994: 113-5).

529 Danet & Bogoch (1994: 114).

enemies of Maat'[530]; the donkey in *pAdoptions* is perhaps to be viewed as a Sethian animal, although Seth's mythical animal image must not be confused with the donkey[531].

The *pAdoptions'* curse resembles the *no-contest clause* of the modern Anglo-American legal system; note that these modern *no-contest clauses* are also called *(in) terrorem* clauses.

The *Amarah stela* (*Stela Brooklyn* 38.544) also has a *terrorem* clause inscribed along its section: *ir p3 nty iw.f mdt im.f iri ỉmn-Rˁ ni-swt nṯrw m-s3.f r s3s3.f Mwt m-s3 ḥmt.f Ḫnsw m-s3 ẖrd.f ḥḳr.f* 'As for the one who will contest it, Amun-Re, King of the Gods, is after him in order to repel him, Mut is after his wife, Khonsu is after his child so that he will starve'[532]. See also David (2006: 102-3, 124) for curses in Ramesside royal decrees; Spiegelberg (1903: 190ff) for sexual curses of the Late Period;

- Neo-Egyptian possessive determinator for kinship and other close relationships (*t3y.w mwt, p3y.w it, p3y.i* 4 *ẖrdw, p3y.i h3y*);
- *wpwt* PN: Neo-Egyptian omission of preposition in the contrast/exclusion compound *wpwt-ḥr* (see *supra* other forms of exception expressions: *inn mntw*; *r-ḥrw-r ink*). The same omission has been noted in Ramesside royal decrees (David 2006: 150);
- *Pndiw p3(y) šriw ink*: kinship relation expressed by # PN + Neo-Egyptian deictic *p3(y)* + N + *ink* locutive independent pronoun possessor #. See lines 6 and 25 *supra,* and *oGardiner/Ashmolean* 272;
- *iw bn st m-di.f m b3kiw m r-ˁ iwn3*: converted present adverbial nexus negated by *bn… iwn3,* followed by a parallel positive sentence (*iw.w m-di.f m snw šriw iw.w m rmṯ nmḥw*);
- *m r3-ˁ*: Neo-Egyptian adverbial modifier in trailing position, see *oPetrie* 18 verso 8;
- Neo-Egyptian spelling (*ˁ3wt, b3ki, sw3ḏ, šriw*);
- *šriw šriw sn sn n t3y.w mwt p3y.w it*: absence of disjuncter between both gender binomials of contestants (note that the feminine follows the masculine, except for the ascendants with possessive *t3y.w mwt p3y.w it*).

  Similar lists are known in the same context already during the Second Intermediate Period, e.g. *Stèle juridique de Karnak* JE 52453, lines 9-10: *s3 nb s3t nbt sn nb snt nbt* (see *supra*). See also Théodoridès (1965: 94-5) who underlines the formula's adaptability to circumstances; Rabinowitz (1958: 146) for similar lists of binomials in Aramaic papyri;
- *p3 nty iw.f ḏd*: cataphoric *p3* substantivizing a relative clause constituting a future apposition (preposition omission) to *šriw šriw sn sn n t3y.w mwt p3y.w it* and to their singular masculine resumption *sw* and *ḥmt.f*;
- *inn wnw m-diw.i* N… *iw.w pšw*: three condition protases # Neo-Egyptian *inn* conditional + *wnw* (existence)[533] + Neo-Egyptian compound preposition *m-diw.i* (possessor) + undetermined N (possessed assets, actor of *wnw*) # followed by one future apodosis (preposition omission) exposing the *descent and distribution* rules with

530 Nordh (1996: 97).

531 See te Velde (1967: *esp.* 8-14 and n. 4 on page 14).

532 Théodoridès (1964: 65).

533 See Černý (1941: 109 e-f, 111): *wnw* + noun 'equivalent of Middle Egyptian '. In *LEG* § 28.5-6, the *wnw m-diw.i* N construction is regarded as a development of *wn*.N; *m-di* became inseparable from *wn*, the noun was 'felt to be a direct object', expressing present tense. For Junge (2005: 172), this construction uses an adjectival form of the existential *wn*.

equal partition between coheirs. As in the conditional sentence *supra*, the attitude of the testatrix towards the reality of the condition is neutral, unmarked; in case there are assets remaining at the time of her death (essential conditioning event, the unknown element of the equation), they will be divided. The testatrix takes into account the possibility of the absence of assets in the future, as one of the essential conditions of a will is the existence of assets at the time of the testator' death[534].

The isotopic # *inn wnw m-diw.i* N # divides the list of assets into categories, beginning with immovable (land), through non-specific movable assets (*ḫt nb*), to specific movables[535]. The same characteristic reference to the unknown importance of the heirloom by the time of its transmission and list of categorized assets are fixtures of modern wills: 'I give, devise and bequeath all of the said rest, residue and remainder of my property which I may own at the time of my death, real, personal and mixed, of whatsoever kind and nature and wheresoever situate, including all property which I may acquire or to which I may become entitled after the execution of this will, in equal shares, absolutely and forever, to (…)'[536].

Note that the 6th dynasty *Balat tablet* 5955 uses another type of conditional provision, with implicit performative form, in its brief operative part concerning attribution of ownership and heir substitution: *ir ꜥnḫ sꜣ.i iw išt.i nb n.f* (…) *ir swt mwt.f iw išt.i nb n msw* [PN] 'in case my son should live, all my assets belong to him (…) but in case he should die, all my assets belong to [PN]'s children';

- *ir nꜣ mdwt i.ḏd.i… st swꜣḏ n* PN: entrustment formula expressed by topicalized expanded noun representing the *dispositions* # *ir* (topicalizer) + *nꜣ* (cataphoric) + N + *i.ḏd.i* (Neo-Egyptian relative form with prothetic *yod*) # followed by an unconverted adverbial generic present nexus (Neo-Egyptian delocutive plural pronoun *st* + stative *swꜣḏ*).

  Frandsen (1974: 60) notes that present # *sw* + stative # pattern in Neo-Egyptian is only attested in judicial texts as an archaism (his examples are almost all from the *Tomb Robberies* papyri and from letters).

  It is not absolutely clear if it is the instrument itself that was confided to the executor's care for safekeeping[537] or the responsibility to execute its provisions as it states that *nꜣ mdwt* are *swꜣḏ* to him (the provisions are marked as topic in order to achieve an 'objective' style again). The appointment of an executor/administrator is also attested in the lawsuits of *pBerlin* P 9010 (6th dynasty), *Mes* and *pBerlin* P 3047 (19th dynasty);
- PN *pꜣy šriw ink irt n.i nfr*: perfect participle *irt* (without prothetic *yod* but with non-pertinent feminine mark) used as adnominal expansion of PN *pꜣy šriw ink*[538].

  Other interpretations[539] neglect the function of this statement: justifying, grounding a positive measure in favor of a person by mentioning its beneficiary's past and present good behavior; similar phraseology is used e.g. in *oGardiner/Ashmolean* 90 v.1-3 with # PN *pꜣ*[*y.i šri*] *nty nfrw n.i* # and in *oPetrie* 18, lines 6-7 with # PN [*pꜣy.i šriw iw.*]*f ḥr irt n.i nfr* # following an independent perfect negative statement concerning another person.

---

534 Finegan (1982: 116-7) has underlined the frequent use of conditional sentences in modern testaments, since it is ultimately contingent on an unknown future.

535 For other categories of assets in testamentary lists, see e.g. 22nd dynasty *Nḫtfmwti statue Cairo* CG 42208 and the *Amarah stela* (Stela Brooklyn 38.544) from the end of the New Kingdom.

536 Tirsma (1999: 249).

537 Eyre (1992: 213).

538 The alternative reconstruction of a converted present (*iw.f ḥr*) *irt* is also possible.

539 For example Cruz-Uribe (1988: 221, n.2) for whom it is a dependent prospective *ir.t(w)* form.

In private autobiographies (e.g. *Denderah*, pl. 8C – First Intermediate Period) and eulogic-propagandist texts (e.g. *pHarris* I, 79, 2-3 – 20th dynasty), the same expression *ỉri nfr* is also used, relating to past action, for auto-justification or praise. The expression represents the accomplishment of Maat, and as such it is used as a justificative assumption (see *supra* the retributive principle). For Eyre (1992: 215), 'The formulae referring to good treatment by children has (*sic*) the appearance of a formal declaration of recognition; in practice the function of a 'will' is to recognize the heir(s)'; but the primary function of a will is to *designate* legatees and *organize* the transmission of assets in a different way from intestate rules and in so doing, the provisions must be motivated;

* 'Classical' degree 0 forms used:

- *m šriw mỉ-ḳdw ꜥḳꜣ sp sn*: extent of the adopted child's rights expressed with # adverbial *mỉ-ḳdw* + intensifiers *ꜥḳꜣ* (intensity expression) and *sp sn* (intensity iteration) #. See *supra* (*m-*)*mitt ꜥḳꜣ sp sn*;
- *wꜣḥ*.PN/*pꜣ ḥḳꜣ*: modal prospective in the protasis of the oath;
- relator *n* in kinship (*šriw šriw sn sn n tꜣy.w mwt pꜣy.w ỉt*), 'citizenship'/residence and dominion relations (*nmḥw n pꜣ tꜣ n Pr-ꜥꜣ*);
- *nk ꜥꜣwt*: imprecatory modal prospective[540].

  It is apparently one of the first uses of the specific sexual threat implying bestial copulation in a Ramesside text, along with Deir el-Bahari graffito n.11 of the 20th dynasty (*nk sw ꜥꜣ nk ꜥꜣ ḥmt(.f)*)[541]. It becomes a stereotyped formula in Late Period donation stelae[542]. Note that a sexual threat is also present in the 21st dynasty copy of a 18th dynasty decree, *stela BM* 138: *ẖꜥ.tw ḥmt.sn ỉrty ḥr nw* 'their wife shall be raped while (their) eyes are watching'.

  Prominent rhythmic factors such as parallelism, binomials, assonance and the iterative use of a verb (*nk; wꜣḥ*) magnify the magical quality of the word, and are thus major tools used in curses. The same prosodic features are noted by Danet and Bogoch (1992b: 152-6) in ancient Anglo-Saxon legal documents using curses;
- *ỉw*.PN *m wꜥ ỉm.w*: converted adverbial nexus (present);
- *ỉr nꜣ mdwt r-ḏr.w sp sn*: # determined noun + *r-ḏr.w* augens + intensity iteration #. We chose to render the isotopy device by a binomial used in modern legalese ('full and complete') that also has a prosodic effect;
- *ỉw.i m ẖꜣrt ỉw pꜣy.i hꜣy mttw*: two converted adverbial nexuses, the first one with prepositional phrase rheme, the second with stative rheme.

  The pleonasm (a form of lexemic isotopy) emphasizes the circumstances in which the positive behavior of the executor has been most helpful (grounding his designation);

* General dialectal features: degree 2.

* Legal formulae:

- adoption: *tw.i ỉ.ỉri.f n.i m šriw* (performative) + *m pꜣ hrw* + *mỉ-ḳdw ꜥḳꜣ sp sn* (extent of rights)

540 See David (2006: 124, 128) for examples of imprecatory prospectives in Ramesside royal decrees.

541 Nordh (1996: 90).

542 See Spiegelberg (1903); Sottas (1913: 152-4, 165-6); Janssen (1968: 171, pl. 25) for the *Dakhla stela Ashmolean Museum* 1894.107b (*nk sw ꜥꜣwt nk ꜥꜣwt ḥmt.f nk ḥmt.f .f*, with incest); Allam (1973: 261-2) for further references.

- *terrorem* clause (threatening oath): *wꜣḥ Ỉmn wꜣḥ pꜣ ḥḳꜣ* (imprecative) + *tw.ỉ ỉrt nꜣ rmṯ m rmṯ nmḥw* (performative) + *mtw šrỉw šrỉw sn sn mdwt ỉm.w* (third party contestation) + *wpwt* PN (exception) + *nk sw ꜥꜣwt nk ꜥꜣwt ḥmt.f* (curse) + *pꜣ nty ỉw.f ḏd bꜣkỉ r wꜥ ỉm.w*
- *descent and distribution* rules: *ỉnn wnw m-dỉw.ỉ* N (condition of existence of assets) + *ỉw.w pšw* + *n pꜣy.ỉ* 4 *ẖrdw* (beneficiaries)
- executor designation: *ỉr nꜣ mdwt ỉ.ḏd.ỉ r-ḏr.w sp sn st swꜣḏ n* PN (executor) + *ỉrt n.ỉ nfr* + circumstances (ground)

4. Colophon

Witnesses: *m-bꜣḥ mtrtyw ḳnw* (12) *ꜥšꜣ ḥry ỉḥ Sṯḫymḥb šmꜥy n Sṯḫy Tꜣywḥry ꜥḥtyw* (13) *Swꜥwyỉmn m-bꜣḥ Tꜣymwtnfr šmꜥy n ꜥnty Tỉntnbḥwt* In presence of very numerous witnesses: (the) stable-master *Sṯḫymḥb*, (the) singer of Seth *Tꜣywḥry*, (the) farmer *Swꜥwyỉmn*; in presence of *Tꜣymwtnfr*, (the) singer of *ꜥnty*[543], *Tỉntnbḥwt*.

* Neo-Egyptian characteristics:
  - Neo-Egyptian spelling (*šmꜥy*); note also the spelling of *ꜥšꜣ* and *mtrtyw*, compared to title deed *m-bꜣḥ mtryw ḳnw ꜥšꜣt*;

* 'Classical' degree 0 forms used:
  - relator *n* in religious dedication relation (*šmꜥy n Sṯḫy/ ꜥnty);*

* General dialectal features: degree 1.

* Legal formula: witnesses: *m-bꜣḥ mtrtyw ḳnw ꜥšꜣ* + function + PN

Categorization of terms of special relevance in the legal register:

- *ỉrỉ sšw*: to make a document, record (a statement). Théodoridès (1965: 81 n.8): 'dresser un acte' as in *Sꜣbꜣstt statue Louvre* E 11673.
- *sš n* PN/N *n* (= *m*) *pꜣ sꜣwt nb*: to write down on behalf of someone an entire patrimony.
- *mꜥḏꜣ*: *acquets*; and *ỉr mꜥḏꜣ ỉrm* (to make *acquets* with someone). See Théodoridès (1964: 50; 1965: 82); Gardiner (1940b: 157-8) 'profit' as in Late Period contracts. Compare with *pTurin* 2021, line II:1-2, the formula *ỉw.ỉ ỉrt rwy r r-3 m pꜣ ỉryw.ỉ nb ỉrm.st*.
  A Neo-Egyptian lexeme. The corn measure classifier (U9 in *EG*'s list of hieroglyphic signs, representing the container and a part of its escaping contents) is used metaphorically to represent a universality of assets in the same way modern legal terminology uses the term *mass(-asset)* or French *masse*, to designate an 'ensemble de biens d'une catégorie particulière soumise à un régime spécial. Ex. la masse des biens communs sous le régime légal'[544], as well as the *masse successorale*. Grain always being dealt with in bulk, the icon may represent valuable universalities of assets treated as single entities. The notion of *acquets* represents a non-prototypical member of the category of [GRAIN/MEASURE] of which *ỉt* 'barley, corn', *bdt* 'emmer,' *ḥḳꜣt, ỉpt* 'grain-measure', and *ḫꜣỉ* 'to measure' are central members, by a metaphoric process mapping the semantic fields of legal *mass-assets* on graminae volume measurements.

543 Read *Nmtỉ* by Allam (1973: 262 n.40).
544 Cornu (2003: 556).

Gardiner (1940b: 158) suggests seeing another metaphorical process in the 'transition of meaning from 'basket for dates'[545] to 'profit'': the 'metaphor we employ in speaking of the 'fruit' of a man's labour (*cf.* also καρπος, *fructus*)'. Once again, ancient Egyptian categorization processes magnify the way human conceptualization works, using material basic elements to organize abstract notions.

- *swꜣḏ* *n*: to hand over, transmit, entrust to someone (with objects *mꜥḏꜣ* and *mdwt*). An abstract transmission (of the rights relative to the assets), and perhaps the material handing over (tradition) of a document are meant here[546]. We have here the only instance of *swꜣḏ* used instead of *ỉw.f n* N/PN concerning the *disposition* of a bequest.
- *ꜥḥꜥ* *rḳi* : contentious binomial, to stand and confront; 'faire opposition'[547] in New Kingdom texts.

  As for *ꜥḥꜥ*, compare with Latin *stare,* French *ester*[548], Semitic לקום[549]. As for the standing metaphor, see David (2007: 8): *stare* is demanding, since the upright position is the one that represents a claim; the accuser stands before the court ('Stand up and fight!')[550]. The use of the classifier representing the [MOTION] category to categorize lexemes relating to the judicial process illustrates the conceptual metaphor '*ACTION IS MOTION*'[551].

  The lexeme *rḳi* is here classified by both the [LEG] and [MOTION] categories classifiers, merged in the frequent couplet of the [LEGS MOTION] category that represents metaphorically the ideas of action and control[552]. The earliest instance of the lexeme belongs to the Middle Kingdom, meaning to tilt or be hostile, and is classified by the arm; the legs in motion appear during the 18th dynasty[553] as classifier of the lexeme, but the arm is still used. The double classifiers appear during the 20th dynasty;
- *dnỉ* : share, portion, fraction.
- *mtry*/ *mtrtyw* : witnesses.
- *ḏdt*: declaration, statement (McDowell 1990: 18).
- *ỉnỉ r swnw* : to acquire for a price.

  The lexeme *swnt* is attested since the Old Kingdom, without classifier.[554] During the Middle Kingdom, it is classified by the [ABSTRACT] category classifier . The [COERCION] category classifier is here appended to the lexeme instead of the usual [ABSTRACT] category classifier , as is sometimes the case in 19th and 20th dynasties papyri (e.g. *pTurin* 1887 v° I, 3: *swnw*). Since sales/exchanges are typical

545 The *Wb* II, 186.15 notes the entry *mḏꜣ* 'Art Mass für Datteln' (the basis of Gardiner's comparison with Coptic ⲙⲁⲗϫⲉ 'a measure of capacity for dry goods').

546 Eyre (1992: 213) opts for a 'physical and symbolic conveyance of the written text'.

547 Théodoridès (1976: 32; 1965: 93-4) for the relationship with the judgement of the dead.

548 Lacau (1949: 35).

549 Rabinowitz (1958: 146), but of course, it is not a Semitic influence as he purports, but an example of a conceptual metaphor.

550 See also *sꜥḥꜥ* 'to accuse' (Gardiner 1935: 144).

551 Winter (1988: 1412).

552 For an in-depth analysis of both classifiers, see David (2007).

553 But see one instance with the legs in motion during the Second Intermediate Period in *ÄW* II, 1528.

554 *ÄW* I, 1089.

synallagmatic contracts, the [COERCION] category classifier may imply the binding character of correlative obligations.

- *sꜥnḫ*: to make live, maintain.
  Interestingly, the maintenance of the children is expressed here by the lexeme *sꜥnḫ* as the maintenance of a woman in an Old Kingdom letter, *pBoulaq* 8, according to Baer's translation (1966: 5-7); Baer compares the formulation to Demotic *sẖ n sꜥnḫ*. But the *recital* of *pNaunakhte*, lines II.2-3, uses *sḫpr* and *rdi grg-pr* in the context of children maintenance.
- *nmḥw* (or): the voiceless, common 'citizen'; a woman/man who is not submitted to any kind of dependency and who possesses private assets.
- *ỉri m rmṯ nmḥw n pꜣ tꜣ n Pr-ꜥꜣ*: to elevate a woman to the status of *nmḥw* of the land of Pharaoh, which means a simple Egyptian 'citizen'.
  Of course this change of status is not meant here as a kind of naturalization, as there is no evidence of any such procedure in Pharaonic Egypt, only eventual assimilation processes[555], and it is not certain that the acquired slave was of foreign origin. See Théodoridès (1965) against the concept of manumission (to free a slave) in this context[556].
- *ỉri spẖr* (*m rmṯ nmḥw n pꜣ tꜣ n Pr-ꜥꜣ*): to register[557], record, publicize (?) (as a *nmḥw* of the land of Pharaoh). The use of the [ABSTRACT] category classifier to categorize *spẖr* needs no further explanation; as for the [COERCION] category classifier, the 'strong arm' represents the empowered hand by virtue of function/status, the action of one who is in charge (see David 2006: 27-8). In this particular case, the instrument that performs the change of status of the slave is the written document, not a stick or a sceptre; the adopter was entitled to do so not because she was an administrative officer but because of her personal status, and the icon is a metaphorical representation of her discretionary power to act and her dominance over other persons. The stick in the hand of a standing man (the personification of the power to act since '*IDEAS ARE PEOPLE*') as an image of POWER is somewhat similar to the French figure of speech 'être sous la férule de quelqu'un' (to be under someone's iron rule, *lit.* under someone's rod).
- *ỉri m šriw* /: to treat as a child/daughter; to adopt.
  One of the most heated debates concerning the *pAdoptions* is on the legal implications of this expression: is it only an image implying concern and affection, or does it represent a true adoption, a legal fiction with personal and patrimonial consequences, the adopted person officially benefiting from a status that entitles him/her to all the rights of a biological child? The expression is used in our text about the testatrix herself and her brother (concerning the children of the slave, the reconstruction *tw.ỉ ỉrt nꜣ rmṯ* [*m šriw.ỉ*?] is plausible). The question is particularly crucial in the case of *Nꜣnfr*: could a man leave all his assets to his companion by testament in case he had no children? Believing it was the case on the basis of *pTurin* 2021, Théodoridès (1962b: 25-6; 1965; 1970: 190) assimilated *ỉri m šriw* in *pAdoptions* to *pTurin* 2021, II.3-4 *ỉw.st ỉry n.ỉ ỉ.ỉryt šr*[*ỉw ỉ.ỉryt*? *šriw*] 'she did for me what a son (or) a daughter would do'; he translated

555 Helck (1977: 306-10).

556 Proposed by De Zulueta (Gardiner 1940: 28) and Cruze-Uribe (1982: 63).

557 Eyre (1992: 208, n. 6) warns against regarding it as 'a formal registration in writing of the free population'; Donker van Heel & Haring (2003: 12-3) note the scant occurrences of *spẖr* in the administrative records.

iri m šriw as 'to treat as a child' in the case of *N3nfr* and 'to adopt' in the case of *Pndiw* who was a collateral and thus would have been excluded from the succession by the other children. Others, e.g. Allam (1972: 281) and Eyre (1992: 207), opt for a true adoption of the testatrix by her companion.
In *oBerlin* P 10627, the 'adoption' is expressed by *ini n.f nmḥw* 'to acquire an orphan on one's behalf'; of considerable importance is the assimilation that this document makes between the 'adopted' child and biological offspring: ('It's him who is/will be pouring water on your hands') *m šriw ꜥ3 n ḥꜥt.f* 'as an eldest son of your flesh.'

- *mdt* 𓀁𓏛 *m*: to contest the right of someone.
- *n3 mdwt* 𓀁𓏛: statement.
- *m-di.f*: in the possession of (for *res*).
- *ḫt* 𓆱: assets.
- *pš* × 𓆱 *n*: to divide between legatees.

9. *pTurin* 2021 r° and *pGeneva* D 409

Date: 20th dynasty, Ramesses XI
Hieroglyphic version: *KRI* VI, 738-42 n.20
Instrument:

* **state –** damaged
* **value – original or exact copy?**: the information in what is left of the papyri seems complete, the pre-material is lost but the document contains the names of settler, beneficiary, witnesses, scribe, the indication of the forum, a *recital* with 'statutory' grounding, bequests, elaborated authentication measures and colophon. It may consist of the copy ordered by the vizier for the temple of Medinet Habu, the seat of the Necropolis administration during the late 20th dynasty.
* **nature – notary instrument** (lost internal characterization) concerning legal rights about assets, before a high official, scribes and witnesses.
* **genre – consentient legal**: formulaic style, ordered layout; neat business hand[558] (with errors and corrections, free of business practice diacritical mark); concerns private interests; locutive/delocutive textemes, degree 2 Neo-Egyptian.

The verso bears two lines belonging to the epistolary genre and naming historical characters belonging to the 21st dynasty, probably a school exercise[559], although Allam (1973: 327) notes that these lines belong to another sheet that has been glued on the papyrus, perhaps to strengthen it. The 23 cm high papyrus is common for literary works and the orientation of the fiber is not specific of legal documents.

The document is of unknown provenance, but Černý & Peet (1927: 38) suggested that *pTurin* 2021 'was found at Medinet Habu with the great mass of cemetery papyri now in Turin, it must be the copy made for the temple'[560]. As for *pGeneva* D 409, it was exchanged by Gardiner[561]. If our document comes from the archives of the temple, one must note the absence of a docket that such an archiving should imply.

Legal step: **external manifestation of will** (performative) concerning the transmission (*rdi*) of private assets with a **notification** purpose (*r rdit rḫ*), and **authenticated** by the vizier.
The deed is recorded before the vizier and in the presence of the family and witnesses, probably in the *ḳnbt* of the temple of Medinet Habu[562]. For Černý & Peet (1927: 37), the procedure is not brought before a court but only before the vizier as there are numerous witnesses who would not have been necessary in the case of a court proceeding; but for Donker van Heel & Haring (2003: 90), it is a court case that took place in the temple of Medinet Habu.

Legal issue: **will**[563] **and/or gift**[564]: absence of *consideration*, unilateral deed concerning the transmission of ensembles of assets (the 2/3 of community property) to the companion and to the children of the testator; use of *dni*, *rdi*; typical clauses (retributive principle, explicit performative for bequests, type and origin of assets, *exemption from hotchpot*

558 Černý & Peet (1927: 31) characterized the script as 'moderately large and not unattractive hand, remarkably free from the extravagant ligatures and cursive strokes of the usual legal and business hands of this period, except in the list of witnesses'; Donker van Heel & Haring (2003: 91) add that it is 'clearly distinct from contemporary cursive hieratic' although less of 'a stately 'uncial'' than *pAbbott* and *pAmherst*.
559 Černý & Peet (1927: 30): 'perhaps written to try a pen'.
560 See also Valbelle (1985: 28).
561 Massart (1957: 172).
562 See line II.1.
563 Théodoridès (1968b); Allam (1977: 94).
564 Mainly because of the absence of future *descent and distribution* rule.

(?)[565], reference by the vizier to warranty against claims). Immediate gifts and testamentary *dispositions* may in fact coexist in the document.
For Černý & Peet (1927: 37), 'the papyrus does not record a dispute of any kind, but (…) a marriage settlement'[566], 'not the actual marriage contract but the record of proceedings before the vizier preliminary to the making of such a contract'. But the fact that there are already common *acquets* does not support this interpretation[567]. For Pestman (1961: 127, 132 n.5, 138-9) it is a case of a 'fictitious lawsuit between the persons entitled and the successor in title'[568]; but 'fictitious lawsuits' may be regarded as sessions of courts acting with notarial functions. For McDowell (1990: 145 n.14) our document represents a 'divorce settlement'; but it could not be the divorce from the first wife, as she is absent, probably already dead, and since the second wife is praised by the testator, a divorce is highly improbable.

Textemic features:

1. *Recital*

Since the first part of the text is missing, essential information is lost, such as an eventual title deed and the pre-material). Fragments of the first page present a locutive texteme, probably the *recital* expressed in a sequential past narrative. These features also appear in the second page; the end of the *recital* is marked, as already noted in *Naunakhte* and in *pAdoptions,* by the use of the direct address to the court stating the main purpose and ground of the procedure; but here the 'statutory' ground is added as a closure to the *recital*, a principle stated by an unnamed king. The reference is brief, without any kind of formal or technico-legal mention (date, instrument, etc.), more as a general legal principle than a quotation from a statute. The reference is placed just before the main provisions of the will, as the superordinated grounding to the dispositions, their justification in the eye of the highest legal and judicial instance, the king, the final argument.

This texteme represents the longest *recital* to be found in our corpus.

Statement quotation: (I)[…] (x + 2) […ʿ]*nḫ-n-niwt Ỉnk*[*swnḏm*…] (x + 3) […] *iw.i ʿḳw r* [*pr n Tꜣṯꜣtriꜣ?...*] (x + 4) […] *pꜣ nṯr ʿꜣ iw.st ḫprw* [*nbt*] *pꜣy.i pr iw.i ḳd* (x + 5) […*n pꜣy.i ?*] *ẖrdw iw.i* […*i*]*rt* (*n*) *nꜣy.w msw* (II.1) *iw pꜣ nṯr rwi* [*iw.i ʿr*]*ḳwi ḥr.st m tꜣ ḳnbt tꜣ ḥwt iw.i irt rwy r r*-3 *m pꜣ iryw.i nb* (2) *irm.st i*[*w.i ʿḳ*] *r pꜣ pr n ʿnḫ-n-niwt Ỉnkswnḏm tꜣy st-ḥmt nty ʿḥʿti m-bꜣḥ ṯꜣt* (3) *iw.i in* 4 *bꜣk*[*iw ir*]*m.st iw.st nfr n.i iw.st šmswy biꜣt.i iw.st iry n.i i.iryt* (4) *šr*[*iw i.iryt?*[569] *šriw*] *iw.i dit n.st ḥmt Nwmwtri ḥmt Bwpymwtḫꜣʿn hnʿ* (5) *n*[*ꜣy*]*.w ms*[*w r pꜣy*]*.s r*-3 *iw.i dwny.st m ḥm Sꜣptriḏḥwty ḥm Gmimn*[*pꜣ*]*ʿš* (6) [*pꜣy bꜣk*]*i* 2 *nty m-di.i m dni m pꜣy.i p*[*š pꜣ*] *iry.i nb irm.st* (7)

565 Although the idea of a double gift to different beneficiaries in the same document is cursorily dismissed by Théodoridès (1968b: 151), it may not have been inconceivable to Egyptians. These gifts may have been viewed as excluded from the partition of the assets after the donor's death (*gift with exemption from hotchpot*).

566 See Eyre (2007: 231): 'settlement associated with remarriage, rather than a will'.

567 Théodoridès (1968b: 149), *contra*: Eyre (2007: 229, 234) 'written marriage settlements of a later period are frequently dated some time after the original consummation of the marriage.'

568 *Contra*: Théodoridès (1968b: 151) for there is no petition, the father is no defendant.

569 Perhaps a sequence close to  could be suggested for the beginning of line 4 instead of the reconstruction usually proposed (*KRI* VI, 739 and Allam 1973: pl. 114)?

[r][570] *iry.st m šriw[* *mi]-ḳd n3 ẖrdw n t3y.i ḥmt ḥ3w[ty]tw*[571] *ʿḳ3 sp sn i.wnw m p3[y].i* (8) *pr iw bwpwy[.i] smn [r] wʿ mr ky ẖr ptri tw.i iw.k(wi) m-b3ḥ ṯ3t* (9) *[ḥnʿ] srw n t3 ḳnbt m p3 hrw r rdit rẖ wʿ nb dnitw.f m n3y.i ẖrdw [m 3ẖt.i?]* (10) *p3y sẖrw nt[y i]w.i irw.f n ʿnẖ-n-[niw]t Ỉnkswnḏm t[3]y st-ḥmt nty m p3[y.i pr] m p3* (11) *hrw*

[… *ʿ]nẖ-n-niwt Ỉnk[swnḏm…]*; and I entered [the house of *T3ṯ3tri3* with the assent of?] the Great God; and she became [lady of] my house. And I built [a home for my?] children; and I […d]id? (it for) their descendants. But the God went away; [and I swo]re about her/it in the court of this temple (= Medinet Habu?), and I made (a division of) 2/3 to 1/3 from all I had made with her. And [I entered] the house of (the) *ʿnẖ-n-niwt Ỉnkswnḏm*, this woman who is standing before (the) vizier. And I acquired 4 servan[ts wit]h her. She was good to me, she suited my character; and she did for me what would do a son [(or) would do? a daugh]ter (**retributive principle**). And I gave her (the) servant *Nwmwtri*, (the) servant *Bwpwymwtẖ3ʿn*, with th[ei]r childr[en for h]er 1/3; and I gave her a bonus[572] with (the) servant *S3ptriḏḥwty*, (the) servant *Gmimn[p3]ʿš*, [these] 2 [serva]nts who were in my possession as a share, as my p[ortion of] all I have made with her, [to] treat her as a daught[er, li]ke the children of my fir[s]t woman, very exactly, who are/were in m[y] house, while [I] did not establish a beloved one [above] (the) other.

But see me approaching (the) vizier [and] officials of this court today, in order to inform each one of my children about his share [in my assets?] (and) these provisions tha[t] I shall make for (the) *ʿnẖ-n-[niw]t Ỉnkswnḏm*, t[h]is woman who is (= lives) in m[y house] today.

'Statutory' ground: *ẖr ḏd [Pr]-ʿ3 ʿ.w.s. imi iry s nb 3bwtw.f m 3ẖttw.f*

And Pharaoh L.P.H. said: 'Let every man do what he wants with his assets.'

* Neo-Egyptian characteristics:

- *iw.i ʿḳw, iw.st ẖprw, iw.i ḳd, iw.i irt, iw.i in, iw.st iry, iw.i dit, iw.i dwny.st*: sequential past narratives (preposition omission) constituting the chain of events;
- Neo-Egyptian morphology of the infinitive (*ʿḳw, ẖprw, in, iry, dwny, irw*);
- exophoric articloid (extratextual deixis) with probable reference to the oracle (*p3 nṯr ʿ3*);
- probably deictic articloid referring to the locus of the forum (*t3 ḥwt*) and deictic *m p3 hrw*;
- cataphoric articloid (the first one in *t3 ḳnbt t3 ḥwt; p3 pr n ʿnẖ-n-niwt; n3 ẖrdw n t3y.i ḥmt*) and substantivizing cataphoric *p3 iryw.i nb*;
- Neo-Egyptian plural (*w*) and feminine singular (*st*) delocutive suffixes;
- Neo-Egyptian possessive determinator for material ownership and ownership right (*p3y.i pr, p3y.i p[š]*) and kinship relations (*n3y.w msw, t3y.i ḥmt; n3y.i ẖrdw*);
- preposition omission: sequential narratives and probably in *[i]rt (n) n3y.w msw;*
- *iw p3 nṯr rwi*: either contrastive use of coordinator *iw* (see *supra oGardiner/Ashmolean* 55) or converted adverbial nexus;
- *p3 iryw.i nb*: substantivized perfect relative form without prothetic *yod,* as is usually the case when the relative is preceded by the articloid[573];
- Neo-Egyptian prepositions (*irm.st; m-di.f*);
- Neo-Egyptian deictic determinator (*t3y st-ḥmt; p3y sẖrw*);

570 Allam (1993: 27) restores [*iw.i*] and believes that the man adopts his wife in order to bequeath assets to her (legal fiction).

571 See Théodoridès (1965: 104) who restored as in *pOrbiney* 5, 9 *t3y.f iḥw ḥ3wty*. For *ḥ3wty* as 'first in time', see *Wb* III, 29 n.19-20.

572 Gift with *exemption from hotchpot*?

573 Winand (1992: 381).

- PN *tꜣy st-ḥmt nty ꜥḥꜥti*: proper noun and apposition with # Neo-Egyptian deictic determinator + noun + relative expansion with stative (relative adjective not in concord)#. Similar constructions are used in PN *pꜣy bꜣki* 2 *nty m-di.i* and *pꜣy sẖrw nt*[*y ỉ*]*w.ỉ irw.f* (relative clause with future, preposition omission; in Middle Egyptian, *ỉw* is avoided after *nty*)[574]. The *recital* monologue uses deictic forms and situational-identificative expressions common in direct addresses to a public;
- *ỉ.iryt*.N: imperfect relative neutrum with prothetic *yod*;
- *ỉ.iryt šr*[*iw ỉ.iryt*? *šriw*] : both genders filiation binomial, with unique case in our corpus of repetitive use of a relative form ;
- *ỉ.wnw*: (im)perfect participle with prothetic *yod*;
- *ỉw bwpwy*[*.i*] *smn* [*r*] *wꜥ mr ky*: converted negative report perfect in a commentary opposed to the evolution mode sequential forms. We have seen the same form in the title deed of *pBoulaq* 10, line 7;
- *ḫr ptri tw.i ỉw.k*(*wi*): final part of the *recital* expounding the main purpose of the procedure, constructed with # proclitic coordinator *ḫr* (contrastive) + Neo-Egyptian presentative *ptri* (marker of involvement) + Neo-Egyptian locutive thematic pronoun + stative (present) #. The cohesive *ḫr* and presentative *ptri* again introduce a climax in the *recital*, ending the sequentials chain of the narrative *sensu stricto* with a segment of a commentary nature expounding the main arguments motivating the testator's decision (compare with *Naunakhte*'s *recital* construction *ḫr ptri tw.i iꜣwt.ki*);
- Neo-Egyptian spelling (*ꜣḫt*{*tw*}, *ptri*);
- anaphoric articloid (*pꜣ nṯr; srw n tꜣ ḳnbt*);
- *ḫr ḏd* [*Pr*]-*ꜥꜣ*: the 'statutory' ground is expressed as a verbal statement introduced by a tag clause with # proclitic coordinator *ḫr* + report perfect form of the *verbum dicendi* #;
- *ꜣbwtw.f*: imperfect relative neutrum with intrusive *w*, object of *iry s nb*;

* 'Classical' degree 0 forms used:

- use of the relator in unclear kind of relation in frozen expression (*ꜥnḫ-n-niwt*) or for ownership (*pꜣ pr n ꜥnḫ-n-niwt* PN), part-whole (*srw n tꜣ ḳnbt*), and kinship relations (*nꜣ ẖrdw n tꜣy.i ḥmt* PN);
- perfect relative forms without prothetic *yod* (*iryw.i; iry.i*). Both prothetic *yod* forms and classic forms are used in the same texteme;
- *ꜥḥꜥti*: stative (feminine actor);
- *ỉw.st nfr n.i*: non-converted adverbial nexus with stative rheme; compare to *iri nfr supra;*
- [*r*] *iry.st m šriw*[*mi*]-*ḳd* N *ꜥḳꜣ sp sn*: # compound preposition [*mi*]-*ḳd* + expanded N + intensifiers *ꜥḳꜣ* (intensity expression) and *sp sn* (intensity iteration) #, compare *supra ỉw.w m-mitt ꜥḳꜣ sp sn*;
- *r rdit rḫ wꜥ nb* (object) *m nꜣy.i ẖrdw*: the purpose of the testator's procedure (the legal step) is the notification of his testamentary provisions, and it is expressed by a variant of the locution *r rdit rḫ.tw* (see *oGardiner/Ashmolean* 90 *supra* for *r rdit rḫ.kwi*). The use of *wꜥ nb m* is attested in Middle Egyptian[575] to indicate 'every one of/amongst'. See also the classical pair of quantifiers *wꜥ*... *ky* (both without expansion);
- *imm iry s nb*: the royal edict is a verbal statement constructed with iussive/3rd person causative imperative *imi* + prospective object *iry*.N *nb*, expressing deontic modality in a general statement (*rdi, s nb*, following relative neutrum).

---

574 For this rather common construction in Ramesside royal decrees, see David (2006: 57).
575 *EG* § 262.

Note the interesting fact that in the surviving normative royal decrees from the Ramesside Period, only one example of this form is attested and not in the operative part[576]; but an order is given in that form in an epistolary royal decree[577] (David 2006: 121, 237, 239). Ramesside royal decrees do not use the imperative in their normative provisions[578]. A similar general grounding principle is provided in a later private document, *Nḫtfmwti statue Cairo* CG 42208 (22nd dyn.)[579].

The reference is made to the *Verbum Regis*, not to a specific, dated, normative text; it consists more of some kind of oral guideline or principle which must have been recorded afterwards. It is referred to in court without any precision concerning the pharaoh; it may be the reigning king, but that is not absolutely sure (see also *pBoulaq* 10, lines 10-11). There is no sign during the Ramesside Period of a reference to a *Lex Scripta* as legally binding text per se. This is reminiscent of the situation in Mesopotamia where the Hammurabi 'code' and other documents of the same type are never referred to as such in court records[580]. The first references to dated normative texts in Egypt seem to belong to the very end of the first millennium B.C., in *pBM* EA 10591, 2nd century B.C. and in the Demotic *pCarlsberg* 301 '*manuel juridique de Tebtynis*', 1st century B.C.[581].

The principle[582] stated by the king is the very general autonomy of decision, *libre disposition des biens* principle at the core of the *consentient* genre of our corpus; the same principle appears in the preamble of Coptic child gifts (e.g. in *pKRU* 87, 94, 8th century B.C.[583]).

* General dialectal features: degree 2.
* Legal formula: *recital* = […] + *iwi sḏm* (narrative of positive behavior of the testator) + *iw.st nfr n.i* (positive behavior of the legatee) + *ḫr ptri* (commentary: purpose) + *ḫr ḏd* [*Pr*]-*ʿ3 ʿ.w.s.* + imperative (main ground)

2. Operative part

***Disposition* of specific bequests**:
tw.i dit [*p3*] *iryw*(*.i*) (12) *nb irm ʿnḫ-n-niwt Ỉnkswnḏm t3 st-ḥmt nty m p3y.i pr n.st m p3 h*[*rw*] *m p3* (III.1) *b3ki* 2 *ʿ*[*ḥ3*]*wtyw b3ki*  2 *ḥmwtt dmḏ* 4 *ḥnʿ msw.w iw p3*(*y.i*) *rwy ḥr p3y.st r*-3 *mtw.i* (2) *dit p3y* 9 *b3kiw i.h3y r.i m p3y.i rwy irm ʿnḫ-n-niwt T3ṯ3ri3 n n3y.i* (3) *ẖrdw ḥnʿ p3 pr it.i mwt m-di.w m r3-ʿ*

576 *Kanais* decree, preamble, line 13: *imi nḥm sw šw m bt3.f* 'Let one who is void of (his) crime save himself'.

577 *pCairo ESP (B)* lines 23-4: *h3b.i n.k* (…) *r-ḏd imi in.tw msdmt nfr nfr* 'I have sent (a message) to you… saying: "Have very good galena be brought"'.

578 See David (2006: 63-5): modal prospective in criminal law decrees. Note *ibid*. reference to Latin and modern statutes also devoid of imperative forms.

579 *mi ḏdtw nt nṯr ʿ3 imi ir s nb{t} sḫrw n išttw.f* 'in conformity with the Great God's words: "Let every man make arrangements for his assets"'.

580 Bottéro (1987: 199); VerSteeg (2000: 15 and his references in n.9).

581 Introduced in *pCarlsberg* 301 by the formula *iw.f sẖ n ḥ3t-sp* x; Chauveau (1991: 119-21) thinks the text of the laws might be quoted *verbatim*. Concerning *pBM* EA 10591 from the Siut archives, he adds that it provided perhaps an excerpt or a summary of the normative text (in the context of litigation), mentioning it by its date (but without reference to the royal legislator), in the format *iw.f sẖ n p3 hp n ḥ3t-sp* x *ḏd*.

582 See Théodoridès (1967b: 118, 120, 125).

583 See Richter (2005: 242): 'The royal laws command that everybody shall do with his property whatever he wants'.

I bequeath all [t]hat (I) made with (the) *ꜥnḫ-n-niwt Ꞽnkswnḏm*, the woman who (lives) in my house, to her tod[ay], consisting of these 2 m[al]e servants (and) 2 female servants, total: 4, with their children, while m(y) 2/3 are with her 1/3[584],
and I bequeath these 9 servants who have befallen me in/as my 2/3 with (the) *ꜥnḫ-n-niwt Tꜣṯꜣriꜣ* to my children, with the house of my father (and) mother (= parental house[585]) already in their possession.
Remark concerning the rights of the children based on 'statutory' ground:
bn st [*ꜣty*][586] *pꜣ in.i nb irm tꜣy.w mwt* (4) [*i*]*w wnw iw.i dit n.w m pꜣ inw.i irm ꜥnḫ-n-niwt Ꞽnkswnḏm ḥr Pr-ꜥꜣ ꜥ.w.s. ḏd imi sfyrw* (5) *n s*[*t nb*] *n.st*
They are not [deprived of] all that I acquired with their mother, [al]though I would have bequeathed to them (my share) from what I acquired with (the) *ꜥnḫ-n-niwt Ꞽnkswnḏm,* but Pharaoh L.P.H. says: 'Give (the) *sfyrw* of [any wom]an to her.'

* Neo-Egyptian characteristics:
- *tw.i dit… m pꜣ hrw… mtw.i dit*: explicit performative[587] (locutive present, preposition omitted), with performativity marker *m pꜣ hrw*, to express the first bequest, the second being constructed with a full-fledged locutive conjunctive (same lexemic constituency). Thus the first bequest concerns the surviving female companion, whereas the second is meant for the children of the first union, limited by the first bequest. It is the first time we encounter such a specific performative bequest disposition, the exact counterpart of which is to be found in the English 'I hereby bequeath' formula. We have seen *supra* in *pAdoptions* the use of the same explicit performative construction for an adoption (*tw.i i.iri.f n.i m šriw m pꜣ hrw*).
Note again the absence of a tag clause to introduce the operative part;
- [*pꜣ*] *iryw*(*.i*) *nb, pꜣ ini.i nb, pꜣ inw.i*: substantivized perfect relatives without prothetic *yod*;
- Neo-Egyptian prepositions (*irm, m-di.f*);
- cataphoric articloid (*tꜣ ḥmt-st nty; pꜣ pr it*), also with relatives;
- Neo-Egyptian possessive determinator for material ownership and ownership right (*pꜣy.i pr, pꜣy.st r*-3, *pꜣ*(*y.i*) *rwy*) and kinship relations (*nꜣy.i ḫrdw, tꜣy.w mwt*). But note suffixed pronouns for kinship *it.i mwt* (without repetition of the suffix) and *msw.w*;
- Neo-Egyptian delocutive suffixes *w* and *st*;
- deictic articloid (*m pꜣ h*[*rw*]);
- anaphoric articloid (*pꜣ bꜣki* 2);
- Neo-Egyptian deictic *pꜣy*;
- perfect participle with prothetic *yod* (*i.hꜣy*);
- Neo-Egyptian adverbial modifier in trailing position *m rꜣ-ꜥ* (see *oPetrie* 18 and *pAdoptions supra*);
- *bn st* [*ꜣty*]: non converted negative generic present adverbial nexus: # Neo-Egyptian negator + Neo-Egyptian delocutive plural dependent pronoun + [stative] #.

584 Théodoridès (1967b: 123) 'ce qui (dans nos acquêts de communauté) représente (mes) deux tiers ajoutés à son tiers'.
585 For Helck (1961-70: 337) is the expression '"*pr* des Vaters der Mutter" nicht ein wirkliches Wohnhaus, sondern ist Umschreibung für den Teil des Erbes der Kinder, der ursprünglich Mitgift der Eltern der Mutter an diese'. For Théodoridès (1968b: 150 n.4), a parental house being an acquet of the community property, the house in question must be viewed as the private property of the testator, 'hérité du père maternel'.
586 Černý & Peet (1927: 34) restore *ḥr ḫm*(*t*); Allam (1973: 324) proposes *iꜣd* or *iwty*.
587 See Vernus (1985: 310).

The segment is meant as a conclusive and apologetic justification of the testator's decision relating to the extent of the children's bequest: 'I do not deprive my children, I would have given more to them if it weren't for the royal decree protecting women';

- *iw wnw iw.i dit*: # converter *iw* + preterit converter *wnw* + future (preposition omitted)#, with a not exploited possibility value[588];
- *ḫr Pr-ʿ3 ʿ.w.s. ḏd imi sfyrw n s[t nb] n.st*: the tag clause of the general principle grounding the decision is not constructed as in the previous line 11 (*ḫr ḏd* [*Pr*]-*ʿ3 ʿ.w.s.*, perfect report), but # proclitic contrastive coordinator *ḫr* + present[589] N (*ḫr*) *sḏm* of the *verbum dicendi* #.
  This is again a quotation of a royal verbal statement with # imperative *imi* + object *sfyrw* + beneficiary #l;
- Neo-Egyptian lexeme, *hapax* (*sfyrw*).

* 'Classical' degree 0 forms used:
- use of the relator in unclear kind of relation in frozen expression (*ʿnḫ-n-niwt*);

* General dialectal features: degree 2.

* Legal formulae:
- *disposition* of specific bequests: *tw.i dit* + object + *n* (first beneficiary) + *m p3 hrw* + *m* (detail of the bequest)... *mtw.i dit* + *n* (second beneficiary)
- 'statutory' reference: *ḫr Pr-ʿ3 ʿ.w.s. ḏd* + imperative

3. Sanction and *authentication* of the deed by the vizier

The nature of the reported dialogue between the vizier and the eldests of the testator's children has been the subject of debate: was the family's active presence needed for the will to be enforceable, in which case it was not an actual will, as the testator's unilateral decision was insufficient to create it, or was their participation only a matter of evidence to prevent future contestation and 'to testify to the fact that the goods of which their father was disposing were not part of the common property of the first marriage'[590]? As the will is authenticated[591] by the court acting as a notary, the vizier is establishing the truth of the testator's assumptions before confirming the deed, corroborating facts (this is usually the reason why the acting person provides the court with a title deed), verifying if the children understand the precise nature of the provisions and examining their position towards them in order to make sure they will not oppose it (reinforcing the warranty against claims quoted by the vizier but lacking in what is left of the testator's statement)[592]. This texteme is not to be found elsewhere in our corpus which may indicate that in this case only we are dealing with an original or exact copy deposited in the official archives; furthermore, the transparency of the authentication procedure

588 For Satzinger (1976: 214, 277) 'Futurum in Praeterito' 'volitiv' 'Irrealis der Vergangenheit', 'mittels eines vorgeschalteten *iw* in Parenthese gesetzt'; Junge (2005: 160) 'future perfect tense'. See also Frandsen (1974: 222), Winand (1992: 494-5).

589 Satzinger (1976: 125-6): gnomic present.

590 Černý & Peet (1927: 37).

591 Théodoridès (1970: 172): 'le Vizir est censé faire lui-même les *sḫr* de son ressortissant ; comme représentant de l'Etat, il les prend sur lui ; il les légalise en les faisant siennes ; il les authentifie et il leur procure la force d'exécution nécessaire.'

592 Allam (1977: 93-4, 96) understands that the agreement of the family is required for the document to be valid as 'Tout membre de la famille nucléaire avait sur les biens de sa famille un certain droit, un droit communautaire'. Compare with Pestman's remark (1994: 24) concerning the intervention of the family in the case of a man transferring his property during the Late Period: 'Le régime de la propriété dans le droit privé égyptien est d'un caractère ambivalent car, s'il admet que les individus peuvent jouir de biens en pleine propriété, il reconnaît en même temps à la famille certains droits sur ces biens.'

may indicate a higher autonomy of the written text as it becomes more detailed in terms of procedure and the express mention of the authority's *fiat*.

The testator is omitted from this part of the procedure, although some of his previous statements are quoted. Note that although the *recital* is a locutive construct, it is monologic; dialogue is only used for the examination of legal heirs and potential opponents to the will. The texteme's interactive (interpersonal focus, allocutive mode, questions-answers, imperative) and argumentative (modals, question for corroboration, rhetorical question) style is nevertheless presented as formal, with repetitive format of questions and answers, with integrated informational focus (relative clauses for elaboration, precise identification references[593], explicitness, and almost literal quotations from the testator's provisions). The two eldest children represent their brothers and answer 'as one mouth'; the personal stance is off limits (absence of 'private verbs' of the type *think, believe*). Thus even here, the dialogue has been carefully produced in writing and seems not to reflect the precise original verbal production. Moreover, the delocutive tag clauses and framework of the dialogue is highly formal (archaisms, isotopy, expliciteness).

The record order and copy testify to the proliferation of documents in the legal sphere and the increased value of written evidence and title in Ramesside society.

Examination of the legal heirs by the vizier:

corroboration of facts concerning the share of the legal heirs:

ḏdt.n ṯꜣt n wꜥb ḥry-kꜣwtyw ꜥḥꜣwtywnfr wꜥb Nbnfr nꜣ ẖrdw (6) *n ỉt-nṯr Ỉmnḫꜥw nty ꜥḥꜥ m-bꜣḥ.f nꜣ snw ꜥꜣytw nꜣy.f ẖrdw*

ỉḫ ḫr.tn tꜣ mdwyt i.ḏd ỉt-nṯr (7) *Ỉmnḫꜥw pꜣy.tn ỉt* (*ỉ*)*n mꜣꜥt m pꜣy* 9 *bꜣkỉw i.ḏd.f di.i st n{t}.tn m pꜣy.i rwy i.pš*[*.i*] *ỉrm* (8) *tꜣy.tn m*[*wt*] *ḥnꜥ pꜣ pr ỉt mwt*

ḏd.w m rꜣ wꜥ

mꜣꜥttw pꜣy.n [*ỉ*]*t st m-di.n n mꜣꜥ*

What (the) vizier said to (the) priest, chief workman *ꜥḥꜣwtywnfr* (and the) priest *Nbnfr*, the children of (the) god's father *Ỉmnḫꜥw* who is standing before him, the eldest brothers of his children:

- 'What can you say (about) the statement that made (the) god's father *Ỉmnḫꜥw*, your father? (I)s it true about these 9 servants of whom he said: "I gave them to you as my 2/3 that [I] divided with your m[other], as well as the house of (my) father (and) mother (= parental house)"?'

They declared as one mouth:

- 'Right is our [f]ather, they are in our possession truly.'

verification of the legal heirs' attitude concerning the liberality to *Ỉnkswnḏm*:

ḏdt.n (9) *ṯꜣt*

[*ỉḫ ḫr.tn*] *pꜣy sḫrw i.ỉrw pꜣy.tn ỉt n ꜥnḫ-n-nỉwt Ỉnksw*[*nḏm*] *tꜣy ḥbsw sꜣwy*

(10) *ḏd.w m* [*r wꜥ*

mꜣꜥttw pꜣ?][594] *ỉryw pꜣy.n ỉt ỉr pꜣ ỉry.f ỉry nym rḫy mdwty ỉm.f sꜣwy ꜣḫttw.f* (11) *ỉmỉ di.f sw*[*n mr.f*]

ḏdt.n ṯꜣt

593 When addressing his children, the vizier refers to the father's complete identification 'the prophet *Ỉmnḫꜥw*, your father' and does the same concerning '*ꜥnḫ-n-nỉwt Ỉnksw*[*nḏm*], this companion of his'.

594 Černý & Peet (1927: 35 n.23) and *KRI* VI, 741: [*sḏm.n pꜣ*] because of the lack of space; but an abbreviated form may be used here.

ir iw bn ḥmt sꜣwt iwnꜣ iw ḫꜣ[rw][595] *nḥsy iw mr.f sw [i]w.f dit n.s* (12) *ꜣḫttw.f [nym i.]irw.f wsfy pꜣ iry.f imi [n.s pꜣ]* 4 *bꜣkiw i[.in.f i]rm ꜥnḫ-n-niwt Ỉnkswnḏm* (13) *ḥnꜥ pꜣ [in.f nb] irm.st i.ḏd.f tw.i dit n.st pꜣy.i rwy [ḥr pꜣ]y.st r-3 iw bn ir šriw šriw* (IV.1) *mdty m pꜣy sḫrw i.ir.i n.st m pꜣ hrw*

What (the) vizier said:

- '[What can you say (about)] these provisions that your father has made in favor of (the) *ꜥnḫ-n-niwt Ỉnksw[nḏm]*, this *ḥbsw*[596] of his ?'

They declared as [one mouth:

- 'Right is?] what has done our father. As for what he has done, who will speak against it? His are his assets. Let him bequeath th[em as he wishes].'

What (the) vizier said:

- 'But (even) if (she) would not have been (the) woman of his, but an Syr[ian] (or) Nubian he would have loved, and he had bequeathed his assets to her, [who is it] who would void the (provision) he took? Give [her the] 4 servants that he [acquired w]ith (the) *ꜥnḫ-n-niwt Ỉnkswnḏm* and [all] that [he acquired] with her, (as) he said: "I bequeath to her my 2/3 [with h]er 1/3 while neither a son (nor) a daughter shall question these provisions that I made for her today."'

***Fiat* of the vizier**:

ḏd ṯꜣt

irw mitt m pꜣ ḏd it-nṯr Ỉmnḫꜥw pꜣy it-nṯr nty ꜥḥꜥ m-bꜣḥ.i

(The) vizier said:

- 'It must be acted in conformity with what stated (the) god's father *Ỉmnḫꜥw*, this god's father who is standing in front of me.'

Record order and copy:

(2) *diw ṯꜣt m ḥr n wꜥb sš n tmꜣ Ptḥmḥbw n tꜣ ḳnbt tꜣ ḥwt Wsrmꜣꜥtrꜥ Mrimn ꜥ.w.s. r-ḏd imi mn pꜣy sḫrw i.ir.i* (3) *ḥr ꜥrw nt ḏmꜥ m tꜣ ḥwt Wsrmꜣꜥtrꜥ Mrimn ꜥ.w.s. iw.tw iry m-mitt n tꜣ ḳnbt ꜥꜣt n niwt*

(The) vizier commissioned (the) priest (and) scribe of (the) mat[597] *Ptḥmḥbw* of the court of the temple of *Wsrmꜣꜥtrꜥ Mrimn* L.P.H., saying: 'Let these provisions that I have acted be recorded upon a roll of papyrus in the temple of *Wsrmꜣꜥtrꜥ Mrimn* L.P.H.'; and a copy (= likewise) was made for the High Court of (the) City (= Thebes).

* Neo-Egyptian characteristics:

- cataphoric articloid (*nꜣ ẖrdw n it-nṯr* PN; *nꜣ snw ꜥꜣytw nꜣy.f ẖrdw; tꜣ mdwt i.ḏd.*N; *pꜣ pr it mwt; tꜣ ḥbsw sꜣwy; tꜣ ḳnbt tꜣ ḥwt* PN; *tꜣ ḳnbt ꜥꜣyt n niwt; pꜣ ḏd it-nṯr; tꜣ ḳnbt tꜣ ḥwt Wsrmꜣꜥtrꜥ Mrimn*) and with substantivized perfect relative forms;
- anaphoric and cataphoric articloid (*tꜣ ḥwt Wsrmꜣꜥtrꜥ Mrimn*);
- Neo-Egyptian possessive determinator for kinship (*nꜣy.f ẖrdw, pꜣy.tn it, tꜣy.tn m[wt]*) and ownership right relations (*pꜣy.i rwy; [pꜣ]y.st r-3*);

595 Asiatic, Syrian; see Spalinger (1984: 636 n.16) concerning *Snims*' will (*stela Cairo* CG 34016, 18th dynasty) where, interestingly, the same *ḫꜣrw nḥsy* association is used, albeit in another context (*Urk.* IV 1069, lines 12-3 *ink nḥsy ntk ḫꜣrw*).

596 'Respectable but secondary relationship' for Eyre (1992: 212), as for Théodoridès (1965: 101). See Toivari-Viitala (2001: 32-8) for a recent analysis of *ḥbs(y/w)t*. One may ask if the [COERCION] and [ROPE/TIE] classifiers that sometimes accompany the lexeme do not imply that the *ḥbs(y/w)t* is perceived as a companion with whom '*the knot has been tied*'?

597 See Eyre (1980: iii): 'accounts scribe'; McDowell (1990: 146-7).

- *iḫ ḫr.tn tꜣ mdwt i.ḏd*.N: direct question in examination context (allocutive mode) constructed with # proclitic interrogative particle *iḫ* (Neo-Egyptian use) + prospective *sḏm.f* (alethic modality) + determined N (preposition *m* omitted) + Neo-Egyptian perfect relative form with prothetic *yod* #.
For *LEG* § 30.3, the *iḫ ḫr.k* formation does not belong to the *iḫ stp.k* pattern ('initial conjunctional main clause') but is a fixed pattern in which *ḫr.k* 'is apparently a Middle Egyptian relative form indicating the present time', following 'mainly the perfect active *ḏd.tw* formation'. Here it follows the *ḏdt.n*.N form and should be distinguished from the 'frozen' *ḫr.f* pattern in trailing position. Examples offered by Groll are all from *pBM* 10052 and those in *Wb* III, 316.10 come from *pMayer* A, thus both from the context of the cross-examination of the *Tomb Robberies*. We thus have in all cases a legal examination dialogue, the form expressing a firm request by the competent authorities to answer their questions.
This first type of open, direct question is aimed at collecting facts ('WH-words question') ; the attitude of the questioner is firm and inviting (use of alethic modality) in order to elicit information;
- Neo-Egyptian perfect relative forms with prothetic *yod* (*i.ḏd*.N, *i.ḏd.f, i.pš*[*.i*], *i.irw*.N, *i.ir.i*) used in the dialogue, as opposed to classical past relative *ḏdt.n*.N belonging to its delocutive framework;
- (*i*)*n mꜣꜥt m* N: second type of question addressed by the competent authority (the vizier) to the children, restricting the scope of the first question. It consists of a question for corroboration ('Yes-No question') in the context of an examination, constructed with # interrogative particle (*i*)*n* + *mꜣꜥt* + preposition *m* + nominal syntagm #[598]. The use of *mꜣꜥt*/*ꜥḏꜣ* (limited lexemic constituency) is typical of legal contexts, as in verdicts;
- *di.i st n*{*t*}*.tn*: introduced by a tag clause *i.ḏd.f* inside the dialogue, a paraphrased quotation of the testator's statement in locutive mode using perfect report instead of the will's conjunctive following the explicit performative;
- Neo-Egyptian deictic *pꜣy* (*pꜣy* 9 *bꜣkiw, pꜣy sḫrw, tꜣy ḥbsw, pꜣy it-nṯr*);
- Neo-Egyptian delocutive plural *st* and feminine *sw* dependent pronouns; feminine singular *.st* and plural *.w* suffixes;
- Neo-Egyptian prepositions *irm* and *m-di.f*;
- *ḏd.w m rꜣ wꜥ*: perfect report tag clause introducing the children answers, with expression implying unanimity (*m rꜣ wꜥ*). Repeated twice after the presentation of the vizier's questions by an archaic relative form. In this reported dialogic texteme, the tag clauses belong to two categories: the nominal, detached, and informative *ḏdt.n ṯꜣt* are opposed to the perfect report forms *ḏd.w*.
Compare with *Snims stela Cairo* CG 34016 (*Urk*. IV, 1068, line 17), probably in a *recital*: *ꜥḥꜥ.n.sn ḥr ḏd m r* [*wꜥ*] 'And they said as [one] mouth'. See also late examples, e.g. in abnormal hieratic sale contract of the 26th dynasty[599] (*iw.w rꜣ wꜥ*) and Demotic joint declaration to a lease (*ḏd… n wꜥ r*)[600];

598 See *LEG*, 61.2.12 '*in* preceding an adjectival sentence pattern' (e.g. *oIFAO* 681 (*i*)*n ꜥḏꜣ nꜣ dd*[*.i*] 'Is it false, the thing I said?') and Groll (1967: 42) 'patterns in which the first member is an abstract noun serving as an adjective' (*ꜥḏꜣ*/*mꜣꜥt pꜣ*(*y*) *sḏm.f* and the interrogative *m mꜣꜥt nꜣ*, all in legal contexts).

599 Malinine (1953: 58-9).

600 Martin (1995: 78).

- *mꜣꜥttw pꜣy.n* [*i*]*t*: adjectival nexus # adjectival rheme + determined N theme # of the type *nfr sw*[601]. Instead of a 'Yes' answer to the question (*i*)*n mꜣꜥt,* the brothers repeat the key-word *mꜣꜥttw* (corroboration of facts). Note how the adjective is spelt.
The format is characteristic of the legal genre of court transcripts (see e.g. *oGardiner/Ashmolean* 53, 7-8 *mꜣꜥtyw pꜣy rmṯ ist*).
The second answer of the brothers legitimizing their father's actions has been reconstructed on the basis of the first as a parallel pattern[602]: [*mꜣꜥttw pꜣ*?] *iryw*.N (# adjectival rheme + cataphoric articloid and relative form (with prothetic *yod*?) theme #). Compare with *pBM* 10052, 14, 7 (*ꜥdꜣ pꜣy ḏd.f nb*) and *pBerlin* P 3047, 14 (*mꜣꜥt nꜣ i.ḏdw sš ni-swt* PN);
- [*pꜣ*] *iryw pꜣy.n it, pꜣ iry.f, pꜣ* [*in.f nb*], *pꜣ ḏd it-nṯr Ỉmnḫꜥw*: substantivized perfect relatives without prothetic *yod*;
- *st m-di.n*: non converted adverbial nexus;
- *n mꜣꜥ*: Neo-Egyptian form of classical *m mꜣꜥt.* Again, the statement of the brothers is about truth, the corroboration of the facts expounded by the testator;
- *tꜣy ḥbsw sꜣwy*: # Neo-Egyptian deictic determinator + N + Neo-Egyptian delocutive singular possessive independent pronoun[603] #, a pattern already observed in this genre;
- *ir pꜣ iry.f iry nym rḫy mdwty im.f*: rhetorical question added by the brothers to their positive answer, in the form of # topicalized and substantivized relative form (without prothetic *yod*) + future [*iry* (instead of *iw* when the actor is not a suffix) + interrogative *nym*[604] (theme) + infinitive with intrusive *y* (omission of preposition *r*)] + object + prepositional adjunct (*.f* resumptive to *pꜣ iry.f*) #. Another case of *nym* as actor of a future form is to be found in *pAnastasi* I 21, 6 (*nym r mḥtw.f*).
The question is asked by the brothers for its persuasive effect, they are not expecting a reply; only the examiner (the vizier) is supposed to ask answerable questions leading to informative answers;
- *sꜣwy ꜣḫttw.f*: nominal nexus expressing rhematic possession, constructed with # Neo-Egyptian delocutive singular possessor independent pronoun (rheme) + N.f possessum (theme) #[605], based on a classical pattern. Note the Neo-Egyptian spelling of *ꜣḫttw*;
- *ir iw bn ḥmt sꜣwt iwnꜣ iw ḫꜣ*[*rw*] *nḥsy iw mr.f sw* [*i*]*w.f dit*: complex condition protasis with negative and positive contrasted nominal segments, constructed with # contrastive conditional *ir iw* + [discontinued negator *bn... iwnꜣ* of nominal nexus (implied theme = *Ỉnkswnḏm*)]$^{\text{negative segment}}$ + [contrastive *iw* + nominal nexus (implied theme[606] + undetermined rheme + converted perfect *iw mr.f* as adnexal expansion[607]) + sequential past [*i*]*w.f dit*]$^{\text{positive segment}}$ #[608].
The 'but (even) if' condition creates an imaginary scenario in order to make a point, to insist on the inescapable solution; the attitude of the vizier towards the reality of the condition is negatively marked;

---

601 See Groll (1967: 34-46), although she does not list this example.
602 Although it probably answers the open question [*iḫ ḫr.tn*] *pꜣy sḫrw i.irw pꜣy.tn it.*
603 See *supra pAdoptions* recto 4 for *sꜣwt*.
604 See Hintze (1952: 205-6) 'nur substantivisch gebraucht'; 'amalgamation of the particle *in* which introduces Cleft Sentences with the interrogative pronoun *m* "who?", "what?"' (Junge 2005: 178).
605 See Junge (2005: 165).
606 Satzinger (1976: 79): 'eingliedriger Nominalsatz'.
607 See Frandsen (1974: 194, 196).
608 See Groll (1967: 95) '*ir iw bn* A *iwnꜣ ø*' and Satzinger (1976: 79) *ir* with 'freie *iw*' + nominal sentence.

- [*nym i.*]*irw.f wsfy pꜣ iry.f*: rhetorical question in the form of a focus-initial cleft sentence[609], apodosis of the preceding, with # interrogative *nym* (rheme and focus) + analytic that-form [*i.*]*irw.f wsfy* (theme) + substantivized relative perfect without prothetic *yod* (object of [*i.*]*irw.f wsfy*) #;
- *i.ḏd.f*: tag clause with prothetic *yod* that-form (probably to be understood as following a missing preposition) opening the second quotation of the testator's will: *tw.i dit n.st pꜣy.i rwy* [*ḥr pꜣ*]*y.st r-3 iw bn ir šriw šriw mdty m pꜣy sḫrw i.ir.i n.st m pꜣ hrw*.
The part of the will that is quoted runs as follows: *tw.i dit* **[*pꜣ*] *iryw*(*.i*) *nb irm ꜥnḫ-n-niwt Ỉnkswnḏm tꜣ st-ḥmt nty m pꜣy.i pr*** *n.st* ***m pꜣ h*[*rw*] *m pꜣ bꜣki* 2 *ꜥ*[*ḥꜣ*]*wtyw bꜣki* 2 *ḥmwtt dmḏ* 4 *ḥnꜥ msw.w iw*** *pꜣ rwy ḥr pꜣy.st r*-3 (in bold the elements not mentioned by the vizier). Again it is not a literal quotation from the will and Théodoridès (1970: 201 n. 327) suggests that the vizier 'l'interprète en y apportant plus de rigueur dans l'expression juridique', the main reason to proceed before a competent authority. But curiously, the vizier quoted a warranty against claims that did not survive in the will itself (*iw bn ir šriw šriw mdty m pꜣy sḫrw i.ir.i n.st m pꜣ hrw*). This section of the record is especially enlighting in terms of Ramesside reference to oral speech (the testator's and perhaps also the vizier's) and of the degree of precision of legal written acts;
- *tw.i dit*: explicit performative (Neo-Egyptian locutive present);
- *iw bn ir šriw šriw mdty*: converted negative future with nominal actor, preposition omitted.
Compare with the *no-contest* clauses in *pAdoptions*: lines 4-5 in the summary of the title deed (*iw bn n.f šriw šriw r-ḥrw-r ink*) and in the will of the testatrix, verso lines 3-4 (*mtw šriw šriw sn sn n tꜣy.w mwt pꜣy.w it mdwt im.w*…). The formulation in *pTurin* 2021 is close to the one used in warranties against claims of coheirs (see *pAshmolean Museum* 1945.95 lines 3 and 5 *iw.f n.*N/f *bn mdt šriw šriw im.f*);
- *šriw šriw*: both genders filiation binomial;
- deictic articloid (*m pꜣ hrw*);
- *ḏd ṯꜣt*: perfect report tag clause introducing the vizier's *fiat* and recommendations.
The commentary form is opposed to the preceding detached archaic *ḏdt.n ṯꜣt* (see *supra ḏd.w m rꜣ wꜥ*);
- *diw ṯꜣt m ḥr*: perfect report of the vizier's action followed by *r-ḏd* tagged speech marker;
- *iw.tw iry*: agentless impersonal sequential past (preposition omitted, Neo-Egyptian form of the infinitive); agentless forms promote decontextualization and generalization characteristic of legal registers.

* 'Classical' degree 0 forms used:
- *ḏdt.n ṯꜣt*: classical relative neutrum *sḏmt.n*.N, an archaism (see *supra*). The vizier's questions are repeatedly introduced by a relatively past nominal tag clause (see *supra*);
- relator for kinship (*nꜣ ẖrdw n it-nṯr* PN), unclear kind of relation in frozen expression (*ꜥnḫ-n-niwt*), administrative or geographic dependence (PN *n tꜣ ḳnbt; tꜣ ḳnbt ꜥꜣyt n niwt; sš n tmꜣ*), and material relations (*ꜥrw nt ḏmꜥ*, marked concord with feminine *ꜥr*(*t*));
- PN *nty ꜥḥꜥ*: stative in relative clause;

609 See Satzinger (1976: 82-3): a 'Cleft Sentence als Konstruktion des Zweiten Gliedes' after protasis 'Wenn es nicht seine Frau sein solte…'. See the examples given by Hintze (1952: 206) and Groll (1967: 52), marked or not by proclitic focalizer *m*.

  - *imi mn pꜣy sḫrw*: iussive/3rd person causative imperative *imi* + prospective object. The direct speech of the vizier is quoted in order to report 'exactly' the words of the certifying authority;
  - *irw mitt*: passive prospective (deontic modality) as a direct speech of the vizier expressing his *fiat*;

* General dialectal features: degree 2.

* Legal formulae:
  - examination by the vizier: *ḏdt.n ṯꜣt* + *iḫ ḫr.tn tꜣ mdwt i.ḏd*.N (direct question) and *(i)n mꜣꜥt m* N (question for corroboration) + *ir iw* (imaginary scenario) followed by [*nym i.*]*irw.f wsfy pꜣ iry.f* (rhetorical question)
  - answer of the brothers: *ḏd.w m rꜣ wꜥ* (unanimity) + *mꜣꜥttw* (elaboration)
  - *fiat* of the vizier: *ḏd ṯꜣt* + *irw mitt m pꜣ ḏd it-nṯr* PN
  - record order and copy: *diw ṯꜣt m ḥr n* N PN (commission) + *r-ḏd* + *imi mn pꜣy sḫrw i.ir.i ḥr ꜥrw nt ḏmꜥ* (record) + *m* (location) + *iw.tw iry m-mitt n* (copy for the temple)

4. Colophon

Functionally, the record order and copy statement may belong to the colophon, but they are presentend as the follow-up to the reported speech and action and not as a technical-formal stipulation detached of a specific order as the following witnesses list; the two provisions have thus been analyzed separately. The question remains why did so many witnesses appear to probate the will in court (the list is not limitative)?

Witnesses: *m-bꜣḥ mttryw ḳnw ꜥšꜣt imy rn.f iry*	
Before very numerous witnesses of which name(s) are:	
(4) *ḥry sꜣw sšw Ḏḥwtymḥb n pꜣ mšꜥ*	chief of guardians of writings *Ḏḥwtymḥb* of the army
(5) *ḥry sꜣw Ḥri sꜣ Ḏḥwtynḫtw n pꜣ mšꜥ*	chief of guardians *Ḥri*, son of *Ḏḥwtynḫtw*, of the army
(6) *idnw Nsyḫnsw n* [*pꜣ*] *mšꜥ*	deputy *Nsyḫnsw* of [the] army
(7) *ḥry iḥ*[*w*] *Mnsnw* [*n*] *ḫn*[*w*]	stable-master *Mnsnw* [of] (the) interi[or][610]
(8) *kꜣṯꜣ*[*nw*] *Bꜣkinꜣst n* [*tꜣ ḥw*]*t*	chariote[er] *Bꜣkinꜣst* of the [templ]e
(9) *sš Ḏḥwtyms*[*w*] *n pꜣ ḫr*	scribe *Ḏḥwtyms*[*w*] of the Necropolis
(10) *sš Ỉwfnḫnsw n pꜣ ḫr*	scribe *Ỉwfnḫnsw* of the Necropolis
(11) [ꜥꜣ] *n ist Bꜣkinm(w)t n* [*pꜣ ḫr*]	[fore]man *Bꜣkinm(w)t* of [the Necropolis]
(12) *nꜣ ḫry-ḥbw n tꜣ ḥwt*	the lector-priests of the temple:
(13) *ḥꜣty-ꜥ Nsyimnipt*	governor *Nsyimnipt*
(14) *sš spꜣt Nsyimnipt*	scribe of (the) district *Nsyimnipt*
(15) *nꜣ ḥry mꜥḏꜣyw n pꜣ ḫr*	the chiefs of (the) police of the Necropolis:
(16) *ꜣṯw Ỉmnḫꜥw n imntt Niwt*	*ꜣṯw*-officer *Ỉmnḫꜥw* of (the) west of (the) City (= Thebes)
(17) *ꜣṯw Pꜣḫꜣrw n imntt Niwt*	*ꜣṯw*-officer *Pꜣḫꜣrw* of (the) west of (the) City
(18) *ꜣṯw Pꜣnḫtipt*	*ꜣṯw*-officer *Pꜣnḫtipt*
(19) *ꜣṯw Ỉmn*[*ḫ*]*tpw*	*ꜣṯw*-officer *Ỉmn*[*ḫ*]*tpw*
(20) *ꜣṯw Ỉmniptnḫtw*	*ꜣṯw*-officer *Ỉmniptnḫtw*
(21) *ꜣṯw ꜥnḫtwmdiimn*	*ꜣṯw*-officer *ꜥnḫtwmdiimn*

610 The perimeter within which the members of the community circulate: the village and work sites (KV, QV).

* Neo-Egyptian characteristics:
- Neo-Egyptian lexemes (*kꜣṯꜣ*[*n*]);
- exophoric articloid (*pꜣ mšꜥ, pꜣ ẖr, tꜣ ḥwt*) or deictic articloid (*tꜣ ḥwt*);
- cataphoric articloid (*nꜣ ḥry-ḥbw n tꜣ ḥwt; nꜣ ḥry mḏꜣyw n pꜣ ẖr*).

* 'Classical' degree 0 forms used:
- *imy rn.f iry*: short formula[611] on the exact model of the inscription of *Ḥꜥpydfꜣ*'s tomb, in a table belonging to the third 'contract' (Griffith 1889: pl. 7, table's first line: *im*(*y*) *rn.f ir*(*y*) + list of names) ; see also *pKahun* VII.1(*imy rn.f mtrw iry imyt-pr tn r-gs.sn*) and I.1 (*imy rn.f rmṯ iry nn r-gs.sn*); also used in *Snims stela Cairo* CG 34016, *Urk*. IV, 1066 line 16 ([*imy*] *rnw.f iry* + N PN). The formula is thus familiar in legal genres and somewhat archaic;
- relator for administrative dependence (*sš n pꜣ mšꜥ*, PN *n pꜣ ẖr, ꜣṯw* PN *n imntt Niwt*) and dominion relations ([*ꜥꜣ*] *n ist*);

* General dialectal features: degree 2.

* Legal formula: witnesses: *m-bꜣḥ mttryw ḳnw ꜥšꜣt imy rn.f iry* + list (title + PN)

Categorization of terms of special relevance in the legal register:

- *ꜥḳ*  *r* [*pr*]: to enter the house of, cohabitate.
  See Pestman (1961: 10) and Toivari-Viitala (2001: 74, n.446). Concerning the [MOTION] superordinate category, see David (2007).
- [*ꜥr*]*ḳ*  *ḥr*: to swear about, repudiate (?). See Allam (1973: 321) '[Ich band] mich darüber (durch einen Eid)'; McDowell (1990: 33-36) 'to swear,' 'to reject, forswear, or deny upon oath,' 'to abjure,' 'to renounce' (a woman, an asset). For Demotic and Coptic, see Richter (2002: 280-1).
  The lexeme *ꜥrḳ* 'to end'[612] is not classified during the Old Kingdom; *ꜥrḳ* 'to swear' is generally classified by  or by  during the Middle Kingdom. The sign  is also used as a phonetic element ('phonetic classifier'[613]) and as a logogram (phonetic + iconic values). New Kingdom *ꜥrḳ* 'to swear' is classified by and  or (and also by 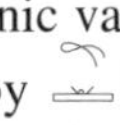 in Ramesside papyri). New Kingdom cases of the use of *ꜥrḳ ḥr* concerning repudiation of a woman are few[614]. It is not clear if the object of *ꜥrḳ* in these texts is the woman herself (to swear about a woman = to repudiate her)[615] or a financial arrangement[616], and if it has to be taken in the sense of *to swear* or *to end*.
  Here, the lexeme belongs to the basic level [BINDING] (although the string is also a 'phonetic classifier' in this case), superordinate [ABSTRACT] and basic level [MOUTH LINKED ACTIVITIES] categories. A public, verbal declaration concerning abstract rights is probably what is signified here by the choice of categorization. Note that the lexeme *ꜥnḫ*

611 See Donker van Heel & Haring (2003: 86-7) 'name-list thereof'.
612 *ÄW* I, 283.
613 *EG* § 54; David (2006: 25 n.25).
614 See the list in Toivari-Viitala (2001:92) besides our *pTurin* 2021; most texts and contexts are unclear.
615 But if there is no formal act at the basis of the union between men and women, why should there be a formal oath at its dissolution? The only reasons should be either financial, and then the 'oath' would only concern financial terms, not the act itself of repudiating a woman, or a promise not to approach the 'divorced' party, a voluntary version of modern restraining orders against domestic violence.
616 See McDowell (1990: 35-6): 'to renounce' a woman; Toivari-Viitala (2001: 90).

'oath' is usually not classified in our corpus, but when it is, the classifier of the [MOUTH LINKED ACTIVITIES] is used, as in *oDeM* 433 or *oIFAO* 388.

- *ḳnbt*: court.
- *iri rwy r r-*3: to divide the community property (= 'to make 2/3 to 1/3').
- *rwy*: two-thirds (the man's share in the community property).
- *r-*3: third (the woman's share in the community property).
- *ꜥḥꜥ m-bꜣḥ*: to stand before (the judges/vizier). See *supra ꜥḥꜥ rḳw*. One also has to stand to take an oath (see *pCairo* JE 65739, line 26).
- *ini* (*bꜣki*): to acquire (a slave).
- *rdi*: to give, bequeath.
- *dwny*: to give a bonus, to advantage someone. Old and Middle Kingdom *dwn* mainly classified by (but also by and) means primarily 'to stretch'; the semantic 'to give a bonus' is apparently known only since the New Kingdom and must be related to (*m*)*twnw* 'bonus, advantage' (see *supra*).
  The fact that our lexeme is classified in the superordinate [MOTION] category is interesting because it is based on an orientation metaphor (FRONT-BACK) also at the basis of English 'advantage' (something moved ahead), or French 'avantage' and 'avancement'.
- *m-di.f*: in the possession of.
- *dni*(*t*): share. Here without the superordinate [ABSTRACT] category classifier (see *supra*).
- *pš*[?]: share, portion.
- *pꜣ iry.i*/*in.i nb irm* (PN): all I have made/acquired with PN (mate), the *acquets*. See *supra* the discussion of *mꜥḏꜣ*.
- *iri m šriw*[]: to treat as a child/daughter. See *supra pAdoptions*.
- *smn*[?]: to establish someone. Compare with *grg-pr* in *Naunakhte*.
- *iw m-bꜣḥ*: to approach (the vizier). See modern legal 'to approach the bench'; *spr* is also used in this sense (McDowell 1990: 15).
- *srw n tꜣ ḳnbt*: officials of the court. McDowell (1990: 66): 'standard word for judge'. Both lexemes are classified in the superordinate [MALE-HUMAN] category.
- *r rdit rḫ*: to let know, to inform.
- *iri sẖrw*: to make provisions.
- *ꜣḫtt*: assets.
- *hꜣy r*: to get a share. See *Naunakhte*.
- *sfyrw*[?]: alimony? *Hapax*. Černý & Peet (1927: 32, 35 n.18) 'dowry (??)' suggest regarding it as a foreign lexeme 'Hebrew ספר, "a writing"?'; Černý (1937-8: 46) reads the plant classifier and corrects his first assumption 'un équivalent de ce qu'Amenkhēw a donné comme sa part à l'occasion du mariage avec sa seconde femme'; Seidl (1957: 20, 56) 'Mitgift (?)' 'Frauen-Anteil (?)'; Pestman (1961: 107 n.6) 'her part in the community of goods'; Helck (1961-70: 530, 532) 'Mitgift' 'Brautgabe'; Théodoridès (1967b: 123 n.67) 'subsistance' and (1968b: 152) 'privilège féminin, mais dont la réalisation demeure soumise à la décision maritale'; Allam (1973: 321, 324 n.28) 'Gut';
- *mꜣꜥt*(*tw*): to be right.

During the Old Kingdom the lexeme is not classified. The papyrus roll appears as a classifier during the Middle Kingdom. Gardiner (*EG*, 474) notes that the adjective 'true' and related lexemes do not use the feather icon 'nor has it been found in M.E. hieratic in any words from this stem' (but the feather appears instead of the personification of *Mꜣꜥt* during this period[617]); the feather as a phonetic element (and classifier?) in our lexeme is New Kingdom practice (*Wb* II, 21).
The superordinate [ABSTRACT] category includes the legal concept of truthfulness, and the feather recalls the metaphor of the scales in the context of the Egyptian 'psychostasy' (for modern legal concepts driven by the same metaphors of weight and balance, see David 2007).

- *wsfy* : to suppress, void (provisions).
  The lexeme *wsf* is not classified during the Old Kingdom; during the Middle Kingdom, it is classified by both or by . Thus, since the Middle Kingdom, the lexeme is categorized in a semantic field of motion, a motion translated by human legs (or reversed for hindered movement) or a bird alighting from flight (*ẖni* is a central member of the basic-level action category [HALT?]). Although human legs are used to translate any type of motion, human or not (David 2007), the choice of the classifier implies that the halt motion is viewed as typically embodied by a bird. Furthermore, physical suppression of motion is used to translate the abstract notion of rendering void someone's will by a metaphorical process. As usual the [ABSTRACT] category classifier completes the idea of a written embodiment of the decision and the fact that it concerns abstract rights.
- *iri mdty* *m sẖrw*: to contest provisions.
- *iri mitt* *m*: to conform to, to act in conformity with.
- *di m ḥr n*: to place in sight of, commission someone. See David (2006: esp. 202-3) for the expression in royal decrees.
- *tꜣ ḳnbt* *tꜣ ḥwt* PN: the court of the temple PN. The [ABSTRACT] category classifier replaces here the classifier of the superordinate [MALE-HUMAN] category.
- *mn* : to record, fix. See Eyre (1980: 11).
- *iri m-mitt* : to make a copy. See David (2006: 110-1) for the expression in royal decrees.
- *ḳnbt* *ꜥꜣt* [ ] *n Niwt*: the high court of the City (Thebes).
- *mttry* : witness.
- *m rꜣ wꜥ*: in one voice, unanimously. See Richter (2002: 62) for Demotic *n wꜥ rꜣ*.

617 *ÄW* II, 1007-10.

10. Elliptic records of movable assets: (social) gifts or else?

Clearly, most of the following documents do not belong to the consentient genre; they are probably brief records concerning private assets transmissions but not private law instruments; they are not constitutive of rights. But one must try to assess their contents in order to complete the picture of private assets transmissions during the Ramesside Period.

As already mentioned, Egyptian documents use the verb *rdi* in many different contexts[618], associated with a broad spectrum of legal issues including successions, donations, partitions, exchanges, etc. A rather large group of short Ramesside ostraca mention the 'giving' to certain persons of a list of mostly consumable products by a private person; these documents may be interpreted as recording gifts, the mention of a *consideration* generally lacking. In 1982, Janssen wrote an article concerning 'reciprocal gift-giving' in Deir el-Medina, where 'gift' is not to be understood as a 'free manifestation of generosity' since 'the receiver is generally obliged to present a counter-gift, either immediately or after a lapse of time.' (p. 254). In Janssen's view, these Ramesside gifts are not isolated; they must be considered in the context of broader social behavior, and since reciprocity means exchange, their true nature is more of a barter than of a liberality. Even though such exchanges certainly do not have the same meaning in the economic context of ancient Egypt as in our modern societies, we must note that gift exchanges on private occasions are also a social requirement for us. They should in this case be viewed as *manual gifts*[619], and of course without the necessity of a written instrument. For Janssen these Egyptian records are not legal documents, but belong to the *aide-mémoire*[620] category, like most of the ostraca relating to legal procedures or contracts; records had to be made because counter-gifts were social obligations.

A non-exhaustive list of 'gifts' ostraca has been provided by Janssen (1982, 1997) and Grandet (2003)[621] and some of them will be examined below. For the most part, this corpus consists of ambiguous documents, lacking contextual information. The intention may be the execution of a broad spectrum of transactions; documents constructed as a series of # PN + list of goods # items might imply virtually anything: transmission or reception of gifts, trade, production of goods, private or public distribution, offerings, consumption…

In examining these records, one must first assess the *common features* of these texts and then distinguish sub-categories based on *significant variation factors*. The records have the following *common features*:

- on ostraca
- cursory
- context-dependent
- containing lists of mainly consumable goods (never the transmission of an entire patrimony or of immovables)
- generally no mention of a *consideration*
- written in a business hand and in a formulaic minimalist style,
- ostraca generally undated although the transmissions of goods may be dated
- lacking a docket

618 See Bleiberg (1996: 23).

619 See Continental Law's *dons manuels* and, more precisely, *présents d'usage*, 'Dons ou cadeaux offerts, conformément aux usages, à l'occasion de certaines fêtes ou cérémonies (…) et soumis, quand ces dons ne sont pas excessifs eu égard aux coutumes et à la situation sociale du donateur, à un régime particulier. Ex. ils sont dispensés du rapport successoral (…)' (Cornu 2003: 682-3).

620 Janssen (1982: 256-7). But, interestingly, the word *sḫꜣ* 'memorandum' is never used in this context.

621 Note that Grandet does not specify if the 'don de biens' is reciprocal or not, except in the case of *oDeM* 948 ('échange de cadeaux'); furthermore, Grandet may use 'don' in a wider sense, not as 'donation'.

- lacking mention of forum, witnesses, scribe, title deed, oath, oracle, performative attribution of ownership, authentication
- not using lexemes related to partitions (*pš, dni*) and lacking a future *descent and distribution* rule
- without internal characterization of the document
- usually only one texteme and absence of pre-material, *recital* and colophon.

We propose the following *significant variation factors* as indicators of textual genres and sub-categories:
- provenance of the document: may indicate if it was an official or private document
- day-by-day record of goods distribution (and absentees), delocutive mode: administrative duty roster
- epistolary formulae, allocutive mode: letter (which may also involve a gift or a transaction)
- narrative forms in delocutive or locutive mode: narrative genre, or *recital* in legal text
- locutive mode, no mention of the writer's proper name: personal *aide-mémoire*
- valuation of assets with # *ỉr n dbn* + quantifier # syntagm: commercial transaction, valuation of shares
- lexemes used[622]: *rdi* opposed to *ỉni* (delivery, acquisition), *ỉṯ3 n* (*consideration*?), *šsp* (reception), *ỉri* (production?)[623]
- # PN + goods # lists without any other precision
- indication of special circumstances, such as religious festival, drinking party, private feast involving personal event, river bank market exchanges, performance of a payable service
- expression of a gratuitous intent
- mention of delivery agents: excludes personal participation in a 'party'
- formalism (such as archaic anaphora, specific phraseology or layout): administrative or legal genre
- dated transmission between parties all named: contextualized information usually excluding an *aide-mémoire* for the writer's private use
- involvement of family members: may imply some kind of familial obligation
- only consumables or other movables involved
- number of donors and recipients: the presence of a unique donor and a unique recipient precludes a festive occasion on which all the invited people bring a present; these may be cases of personal allowance, gift, bequest, or transaction
- notification formula # *r rdit rḫ.tw* #: indicates that the list is brought to the attention of one or more persons, which excludes an *aide-mémoire* for the writer's private use
- manifestation of will (invitation to transmit an item or performative form): legal or epistolary text
- degree of Neo-Egyptian: indicates the register used, more or less formal
- administrative/business practice features (e.g. abbreviations) and diacritical marks; bichromy.

622 These texts use a fairly limited number of 'legal terms' such as *r rdit rḫ.tw; rdi; ỉr n; ỉni; ỉṯ3; r(3); 3ḫt/nkt*, which are rather common lexemes and are either not classified or quite conventional; since the purpose of this section is primarily to categorize texts, the categorization features of the lexemes are not presented here.

623 Note that the lexeme *sw3ḏ* (*traditio*) is never used.

Obviously, we are not dealing with an homogenous *genre* but with a mixed bag of documents, the purpose and nature of which is quite elusive in most cases; and if some of these texts represent a partial record of a legal transaction or transmission of assets, they are clearly distinct from the wills and gift deeds previously analyzed, lacking their distinctive textemes and clauses. The language used is mainly a bureaucratic, formulaic register, even in the case of possible personal 'memo' notes; the people who wrote them were used to reading and writing bureaucratic records; this is not a case of idiosyncratic registers reflecting the personality and style of their writers. Even when writing or drawing on ostraca, the Egyptians rarely depart from the canonic way of dealing with these activities: totally free sketches and notes are virtually non-existent[624]. Once again, the following analysis is limited to the establishment of a distinction between these 'gifts' records and the liberalities belonging to the consentient genre as studied *supra*.

a. Administrative duty roster

oGlasgow D 1925.76 (*oColin Campbell* 11) and *oGardiner/Ashmolean* 52

Date: 20th dynasty, Ramesses III
Hieroglyphic version: *KRI* VII, 293-5 n.272 A 376
Features: damaged ostraca of unknown provenance. Gifts for Janssen (1982: 257, n.21), but clearly administrative supplies delivery journal, duty-roster/*wrš*-list[625], on the basis of day-by-day structure and the distribution and absentees entries. Their structure is the following:

day-by-day dating (no regnal year) + PN (beneficiary/absent) + goods or *iw*/*šsp* 'what came/was received' + *m-ḏrt* PN[626] 'by (the) hand of (delivery agent)' + goods (+ total).

Concerning the delivery agency of named policemen (middlemen), Černý (2001: 281) notes that 'It is surprising how often objects of varying kinds are said to have been '*received*', '*gone out*' or '*brought*' (...) '*by the hand of*' a Medjay. With a few exceptions they are foodstuffs, probably in repayment of supplies from workmen.'[627] The reason for using an agent may be that the parties do not live in the same area, that the agent was a promoter of the deal, or because the agent is also a witness to the delivery.

Note the degree 1 Neo-Egyptian (absence of nexus), the absence of *consideration* mention, administrative practice features (corrections, abbreviation, bichromy), delocutive texteme, staple commodities delivered including wood. Thus we are not dealing with private sphere 'reciprocal gift-giving' here but with the public distribution of supplies.

624 Except perhaps for the one-of-a-kind and minimalist drawing of *oDeM* 2928.

625 McDowell (1993: 16) notes that it 'picks up the roster one month after the similar O Glasgow D.1925.67 leaves off.'; 'Supplies/Turnus' for *KRI* VII, 293.

626 For the formulae # date *šsp m-ḏrt* PN # and # (date) *iw m-ḏrt* PN # in headings of 'accounts of necropolis supplies', see Donker van Heel & Haring (2003: 126-7, 132). We are not dealing with headings here.

627 See also Janssen (2005: 104-5); Haring (2003: 144) notes that # *m-ḏrt* PN # appears in the headings of documents concerning administrative matters.

b Epistolary genre[628]

pDeM 11

Date: 20th dynasty, Ramesses V
Hieroglyphic version: *KRI* VI, 268-9 n.36.1
Features: the sole papyrus in 'reciprocal gift-giving' documents, it is damaged and originates from Deir el-Medina 'dans un espace trapézoïdal' 'entre une pyramide et une chapelle' au sud de la chapelle 1166'[629]. Probably a model of a private letter addressed by a scribe to another scribe and mentioning a request for transmission of movables; it is unclear if a *consideration* is mentioned[630]. Contains a gift for Janssen (1982: 258, n.25), although he agrees that it 'may belong to another category' of texts (see *infra* the *Contract-related records* chapter). It has the following structure:

Epistolary formulae: heading with sender and addressee, complimentary preamble: (R.1) *sš* PN *nḏ-ḫrt [n] sš* PN *m ꜥ.w.s. m ḥs[t P3]* (2) *Rꜥḥr3ḫty [r-n]ty* (…) (The) scribe PN greets (the) scribe PN in L.P.H. (and) in fav[our of *P3*] *Rꜥḥr3ḫty*, [to (let you know) t]hat: (…) **Content**: (V.2) (…) *im[y di]w.k wꜥ ḥꜥti n* (3) [PN?] *m Niwt p3y ḳ(n)iw i[w].k [h3bt]w.f r int.w m [...ḫ3]rwry m p3[y] sp* (…) *wnn t3 šꜥ(t)* […] (5) *p3y [nty] ḫ3rwy* 3 *m-im* (6) [… *mtw.k dit*] *in.tw.w n.i* […] Caus[e that you will g]ive one bed to [PN?] in (the) City (Thebes), (and) this chair. You [shall send h]im to bring/acquire them from [… Sy]rian woman on thi[s] occasion (…). As soon as this letter [reaches you, you are to go to] this [place wh]ere (the) 3 Syrians are [and cause] that they will be brought to me […]

Bakir notes that 'real letters, as distinguished from the models, (…) [have] only one address visible on the outside, when it is folded and sealed' (1970: 36); here an address is missing. He adds that the heading formula used here is not employed when writing to inferiors (*ibid.*, 47). Note that the recto is a palimpsest, there is a correction, and the movables to be transmitted are pieces of furniture, not staple commodities; the use of *ini* and *rdi* is ambiguous (*consideration*?), but in any case we do not have a concomitant or *a posteriori* record here of 'reciprocal gift-giving', rather an invitation to take some measures, thus a manifestation of will in a letter.

c. Notified records

Of the 'reciprocal gift-giving' documents, a small percentage use the impersonal notification formula *r (r)dit rḫ.tw* (or an allocutive version of it), which means in our view that the text is intended to receive some kind of publicity or to be brought to the attention of someone, and is not a simple personal note meant to remain such. The notification of what someone has given would seem a curious way of making a 'gift', even if reciprocity is intended. Other short texts,

628 Other documents may also belong to the epistolary genre since they are written in the allocutive mode, sometimes also using narrative forms, but they do not have any specific epistolary formula: see *infra* o*Glasgow D* 1925.66, *oDeM* 945 and 934.
629 Černý & Posener (1978: vii and n.2).
630 For Cooney (2006: 50 n. 45), 'sale of a *ḥꜥtj* bed in the town'.

not mentioned by Janssen, could represent the same type of notifications, e.g. *oBerlin* P 10637, *oCairo* CG 25612 (that uses a similar opening as *oDeM* 239: *rꜣ n ṯꜣy mḏꜣt* PN).

c.1 Remuneration for service: *oDeM* 941

Date: 20th dynasty (Wimmer 2004: 517)
Hieroglyphic version: Grandet (2003: 378)
Features: incomplete limestone ostracon, provenance unknown, and although for Grandet it is a 'mémoire relatif à un don de biens'[631], on the basis of its structure it probably consists of the notification of the production and transmission of goods in the context of a paid service:

(1) *r rdit rḫ*[*.tw pꜣ* ?] (2) *i.irt n.f* + movable(s?)
For informati[on (relative to) w]hat has been made for him: (movable(s?))
(3) *r rdit rḫ.tw pꜣ i.di.f n* [PN *r.st*?] (4) + list of goods
For information (relative to) what he gave to [PN for it?]: (list)

The notification formula implies that the document is not a mere *aide-mémoire*, but a record that is intended to be seen by a third party, made in a delocutive mode and degree 2 Neo-Egyptian. Only one 'donor' and one recipient are implied, and only the latter is probably named. The goods that are the object of the transaction are not simple staple commodities like those offered in the context of a social gathering. The production of goods is implied by *i.irt n.f* + movable asset(s), and *pꜣ i.di.f n* [PN] could relate to the price paid for it, thus a *consideration*. The 1st notification formula is reminiscent of Janssen's[632] 5th category of transactions 'recompense for the manufacture of an object', typically # *r rdit rḫ.tw bꜣkw nb i.irw* PN *n* PN #, and one of its variants # *r rdit rḫ.tw pꜣ i.ir*.PN *n* PN #. The 2nd notification formula is closer to Janssen's[633] 2nd category which may indicate a 'barter'[634] # *r rdit rḫ.tw ꜣḫt nb i.diw* PN *n* PN # and one of its variant # *r rdit rḫ.tw pꜣ diw nb* PN *n* PN #. See *infra* similar records in the *Contract-related records* chapter.

c. 2 Regular allowances or remuneration: o*Glasgow D* 1925.66 (*oColin Campbell* 1)

Date: 19th-20th dynasties
Hieroglyphic version: McDowell (1993: pl. 1)
Features: incomplete limestone ostracon of unknown provenance. Helck (1961-70: 664) and Allam (1973: 79) suggest that the text may be regarded as an epistolary document (allocutive notification formula[635], narrative sequential *iw.i ḥr dit*, but absence of introductory and closing epistolary formulae); it is addressed to an unnamed recipient and relates to the recurrent transmissions of staple commodities, without expressed *consideration*. Although for Janssen (1982: 258) it concerns gifts, it may represent

631 Grandet (2003: 114).
632 Janssen (1975: 502-3).
633 Janssen (1975: 497-9).
634 Donker van Heel & Haring (2003: 148-9) regard the second formula in headings as referring to accounts of transfer in which the giver keeps the record in expectation of a 'recompense'; but if the preposition *r* follows the PN, this may be a case of 'accounts of payment category' (*ibid.*, 153).
635 As in *oGardiner/Ashmolean* 90, lines 4-7.

regular material support to a woman by an ex-companion[636] or relative[637] living at some distance, or even a payment made in several parts in the framework of an unknown transaction. It has the following structure:

(R.1) *(r) dit rḫ.kwi [rdyt n ?]* (2) PN *m[-ḏrt mḏ3iw]* (3) PN + list of consumables (To) inform you[638] [about what was given to?] PN by [the hand of policeman] PN: (list) (4) *wḥm m-ḏrt mḏ3iw* PN + list of consumables Again by (the) hand of policeman PN: (list) *(r) dit rḫ.t p3y di.i in.[t]w* (5) *n.t m-ḏrt mḏ3iw* PN + list of consumables (To) inform you[639] of that which I caused that [b]e brought to you by (the) hand of policeman PN: (list) (7) *wḥm m-ḏrt mḏ3iw* PN + list of consumables Again by (the) hand of policeman PN: (list) (11) *iw.i ḥr dit in.tw n.t* + list of consumables And I caused that be brought to you: (list) (V.1) *ns t3 rnpt iw bn tw.t ḥr dit s3[.t ?]* (2) *ḥr.sn* It belongs to this year, while you do not get sat[isfaction?] from them.

Note the change in the gender of the addressee of the notification, probably an error; it seems that only one unnamed 'donor' is implied, but perhaps two 'donatees' (creditors ?)[640], the first perhaps named in line 2, the second remaining an anonymous 'you'. In the case of 'reciprocal gift-giving' at parties, it would be quite unusual to use someone's agency[641]. The final reference to an annual benefit of some sort may also indicate the granting of an allowance, as is the case for instance in *oUniversity College* 19614.

c.3 Regular allowances: *oBerlin* P 12406 and *oGlasgow D* 1925.71 (*oColin Campbell* 6)

Date: 20th dynasty, Ramesses III-VI
Hieroglyphic version: Munich Deir el-Medine online and *KRI* VII, 361-2 n.61 A 31
Features: incomplete limestone ostraca, both of unknown provenance but certainly from Deir el-Medina. They concern the notification of repeated transmissions of goods by a son to his father, without expressed *consideration*. Both texts begin with the same notification formula (*r dit rḫ.tw 3ḫt nb(t) i.dit/w Wsḫtnnmtt n p3y.f it*), but the occasions of the transmissions and the quantities vary in each text (they may concern different periods). The texts have the following structure:

***oBerlin* P 12406**

636 Helck (1961-70: 664) 'Aufstellung der Leistung eines Mannes an seine Frau, hier als Brief an sie gerichtet', regarding the delivery by a policeman as an indication that 'der Sender also eine höhere Stellung eingenommen haben muß'.
637 McDowell (1993: 4).
638 Masculine.
639 Feminine.
640 Which would explain the two notification formulae acting also as dividers between two groups of transfers intended for different recipients.
641 This point has been noted by Janssen (1982: 258) who underlines that it cannot be explained, but that the fact that these 'gifts' were recorded demonstrates their economic relevance; nevertheless, their relevance as an economic factor may be of a nature other than that of reciprocal social gifts.

(R.1) *r dit rḫ.tw ꜣḫt nb i.dit* PN *n* (2) *pꜣy.f it m-ḏr irwy.f* PN *m ḥmt* […]
For information (relative to) all items that PN gave to his father(-in-law?)[642] after he made PN a woman:
(3) festival + list of goods (with intermediate totals in the form # *ir n* + quantifier #)
(9) *wḥm* [*m* + festival] + goods
Again [at (festival)]: (list)
(V.1) *wḥm m* + festival + list of goods
Again at (festival): (list)
(6) *r dit rḫ.tw tꜣ ḫrt* (7) *i.dit n.f* PN *mn-ḏr ṯs.f*
For information (relative to) the assets[643] that PN gave him after he was promoted (?)[644]:
(8) *rdyt n.f m tꜣy.f ḥs* + goods
What was given to him in his honor: (list)
(12) *rdyt n.f m tꜣy.f diw* + goods
What was given to him from his portions: (list)

***oGlasgow D* 1925.71**

(R.1) *r dit rḫ.tw ꜣḫt nbt i.diw* PN (2) *n pꜣy.f it* [*šꜣ*(ʿ) *rnpt* 2?][645] + consumables
For information (relative to) all assets that PN gave to his father(-in-law?) [up to year 2?]: (list)
(3) festival + consumables + festival: (list)
(5) *rdy n.f m nꜣ mkw i.diw n.*(*n*?)[646] *Pr-ꜥꜣ ꜥ.w.s.* + list of consumables
What was given to him from the rewards that Pharaoh L.P.H. gave to (us?): (list)
(6) *wḥm ꜥn* + goods
Repeated again: (list)
(V.1) *iw.i dit n.f* + consumables + *m diw r* (2) *tnw ꜣbd m rnpt* 1 *nfryt r rnpt* 2 (3) + *ꜣbd* x *r ꜣbd* y + *ir n ꜣbd* 10 + total quantity
And I gave to him (goods) from (my) rations every month from year 1 till year 2, month x to month y, making 10 months (total)
(4) *wḥm dit n.f* + goods and total
Again given to him: (list and total)
(5) [*ditto*] *wḥm dit n.f* + quantity
[*ditto*] again given to him: (quantity)
(6) […*i.diw*] *Pr-ꜥꜣ ꜥ.w.s. iw.i irt rnpt* 1 *n* (7) […] *hrw bꜣki i.diw n.*(*n*?)[647] *Pr-ꜥꜣ ꜥ.w.s.*
[… that gave] Pharaoh L.P.H. And I spent 1 year of […] day of service that Pharaoh L.P.H. gave to (us?).
(8) *ḫr* […] *iw.i dit n.f wꜥ* […]
But […] And I gave him one […]

642 Janssen (1982: 256) and Wimmer (2006: 163).
643 'Besitz (?)' for Deir el-Medine online; see *Wb* III, 319.15 (for *ḫt*).
644 'er befördert (?) wurde' in Deir el-Medine online.
645 McDowell (1993: pl.VIIIa, a).
646 Following MacDowell, *ibid.*
647 Following MacDowell, *ibid.*

Janssen (1982: 256) presented the two documents as cases of 'reciprocal gift-giving,' underlining that 'on special occasions (the birth of a child and festivals such as New Year's Day) the people of Deir el-Medîna presented each other with small quantities of food and, in a few instances, with objects in daily use'. Janssen and Toivari-Viitala[648] also added that *oBerlin* 12406 may well represent the record of the 'gift'[649] made by a man to the 'father of the bride', since the man 'makes PN as a woman'.

The *oGlasgow D* 1925.71 may be the record of support to an elderly parent who retired for the profit of his son, the latter becoming his father's 'staff of old age'[650].

Both texts are notifications, the opening formula being close to Janssen's category II of transactions ('barter' notification?) # *r rdit rḫ.tw ꜣḫt nb i.diw* PN *n* PN #[651]. They are written in cursory style[652] degree 2 Neo-Egyptian, and in the delocutive mode (using the formula *rdyt n.f*), but with the addition of a locutive sequential narrative segment in *oGlasgow D* 1925.71. They provide the occasions (family events or festivals) of transmissions which are directed at a unique close-family recipient, only the 'donor' is named, and the items transmitted do not only consist of foodstuff. These are not 'group-events' where everyone brings some food to a party, but rather transmissions implied by family ties and perhaps recorded in order to prove or officialize in an unfortunately lost context the donor's good behavior or the execution of some kinship-related obligation.

c.4 *oBerlin* P 14328

Date: 20th dynasty, Ramesses IV
Hieroglyphic version: Munich Deir el-Medine online
Features: damaged limestone ostracon from Deir el-Medina ('Raum XI NE') recording the notification of names and associated goods, gifts taken home by a man after a drinking party for Janssen (1997: 79-82). It has the following structure:

(R.1) *r rdit rḫ.tw pꜣ nkt* (2) *i.ṯꜣ.n rmṯ ist* PN *m-dit* (3) *swr* [*m*?] *pꜣy.f pr* + list of # PN + goods #
For information (relative to) the items that workman PN took after drinking [from?] his house: PN + goods (several times)

Although a circumstance is expressed (after drinking at one's house), the situation is far from clear. The mode is delocutive, the list of people and goods does not indicate whether these people brought/gave the goods to the named workman or if they also took some items, the lexeme *rdi* is not used here (no 'gift' mention) and *ṯꜣi* is ambiguous (seized, kept?). The presence of the notification formula preceding a # PN + goods # list is uncommon and implies that the list may not be a simple personal memo note.

648 (1998: 1159; 2001: 62). Toivari-Viitala (1998: 1159, n. 16) also contends that the verso of *oBerlin* may be interpreted as 'a record of what the father-in-law gave as a gift to his son-in-law when the latter was promoted as a workman.'
649 The famous *fꜣi gꜣyt* of *pDeM* 27 line 2, 'presentation of tribute/bundle' or alleged 'bride-wealth'.
650 McDowell (1993: 12). For *KRI*, it is a payment of a son to his father.
651 Janssen (1975: 497-9). See also Donker van Heel & Haring (2003: 148-53) 'account of transfer' headed by the notification formula # *r rdit rḫ.tw ꜣḫt nb i.di* PN *n* PN # with both parties' names (but the record being made in all likelihood by the giver), list of goods and their value.
652 Note the administrative practice *ditto* mark.

d. Locutive elements in narrative context

oQueen's College Oxford 1115

Date: 20th dynasty, Ramesses IV
Hieroglyphic version: *KRI* VI, 167-8 n.92A133
Features: complete limestone ostracon of unknown provenance. Records recurrent transmissions of consumables (gifts for Janssen 1982: 258)[653], without expressed *consideration*. It has the following structure:

(R.1) Goods + *m-ḏrt in mw* PN (2) *p3y.i* + festival
iw.i dit iṯ3.tw (3) + consumables + *iw.st wḥmw* (4) *iy r p3 ḫtmw iw.i dit* + bread + *iw ky ḥr ḥt.f iw* (5) + bread + PN *im.f*
(Goods) by (the) hand of (the) water-carrier PN (during) my (festival).
And I caused that be taken (list) when she repeated (the) coming to the *ḫtm* outpost; and I gave (bread), another being in it, (bread) of PN being in it;
Festival + *iw.i dit* + goods
(festival:) and I gave (list);
(6 and 7) *wḥmw dit* + festival + goods
again giving of (festival): (list)
(V.I.6) *wḥmw dit n.s p3y.i* + festival (7) + goods
again giving to her (during) my (festival): (list)
(V.II.4) *wḥmw dit n.s m-ḏrt in mw* PN (5) + goods
again giving to her by (the) hand of (the) water-carrier PN: (list)
(6) *wḥmw dit m-ḏrt mḏ3y* PN (7) + goods
again giving by (the) hand of (the) policeman PN: (list)

The unique 'donor' is not named and neither is the recipient, but apparently only one 'donor' and one recipient are implied. The transmissions of food to the woman are made during festivals by named delivery agents (water-carriers, policeman), not in person by the donor. It cannot be determined if the allowances are made in the context of reciprocal exchanges of gifts or as a personal execution of some obligation.
Although close to the preceding cases of records of personal allowances that made use of locutive narrative sequential forms (o*Glasgow D* 1925.66 and 1925.71), this document does not involve a notification formula. We have already noted the use of locutive narrative forms in the *recital* of unilateral deeds, but here there is no use of *ir ink* formula and no address to a third party. The texts could represent arguments noted in case of contestation, but this is not certain.
Note that the format and object are also close to those of *oBerlin* P 12635 (20th dynasty, Ramesses IV), a damaged limestone ostracon from Deir el-Medina recording recurrent transmissions of consumables by an unnamed father to his unnamed daughter on various occasions and feasts (recto), as well as to an unnamed man (verso). This document was not referred to by Janssen. Interestingly, in lines 9-10 it records *r-ḏb3 p3y.i* […] '(goods) in exchange of my […]' and in verso 12 *wḥm iṯ3 n p3 ṯbw* 'Again, what was taken for the sandals: (list of consumables)'; these may indicate that a transaction with *consideration* was implied.

653 'Provisions for Feasts' for *KRI* VI, 167.

e. Valuation of items

In two cases the given items were evaluated using the formula # *ir n* + value unit + quantifier #. It could indicate a commercial transaction *sensu stricto,* a valuation of bequests or expenses (see *supra* cases of valuation of items, e.g. *oGardiner/Ashmolean* 272, lines 5-6 and *pBoulaq* 10 line 3) rather than 'reciprocal gift-giving.' But as the same *ir n* can be used instead of *dmḏ* to express totals of previously listed items (e.g. in *pAshmolean Museum* 1945.95 line 3), the first possibility is doubtful.

e.1 Transaction or bequest: *oDeM* 946 r°

Date: end 19th to 20th dynasty, from Seti II to Ramesses V
Hieroglyphic version: Grandet (2003: 387)
Features: incomplete pottery ostracon, discovered in the *Grand Puits*. It records a transmission of garments, without expressed *consideration*. It has the following structure:

(1) *rdyt rmṯ ist* [PN... *n*[654]] (2) PN + (3) list of garments + *ir n* [*dbn*...]
What gave (the) workman [PN... to] PN: (list + valuation or total)

Interestingly, the verso bears part of a dated administrative journal, unconnected for Grandet (*ibid.*). The text is written in delocutive mode, in a degree 1 Neo-Egyptian (no nexus expressed), and probably both parties were named; use of *rdyt* N PN *n* or *rdyt* (*n*) N PN *in* PN. For Grandet, it is a 'mémoire relatif à un don de biens'[655]; the fact that the cost of the garments was probably evaluated, and that only one 'donor' and one recipient were apparently concerned may indicate that it is a record of either a payment in the context of a sale[656] or a bequest.

Note a similar case, *oCairo* 25583 (19th dynasty, Seti II for *KRI* or 20th dynasty, Ramesses III or later for Janssen 1975: 32)[657], an almost complete limestone ostracon from the temple excavations at Deir el-Medina; it records a transmission of goods by a man to a woman without expressed *consideration* and bears [ꜣ]*ḫt n rmṯ ist* PN *r.didi.f ꜥnḫ-niwt* PN + list of goods + *ir n oipe* x (in three cases) + *dmḏ oipe* y '[A]ssets of (the) workman PN that he gave (to the) *ꜥnḫ-n-niwt* PN: (list), worth x *oipe*, total: y *oipe*'. Various types of goods are transmitted, even necklaces and an amulet, bedsheets and even a rope, some of them being evaluated, a different context from an exchange of gifts between good neighbors.

654 Another possible reconstruction: *rdyt* (*n*) *rmṯ ist* [PN... *in*] PN 'What was given (to the) workman [PN... by] PN' as the preposition *n* is often omitted (see *rdyt* (*n*) in partitions).

655 Grandet (2003: 119).

656 For Donker van Heel & Haring (2003: 151), the heading formula *rdyt* PN *n* PN belongs to accounts of transfer (personal transactions), sometimes payments for objects produced by craftsmen or their delivery by the same. Many other examples of the formula are provided *infra*, to which *oDeM* 937 of the 20th dynasty, (Ramesses III?) may be added.

657 'Payment or Bequest' for *KRI* IV, 329; difficult to determine if related to gifts, contributions for upkeep or exchange for Toivari-Viitala (2001: 129); not proposed by Janssen as a reciprocal gift-giving. For Donker van Heel & Haring (2003: 149), we are dealing with a private matter heading of transfer account 'without *r rdit rḫ.tw*'.

e.2 Transaction: *oDeM* 938

Date: 20th dynasty, Ramesses IV-XI
Hieroglyphic version: Grandet (2003: 375)
Features: incomplete pottery ostracon, discovered in the *Grand Puits*, recording the transmission of cereals without expressed *consideration*. For Grandet, 'mémoire relatif à un don de biens'[658]. It has the following structure:

(1) [*rdyt* PN *n mḏ*]*ꜣy* PN + (2) list of goods, each with # *ỉr n dbn* x #
[What PN has given to the police]man PN: (list), worth x *dbn*
(5) […] *dbn* x *ḥr-ꜥ.f*
[…] x *dbn* at his charge

Both 'donor' and recipient were probably named in a delocutive texteme; the valuation of the goods in *dbn* and the mention 'at his charge' indicate that it is probably a commercial transaction and not a gift. The possible use of the formula # *rdyt* PN *n* policeman PN#[659] may support this option.

f. Delivery of goods

In two cases referred to by Grandet[660] as 'mémoires relatifs à des dons de biens', there is only the issue of a delivery (*ỉnỉ*) of goods, and the lexeme *rdỉ* is not used in these records; the delivery could be the result of any kind of transaction, partition, allowance, payment of debt… In both cases the texteme is allocutive and the texts are addressed to the beneficiary of the transmission; the 'donor' and the recipient are unnamed. The delivery agents are named (see *infra* for other texts naming delivery agents but using the lexeme *rdỉ*). Nothing proves the assumption that they record gifts, they only concern an indirect transmission.

oDeM 936

Date: ?
Hieroglyphic version: Grandet (2003: 373)
Features: complete limestone ostracon of unknown provenance, recording an isolated dated transmission of consumables to an unnamed recipient by a named agent without expressed *consideration*, with the following structure:

(1) *inyt n.k m-ḏrt mḏꜣy* (2) PN *m* + date + (3) list of consumables
What was delivered to you by (the) hand of policeman PN on (date): (list)

oDeM 947

Date: ?
Hieroglyphic version: Grandet (2003: 388)

658 Grandet (2003: 110).
659 Donker van Heel & Haring (2003: 151).
660 Grandet (2003: 109, 120).

Features: incomplete limestone ostracon discovered in the *Grand Puits*; the record is addressed to an unnamed beneficiary of recurrent transmissions of bread (one of these being dated), without expressed *consideration*, by named agents and with the following structure:

(R.1) *wḥm m-ḏr in n.k* P[N] + (2) goods
Again, after P[N] brought you (list)
(3) [*wḥm*] + date + *m-ḏrt* (4) [*inw-mw* P]N (V.1) + breads
[Again] (date): by (the) hand of [the water-carrier P]N: (list)

g. Lists of proper names and goods of the type # PN + goods

These ostraca are the most elliptic records included in Janssen's category of 'reciprocal gift-giving,' and they are his best candidates for membership of the category. They consist of several proper names preceding lists of mainly foodstuffs. Nothing proves that they are private records; they could be administrative. There is no way to determine if the people named are 'donors' or recipients. Since these documents have the same # PN + goods # structure, they are only listed below (but note *supra oBerlin* P 14328 and its notification formula):

- ***oOIC* 17005 (*oNelson* 14)**[661]: 19th dynasty.
- ***oDeM* 222**[662]: 20th dynasty, Ramesses III. Note in line V.22 the date followed by *m hrw pn* [...], thus probably an official document.
- ***oDeM* 666**[663]: 20th dynasty, Ramesses III.
- ***oLouvre* E 3262b, f, g**[664]: 20th dynasty, Ramesses III. Note that a date appears in fragments f/g.
- ***oDeM* 134**[665]: 20th dynasty, Ramesses III-IV. Note the red dots, *ditto* marks, total and correction, implying administrative practice and copy or verification of the list.
- ***oPetrie* 31/*oUC* 39630**[666]: 20th dynasty, Ramesses III-IV. Note the red lines, abbreviations, total (administrative practice).
- ***oDeM* 643**[667]: 20th dynasty, Ramesses III-IV.
- ***oCairo* 25660 & *JE* 37649**[668]: 20th dynasty, Ramesses IV.
- ***oFaulkner* 1**[669]: 20th dynasty, Ramesses IV ?
- ***oCairo* 25650**[670]: 20th dynasty, Ramesses IV. Note the mention of total.
- ***oGardiner/Ashmolean* 178**[671]: 20th dynasty, Ramesses IV? Note the mention of *ḥ3w* 'expenses'(?) and # *n* PN + goods # in v° I.2.

661 Unpublished (Černý's *Notebook* 107.32-4); Janssen (1982: 257, n.21).
662 *KRI* V, 480-2 n.A63: 'List of Workmen Provisions'; Janssen (1982: 257; 1997: 61-7).
663 *KRI* V, 617 n.A333; Janssen (1982: 258; 1997: 56, n.4).
664 *KRI* VII, 314 n.280 A409 (rations supplies); Janssen (1997: 56, n.4).
665 *KRI* VI, 172 n.94 A142 (bread account); Janssen (1982: 258; 1997: 59-61).
666 *KRI* VI, 169-70 n.93.A135 (food list); Janssen (1982: 257; 1997: 75-8) 'makes the impression of having been noted down on the spur of the moment, that is, during the party itself, perhaps as the guests arrived'.
667 *KRI* V, 602-3 n.A293: 'Grain-related supplies'; gifts for Janssen (1982: 258; 1997: 67-8) and McDowell (1999: 78-9).
668 *KRI* VI, 168-9 n.93.A134 (*oCairo* 25660) 'Food for people', and Černý's *Notebook* 106.98 (*oCairo JE* 37649) ; Janssen (1982: 258; 1997: 69-72).
669 Unpublished (Černý's *Notebook* 31.79a); Janssen (1997: 78-9).
670 *KRI* VI, 172 n.94A140 (bread account); Janssen (1997: 56, n.4).
671 Unpublished (Černý's *Notebook* 45.81); Janssen (1997: 56, n.4).

- *oPrague* H 24[672]: 20th dynasty ?

h. Mention of specific circumstances, events

Apart from already presented ostraca giving details of the occasion of the 'gifts' (*oBerlin* 12406, *oQueen's College Oxford* 1115, *oBerlin* 14328), a few ostraca mention special circumstances apparently linked to the transmission of the goods. Since religious feasts may be either the occasion of the 'gifts' or a mere indication of the date, this particular kind of circumstances might not always be informative[673].

h.1 *oMichaelides* 48 r°

Date: 20th dynasty, Ramesses II?
Hieroglyphic version: *KRI* III, 556-7 n.234.A70
Features: damaged limestone of unknown provenance, record of goods without expressed *consideration*, on the occasion of religious feasts and probably also at a private purification ceremony of a daughter. Believed to be a list of gifts by Janssen (1982: 255-6)[674]. It has the following structure:

(R.I.1) Goods + [*ḥb*] *n* PN (God) + (2) list of goods
Goods; [festival] of (God): (list)
(4) [*pꜣ*]*y.f ḥb n* PN (God) + (5) list of goods
[H]is festival of (God): (list)
(II.1) *pꜣ swʿb n tꜣy.f šr*[*i͗*] + (2) list of goods
The purification of his daught[er]: (list)
(5) *wḥm ky ḥb n* PN (God) + list of goods
Again another festival of (God): (list)

The ordered layout, delocutive texteme of degree 1 Neo-Egyptian (absence of nexus), the use of abbreviations (*wḥm*, *dmḏ*), the formulaic style are all marks of an 'administrative' document, but one should note the absence of names of the parties involved, as well as of the lexeme *rdi*. We do not know how many parties ('donors'/beneficiaries) are involved and there is no mention of anyone's agency. The record could represent anything: consumption of goods, production, any kind of private transmission, public distribution, offerings to the gods (the purification of one's daughter being either the occasion or the date of these events). Note that not only foodstuffs are involved in this case.

h.2 *oDeM* 942

Date: 19th dynasty, Ramesses II?
Hieroglyphic version: Grandet (2003: 379-80)
Features: incomplete limestone ostracon discovered in the *kom* of the *Grand Puits*, consisting of a record addressed to an unnamed party of various transmissions of consumables

672 Unpublished (Černý's *Notebook* 26.31); Janssen (1997: 56, n.4).
673 Add *oIFAO* 1322 + *oVarille* 38 + *oCairo* CG 25705: *rdyt* PN + list of foodstuff + *n pꜣ swri n Ḥwtḥrt* (for the drinking(-party) of *Ḥwtḥrt*) + list # PN + foodstuff # (Janssen 1997: 56-9).
674 'Liste von Lebensmitteln für die Feste verschiedener Götter' for Goedicke & Wente (1962: 20) 'Supplies for Various Festivals' for *KRI* III, 556.

without expressed *consideration*, a 'Mémoire relatif à un don de biens' for Grandet[675]. It has the following structure:

(R.2) *m* + date (*diw ḥryw rnpt mswt Stẖ*) (3) *m-ḏrt* PN + (4) list of goods (6) *dmḏ* + quantifier On (date: epagomenal day, birth of *Stẖ*), by (the) hand of PN: (list). Total: (x) (7) [*m-ḏrt* ?] *rẖty* PN + (8) list of goods [By the hand of?] washerman PN: (list) (V.1) *m* + date (*diw ḥryw rnpt mswt Nbtḥwt*) (3) *rdyt n.k k3ry* (4) PN + list of goods On (date: epagomenal day, birth of *Nbtḥwt*), what (the) gardener PN has given to you: (list)

Dated transmissions of foodstuff by named delivery agents to unnamed party probably given by the unnamed author of the record, using the lexeme *rdi* (*rdyt n.k* N); delocutive/allocutive textemes, degree 1 Neo-Egyptian (no nexus), use of *dmḏ* abbreviation.
Donker van Heel & Haring (2003: 128-30) present the use of the formula # date + *m-ḏrt* PN # in the context of delivery account headings concerning supplies for the Necropolis. Again, the date may record a religious festival as the occasion or be a simple dating of the transmission.

h.3 *oCairo* 25624 & 25365

Date: 20th dynasty, Ramesses III
Hieroglyphic version: *KRI* V, 516-7 n.A123
Features: incomplete pottery ostraca of unknown provenance, recording the transmission of goods, gifts for Janssen (1982: 258; 1997: 69-72)[676]. It has the following structure:

(R.I, etc.) # PN + goods # (several times) (II.1) Date + (3) *rdy n.f* PN *n* (4) *p3 sw3 r mw n Ḥnwt-ẖn* + list of goods Date: what PN gave to him for the crossing through (the) waters of (the) Mistress of the Interior (toponym?): (list)

Although the recto's first column is a simple list of the type # PN + goods # (see *supra*) not including exclusively foodstuff, its second column has a brief date and a delocutive texteme possibly referring to a remuneration of service with *rdy n.f* PN. The lists of these two columns may of course be unrelated.

h.4 *oTurin* 57010

Date: 20th dynasty, Ramesses III
Hieroglyphic version: *KRI* V, 517 n.A124
Features: damaged pottery ostracon of unknown provenance, recording names and associated goods. Gifts for Janssen (1997: 56, n.4)[677]. It has the following structure:

675 Grandet (2003: 115).
676 Supplies for *KRI*, V, 516.
677 Supplies for *KRI* V, 517 and Helck (2002: 287).

(R.1, etc.) # PN + goods # (several times)
(V.1) Date + *m hrw pn* […] (2) *ỉr.n* PN *n tꜣy.st šri* (3) list of goods
Date: on this day, […] that PN has done for her daughter: (list)

As in the preceding document, we may have here two unconnected types of records: on the recto, of the # PN + goods # type; on the verso, a formally dated delocutive texteme (with archaic anaphora, a somewhat rare feature in the 'reciprocal gifts' corpus, see *oDeM* 222, 282, 934 and 939) with an unknown action that a mother did for her daughter in relation to various objects. In cases of kinship relations, a large range of allowances, bequests, gifts, benefices of all sorts may be meant; the reasons for the record may be equally varied.

h.5 *oBerlin* P 10631

Date: 20th dynasty
Hieroglyphic version: Erman (1911: pl. 36)
Features: complete but somewhat damaged pottery ostracon of unknown provenance, recording transmissions of goods without expressed *consideration*. Gifts for Janssen (1982: 258). It has the following structure:

(1) *rdyt n.s pꜣ ỉw ḥsmn n* PN (2) *m-ḏrt rmṯ* {*rmṯ*} *ỉst* PN (3) + list of goods
What was given to her (on the occasion of/during?) the coming of menstruation of PN by (the) hand of (the) workman PN: (list)
(8) *rdyt n.s m ỉn*[…] *sš* PN + list of goods
What was given to her from/at (?)[…] scribe PN: (list)
(9) *rdyt n.f* + list of goods
What was given to him (?): (list)

Delocutive texteme of degree 1 Neo-Egyptian, named delivery agent, use of *rdyt n.f*, brief mention of private circumstance, change in gender of the beneficiary (?), unnamed recipient and 'donor', various goods implied, not exclusively foodstuff.

h.6 Trade?: *oDeM* 943

Date: ?
Hieroglyphic version: Grandet (2003: 381)
Features: incomplete pottery ostracon discovered in the *Grand Puits*, recording various transmissions of goods without expressed *consideration*. For Grandet, 'mémoire relatif à un don de biens'[678]. It has the following structure:

(1) […] list of goods (3) *ỉw pꜣy.n dꜣỉw* 2 *r pḥt.f*
[…] (list), our 2 *dꜣỉw*-garments being for his buttocks.
(4) [… *rdyt* ?] *n.f* + list of consumables + *rdyt n.f* + list of goods (5) *ỉw.f* (*r*) *mryt*
[…What was given?] to him: (list); given to him: (list); he came (to) (the) river-bank.
(6) […] *rdyt* [*n.f* (list)?]
[…] what was given [to him: (list)?]

678 Grandet (2003: 116).

Unnamed parties; note the plural locutive besides the delocutive forms. Use of *rdyt n.f*, and there appears to be a reference to products transmitted in Deir el-Medina's market place, at the river-bank; it may thus be a case of trade. Obviously the 'donors' recorded the items already given to the other party in order to keep track of the transaction.

h.7 *oDeM* 952 (*oIFAO* 1069)

Date: ?
Hieroglyphic version: Grandet (2003: 396-8).
Features: incomplete ostracon bought in Gurna, recording the transmission of consumable products without expressed *consideration*. Janssen (1982: 254-5) presented a summary of this text as his first case of 'reciprocal gift-giving'[679]. It has the following structure:

(R.1) [*wḥm*?] *rdyt n.f m pꜣ* (2) *msw n tꜣy.f šrit* (3) + list of goods
[Again?] what was given to him at the birth[680] of his daughter: (list)
(V.1) [*wḥm*] *m pꜣy.st sw* 3 (2) + list of goods
[Again] at her day 3: (list)
(8) *wḥm m pꜣ sw* 14 (9) + list of goods
Again at the day 14: (list)
(11) *wḥm m pꜣ swri ꜥꜣ* (12) + list of goods
Again at the great drinking(-party): (list)

Unnanmed parties in a delocutive texteme using *rdyt n.f*; it could be an administrative record of benefits offered by the community on the occasion of the event, as well as a private memo by one of the members of the community.

i. Allocutive records

Allocutive records have already been encountered, either epistolary documents (*pDeM* 11, perhaps also *oGlasgow* 1925.66), or deliveries of goods (*oDeM* 936, 947), sometimes also with the mention of specific circumstances (*oDeM* 942). Here are two additional cases of records addressed directly to an unnamed party. The reason for the record may be that a *consideration* is expected from the addressee or that allowances should be traceable in view of future contestation; these are more probably accounts of transfers communicated to the recipient, perhaps epistolary documents[681], than private memos concerning liberalities.

oDeM 945

Date: 19th dynasty, Ramesses II?
Hieroglyphic version: Grandet (2003: 385)
Features: complete text on the recto of a limestone ostracon (the verso 'semble avoir été écrit sur la face vierge d'une ancienne lettre à moitié effacée'[682]) discovered in the *kom* of the *Grand Puits*, recording recurrent transmissions of consumables and addressed to an

679 'Liste de biens donnés en cadeau à l'occasion d'un accouchement' for Grandet (2003: 124).
680 Janssen (1982: 254-5): confinement.
681 But as in *oGlasgow* 1925.66, there are no traces of specific epistolary formulae in the documents.
682 Grandet (2003: 118).

unnamed party. For Grandet, 'mémoire relatif à un don de biens'[683]. It has the following structure:

(R.1) *rdyt n.k m* + date (2) *m p3 ky sw* 10 *m-ḏrt* (3) *in-mw* PN + consumables
What was given to you on (date) from the other 10 days (period?) by (the) hand of (the) water-carrier PN: (list)
(4) *wḥm in(yt) n.k m* + date + (*m-ḏrt*) PN + (5) consumables
Again brought to you on (date), (by the hand of) PN: (list)
(5) *wḥm n.k m* + date *m-ḏrt* (6) PN + consumables
Again to you on (date), by (the) hand of PN: (list)
(7) *inyt n.k m-ḏrt rḫty* PN + (8) consumables
Brought to you by (the) hand of (the) washerman PN: (list).
(V.1) *mtw.k dit in(.tw) n.i* + list of goods + (4) [...] *ḏd.k* [...] *p3 wn* [...]
and you caused that be given to me: (list); [...] you said [...] because [...]

It could be a brief epistolary document in degree 2 Neo-Egyptian (albeit without any introduction formula or proper names), and there is no certainty that the recto and the verso are unrelated (the first line of the verso could express the *consideration* in a sale). Dated deliveries of goods to the addressee are made by named agents, using *rdyt n.k/inyt n.k*. For Donker van Heel & Haring (2003: 152), # *rdyt n.k m* + date *m-ḏrt* PN # is a variation of the heading # *rdyt n* PN *m* + date # that belongs to accounts of transfer, personal transactions, sometimes for a commercial purpose.

***oDeM* 934**

Date: 19th dynasty (Wimmer 2004: 517)
Hieroglyphic version: Grandet (2003: 371)
Features: damaged limestone ostracon, discovered in the *kom* of the *Grand Puits*, recording recurrent bread transmissions to one named and one unnamed party (the addressee of the record) without expressed *consideration*. For Grandet, 'mémoire relatif à un don de pain'[684]. It has the following structure:

(R.1) [*rd*]*yt n.k m* + date (without reign) (2) *m-ḏrt* PN + list of bread
[What was g]iven to you on (date) by (the) hand of PN: (list)
(3) *wḥm* (4) *m hrw pn n* PN + list
Again on this day, to PN: (list)
(V.2) *wḥm n.k* (3) *m* + date (without reign) *m-ḏrt* PN + bread
Again to you on (date) by (the) hand of PN: (bread)

Dated transmissions in degree 1 Neo-Egyptian (absence of nexus), using the archaic anaphora *m hrw pn* instead of repeating the date[685]; delivery by a named agent. The formula used is similar to the 1st category of transactions ('barter') formula # *rdyt n* PN # of Janssen (1975: 497)[686]. Identity of the 'donor' unknown.

683 *Ibid.*
684 *Ibid.*, p. 108.
685 Megally (1977: 65-6).
686 See again Donker van Heel & Haring (2003: 152).

j. Favor

oDeM 948

A unique case of a transmission expressly described as 'by favor', probably meaning without *consideration*; this could be regarded as a true gift, although it is impossible to say if it is made in the context of private relationships or in a more public sphere.

Date: 19th dynasty, Ramesses II?
Hieroglyphic version: Grandet (2003: 389-90)
Features: complete limestone ostracon discovered in the *kom* of the *Grand Puits*, recording a gift (*rdyt m ḥrt-ib*) of consumable products. For Grandet, 'mémoire relatif à un échange de cadeaux'[687]. It has the following structure:

(R.1) [*r*]*dyt m ḥrt-ib m-ḏrt* PN + (2) list of consumables
[Wh]at was given by favor by (the) hand of PN: (list)
(4) *rdyt n.f* + list of consumables
What was given to him: (list)
(V.1) *ky* + goods *rd n.f*
Another (time): (goods) given to him.

Degree 1 Neo-Egyptian delocutive texteme, use of *rdyt n.f*; named delivery agent (although the recipient and 'donor' are not). Interestingly, even expressly mentioned favors are recorded.

k. Use of delivery agents

Several cases of the agency of a middleman in the transmission of goods have already been mentioned (*oGlasgow D* 1925.76 & *oGardiner/Ashmolean* 52, o*Glasgow D* 1925.66, *oQueen's College Oxford* 1115, *oBerlin P* 10631 and 12635, *oDeM* 934, 936, 942, 945, 947, and 948). It is difficult to reconcile this feature with the idea of a party where every participant brings a gift; the delivery agent may act as a witness in some kind of transaction. However, it does not preclude the transmission of a gift emanating from a distant 'donor'.

k.1 *oDeM* 935

Date: end of 19th – beginning of 20th dynasty
Hieroglyphic version: Grandet (2003: 372)
Features: fragmentary limestone ostracon discovered in the southern *kom*, recording recurrent oil transmissions without expressed *consideration*. For Grandet, 'mémoire relatif à un don de biens'[688]. It has the following structure:

(1) [...] *rdyt* [(2) *n* PN] + list of consumables
[...] What was given [to PN]: (list)
(3) [...] *wḥm m-ḏrt* PN

687 Grandet (2003: 121).
688 Grandet (2003: 109).

[…] Again by (the) hand of PN

With *rdyt n*.PN and degree 1 Neo-Egyptian (absence of nexus) in a delocutive texteme; the recipient was probably named, but not the 'donor'.

k.2 *oDeM* 940

Date: 19th dynasty (Wimmer 2004: 517), although 20th dynasty, Ramesses III for Grandet
Hieroglyphic version: Grandet (2003: 377)
Features: incomplete limestone ostracon discovered in the *kom* of the *Grand Puits*, recording a transmission of consumables without expressed *consideration*. For Grandet, 'mémoire relatif à un don de biens'[689]. It has the following structure:

(1) [*rdyt n.f m-ḏrt m*]*ḏ3y* PN + (2) list of consumables
[What was given to him by the hand of the pol]iceman PN: (list)
(4) [*wḥm*?] *rdyt n.f m-ḏrt* PN
[Again?] what was given to him by (the) hand of PN: (?)

Rdyt n.f and degree 1 Neo-Egyptian (absence of nexus) in a delocutive texteme; no party named apart from the middleman.

k.3 *oDeM* 944

Date: 20th dynasty, Ramesses III-VI
Hieroglyphic version: Grandet (2003: 384)
Features: incomplete pottery ostracon, provenance unknown, recording recurrent transmissions of cereals without expressed *consideration*. For Grandet, 'mémoire relatif à un don de grain (?)'[690]. It has the following structure:

(1) *rdyt sš* PN *n* (2) *sš ḳd* PN + cereals
What (the) scribe PN gave to (the) draughtsman PN: (cereals)
(3) *wḥm* (cereals)
Again: (cereals)
(7) *wḥm m-ḏrt* PN (cereals)
Again by (the) hand of PN: (cereals)

Rdyt PN *n*.PN and degree 1 Neo-Egyptian (absence of nexus) in a delocutive texteme in which all parties are named (there is only one 'donor' and one recipient). The record corresponds to Janssen's 1st category of transactions ('barter') formula[691] # *rdyt* PN *n* PN #.

689 *Ibid*., p. 113.
690 *Ibid*., p. 117.
691 Janssen (1975: 497). See again Donker van Heel & Haring (2003: 152).

I. Formalism

If these records only belong to the category of *aide-mémoires*, it is somewhat surprising that instead of the idiosyncratic features of scribbled personal notes they all use the same kind of format and expressions. Some of them even use the archaic anaphora that belongs to official and administrative records and to a high register of expression, sometimes without preceding mention of a date of transmission (we have already noted the *m hrw pn* archaism in *oDeM* 222 and 934, *oTurin* 57010). Note also the absence of prothetic *yod* and the very classic *rdyt* participle or *rdyt* PN relative form; of course, the quasi-omnipresent degree 1 of Neo-Egyptian is a direct consequence of the absence of nexus.

oDeM 282

Date: 20th dynasty, Ramesses IV
Hieroglyphic version: *KRI* VI, 172 n.94 A141
Features: damaged pottery ostracon, exact provenance in Deir el-Medina unknown, recording transmissions of goods without expressed *consideration*. Gifts for Janssen (1997: 56, n.4)[692]. It has the following structure:

(1) [...] PN + goods (several times)
(3) [*rdy*]*t n* PN *m hrw pn* (4) [...] + goods
[What was give]n to PN on this day: (list)

Again a series of # PN + goods # (see *supra*); use of *rdyt n* PN and degree 1 Neo-Egyptian (absence of nexus) in a delocutive texteme; abbreviations; absence of date (lost?), recipient named.

oDeM 939

Date:?
Hieroglyphic version: Grandet (2003: 376)
Features: incomplete limestone ostracon discovered in the southern *kom*, recording a transmission of goods without expressed *consideration*. For Grandet, 'mémoire relatif à un don de biens'[693]. It has the following structure:

(R.1) [*rd*]*yt m hrw pn* + list of goods
[What was give]n on this day: (list)
(V.1) *n* PN [...] + (2) list of goods
To PN: (list)

Use of *rdyt* and degree 1 Neo-Egyptian (absence of nexus) in a delocutive texteme; absence of date before the archaic anaphora; only recipient named.

692 Bread account for *KRI* VI, 172.
693 Grandet (2003: 112).

m. Administrative distribution of metal

oGardiner/Ashmolean 63

Date: 20th dynasty, Ramesses IX
Hieroglyphic version: *KRI* VI, 664 n.67 A38
Features: damaged limestone ostracon of unknown provenance, recording the distribution of specified quantities of copper. Gifts for Janssen (1997: 56, n.4)[694]. It has the following structure:

(1) *ꜥḥꜥ n ḥmt dbn* + quantifier (2) *nty* ꜥ (= *n*) *sꜣw* PN Amount of copper *dbn* x that is for (the) guardian PN; (3) *ḥmt dbn* + quantifier (4) *nty* (ꜥ) (etc.) copper *dbn* x that is (for) (etc.)

These are apparently not private transmissions (quantities of copper as mutual social gifts seem out of place) but administrative distributions of copper. The phraseology is different from the usual *rdyt n.f*/PN.

694 'Statement on Copper' for *KRI* VI, 664; 'Accounts of the distribution of a specific quantity' for Donker van Heel & Haring (2003: 140) as well as 'division accounts' with the phrase 'what is for PN' (*nty n* PN) (*ibid.*, 157).

11. Table of syntactic forms and particularities in wills and gifts

The following table is a summary of the forms found in the remaining fragments of the wills and gifts analyzed *supra*. The number of occurrences is only an indication in view of what has survived of the texts. Concerning *Naunakhte*, only Doc. I (*pAshmolean Museum* 1945.97) has been taken into consideration for the comparison with the other texts (Docs. II and III are compared *infra* with the other partition documents in a separate table); the material partition report of *pBoulaq* 10 is also excluded but included in the table of partition documents.

Abbreviations:

A = active
Ad = *adscriptus*/addition
Au = authentication
Col = colophon
C = contents
D = docket
DDR = *descent and distribution* rule
Neg = negative
O = operative part
P = pre-material
Pa = passive
Prep = preposition
Q = illustrative constructed quotation
R = *recital*
Ram. = Ramesses
S = sanction and authentication
T = title deed
x = more than 10 instances

Form	Degree	*oDeM 108* **19th d. Seti I**	*oG 90* **19th d. Ram. II**	*oG 55* **19th-20th d. Ram. II-III**	*oG 272* **20th d. Ram. III**	*Naunakhte* **20th d. Ram. V**	*pBoulaq 10* **20th d. Ram. VI**	*oPetrie 18* **20th d. Ram. VII**	*pAdoptions* **20th d. Ram. XI**	*pTurin 2021* **20th d. Ram. XI**
ir N… *iw.f r sḏm* (topicalized assets/heirs & indep. future, A, in DDR, general bequest or retributive principle)	0					3 (R, O)				
iw.f sḏm (prep. omission)	1	1 (O)							2 (T, O)	
bn iw.f r sdm (indep. future, A, neg.)	2					5 (R, O)		2 (Ad)		
bn iw.f sḏm (prep. omission)	2					1 (Ad)				
determined N + *nty iw.i irw.f* (relative future clause, A, prep. omission)	2									1 (R)
iw bn ir N *sḏm* (converted future, A, neg., prep. omission)	2									1 (S)
iw wnw iw.i sḏm (converted *futurum in praeterito*, not exploited possibility)	2									1 (O)
ir + nominal syntagm + *iry nym sḏm* (topicalized action & rhetorical question with future, A)	2									1 (S)

Form	Degree	*oDeM 108* 19th d. Seti I	*oG 90* 19th d. Ram. II	*oG 55* 19th-20th d. Ram. II-III	*oG 272* 20th d. Ram. III	*Naunakhte* 20th d. Ram. V	*pBoulaq 10* 20th d. Ram. VI	*oPetrie 18* 20th d. Ram. VII	*pAdoptions* 20th d. Ram. XI	*pTurin 2021* 20th d. Ram. XI
p3 nty iw.f ḏd (substantivized relative future clause)	2								1 (O)	
ir N… *iw.f n.f*/PN (topicalized assets & bequest implicit performative, A)	0	4 (O)	2? (C)			1 (O)		1 (O)		
N *n* PN	0	2 (O)								
iw.f PN (prep. omission)	1	1 (O)								
iw.f n PN (indep. present recognition of ownership, A)	0			1 (R?)						
iw.f ḫry 100 *n sḫ(t)* (penalty implicit performative in oath apodosis, A)	0					1 (Ad)		1 (Ad)		
tw.i sḏm (*m p3 hrw*) (indep. locutive present, explicit performative)	2								1 (O)	1 (S)
tw.i i.iri.f	2								1 (O)	
tw.i sḏm m p3 hrw… mtw.i sḏm (with conjunctive in 2nd bequest)	2									1 (O)
N *nb nty tw.tw ḥr sḏm* (relative present clause, generic)	2					1 (R)				

Form	Degree	*oDeM 108* 19th d. Seti I	*oG 90* 19th d. Ram. II	*oG 55* 19th-20th d. Ram. II-III	*oG 272* 20th d. Ram. III	*Naunakhte* 20th d. Ram. V	*pBoulaq 10* 20th d. Ram. VI	*oPetrie 18* 20th d. Ram. VII	*pAdoptions* 20th d. Ram. XI	*pTurin 2021* 20th d. Ram. XI
ir N… *iw.f m-mitt* (topicalized document & indep. present, instrumental conformity formula)	0					1 (Ad)				
nꜣ nty + adverbial rheme (substantivized relative present clause, generality)	1					1 (R)				
ir N… *st swꜣḏ* (topicalized statement/doc. & indep. present, entrustment form.)	1								1 (O)	
bn sw + converb (indep. present, neg.)	2									1 (O)
iw bn st m-di.f m N *iwnꜣ* (converted present, neg., motive related to status)	2								1 (O)	
ḫr Pr-ꜥꜣ (*ḫr*) *ḏd* (coordinated indep. present tag clause, A)	1									1 (O)
ḏd(*w*)*.f*/N (indep. delocutive perfect tag clause, A) *ḫr ḏd Pr-ꜥꜣ*	2 2					3 (R, O)		1 (R)	1 (O)	3 (S) 1 (R)

Form	Degree	*oDeM 108* 19th d. Seti I	*oG 90* 19th d. Ram. II	*oG 55* 19th-20th d. Ram. II-III	*oG 272* 20th d. Ram. III	*Naunakhte* 20th d. Ram. V	*pBoulaq 10* 20th d. Ram. VI	*oPetrie 18* 20th d. Ram. VII	*pAdoptions* 20th d. Ram. XI	*pTurin 2021* 20th d. Ram. XI
sḏm.f/N (indep. perfect report, A)	2					1 (O)			1 (R)	2 (S)
irwy.f	2					1 (Ad)		2 (Ad)		
irwy.i sḏm (analytic)	2					1 (R)				
(m)bwpwy.f/N *sḏm* (indep. perfect report, A, neg.)	2						1 (T)	1 (R)		
iw sḏm.f (converted perfect, A)	2						2 (T)			1 (S)
(*ḥr*) *iw* (*m*)*bwpwy.f sḏm* (converted perfect, A, neg.)	2						2 (T)			1 (R)
pꜣ nty bwpw.f sḏm (substantivized relative perfect clause, neg.)	2					1 (R)				
iw.f (*ḥr*) *sḏm* (sequential narrative past)	2					1 (R)	2 (T)	4 (R)	x (T, R)	x (R, S)
iw.f tmt sḏm (sequential narrative past, neg.)	2								1 (R)	
ꜥḥꜥ.n iryw PN (narrative past)	1								1 (T)	
sḏm.f/N (indep. modal prospective, A)	0		1 (C)						2 (O)	
nk N (imprecatory)	0								2 (O)	
irw mitt (indep. modal prospective, P, vizier's *fiat*)	0									1 (S)

Form	Degree	*oDeM 108* 19th d. Seti I	*oG 90* 19th d. Ram. II	*oG 55* 19th-20th d. Ram. II-III	*oG 272* 20th d. Ram. III	*Naunakhte* 20th d. Ram. V	*pBoulaq 10* 20th d. Ram. VI	*oPetrie 18* 20th d. Ram. VII	*pAdoptions* 20th d. Ram. XI	*pTurin 2021* 20th d. Ram. XI
(*wꜣḥ* PN…) *mtw.i/f sḏm* (indep. modal prospective & conjunctive, as crime protasis in *promissory* oath)	2					1 (Ad)			1 (O)	
bn iw.i r ḫnw… mtw.i r ḫnw (with neg. future)	2							1 (Ad)		
iḫ ḫr.tn (allocutive 'WH-words' question with modal prospective, A)	1									1 (S)
sḏm.f (depend. modal prospective, A)	0		3 (C)			2 (O)		1 (Ad)	1 (R)	1 (R)
imi sḏm.f/N (iussive/3rd person causative imperative + depend. prospective)	0						1 (T)			2 (R, S)
imi tw (imperative + allocutive dependent pronoun)	0								1 (T)	
sḏm (imperative)	0							1? (R)		3 (O, S)
sḏm (stative)	0		1 (C)					4 (R)	4 (T, O)	3 (R, S)
šwy	1					1 (Ad)				
sḏm (perfect participle, A)	0					1 (R)	1 (T)		2 (T)	
irt (masc.)	1								1? (O)	
r.sḏm	2			1 (R?)			1? (T)			
i.sḏm	2									1 (O)

Form	Degree	*oDeM 108* 19th d. Seti I	*oG 90* 19th d. Ram. II	*oG 55* 19th-20th d. Ram. II-III	*oG 272* 20th d. Ram. III	*Naunakhte* 20th d. Ram. V	*pBoulaq 10* 20th d. Ram. VI	*oPetrie 18* 20th d. Ram. VII	*pAdoptions* 20th d. Ram. XI	*pTurin 2021* 20th d. Ram. XI
i.wnw ((im)perfect participle, A)	2									1 (R)
sḏm (perfect participle Pa or stative)	0				2 (O)	3 (P, O, Col)			2 (T, P)	
ir n dbn + quantifier	0				2 (O)	1 (O)				
p3 sḏm nb (substantivized perfect participle)	1					1 (R)				
sḏm.f/N (perfect relative)	0	1 (O)								5 (O, S)
sḏm.n.N	0							1 (P)		
ḏdt.n.N/*rdyt.n.f*	0				1 (P)		1 (T)			3 (S)
rdy.n.f (relative neutrum)	1						1 (T)			
iry(w).i	1									3 (R, O)
i.sḏm.f/N	2			1 (R?)		4 (O, D)		1 (R)	3 (T, O)	5 (S)
r.nwy.i, r.di.f (?)	2					3 (O)				
i.irt.N (intrusive *t*)	2					1 (Ad)				
p3 sḏm.f/N (*nb*) (substantivized perfect relative form)	2									8 (R, O, S)
3bwtw.f (imperfect relative neutrum)	1									1 (R)
i.iryt.N	2									1 (R)
wnn.N(imperfect that-form)	0		1 (C)							
i.irw.i sḏm	2								1 (O)	
sḏm.N (perfect that-form)	0						1 (T)			
i.sḏm.f	2							1 (R)		1 (S)
i.ir(w).i sḏm	2			1 (R?)					1 (T)	

Form	Degree	*oDeM 108* 19th d. Seti I	*oG 90* 19th d. Ram. II	*oG 55* 19th-20th d. Ram. II-III	*oG 272* 20th d. Ram. III	*Naunakhte* 20th d. Ram. V	*pBoulaq 10* 20th d. Ram. VI	*oPetrie 18* 20th d. Ram. VII	*pAdoptions* 20th d. Ram. XI	*pTurin 2021* 20th d. Ram. XI
i.ir.f sḏm (prospective that-form)	2					1 (O)				1 (S)
m-n-ḏr sḏm.f (temporalis with prospective that-form)	1			1 (R?)						
m-di sḏm.f	2						2? (T)			
sḏm/t (infinitive)	0	3 (P, O)	3 (P, C)		1 (O)	x(P,R,O,Ad)	x (T, P, O)	7 (R, Ad)	10 (T, R)	x (R, O, S)
sḏmw	1			1 (R?)		1 (Ad)		3 (Ad)	4 (T, R)	3 (R)
sḏm (fem.)/*sḏmt* (masc.)	1					9 (R, O)			4 (T, R)	1 (R)
h3y, iṯ3y, iry…	1					1 (O)			1 (R)	6 (R, S)
r rdit rḫ.tw (impersonal notification)	0					2 (O)	2 (T, O)			
r dit rḫ.k(wi) (allocutive notification)	0		1 (C)							
r rdit rḫ wʿ nb	0									1 (R)
(*ḫr*) *ptr*(*i*) + N syntagm (presentative with nominal object, involvement)	1		1 (C)				1 (T)			
ḫr ptri tw.i + stative/prep + N (coordinated presentative with present, involvement and climax)	2					1 (R)	1 (T)			1 (R)
ḫr ptri bn st ḥr sḏm (coordinated presentative with negative present, involvement and climax)	2					1 (R)				

Form	Degree	*oDeM 108* 19th d. Seti I	*oG 90* 19th d. Ram. II	*oG 55* 19th-20th d. Ram. II-III	*oG 272* 20th d. Ram. III	*Naunakhte* 20th d. Ram. V	*pBoulaq 10* 20th d. Ram. VI	*oPetrie 18* 20th d. Ram. VII	*pAdoptions* 20th d. Ram. XI	*pTurin 2021* 20th d. Ram. XI
ḫr ptri di.tw. N/*iry(.i)* + adverbial focus (coordinated presentative with topic-initial cleft sentence) *ptr i.irw.i sḏm* + adverbial focus	1 2						1 (T)		1 (R) 1 (T)	
m.k (presentative) + adverbial nexus… *mtw.f sḏm* (conjunctive)	2				1 (O)					
w3ḥ PN… *mtw.*N *sḏm* (indep. modal prospective & conjunctive as crime apodosis of *terrorem* cl.)	2								1 (O)	
inn iw.f sḏm… iw.f m N (condition protasis with future + adverbial nexus apodosis; neutral attitude towards reality)	2								1 (R)	
inn wnw m-diw.i N… *iw.f sḏm* (condition protasis of existence & possession + future apodosis; neutral attitude towards reality)	2								3 (O)	

Form	Degree	*oDeM 108* 19th d. Seti I	*oG 90* 19th d. Ram. II	*oG 55* 19th-20th d. Ram. II-III	*oG 272* 20th d. Ram. III	*Naunakhte* 20th d. Ram. V	*pBoulaq 10* 20th d. Ram. VI	*oPetrie 18* 20th d. Ram. VII	*pAdoptions* 20th d. Ram. XI	*pTurin 2021* 20th d. Ram. XI
ir iw bn nominal nexus *iwnꜣ iw* nominal nexus *iw.f dit… nym i.irw.f sḏm pꜣ iry.f* (condition protasis with contrasted nominal segments & sequential past; rhetorical question apodosis with focus-initial cleft sentence; negative attitude towards reality)	2									1 (S)
in mꜣꜥt m + nominal syntagm (question for corroboration, present)	2									1 (S)
sḏm.N + adverbial focus (topic-initial cleft sentence)	0		1 (C)							
ḫr i.di.tw + adverbial focus	1						1 (T)			
i.ir.f sḏm + adverbial focus	2					1 (O)			1 (O)	
iw i.ir.i ir.f + adverbial focus (converted topic-initial cleft sentence)	2			1 (R?)						
N *pꜣ nty* + adverbial nexus (focus-initial cleft sentence)	2						1 (T)			
ir N… N (topicalized assets + nominal nexus with deleted pronominal theme, recognition of ownership)	1			1 (R?)						

Form	Degree	*oDeM 108* 19th d. Seti I	*oG 90* 19th d. Ram. II	*oG 55* 19th-20th d. Ram. II-III	*oG 272* 20th d. Ram. III	*Naunakhte* 20th d. Ram. V	*pBoulaq 10* 20th d. Ram. VI	*oPetrie 18* 20th d. Ram. VII	*pAdoptions* 20th d. Ram. XI	*pTurin 2021* 20th d. Ram. XI
ỉr N… *mtw.f ḏd* (+ curse?) (topicalized collaterals + conjunctive tagged speech marker, *no-contest* clause)	2								1 (T)	
ink N (nominal nexus, identity)	0					1 (R)				
participle + *sw* (nominal nexus, accusation)	1							1 (R)		
mꜣʿtw + nominal syntagm (nexus with adjectival rheme, corroboration of facts & legitimization)	1									2 (S)
ỉw pꜣy.ỉ N <*sw*> (converted nominal nexus, identity)	2								1 (R)	
N *ỉw mr.f sw* (nominal nexus with implied theme and N rheme with adnexal expansion)	2									1 (S)
bn N *sꜣwt iwnꜣ* (negative nominal nexus with implied theme)	2									1 (S)
sꜣwy N*.f* (delocutive rhematic possession)	1									1 (S)

Form	Degree	*oDeM 108* 19th d. Seti I	*oG 90* 19th d. Ram. II	*oG 55* 19th-20th d. Ram. II-III	*oG 272* 20th d. Ram. III	*Naunakhte* 20th d. Ram. V	*pBoulaq 10* 20th d. Ram. VI	*oPetrie 18* 20th d. Ram. VII	*pAdoptions* 20th d. Ram. XI	*pTurin 2021* 20th d. Ram. XI
iw ink sw (converted locutive rhematic possession)	2								1 (R)	
y3 mntst r.intw st (indep. perfect participial statement, assertive)	2			1 (R?)						
ḫr iw m (= *in*) N PN *rdit* (coordinated & converted perfect participial statement)	2						1 (T)			
bn st ink (converted & negated possession, thetic statement)	2							1 (R)		
iw bn N (converted non-existence)	2								1 (T)	
iw mn N	2								1 (R)	
.nn (locutive plural suffix)	1								1 (R)	
.w (delocutive plural suffix)	1	2 (O)	1 (C)	2 (R?)	1 (O)	x (R, O, Ad, D)	4 (T, P, O)	1 (O)	x (T, R, O)	8 (R, O, S)
.st (delocutive feminine suffix)	1			4 (R?)		8(P,R,O,Ad)	10 (T)	4 (R, Ad)	7 (T, R, O)	x (R, O, S)
.sw								1 (R)		
st (delocutive plural dependent pronoun)	1					1 (R)	2 (T)		1 (O)	3 (O, S)

Form	Degree	*oDeM 108* 19th d. Seti I	*oG 90* 19th d. Ram. II	*oG 55* 19th-20th d. Ram. II-III	*oG 272* 20th d. Ram. III	*Naunakhte* 20th d. Ram. V	*pBoulaq 10* 20th d. Ram. VI	*oPetrie 18* 20th d. Ram. VII	*pAdoptions* 20th d. Ram. XI	*pTurin 2021* 20th d. Ram. XI
sw (delocutive feminine dependent pronoun)	1							1 (R)		1 (S)
mnt(*y*)*st* (independent delocutive feminine pronoun)	1			1 (R?)			1 (T)			
s3wy (independent delocutive masculine pronoun)	1									2 (S)
s3wt	1								1 (T)	1 (S)
hrw pn, *nṯr pn* (archaic anaphora)	0	1 (P)				2 (P, Ad)	1 (P)	1 (P)	3 (T)	
ḳnbt tn (archaic cataphora)	0					1 (P)				
p3, *t3*, *n3* (anaphoric articloid)	1								2 (R, O)	4 (R, O, S)
n3 n	1		1 (C)							
p3, *t3*, *n3* (cataphoric articloid)	1	2 (O)	1 (C)	2 (R?)		9 (R, O,Ad)	9 (T, O)	3 (R, O, Ad)	5 (R, O)	x (R, O, S, Col)
n3 n	1	1 (O)	1 (C)							
p3, *t3*, *n3* (exophoric articloid)	1	1 (O)				3 (P, Col, Ad)	1 (O)	2 (R)	2 (O)	9? (R, Col)
p3, *t3*, *n3* (deictic articloid)	1						4 (T)		4 (T, R, O)	7? (R, O, S, Col)

Form	**Degree**	***oDeM 108*** **19th d.** **Seti I**	***oG 90*** **19th d.** **Ram. II**	***oG 55*** **19th-20th d.** **Ram. II-III**	***oG 272*** **20th d.** **Ram. III**	***Naunakhte*** **20th d.** **Ram. V**	***pBoulaq 10*** **20th d.** **Ram. VI**	***oPetrie 18*** **20th d.** **Ram. VII**	***pAdoptions*** **20th d.** **Ram. XI**	***pTurin 2021*** **20th d.** **Ram. XI**
p3, t3, n3 (non-phoric articloid)	1						1 (T)			
p3y (demonstrative)	1					3 (O)		1 (R)	1 (R)	9 (R, O, S)
p3y N *ink* (deictic + locutive possession) *p3y* N *r ink* *p3* N *ink*	1 1 1				1 (O)				1 (R) 1 (T) 1 (O)	
p3y N *s3wy* (deictic + delocutive possession)	1									1 (S)
p3 s3wt nb (delocutive possession with totalizing *nb*)	1								1 (T)	
p3y quantifier N *ink*/*tn-myw* (deixis, number and (al)locutive possession)	1					3 (R, O)				
N (*nb*) *ink* (locutive possession)	1							2 (R, O)		
p3y.f (possessive) *n3.f* *p3(y.i)*	1 1 1	1 (O) 1 (P)	4 (C)	5 (R?)	1 (O)	x (O, Ad)	x (T, P, O)	4 (R, O)	x (T, R, O)	x (R, O, S) 1 (O)
p3y.f N + quantifier (delocutive possession and number)	1						1 (T)			
nbt/*nbw* marked concord *(3)ḫt nb, st nb* (no concord)	0 1	 1 (O)		 1 (R?)		2 (O) 2 (R, O)		 2 (O)		

Form	Degree	*oDeM 108* 19th d. Seti I	*oG 90* 19th d. Ram. II	*oG 55* 19th-20th d. Ram. II-III	*oG 272* 20th d. Ram. III	*Naunakhte* 20th d. Ram. V	*pBoulaq 10* 20th d. Ram. VI	*oPetrie 18* 20th d. Ram. VII	*pAdoptions* 20th d. Ram. XI	*pTurin 2021* 20th d. Ram. XI
Fem N + *nty* (no concord)	1						2 (O)			1 (O)
n (relator)	0	7 (P, O)	6 (P, C)		1 (P)	x (P, R, O, Col, Ad, D)	x (T, P, O)	6 (O, Ad)	x (T, P, R, O, Col)	x (R, O, S, Col)
Fem N *nt* (concord)										1 (S)
r-nty (introductory purpose marker)	1				1 (P)				1 (R)	
m-ḏd (tagged speech marker)	0					2 (Ad)			1? (T)	
r-ḏd	1							2 (Ad)		1 (S)
ḫr(.f m) p3 hp (present trailing tag clause)	1						1 (T)			
mtw.f ḏd (conjunctive)	2								1 (T)	
ir(y) (topicalizer)	0	3 (O)	1 (C)			2 (R)				
ḫr ir(y) (+ coordinator)	0	3 (O)		1 (R?)		3 (O)	1 (T)			
iw ir (+ contrastive coordinator)	1			1 (R?)						
ir ink (opening locutive prominent topic of *recital*)	1					1 (R)		1 (R)		
gr ink (closing locutive stress marker)	1					1 (R)				
gr mntyst (delocutive)	1						1 (T)			
imy rn.f iry + list of people	0									1 (Col)
r-ḥrw-r ink (locutive exclusion)	1								1 (T)	
inn mntw (delocutive)	1								1 (R)	
wpwt PN	1								1 (O)	

Form	Degree	*oDeM 108* 19th d. Seti I	*oG 90* 19th d. Ram. II	*oG 55* 19th-20th d. Ram. II-III	*oG 272* 20th d. Ram. III	*Naunakhte* 20th d. Ram. V	*pBoulaq 10* 20th d. Ram. VI	*oPetrie 18* 20th d. Ram. VII	*pAdoptions* 20th d. Ram. XI	*pTurin 2021* 20th d. Ram. XI
n/m prepositions confusion *m/ir?*	1 1								3 (T) 1 (T)	1 (S)
m (= *in*) focus marker	1						1 (T)			
m r3-ꜥ (adverbial modifier in trailing position)	1							1 (Ad)	1 (O)	1 (O)
m-mitt (phrasal coordinator) *mitt*	0 1					7 (O)		2 (O) 1 (Ad)		
iw (contrastive coordinator)	1			1 (R?)						3? (R, S)
bn N *bn* N (positive disjuncter)	1								1 (R)	
m-di.f/N (compound preposition) *m-dit.st* *m-diw.i*	1 1 1			1 (R?)					1 (R) 3 (O)	3 (R, O, S)
irm.f/N (preposition)	1			1 (R?)			1 (T)		4 (T, R)	9 (R, O, S)
ḏt nḥḥ (binomial) *ḏt r nḥḥ*	0 0					1 (P)			2 (T, P)	

Form	**Degree**	***oDeM 108*** **19th d.** **Seti I**	***oG 90*** **19th d.** **Ram. II**	***oG 55*** **19th-20th d.** **Ram. II-III**	***oG 272*** **20th d.** **Ram. III**	***Naunakhte*** **20th d.** **Ram. V**	***pBoulaq 10*** **20th d.** **Ram. VI**	***oPetrie 18*** **20th d.** **Ram. VII**	***pAdoptions*** **20th d.** **Ram. XI**	***pTurin 2021*** **20th d.** **Ram. XI**
šri(w) šri(w) (filiation binomial) *bn šriw bn šriw* (+ disjuncter) *šriw šriw sn sn n t3y.w mwt* *p3y.w it* *iw mn šriw šriw* (negative)	1 1 1 2		1 (C)						1 (T) 1 (R) 1 (O) 1 (R)	1 (S)
(*m*) *dw3w r-s3 dw3w* (mortis causa binomial)	1								1 (T)	
preposition omission	1	3 (P, O)		1 (R?)		1 (Ad)	4 (T, O)	4 (R, Ad)	x (T, R, O)	x (R)
preposition redundancy	1					1 (Ad)	2 (T, O)		2 (T, R)	

B. Partitions

The following texts do not belong to the *consentient legal* genre: they are not constitutive of rights or obligations, they do not represent expressions of will by a testator or donor. They may represent a preliminary *allotment* of assets (the scriptural constitution of *allotments*) induced by a will or a gift, or the report concerning the actual, material execution of the partition. They have been included in our survey as representative of the consequences of such deeds as Docs. II and III were included in *Naunakhte*'s file *supra*; contestations of wills, on the other hand, were not encompassed since the *contentious legal genre* will be examined separately on another occasion. The remarks made about the textemes of *pDeM* 23 and 25 are also relevant here: informational (with high noun and proper noun frequency, relational expansions, agentless passives, delocutive mode, absence of nexus, prepositional phrases, quantifiers, well organized with isotopic listing layout denoting structural elaboration, using lexemic/graphic dividers) but often lacking contextual precision thus not completely detached; usually non narrative, high authoritative register.

1. *oGardiner/Ashmolean* 89

Date: 19th dynasty, Ramesses II
Hieroglyphic version: *KRI* III, 724 n.9
Instrument:

* **state** – damaged
* **value – copy or draft?:** material used, seems complete except for the date which does not always appear in *memoranda*[695], limited to the partition list and its brief heading
* **nature** – ***sḫ3 memorandum*** concerning private assets (internal characterization), the sole '*sḫ3* document' in our corpus
* **genre – accounting**[696]: business hand but absence of correction or business practice diacritical marks; delocutive mode, degree 1 Neo-Egyptian, formulaic style, ordered layout of list, no mention of specific legal procedures, forums or institutions, absence of *recital* and colophon; concerns only each heir's share of hides, its quality and approximate size; uses accounting documents' term *ʿḥʿ*; of unknown provenance.

Step in the process: after-the-fact record of the taking (*iṯi*)[697] of movable assets, thus material execution of partition[698]

Legal issue: inheritance (*iwʿt*)[699], execution of a will or intestate succession; *rdi, iṯi*; it does not relate to the entire patrimony of the testator, only hides, and the 'seizers' are probably the sons and daughters of the testator. The reference to an excess (*exemption from hotchpot*?) and a global amount owed is unclear due to the damaged state of the document, but is indicative of a document dealing with the succession as a global estate and its valuation.

---

695 See for instance *oLeipzig* 5 (epistolary genre). Example of a dated administrative memorandum: *oBM* EA 50729 (brief date + *hrw pn sḫ3w*) concerning absence from work.

696 Megally (1977: 62): *sḫ3 n* 'rappel', sometimes introducing an independent 'pièce comptable' as for *oGardiner/Ashmolean* 89.

697 An active 'recipient', not as in the other cases.

698 Note that contrary to *pDeM* 23 and 25 (see *supra Naunakhte*), the document does not use the notification and the # *rdyt n* PN # formulae; and it is not constructed with a report form as the material partition of *pBoulaq* 10 (*pšw.w n.sn m* + date).

699 Donker van Heel & Haring (2003: 109 n.151) note that the lexeme *iwʿt* is written here as *iwʿ(.y)t* 'troop' or 'battalion' but that all persons concerned are necropolis workmen, and that it is an account of a division of private property (*ibid.*, 157).

Textemic features:

1. Pre-material

Title: (R.1) *sẖ3 n n3 n dḥrw* (2) *n t3 iwꜥt n ꜥ3mk* *Memorandum* of the hides of the inheritance of *ꜥ3mk*

* Neo-Egyptian characteristics:
  - cataphoric articloid (*n3 n dḥrw n t3 iwꜥt n ꜥ3mk*) ;

* 'Classical' degree 0 forms used:
  - use of the relator *n* (absence of concord) in object relation (*sẖ3 n n3 n dḥrw*), with plural articloid (*n3 n dḥrw*), part/whole (*dḥrw n t3 iwꜥt*) and source of rights relations (*t3 iwꜥt n ꜥ3mk*);

* General dialectal features: degree 1.

* Formula: *sẖ3 n* + object.

2. Content

Partition list (3) *ꜥ3mk iṯt.f nfr nfr sw rdi šri* *ꜥ3mk*[700], what he took: it is very good (quality), a small (sized) transmission (4) *Ḥ3y iṯt.f šri sw rdi ḥry-ib* *Ḥ3y,* what he took: it is inferior (quality), a medium (sized) transmission (5) *Twrb3y iṯt[.f nfr? sw rdi] ḥry[-ib]* *Twrb3y,* what [he] took: [it is good? (quality), a] medi[um (sized) transmission] (6) *ỉpy iṯt[.f… sw rdi…]* *ỉpy,* what [he] took: [it is… (quality), a… (sized) transmission] (7) *[Snnḏ]m iṯ[t.f… sw rdi]* *[Snnḏ]m* , what [he] took: [it is… (quality), a… (sized) transmission]; (8) *nty m-ḫ3w m m-ꜥ* (9) *ꜥ3mkt* (10) *dḥr* 1 *ḥry-ib* what is in excess[701] from *ꜥ3mkt*[702]: 1 hide, medium (sized) (V.1) […] (2) [*ꜥḥꜥ?*] *ḥr t3 iwꜥt* (3) [*n?*] *Ḳ3ḥ3 dḥry* 1 [… amount owed?] by this succession [to?] *Ḳ3ḥ3*: 1 hide (**estate's debt?**) (4) [*ꜥḥꜥ?*] *ḥr ꜥ3fy r p3 iṯty* (5) *t3 iwꜥt n ꜥ3mkt* (6) [… *dḥrw?*] 2 *ꜥḥꜥ* ½ [amount owed?] by *ꜥ3fy* for the taking of the inheritance of *ꜥ3mkt*: 2 [hides?…] (**amount due to the estate?**). Global amount owed:[703] ½.

* Neo-Egyptian characteristics:
  - cataphoric articloid (*p3 iṯty t3 iwꜥt n* PN);

700 Kitchen (*RITA*, 486) sees in line 3 *ꜥ3mk* a redundant repetition of line 2 *ꜥ3mk* and the entire construction as # *iṯt.f* + qualification + PN (the possessor in apposition) #.

701 This may refer to an *exemption from hotchpot* (see *oGardiner/Ashmolean* 272, lines 3-4: *twnw* PN… *m-ḫ3w n n3y.f snw r-ḏrw*).

702 For *ꜥ3mk* apparently as line 2 *t3 iwꜥt n ꜥ3mk* is followed in verso line 5 by *t3 iwꜥt n ꜥ3mkt*. But is *ꜥ3mk* in recto line 3 the same person as in recto line 2 or a son of his (although the existence of such an homonym is not attested in Davies 1999: chart 19)?

703 *ꜥḥꜥ*: '(out?)standing' (*RITA*, 487); 'montant global dû' in *pLouvre* E 3226 (Megally 1977: 56-61); 'amount standing' (Collier & Quirke 2006: 302).

- preposition redundancy: *m m-ˁ* (but note classical *m-ˁ* instead of *m-di*);
- *nty m-ḥ3w*: probably a new entry in the account unrelated to the preceding entry, without articloid but not spelled as the classical *ntt* used as noun;

* 'Classical' degree 0 forms used:
  - PN *iṯt.f nfr/šri sw rdi šri/ḥry-ib*: # PN topicalized + *sḏmt.f* (perfect relative neutrum) + adjectival nexus *nfr sw* (quality) + nominal apposition *rdi* (participle used as a noun?) with attributive expansion (size) #;
  - relator *n* used in source of rights relation (*t3 iwˁt n* PN);
* General dialectal features: degree 1.
* Formula: PN (possessor) + *iṯt.f* + *nfr/šri sw* (quality) + *rdi šri/ ḥry-ib* (size)

Categorization of terms of special relevance in the legal register:

- *sḫ3* *n*: *memorandum* of. See Megally (1977: 61-3), Fitzpatrick (1983), McDowell (1990: 16-8), Donker van Heel & Haring (2003: 108-10).
  It can be used as a heading of a brief notation, of a larger document or letter. For Donker van Heel & Haring (*ibid.*), it is the name of a textual genre; but as it appears in the pre-material of epistolary[704], accounting/administrative[705], or legal charge[706] documents, it appears to be something of a general term used in written documents of diverse types[707].
  The lexeme is attested since the Middle Kingdom[708] and classified by the classifier of the [MOUTH LINKED ACTIVITIES] category; it is used to conceptualize an essentially mental process (remembrance) as for *k3i* 'to think', *ḫmt* 'to expect, think', although verbal associations are not excluded.
- *iwˁt*: inheritance.
  Attested since the Old Kingdom, without classifier (the leg-bone with meat is a 'phonetic classifier'); during the Middle Kingdom, sometimes with the papyrus roll classifier which becomes the regular classifier of the lexeme during the New Kingdom. Perhaps more precisely, due to the classifier and the plural grapheme, the ensemble of heirs.
- *iṯi*: to take.
- *iṯty* *iwˁt*: the taking of inheritance. The expression *iṯi iwˁt* is already attested during the Old Kingdom in *PT* 2142 (Spell 693).
- *rdi*: transmission, giving.

704 For example *oLeipzig* 5 (*sḫ3w n* N PN).
705 For example *oBM* EA 50729 (date + *hrw pn sḫ3w p3y.f wsf*).
706 For example *pMallet* line I, 1 (*sḫ3 n smy n* N PN).
707 See also the probable abbreviated form of *sḫ3* used as checkmark in margins (Donker van Heel & Haring 2003: 108 a).
708 *ÄW* II, 2303 'Aktenstück mit Notizen, Memo, Memorandum'.

2. *oLouvre* E 13156 (*oLouvre* E 2425, *oAnastasi*)

Date: 19th dynasty, Ramesses II
Hieroglyphic version: *KRI* III, 547 n.232 A56
Instrument:

* **state –** complete

* **value – draft/copy/excerpt?:** material used, lacking a date and other precise references to the context, cursory note

* **nature – record concerning private assets** (absence of internal characterization)

* **genre – accounting or bureaucratic note:** of both private and public interest as it concerns immovables; business hand with several corrections, but absence of business practice diacritical mark; mostly delocutive texteme but includes a narrative addition related to the outcome of one share and one heir's declaration introduced by locutive reference (to the scribe?), degree 2 of Neo-Egyptian; ordered layout, no mention of specific legal procedures, forums or institutions, absence of *recital* and colophon, absence of date, but all parties named; of unknown provenance

Step in the process: preliminary *allotment* of immovable assets (*tp n pšw, nty n*)

Legal issue: probably the execution of a will/intestate succession (absence of *consideration*; *pšw*; family relations, number and description of shares[709], but concerns only the immovable assets and not the entire patrimony). The document does not seem to consist of a *partage d'ascendant* (see *supra*) as there is no mention of the declaration of the testator, and lines 8-9 refer to an arrangement between two heirs. Of course, the document may also relate to the conclusion of a litigation process.

Textemic features:

1. Pre-material

Title: (1) *tp n pšw p3 wḏ3 n Nbimntt n* (2) *s3t.f 3st ḥnʿ Ḥnwtḏww*	
Key of division of the storehouse of *Nbimntt* for his daughter *3st* with *Ḥnwtḏw*:	

* Neo-Egyptian characteristics:
  - cataphoric articloid (*p3 wḏ3 n Nbimntt*);

* 'Classical' degree 0 forms used:
  - relator *n* used in nature (*tp n pšw*) and ownership relations (*wḏ3 n Nbimntt*);

* General dialectal features: degree 1.

* Formula: *allotment* heading: *tp n pšw* + object

2. Content

Partition list:	
(3) *wḏ3 1 ir n pš 2 nty im.f*	1 storehouse, making 2 shares that are in it;
št3t 1 m b3kw m (4) *p3 ḏw iw.st pšw 2 mi ḳd p3 wḏ3 ʿk3*	1 cave/cellar cut into the mountain. It is 2 shares like this storehouse, exactly;
subtitle: (5) *tp n pšw t3 št3t m pšw 2*	
key of division of this cave/cellar in 2 shares:	
partition list:	

709 But absence of the dimension of the immovables (see *pBoulaq* 10).

nty n rmṯ ist Nfrḥtp wsḫt [1]	what is for (the) workman *Nfrḥtp*: 1 room;
(6) *nty n ʿnḫ-n-niwt Ḥwtiyt wsḫt* 1	what is for (the) *ʿnḫ-n-niwt Ḥwtiyt*: 1 room;

(7) *n Ỉmnmipt ḥnʿ M33nty m pšwt.w n t3y.w mwt m pš.w* (8) *wḏ3 n ḫny*
(what is) for *Ỉmnmipt* and *M33nty*, as the share of their mother in their division: inner storeroom.

* Neo-Egyptian characteristics:
- anaphoric articloid (*t3 št3t*);
- exophoric articloid for specific geographic feature of the Necropolis area (*p3 ḏw*);
- *nty n* PN: relative phrase used as a substantive, without articloid, but also not in the classical form *ntt*. The phrase does not represent a performative formulation by the testator or donor as does # *iw.f n* PN # in the context of the operative part of a will or gift. See *pTurin* 2070 and *oDeM* 586; also *nty m-ḫ3w* in *oGardiner/Ashmolean* 89;

* 'Classical' degree 0 forms used:
- relator *n* used in nature (*tp n pšw*), value (*ir n pš* 2), unclear kind of relation in frozen expression (*ʿnḫ-n-niwt*), source of rights (*pšwt.w n t3y.w mwt*), and location relations (*wḏ3 n ḫny*);
- *ir n pš* 2: # passive perfect participle *ir* + relator *n* + unit + quantifier #;
- delocutive Neo-Egyptian suffix *.w* (plural) and *.st* (feminine);
- Neo-Egyptian possessive determinator for kinship relations (*t3y.w mwt*; but see *s3t.f*);

* General dialectal features: degree 1.

* Formula: *allotment*: *tp n pšw* + object + immovable + quantifier and *nty n* PN (beneficiary)

3. Addition

The renunciation by a brother of his share in favor of his sister. This arrangement constitutes a narrative with a quotation following the main texteme. Compare with *oBerlin* P 12636, lines 8-10.

Renunciation in favor of a sibling:
iw rmṯ ist Nfrḥtp ḥr dit t3y.f pšw m (= *n*) *t3* (9) *snt.f Ḥwtiyt iw.st ḥr ḏd n.i*[710] *bn sw ḥr mdn m-di.i* (?)
And (the) workman *Nfrḥtp* gave his share to this sister of his *Ḥwtiyt*, and she said to me: 'It is not inscribed in my possession (?).'

* Neo-Egyptian characteristics:
- sequential narrative past with preposition (*iw rmṯ ist* PN *ḥr dit*; *iw.st ḥr ḏd* used as a tag clause) expressing a development in the division process.
  Note that the sequential does not follow a nexus, only a long nominal segment; ostraca constituting short notes about some contractual deals may also show a sequential form after a nominal segment without nexus, e.g. *oDeM* 619: Date + 'This day of giving the donkey to (the) water-carrier PN for its hire.' + date (26 days later) + 'And I took it (*iw.i nḥm.f*), making 26 days worth 1 ½ sack'. The sequential represents the event mode, as opposed to a given situation;
- Neo-Egyptian possessive determinator for ownership relation (*t3y.f pšw*);

710 Allam (1973: 203, n. 6) notes that there are traces of a previous *n.s* instead of *n.i* (the writer) after *iw.st ḥr ḏd*.

- *m* (= *n*) *tꜣ snt.f*: preposition confusion;
- *tꜣ snt.f* PN: # cataphoric articloic + N + possessive suffix (kinship) + PN #: hyperdetermination;
- *bn sw ḥr mdn*: # Neo-Egyptian negator *bn* + dependent pronoun + *ḥr* + infinitive *mdn* #, negative present quoted direct speech;
- *m-di.ỉ*: Neo-Egyptian preposition.

* 'Classical' degree 0 forms used: -
* General dialectal features: degree 2.
* Formula: *ỉw*.N/*f ḥr sḏm* + quoted direct speech

Categorization of terms of special relevance in the legal register:

- *pš(w/t)*: division, share.
- *tp n pšw*: detail/ensemble/key of division. The expression comes at the beginning of two lists. Černý (1931: 493, n.7) suggests translating it by 'accomplissement' or 'manière' of division, followed in that by Janssen (1975b: 294) who criticizes Allam (1973: 202) for his translation 'details' of division; Malinine (1953: 38-40, n. 11) proposes 'convention de partage' when *tp n pš* appears in Demotic texts of the 25th – 27th dynasties; 'specification of dividing' for Donker van Heel & Haring (2003: 135) in the heading of a collective Necropolis administration document. Other examples of this heading are given by Janssen (1975b: 294) and Donker van Heel & Haring (*ibid.*): *oDeM* 435, a division of tools; *oPetrie* 5, a division of yarn; *oCairo* CG 25555, a division of a storehouse; *oCairo* CG 25667, an 18th dynasty letter concerning the distribution of offerings; as a subtitle: *pTurin* 1894, a distribution of oil).
  Černý recalled (*op. cit.*) that several expressions beginning with *tp n* are translated 'example of' and it is difficult to assess with absolute confidence what # *tp n* + N # means in each instance. In our analysis of # *tp n* + N # in the corpus of Ramesside decrees[711] we concluded that the expression may have diverse meanings: unit/specimen in a group/category (specific, metonymic), the group itself (generic), a paradigmatic exemplar or beginning of (metaphoric), a modus of.
- *mdn*: to be inscribed, carved.
  For a discussion of the meaning of *mdn* 'to be quiet' (*Wb* II, 182), see Kruchten (1981: 153.E) who tentatively suggests the etymology *dn* 'couper, partager' (see *dni* – share). Others[712] translate it as 'to be recorded', on the basis of *mtn,* thought to be a Neo-Egyptian lexeme (*Wb* II, 170-1) often classified by the finger and the strong hand in the [FINGER ACTIONS] basic level category or by (Gardiner's double T14 signs are here used as phonetic *mt*), but with probable origin in Middle Kingdom[713].
  A formulation close to our text is to be found in *pBerlin* P 10496 r°, 13 (dispute concerning a tomb, reign of Ramesses III): *ỉw bn sw mdnw tw ḥr rn n rmṯ nbt* '(a coffin) that has no name of any person inscribed upon it' (with the basic level [BINDING] category string classifier). In our text, *mdn* is categorized with the help of the superordinate [ABSTRACT] category classifier. Both classifiers seem to confirm the 'record' semantics of the lexeme.

711 David (2006: 42-3 n.67, 163 n.3).
712 Helck (1961-70: 339); Allam (1973: 203); *RITA*, 379.
713 *ÄW* II, 1157: *mtnt* 'Abzeichen', *CT* Spell 9 (with or without papyrus roll classifier).

3. *oDeM* 112 and 964

Date: 20th dynasty, Ramesses III-IV (Demarée 2006: 59)
Hieroglyphic version: *KRI* III, 546 n.232 A.55 (*oDeM* 112) and Grandet 2003: 415, 417 (*oDeM* 964)
Instrument:
 * **state** – damaged
 * **value – draft/copy/excerpt?**: material used, undated, essentially context-dependent lists
 * **nature – records concerning private assets** (absence of internal characterization)
 * **genre – accounting or bureaucratic**[714]**:** of both private and public interest as they concern parts of immovables, essentially doors; same business hand[715] in both documents with one correction in *oDeM* 964, use of abbreviation for *dmḏ* and of *ditto* mark only in *oDeM* 112; delocutive texteme, degree 1 Neo-Egyptian; ordered layout, no mention of specific legal procedures, forums or institutions, absence of pre-material, *recital* and colophon, but all parties named; *oDeM* 112 was found in the southern *kom* and *oDeM* 964 in the *Grand Puits*.

Step in the process: partition with transmission (*rdyt*) of parts of immovable assets; each list might represent a different phase, one being the record of *allotment* concerning all the heirs (*oDeM* 964), the other the after-the-fact record of the physical distribution of the items to two of them. As a matter of fact, *oDeM* 964 is a more elementary record; it may not use the formula # *rdyt n* PN #, does not include totals or *ditto* marks, and it groups the two women's shares as opposed to the other recipients; furthermore, the entries are not all identical.
 For Grandet (2003 : 8) the two documents record a procedure of successive partition of assets with 'le déplacement en groupe des héritiers à la maison du défunt, autant de fois que nécessaire, pour s'y partager à chaque fois une quantité équivalente de biens, jusqu'à ce qu'il n'y en ait plus aucun à partager' (as in *pDeM* 23 and 25).

Legal issue: probable execution of the will or intestate succession of the recipients' father *Nḫmmwt* as the recipients are siblings[716].
Textemic features:

1. *oDeM* 112

Partition list:	
(1) *rdyt n T3mkw*	What was given to *T3mkw*:
(2) *t3 št3yt mryt sb3* [1]	the cave/cellar of the river-bank: [1] door;
(3) *p3 wḏ3 ḥry ditto*[717] 1	the upper storehouse: *ditto* 1
(4) *t3 ḥb mryt ditto* 1	the river-bank's festival kiosk[718]/court[719]: *ditto* 1
(5) *t3 ʿt m Sḫt*[720] *ditto* 1	the hut/workplace in (the) Field (= KV): *ditto* 1

714 For Cooney (2006: 44 n.14 and 45 n.17), *oDeM* 112 represents a 'multi-transaction' receipt and legal text 'mentioning the private sector funerary arts market'; in (2007: 58, 65) she characterizes *oDeM* 112 as a 'transaction receipt and legal text (inheritance)' and *oDeM* 964 as a matter of inheritance without substantiating these definitions.
715 Grandet (2003: 5, 135).
716 Černý (2001: 89); Toivari-Viitala (2001: 99).
717 The *ditto* mark, a simple crooked draw, appears during the New Kingdom (Helck 1975: 121).
718 Černý (2001: 95); Grandet (2003: 6).
719 *RITA*, 379.

(6) *Ḫnsw ditto* 1 *rdit.n.f n.s*	*Ḫnsw*: *ditto* 1, that he gave to her[721]
(7) *ꜣnwynḫt sbꜣ n mḫri* (8) 1 *rdit.n.f n.s*	*ꜣnwynḫt*: 1 door of granary, that he gave to her[722]
total: (9) *dmḏ* 6	Total: 6
(V. 1) *rdyt n Tꜣsꜣkt*	What was given to *Tꜣsꜣkt*:
(2) *tꜣ ꜥḥꜥt ditto* 1	the tomb: *ditto* 1
(3) *wḏꜣ n Ꞽny ditto* 1	storehouse of *Ꞽny*: *ditto* 1
(4) *wḏꜣ n Pndwꜣ ditto* 1	storehouse of *Pndwꜣ*: *ditto* 1
(5) *ꜥt m tꜣ St-Nfrw ditto* 2	hut/workplace in the Place of Beauty (= QV): *ditto* 2
(6) [*s*]*bꜣ n mḫri ditto* 1	[do]or of granary *ditto* 1
total: (7) *dmḏ* 6	Total: 6
addition[723]: (8) *pꜣ wḏꜣ n Ḥwy* 1	the storehouse of *Ḥwy:* 1
(9) *tꜣ ḫb n mryt* 1	the river- bank's festival kiosk/court: 1
(10) *pꜣ wḏꜣ n ḥry* [1]	the upper storehouse: [1]

* Neo-Egyptian characteristics:
- cataphoric articloid (*tꜣ šṯḫꜣyt, pꜣ wḏꜣ, tꜣ ḫb, tꜣ ꜥt*); note its absence with *wḏꜣ n* PN, *ꜥt m tꜣ St-Nfrw*, [*s*]*bꜣ n* N;
- exophoric articloid for toponym of the Necropolis area (*tꜣ st-nfrw*); but note its absence with *Sḫt*;

* 'Classical' degree 0 forms used:
- list form: # *rdyt* (perfect passive participle) *n* PN (recipient) + object + number of units # (agentless attribution). This formula represents the major difference between the two ostraca on the linguistic level; it may constitute an indication of the purpose of the text, the record posterior to the execution of the partition indicating its final outcome, as opposed to the preliminary *allotment* of all the shares recorded in *oDeM* 964, but one may not completely dismiss the possibility that *oDeM* 964 was written in a more schematic style but for the same purpose or that the formula is in lacuna concerning the two names preceding those of the women. Contrary to *pDeM* 23 and 25, the notification formula is not used here.
  For Donker van Heel & Haring (2003: 158-9), 'one of the older formulas introducing transfers of personal property composed with *rdy.t* (...) could also be used in division accounts: *rdy.t n* NN "what was given to NN"';
- use of the relator *n* for location (*sbꜣ n mḫri, tꜣ ḫb n mryt, pꜣ wḏꜣ n ḥry*) and ownership relation (*wḏꜣ n* PN). But note also *tꜣ štꜣyt mryt, pꜣ wḏꜣ ḥry, tꜣ ḫb mryt* without relator;
- past relative form (*rdit.n.f*) without prothetic *yod* but in feminine form, although the referent is a maculine noun (*sbꜣ*);

* General dialectal features: degree 1.

* Formula: *rdyt n* PN (recipient) + object + quantifier

---

720 Note that in *oDeM* 964, line 7 it appears as *Sḫt-ꜥꜣt*.

721 Probably the renunciation of part of a share in favor of a sibling, as the second text shows that *Ḫnsw* got 5 doors. Obviously the other parties' names are not on the same level as the women's, and are only brought up as the origin of two more doors in *Tꜣmkw*'s total of received items.

722 *Idem*.

723 Grandet (2003: 7): 'probablement des portes ajoutées après coup'.

2. *oDeM* 964

Partition list:

(1)[… *Ḫn*]*sw*	[… *Ḫn*]*sw*:
pꜣ wḏꜣ n mryt sbꜣ 5	the river-bank's storehouse: 5 door(s)
(2) [… *ꜣnwynḫt*?]	[… *ꜣnwynḫt*?]:
pꜣ wḏꜣ n Swnr 5	the storehouse of *Swnr*: 5
(3) [*sb*]*ꜣ n mḫri* 3	[doo]r(s) of granary: 3
(4) *Tꜣsꜣkti Tꜣmkw*	*Tꜣsꜣkti* (and) *Tꜣmkw*:
(5) *sbꜣ* 1 *m tꜣ štꜣyt rsyt*	1 door in the southern cellar
(6) [*p*]*ꜣ wḏꜣ n Ỉny* 1	[th]e storehouse of *Ỉny*: 1
(7) [*tꜣ ꜥt m*] *Sḫt-ꜥꜣt* 1	[the hut/workplace in] (the) Great Field (KV): 1
(8) [*tꜣ ꜥt m tꜣ*] *St-Nfrw* 2	[the hut/workplace in the] Place of Beauty: 2
(9) [*pꜣ wḏ*]*ꜣ n P*[*n*]*dwꜣ* 1	[the storehou]se of *P*[*n*]*dwꜣ*: 1
(V.1) [*tꜣ ḥb*?] *nty ḥr mr*[*yt*] 1	[the festival kiosk?] that is on the river-[bank]: 1
(2) [… *šꜥd* ?] *ỉwf pḫꜣ* 1	[… to slice?] meat: 1 platter
(3) [*pꜣ wḏ*]*ꜣ ḥry* 1 (10 crossed out)	[the] upper [storehou]se: 1
(4) […] *n Ḳnḥrḫpšf* 1	[the…] of *Ḳnḥrḫpšf*: 1
(5) *pꜣ* [*wḏ*]*ꜣ n Ḫꜥmdwꜣwy* 1	the [storehou]se of *Ḫꜥmdwꜣwy*: 1

* Neo-Egyptian characteristics:
  - cataphoric articloid (*pꜣ wḏꜣ*);
  - exophoric articloid (*tꜣ štꜣyt rsyt*);
* 'Classical' degree 0 forms used:
  - list form: # PN + object + quantifier #;
  - use of the relator *n*, for location (*pꜣ wḏꜣ n mryt,* [*sb*]*ꜣ n mḫri*) and ownership relation (*pꜣ wḏꜣ n* PN);
  - *ỉwf pḫꜣ* 1: # generic noun + *Badal* apposition (non-specific noun + quantifier) #;
* General dialectal features: degree 1.
* Formula: PN (recipient) + object + quantifier

Categorization of terms of special relevance in the legal register:

- *rdyt*: what was given, bequest.

4. *oBerlin* P 12636 v°

Date: 20th dynasty, Ramesses III
Hieroglyphic version: *KRI* VII, 288 n.A364
Instrument:

* **state –** fragmentary
* **value – draft/copy?:** material used, brief date, addressor/addressee (a woman) unnamed and lacking other precise references to the context, but perhaps complete in terms of the information that this type of document aims to communicate
* **nature – communication concerning private assets** (absence of internal characterization)
* **genres – epistolary? and accounting:** concerns private interest; business hand, absence of error/correction and of business practice diacritical mark, but expresses an account with balance of shares; delocutive/allocutive textemes, degree 2 Neo-Egyptian; formulaic style but absence of introductory and closing epistolary formulae; with narrative quotation addition to dated notification by unnamed addressor to unnamed addressee, other parties named; no mention of specific legal procedures, forums or institutions, absence of *recital* and colophon; palimpsest, found in Deir el-Medina in unknown spot.

The structure is reminiscent of *oGlasgow* D 1925.66, although *oBerlin* P 12636 v° deals also with shares and does not state regular allowances as does *oGlasgow* D 1925.66.

Step in the process: **notification** (*r* [*r*]*dit rḫ.tw*) of a transmission (*i.diw*) of movable assets, mentioning a partition (*pšw*)

Legal issue: separation of a couple, will or intestate succession, or even transaction? No *consideration* mentioned, partition with perhaps an *exemption from hotchpot* or debt.

The text is categorized as an 'account of private transfer' on the basis of the heading formula by Donker van Heel & Haring[724] who add that the last part of the text obviously refers to 'a division of property between a man and a woman (possibly his wife).'[725]

Textemic features:

1. Pre-material

Date: (1) *rnpt-sp* 20 *ꜣbd* 4 *šmw sw* 10 […]	Year 20, 4th month of summer, day 10 […]

* Neo-Egyptian characteristics: -
* 'Classical' degree 0 forms used: date format.
* General dialectal features: degree 1.
* Formula: date

2. Content

Notification of list of assets:	
(2) *r* [*r*]*dit rḫ.tw ꜣḫt i.diw rmṯ ꞽpwy n Nbwiry*	
For [in]formation (relative to) assets that (the work)man *ꞽpwy* gave to *Nbwiry*:	
(3) [*ḥmt*?] *dbn* [6?...][726]	[copper?: 6?] *dbn* […]

724 (2003: 149).
725 *Ibid.*, p. 158. Similarily: Davies (1999: 52); Toivari-Viitala (2001: 114).

(4) […]	
(5) […] *g3y* 2	[…] *g3y*-vessel: 2
(6) […]	
(7) *k3ḥsw n st-ḥmt* 1	wooden *k3ḥsw* for woman: 1,
Balance: *wḏ3t.f m ẖ3r* 2 *m t3y.i* (8) *pšw*	his (*Ipwy* ?) deficit[727] (consisting) of 2 sacks from my share.

* Neo-Egyptian characteristics:
- *i.diw*.N: perfect relative form with prothetic *yod*, attributive expansion;
- Neo-Egyptian lexeme (*g3y*);
- Neo-Egyptian possessive determinator for ownership (*t3y.i pšw*);

* 'Classical' degree 0 forms used:
- *r* [*r*]*dit rḫ.tw*: the notification formula implies that the document is not a simple *aide-mémoire*, but a record that is intended to be seen by a third party, the fact being confirmed by the use of the allocutive mode in the following texteme;
- *wḏ3.f m ẖ3r* 2 *m t3y.i pšw*: circumstantial adverbial nexus stating the overall balance of the partition;

* General dialectal features: degree 2.

* Formulae: - notification: *r rdit rḫ.tw 3ḫt i.diw* N PN *n* PN + list
- balance: list + *wḏ3t.f m* (deficit) + measurement unit + quantifier + *m t3y.i pšw*

3. Addition

***Exemption from hotchpot*? Debt?**:
iw.f ḥr ḏd n.(?) *ir iw.i ḥr pšw* (9) *n3 sb3 iw.i ḥr dit n.*(?) *wꜥ sb3* (10) *m-s3 t3y.* *pšw*
And he said to you (*Nbwiry*?): 'When I am dividing these door(s), I am giving to you one door after (= "in excess of"?) your share.'

* Neo-Egyptian characteristics:
- sequential narrative past *iw.f ḥr ḏd*: used as a tag clause introducing the quotation of someone's speech; it still retains the preposition (see *oLouvre* E 13156). The event is a verbal arrangement concerning the given partition;
- *ir iw.i ḥr pšw… iw.i ḥr dit*: temporal/conditional protasis - apodosis system, where the prepositions *ḥr* are retained in the protasis and the apodosis, thus not to be confused with *r*[728] but both present[729]. As presented here, the attitude of the speaker towards the reality of the condition is neutral, unmarked.

726 Following Černý (Notebook 32.37).

727 'Er ist unbeschädigt' for Allam (1982: 57).

728 Winand (1992: 521) shows that for the reigns of Ramesses III-VIII, it is the first present that retains the highest percentage of *ḥr* prepositions.

729 Concerning the protasis, Satzinger (1976: 73) states that the '*ir iw.f* ( ) *sḏm*' non-literary text constructions always have a potential future connotation; for *LEG*, 258 and 435, it is constructed with the '*iw.f* (*ḥr*) *stp.f* of the future' (negated by *tm* in *pStrassburg* 39 v°, 12-14, thus neither the future *iw.f r sḏm* nor a converted form; see also Groll 1969: 97 and Frandsen 1974: 100-2), whereas the apodosis is composed of the third future or the prospective (obviously not the case here). For Junge (2005: 262), the protasis uses a converted present, and the apodosis a third future, imperative or prospective 'expressing anticipated or expected actions' (but apparently not limited to these forms).

The addition may represent an *exemption from hotchpot*, although there is no mention of siblings or of the term 'bonus' (*twnw*) as in the other texts of this nature; it may also represent the expression of a debt towards *Nbwỉry*, as the balance of the account between the two parties was characterized by a deficit;

- use of the deictic articloid (*n3 sb3*) in direct speech context;
- Neo-Egyptian possessive determinator for ownership (*t3y.*[hieroglyph] *pšw*);

* 'Classical' degree 0 forms used: -
* General dialectal features: degree 2.
* Formula: *ỉw.f ḥr ḏd* + quoted direct speech

Categorization of terms of special relevance in the legal register:

- *r rdit rḫ*[hieroglyph]*.tw*: to let be known, for information (relative to).
- *dỉ*: to give.
- *3ḫt* [hieroglyph]: assets.
- *pšw* ×[hieroglyph]: a share; to divide.
- *wḏ3t* [hieroglyph]: balance, arrears, deficit. See Megally (1977: 69-78) 'reste (dû)', 'reliquat', 'solde'; Donker van Heel & Haring (2003: 141-2) for administrative accounts of deficits; Collier & Quirke (2006: 302) 'remainder'.
  Neo-Egyptian form of the lexeme *ḏ3t* already used during the Middle Kingdom (see e.g *pKahun* VI.10 r°, line 13 *ḏ3t ntt ʿḥʿ* 'the remainder that stands') without classifier. The accounting operation is classified during the New Kingdom in the superordinate [ABSTRACT] category.

5. *oDeM* 586

Date: 20th dynasty, Ramesses III (*KRI*)-IV (Demarée 2006: 60)
Hieroglyphic version: *KRI* V, 583 n.232 A 253
Instrument:

* **state** – almost complete?[730]
* **value – draft/copy/excerpt?:** material used, named parties, lacking a date and beginning (?), essentially context-dependent list
* **nature – record concerning private assets** (absence of internal characterization)
* **genre – consentient legal or accounting/bureaucratic:** of both private and public interest as it concerns immovables; business hand, absence of error/correction, accounting practice feature; ordered layout and formulaic style, degree 1 Neo-Egyptian, delocutive texteme; no mention of specific legal procedures, forums or institutions, absence of pre-material, *recital* and colophon, but all parties named; found in an ancient hypogea of Qurnet Murai North, pit n.1446[731].

Step in the process: excerpt of an **external manifestation of will** with performative (*partage d'ascendant*, *dni*) or preliminary *allotment* (*nty n* PN) of immovable assets

Legal issue: either essential part of a **will**[732] (uncertain in the absence of pre-material, *recital*, specific clauses, locutive forms and lack of evidence that *nty n* PN and N *ny-sw* PN are performatives in the absence of specific context) or execution of a will/intestate succession. No mention of *consideration* or of the origin of the shares, the partition does not involve an entire patrimony, and the relationship between the two women is unknown.

The document may be related to *pDeM* 30[733], although this division of property involves *Mwt* and a man, *T3wrḥtpw*, not our *T3wrḥtpti*.

Textemic features:

Partition list:

(1) [?] *gs.f ny-sw Mwt*	[?] Its half, it belongs to *Mwt.*
(2) *nty n T3wrḥtpti*	What is for *T3wrḥtpti:*

(3) *p3 wḏ3 n Wsir ny-sw T3wrḥtpti*
the storehouse of Osiris, it belongs to *T3wrḥtpti*
(4) *p3 wḏ3 nty r-gs pr Ptḥ ny-sw T3wrḥtpti*
the storehouse that is beside (the) house of Ptah, it belongs to *T3wrḥtpti*
(5) *t3 ʿt nty r-gs pr Ỉmn-Rʿ ditto ditto*
the hut/workplace that is beside (the) house of Amun-Re *ditto ditto*
(6) *p3 wḏ3 nty r-gs t3 ʿḥʿ Sb3 ny-sw T3wrḥtpti*
the storehouse that is beside the tomb of *Sb3*, it belongs to *T3wrḥtpti*
(7) *ỉr t3 ḥb šri nty r-gs* [...] *ditto T3wrḥtpti*
As for the little shrine that is beside [...], *ditto T3wrḥtpti*
(8) *ỉr p3 mr nty ḥr ʿḥʿ n Ỉmnmipt ny-sw T3wrḥtpt*[*i*]
As for the pyramid that is on (the) tomb of *Ỉmnmipt,* it belongs to *T3wrḥtpt*[*i*],
(9) [?] *m dni* 1 *m* 2 *wʿ Mwt wʿ* [*T3wrḥtpti*]

730 Allam (1973: 140) believes that *oDeM* 586 is part of a larger text split in two, the other part belonging to an unknown sherd.
731 Bruyère (1953: 111).
732 Will for McDowell (1999: 176) and Cooney (2007: 62): 'inheritance record or last will and testament'.
733 Donker van Heel & Haring (2003: 30 n.164) suggest that *oDeM* 586 was a draft of *pDeM* 30's redaction.

[?] as 1 share from 2, one of *Mwt* (and) one of [*T3wrḥtpti*][734].

* Neo-Egyptian characteristics:
- cataphoric articloid (*p3 wḏ3, t3 ꜥt, t3 ꜥḥꜥ, t3 ḥb, p3 mr*) but note *nty ḥr ꜥḥꜥ n Ỉmnmipt* and *pr* PN without the articloid;
- *nty n* PN: relative phrase used as a substantive, without articloid, but also not in the classical form *ntt*. It does not seem that this formula is to be regarded as a performative form given the lack of suitable context and positive examples; see *supra oLouvre* E 13156 (where the form was also not regarded as a performative);
- # (*ir*) + determined N (possessed) + *ny-sw* (anaphoric, invariable) + PN (possessor) #: repeated possession nexus[735], with topicalizer in the two last instances of the series. Either performative expression or constative, unclear in the absence of co- and contextual information. On the *Amarah stela* (*Stela Brooklyn* 38.544) of late 20th dynasty, a brother declares: *ir ḫt nbt n imy-r šnwt* PN *p(3y).n it m 3ḥwt m sḫt m ḥm ḥmt m šnw ns-sw šmꜥyt n Ḫnm* PN *n s3 n s3.s iwꜥw n iwꜥw.s* ' As for all assets of (the) overseer of (the) granary PN, our father, consisting of fields, of pastures, of male (and) female servants, of trees, they belong to (the) singer of *Ḫnm* PN, for (the) son of her son, (the) heir of her heir'. The stela does not belong to the consentient legal genre, and the statement may be a constative (confirmation of a decision taken by another party) or the record of a performative statement (renunciation/gift);

* 'Classical' degree 0 forms used:
- relator *n* used in religious dedication (*p3 wḏ3 n Wsir*) and ownership relations (*ꜥḥꜥ n Ỉmnmipt*);

* General dialectal features: degree 1.
* Formula: (*ir*) N *ny-sw* PN (ownership)

Categorization of terms of special relevance in the legal register:

- *ny-sw* PN: belongs to PN (ownership).
- *dni* (logogram ⊏): share, portion, fraction.

734 Joint property (see Donker van Heel & Haring 2003: 30 n.164).
735 See *LEG* § 2.3.4.

6. *pDeM* 30

Date: 20th dynasty, Ramesses III-IV (see Helck 2002: 403)
Hieroglyphic version: Černý (1986 : pl. 21).
Instrument:

* **state –** complete but unfinished or broken off papyrus
* **value – original/copy/excerpt**?: material used, only pre-material with brief date and named parties, and introduction of the partition list
* **nature – record concerning private assets** (absence of internal characterization)
* **genre – administrative**: private and public interest as it concerns immovables; business hand 'spécialement cursive'[736], absence of error/correction and business practice diacritical marks; unspecific layout and formulaic style, degree 1 Neo-Egyptian, delocutive texteme; no mention of specific forums or institutions, absence of *recital*, substance of partition list, and colophon, but all parties named and brief date without archaic anaphora; degree 1 Neo-Egyptian (absence of nexus), delocutive texteme; found among other documents, probably in the area east of Hathor temple precinct[737]

Step in the process: after-the-fact record of the execution of a partition (*pš*) and transmission (*rdyt*) of immovable assets
Legal issue: probably the execution of a will or intestate succession[738]. See *supra oDeM* 586 (in *pDeM* 30, the parties are one woman *Mwt* and two men including *Tꜣwrtḥtpw*).
Textemic features:

1. Pre-material

Date: (1) *rnpt-sp* 6 *ꜣbd* 4 *prt sw* 29	Year 6, 4th month of winter, day 29
Title: *pš nꜣ s{ꜣ* for *w}t* (2) *n Pꜣrꜥḥtpw*	Division of the immovable assets of *Pꜣrꜥḥtpw*
beneficiaries: *n Tꜣwrtḥtpw ḥnꜥ* (3) *ꜥnḫ-n-niwt Mwt ḥnꜥ Nsyimn*	for *Tꜣwrtḥtpw* and (the) *ꜥnḫ-n-niwt Mwt* and *Nsyimn*

* Neo-Egyptian characteristics:
  - cataphoric articloid (*nꜣ swt*);
* 'Classical' degree 0 forms used:
  - use of relator in ownership (*nꜣ swt n* PN) and unclear kind of relation in frozen expression (*ꜥnḫ-n-niwt*);
  - use of the coordinator *ḥnꜥ* between PNs;
* General dialectal features: degree 1.
* Formula: date + *pš nꜣ swt* + PN (owner) + *n* (beneficiaries)

2. Content

Partition (list)	
(4) *rdyt ꜥnḫ-niwt Mwt*	What was given (to the) *ꜥnḫ-niwt Mwt*:

736 Černý (1986: 6).
737 Bruyère (1952: 151-2).
738 Inheritance settlement for Toivari-Viitala (2001: 41); division account of private property for Donker van Heel & Haring (2003: 157), with heading formula similar to headings of collective administration documents.

* Neo-Egyptian characteristics:
  - preposition *n* and relator (in frozen expression) omission (*rdyt ʿnḫ-niwt*);
* 'Classical' degree 0 forms used:
  - *rdyt*: perfect passive participle for agentless past transmission.
* General dialectal features: degree 1.
* Formula: *rdyt* + N PN (recipient).

Categorization of terms of special relevance in the legal register:

- *pš*: division.
- *st* : immovable asset.
- *rdyt*: what was given.

7. *pTurin* 2070 v°, col. II

Date: 20th dynasty, Ramesses VI-IX (Demarée 2006: 60)
Hieroglyphic version: *KRI* VI, 427-8 n.23 A5
Instrument:

* **state –** fragmentary
* **value – original/copy?:** material used, perhaps dated, all parties named as well as perhaps the scribe, apparently including the essential elements for that type of document
* **nature – record concerning private assets** (absence of internal characterization)
* **genre – entry of an administrative journal**[739]: Muszynski (1977) notes the fact that the text is part of a 'journal of Deir el-Medina' (*recto*) and is recorded on the *verso* after an accounting list. See the private and public interests as it concerns immovables; business hand, perhaps the same author as *pTurin* 1885 v°[740], and the same as the hand of the recto (the recto is a palimpsest), with errors and a correction, absence of administrative practice features but bichromy; ordered layout, formulaic style, degree 2 Neo-Egyptian, delocutive texteme with brief locutive quotation in oath; perhaps related colophon with brief date and named recording scribe, no mention of specific forums or institutions, absence of *recital*; of unknown provenance

Step in the process: **notification** (*r rdỉt rḫ.tw*) of *allotment* (*nty n* N PN) of immovable assets before partition ([*ỉ*]*w.w pš.w*)
Legal issue: probably a succession (division by 'them', thus not by *Nḫtmỉnỉ* himself[741], repayment of a debt of the estate, family ties) although it only concerns immovables, but also a dispute (oath of the heirs, but absence of indication of the forum)[742].
Textemic features:

1. Content

Notification of partition list: (1) *r rdỉt rḫ.tw swt{t} n Nḫtmỉnỉ* [*nty ỉ*]*w.w pš.w* For information (relative to) immovables of *Nḫtmỉnỉ* [that] they will divide: (2) *nty* (*n*) *ꜥnḫ-n-nỉwt Mrwt* [*r-ḏ*]*bꜣw tꜣ st n pꜣy.st ỉt* (3) *ỉw.st wnm pꜣy.st* […][743] *ỉrm Nḫtmỉnỉ* (4) *tꜣ ꜥt{t} nty r-gs pr Ỉꜥḥ<ms> Nfr*[*t*]*rỉ ꜥ.w.<s.> n Mnst ỉw pꜣ ky* […] (**repayment of estate's debt**)[744]

739 Note that even the Middle Kingdom administrative journals found in Kahun contain 'day-by-day copies of business letters and transactions' (Collier & Quirke 2006: ii); concerning Deir el-Medina,Valbelle (1985: 38, n. 5) notes that 'La réunion de textes traitant d'affaires privées et d'informations concernant la communauté n'est par rare'.

740 Muszinski (1977: 192 n.23).

741 Muszynski (1977: 192) notes that 'Le fait que ce partage ait été noté dans le "Journal" du village de Deir el-Medineh montre qu'il est survenu suite au décès de Nekhtmini. Il importait en effet à l'administration de connaître l'identité des nouveaux propriétaires des biens immobiliers du défunt.'

742 Toivari-Viitala (2001: 41,100) recognizes a property or inheritance settlement.

743 Janssen (1974) supplies *ḥmꜣy* 'salt,' a restoration not accepted by Allam (1974) and Muszynski (1977).

744 Interestingly, a similar clause appears in *pBoulaq* 10 v°, lines 13-15: *tꜣy.f štꜣt ỉm.f nty n.f r-ḏbꜣ wttyw* [*sšw m ḳdwt*?] 2 *nty m pꜣ ḫnw dỉwyw* (*n*) *Tꜣgmyt* 'his cave/cellar in it which was for him in payment of 2 [painted?] coffins that are in the cellar/chapel, that were given (to) *Tꜣgmyt*'. See also a similar note in *pTurin* 1885 *infra*. Muszynski (1977: 195) notes that in *pTurin* 2070, the woman is 'titulaire d'une créance grevant la succession du défunt.'

what is (for the) *ꜥnḫ-n-niwt Mrwt* [in com]pensation of the immovable of her father because she consumed her […] with *Nḫtmini*[745]: the hut/workplace that is beside (the) temple of *Iꜥḥ<ms> Nfr[t]ri* L.P.<H.> of *Mnst*[746], while the other […];

(5) *nty n tꜣy.st šriwt m pš pꜣ mr nty m tꜣ ꜥḥꜥt* […]

what is for her daughter as a share: the pyramid that is in the tomb [of PN?];

(6) *nty (n) Pntꜣwrt sꜣ Nḫtmini pꜣ mr nty r-gs tꜣ štꜣyt* 2 *ḥnꜥ* […] (7) *n Pnbwy*

what is (for) *Pntꜣwrt*, son of *Nḫtmini*: the pyramid that is beside the 2 caves/cellars and [the…] of *Pnbwy*;

n[ty] (n) Nbnḫtw sꜣ Nḫtmini tꜣ štꜣyt nty r-gs tꜣ ꜥḥ[ꜥ]t (8) *ḥnꜥ pꜣy.st rwr nt[y im.st?]*

what is (for) *Nbnḫtw*, son of *Nḫtmini*: the cave/cellar that is beside the to[m]b and its door/forecourt tha[t is in it?].

* Neo-Egyptian characteristics:

- *swt{t}n* PN [*nty i*]*w.w pš.w*: adnominal relative expansion with future (preposition omission) and Neo-Egyptian delocutive plural actor.
  In Middle Egyptian[747], *iw* is avoided after *nty*, but this construction is common in Neo-Egyptian[748]. As for the form following *nty*, Muszynski[749] did not exclude the reconstruction [*nty tw.*]*tw (ḥr) pš.w* but prefered the future since the scribe 'se met dans la peau' of the protagonists and relates what they intend to do (future), then reports what has been done in past tense. In fact, as the following # *nty (n)* PN # are used in *allotments* formulae before actual execution (see *oLouvre* E 13156, *oDeM* 586), and the oath may indicate the end of a litigation on it, we may assume that the partition has not yet been executed;
- *nty (n* N) PN: see *supra*. The preposition is omitted three times out of four;
- cataphoric articloid (*tꜣ st n pꜣy.st it; tꜣ ꜥt{t} nty r-gs pr; pꜣ mr nty m tꜣ ꜥḥꜥt; tꜣ štꜣyt nty r-gs tꜣ ꜥḥ[ꜥ]t*);
- Neo-Egyptian possessive determinator for kinship (*pꜣy.st it; tꜣy.st šriw*) and location (*pꜣy.st rwr*);
- Neo-Egyptian delocutive suffixes *st* (feminine) and *w* (plural);
- Neo-Egyptian preposition *irm*;

* 'Classical' degree 0 forms used:

- *r rdit rḫ.tw swt{t} n Nḫtmini*: see *supra*;
- use of the relator *n* in ownership (*swt n* PN; *tꜣ st n pꜣy.st it*), unclear kind of relation in frozen expression (*ꜥnḫ-n-niwt*), location relations (*pr Iꜥḥ[ms] Nfrtri n Mnst*);
- *iw.st wnm*: converted adverbial nexus with stative rheme following the determined *tꜣ st n pꜣy.st it*. It was regarded by Muszynski (1977: 194 n.28) as a 'virtual relative clause' but the preceding noun is determined excluding the adnominal function of the adverbial nexus;

* General dialectal features: degree 2.

* Formulae: - notification: *r rdit rḫ.tw swt n* PN [*nty i*]*w.w pš.w* (future partition)
- list: *nty (n)* N PN (beneficiary) + object + quantifier
- repayment of estate's debt: *nty (n)* N PN (recipient) + [*r-ḏ*]*bꜣw* + object

745 For Janssen (1974: 26), *Mrwt* was *Nḫtmini*'s second 'wife' (see *oGardiner/Ashmolean*157). See the discussion of *Mrwt* and her daughter's presence in the list in Muszynski (1977: 193-7).

746 Temple West of Gurna (Muszynski 1977: 189 (r)).

747 *EG* § 107,2; 328 Obs. and 468,4.

748 See references in David (2006: 57).

749 1977: 188 (l).

2. Addition

***Promissory* oath of the heirs (warranty with penalty)**
ỉryw.w ꜥnḫ n nb ꜥ.w.s. m-ḏd ỉw ỉw.n pn[*ꜥꜥ*?] (9) *ỉw.w r-ẖry* 100 *n sẖ* [*šꜣ*]*ti šww m pš.w*
They took an oath of (the) Lord L.P.H. saying: 'Should we reve[rse] (our undertaking)', they are liable to 100 blows of (the) [r]od (and) deprived of their share.

* Neo-Egyptian characteristics:
- *ỉrwy.w*: perfect delocutive report expressing legal formality, the normal introduction to the oath formula;
- Neo-Egyptian delocutive suffix *w* (plural);
- *ỉw ỉw.n pnꜥ… ỉw.w r-ẖry* 100 *n sẖ*: instead of the usual conjunctive *mtw.n pnꜥ* (see *supra*), probably a scribal error[750] for *mtw.n*. Note the preposition *r-ẖry* of the performative penalty apodosis (in all the preceding oaths, only *ẖry* was used);

* 'Classical' degree 0 forms used:
- *m-ḏd*: tagged speech marker introducing the quotation of the *promissory* oath;
- use of the relator *n* in address relation (*ꜥnḫ n nb*) and between quantifier and noun (100 *n sẖ*);

* General dialectal features: degree 2.

* Formula: *promissory* oath: *ỉrwy.f ꜥnḫ nb ꜥ.w.s.* (report) + *m-ḏd* (tag clause) + *ỉw ỉw.n pn*[*ꜥꜥ*?] (perjury) + *ỉw.w r-ẖry* 100 *n sẖ* [*šꜣ*]*ti šww m pš.w* (penalty)

3. Colophon or beginning of another entry?

Date: (10) *rnpt-sp* 7 *ꜣbd* 3 *ꜣḫt sw* 9 […] Year 7, month 3 of the inundation, day 9 […]
Recording: [*ỉrw ỉn*?][751] *sš Ḥri n pꜣ ẖr ḥnꜥ Mr*[…] (11) *wnw wꜥ mꜣỉw*[…]
[Done by?] the scribe *Ḥri* of the Tomb with *Mr*[…] ??[…].

* Neo-Egyptian characteristics:
- exophoric articloid for specific administrative unit of the Theban area (*pꜣ ẖr*);

* 'Classical' degree 0 forms used:
- relator *n* in administrative department dependence relation (*sš* PN *n pꜣ ẖr*);

* General dialectal features: degree 1.

* Formula: date + redactor identification: [*ỉrw ỉn*] *sš* + PN + department

Categorization of terms of special relevance in the legal register:

- *r rdỉt rḫ.tw*: to let be known, for information (relative to).
- *st*: 'place', immovable property.
- *pš*: to divide, a share.
- [*r-ḏ*]*bꜣw*: in exchange for, compensation, payment.
- *wnm*: to eat, consume.

750 *LEG* § 37.1 suggests a future form, the construction being 'explained as the omission of the opening sentence of an oath', but we have seen that it is not the normal construction in such cases.

751 On the model of the colophon of the will of *Naunakhte*, *pAshmolean Museum* 1945.97 (V.8).

For Janssen (1974) and Toivari-Viitala (2001: 80-1), the expression *wnw irm* 'to eat together with' 'might thus have been employed as a designation for a conjugal union.' Janssen adds that the missing word might be *ḥmꜣy* 'salt', and that the expression 'to eat salt with someone' might indicate a legally established union; but as there is no other example of such an expression, the matter remains unresolved[752]. However, since the end of the Old Kingdom (*pBerlin* P 9010; *Dakhla royal decree* of Pepy II), the verb *wnm* already has the metaphoric value of 'consuming revenues'[753] (*ususfruct*). The use of alimentary metaphors is well known in the ancient Egyptian legal conceptual system (see David 2006: 24-5) as well as in modern legal systems, and is based on the conceptual metaphor '*IDEAS ARE FOOD*'[754].

The lexeme *wnm* 'to eat' is classified since the Old Kingdom in the [MOUTH LINKED ACTIVITIES] category by the classifier (or in the *PT* by and/or classifiers, the last representing protoypical food – bread – for the [FOOD] category).

- *iri ʿnḫ n nb*: to take an oath of (the) Lord.
- *pnʿ*[ ]: to reverse (an undertaking).
- *r-ḫry* *sḫ*: liable to blows.
- *šwy* × *m pš* ×: deprived of a share.

752 See the objections of Allam (1974) and of Muszynski (1977: 194-5 n.28).

753 See also *pBerlin* P 3047 lines 15-16 and 32; Helck (1963: 68, 70); Middle Kingdom *Ḥʿpydfꜣ*'s contracts.

754 Lakoff & Johnson (1980: 46-7).

8. *pTurin* 1885 v°

Date: 20th dynasty, Ramesses VI-VII
Hieroglyphic version: *KRI* VI, 371 n.A15 (col. 2) and 424 n.20 A1 (col. 3); corrections of Von Beckerath (2000: 1 n. 5)
Instrument:
* **state –** fragmentary papyrus
* **value – original/copy**[755]**?**: material used, brief date with archaic anaphora, named parties and executors, apparently including the essential elements for that type of document
* **nature – record concerning private assets** (absence of internal characterization)
* **genre – entry of an administrative journal**: although it concerns private interests (essentially the transfer of garments, honey, and *sft*), it is included in a journal of the necropolis; by a business hand, script similar to the hand of *pTurin* 2070[756], few errors, absence of correction, use of accounting abbreviations, no other business practice diacritical marks; ordered layout, formulaic style, degree 1 Neo-Egyptian, delocutive texteme; briefly dated with archaic anaphora, parties and executors named, no mention of specific forums or institutions, absence of *recital* and colophon, one item being valuated as it is given in repayment of a debt of the estate; from Deir el-Medina tombs 1336, 1337 and 1340 along with other papyrus fragments[757].

Step in the process: after-the-fact record of the execution of a partition (*pš*) and transmission (*rdyt*) of movable assets
Legal issue: succession: no indication of a will but partage by two executors in favor of the children of a man obviously not present, with repayment of a debt of the estate, concerns mainly each heir's share of garments (and their quality), of honey or *sft*, and not the entire patrimony.
Close to *pDeM* 30, although our papyrus concerns movable assets.
Textemic features:

1. Pre-material

Date: (II.2) *rnpt-sp* 7 *ꜣbd* 2 *šmw sw* 4[758]	Year 7, 2nd month of summer, day 4.
archaic anaphora: *hrw pn*	This day
Title:	
object of the procedure: *pš ꜣḫt n sš Ỉmnnḫt*	of (the) division of assets of (the) scribe *Ỉmnnḫt*
beneficiaries: (3) *n nꜣy.f ẖr{t}dw*	for his children
executors: *in sš Ḥri n pꜣ ḫr ḥnꜥ ꜥnḫ-n-niw{w}t Tꜣwrtmḥb*	
by (the) scribe of the Necropolis *Ḥri* and (the) *ꜥnḫ-n-niwt Tꜣwrtmḥb*	

* Neo-Egyptian characteristics:
  - Neo-Egyptian possessive determinator for kinship (*nꜣy.f ẖr{t}dw*);
  - exophoric articloid for specific administrative unit of the Theban area (*pꜣ ḫr*);

755 For Von Beckerath (2000: 2), an 'Entwurf' but the distinction between an official partition document – supposing that there was such document – and an administrative notice in the community's journal is blurred.
756 Muszynski (1977: 192 n.23).
757 Bruyère (1937: 79-80).
758 Wente & Van Siclen (1976: 240).

* 'Classical' degree 0 forms used:
- archaic anaphora *hrw pn*;
- use of the relator *n* in ownership (*ꜣḫt n sš Ỉmnnḫt*), administrative department dependence relation (*sš* PN *n pꜣ ḫr*) and unclear kind of relation in frozen expression (*ꜥnḫ-n-niwt*);
- use of the coordinator *ḥnꜥ* between two N PN;

* General dialectal features: degree 1.

* Formula: date + *hrw pn* + *pš ꜣḫt* (object) + *n* NPN (*de cuius*) + *n* (beneficiaries) + *in* (executors)

2. Content

Partition list:

(4) *rdyt n ꜥnḫ-n-niw{w}t Tꜣwrtmḥb m pš m nꜣy.f ḥbsw*

What was given to (the) *ꜥnḫ-n-niwt Tꜣwrtmḥb* as a share from his garments:

(5) *šmꜥt thꜣ dꜣiw* 1	fine used *dꜣiw*-garment: 1
(6) *šmꜥt thꜣ rwḏw* 5	fine used *rwḏw*-garment: 5
(7) *šmꜥt ḏꜣy* 1	fine *ḏꜥy*-garment: 1
(8) *šmꜥt rwḏw* 2	fine *rwḏw*-garment: 2
dmḏ ḥbsw šbnw 2?	Total of various garments: 2?
(9) *ḫt tꜣy ꜣtpw* 1	wooden heavy chest: 1
(10) *tmꜣw* 3	mats: 3
rdyt [*m tꜣy.f bit*?]	What was given [from his honey?]:
(11) [*sš*] *Ḥr n* [*pꜣ ḫr*[759] *bit hnw…*]	[scribe] *Ḥr* of [the Tomb: …honey jar]
(12) *Tꜣwrtmḥb bit* (*hnw*) 2	*Tꜣwrtmḥb:* 2 honey (jars)
(13) [N PN] *n pꜣ ḫr bit hnw* 1	[N PN] of the Tomb: 1 honey jar
Tꜣ[*imn*]*nḫtw hnw* 1	*Tꜣ*[*imn*]*nḫtw:* 1 jar
Pꜣidnw hnw 1	*Pꜣidnw*: 1 jar
Tꜣ […]	*Tꜣ* [: …jar]
Tꜣgr<m>pt (*hnw*) 1	*Tꜣgr<m>pt*: 1 (jar)
Pntꜣwrt hnw 1	*Pntꜣwrt*: 1 jar
(14) *rdyt* [*n* PN] *sft hnw* 4	What was given [to PN:] 4 jars of *sft*
Ḥnr hnw ¼	*Ḥnr*: ¼ jar
Pꜣidnw h[*nw…*]	*Pꜣidnw*: […] j[ar]
[PN] *hnw* […]	[PN]: […] jar

(added at top) *rdyt n Tꜣ r-ḏbꜣw tꜣy.f gꜣw*[*t*] *isy* 1 *ir n dbn* 10 (**repayment of estate's debt**)

What was given to *Tꜣ* in payment of his chest: 1 tamarisk wood[760], worth 10 *dbn*.

(III.1) *rdy*[*t n* ꜥ]*nḫ-n-niw{w}t Ḥnr* […]:	What was give[n to the ꜥ]*nḫ-n-niw{w}t Ḥnr*: […]
(2) *rdy*[*t*] *n.s m ḥb<s>w* [blank]	What was give[n] to her from (the) garments: [blank]

* Neo-Egyptian characteristics:
- Neo-Egyptian possessive determinator for ownership (*nꜣy.f ḥbsw, tꜣy.f gꜣw*[*t*]);
- exophoric articloid for specific administrative unit of the Theban area (*pꜣ ḫr*);

* 'Classical' degree 0 forms used:

759 *KRI* VI, 371 n. 9 [a-a] and Leiden Deir el-Medina database, following Černý MSS.3.714.

760 Janssen (1975: 200).

- list: # *rdyt* (perfect passive participle) *n* N PN (recipient) + object + quantifier #;
- *rdyt n* PN *r-ḏb3w* + movable: variation of the 1st category of transactions ('barter') in Janssen's typology (1975: 496) mentioning only one of the parties. Here it is again apparently a repayment of a debt of the estate;
- use of the relator *n* in administrative department dependence relation (*sš* PN *n p3 ẖr*), value (*ỉr n dbn* 10), and unclear kind of relation in frozen expression (*ʿnḫ-n-nỉwt*);
- *bit hnw* 1, *sft hnw* 4: # generic noun + *Badal* apposition (non-specific noun + quantifier)#;
- *ỉr n dbn* 10: see *supra*.

* General dialectal features: degree 1.

* Formulae: - partition list: *rdyt n* N PN (recipient) + object + quantifier
  - repayment of estate's debt: *rdyt n* PN (recipient) + *r-ḏb3w* + movable

Categorization of terms of special relevance in the legal register:

- *pš* [hieroglyphs]: division, share.
- *3ẖt* [hieroglyphs]: assets.
- *rdyt* [hieroglyphs]: what was given.
- *r-ḏb3w* [hieroglyphs]: in exchange, compensation, payment.

9. Table of syntactic forms and particularities in partitions

The following table is a summary of the forms found in the remaining fragments of the partition documents analyzed *supra*. The number of occurrences is purely an indication in view of what has survived of the texts.

Abbreviations:

A = active
Ad = *adscriptus*/addition
Col = colophon
Neg = negative
O = operative part
P = pre-material
Pa = passive
Prep = preposition
R = Ramesses
x = more than 10 instances

Form (degree)	***oGardiner* 89 19 th d. R. II**	***oLouvre* E 13156 19 th d. R. II**	***oDeM* 112/964 20th d. R. III-IV**	***oBerlin* P 12636 20th d. R. III**	***oDeM* 586 20th d. R. III-IV**	***pDeM* 30 20th d. R. III-IV**	***pDeM* 23/25 20th d. R. V**	***pBoulaq* 10 20th d. R. VI**	***pTurin* 2070 20th d. R. VI-IX**	***pTurin* 1885 v° 20th d. R. VII**
iryw.f (indep. perfect report, A) (2)									1 (O)	
sḏm.f (indep. perfect report, Pa) (2)								1 (Ad)		
iw.f ḥr sḏm (sequential narrative past) (2)		2 (Ad)		1 (Ad)						
nty iw.f sḏm (relative clause with future, prep. omitted) (2)									1 (O)	
r rdit rḫ.tw (0) (impersonal notification)				1 (O)			2 (O)		1 (O)	
rdyt (perfect participle, Pa, used as N) (0) *rdy* (1)			2 (O)			1 (O)	x (O) 9 (O)			6 (O)
ir (perfect participle, Pa) (0) *diwyw* (1)								1 (Ad)		1 (O)

Form (degree)	***oGardiner* 89 19th d. R. II**	***oLouvre* E 13156 19th d. R. II**	***oDeM* 112/964 20th d. R. III-IV**	***oBerlin* P 12636 20th d. R. III**	***oDeM* 586 20th d. R. III-IV**	***pDeM* 30 20th d. R. III-IV**	***pDeM* 23/25 20th d. R. V**	***pBoulaq* 10 20th d. R. VI**	***pTurin* 2070 20th d. R. VI-IX**	***pTurin* 1885 v° 20th d. R. VII**
rdit.n.f (perfect relative,masc) (1) *i.diw*.N (2)			2 (O)	1 (O)						
iṯt.f (perfect relative neutrum) (0)	5 (O)									
sḏm (stative) (0)									1 (O)	
ir iw.f ḥr sḏm… iw.f ḥr sḏm (condition, present protasis & apodosis; neutral attitude towards reality) (2)				1 (Ad)						
(*w3ḥ* PN…) *mtw.i pnᶜ* (*r mdt*)… *iw.f* (*r-*)*ḫry* 100 *n sḫ*(*t*) (omitted indep. modal prospective, conjunctive in crime protasis, performative in penalty apodosis of *promissory* oath) (2) *iw iw.i pnᶜ*… (protasis) (2)								1 (Ad)	1 (O)	
bn sw + converb (ind. pres., neg)(2)		1 (Ad)								
nfr sw (adjectival nexus) (0)	2 (O)									
(*ir*) determined N + *ny-sw* + PN (topicalized possession nexus) (1)					7 (O)					
nty + prep. (used as N) (1) no prep. (1)	1 (O)	2 (O)			1 (O)				1 (O) 3 (O)	
ḥrw pn (archaic anaphora) (0)										1 (P)

Form (degree)	***oGardiner* 89 19 th d. R. II**	***oLouvre* E 13156 19 th d. R. II**	***oDeM* 112/964 20th d. R. III-IV**	***oBerlin* P 12636 20th d. R. III**	***oDeM* 586 20th d. R. III-IV**	***pDeM* 30 20th d. R. III-IV**	***pDeM* 23/25 20th d. R. V**	***pBoulaq* 10 20th d. R. VI**	***pTurin* 2070 20th d. R. VI-IX**	***pTurin* 1885 v° 20th d. R. VII**
pꜣ, tꜣ, nꜣ (deictic articloid) (1)				1 (Ad)						
pꜣ, tꜣ, nꜣ (cataphoric articloid) (1)	4 (P,O)	2 (P,Ad)	9 (O)		7 (O)	1 (P)	2 (O)	9 (Ad)		
pꜣ, tꜣ, nꜣ (anaphoric articloid) (1)		1 (O)						1 (Ad)		
pꜣ, tꜣ, nꜣ (exophoric articloid) (1)		1 (O)	2 (O)					1 (Ad)	1 (Col?)	3 (P,O)
.w (delocutive plural suffix) (1)		3 (O)						2 (Ad)	5 (O)	
.st (delocutive feminine suffix) (1)		1 (O)						1 (Ad)	4 (O)	
pꜣy.f (possessive) (1)		2 (O,Ad)		2 (O,Ad)			2 (O)	4 (Ad)	4 (O)	3 (P,O)
pꜣ N*.f* PN (hyperdetermination) (1)		1 (Ad)								
n (relator) (0)	5 (P,O)	7 (P,O)	x (O)		2 (O)	2 (P)	5 (O)	9 (Ad)	6 (O,Col?)	7 (P,O)
(N) PN *ḥnꜥ* N PN (0) (coordinator) *pꜣ* N *ḥnꜥ pꜣ(y.f)* N (1)						1 (P)		1 (Ad) 3 (Ad)	1 (O)	1 (P)
wḥm(w) ky (n) pšt (section divider & coordinator) (0)							5 (O)			
m-ḏd (tagged speech marker) (0)								1? (Ad)	1 (O)	
m-di.f (compound prep.) (1)		1 (Ad)								
ỉrm PN (prep.) (1)									1 (O)	
prep. redundancy (1)	1 (O)									
prep. omission (1)						1 (O)	22 (O)		4 (O)	
n/m prep. confusion (1)		1 (Ad)								

Part Two: Contract-related records

Once again, Deir el-Medina constitutes by far the most abundant source of contract-related records: the village and its surroundings are an exceptionally well-preserved archaeological site with habitational, administrative[761], religious, and funerary components, as well as an especially rich location in terms of written material. This highly specific community is not a typical sample of the Ramesside Egypt population since it is a relatively highly literate group. Thus if no real written contract is to be found in Deir el-Medina, we may conclude that it reflects the situation in Ramesside Egypt[762].

The first issue to consider is again the one related to the *genre of the documents*: are we witness to instruments belonging to the *consentient legal genre* and expressing a *mutual assent* of the parties[763] to contract? Are there elements in written contracts[764] essential to classifying them as such? Are they autonomous and authoritative contracts? And if these contract-related records are not contracts, are there linguistic-pragmatic elements to indicate their nature?

The issue is related to the general one of *orality* of legal matters in New Kingdom Egypt, as we have seen *supra*. We know that Ramesside contracts were mostly verbal[765], either *consensual* or *real*[766]. A good example of a verbal transaction in the context of a cash purchase from a peddler is given by 19th dynasty *pCairo* JE 65739 (lines 4-6 and 13-14), a lawsuit protocol of the period of Ramesses II[767]:

---

761 Although no administrative compound has yet been precisely located; see the last discussion of the *ḫtm n pꜣ ḫr* issue by Burkard (2006), its functions, and the adoption by the author of the thesis proposed by Ventura (1986: 106).

762 The only comparable archaeological site in terms of a documentary source for pre-Demotic Egypt is Middle Kingdom Kahun with its large repertoire of 'private sphere' written material.

763 *Bilateral* contracts.

764 The term contract is used here in a broad sense that includes sales and conveyances.

765 Menu (1998: 293) notes that written contracts are more frequent during the New Kingdom than earlier, but they are still of the 'contrat dialogué' type or in the form of a 'procès-verbal constatant les prestations réciproques'. The essential loan clauses during the New Kingdom are slowly recorded in order to give the contract a more official character, constraint, and as evidence, although the verbal contract is still used (1982: 232, 240-1, 248); she contends the same is applicable to sale contracts (1988: 166).
Pestman (1985: 198-200; 1994: 21) remarks that even during the Late Period, the phase of the agreement leading to a Demotic contract was mainly oral, and that when a written act followed, it did not usually refer to the agreement phase and had value only as evidence. Depauw (1997: 144) concludes that there are so few Demotic exchange documents probably because these agreements were 'usually settled orally' (or by means of mutual sales or cession documents for instance). See also the abnormal hieratic *stela Cairo* 27.6.24.3 (22nd dynasty?) for verbal transactions and Manning (2003: 824, n.26 and 843).
Concerning the evidence of private commercial activity in ancient Egypt, see Warburton (2007).

766 Théodoridès (1979 : 83) concluded at the end of a lengthy study that the Egyptian documents show in each case of a sale transaction a 'commencement d'exécution, tout à fait comme si, pour que la vente prît corps, il fallût indispensablement au moins le payement du prix ou la tradition de la chose, indépendamment des formalités d'authentification,' sufficiently proving for him the non *consensual* character of the transaction. *Contra*: Menu (1988: 166) who believes that already during the Old Kingdom 'on peut admettre que la vente consensuelle était née'; she wrote (1985: 252) concerning the *Giza boundary stone Cairo JE* 42787 of the 5th dynasty (?) that the buyer 'devient propriétaire dès la rédaction de l'acte', although in fact he became the owner as soon as he paid the price.

767 The document is viewed differently by Mrsich (1995: 298-9) as the written protocol by the administration controlling the market of the slave's acquisition by co-buyers, thus an *authentic* record and not a lawsuit as usually contended.

[*iw.f ḥr*] *ḏd n.i in n.t tꜣy ꜥḏt šrt* (or *ꜥḏ{t}t*) *mtw.t dit n.i swnwt.st i.n.f n.i iw.i ḥr šsp tꜣ ꜥḏw šrt* (or *ꜥḏwt*) *iw.i ḥr dit n.f* [*swn*]*wt.st* (…) *iw.i ḥr ditw.w n šwty Rꜥiꜣ* (…) *iw.f dit n.i tꜣy ꜥḏw šrt* (or *ꜥḏwt*) [He (the merchant) sa]id to me: 'buy yourself this maid and you will give me her price', so he said to me; and I received/accepted the maid, and I gave him her [pr]ice.(…) And I gave them (the items constituting the payment) to (the) merchant *Rꜥiꜣ* (...), and he gave me this maid.

The essential elements of the sale[768] are: '(1) parties competent to contract, (2) *mutual assent*[769], (3) a thing capable of being transferred, and (4) a price (…) paid or promised'[770]. Transposed to our Egyptian sale (or money-barter[771]), all of these elements are present[772] in the verbal agreement[773].

There is no mention here of any solemnity or significant gesture during the verbal exchange constituting the contract[774]. Nevertheless, some authors have postulated that symbolic acts were performed in the context of transactions on the basis of limited evidence[775]; but what may be true for other legal acts[776] is insufficiently proved in the case of transactions.

---

768 These are elements 'du contrat sans lesquels celui-ci ne peut valablement exister, éléments consitutifs nécessaires à sa formation (consentement, capacité, etc.; (…)) ainsi que de ceux, spécifiques, qui déterminent le type d'un contrat et sans lesquels l'accord ne peut avoir le caractère qu'on veut lui attribuer. Ex. Le loyer dans le bail (*essentialia negotii*).' (Cornu 2003: 359). Thus e.g. in the Belgian legal system, the essential elements of a sale contract are the property transfer and the price, with 'consentement, capacité, objet' its validity conditions.

769 The buyer in this case actually is not quoted as verbally accepting the deal; it is more a case of a preliminary contact of the seller followed by a tacit acceptance with exchange of the girl and her price.

770 Garner (2004: 1364).

771 For this notion, see Janssen (1975: 495).

772 The papyrus adds the quality of the buyer and her potential sources of income: '[I am the wife of the superintendent of the district Simūt], and I came to dwell in his house, and I worked and […] and provided my dress.' (Gardiner 1935: 141).

773 Note that in the modern Anglo-American legal system, 'rules of law utilizing the concept 'contract' rarely refer to the writing itself. Usually, the reference is to the agreement; the writing being merely a memorial of the agreement.' (Garner 2004: 341, quoting Calamari & Perillo 1998: § 1.1, at 3).

774 Compare with the situation during the first part of the Old Babylonian Period when oral transactions required *verba solemnia*, symbolic acts and the presence of witnesses, although towards the end of the period there is a marked decrease in ritual practice (Goddeeris 2002: 17-8).

775 For instance, Shupak (1992: 6-8, 18 n. 69) on the basis of the *Eloquent Peasant* and the exchange of *oDeM* 73 r° (an unsatisfactory donkey had been delivered to a man, later exchanged and the seller *ꜥnḫ ḥr pḥw.st* 'swore on its back'). She referred to Allam (1973: 89, n. 4) who stated that 'der Schwörende bei der Eidesleistung tatsächlich nahe dem Tier zu stehen hatte, zum Zeichen der Übertragung des Eigentums am Tier.' But the oath 'on the back of the donkey' followed the exchange, probably in order to close a dispute, and was not part of the original deal. Furthermore, the 'gesture' may not be one, as Janssen noted (2005: 36) that the expression reminds the clause *bn ꜥḥꜥ ḥr pḥwy.f* 'nobody shall stand on its back' involved in warranties against claims (see also McDowell 1990: 37). Note the interesting point made by Vleeming (1991: 133) concerning donkey marks branded on the hind quarters and early Demotic cattle contracts, the meaning of the clause being perhaps that the owner's mark is the sole mark that should appear on the donkey's hind quarters.
Haring (2006: 110) also contends that important transactions 'would have been effected with appropriate oral expressions, significant gestures, and witnesses present', but does not give examples of such gestures.

776 In the Old Kingdom tomb of *Wpmnfrt*, all 15 witnesses to the unilateral declaration by the tomb's owner *wḏt-mdw* are sitting on the floor with the right hand to the heart and the left resting on the thigh; Menu (2004: 247) suggests that it may be the gesture of an oath. Dominicus (1994: 94-5) notes gestures associated with oaths such as raising the arm, or putting a hand to the mouth, both apparently since the 18th dynasty.

Nowhere is a highly formal, multisensory legal procedure such as the Roman *mancipatio* to be found in the texts; there is no example of object transmission as a symbol of conveyance nor 'memory of a title to property' as in medieval law[777] that can serve our discussion; no semiotic act[778] can be ascribed with certainty to a private transaction[779].

Nor is the presence of witnesses to the agreement mentioned in *pCairo* JE 65739; the court summons witnesses who should confirm the source of the items given in exchange for the maid but not the agreement itself. Haring (2003b: 260) mentions witnesses and oaths in Deir el-Medina records of transactions as evidence of basic oral practice in the village, and although they are evidently signs of orality, we will see that witnesses do not usually appear in these records unless an oath has been taken and a dispute has arisen.

No Ramesside *authentic* contracts (recorded before a court acting as a notary, thus formalized) have been found, and the few mentions of the *ḳnbt* in the records related to private transactions should probably be explained as a litigation procedure with an oath taken (e.g. *oMichaelides* 1 and *oTurin* 57389). Agreements were reached mostly between members of a small community; people knew each other well and transactions were based on mutual trust; the logic behind the notarial will relates to the fact that the will is to be enforced after the death of its author, thus beyond his control, involving often entire patrimonies and always an 'abnormal' *devolution* threatening the legal heirs, issues absent in the case of a relatively simple contract. Nevertheless, Seidl (1957: 27-8) believed that *oCairo* CG 25553 and *oDeM* 225[780] were probably drafts of a court protocol giving full authority to the obligations of the parties in the course of a 'Scheinprozeβ'[781]; McDowell (1990: 155) believes the court acted as a notary for transactions in *oBrussels* E 6311[782], *oGardiner/Ashmolean* 36[783], and *oPrague* H 12[784]. Allam (1973b: 43-4) deals with 'Freiwillige Gerichtsbarkeit' in cases in which the court (or a commission) has a preventive role, such as *oBrussels* E 6311, *oGardiner/Ashmolean* 36, *oBodleian Library* 253[785], *oCairo* CG 25555 r°[786], *oFlorence* 2620[787], as well as in cases of

Of course the god's oracular expression must have had a motional component. And the ownership metaphor 'under the feet' may also denote some symbolic practice attached to legal acts (Théodoridès 1972; David 2006: 128-9 and 2007: 7).

Note also the overall communicative importance of gestures as reflected in the hieroglyphic system.

777 See Clanchy (1993: 38).

778 See Mattila (2006: 33) concerning the symbolic rituals involved in legal operations, some belonging to the past and reinforcing a speech act (performative utterance), others characteristic of our times and replacing speech acts altogether, such as a silent handshake, or the handing of a credit card with the purchases to the assistant and the collection of a receipt without even exchanging a word.

779 Théodoridès (1966: 47) notes that when the *ḳnbt* acts as a notary to authenticate instruments, there is no sign of strict formalism, of a ritual with prescribed gestures and solemn utterances.

780 *oCairo* CG 25553 refers to a dispute in court (one party is found 'guilty', has to swear an oath, and an *ꜣṯw*-officer is committed to pursue the collection of the debt), as does probably *oDeM* 225 (with locutive *recital*; the same affair may be recorded in *pDeM* 26 A r° 1-8, see McDowell 1990: 122).

781 We have already dealt *supra* with the issue of 'pseudo-process'; a court has, of course, both litigation and notarial functions and may use examination procedures in both of them.

782 She notes on p. 13 that the report in court was made 'evidently to have it [a transaction] notarized and not to raise a dispute'. But see the use of *smi*, the debt issue, and the locutive *recital*, elements that may indicate litigation in court.

783 She adds on p. 22 that it may concern either a transaction or an inheritance. Note the *wpwtw* in court and the debt/partition issue.

784 Notification of payments to the court; rather damaged, context unclear.

785 Request to foreman and scribe before two witnesses, oath, thus probably in the context of a litigation process posterior to the cohabitation of a couple; it does not constitute a 'prenuptial contract' (Gardiner 1956: 17).

786 Oracle followed by oath and statement by foreman about disputed right.

successions and partitions (*oDeM* 108, *Naunakhte*, *oPetrie* 18, *pBoulaq* 10 v°, *pTurin* 2070, and *oLouvre* E 13156). These documents are not *authentic* contracts, nor even contracts, although some of them may refer to contractual relationships.

The records studied in this chapter do not contain any internal characterization such as 'contract' in their heading, and the legal issue[788] is never qualified (the same situation as with wills and gifts, see *supra*); nor are the parties designated as 'vendor/buyer, lessor/lessee'; but these are not essential criteria for a determination of the contractual nature of the records or their inclusion in the consentient genre. We have seen that for a contract to exist it must comply with *essentialia*, the 'associated criteria' or minimal conditions of a contract, meaning that a valid agreement has been reached by competent parties by *mutual assent*, relating to an object and a number of essential issues, such as the undertakings or commitments associated with each type of contract. Today, the terms of the contract may be reduced to writing, but it is not mandatory for many types of contracts; if this was the case, one would expect the main points of the agreement to be reflected in the instrument: the names of the parties, their assent (even implied), the object of the contract and main modalities (date of the agreement and of the transmission of the object, conditions and time of payment, hire period, warranties). The format may vary intrinsically, since 'a written contract may consist of an exchange of correspondence, of a letter written by the promisee and assented to by the promisor without signature, or even of a *memorandum* or printed document not signed by either party'[789]; but we would expect at least an expository texteme and an operative part. The point is that the obligations created by the agreement should be enforceable, the instrument representing a memorial and evidence of the agreement as well as an operative fact having legal consequences. Returning to Egypt, it would appear that New Kingdom transactions did not have to be written down and that the records left by the Deir el-Medina community are lacking essential contractual elements to represent contracts, or even evidentiary instruments in many cases. Take for instance the minimalistic *oDeM* 64:

Date + *dit p3 ꜥ3t r b3kw.f n* PN *m rnpt* 29 (Date), giving the donkey for his service/rent[790] to PN in year 29.

787 The oath of *oFlorence* 2620 may be taken in order to conclude a litigation (see *infra*): date + *m hrw pn sw3ḏ p3 wḏ3 n rmṯ ist* PN *n rmṯ ist* PN *m-b3ḥ sš* PN *idnw* PN *idnw* PN *3ṯw* PN *m-b3ḥ s3w* PN *iw.f ir ꜥnḫ n nb{k} r-ḏd w3ḥ Ỉmn w3ḥ p3 ḥk3 ꜥ.w.s. mtw rmṯ mdt ḥr p3y iwtn iw(.i) ẖry* 100 (*sḫ*) *šw.k m-im.f iw*[*.f*] *ir*[*t m-mitt*] *ꜥḳ sp sn* ' Date + on this day of handing over the storehouse of (the) workman PN to (the) workman PN before (the) scribe PN, (the deputy PN, (the) *3ṯw*-officer PN, before (the) guardian PN; and he took an oath of (the) Lord saying: "May Amun be clement, may the Ruler L.P.H. be clement, should people contest this plot, (I) am liable to 100 (blows and) deprived of it". And [he] di[d] (the) like very exactly.'

788 The issue is puzzling as we have already noted *supra*, because of the terminology used. Bleiberg (1996: 23) remarks that 'the Egyptians of the Ramesside Period most commonly used the verbs *ini*, "to bring, to acquire," or *rdi*, "to give," followed by *ḥr, r isw*, or *r ḏb3*, all of which could be understood as "in exchange for." The psychological difference between buying and selling is not recognized if the actions of both parties in a transaction are described with the same verb.' (for a discussion of the main verbs used to express the transfer of donkeys – *rdi, ini, iṯ3, nḥm, swḏ*–, see Janssen 2005: 74-7).
Depauw (1997: 144) notes that Demotic documents using the formula *dy.y n.k* or *mtw.k* may also be variously interpreted depending on the relationship of the parties (kinship) or the mention of a share (*dnit*), as gifts, payments of services, or inheritance, indicating the same fundamental ambiguity as in our corpus.

789 *Restatement (Second) of Contracts* § 95 cmt. c (1979) as quoted in Garner (2004: 350).

790 Hire for Neveu (1986), Janssen (1993 and 2005: 81-2), and Janssen, Frood & Goecke-Bauer (2003: 26). Janssen believes that each time *r b3kw.f* is used, a *consideration* is expected, even though not always explicitly valued; this is not absolutely certain.

One of the parties is not named, the price is omitted (but the contract may also be a gratuitous contract for permissive use[791], in which case no *consideration* is expected), the loan period is missing; the cursory record is more a brief descriptive note with unique elusive texteme than an enforceable and thus complete legal document defining rights and duties agreed upon by the parties. The purpose of briefly jotting down the note is not to ascertain the agreement of the parties or to determine the nature of their obligations in case of dispute; it could not have an evidentiary function in a legal context[792].

Malinine regarded[793] *oDeM* 56 as a 'partie de l'acte authentique de vente proprement dite'. The text runs as follows:

> date + *ʿnḫ nb ʿ.w.s. ḏd.n iry-ʿꜣ* PN *wꜣḥ Ỉmn wꜣḥ pꜣ ḥḳꜣ ʿ.w.s.* 50 *n dbn n ḥmt pꜣy* *bn mdw.i im.f m dwꜣ sꜣ dwꜣ* (Vs.) *m-bꜣḥ rmṯ ist* PN
>
> (Date), oath of (the) Lord L.P.H. that said (the) doorkeeper PN: 'May Amun be clement, may the Ruler L.P.H. be clement, 50 *dbn* of copper is (the value/price of)[794] this [bovine], and I shall not contest it in (the) future.' Before (the) workman PN.

Even here, we only have a dated unilateral oath relating to the valuation of a head of cattle and a *waiver of suit*, not a written agreement between two named parties[795]; the oath may well conclude a litigation process (see *infra*). It does not directly address the transaction.

Concerning the issue of *mutual assent*, we have noted that in the verbal agreement of *pCairo* JE 65739 it is tacitly expressed by the exchange of objects[796] and the record does not contain a formula such as 'we agreed to the transaction'[797]. In fact, the agreement of the parties is never expressly noted in our documents[798]. Concerning sources anterior to the Ramesside Period, the Old Kingdom oath of the vendors in *Giza boundary stone Cairo JE* 42787 (5th dynasty?) and *pCairo* JE 66844-1/6 (5th-6th dynasty) is a promise concerning the future satisfaction (*ḥtp*)[799] of the buyer, and thus a guarantee, not the expression of mutual agreement

791 *Commodatum*, see Garner (2004: 290-1).

792 Although it could be part of an administrative record of the transfer of an animal belonging to the administration; in this case, the note could theoretically be used for consultation as an official record (more probably if the note was transferred into a register).

793 (1947: 111). He also believed that *oDeM* 57 was 'le fragment d'un contrat'.

794 Malinine (1947: 102) suggests translating the line as '(J'ai reçu?) les 50 (4) deben de cuivre (équivalent au prix) de ce boeuf', a *quittance*; but he also proposes (p. 104) the translation 'ce bœuf représente (ou bien – a le prix de) 50 deben' which constitutes a promise not to discuss further the price of the bovine.

795 For Malinine (1947: 106), a sale required two records: a declaration by the buyer stating the transfer of ownership and his payment, and the oath of the vendor concerning the payment in full and a warranty to the buyer. Note that abnormal hieratic and Demotic contractual dispositions (records of an oral agreement) are constructed as unilateral locutive statements (of the debtor/vendor/lessee/lessor): see Malinine (1953), Pestman (1994: 21-2) and Depauw (1997: 140-8).

796 Menu (1971: 161 n.6) notes that 'L'accord sur le prix concrétise le consentement des parties à la vente, ceci jusque dans les contrats démotiques de l'Epoque Ptolémaïque'.

797 See also *oPetrie* 14, the protocol of a dispute concerning a verbal sale contract. It is also the case in *pBerlin* P 9784-5 (18th dynasty): proposal by one of the parties (once with the words *in n.k* as in *pCairo* JE 65739), payment by the other, sometimes with the added mention of quittance by the recipient of the payment, using once a binomial expression: *twy mḥ.k grḥ.k m tꜣ swnw tꜣy[.i ḥ]m* 'I am fully and completely (paid) with the price of m[y serv]ant' (*pBerlin* P 9784, lines 25-6).

798 Note in *pAnastasi* V 13,2-14,6, a letter in which a party is offering settlement in a dispute (?), probably not a sale, the expression *hꜣ[n].nn dy tw[t].n*, perhaps a binomial, translated by Caminos in *LEM*, 242 as 'Let us concur here and be agreeable'.

799 Menu (1985: 251): 'jouissance paisible'.

on the basis of the contract[800]. The satisfaction of the craftsman working to furnish or decorate the tomb is noted in a great number of Old Kingdom autobiographies[801] (these texts do not represent contracts but relate to transactions), but it concerns the pleasure caused (*sḥtp*) by a generous gratification[802], the level of which had not necessarily to be agreed upon at the conclusion of the contract[803]. Similarily, it is not the expression of *mutual assent* but the satisfaction of a cocontractant that is mentioned earlier in 12th dynasty *Ḥꜥpydfꜣ tomb,* lines 276, 282, 289, etc., with a satisfaction clause concluding each *ḫtmt* (sealed document): *ꜥḥꜥ.n.sn hrw ḥr.s* 'And they were/he was satisfied therewith'[804]. Although the texts are presented from the tomb owner's point of view and the bilateral nature of the agreements is downplayed, the satisfaction of the other party is noted, but it is not clear if it concerns the transaction[805] or *Ḥꜥpydfꜣ*'s generous payment. Double *assertory* oaths before an administrative authority announce the satisfaction of the parties with a sale with payment deferred in Middle Kingdom *pKahun* II.1 and with a *datio in solutum* as settlement of a dispute in the 17th dynasty *Stèle juridique de Karnak* JE 52453; the satisfaction is here with the agreements, but the *Stèle,* line 21, specifies that the purpose of the oath is to prevent withdrawal from the agreement, thus a warranty. In the *pBerlin* P 9784 lines 25-6 (18th dynasty), the satisfaction of one of the parties is dependent on the complete payment of the object of the contract[806].

Performative formulae[807] expressing personal commitment are found in our records exclusively in unilateral promises under oath: the penalty included in the warranty clause, as already seen *supra*, takes the performative form 'I am liable to 100 blows, etc.'[808] But nowhere in the Deir el-Medina records is there phraseology of the type 'it is this day mutually agreed between the parties' or 'we hereby agree', the equivalent of the testamentary performative expression 'I hereby bequeath' (Ramesside *tw.i dit m pꜣ hrw*).

---

800 *Contra*: Helck (1986: 1225).

801 Müller-Wollermann (1985: 142-4); Malek (1986: 74); Goedicke (1986); Strudwick (2005: 251-60). See e.g. *Mmi*'s *Leipzig statue* 2560, 5th dynasty: *rdi.n(.i) irt twt pw in ḳsty ḥtp ḥr isw.s irt.n(.i) n.f* 'It is by a sculptor satisfied by its remuneration that I made to him that I let this statue be done.'

802 Edel (1955: 53).

803 But see *Nfrḥrnptḥ*'s *lintel*: *ḫrty-nṯr Ppi ḥtp ḥr ḫtm irt.n(.i) ḥnꜥ.f* 'The necropolis workman *Ppi* was satisfied with the sealed document that (I) made with him'; it records what appears to be general satisfaction with the deal. But Müller-Wollermann (1985: 145) thinks that the prior consent of the parties to the payment on the basis of a fixed rate may be inferred from the insistence upon the partner's satisfaction. Nevertheless, Helck (1986: 1225) infers from a declaration such as *Ḥtpḥrꜣḫti*'s in his Saqqara tomb (*Urk.* I, 50 line 8: *n sp iry ḫt nb m wsr rmṯ nb*) that 'Ein Vertrag kann also nicht unter Zwang geschlossen warden, sondern setzt freiwillige Zustimmung beider Seiten voraus'; but the tomb owner's statement belongs to the 'doing *mꜣꜥt*' litany and thus only reflects a moral justification, not actual practice. See also Pirenne (1934: 321-2) 'les ouvriers étaient libres et engagés par contrat' but he also stresses their satisfaction concerning their remuneration.

804 Spalinger (1985: 14-5) notes that the 6th sealed document adds an interesting precision that may be interepreted as a formal gathering of the parties with the texts being read aloud: *ꜥḥꜥ.n.f hrw ḥr.s r-gs ḳnbt nt ḥwt-nṯr* 'And he was satisfied therewith besides (the) temple staff'.

805 As Théodoridès (1971) perceives it.

806 For clauses expressing the satisfaction of the vendor concerning the full payment of the price after the New Kingdom, see Malinine (1953: 39) and Menu (1985b: 78) for abnormal hieratic; for Demotic contracts (e.g. *pLouvre* E 7832) see Menu (1985b: 86). See also Menu (1988: 169, 173-4) 'clause de satisfaction' of the seller concerning the payment and Cruz-Uribe (1985: 39-46) 'MTY-clauses'.

807 Concerning performatives in relation to contracts in the Anglo-American legal system, see e.g. Samek (1965).

808 For example in *oDeM* 564: *mtw.i tmt pꜣy* 4 *ḥꜣpwti n rmṯ ist* PN *m ꜣbd* 3 *prt sw* 10 *iw.i ḫry sḫt* 100 *iw.w r.i m ḳb* 'Should I not (give/repay) these 4 balls of yarn (see the *Leiden database*) to (the) workman PN on (the) 3rd month of winter, day 10, I am liable to 100 blows (and) they are against me as double'. For a comparison with the *stipulatio duplae* in Roman Law, see Allam (1967: 16).

Note that the notification formulae (*r rdit rḫ.tw*) are used in these records, apparently always in the absence of mention of witnesses[809].

An interesting point is that a mention of the document to be used as evidence for the transaction only appears in letters dealing with contractual relationships, although it does not seem to be an automatic provision of this type of document. See for instance the 21st dynasty epistolary *pBerlin* P 8523 concerning the renewing of a lease: the document ends with *mtw.k sꜣwy tꜣy.i šꜥt ỉryw.st n.k mtry* 'and you shall keep my letter, it will constitute evidence in your favor'[810]. For Eyre[811], the mention in *pBerlin* P 8523 probably refers to the 'use of the text for advice and reference, rather than as a legal document proving the validity' of the transaction, as in literary compositions, although some texts and later Demotic practice may allude to the use of documents as evidence[812]. In the Deir el-Medina community, many agreements would not require documentary evidence if they were of an uncomplicated nature, dealing with standard and repetitive transactions; keeping track of the donkeys hired and goods exchanged between kin did not require any reference to the provisions of a contract, laconic notes would amply suffice[813].

Then what is the nature of our contract-related records?

For Malinine[814] and Janssen[815], the majority of ostraca recording transactions are simple *memos* and not actual legal deeds. They were all intended to jog the author's memory on the most important points at some later stage'; but Janssen concedes[816] that ostraca did possess some value as legal documents, that they were used to record transactions relating to expensive commodities in order to avoid later disputes. Théodoridès[817] believed that the Deir el-Medina ostraca 'ne fournissent que des extraits, voire des résumés (ou des brouillons) des pièces authentiques qui sont perdues'; for Helck[818], the Deir el-Medina documents dealing with purchases represented 'Kaufquittungen.' Menu[819] recognizes that the Deir el-Medina

---

809 For example *oMichaelides* 5, *oDeM* 767.

810 Similar formulae are to be found in *pAnastasi* V 13,2-14,6 (19th dynasty dispute concerning bull and settlement proposal?), *pBM* EA 10100 (20th dynasty assignation of workmen), *pBN* 198 III and 199 I (20th dynasty, commissions), *pMallet* IV (20th dynasty, corvée), *pBankes* I (20th dynasty abduction of a slave); the mention in *oEdgerton* 1, a request for payment for a donkey already in the possession of the buyer, is slightly different (Janssen 2005: 53): 'You should let (me) keep the documentary evidence' (*sšw mtrw*). See also probably *pBoulaq* 8, 6th dynasty, as restored and translated by Baer (1966: 2, 5): *ỉw swt dỉ.n* PN *ꜥ.f m sꜥnḫ.s* [*r* 𓏛] *tn rdit.n(.ỉ) ỉnt.f n(.ỉ)* '[PN], however, has put his legal obligation to maintain her (on record) [in] this [let]ter that I made him bring me.' (*contra*: Goedicke 1967b). Compare with the use of epistolary documents as evidence in Mesopotamia, in which the formula 'Conserve mon billet en témoignage pour moi' is well attested at the beginning of the second millennium B.C. (Charpin 2008).

811 (1980: 15).

812 Manning (2003: 821 and n. 13, 843 and n.127).

813 See Goody (1986: 145) for the necessity of written contracts in urban situations and with complicated variable arrangements.

814 (1947: 94): 'aide-mémoire personnel' since the Egyptian procedure did not encourage the record of individual acts or at least did not consider them as absolutely indispensable.

815 (1982: 256). Janssen mostly bases his appreciation of the documents as *aide-mémoire* on the fact that a mention of witnesses is generally lacking, but there is no conclusive proof of the fact that witnesses had to appear in order to conclude or record a valid New Kingdom contract. We have seen no sign of formalism (protecting the assent of the parties, for evidence or publicity) in the verbal agreement of *pCairo* JE 65739; a mention of the presence of witnesses by the transmission of the object of the contract or its conclusion is rarely made (e.g. *oGardiner/Ashmolean* 185, *oDeM* 593), all other mentions of witnesses pertain to an oath/litigation context.

816 (1975: 511-3).

817 (1977: 69).

818 (1980).

819 (1998 : 303).

documents are not actual sale contracts, except for the few cases using the verb *ỉnỉ* assembled by Janssen (1975 : 504)[820], but 'des aide-mémoire, des procès-verbaux venant à l'appui de ventes matérielles réalisées verbalement'. She adds[821] that the ostraca containing the mention of a price may be records of exchanges, of remunerations ('louage d'ouvrage ou de services entre particuliers'), 'listes-types' (price-lists), used perhaps as 'monnaie scripturale', as evidence, or in order to 'faciliter la comptabilité publique'. Haring[822] recognizes that 'private transactions – loans, property transfers and divisions, payments, and donkeys hires – became the subject of more or less formalized types of texts' but that 'private business documents as a genre still lacked their own specific forms, that is, that they were not yet a true genre.' He also suggests regarding most of the donkey hire ostraca as *aide-mémoire,* 'written supplements to oral practice'[823]. And private business documents are usually termed 'accounts of transfer' in the Leiden database, never 'contracts'.

Recent works deal with the categorization of textual genres of business and administrative documents in Deir el-Medina in order to improve our knowledge of these enigmatic records. Donker van Heel & Haring[824] categorize Deir el-Medina's documents dealing with private transactions in five categories: *accounts of debt, accounts of transfer, accounts of payment, accounts of division,* and *records of donkey hire*, using the heading formula to make the classification[825]. In a recent article dealing with the textual evidence of an informal workshop for the production of private art in Deir el-Medina[826], followed by a monograph on the same subject[827], Cooney classifies her material in six categories based on the genre of the documents mentioning the 'private sector funerary arts market'. She accounts for the following genres:

- *workshop records*: 'organizational tool and protective record' made by the producers, mentioning an amount in *dbn* representing the costs and labor, usually neither the final price on the market nor the goods exchanged for this price. These records were 'not meant to track payment but to track the amount and type of craftwork performed', the 'details how craft labor was organized'[828], and to protect the craftsmen in case of any dispute between them or with their clients[829]. Artisans are often mentioned by title, but often the craftsman keeping the record is not named, only the purchaser[830]
- *receipts*: after an item is transferred by the producer to the buyer, the receipt records all commodities given by both sides; Cooney believes it was usually kept by the buyer to protect him in case of a dispute, but that it could also protect the producer, and ideally included the names of both parties, although 'many receipts include no names or titles'. The opening formula includes the items bought, sometimes names, and the payment

820 I do not think that what Janssen had in mind was the genre of the texts, but the fact that they concerned sale transactions expressed with the verb *ỉnỉ* 'to buy,' and although still 'barter' transactions, they had been especially distinguished by the scribes 'to stress that one party received the principal object.'

821 (2004: 256-7).

822 (2003b: 263).

823 Haring (2003b: 266).

824 (2003).

825 (*ibid.*, pp.146-62); they add on p. 162 that accounts of transfers, payments, debts and property divisions were not dated 'because they were affairs that had been completed', as opposed to donkey hires.

826 Cooney (2006: 44-5).

827 Cooney (2007: esp. 46-67).

828 Cooney (2006: 45, 48).

829 Cooney (2007: 47).

830 Cooney (2007: 46-7).

with or without total. Nevertheless, Cooney adds that all 'these text categories are artificial' and she classifies a text as a receipt when it concerns 'one major purchase'[831]

- *multi-transaction receipts*: more complicated transactions often involving multiple traders, many items, and complex sequences of exchanges, sometimes over time; it is her largest category. The records include arithmetical accounting, sometimes valuations in *dbn* or *ḫ3r* of grain, and even outstanding balances. When only one person is named, it is probably not the keeper of the record but the other party, in order to offer some protection to the keeper in case of litigation[832]
- *letters*: most of them between artisans, with details about acquisition and production but rarely including prices[833]
- *official records*: daily journals of the necropolis; the brief mentions of funerary art do not generally include prices, and do not deal with transactions but with absence from work due to craftwork executed by a workman for his superior[834]
- *legal texts*: mainly disputes, but also wills.

She also uses the expression 'private fiscal documents'[835] without further qualifying the category.

Some of the textual categories used by authors are problematic. For instance, the notion of a *receipt* as a 'written acknowledgment that something has been received' (Garner 2004: 1296), kept as evidence by the transmitter (the buyer in the case of payment for a manufactured good). It is clear that the modern mechanism implied by the receipt (*prima facie* evidence of payment or transmission of goods), with the signature of the recipient, does not apply to Ramesside Egypt: it belongs to a legal system in which written evidence is either preeminent or pervasive and in which documentary evidence may consist of a private deed produced without the sanction of a public authority. In Ramesside Egypt, business agreements are mainly verbal, written documents remaining unsigned[836]. Documentary evidence in a legal context is apparently only offered by official records (authentified deeds, official registers, court and administrative proceedings), and the use of receipts as evidence is not attested in legal proceedings or other types of sources. Thus records concerning the transfer of items are either personal records of the transmitter or the recipient without special evidenciary value (although they may be useful in the event of a dispute to recall the details of the transfer), or as administrative documentation of transfers of some sorts (descriptive documents). In conclusion, we will not use the notion of receipt in our treatment of the material.

Another problematic point concerns speculations as to the identity of the keeper of the record. Nothing definitive can be said on the subject.

Although we do not appear to be dealing in this chapter with true contracts, the documents should not be regarded as memos written by relatively untrained individuals[837] in a free fashion; they have a formulaic style, although they are rarely composed in an absolutely identical manner, and they use a 'bureaucratic' register. This remark has already been made

831 Cooney (2007: 51). On p. 53 she mentions another issue concerning the records she categorizes as receipts: 'One might expect the seller to be mentioned far more frequently as the buyer was less likely to record his own name in a text meant for his own archives; however, in reality, this is not the case.'

832 Cooney (2007: 54-6). She adds that receipts and workshop records are sometimes difficult to distinguish,when almost only craft items are exchanged.

833 Cooney (2007: 59-60, 66).

834 Cooney (2007: 60-2).

835 Cooney (2006: 46-7).

836 Not before the beginning of the Late Period, see Baines & Eyre (1983: 75).

837 Baines & Eyre (1983: 74): 'the writer was the primary witness; mostly he was one of the professional scribes' (and in most cases anonymous).

supra regarding the *(social) gifts or else* categories of documents. The people who wrote them were trained to write in a certain way, and we may surmise that if they were recording contracts, they would use the same approach. There does not appear to have been one valid model for each legal act that was copied word-for-word (formalism)[838]; nevertheless, the written records are not improvisations, but draw on a 'more or less stable core with variations' in formulae, to use the formulation of Lord[839] concerning oral traditional poetry. Of course, although multiformity may be an indication of a primary oral register, it is evident that the formulae are too impersonal, brief, expository, and similar to suggest the transcription of a verbal discourse. It seems that in ancient Egyptian society, scribes were mainly trained to be literate in a core curriculum of standard key texts serving as mental templates, memorized and recited, being able to rewrite the tradition without any need for physical texts[840], and using the same style for official as well as for private sphere documents. Interestingly, we know of textual collections designed for the training of Egyptian scribes, but they are mostly literary or epistolary models and not of the cursory type we encounter in this chapter. The trainees must have learned this notational bureaucratic style directly from actual records; there was no need to invent special exercises in their usage for such brief and strightforward material.

It is important to remark that our records may not represent only one genre, as some of the documents considered may be administrative records and not private sphere productions, especially the 'donkey hire texts' mentioning the transmission of a donkey to a named recipient, but without the name of the transmitter or mention of a price. The donkey may have been transmitted by the administration to the workers like any other tool for public service[841], and the transfers recorded by the administration and for its benefit; the record would thus belong to a bureaucratic genre, not to the consentient genre of the private sphere[842]. The issue thus concerns the ownership of the items transferred; Helck[843] correctly noted that even when two individuals' names are written down in a hire record it does not mean that the object of the transaction belongs to one of them. It may belong to a temple[844] or to a state administration[845]. Eyre[846] has also noted that donkey hire texts exemplify the difficulty of distinguishing between private business affairs and official business and that what appear to be private transactions

838 For the same conclusion concerning loans during the Late Period, see Menu (1982: 289).

839 (1987: 67).

840 Carr (2005: 8, 68-77). Janssen (1975: 495) regards the numerous variants of a formula as a case of free wording; the scribes did not have to follow a legally prescribed example and usage led to similar expressions (opinion followed by Baines and Eyre 1983: 74). But one must add that their training strictly limited this 'freedom' of wording. See also Donker van Heel & Haring (2003).

841 See e.g. *oDeM* 64 *supra*; *oDeM* 400: date + *dit pꜣ ꜥꜣt n sš* PN *n pꜣ ḫr* 'Giving the donkey to (the) scribe of the Tomb PN'.
For Allam (1996: 218), the absence of any mention of a *consideration* may lead us to believe that 'c'était la communauté même qui disposait d'un troupeau d'ânes' and a scribe was probably in charge of the transfers in the name of the crew. Janssen (2005: 110) admits that there might be 'a pool of donkeys available to the *smdt*', adding that 'the memorandum quoted in Pap. Turin 2084 + 2091, II, 8, "concerning the six donkeys of the Tomb"' may represent an isolated reference to donkeys 'belonging to the organization of the Tomb-builders, not to the individual members.' See also Janssen, Frood & Goecke-Bauer (2003: 27).

842 It is still strange that no journal of animals transmissions has been found, only brief ostraca dealing with either one or a few transfers.

843 (1961-70: 501).

844 See e.g. *pTurin* 1881 col. 8 & 9 and probably also the *pCairo* CG 58057.

845 See also Menu (1982: 170-1, 264; 2004: 206, 220). Concerning a similar ambiguity as to the ownership of the assets dealt with in Old Kingdom documents, see Goedicke (1986: 79). Most known Demotic period hire transactions of animals for plowing or hauling belong to the public sphere 'where royal farmers were provided with public (or commandeered) animals' (Manning 2003: 847).

846 (1980: 56).

may be cases of work done 'for the personal use and profit of the vizier himself.'[847] Of course, as the 'bureaucratic style' is used both in the private and public spheres, and since the records dealt with are somewhat brief, the distinction cannot easily be made. But a fine-tuned analysis may be helpful here: the quasi-absence of notification formula in the case of donkey-hire[848] could be explained by the administrative character of the transaction or the private/administrative-internal use of the record; the number of parties named and the absence of *consideration* may be key elements to be taken into account in any determination of the nature of the texts.

Finally, the scant material concerning private transfers and agreements during the preceding periods is not easy to evaluate; but the basic transactions also appear to have been verbal[849], although a record of the payment (and of the vendor's oath) may exist. The monumental versions of so-called sales and other contracts[850] are mostly simple mentions, emendated copies or excerpts of unilateral declarations; see e.g.

- the *Kꜣmnfrt* (?) *Cairo block* CG 1432 of the 5th dynasty, concerning a funerary foundation, thus certainly involving agreements with priests, but presented in the form of a unilateral verbal act (*wḏt-mdt*) on the model of royal decrees protecting the assets and workers of a temple;
- the *Giza boundary stone Cairo* JE 42787 of the 5th dynasty(?), dealing with the sale of a house[851], presenting separately the declaration of the buyer concerning the payment, sealed (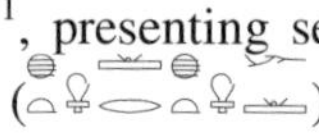)[852] before the *ḏꜣḏꜣt* administrative council and witnesses,

847 *Ibid.*, p. 123 and p. 188: 'It is often impossible to tell if a simple record of the commissioning of such work refers to an official or to a private project.' See also Valbelle (1985: 30): 'le scribe ne faisait pas la distinction qui nous paraît aujourd'hui naturelle entre affaire privée et affaire publique, mais seulement entre affaire interne à la communauté et affaire concernant les autorités.'

848 Donker van Heel & Haring (2003: 159).

849 See Goedicke (1970: 195, 197 and 1986: 79); *contra*: Helck (1980: 370). We may conceive these transactions on the model of the Old Kingdom market scenes such as the one presented in *LD* II, 96 (s) from a Saqqara tomb of the 4th dynasty (?): a man sitting behind a vegetable basket, seizing a necklace presented by another man, the caption above reading *di mꜣꜣ(.i) di isw* ' let (me) see, give a price'. See also the double statement introduced by *ḏd.f* in the *Giza boundary stone Cairo JE* 42787 and the locutive/allocutive parts introduced by *ꜥḥꜥ.n ḏd.n.f* in *Ḥꜥpyḏfꜣ*'s sealed documents, about which Théodoridès (1971: 226) notes that 'Les contrats ont indiscutablement été conclus *oralement*, et quoique insérés dans un moule identique, ils ont été mis sous une forme qui ne l'est pas.'

850 Helck (1986: 1225-6) classifies the contracts in two groups in his 'Werkverträge und andere Privatverträge' entry for the *LÄ*: 'Werkverträge' with craftsmen (*ḫtm* or 'gesiegelte Urkunde') and with *kꜣ*-priests (*wḏt-mdt*), and 'Kaufverträge' (usually with *r isw*). See also Menu (1982: 223-8) concerning the loan (*tꜣbt*) during the Old and Middle Kingdoms, in the form of 'avances des céréales accordées par des fonctionnaires à des particuliers (…) remboursables (…) probablement dès que possible (…). Ce prêt, conçu comme un « service public » est sans doute gratuit.'; Goedicke (1986).

851 *Contra*: Goedicke (1970: 150-1; 1986: 76-8) for whom it consists of a work-contract.

852 There is no unanimity concerning either the reading or the meaning; it appears that the sealing is a prerogative of the administration during the Old Kingdom, as there is no evidence of private sealing before the end of this period (Goedicke 1986: 75-6). See Grdseloff (1951: 155) for a picture of a wooden stamp-seal bearing the text # *ḫtmt ḫt* + location + title + PN # (probably from Middle Kingdom Lahun); the author compares it to the inscription of *Tfḫꜣi*'s *false door Cairo* JE 56994 (6th dynasty) 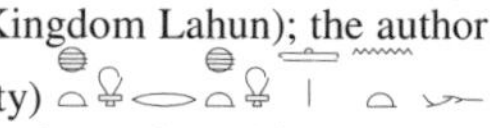 reading it *ḫtm r ḫtm nt ḫt* 'scellé sur le contrat-"bois"'. For Fischer (1961: 50), *ḫtm r ḫtmt* (*n*) means 'to legally convey something to someone in a sealed document', an example of Old Kingdom legal phraseology, equivalent to *rdi r isw n* and *iri n*. For Théodoridès (1979: 75), the *ḫtm*(*w*) *r ḫtm-ḫt* expression means 'scellé au (ou « pour le ») service du cadastre (?)'. For Boochs (1982: esp. 49), the reading is *ḫtm r-ḫt* 'to seal what is in a document' and concerns 'eines zeitlich begrenzten Arbeits- oder Abhängigkeitsverhältnisses gegen Entgelt'.

followed by an oath of the seller before other witnesses in order to guarantee the buyer's satisfaction after the payment in full;

- *Ḥ*ʿ*pydf*ꜣ *tomb* in Siut (12th dynasty), recording 10 *ḫtmt* (sealed documents) with priests in order to perpetuate *Ḥ*ʿ*pydf*ꜣ's cult, constituting in fact onerous *donations mortis causa mortis*[853]; it is the tomb owner declaration that is noted[854];
- the *Stèle juridique de Karnak* JE 52453 of the 17th dynasty is the lapidary version of both a detailed unilateral *imyt-pr* enacting the sale of an administrative function (an *authentic* document) and the record of a *datio in solutum* (*swnt*).

Pre-Ramesside hieratic documents may also be copies or excerpts of unilateral declarations related to contracts, sometimes embedded in administrative or accounting documents:

- *pCairo* JE 66844-1/6[855] of the 5th-6th dynasties[856], concern the sale of houses, with the same successive declarations of the buyer and oath of the seller as warranty and quittance, without mention of witnesses; the qualification of *ḫtm*[*t*] is used in one of the texts;
- *pKahun* I.2 (*pUC* 32167) of the 12th dynasty, a brief administrative mention[857] of an onerous transfer (*swnt*) of labor between brothers with the assent of the scribe of a bureau controlling the placement of personnel (the *ḫ*ꜣ *n didi rmṯ*);
- *pBerlin* P 9784 of the 18th dynasty, probably an administrative record of transfer of days of service of personnel, as well as the sale of fields, before witnesses, the basic agreements being always verbal and the seller expressing quittance and taking an oath of warranty before witnesses;
- *pGurob* II,1-2 of the 18th dynasty, two onerous transfers (*swnt*) of days of service, with oath of warranty and quittance of the sellers before the *ḳnbt*;
- the *Bryce tablet* of the 18th dynasty, a brief note concerning the payment (*swnt*) of days of service.

Note that other texts[858] may mention contracts in the context of a litigation process (*pKahun* II.1), of a royal function's (dis)investiture (*Ahmose's Karnak stela*)[859], or of a private

---

Recently, Russo (2007: 208) compared *ḫtmt nt ḫt* of the Old Kingdom (public responsibility), *ḫtm* of the First Intermediate Period (private responsability), and *ḫtmt db*ꜣ*w* of the 12th dynasty ('private accord in exchange for a payment' between an official and his funerary priests).

Note that there is no reference in our Ramesside material to sealed documents, nor to witnesses' signatures (see Baines & Eyre 1983: 75).

853 See Théodoridès (1971: 242).

854 For Théodoridès (1971: 230), the records are summaries engraved in the tomb, evidencing the tomb's owner interest in *synallagmatic* contracts. Some parts of the text betray 'la mise en discours indirect de ce qui, dans l'original, au moment de la confection de l'acte, a dû se trouver en style direct' (p. 224); missing are the date and formal mentions, the acting authority, the recording administration, the seal, the oath of the parties, and the names of the witnesses (pp. 234-7). But for Spalinger (1985: 7), the records are not abbreviated versions of the originals, but 'almost complete records of the original texts with a few omissions (...) due to the nature of the final carved copy.'

Compare with Russo (2007: 197) concerning *stela BM* EA 1164 of the 11th dynasty, bearing a 'synopsis of the contracts' 'in the final lines'.

855 Regarded by Posener-Kriéger (1979: 328) as actual legal documents, *swnt* acts, 'conventions d'échange' preceding the sale deed, not the definitive sale instruments since they appear on accounting rolls and do not mention witnesses.

856 4th dynasty for Strudwick (2005: 185).

857 See Menu (1982: 118-9).

858 As for *S*ꜣ*b*ꜣ*stt*'s *statue Louvre* E 11673, the line concerning the presumed transfer of function is too badly damaged to decide if this is indeed the issue.

cultic context (e.g. *Block Saqqara* RM 22-11-1956 of the 5-6th dynasties; *Architrave Cairo* CG 1634 of the 6th (?) dynasty; *Louvre stela* C 34 of 12th dynasty)[860].

Again, the records presented *infra* do not belong to the consentient legal genre and they do not represent contracts. A brief sketch of the main categories of documents dealing with contractual relations and not obviously belonging to a litigation procedure before a court or the oracle is provided *infra* as a further attempt to determine the genre of the texts, using linguistic-pragmatic criteria. Some of the criteria used to identify and categorize the documents are the same as those previously mentioned concerning wills, gifts, and partitions (see e.g. certain *significant variation factors* listed *supra* in the *(social) gifts or else?* subchapter), with additions relevant to contract-related records; they are listed for each category and sub-category of records. Texts mentioning only 'giving items' or items without other precisions have generally been omitted (see the *(social) gifts or else?* chapter for further documents possibly linked with business transactions); the following list is thus not exhaustive. Janssen's categories of transactions based on their main formula[861] do not correspond to our classification of the records, as he did not attempt to classify the genre of the instruments but only the transactions they concern.

The records use lexemes and expressions already encountered in our corpus with a few additions: *rdỉ, ꜣḫt, r rdỉt rḫ.tw, smỉ, ỉrỉ ꜥnḫ, ḏd, r(ꜣ), sw(ꜣ)ḏ, (ꜥḥꜥ) ḥr pḥwy, mdt, ḫry, šw, m dwꜣ sꜣ dwꜣ, m-dỉ.f, ỉnỉ, ỉṯꜣ, nḥm, mỉty, r-ḏbꜣ, ỉsw, šbw/t, šꜥꜣyr, swnt, r bꜣkw.f, m-ḳb, ḥḏ*, etc. Since the purpose of this section is primarily to categorize texts, the categorization features of the lexemes are not presented here.

1. Epistolary genre

Features: epistolary formulae, allocutive mode, imperative, epistolary register (degree 2/3 Neo-Egyptian), and textemic texture; other concerns besides the contractual relation; often includes directives to an executant concerning diverse types of transactions (*rdỉ, ỉnỉ, ỉrỉ*, etc.), sometimes with explicit *consideration*; may mention a request of payment or that the record should be used as evidence (see *supra*). Related either to private or official concerns.[862] The relationship between the writer and the addressee may vary (debtor, partner, servant, agent, inferior, etc.), and is generally unclear.

pBerlin P 8523 could qualify for the title of written 'contract' embedded in a letter (renewal of a lease between the writer and the addressee[863]), but it is dated after the Ramesside Period (21st dynasty), and it may concern a land belonging to a temple[864].

---

859 The situation described on the stela is far from clear: it concerns the transfer of a function for Menu (1971: 155-6 'transfert à titre onéreux') and Harari (1959: 'donation'), but a disinvestiture or 'résiliation' for Gitton (1975: 102 'renonciation à la fonction' and 1976) and Grimal (1988: 263).

860 Although the first two are regarded as 'actes de vente' by Menu (1985: 251, 255-7).

861 (1975: 495-509).

862 Eyre (1984: 203) notes in relation to letters that one cannot clearly distinguish 'between purely private agricultural transactions and official or semi-official functions'.
Interestingly, Depauw (1997 : 148) notes that Demotic private receipts (confirmation of payment in money or in kind) normally use the epistolary form and 'it is often not clear whether the parties act on their own behalf or are representatives of institutions'. Furthermore, he adds (p. 140) that sales of small items in Demotic texts are 'usually phrased in epistolary style, sometimes even on ostraca'; the same is said concerning loans on p. 146.

863 Who is of an inferior status and thus not in a position to discuss the terms of the lease. The dispositions are brief, which may be explained by the fact that the document concerns the renewing of a prior lease. See Allam (1973: 274-5): 'Pachturkunde'.

864 *Contra*: Théodoridès (1963); see Eyre (1994: 130-1).

Example[865]: *oDeM* 125: 19th dynasty, Ramesses II (*KRI* III, 543 n.231 A 47)[866]:

ky ḏd n PN *iḫ di.* *ḥr.* *mtw.* *wḫ3 n.i wꜥ mss r-ḏb3*[*w*] *p3 š3ḳw mtw.* *di.* *grg n.* *sw* 10
Another communication for PN: Please pay attention and you will claim for me one tunic in exchang[e] for this ring, and I will provide for you 10 days.

2. Record of oaths: contentious legal genre?

Some oaths are taken out of a judicial setting[867] and some are not even related to a legal issue[868]; but in the context of a transaction, were oaths an integral part of a contract or exclusively taken in case of dispute? Can the record of an oath related to a transaction represent a written Ramesside contract?

Malinine[869] was convinced that the vendor's guarantee was part of the verbal and solemn exchange of statements constituting a sale[870]; the oath was taken before witnesses in an administrative bureau and afterwards recorded in the form of a procès-verbal (*authentic* act) with excerpts delivered to the parties. Thus there were both contractual and judicial oaths[871]

865 See also e.g. ***oDeM* 118**, 19th dynasty, Ramesses II ('pouvoir à une tierce personne' given in order to negotiate a transaction for Allam 1996: 200); ***oGardiner/Ashmolean* 112**, 19th dynasty, Seti II; ***oEdgerton* 1**, 20th dynasty, Ramesses III?; ***pDeM* 11** (?), 20th dynasty, Ramesses V (see *supra (social) gifts or else?*); ***oGardiner/Ashmolean* 164 v°**, 20th dynasty, Ramesses IX (a letter to the king concerning work in the tomb on recto, and on verso a dated address to a scribe (another letter?) followed by a brief dated note concerning the transfer of a donkey, quite unconnected with the recto, probably by another hand; 'brief note on donkey hire' for Donker van Heel & Haring 2003: 159 n. 143; donkey hire or sale for Janssen 2005: 17); ***oIFAO* 1305**, 20th dynasty (brief letter in which the writer recommends the addressee to take care of a donkey, with final brief dated note concerning the transfer of a donkey by another hand (?); the last two lines dealing with the transfer of a donkey are a later addition to the letter for Janssen 2005: 55); ***oDeM* 411**, 20th dynasty (the Leiden database suggests that it may be a letter, but the sole indicator of epistolary genre here would be a directive expressed in the allocutive mode and using the future; debt in the context of a transaction for Allam 1973: 119; possibly category VI sale of an animal for Janssen 1975: 505).

866 'Target trading' for McDowell (1999: 75).

867 See Wilson (1948: 131-5, 140-2); Seidl (1957: 29-30 n.104): 'promissorische Eide auch in Privaturkunden vorkommen, die keine Mitwirkung eines Gerichts erkennen lassen'.

868 For instance the 'assertions of emotion' examples noted by Wilson (1948: 134-5).

869 (1947: 106, 111).

870 See also Menu (1988: 167) concerning the sale; she notes that 'la vente comporte, de la part du vendeur, une obligation de garantie vis-à-vis de l'acheteur. Le vendeur promet à l'acheteur de renoncer à toute réclamation et d'écarter tous les tiers qui pourraient revendiquer la chose vendue'. For Menu (1998: 40-1), the oath had the value of a 'serment d'engagement ayant des effets promissoires et pouvant avoir des effets novatoires' during the Ramesside Period.

871 See also Menu (1982: 229), but her examples of contractual oaths (e.g. *oPetrie* 67 and *oDeM* 564) may belong to a litigation process that was not expressly mentioned. For Allam (1996: 199); 'une obligation pouvait être consignée essentiellement sous la forme d'un serment, lequel était aussi devenu un acte en lui-même pouvant couvrir toute sorte d'engagement.' He admits the 'contractual oath' in the case of *oDeM* 56 and *oTurin* 57173; but he shows (1967b; 1973: 172; 1994: 25) that the brief *oGardiner/Ashmolean* 104 may record an oath taken in the context of litigation, and takes the same view about *oGardiner/Ashmolean* 196 since 'the penalty of double payment is generally to be stipulated at court when a defendant backs up his promise to pay off his debt' (1994: 25).

See also Donker van Heel & Haring (2003: 171-2) who note that oaths were taken 'with sales, hires and in court' and that 'we also find the oath as a type of document in itself, that is, as a genre in the scribal tradition.' The fact that statements in court are often introduced by the formula *ḏd*(*t.*)*n* PN as are some oaths (*ibid.*, pp. 173-4) perhaps confirm our intuition, and the authors themselves admit (*ibid.*, pp. 174-5) that some oath documents may be abbreviated court proceedings, although in the case of donkey hire, 'the oath and the contractual oath was an integral part of the agreement between the parties (see *supra* his remarks concerning *oDeM* 56 and 57). A similar picture is presented for the Ancient Near East by Westbrook (2003: 66) who considers that there were two ways of creating a binding contract, either orally (the enforceability arising from the performance by one party) or by oath (unilateral obligation, the enforceability stemming from its form).

But the Ramesside sources are lacunary; they do not include *authentic* acts, only cursory records not readily understandable in the absence of extra-textual information. We have seen that the verbal agreement recorded in *pCairo* JE 65739 does not include oaths by the parties; evidence of contractual provisions could be supplied by epistolary documents, no oath being taken.[872] The fact that a forum or a litigation process is not expressly mentioned in our brief records related to oaths does not necessarily imply that a dispute and its settlement are excluded[873]. Furthermore, we have already seen that *promissory* oaths taken in the context of inheritance[874] and partitions[875] were generally related to disputes and were never taken by a testator during the record of the testamentary provisions by the court (*authentic* will)[876]. Concerning the abbreviated, contract-related records, the circumstances of the oath were not explicitly revealed, but a conflictual setting could generally be assumed. As shown *infra*, the oaths in contract-related records concern mainly the guarantee of execution in time of his obligation by a debtor and warranties against claims; the records referred to *infra* include a unilateral promise, not an exchange of promises, and they do not suggest the existence of such an exchange. In most cases, the explanation may be that they are part of a dispute settled by a promise to respect his undertaking[877] sworn by the losing party. An oath could perhaps be taken as a preventive measure in particular cases to forestall a dispute, but the oath does not appear to constitute an integral part of the contract. It is interesting to note that prior to the Ramesside Period warranties against claims could be given without resorting to an oath, by a unilateral verbal declaration of satisfaction[878], or by a clause in a written act during all periods[879].

---

may have been a transaction formality and its written version a document for future reference or even proof'.

872 Nevertheless, compare abnormal hieratic (25th -26th dynasty) and early Demotic (26th dynasty) contracts with oath (Malinine 1953: xviii).

873 A similar documentary texture of missing mentions, fictions, and appearance was noted by Pestman (1995) in Demotic contracts.

874 In *Naunakhte*, *adscriptus* of Document I, the *promissory* oath concludes the contestation by a desinherited son of a will; Document IV may be a case of a compromise ending a dispute between a father and a son related to an item inherited by the latter; in *oPetrie* 18's additional note to the will settling a contestation(?).

875 In *pBoulaq* 10, perhaps because a dispute had arisen during the material partition between its beneficiaries; in *pTurin* 2070 v°, probably in the context of an inheritance settlement.

876 The case of the *terrorem clause* of the *pAdoptions* is particular as it is a curse, its main aim being to threaten potential objectors to the will while reinforcing its performativity.

877 Allam mentions (1967b: 50) the use during the Ramesside Period of an oath imposed on the party that lost a case (in court or in an oracular context) concerning ownership, as well as in later documents written in abnormal hieratic (1994: 22-3). For oaths not to contest a settled lawsuit in Mesopotamia, see for instance Greengus (1969: 531, n. 136).

878 Given by a party to an agreement by the closing of a deal (?) or receipt of full and generous payment and thus expressing some sort of warranty against personal claim (12th dynasty *Ḥʿpydf3 tomb,* lines 276, 282, 289, etc.). This expression of satisfaction should be compared with two isolated examples of double *assertory* oaths taken before an administrative authority (Middle Kingdom *pKahun* II.1 and 17th dynasty *Stèle juridique de Karnak* JE 52453) which have the value of a warranty against both parties' claims as expressly mentioned in the *Stèle*. These oaths may have been occasioned by the settlement of a dispute in both cases.

879 Warranty against claims by a third party or a general warranty in wills (e.g. 5th dynasty *Wpmnfrt tomb*; *pTurin* 2021, a testamentary disposition quoted by the vizier), in *imyt-pr* related to testamentary dispositions

The context of the oath may not always be a litigation before a court, but a more informal arbitration[880] or mediation by a scribe or other prominent member of the community in order to resolve a dispute, hence there is no mention of a court. The oath should not be regarded as a tool exclusively used in a court, even in legal contexts; although it may appear to be imposed on a party and thus incompatible with a negotiated compromise[881], it is a solemn way of effecting a promise, possibly obtained by conciliation, the breaking of which would have serious consequences. Settlements signed in the context of modern arbitration procedures may also involve large sums of money that would appear to be stiff penalties if we did not know about the negotiation procedure that preceded them. In our material, the choice of a negotiated settlement was made by the two parties, whereas litigation before a court in matters of private transaction was the consequence of a unilateral motion.

See, for instance, the case of *oDeM* 73 r° (20th dynasty, Ramesses III)[882]:

> Date + *hrw pn ḏd ỉr.n ḳd* PN *ḥnꜥ* PN *m-bꜣḥ sš nt tmꜣ* PN *ỉw.tw ḥr swꜣḏ n.f pꜣ ꜥꜣt bỉn ỉw.f dỉt.f wꜥ ꜥꜣtt r-ḏbꜣw.f ỉryw.f ꜥnḫ n nb ꜥ.w.s. ḥr pḥw.st*
> (Date), this day of (the) statement that did (the) potter PN with PN before (the) scribe of (the) mat PN. And one handed over to him the bad donkey and he gave him one she-ass in exchange of it. He took an oath of (the) Lord L.P.H. on its back.

McDowell[883] recognizes the legal authority of the *ḥwtyw* (captains of the workers' gangs) to deal as arbiters independently of their role as judges in the forum of the *ḳnbt*, and she proposes several possible examples of arbitration cases, although she assumes that *oDeM* 73 r° does not concern a dispute, the issue being already resolved (but this is a concise presentation of the case in the record, the solution being probably the result of a negotiation that has not been reported in the document).

Nothing proves that the oath was an integral part of a contract during preceding periods: the Old Kingdom documents show that separate records and/or groups of witnesses testify for the declaration of the buyer and the oath of the vendor (*Giza boundary stone Cairo* JE 42787 and *pCairo* JE 66844-1/6)[884]. A double *assertory* oath of the parties expresses their satisfaction in the case of a sale on credit of a function in Middle Kingdom *pKahun* II.1 (during a procedure before an official)[885], and of a *datio in solutum* resulting from a settled contentious situation in

(e.g. 18th dynasty *Snims Cairo stela* CG 34016) or sale contracts (e.g. 17th dynasty *Stèle juridique de Karnak* JE 52453), as well as in Late Period contracts (e.g. 25th dynasty *pLouvre* E 3228e); see *supra* also in agreements concluding a dispute (*Naunakhte*'s Doc. IV).

880 For arbitration before the New Kingdom, see Pirenne (1934: 325-6, 332) and Mrsich (2005: 98-9, 258-9 *et passim*). Concerning arbitration in Deir el-Medina, see McDowell (1990: 146-8; 1995 on *oAshmolean* 655); but for her, disputes concerning property are dealt with by the oracle or representatives of the vizier, not by individual officials or the *ḳnbt*.

881 McDowell (1990: 177).

882 For Helck (1961-70: 499), it is a 'Verkaufsurkunde', but for Allam (1973b: 33, 35) and Janssen (1975: 9 and 2005: 36), it is a case of litigation.

883 (1990: 146-8).

884 The Old Kingdom oath of the vendor guarantees general order and the buyer's satisfaction; it does not expressly address contestation: *ꜥnḫ nỉ-swt dỉ(.ỉ) wn mꜣꜥ ḥtp.k ḥr.s* in the *Giza boundary stone*; *ꜥnḫ nỉ-swt dỉ(.ỉ)/Nṯrsn wn mꜣꜥ ḥtp ḥr.s* in *pCairo* JE 66844-1/6. Goedicke (1986: 78) rightly remarks that in case of isolated documents such as these, 'we have no way to decide if the incorporation of a promissory oath was usual or exceptional.' He adds that on registration with the administration of the necropolis (sealer), 'the verbal agreement between the two parties is transformed into a "contract"'; in fact, the original agreement was verbal, and either a dispute brought the parties before the *dꜣḏꜣt*, or the deal concerned real estate thus justifying an administrative record. See also Théodoridès (1979 : 72-3).

885 Wilson (1948: 144) believed that the agreement of *pKahun* II.1 resulted from an 'adjustment of a dispute'.

the 17th dynasty *Stèle juridique de Karnak* JE 52453[886]. The group of 18th dynasty *pBerlin* P 9784-5[887] and *pGurob* II.1-2 seems, at least partly, to refer to disputes and to procedures before the court, and *promissory* oaths are taken in order to guarantee compensation, after payment in full by the other party, in the event of contestation.

Interestingly, the same issue has been treated in the context of Greek oaths, and Carawan (2007) concludes that contracts did not require oaths in ancient Greek society and that oaths were only used in the event of disagreements. See also the no-claim documents representing the bulk of Old-Babylonian texts relating to litigation (Goddeeris 2002: 111).

The various guarantees expressed by the oaths are as follows[888]:

2.1 General warranty against claims: oath of the vendor after payment in full by the buyer[889]

Features: brief dated delocutive record (except for the quotation of a locutive oath), formulaic style, both parties named (# *rdit* N PN *n* N PN #), mention of object and *consideration* (*r-ḏbꜣ*, list of items with valuation and total), followed by oath (tag clause, general warranty, penalty), no mention of forum or witnesses. The register is mostly degree 1 Neo-Egyptian for the pre-material but degree 2 in the body of the text (mainly the oath). The record concerns the making of a payment[890] and the oath is taken after execution of the buyer's obligation; it does not concern the *mutual assent* to the contract. The penalty of the double is often associated with a trial[891], but there is no express mention of litigation[892]; as the payment is complete, the record may represent both warranty and quittance[893].

886 See Théodoridès (1957: esp. 49-51; 1962: 99) concerning the *Stèle juridique de Karnak* JE 52453. The purpose of the double oath is noted on the *Stèle,* line 21: *ỉw.tw r rdit ʿrḳ.sn ḥr.s m ʿnḫ n nb ʿ.w.s. sꜣ ʿnn.sn st ḥr*[*.s*] *r* [*n*]*ḥḥ* 'One will cause that they swear about it an oath of the Lord L.P.H. preventing they ever would withdraw it because of [it].' Thus the *assertory* oath is also a warranty.

887 See Navailles & Neveu (1989) concerning the formulation of the oath as in *pBerlin* P 9784, lines 26-7: *ỉr šmw pꜣ hrw* 2 *nty twy rdỉ n.k m ḥm* PN *ỉr{n} snỉw ḥr snỉw* 'If the 2 days are hot (contested) that I have given you as (the service of) the servant PN, a *snỉw* should be done (compensated) for a *snỉw*' and in *pBerlin* P 9785, lines 16-7 *ỉr šmm.f m dwꜣ sꜣ dwꜣ* [...] *pw ỉr mdwt.tw ỉm.s ỉn rmṯ nbt ỉr gꜣb ḥr gꜣb* 'If he contests in the future [...] or if it is contested by anyone, an equivalent should be done (compensated) for an equivalent'.

888 *oGardiner/Ashmolean* 104, 20th dynasty, Ramesses III (*KRI* V, 555 n.227 A194) is an oath in an unclear situation ('should I contest this donkey', no further contextual details). For Allam (1967b, 1973: 171-2; 1973b: 20; 1994: 25), it was taken in the context of a sale, perhaps after litigation before a court, being an 'Abstandsurkunde' (the absence of the name of the other party is not important for Allam as he would get the record; as for the failure to mention the payment of the price, Allam believes that it means a credit operation); Donker van Heel & Haring (2003: 171-5): 'oath' as a genre of texts with heading formula # date + *ḏdt.n* PN #; Janssen (2005: 24): oath/promise concerning a donkey.

889 Compare with 18th dynasty *pBerlin* P 9784-5 and *pGurob* II.1 & 2 where full payment is associated with the oath of warranty.
Note that a similar oath is given by the vendor in abnormal hieratic contractual dispositions, although after a locutive declaration of the vendor (Malinine 1953: 36-7); in Demotic *sḫ n ḏbꜣ ḥḏ* documents, the vendor states that he has been paid, the property transferred, that he has no further rights and claims, and that he is willing to assist the buyer against the claims by a third party, even through an oath (Depauw 1997: 141). But in the context of Demotic sales of immovable assets, two distinct documents may attest payment and warranty against claims (Allam 1967b: 48-9; Zauzich 1980).
See also the withdrawal of the losing party after trial in *Naunakhte*, *pAshmolean* 1945.97 V, line 12 *supra* and Demotic *sḫ n wy* (Depauw 1997: 143; Manning 2003: 831-2).

890 Donker van Heel & Haring (2003: 153-7) 'account of payment' headed by the formula # *rdyt n* PN *ỉn* PN *r ḏbꜣ* #, dated because of the oath taken by the seller.

891 Allam (1994: 25).

Example: *oTurin* 57173, 19-20th dynasty, Ramesses II-IV (*KRI* V, 457-8 n.216 A24):

Date + *rdit rmṯ ist* PN *n mḏ3y* [PN] *r-ḏb3w p3y.f ꜥ3t* (items + *ir n ḥmt dbn* x) *iry.f ꜥnḫ n nb ꜥ.w.s. r-ḏd w3ḥ Imn w3ḥ p3 ḥḳ3 ꜥ.w.s. bn mdty.i m p3y ꜥ3t bn mdty ky im.f mtw ir.f iw.f r.i m-ḳb* (Date), giving of (the) workman PN to (the) policeman [PN] in payment of his donkey: (list of items + worth x copper *dbn*). He took an oath of (the) Lord L.P.H. saying: 'May Amun be clement, may the Ruler L.P.H. be clement, I will not contest this donkey (and) neither will another contest it; should he do (so), he is against me for (the) double.'

2.2 Oath of a party declaring the value of an object and renouncing any right to contest it:

Features: cursory dated and delocutive record (except for the quotation of a locutive oath), formulaic style, only the promising party named, valuated price, with short pre-material introducing the oath (tag clause, *assertory* and *promissory* oath, without penalty), without mention of forum, before a witness or the addressee (?). The register is mostly degree 1 Neo-Egyptian with one degree 2 form in the oath.

Example: *oDeM* 56, 20th dynasty, Ramesses III (*KRI* V, 502 n.220 A102)[894]: see *supra*.

2.3 Guarantee of future payment, restitution, or delivery on time[895] by the debtor:

Features: brief dated delocutive record (except for the quotation of a locutive oath), sometimes with formal arachaic anaphora, formulaic style, both parties named, term of payment/delivery, oath (tag clause, penalty). The register is mostly degree 1 Neo-Egyptian for the pre-material, but degree 2 in the body of the text (oath). Of course, the oath acknowledges the existence of an inexecuted obligation, its main concern being to guarantee its timely execution. Sometimes litigation is alluded to[896] or a court may be mentioned[897], and there are many examples of this type of oath in records of court proceedings[898].

Example[899]: *oDeM* 57, 20th dynasty, Ramesses III (*KRI* V, 554 n.227 A192)[900]:

892 But Janssen (1975: 169) notes: 'record of a legal proceeding concerning a donkey' and in (2005: 46) classifies the text in his category of 'Sales Transactions?'.

893 Allam (1967b: 48 and 1973: 249-50): in the context of a sale, 'Quittung' and oath as both 'Verzichts- od. Abstandserklärung' and 'Eviktionsklausel'

894 Malinine (1947: 111): 'partie de l'acte authentique de vente proprement dite'; Lurje (1971: 184): 'Eidliche Bestätigung des Verkaufs eines Ochsen'; Allam (1967b: 48): 'Quittung' concerning the payment with warranty disposition of the vendor marking the transfer of ownership; Donker van Heel & Haring (2003: 171-5): 'oath' as a genre of texts with heading formula # date + *ꜥnḫ n nb ꜥ.w.s. ḏd.n* PN #.

895 This category of oaths taken by the debtor to guarantee the timely execution of his obligation (in operations such as credit, hire, loan, deposit, etc.) is reminiscent of the abnormal hieratic and early Demotic contractual dispositions expressed as a unilateral declaration of the debtor before witnesses, with or without an oath, but making the same guarantee (Malinine 1953). See also Depauw (1997: 147) concerning Demotic loans of money formulated as the acknowledgement of a debt.

896 With use of *smi* (*oIFAO* 388, *oIFAO* 290, *oDeM* 433); the debtor is made to swear (*oIFAO* 765).

897 *oMichaelides* 1.

898 For example *oBerlin* P 10655, *oCairo* CG 25553.

899 See also e.g. ***oDeM* 61**, 19th dynasty, Ramesses II ('Gelddarlehen,' 'Entwurf zu einem Schuldanerkenntnis' for Lurje 1971: 165, 182; 'Vereinbarung eines Rechtsgeschäfts (...) wo ein Schuldner seiner Gläubiger eine Leistung zu erbringen verschpricht' for Allam 1973b: 24; loan of fungible goods for Menu 1982: 230, 236-7); ***oDeM* 58**, 19th dynasty, Ramesses II ('Entwurf zu einem Schuldanerkenntnis' for Lurje 1971: 182; 'oath'

Date + *iryw* PN *ꜥnḫ n nb ꜥ.w.s. r ḏbꜣw n idnw* PN *r-rꜥ ḥb Ḏḥwty mtw.i tm ir ḥtm n.f pꜣ ḥḏ nty m-di.f*
(Date). PN took an oath of (the) Lord L.P.H. for (the) payment to (the) deputy PN until (the) festival of Thot: 'Should I not do (so)', the money[901] that is in his possession must be confiscated for him.

---

as a genre of texts with heading formula # date + *ꜥnḫ n nb ꜥ.w.s. ir.n* PN # for Donker van Heel & Haring 2003: 171-5); ***oDeM* 364**, 20th dynasty, Ramesses III (the delivery term is probably lost and it may belong to an administrative genre; 'prêt d'usage' with no mention of a *consideration* for Menu 1982: 254; 'just a brief note, not a real oath' for Donker van Heel & Haring 2003: 172; oath/promise concerning a donkey for Janssen 2005: 26); ***oDeM* 564**, 20th dynasty, Ramesses III (contractual oath for Menu 1982: 229; 'oath' as a genre of texts with heading formula # date + *ḏdt.n* PN # for Donker van Heel & Haring 2003: 171-5); ***oDeM* 782**, 20th dynasty, Ramesses III (the term of payment must have been mentioned in the lacuna; 'oath' as a genre of texts with heading formula # date + *hrw pn irt ꜥnḫ n nb ꜥ.w.s. in* # and *r ḏbꜣ* for Donker van Heel & Haring 2003: 171-5; oath/promise concerning a donkey for Janssen 2005: 26); ***oGardiner/Ashmolean* 106**, 20th dynasty, Ramesses III ('Kauf oder Miete' for Allam 1973: 173-4, but he admits in 1973b: 29 that the oath may conclude a litigation; 'oath' as a genre of texts with heading formula # date + *ḏd.n* PN # for Donker van Heel & Haring 2003: 171-5; oath/promise concerning a donkey for Janssen 2005: 24-5); ***oGardiner/Ashmolean* 68** (?), 20th dynasty, Ramesses III (the term is not expressed; oath before a court in order to obtain the payment of work already done for Allam 1973: 166-7; category IV of 19th dynasty manufacture of products for Janssen 1975: 502); ***oMichaelides* 1**, 20th dynasty, Ramesses III ('Kreditkauf' with oath before the court in the context of a dispute or the court's intervention in order to guarantee the seller for Allam 1973: 204-5; dispute settlement for McDowell 1990: 64-5; 'court proceedings record' with heading formula # date + *hrw pn ḏd ir.n* PN *m-bꜣḥ tꜣ ḳnbt* # without the initial complaint but with an oath and list of court members, about the payment of a donkey, for Donker van Heel & Haring 2003: 162-7; oath/promise concerning a donkey for Janssen 2005: 28); ***oMichaelides* 2**, 20th dynasty, Ramesses III (the delivery term is probably lost; 'Aktennotizen in denen die Verborgung "aktenkundig" gemacht wird' where the name of the owner is not given, thus 'Quittung (…) die in der Hand des Eigentümers blieb' for Helck 1961-70: 295-6); ***oAG* 77**, 20th dynasty, Ramesses III-V (oath/promise concerning a donkey for Janssen 2005: 23); ***oTurin* 57389** (?), 20th dynasty, Ramesses III-V(term probably lost; too damaged, but mention of a court); ***oIFAO* 290**, 20th dynasty, Ramesses IV? (oath/promise concerning a donkey for Janssen 2005: 26-7); ***oDeM* 433**, 20th dynasty, Ramesses IV (legal dispute for Janssen 1975: 492; 'serment judiciaire' following the creditor's action for Menu 1982: 229; 'record of a court hearing' concerning a trade for McDowell 1990: 7-8; 'court proceedings record' with heading formula # date + *smi in* PN PN *r-ḏd* # and an oath for Donker van Heel & Haring 2003: 162-7); ***oPetrie* 67 = *oUC* 32054**, 20th dynasty, Ramesses IV-VI (oath that may conclude a litigation for Allam 1973b: 33; contractual oath for Menu 1982: 229; 'oath' as a genre of texts with heading formula # date + *ḏdt.n* PN # for Donker van Heel & Haring 2003: 171-5); ***oIFAO* 388**, 20th dynasty, Ramesses V (oath that may conclude a litigation for Allam 1973b: 68; may be a court case with no mention of *ḳnbt* for McDowell 1990: 144; 'court proceedings record' with heading formula # date + *smi in* PN # and an oath for Donker van Heel & Haring 2003: 162-7); ***oGardiner/Ashmolean* 137**, 20th dynasty, Ramesses V (an oath that may conclude a litigation for Allam 1973b: 29; perhaps a loan of fungible goods for Menu 1982: 237-9; business dispute for McDowell 1990: 135; 'oath' as a genre of texts with heading formula # date + *iry* PN *ḥnꜥ* PN *ꜥnḫ n nb* # for Donker van Heel & Haring 2003: 171-5); ***oIFAO* 765**, 20th dynasty, Ramesses V? (oath/promise concerning a donkey for Janssen 2005: 27); ***oDeM* 59**, 20th dynasty ('contrat, très rudimentaire, pourrait être interprété comme un prêt' or a deposit of fungible goods for Menu 1982: 234-5); ***oDeM* 245**, mid-20th dynasty? (the term of payment is probably in lacuna; 'Prozeβakt' for Helck 1961-70: 491, 493-4; 'Rechtsstreit zwischen Vermieter V und Mieter M über einen Esel' for Allam 1973: 111-2; 'prêt d'usage' mentioning a *consideration* for Menu 1982: 263-4; oath/promise concerning a donkey for Janssen 2005: 25-6).

900 Malinine (1947: 111): 'simple brouillon' or 'fragment' 'd'un acte de prêt' ; Lurje (1971: 183): 'Entwurf zu einem Schuldanerkenntnis'; Menu (1982: 233-4): 'prestation à effectuer en échange d'une autre déjà reçue', 'paiement différé' concerning fungible goods; Donker van Heel & Haring (2003: 171-5): 'oath' as a genre of texts with heading formula # date + *iry* PN *ꜥnḫ n nb ꜥ.w.s.* #.

901 *ḥḏ*: 'silver' for 'money, payment' (Peet 1932; Janssen 1975: 499-501), 'valeur' and 'moyen de payement' (Théodoridès 1969 : 185-8), 'Leistung' (Allam 1967), 'contrepartie versée en échange d'une chose' (Menu 2004: 226); *consideration.*

2.4 General warranty against claims: oath of a donkey transmitter on the day of the *traditio*

Features: brief dated delocutive record (except for the quotation of a locutive oath), sometimes with formal archaic anaphora (the date of the transmission), formulaic style, both parties named, object (donkey), oath (tag clause, general warranty using *bn ʿḥʿ rmṯ nb/wʿ ḥr pḥwy.f m dw3 s3 dw3*[902], penalty), witnesses, use of the lexeme *sw3ḏ* (*traditio*), sometimes mention of a *consideration* (valuated price). A litigation procedure[903] may be mentioned, or the penalty of the double[904]. The register is mostly degree 1 Neo-Egyptian for the pre-material, but degree 2 in the body of the text. The transmission relates to a sale (depending mostly on the extent of the *consideration*, but it is not always expressed), as none of the records is expressly related to hire in some way (some of them are badly damaged).

Example[905]: *oDeM* 62, 20th dynasty, Ramesses III (*KRI* V, 527 n.223 A141)[906]:

Date + *hrw pn* [*s*]*w3ḏ p3 ʿ3t* [*n rm*]*ṯ ist* PN [*n in-*]*mw* PN [*r swnt*].*f m dbn* (?) *n ḥmt r* […] PN *r-*[*š3*]*ʿ dw3* […] *iry.f* [*ʿnḫ n nb ʿ.w.s.*] *r-ḏd bn ʿḥʿ rmṯ nbt ḥr pḥ{t}wy.f m dw3* […]*ḏb3 sw ʿn i.n.f m-b3ḥ* [*mtrw*?]
(Date), this day of handing over the donkey [of the work]man PN [to the] water[-carrier] PN [for] its [price] consisting of (?) *dbn* of copper for […] PN u[nt]il tomorrow (?) […]. He took [an oath of the Lord L.P.H.] saying: 'Nobody shall stand on its back in (the) future; [should he do so, I am] paying it back,' so he said before [witnesses?].

3. Locutive elements in records

3.1 Private memos and accounts concerning animal transfers, or administrative notes of a scribe in function?

Features: brief dated record mostly without archaic anaphora, only one party named, object transmitted, formulaic style; sometimes with narrative texteme, computations of hire days with totals (with or without *r b3kw.f* or *r sk3*), lists of valuated items offered in payment, accounting terms, abbreviations and diacritical marks; absence of notification formula or performative form, no mention of witnesses or forum. The register is mostly degree 1 Neo-Egyptian for the pre-material, but degree 2 in the body of the text. The notes relate to transmissions (*rdi, ini, iṯ3, nḥm*) of hired animals. Only in one case is an oath mentioned[907].

---

902 Except in *oTurin* 57159, where it is probably in lacuna. Note that similar oaths are attested in trials (see e.g. *oAshmolean* 1933.810 and *oGardiner/Ashmolean* 182).

903 See *smi*in *oGardiner/Ashmolean* 196.

904 In *oGardiner/Ashmolean* 196.

905 See also e.g. ***oGardiner/Ashmolean* 196**, 20th dynasty, Ramesses III (but *traditio* not mentioned; 'Kauf' for Allam 1973b: 18 or oath that may settle litigation in Allam 1994: 25; 'oath' as a genre of texts with heading formula # date + *ʿnḫ n nb ʿ.w.s. ḏd.n* PN #, 'resembles a record of court proceedings' for Donker van Heel & Haring 2003: 171-5; oath/promise concerning a donkey for Janssen 2005: 25); ***oIFAO* 1403**, 20th dynasty, Ramesses IV-V(sale (?) for Janssen 2005: 45); ***oTurin* 57159** (?), 20th dynasty, Ramesses III (sale (?) for Janssen 2005: 46).

906 Lurje (1971: 185): 'Mietvertrag'; Allam (1973: 86): 'Akt der Übergabe eines Esels', 'Kauf' and (1973b: 24): 'Eid im Zusammenhang mit einer Vereinbarung (...) um die Verzichts- und die Eviktionsklausel (...) zu bekräftigen'; Janssen (1975: 169): 'bill of sale for a donkey', also in (2005: 44); Donker van Heel & Haring (2003: 159-62): 'record of donkey hire' with heading formula # date + *hrw pn swḏ p3 ʿ3 n* PN *n* PN #, with oath.

907 *oPetrie* 34.

The status of the narrator cannot be established with certainty: is it a private owner of animals for hire[908] or a scribe representing the administration[909] keeping track of assets perhaps belonging to the state?

Example[910]: *oIFAO* 1425, 20th dynasty, Ramesses VI (*KRI* VI, 372 n.51 A16):

Date + *dit pꜣ*  *n* PN *r skꜣ iw.f intw.f n.i m* + date [... *iw.f*] *ẖry* [...] *sw* 8 *wḥm ditw.f* [...*m*] date *iw.f intw.f* + date *ir n sw* 15
(Date), giving the [bovine] to PN for ploughing; and he brought it back[911] to me on (date) [... it was] under [...] 8 days.
Again giving it [...on] (date); and he brought it back (on date), making 15 days.

3.2 Business accounts concerning manufactured goods: private memos, accounts relating to a legal or administrative procedure, workshop records?

Features: generally dated record without archaic anaphora, one or two parties named (in which case it is not clear if the narrator is one of them), object (manufactured goods, sometimes with *bꜣkw* and/or *iri*) transmitted or due (*rdi, šsp, swn,* work *nty m-di* PN, *ꜣḫt n* PN$_1$ *nty m-di* PN$_2$), formulaic style, sometimes with narrative texteme or notification formula, lists of

908 Only in *oPetrie* 2 is the possessive determinator used with the object of the record: 'And I gave my donkey for its service'.

909 Explaining the use of the archaic anaphora in *oPetrie* 2 and *oDeM* 619?

910 See also e.g. ***oMunich* 1547 v°** (?), 19th dynasty, Ramesses II ('may originally also have contained the contract of the sale of a donkey' of category VI for Janssen 1975: 504 n.52 but donkey hire or sale for Janssen 2005: 22-3); ***oDeM* 557**, 20th dynasty, Ramesses III ('Miete eines Esels' for Allam 1973: 130-1; 'prêt d'usage' mentioning a *consideration* for Menu 1982: 263); ***oStrasbourg* H 182**, 20th dynasty, Ramesses III ('record of donkey hire' with heading formula # date + (*hrw pn*) *dit pꜣ ꜥꜣ n* PN #, in which the transfer, the length of the hire period and the payment are noted for Donker van Heel & Haring 2003: 159 n. 143; donkey hire for Janssen 2005: 16); ***oDeM* 67**, 20th dynasty, Ramesses III ('Aktennotizen' 'Quittung' for Helck 1961-70: 295-6; 'record of donkey hire' with heading formula # date + (*hrw pn*) *dit pꜣ ꜥꜣ n* PN *r bꜣkw.f* #, omitting the name of the lessor but with deposition that no payment was made for Donker van Heel & Haring 2003: 159-62; a settled debt of category VII for Janssen 1975: 507 and donkey hire for Janssen 2005: 8); ***oGardiner/Ashmolean* 261**, 20th dynasty, Ramesses III (but (erroneous?) allocutive form; 'record of donkey hire' with heading formula # date + (*hrw pn*) *dit pꜣ ꜥꜣ n* PN #, in which the transfer and the length of the hire period are noted for Donker van Heel & Haring 2003: 159 n. 143; donkey hire or sale for Janssen 2005: 17); ***oDeM* 305**, 20th dynasty, Ramesses III ('Aktennotizen' 'Quittung' for Helck 1961-70: 295-6); ***oPetrie* 34**, 20th dynasty, Ramesses III (with mention of the debtor's oath guaranteeing payment on time, perhaps in litigation context; 'Eselmiete' for Allam 1973: 239-40, 1973b: 24, and Lurje 1971: 185; 'prêt d'usage' mentioning a *consideration* for Menu 1982: 261; 'record of donkey hire' with heading formula # date + *hrw n dit pꜣ ꜥꜣ n* PN *r skꜣ* #, without the lessor's name, probably in a legal dispute for Donker van Heel & Haring 2003: 159-62); ***oGardiner/Ashmolean* 152**, 20th dynasty, Ramesses III ('Tausch- bzw. Kaufvereinbarung', a 'Kreditgeschäft' for Allam 1973: 181-2; sale (?) for Janssen 2005: 43); ***oDeM* 619**, 20th dynasty, Ramesses III-IV(with archaic anaphora; 'prêt d'usage' mentioning a *consideration* for Menu 1982: 262; 'record of donkey hire' with heading formula # date + (*hrw pn*) *dit pꜣ ꜥꜣ n* PN *r bꜣkw.f* #, omitting the name of the lessor for Donker van Heel & Haring 2003: 159-62); ***oAG* 55**, 20th dynasty, Ramesses IV-VII (with two parties named; donkey hire for Janssen 2005: 4); ***oPetrie* 2**, 20th dynasty, Ramesses IV-VI (with archaic anaphora; 'Aktennotizen' 'Quittung' for Helck 1961-70: 295-6; 'prêt d'usage' not mentioning a *consideration* for Menu 1982: 257; 'record of donkey hire' with heading formula # date + *hrw pn iṯꜣ ir.n* PN *pꜣ ꜥꜣ* #, without the name of the lessor for Donker van Heel & Haring 2003: 159-62).

911 For *ini* 'to bring back', see Janssen (2005: 75): 'if a sale is recorded *ini* means simply "to bring", whereas if an animal is hired, it is the return to the owner which is expressed by *ini*.'

valuated items offered in payment (with or without *r-ḏbꜣ*, *ḥḏ n*), accounting terms and abbreviations; absence of performative form, no mention of witnesses or forum. The register is mostly degree 1 Neo-Egyptian for the pre-material, but degree 2 in the body of the text. There is no evidence of a dispute in these records; they may constitute private memos (when the narrator is not named and there is no notification formula), accounts relating to some legal or bureaucratic procedure[912], workshop records involving craftsmen[913]. In some cases locutive elements may relate to a scribe in an official function establishing an administrative record involving him in transactions of manufactured goods.

Example[914]: *oDeM* 556, 20th dynasty, Ramesses III (*KRI* V, 592 n.233 A 271)[915]:

---

912 For instance *oDeM* 556 with its notification formula.

913 Cooney (2007: 46-50).

914 See also e.g. ***oMichaelides* 13**, 19th dynasty, Merneptah (transactions with record of goods, the ostracon serving as a 'Buchführung' for Allam 1973: 209-10; 'pure barter transaction' of category I for Janssen 1975: 510; workshop record 'mentioning the private sector funerary arts market' for Cooney 2006: 44 n.12; 2007: 50, 335-7); ***oBrooklyn* 37.1880** and ***oBM* EA 5644**, 19th dynasty, Merneptah/Siptah (but *oBM* 5644 does not use the locutive mode and for the dating, see Demarée 2002: 20; Janssen's category I 'barter'; *oBM* EA 5644 is an 'account of payment' headed by the formula # *rdyt n* PN *in* PN *r ḏbꜣ* # for Donker van Heel & Haring 2003: 153-7; 'multi-transaction' receipt 'mentioning the private sector funerary arts market' for Cooney 2006: 44 n.14; 2007: 57, 314-5); ***oMichaelides* 14**, 19th dynasty, Seti II (transactions with record of goods, the ostracon serving as a 'Buchführung' for Allam 1973: 211-2; case of joint property of category I for Janssen 1975: 532; 'account of payment' headed by the formula # *rdyt n* PN *in* PN *r ḏbꜣ* # for Donker van Heel & Haring 2003: 153-7; 'multi-transaction' receipt 'mentioning the private sector funerary arts market' for Cooney 2006: 44 n.14; 2007: 58, 90, 337-8); ***oLouvre* E 3263**, 19th dynasty, Ramesses II (Janssen's category I 'barter'; 'account of transfer' headed by the classical formula # *rdyt* PN *n* PN # with both parties names, list of goods and their value, perhaps a payment for work done for Donker van Heel & Haring 2003: 148-53); ***oDeM* 261**, 20th dynasty, Ramesses III (Janssen's category VII notification of debt and 'open credit system' for Janssen 1994: 132; 'account of debt' headed by # *r rdit rḫ.tw ꜣḫt n* PN *nty m-di/ꜥ* PN # with no date mentioned but indicating the names of the parties and a list of goods with their quantities for Donker van Heel & Haring 2003: 146-8); ***oDeM* 428**, 20th dynasty, Ramesses III (Janssen's category VII notification of debt and 'open credit system' for Janssen 1994: 133; 'account of debt' headed by a # *ꜣḫt n* PN *nty m-di/ꜥ* PN # formula with no date mentioned but indicating the names of the parties and a list of goods with their quantities, an abbreviated form of the notification of debt formula for Donker van Heel & Haring 2003: 146-8); ***oDeM* 232** (?), 20th dynasty, Ramesses III (Janssen's category VII notification of debt); ***oDeM* 579** (?), 20th dynasty, Ramesses III (Janssen's category II 'barter' notification (?); 'account of transfer' headed on the recto by # *rdyt* PN # with only the giver's name and a list of goods, the verso headed by # *r dit rḫ.tw ꜣḫt nb i.swn.i* # with a list of goods and their value, perhaps without connection, for Donker van Heel & Haring 2003: 148-53; 'multi-transaction' receipt 'mentioning the private sector funerary arts market' for Cooney 2006: 44 n.14; 2007: 58, 331-2); ***oBM* EA 5633**, 20th dynasty, Ramesses III? (Janssen's category II 'barter' notification (?); 'multi-transaction' receipt 'mentioning the private sector funerary arts market' for Cooney 2006: 44 n.14; 2007: 57, 85, 310); ***oGlasgow* D 1925.70**, 20th dynasty, Ramesses IV (Janssen's category II 'barter' notification (?); 'Zusammenstellung von Leistungen' for Allam 1973: 79-80; 'account of transfer' headed by the notification formula # *r rdit rḫ.tw ꜣḫt nb i.di* PN *n* PN # with both parties named, list of goods and their value for Donker van Heel & Haring 2003: 148-53); ***oGardiner/Ashmolean* 119**, 20th dynasty, Ramesses IV (Janssen's category V of 20th dynasty manufacture of products; workshop record 'mentioning the private sector funerary arts market' for Cooney 2006: 44 n.12, 2007: 49, 88, 290); ***oBerlin* P 12343**, 20th dynasty, Ramesses IV (mentions a transaction dealt with in *oGardiner/Ashmolean* 136; Janssen's categories V of 20th dynasty manufacture of products and VII (notification of debt); exchange between carpenter and painter for McDowell 1999: 81-2; workshop record 'mentioning the private sector funerary arts market' for Cooney 2006: 44 n.12; 2007: 44-5, 49, 89-90, 126, 147-8, 304-6); ***oGardiner/Ashmolean* 135**, 20th dynasty, Ramesses IV? (joint property for joint manufacture for Janssen 1975: 532; 'account of transfer' headed by # (date +) *šsp m-ḏrt* PN (*in* PN) # with middlemen named but not the giver, list of goods and their value, a payment for Donker van Heel & Haring 2003: 148-53); ***oBM* 50737**, mid-20th dynasty; ***oBM* 50736**, 20th dynasty, Ramesses VI (Janssen's category V of 20th dynasty manufacture of products); ***oDeM* 146**, 20th dynasty, Ramesses IX (Janssen's category V of 20th dynasty manufacture of products; 'carpenter's bill' for McDowell 1999: 80; workshop record 'mentioning

r rdit rḫ.tw ꜣḫt nb i.diw rmṯ ist PN *n ḥmww* PN *r pꜣ wt wꜣw n st-ḥmt ink sw m ḫt* + list of items with valuation in *dbn*. For information (relative to) all assets that gave (the) workman PN to (the) carpenter PN for the *wt wꜣw* of (this) woman of mine, it being (made) of wood: (list).

3.3 Narratives in contentious legal genre?

Features: dated records (sometimes with archaic anaphora), one or two parties named but the locutor is not necessarily one of them, object (transmission of an animal or item, payment sometimes with *r-ḏbꜣ* and lists of items), formulaic style, some of these records are constructed with a notification formula[916], accounting terms, and abbreviations. Features of *recital* such as locutive narrative, *ḫr ptr*, allocutive elements, quotations, introduction formula with *ḏd/rꜣ n* PN, background elements of transactions; but absence of *ir ink*, forum, witnesses, oath, or verdict. The register is mostly degree 1 Neo-Egyptian for the pre-material, but degree 2 in the body of the text.

Example[917]: *oGardiner/Ashmolean* 140, 20th dynasty, Ramesses III (*KRI* V, 490-1 n.219 A 81)[918]:

Date + *hrw pn dit tꜣ ꜥꜣt n ḥry-mḏꜣy* PN *in ꜥꜣ n ist* PN *r-ḏd ḫꜣꜥ st ḥr rsy ḫry nꜣ wdnw n Rꜥttꜣwy ḫr ir* [...] *iw.f dit* [*in*]*tw n.i nꜣy.i ḫꜣr* ½ *iw.i* [...] date + *ḏdw* (*iry-*)*ꜥꜣ* PN *hꜣbw ꜥꜣ n ist* PN *n ḥry-mḏꜣy* PN *m-ḏd imi didy.tw n.i tꜣy.i ꜥꜣt i.diw.i n.k iw.st iwrti* [*ḫr*] *ptr in*(*.i*) *st iwrti iw.k* [...]

---

the private sector funerary arts market' with the amount due in *dbn* for Cooney 2006: 44 n.12, 45; 2007: 47, 50, 86, 145, 323-4); ***oGardiner/Ashmolean* 105**, 20th dynasty? (Janssen's category III 'barter' notification; 'account of payment' headed by the notification formula # *r rdit rḫ.tw pꜣ ḥḏ i.di n.i* PN *r ḏbꜣ* # for Donker van Heel & Haring 2003: 153-7; workshop record 'mentioning the private sector funerary arts market' for Cooney 2006: 44 n.12; 2007: 49, 105, 93, 289-90); ***oGardiner/Ashmolean* 39**, 20th dynasty? (Janssen's category II 'barter' notification (?); 'account of payment' headed by a variant of the notification formula # *r rdit rḫ.tw ꜣḫt nb i.di* PN *n* PN *r* #, the recipient's name being absent for Donker van Heel & Haring 2003: 153-7); ***oDeM* 767**, 20th dynasty? (but without names).

915 Janssen's category II ('barter' notification?); Donker van Heel & Haring (2003: 153-7) 'account of payment' headed by the notification formula # *r rdit rḫ.tw ꜣḫt nb i.di* PN *n* PN *r* # with both parties named, payments for the production of goods; Cooney (2006: 44 n.13, 2007: 54, 331): 'receipts mentioning the private sector funerary arts market'.

916 For example *oCairo CGC* 25612, *oDeM* 319 and many more. Janssen (1975: 497-502) considers that the choice of the formula is a question of the scribe's personal habits only in records of sale.

917 See also e.g. ***oDeM* 319**, 19th dynasty, Seti II; ***oDeM* 933**, 19th dynasty, Seti II/Siptah (payment for undisclosed item/service, or in the context of a loan; promise of payment with interest (*mst*) for Grandet 2003: 370); ***oCairo CGC* 25612**, 19th dynasty? ('claimant's deposition written down for his own use or to be submitted to the authorities' for McDowell 1990: 18 n.37; 'deposition' with heading formula # *r n* PN (*tw.i dit rḫ*) # introducing an account, perhaps of division, for Donker van Heel & Haring 2003: 167-71and gift of assets about which the entire community is informed for Haring 2003: 150-1); ***oMichaelides* 5**, 20th dynasty, Ramesses III ('Miete' for Allam 1973: 206-7; 'record of donkey hire' with heading formula # date + *swḏ pꜣ ꜥꜣ n* PN *n* PN *r dit.f n* PN #, with notification of payment for Donker van Heel & Haring 2003: 159-62); ***oAshmolean* 1945.39**, 20th dynasty, Ramesses III (Janssen's category II 'barter' notification (?); 'Leistungen und Forderungen des einen Geschäftspartners gegenüber dem anderen' for Allam 1973: 24-6 and 'Klageschrift' in the context of a dispute in 1973b: 13 n.15; 'account of payment' headed by a variant of the notification formula # *r rdit rḫ.tw ꜣḫt nb i.di* PN *n* PN *r* # with both parties named for Donker van Heel & Haring 2003: 153-7; 'receipts mentioning the private sector funerary arts market' for Cooney 2006: 44 n.13; 2007: 53, 285); ***oCairo CGC* 25722** (?), 20th dynasty.

918 Allam (1973: 180-1 and 1973b: 41): dispute; Donker van Heel & Haring (2003: 159-62): 'record of donkey hire' with heading formula # date + *hrw pn dit tꜣ ꜥꜣt n* PN *in* PN #, with names of both parties.

(Date), this day of giving the she-ass to (the) chief policeman PN by (the) chief workman PN saying: 'Leave it in (the) south charged with the offerings for *Rꜥtt3wy*.' And as for [...] he caused that one should bring to me my ½ *ẖ3r*; and I [...]. (Date, the) doorkeeper PN said: '(The) chief workman PN sent (a message) to (the) chief policeman PN saying: "Let one give to me my she-ass that I gave to you while it was in foal. [But] see, I brought it when it was in foal and you [...]"'

4. Delocutive records concerning animal transfers without mention of *consideration*[919]

4.1 Administrative record keeping track of animals belonging to the administration?

Features: brief[920] dated note (sometimes with archaic anaphora), only the recipient named (usually a member of the service personnel *smdt*, but also scribes and workmen), object (transmission of an animal expressed by *rdi, ini, swḏ, šsp, nḥm,* usually with mention of *r b3kw.f*), formulaic style; no mention of *consideration*, accounting, notification, dispute, forum, oath, witnesses. Of course, some of the texts may also be brief private records in order to keep track of privately owned animals. The register is mostly degree 1 Neo-Egyptian.

Example[921]: *oDeM* 400, 20th dynasty, Ramesses III (*KRI* V, 554 n.227 A191)[922]:

Date + *dit p3 ꜥ3t n sš* PN *n p3 ẖr* (Date), giving the donkey to (the) scribe of the Tomb PN.

919 Note that Janssen (1975: 496-7) assumes a sale even in the case of a simple *rdyt n.f*/PN unless 'the payment is being made for work.' For Menu (1982: 265-6), when no *consideration* is mentioned (even with *r b3kw.f*), the lender may be the administration; the mention of the lender must concern an intermediary between the community and the recipient.

920 Donker van Heel & Haring (2003: 159) note that it is 'the briefest variant that represents the actual hire as a textual genre', while 'further elaborations tend to transform the deposition about the hire itself into the starting-point of different type of text, e.g. an account or a record of court proceedings.'

921 See also e.g. ***oDeM* 63**, 19th dynasty and ***oDeM* 64** and **65**, 20th dynasty, Ramesses III ('Aktennotizen' 'Quittung' for Helck 1961-70: 295-6; 'prêt d'usage' not mentioning a *consideration* for Menu 1982: 255, 251-2; 'brief note on donkey hire' for Donker van Heel & Haring 2003: 159 n. 143 and for Janssen 2005: 7-8); ***oDeM* 72**, 20th dynasty, Ramesses III ('Aktennotizen' 'Quittung' for Helck 1961-70: 295-6; 'prêt d'usage' not mentioning a *consideration* for Menu 1982: 250-1; 'brief note on donkey hire' for Donker van Heel & Haring 2003: 159 n. 143; donkey hire or sale for Janssen 2005: 19); ***oDeM* 425**, 20th dynasty, Ramesses III (with only the name of the person to whom the donkey was brought; 'prêt d'usage' not mentioning a *consideration* for Menu 1982: 255; donkey hire or sale, an exceptional case of a record of 'the return of the animal and the name of the owner' for Janssen 2005: 20); ***oDeM* 632**, 20th dynasty, Ramesses III-V? (but with one narrative form; 'record of donkey hire' with heading formula # date + (*hrw pn*) *dit p3 ꜥ3 n* PN *r b3kw.f* #, omitting the name of the lessor for Donker van Heel & Haring 2003: 159-62; donkey hire for Janssen 2005: 12-3); ***oDeM* 774**, 20th dynasty, Ramesses III-V('brief note on donkey hire' for Donker van Heel & Haring 2003: 159 n. 143; donkey hire or sale for Janssen 2005: 21); ***oDeM* 66**, 20th dynasty, Ramesses IV (with goods for tending it; 'Aktennotizen' 'Quittung' for Helck 1961-70: 295-6; 'prêt d'usage' mentioning a *consideration* for Menu 1982: 259-60; 'record of donkey hire' with a variant of heading # date + *dit p3 ꜥ3 n* PN #, where only the transfer and the payment are noted for Donker van Heel & Haring 2003: 159 n. 143; donkey hire or sale for Janssen 2005: 18); ***oGardiner/Ashmolean* 121** and ***oDeM* 71**, 20th dynasty, Ramesses IV ('Aktennotizen' 'Quittung' for Helck 1961-70: 295-6; 'prêt d'usage' not mentioning a *consideration* for Menu 1982: 251; 'brief note on donkey hire' for Donker van Heel & Haring 2003: 159 n. 143 and Janssen 2005: 4, 9); ***oOIC* 16994** (?), 20th dynasty, Ramesses IX-XI (donkey hire or sale for Janssen 2005: 18).

922 Menu (1982: 252): 'prêt d'usage' not mentioning a *consideration* ; Janssen (2005: 19-20): donkey hire or sale.

In some cases[923], a hire period is added (*ir n/iw.f irt hrw* x), perhaps a sign of an onerous private transaction.

4.2 Administrative record keeping track of animals privately owned?

Features: brief dated record (sometimes with archaic anaphora), both parties named[924], object (transmission of an animal expressed by *rdi, iṯꜣ, ini, nḥm* usually with mention of *r bꜣkw.f* and sometimes with hire period or delivery agent with # *m-ḏrt* PN #), formulaic style; no mention of *consideration*, accounting, notification, dispute, forum, oath, witnesses (except for *oGardiner/Ashmolean* 185 and when a middleman is involved). The presence of names of both parties and cases of archaic anaphora, of mention of witnesses or recording scribe make the classification as a private memo unlikely. The register is mostly degree 1 Neo-Egyptian.

Example[925]: *oCairo CG* 25557, 20th dynasty, Ramesses III (*KRI* V, 569 n.231 A 228)[926]:

923 See e.g. ***oDeM* 407, 53** and **70**, 20th dynasty, Ramesses IV ('Aktennotizen' 'Quittung' for Helck 1961-70: 295-6; 'prêt d'usage' not mentioning a *consideration* for Menu 1982: 252-5; 'record of donkey hire' with variant of heading formula # date + (*hrw pn*) *dit pꜣ ꜥꜣ n* PN *r bꜣkw.f* #, omitting the name of the lessor for Donker van Heel & Haring 2003: 159-62; donkey hire for Janssen 2005: 7, 9, 10); ***oPetrie* 78**, 20th dynasty, Ramesses III ('Eselkontrakt' for Helck 1961-70: 872; 'prêt d'usage' not mentioning a *consideration* for Menu 1982: 253-4; 'record of donkey hire' with heading formula # date + *dit pꜣ ꜥꜣ n* PN #, where only the transfer and the hire period are noted for Donker van Heel & Haring 2003: 159 n. 143); ***oDeM* 432**, 20th dynasty, Ramesses III (with a report of the animal's death following mistreatment; 'Eselkontrakt' for Helck 1961-70: 872).

924 Sometimes the object is specifically described as owned by one of the parties ('the donkey of PN' or 'giving his donkey' e.g. *oCairo CG* 25557, *oGardiner/Ashmolean* 185, *oDeM* 451, *oGardiner/Ashmolean* 128); but in other cases the transmitter may be an intermediary between the community and the recipient (Menu 1982: 265).

925 See also e.g. ***oGardiner/Ashmolean* 185**, 20th dynasty, Ramesses III ('brief note on donkey hire' with mention of witnesses for Donker van Heel & Haring 2003: 159 n. 143 and for Janssen 2005: 5 'the only text of a simple transfer which records witnesses; hence it seems to be a real contract'); ***oDeM* 68**, 20th dynasty, Ramesses III ('Aktennotizen' 'Quittung' for Helck 1961-70: 295-6; 'prêt d'usage' not mentioning a *consideration* for Menu 1982: 253; 'brief note on donkey hire' for Donker van Heel & Haring 2003: 159 n. 143; donkey hire or sale for Janssen 2005: 19); ***oDeM* 451**, 20th dynasty, Ramesses III (with hire period; 'Aktennotizen' 'Quittung' for Helck 1961-70: 295-6; 'prêt d'usage' not mentioning a *consideration* for Menu 1982: 257-8; 'record of donkey hire' with heading # date + *hrw pn dit i.ir* PN *pꜣy.f ꜥꜣ r bꜣkw.f n* PN # for Donker van Heel & Haring 2003: 159-62; donkey hire for Janssen 2005: 10-1); ***oTurin* 57151**, 20th dynasty, Ramesses III (donkey hire or sale for Janssen 2005: 23); ***oDeM* 779**, 20th dynasty, Ramesses III ('brief note on donkey hire' for Donker van Heel & Haring 2003: 159 n. 143 and Janssen 2005: 13-4); ***oMichaelides* 84**, 20th dynasty, Ramesses III ('Aktennotizen' 'Quittung' for Helck 1961-70: 295-6; donkey hire or sale for Janssen 2005: 22); ***oDeM* 648**, 20th dynasty, Ramesses III ('prêt d'usage' not mentioning a *consideration* for Menu 1982: 255-6; 'brief note on donkey hire' for Donker van Heel & Haring 2003: 159 n. 143 and Janssen 2005: 13); ***oDeM* 963**, 20th dynasty, Ramesses III; ***oDeM* 702**, 20th dynasty, Ramesses III-IV ('prêt d'usage' not mentioning a *consideration* for Menu 1982: 256; 'brief note on donkey hire' for Donker van Heel & Haring 2003: 159 n. 143; donkey hire or sale for Janssen 2005: 21); ***oDeM* 959**, 20th dynasty, Ramesses III-IV (with unrelated (?) locutive form on the verso; donkey hire for Janssen 2005: 14-5); ***oGardiner/Ashmolean* 128**, 20th dynasty, Ramesses IV ('Aktennotizen' 'Quittung' for Helck 1961-70: 295-6; 'prêt d'usage' not mentioning a *consideration* for Menu 1982: 257; 'brief note on donkey hire' for Donker van Heel & Haring 2003: 159 n. 143 and Janssen 2005: 4-5); ***oMichaelides* 3**, 20th dynasty, Ramesses V-VI (the scribe is named in brief colophon; 'brief note on donkey hire' for Donker van Heel & Haring 2003: 159 n. 143 and Janssen 2005: 15).

926 Menu (1982: 256): 'prêt d'usage' not mentioning a *consideration* ; Donker van Heel & Haring (2003: 159 n. 143): 'brief note on donkey hire'; Janssen (2005: 5-6): donkey hire.

Date + *hrw pn dit pꜣ ꜥꜣt n* PN *n šꜥd-ḫt* PN *r-bꜣkw.f* (Date), this day of giving the donkey of PN to (the) woodcutter PN for his service/rent.

5. Delocutive records concerning onerous transactions: private memos and accounts, or administrative records?

These documents are difficult to assess. They have in common the delocutive mode and the mention of a *consideration*[927] for the transfer of objects in the context of hiring, sale/exchange, workshop production, and contract labor.

5.1 Only one party named

Features: delocutive record sometimes dated (rarely with archaic anaphora or reign that would indicate a more formal record), only one party named (buyer or seller of manufactured good, recipient of animal)[928], object (transmission expressed by *rdi, šsp, ini, iṯꜣ,* of manufactured goods or of an animal, sometimes with mention of *r bꜣkw.f/skꜣ*, hire period, rent per day, or delivery agent), *consideration*[929] (*r šꜥꜣyr, mtnw, ḥḏ, r-ḏbꜣ, r šbt,* lists of valuated[930] commodities and manufactured goods); formulaic style, sometimes accounting terms, abbreviations, diacritical marks, and use of bichromy[931], narrative forms, notification formula[932]; no mention of forum, witnesses (except for delivery agents), oaths, disputes. The register is mostly degree 1 Neo-Egyptian for the pre-material, but degree 2 in the body of the text.

Example[933]: *oCairo CG* 25604, 20th dynasty, Ramesses III (*KRI* V, 526 n.223 A137)[934]:

---

927 Janssen (1975: 495-7) deals with transactions formulated with the help of the key-words *r ḏbꜣ* as 'the simplest formula' for sales (his first category of transactions formulae), but admits variants lacking *r ḏbꜣ* such as *rdyt* (PN) *n* PN. He notes that sometimes only one party's name is mentioned, without seeing any opposition between the one PN and 2 PN formulae.

928 For Eyre (1984: 204), such documents are 'essentially receipts which remained in the hands of the owners, and tend only to name the costumers'.

929 Payment in full or partial payment with mention of amount still due.

930 Cooney (2007: 65-6) suggests that the price equivalent in *dbn* or grain of funerary art noted without a list of commodities given in payment may indicate a workshop record relating to the commission of the item as opposed to a receipt listing the precise nature of commodities given in payment.

931 See *oDeM* 553.

932 In *oTurin* 57368, *oDeM* 423.

933 See also e.g. ***oDeM* 49**, 19th dynasty, Ramesses II (with locutive quotation at the end of the text; 'Kauf von Erzeugnissen handwerklicher Arbeit', 'Zahlungsurkunde' for Lurje 1971: 186; Janssen's categories IV of 19th dynasty manufacture of products and VII of debt notification; 'Zahlung' for work for Allam 1973: 81; 'account of payment' headed by a variant of # *rdyt n* PN *in* PN *r ḏbꜣ* # with only one party named for Donker van Heel & Haring 2003: 153-7; workshop record and 'multi-transaction' receipt 'mentioning the private sector funerary arts market' for Cooney 2006: 44 n.12 & 14; 2007: 50, 58, 86, 94, 322); ***oDeM* 31**, 19th dynasty, Ramesses II (formally dated with reign and archaic anaphora; Janssen's category I 'barter'; 'Rechnung (…) im Rahmen eines Kreditgeschäfts' for Allam 1973: 80-1; workshop record 'mentioning the private sector funerary arts market' for Cooney 2006: 44 n.12; 2007: 50, 85-6, 321); ***oDeM* 928**, 19th dynasty (with archaic anaphora); ***oDeM* 242**, 19th dynasty ('Aktennotizen' 'Quittung' for Helck 1961-70: 295-6; probably hire of a donkey for Janssen 2005: 60-1); ***oOIC* 19154 = *oEdgerton* 10**, 20th dynasty, Ramesses III (dispute about a donkey for Janssen 1975: 169, donkey hire in Janssen 2005: 6); ***oGardiner/Ashmolean* 154**, 20th dynasty, Ramesses III ('brief note on donkey hire' for Donker van Heel & Haring 2003: 159 n. 143; donkey hire or sale for Janssen 2005: 16); ***oTurin* 57362** (?), 20th dynasty, Ramesses III; ***oTurin* 57368**, 20th dynasty, Ramesses III (Janssen's category III 'barter' notification; 'account of transfer' headed by the notification formula # *r rdit rḫ.tw pꜣ ḥḏ i.di* PN *n* PN # with only one name, list of goods and their value, a payment for work done for Donker van Heel & Haring 2003: 148-53;

Date + *dit tꜣ ꜥꜣt n (iry-)ꜥꜣw* PN *r pꜣy.st šꜥꜣyr* (Date), giving of the she-ass to (the) doorkeeper PN for its price.

5.2 Both parties originally named

Features: delocutive record usually dated (and sometimes with archaic anaphora), both parties named (or more parties present); object produced (*iri*), transmitted or due (*rdi, šsp, ini, iṯꜣ, nḥm, ꜣḫt n* PN_1 *nty m-di* PN_2 of manufactured goods, servant, or of an animal, sometimes with mention of *r bꜣkw.f/skꜣ*, hire period, rent, or delivery agent), mentioning a

'receipts mentioning the private sector funerary arts market' for Cooney 2006: 44 n.13; 2007: 54, 87, 91-2, 350-1); ***oBM* EA 5649**, 20th dynasty, Ramesses III (Janssen's category VI sale; 'account of payment' headed by a unique formula # *rdyt r ḏbꜣ pꜣ iḥ in.n* PN #, with the name of the seller only for Donker van Heel & Haring 2003: 153-7; 'receipts mentioning the private sector funerary arts market' for Cooney 2006: 44 n.13; 2007: 52-3, 85, 311); ***oGardiner/Ashmolean* 44**, 20th dynasty, Ramesses III (2nd name lost?; Janssen's category I 'barter'; 'receipts mentioning the private sector funerary arts market' for Cooney 2006: 44 n.13; 2007: 52-3, 287-8); ***oDeM* 553**, 20th dynasty, Ramesses III (Janssen's category I 'barter'; 'account of payment' headed by the formula # *rdyt n* PN *r ḏbꜣ* # for Donker van Heel & Haring 2003: 153-7; 'receipts mentioning the private sector funerary arts market' for Cooney 2006: 44 n.13; 2007: 54, 96, 149, 330-1); ***oDeM* 73 v°**, 20th dynasty, Ramesses III (no PN on the verso, recto related?; receipt for the delivery of a coffin of category I 'barter' for Janssen 1975: 10; 'account of payment' headed by # *rdyt n.f r ḏbꜣ* # without naming the parties involved for Donker van Heel & Haring 2003: 153-7; 'receipts mentioning the private sector funerary arts market' for Cooney 2006: 44 n.13; 2007: 53, 146, 323); ***oDeM* 423**, 20th dynasty, Ramesses III ('account of transfer' headed by # *r rdit rḫ.tw pꜣ ḥḏ i.di* PN *n* PN # with both parties names, list of goods and their value, perhaps a payment for work done for Donker van Heel & Haring 2003: 148-53); ***oIFAO* 389**, 20th dynasty, Ramesses III ('Werkvertrag' for Allam 1973: 196; 'account of payment' headed by a unique formula # *nty n* PN *r ḏbꜣ* #, mentioning only the seller's name for Donker van Heel & Haring 2003: 153-7); ***oTurin* 57457** (?), 20th dynasty, Ramesses III-IV; ***oDeM* 958**, 20th dynasty, Ramesses III-IV (donkey hire or sale for Janssen 2005: 22); ***oDeM* 113**, 20th dynasty, Ramesses IV ('Kaufurkunde' for Lurje 1971: 186; concerns *snw* 'account (?)' for Janssen 1975: 508-9; 'account of payment' headed by the unique formula # date + *swn n* PN *ḥr pꜣ iḥ* #, with the name of the seller only for Donker van Heel & Haring 2003: 153-7); ***oMichaelides* 6**, 20th dynasty, Ramesses IV (first loan made by an unnamed party; 'Sammelbericht' of a loan, payment of a salary (?), and 'Memorandum über die Verteilung (?) von Gegenständen durch Staatliche Funktionäre', an original document of 'eine amtliche Eintragung der staatlichen Ausgabestelle' for Allam 1973: 207-8; 'account of payment' headed by # *rdyt n* PN *r ḏbꜣ* # for Donker van Heel & Haring 2003: 153-7); ***oCairo* CG 25590**, 20th dynasty, Ramesses IV (Janssen's category I 'barter'; 'Kreditgeschäft', 'Rechnung' for one of the parties for Allam 1973: 66; 'account of payment' headed by # *rdyt n* PN *r ḏbꜣ* # for Donker van Heel & Haring 2003: 153-7); ***oMichaelides* 8** (?), 20th dynasty, Ramesses IV (it is difficult to assess the role of the PNs in the transactions; Janssen's category II 'barter' notification (?); 'account of payment' headed by a variant of the notification formula # *r rdit rḫ.tw ꜣḫt nb i.di* PN *n* PN *r* # without the parties' names for Donker van Heel & Haring 2003: 153-7); ***oGardiner/Ashmolean* 260**, 20th dynasty, Ramesses IV-VII? ('brief note on donkey hire' with mention of hire rate for Donker van Heel & Haring 2003: 159 n. 143 and Janssen 2005: 5); ***oDeM* 780** (?), 20th dynasty, Ramesses IV-V (donkey hire for Janssen 2005: 14); ***oDeM* 1068 r°**, 20th dynasty, Ramesses V? (donkey hire for Lurje 1971: 184, Neveu 1986: 152, McDowell 1999: 86, and Janssen 2005: 15); ***pBeatty* I v° D = *pBM* 10681**, 20th dynasty, Ramesses V (with archaic anaphora; 'Geschäftsnotizen' for Seidl 1957: 53; 'Quittung über die Zahlung des Wertes eines Ochsen' for Lurje 1971: 185 and Allam 1973: 293-4; 'sale of an ox' for Janssen 1975: 94); ***oDeM* 960**, mid-20th dynasty (only delivery agent named?; sale (?) for Janssen 2005: 45); ***oDeM* 185**, 20th dynasty (but without PN; 'receipt' for sale of a produced item for Toivari-Viitala 2001: 127; 'account of payment' in an exchange of garments for Donker van Heel & Haring 2003: 158); ***oDeM* 772**, 20th dynasty? ('account of payment' headed by # *rdyt n* PN *r ḏbꜣ* # for Donker van Heel & Haring 2003: 153-7); ***oDeM* 930, 931** and **949**, 20th dynasty? (no names preserved); ***oDeM* 962** (?), 20th dynasty? (no names; payment receipt for Grandet 2003: 413).

934 Donker van Heel & Haring (2003: 159 n. 143): 'brief note on donkey hire'; Janssen (2005: 17-8): donkey hire or sale.

consideration[935] ((*r tꜣ*) *mtnw*, *ḥḏ*, *r-ḏbꜣ*, *r swnt*, lists of sometimes valuated commodities and manufactured goods); formulaic style, sometimes accounting terms, abbreviations, and conventional marks, narrative forms, notification formula[936], mention of witnesses[937], but no mention of forum, oaths, disputes. The register is mostly degree 1 Neo-Egyptian for the pre-material, but degree 2 in the body of the text.

Example: *oBerlin* P 1268 r°, 20th dynasty, Ramesses III (*KRI* VII, 284-5 n.268 A 358)[938]:

Date + *mity*[939] *n pꜣ ḥḏ n tꜣ ꜥꜣt n* PN *in{n} in-mw* PN *n rmṯ ist* PN (items) + *ir.n sš-ḳd* PN *m pr sš* PN + *dmḏ* (Date), copy record of the money for the she-ass of PN that brought (the) water-carrier PN to (the) workman PN: (list). It is in (the) scribe PN's house that (the) draughtsman PN made (it). Total: (valuation).[940]

935 Payment in full or partial payment with mention of amount still due. Sometimes the value of the manufactured goods is noted without express mention of any payment made or due (e.g. *oGardiner/Ashmolean* 136).

936 For example *oDeM* 244, *oDeM* 399, *oGardiner/Ashmolean* 126.

937 For example *oDeM* 410.

938 Janssen's category VI (sale); Donker van Heel & Haring (2003: 148-53) 'account of transfer' headed by a later variant of the classical formula # date + *mity n pꜣ nkt rdi.n* PN *n* PN # with a list of goods and their value, a payment, and p. 96: 'account of payment'; Cooney (2006: 44 n.14; 2007: 57, 96, 302-3) 'multi-transaction' receipt 'mentioning the private sector funerary arts market'.

939 Internal characterization of the instrument's value. For the discussion of the lexeme, see Donker van Heel & Haring (2003: 94-7) concluding that 'The copy in question may be the (single) written version of an oral statement or the recording of any type of information, so that its meaning is weakened to 'text''.

940 See also e.g. ***oDeM* 233**, 19th dynasty, Ramesses II (characterized as *mitt*, dated with reign; 'Kauf von Erzeugnissen handwerklicher Arbeit', 'Bezahlung für die Anfertigung eines Sarges' for Lurje 1971: 186; Janssen's category IV of 19th dynasty manufacture of products; 'account of transfer' headed by # date + *mity n pꜣ nkt rdi.n* PN *n* PN # with a list of goods and their value, a payment for Donker van Heel & Haring 2003: 148-53; 'receipts mentioning the private sector funerary arts market' for Cooney 2006: 44 n.13; 2007: 54, 73-4, 97, 159, 328-9); ***oDeM* 50**, 19th dynasty, Ramesses II (Janssen's category IV of 19th dynasty manufacture of products); ***oGardiner/Ashmolean* 133**, 19th dynasty, Ramesses II (with one locutive suffix; 'account of payment' headed by # *rdyt.n* PN *n* PN *r ḏbꜣ* # for Donker van Heel & Haring 2003: 153-7; 'multi-transaction' receipt 'mentioning the private sector funerary arts market' for Cooney 2006: 44 n.14; 2007: 56-7, 93, 290-2); ***oBM* 65935**, 19th dynasty, Merneptah-Seti II (Janssen's category IV of 19th dynasty manufacture of products); ***oGardiner/Ashmolean* 123**, 19th dynasty, Amenmesse ('Bezahlung einer Sklavenmiete' for Allam 1973b: 20 and 1996: 198; Janssen's category III 'barter' notification; 'Receipt of payment' for Toivari-Viitala 2001: 42); ***oVarille* 13**, 19th dynasty, Amenmesse (with one locutive determinator?; Janssen's category IV of 19th dynasty manufacture of products; workshop record 'mentioning the private sector funerary arts market' for Cooney 2006: 44 n.12; 2007: 42, 50, 97, 144-5, 354-5); ***oDeM* 215**, 19th dynasty, Siptah-Tausert (Janssen's category IV of 19th dynasty manufacture of products; 'account of payment' headed by a variant of # *rdyt.n* PN *n* PN *r ḏbꜣ* # for Donker van Heel & Haring 2003: 153-7; 'receipts mentioning the private sector funerary arts market' for Cooney 2006: 44 n.13; 2007: 40, 53, 67, 326); ***oGardiner/Ashmolean* 9**, 19th dynasty; ***oDeM* 244**, 20th dynasty, Ramesses III ('Aktennotizen' 'Quittung' for Helck 1961-70: 295-6; 'prêt d'usage' mentioning a *consideration* for Menu 1982: 258; 'record of donkey hire' headed by # date + *hrw pn itꜣ pꜣ ꜥꜣ n* PN *r bꜣkw.f m* #, with notification of payment account for Donker van Heel & Haring 2003: 159-62; donkey hire for Janssen 2005: 11); ***oDeM* 410**, 20th dynasty, Ramesses III (Janssen's category I 'barter'; 'account of payment' headed by # *rdyt n* PN *in* PN *r ḏbꜣ* # for Donker van Heel & Haring 2003: 153-7); ***oDeM* 424**, 20th dynasty, Ramesses III ('Aktennotizen' 'Quittung' for Helck 1961-70: 295-6; 'record of donkey hire' headed by # date + *hrw pn dit ir.n* PN *tꜣ ꜥꜣt n* PN #, with names of both parties, followed by an account of payment for Donker van Heel & Haring 2003: 159-62; donkey hire or sale for Janssen 2005: 20); ***oTurin* 57150**, 20th dynasty, Ramesses III (Janssen's category VI sale); ***oAberdeen* 1317 v°**, 20th dynasty, Ramesses III (but with brief locutive narrative on recto; Janssen's category I 'barter' and 'open credit system' in 1994: 134; 'Tausch' for Allam 1973: 17; 'account of transfer' headed by # *rdyt* PN *n* PN # with both parties names, a list of goods and their value, an 'account

of payment' headed by # *rdyt* PN *n* PN *r ḏbȝ* # for Donker van Heel & Haring 2003: 148-57); ***oGardiner/Ashmolean* 103** (second part on the verso), 20th dynasty, Ramesses III (Janssen's category I 'barter'; sale 'account of payment' headed by # *rdyt.n* PN *n* PN *r ḏbȝ* # for Donker van Heel & Haring 2003: 153-7); ***oGardiner/Ashmolean* 126**, 20th dynasty, Ramesses III (Janssen's category III 'barter' notification; 'account of payment' headed by the notification formula # *r rdit rḫ.tw pȝ ḥḏ i.di* PN *n* PN *r ḏbȝ* # for Donker van Heel & Haring 2003: 153-7); ***oGardiner/Ashmolean* 162**, 20th dynasty, Ramesses III (Janssen's categories II 'barter' notification (?) and VII notification of debt, 'open credit system' for Janssen 1994: 131; 'account of transfer' headed by the notification formula # *r rdit rḫ.tw ȝḫt nb i.di* PN *n* PN # with both parties' names, a list of goods and their value, also recording a debt for Donker van Heel & Haring 2003: 148-53; 'multi-transaction' receipt 'mentioning the private sector funerary arts market' for Cooney 2006: 44 n.14; 2007: 55-7, 84, 297); ***oBerlin* P 10626**, 20th dynasty, Ramesses III (Janssen's category VII of notification of debt); ***oDeM* 671** and **765**, 20th dynasty, Ramesses III-IV ('prêt d'usage' mentioning a *consideration* for Menu 1982: 258-9; 'account of debt' based on Janssen's (1994) 'open credit system' and headed by a variation of # *r rdit rḫ.tw ȝḫt n* PN *nty m-di/ꜥ* PN # with no date mentioned, but with the names of the parties and a list of goods with their quantities for Donker van Heel & Haring 2003: 146-8); ***oDeM* 775** (?), 20th dynasty, Ramesses III-V? ('brief note on donkey hire' for Donker van Heel & Haring 2003: 159 n. 143); ***oLeiden* F 2002/10.1**, 20th dynasty, Ramesses III-VI (oath/promise concerning a donkey for Janssen 2005: 27, but the promise is not formulated as an oath; sale for Demarée 2008: 89); ***oDeM* 627** (?), 20th dynasty, Ramesses III-IV (donkey hire for Janssen 2005: 12); ***oTurin* 57456**, 20th dynasty, after Ramesses III? ('records the sale of an ox' for McDowell 1999: 74-5; 'account of transfer' headed by # date + *rdyt n* PN *in* PN # with both parties' names, a list of goods and their value, a sale for Donker van Heel & Haring 2003: 148-53); ***oGardiner/Ashmolean* 136**, 20th dynasty, Ramesses III-IV (*oBerlin* P 12343 mentions some of the work done here; Janssen's category V of 20th dynasty manufacture of products; workshop record 'mentioning the private sector funerary arts market' kept by that artisan to keep track of his craftwork for several clients for Cooney 2006: 44 n.12; 2007: 45, 49, 88-9, 97, 100, 103-4, 126, 144, 293-4); ***oDeM* 195** and ***oBerlin [D]***, 20th dynasty, Ramesses IV ('Dem Zimmermann diente unser Ostrakon folglich zur Buchführung' for Allam 1973: 74; Janssen's category I 'barter'; receipt of purchase for Toivari-Viitala 2001: 39; 'account of transfer' headed by # *rdyt* PN *n* PN # with both parties names, a list of goods and their value, perhaps a payment for work done for Donker van Heel & Haring 2003: 148-53); ***oPetrie* 3 = *oUC* 39606**, 20th dynasty, Ramesses IV ('Receipt for the sale of an ox' of category VI for Janssen 1975: 9); ***oVienna* H 2**, 20th dynasty, Ramesses IV (Janssen's category VI sale; 'receipts mentioning the private sector funerary arts market' for Cooney 2006: 44 n.13; 2007: 54, 87, 355); ***oBerlin* P 11260**, 20th dynasty, Ramesses IV (exchange of craftsmanship; Janssen's category V of 20th dynasty manufacture of products; workshop record 'mentioning the private sector funerary arts market' for Cooney 2006: 44 n.12; 2007: 46, 49, 89, 104, 119, 157, 303-4); ***oBerlin* P 14262, 14357 ('C')** and **14365**, 20th dynasty, Ramesses IV (only one party named and *oBerlin* P 14365 is a locutive version; Janssen's category III 'barter' notification; 'account of payment' headed by the notification formula # *r rdit rḫ.tw pȝ ḥḏ i.di* PN *n* PN *r ḏbȝ* #, perhaps records of proceedings for each party for Donker van Heel & Haring 2003: 27 n.150, 153-7); ***oDeM* 402**, 20th dynasty, Ramesses IV (Janssen's category VII of notification of debt and 'open credit system' for Janssen 1994: 132; 'account of debt' headed by # *r rdit rḫ.tw ȝḫt n* PN *nty m-di/ꜥ* PN # with no date mentioned (but not in this case!), with the names of the parties and a list of goods with their quantities for Donker van Heel & Haring 2003: 146-8; 'multi-transaction' receipt 'mentioning the private sector funerary arts market' for Cooney 2006: 44 n.14; 2007: 58); ***oOIC* 19123**, 20th dynasty, Ramesses IV (donkey hire for Janssen 2005: 6); ***oDeM* 781**, 20th dynasty, Ramesses IV-IX ('brief note on donkey hire' for Donker van Heel & Haring 2003: 159 n. 143; donkey hire or sale for Janssen 2005: 21); ***oDeM* 399**, 20th dynasty, Ramesses V (Janssen's category III 'barter' notification; 'account of payment' headed by the notification formula # *r rdit rḫ.tw pȝ ḥḏ i.di* PN *n* PN *r ḏbȝ* # for Donker van Heel & Haring 2003: 153-7; 'receipts mentioning the private sector funerary arts market' for Cooney 2006: 44 n.13; 2007: 54, 71, 329-30); ***oGardiner/Ashmolean* 66**, 20th dynasty, Ramesses V ('Kauf' for Allam 1973: 165; Janssen's category I 'barter'); ***oDeM* 255**, 20th dynasty, Ramesses V (Janssen's category V of 20th dynasty manufacture of products); ***oGardiner/Ashmolean* 33 v°**, 20th dynasty, Ramesses V (Janssen's category VII of notification of debt and 'open credit system' for Janssen 1994: 133; 'account of transfer' headed by the notification formula # *r rdit rḫ.tw pȝ ḥḏ i.di* PN *n* PN # with both parties names, a list of goods and their value, a unique (?) case of debt with that type of heading for Donker van Heel & Haring 2003: 148-53); ***oGardiner/Ashmolean* 163**, 20th dynasty, Ramesses V ('Buchführung' for one of the parties concerning payments for Allam 1973: 103, 182-3; Janssen's categories II and III sale notification (?); 'account of payment' headed by a variant of the notification formula # *r rdit rḫ.tw ȝḫt nb i.di* PN *n* PN *r* # with both parties named for Donker van Heel & Haring 2003: 153-7; workshop record 'mentioning the private sector funerary arts market' for Cooney 2006: 44 n.12; 2007: 49, 70, 84, 142, 297-8); ***oGardiner/Ashmolean* 204**, 20th dynasty, Ramesses V ('Schuld', 'Teiltilgung eines Darlehens durch eine Schuldnerin' for Allam 1973: 189-90 and 1973b: 20; Janssen's category VII of notification of debt and 'open credit system' for Janssen 1994: 129-30; 'multi-transaction' receipt 'mentioning the private sector funerary arts market' for Cooney 2006: 44 n.14; 2007: 54, 57, 84, 300); ***oPetrie* 17**, 20th dynasty, Ramesses V (Janssen's category V of 20th dynasty manufacture of products; workshop record 'mentioning the private sector funerary arts market' for Cooney 2006: 44 n.12; 2007: 50, 78, 93, 345-6); ***oBerlin* P 10665**, 20th dynasty, Ramesses V? (Janssen's category III 'barter' notification; 'Zahlungen' for Allam 1973: 32-3; 'account of transfer' headed by the notification formula # *r rdit rḫ.tw pꜣ ḥḏ i.di* PN *n* PN # with both parties' names, a list of goods and their value, with payment formula using *rdi r ḏbꜣ* for Donker van Heel & Haring 2003: 148-53); ***oDeM* 624**, 20th dynasty, Ramesses IV-V? ('verbriefte Miete' by an ostracon that 'als Urkunde aufbewahrt wurde' for Allam 1973: 143-4; 'prêt d'usage' mentioning a *consideration* for Menu 1982: 261-2; 'Breaking the lease' and record of 'interim transaction' for McDowell 1999: 86-7; 'record of donkey hire' headed by # date + *dit ꜥꜣ n* PN *n* PN *r bꜣkw.f* # for Donker van Heel & Haring 2003: 159-62; donkey hire for Janssen 2005: 11-2); ***oDeM* 69**, 20th dynasty, Ramesses VI ('Aktennotizen' 'Quittung', 'Eselkontrakt' for Helck 1961-70: 295-6, 872; 'prêt d'usage' mentioning a *consideration* for Menu 1982: 260; 'record of donkey hire' headed by # *dit pꜣ ꜥꜣ n* PN *n* PN *r bꜣkw.f ḥnꜥ* #, omitting the date, but with payment received for Donker van Heel & Haring 2003: 159-62; donkey hire for Janssen 2005: 8-9); ***oDeM* 403**, 20th dynasty, Ramesses VI (Janssen's category VII of notification of debt; 'account of debt' based on Janssen's (1994) 'open credit system' and headed by a # *ꜣḫt n* PN *nty m-di/ꜥ* PN # with no date mentioned, but with the names of the parties and a list of goods with their quantities, an abbreviated form of the notification of debt formula for Donker van Heel & Haring 2003: 146-8); ***oDeM* 593**, 20th dynasty, Ramesses VI (one PN missing?; 'Grundstücksverkauf' for Helck 1961-70: 345; sale for Janssen 1975: 396); ***oStrasbourg* H 84**, 20th dynasty, Ramesses VII (Janssen's category V of 20th dynasty manufacture of products; workshop record 'mentioning the private sector funerary arts market' for Cooney 2006: 44 n.12; 2007: 48, 50, 90, 347-9); ***pTurin* 2024, 2052** and **2077**, 20th dynasty, Ramesses IX (verso 4 related to *pTurin* 2082 Giornale 17B 8); ***pTurin* 2082 (Giornale 17B) v° 8-9**, 20th dynasty, Ramesses IX ('facture détaillée de l'équipement funéraire commandé par une chanteuse d'Amon à un scribe de la Tombe et (...) de l'achat en commun de bovidés par l'Equipe' for Valbelle 1985: 81; workshop record 'mentioning the private sector funerary arts market' for Cooney 2006: 44 n.12); ***oBerlin* P 12405**, 20th dynasty, Ramesses IX-XI (Janssen's category II 'barter' notification (?); workshop record 'mentioning the private sector funerary arts market' for Cooney 2006: 44 n.12; 2007: 46, 49, 152, 306-7, adding in 2006: 51 that it is 'partly a receipt and partly a workshop record'); ***oPetrie* 51**, 20th dynasty, Ramesses VI-XI ('credit position' of a person 'to prove to a third party' one's ability to make an expensive purchase, category VII notification of debt for Janssen 1975: 507-8, and 'open credit system' in Janssen 1994: 129-30; 'account of debt' headed by # *ꜣḫt n* PN *nty m-di/ꜥ* PN # with no date mentioned, but with the names of the parties and a list of goods with their value, an abbreviated form of the notification of debt formula for Donker van Heel & Haring 2003: 146-8); ***oBM* EA 65941 = *oNash* 4**, 20th dynasty (Janssen's category VII of notification of debt and 'open credit system' for Janssen 1994: 133-4; 'transaction receipt mentioning the private sector funerary arts market' for Cooney 2007: 55, 57, 92, 312-3).

Occurences of classifiers in the Ramesside private law instruments

The abbreviation for the text corresponds to its category (WG for wills and gifts, P for partitions) followed by its number in the chapter. Note that the definition of the classifier and the name of the category adopted here relate exclusively to the lexemes and categories as they appear in our Ramesside corpus.

Abbreviations:

WG I = *oDeM* 108
WG II = *oGardiner/Ashmolean* 90
WG III = *oGardiner/Ashmolean* 55
WG IV = *oGardiner/Ashmolean* 272
WG V = *pAshmolean Museum* 1945.97 & 1945.95 and *pDeM* 23 & 25 (*Naunakhte*)
WG VI = *pBoulaq* 10
WG VII = *oPetrie* 18
WG VIII = *pAshmolean Museum* 1945.96 (*pAdoptions*)
WG IX = *pTurin* 2021 r° and *pGeneva* D 409
P I = *oGardiner/Ashmolean* 89
P II = *oLouvre* E 13156
P III = *oDeM* 112 and 964
P IV = *oBerlin* P 12636 v°
P V = *oDeM* 586
P VI = *pDeM* 30
P VII = *pTurin* 2070 v°, col. II
P VIII = *pTurin* 1885 v°

Relation classifier/ category	**Lexeme classified**	**Translation**	**Occurrences in texts**	**Alternative**
𓏛 - Y1 (papyrus roll) metonymic/metaph. classifier of [ABSTRACT] superordinate categ.	*(ꜣ)ḫt*	assets, material property	WG I; WG III; WG V; WG VI; WG VII; WG VIII; WG IX; P IV; P VIII	

Relation classifier/ category	**Lexeme classified**	**Translation**	**Occurrences in texts**	**Alternative**
	m-b3ḥ	in presence of, before	WG I; WG IX	
	(r) rdit rḫ.tw/k	to let know, for information (relative to)	WGII; WG V; WG VI; WG IX; P IV; P VII	
	grg-pr	establishment, equipment	WG V	
	m-mitt, iri mitt m	conform, to act in conformity with	WG V; WG IX	
	(iri) m-mitt	(to make a) copy	WG IX	
	(r-)ḫry (sḫ)	liable to (a beating)	WG V; WG VI; P VII	ø WG VII
	nfrw	Good, Right, Justice	WG VI	
	sʿnḫ	to maintain, sustain	WG VIII	
	(iri) sḫrw	(to make) provisions	WG IX	
	mn	to record, fix	WG IX	
	mdn	to be inscribed, carved	P II	
	ḳnbt ʿ3t	high court	WG IX	
	wḏ3t	balance,arrears, deficit	P IV	
	m3ʿt(tw)	to be right	WG IX	
 - G41 (alighting bird) metonymic/metaph. classifier of [HALT?] basic level categ. +	*wsfy*	to suppress, void (provisions)	WG IX	
 - A24 metonymic/metaph. classifier of [COERCION] superordinate categ.	*iṯi (iwʿt)*	to take, taking (of an inheritance)	P I	
 + 	*(r-)ḏb3(w)*	in payment, exchange, compensation	WG V; WG VI; P VII; P VIII	
	iri spḫr m	to register, publicize as	WG VIII	
 - D40 (arm + stick) metonymic/metaph. classifier of [COERCION] superordinate categ.	*(ini r) swnw*	to acquire for a price	WG VIII	

Relation classifier/ category	Lexeme classified	Translation	Occurrences in texts	Alternative
× - Z9 (crossed sticks) metaphoric classifier of the [UNION/DIVISION] superord. categ. + 𓏛	*p(s)š(t)*	to divide (assets); share	WG I; WG II; WG IV; WG V; WG VIII; WG IX?; P II; P IV	×𓂝 WG III; WG V; WG VI; P VI; P VII; ×𓀜 WG V; 𓏛𓂝 P VIII
× + 𓅪 - G37 (sparrow) metaphoric classifier of the [INFERIORITY/ PERTURBATION] superord. categ.	*šw(y) m (ꜣḫt, pš)*	deprived of (assets, share), disinherited	WG V; WG VI; WG VII?; P VII	
𓏸 - Aa2 (for ×)	*ḥsb*	account, balance	WG I	[𓏛 ?] WG I
𓍱 - V12 (string) metonymic classifier of [BINDING] basic level categ.	*iri hꜣrwy*	to make a dated record of a legal matter	WG V	
	ꜥwty hꜣrwyt	dated record of legal matter, *authentic* act	WG V	
	(iri) sš (n)	(to) record, written provision (on behalf of)	WG V; WG VIII	
	hp	legal norm, law, rule	WG VI	
𓍱 + 𓏛𓀀	*ꜥrḳ ḥr*	to swear about, repudiate?	WG IX	
𓀀 - A1 (seated man) [MALE-HUMAN] superordinate categ.	*ḳnbt*	court	WG V; WG IX	𓀜𓀀 WG VI; 𓏛WG IX
	sr	official, judge	WG VI; WG IX	
	iwꜥt	inheritance	P I	
𓀀+ 𓂭 for 𓂮 - D50 x 2 (2 fingers) metaphoric classifier of the [CONTROLLED ACTIVITIES?] basic level categ.	*mtr*	witness	WG I	ø WG IV; + 𓀀 WG VIII; 𓀀 WG IX
	(m-mitt) ꜥḳꜣ	exactly (conform)	WG V	
𓀀𓁐 - A1 + B1 [BOTH SEXES] superordinate categ.	*hrw n bꜣkw*	workday, day of service (lit. 'day of servants')	WG II	
𓀔 - A17 [CHILDHOOD] superordinate categ. + 𓁐/𓀀	*nmḥy/w*	voiceless, simple (female/male) 'citizen'	WG V; WG VIII	𓀔 WG VIII

Relation classifier/ category	Lexeme classified	Translation	Occurrences in texts	Alternative
𓀁 - A2 [MOUTH LINKED ACTIVITIES] basic level categ.	*thꜣmw*	to claim, summon?	WG III	
	(*iri*) *md*(*w*)*t* (*m*)	to contest, contestation, statement	WG V; WG VIII; WG IX	WG VI
	sẖꜣ n	*memorandum* of	P I	
	wnm	to consume	P VII	
𓂻 - D54 (legs) metonymic/metaph. classifier of [MOTION] superordinate categ.	*ꜥḳ r/hꜣy ḥr pšw/t*	to enter into a share/division, to inherit a share	WG IV; WG V	
	hꜣy (*ḥ*)*r pšt*	to get/inherit a share	WG IX	
	ꜥḳ r [*pr*]	to enter the house of, cohabitate	WG IX	
	(*wḥm*) *sprw* (*r ḳnbt*)	(re)presentation (to the court)	WG V	
	wḫꜣ	to claim	WG VI	
	ꜥḥꜥ	to stand	WG VIII; WG IX	
	iw (*m-bꜣḥ*)	to approach (the vizier)	WG IX	
𓂼 - D55 (inverse of D54)	*pn*(*ꜥ*) (*rꜣ r mdwt*)	to reverse (an undertaking in order to contest)	WG V	𓂡 WG VI; P VII
𓂻 + 𓂾 - D56 (leg) metaphoric classifiers of the [LEGS MOTION] basic level categ.	*rḳi*	to confront	WG VIII	
𓉐 - O1 (house) [HABITAT] superord. categ.	*st*	immovable property	WG V; WG VI; WG VII; P VI; P VII	
	ḫnw (*n pr/ꜣḫt*)	to approach (a house, assets)	WG VII	
𓍗 - U9 (grain container) [GRAIN/MEASURE] basic level categ.	(*iri*) *mꜥḏꜣ* (*irm*)	(to make) *acquets* (with someone)	WG VIII	

Relation classifier/ category	Lexeme classified	Translation	Occurrences in texts	Alternative
ø	*(r)di*	to give, transmit, bequeath	WG I; WG III; WG V; WG VI; WG IX; P I; P IV	*rdyt* 𓏛 WG V; WG VI; P III; P VI; P VIII
	di m ḥr n	to place in sight, commission	WG IX	
	iri	to do, acquire	WG IX	
	iri imyt-pr	to make a (written) deed of transfer	WG I	
	iri ḫrt	to look after	WG V	
	iri ꜥnḫ	to take an oath	WG V; WG VII; P VII	
	iri m rmṯ nmḥw n pꜣ tꜣ n Pr-ꜥꜣ	to elevate to the status of *nmḥw* of the land of Pharaoh	WG VIII	
	iri m šri	to treat as a child, to adopt	WG VIII; WG IX	
	iw.f/N *n* PN	to be for, to belong to	WG I; WG II; WG III; WG V; WG VII	
	ny-sw PN	to belong to	P V	
	rwy	2/3 (the man's share in the community property)	WG III; WG V; WG IX	
	r-3	1/3 (the woman's share in the community property)	WG V; WG IX	
	iri rwy r r-3	to divide the community property	WG IX	
	m-di(t).f	in his possession	WG III; WG VIII; WG IX	
	ini	to bring (in the community property); acquire	WG III; WG V; WG VIII; WG IX	
	ḏd	to say, state, declare; communication, statement	WG II; WG IV; WG V; WG VIII; WG IX	
	sḏm (rꜣ)	hearing (of a deposition, statement)	WG V	𓏛𓀁 WG V; 𓏛 WG VI
	(m)twnw (m-ḥꜣw n)	bonus, advantage (in excess of)	WG IV	𓀁 WG V; *dwny* 𓂻 WG IX
	swꜣḏ (n)	to hand over (to), *traditio*	WG V	𓏛 WG VIII
	dni(t)	share, portion	WG VI; WG IX; P V	𓏛 WG VIII
	m rꜣ wꜥ	unanimously	WG IX	
	tp n (pšw)	detail/ensemble/key of (division)	P II	
[𓏛?]	*smn*	to establish someone	WG IX	
[𓆰?]	*sfyrw*	alimony?	WG IX	

Conclusions

At the conclusion of this *tour d'horizon* of the Ramesside private law instruments, it remains to summarize the material and to compare it with our findings concerning the legal register of the normative genre of Ramesside royal decrees.

During the Ramesside Period, the *consentient legal genre* encompasses exclusively private wills and gift deeds without expressly distinguishing between *inter vivos* and *mortis causa* dispositions. The apparent lack of homogeneity of these documents may be attributable to some discrepancy in the value and nature of the instruments: a number of them, written on papyrus in a more elegant hand than the normal business one, are longer and more complete provisions notarized in court, and thus official finalized productions; on the other hand, records on ostraca are briefer, less orderly, records that may have been excerpts from more extensive official documents, partial records, drafts or copies of provisions. Apart from the brief epistolary testamentary provisions of *oGardiner/Ashmolean* 90, there is no *olographic* will in our corpus; the provisions on ostraca generally record public procedures before witnesses, using a legal register similar to that of the notarial wills.

Thus the *consentient* legal genre must be divided into two subcategories: testamentary and gift dispositions recorded either in letters (merging the *consentient legal* and *epistolary* genres in a *quasi-olographic* deed) or in the context of a public procedure (with some affinities with the *contentious legal* genre); the public record of wills and gifts probably occurs in ticklish cases to prevent already looming litigation[941]. Each subcategory uses a specific textemic and pragmatic structure associated with distinctive linguistic strategies. Apart from the question of the level of completeness of the texts (mainly a papyri versus ostraca issue, although the completeness of the papyri is also sometimes in question), the textemic and lexico-semantic usage in the non-epistolary records is fairly consistent. It is composed of a delocutive expositive *pre-material* texteme (date, title with object or legal step involved, disponor, instrument, beneficiaries, sometimes forum, addressee, and attendant), generally followed by the *recital*, a locutive monologic texteme (narrative preamble and justificatory commentary based on a retributive principle), the *operative part* (main provisions: *descent and distribution* rule, *disposition* of specific bequests/shares or general bequest, specific clauses), in one case a *sanction and authentication* texteme (reported dialogue, *fiat* and final order of the authenticating authority), and a *technical meta-comment* (colophon).

The will or gift deed *sensu stricto* may be preceded by a *title deed* (excerpt of a will or court proceedings) and followed by an addition concerning the outcome of the procedure (assessment in court of the conformity of the written deed with the will of the testator in order to close a probable contestation of the will, thus an addition belonging to the *contentious* legal genre; material partition report concerning the execution of the deed; warranties given by beneficiaries of the distribution or an objector to the deed, again perhaps to settle a dispute). Only in one case is a label attested on the verso for archiving purposes.

Each texteme is associated with a specific syntactic construct corresponding to a particular communicative function.

The expositive *pre-material* of all non-epistolary deeds has features associated with an informative purpose: high frequency of nouns and proper nouns (which may appear in

941 See similar remarks by Greengus (1969: 530) concerning the notorization of Old Babylonian marriage contracts.

hierarchically ordered lists), of nominal verbal forms, and of prepositional phrases, absence of nexus, explicit references including dating (an important feature as the deeds are revocable). During the entire period covered, it is a carefully produced, delocutive, situation-independent texteme, conveying authority through the use of classical high dialect forms, using archaic anaphora/cataphora, relators, classical binomials, and blessing formulae in a formulaic style free of more vernacular prothetic *yod* forms. The general dialectal features are of a degree 1 Neo-Egyptian. Similar features are observable in the date and authority formula of the pre-material of royal decrees. Archaic reference cohesive devices and binomials are also a trademark of modern private deeds, as is their generally context-detached, official-looking, formulaic, and informational pre-material.

The *recital*, an aetiological locutive texteme functioning as a preamble, is introduced before the end of the 20th dynasty by a report tag clause presenting the quotation as a genuine speech of the disponor. It begins with a conventional and brief narrative construct based on a storyline with a predictable structure and formulaic expressions, expounding the causal chain of events that determined the disponor's course of action (the evolution mode). Opening with a conventional marker of personal involvement (*ir ink*), it uses markers of interaction with the public (allocutive reference, humility formulae, deictics), a dynamic verbal style (perfect report, sequential preterit, present), impersonal generalizations, filiation binomials, isotopic and contrasted style, as well as unspecific referents (the texteme is relatively context-dependent). A dramatic climax introduced by *ḫr ptri* opens a commentary segment designed to rationalize and motivate the disponor's decision (the commentary mode); the grounding relies mainly on the present state of vulnerability of the disponor (usually the 'old age argument') and the retributive principle; a so-called 'statutory' ground is added in the case of our last document, *pTurin* 2021 (Ramesses XI's reign), in the form of a cursory general principle expressed by an unnamed king. Again, topicalization, contrast, and isotopy are used to organize and solemnize the motivation, using past, present, and sometimes future forms. This argumentative texteme has a moderately low register (degree 2 Neo-Egyptian), with prothetic *yod* forms (but not exclusively), more appropriate to 'free speech', but it certainly does not reflect the actual speaker's jargon nor his original detailed speech and arguments. The contrasted retributive principle is already in use during the Old Kingdom whereas the old-age argument is to be found during the Middle Kingdom. Contrasted negative-positive style is common in preambles of royal normative decrees from all periods. Narrative preambles are often present in modern normative, consentient, and contentious legal genres.

The *operative part* is the body of legal provisions at issue in the deed. It is presented as a monologue by the disponor (sometimes with perfect report tag clauses) but certainly structured and formatted by the recording authority. The intimate blend of delocutive-objective (formal, of a higher dialect) and locutive-subjective (in some cases with markers of direct interaction with the public, features of involvement) constructions is typical of private legal documents originating in not fully literate societies. Wills are constructed around two temporal poles: immediate present and future. On the one hand, the texteme consists of future delocutive constructions (*descent and distribution* rule, disinheritance, exclusions from estates or assets); the future is usually the only mark of *mortis causa dispositions*. On the other hand, performative constructs (adverbial and present constitutive acts of attribution of ownership right) are used to express a general bequest to a unique legatee, the *disposition* of specific bequests to named legatees, *advancement* and adoption clauses. The performative constructions are either delocutive in the earlier texts (implicit performative (*iw.f/*)N *n* PN), as already during the Old Kingdom, or locutive during the late part of the 20th dynasty (explicit performative *tw.i sḏm* with marker of performativity *m p3 hrw*), although explicit performatives are already recorded in Middle Kingdom testamentary provisions. Other clauses are variously constructed: gifts with *exemption from hotchpot*, general *terrorem* clause (threatening oath using the imprecatory modal prospective), designation of executor, remark based on 'statutory' ground. Once again the focus of the texteme is not narrative or argumentative but informational; the texteme is enunciated in the commentary mode, sometimes with notification formulae, always high noun frequency and topicalization, listing structure for clarity and itemization, categorization of assets, cohesive devices, relatively explicit referentiality (proper names and relative clauses), high specificity. The 'legal' texture is abstract (agentless passives, prominence of inanimate objects of bequests), usually built on contrast and complex sentence structure with embedded restrictions to the rule, and authoritative (high dialect of degree 1 Neo-Egyptian until Ramesses II's reign, then degree 2 with both classical and prothetic *yod* forms, ordered isotopic layout, formulae, strong rhythmic features for solemnity, archaisms such as in one case a *mortis causa* binomial).

A unique *sanction and authentication* texteme appears in *pTurin* 2021 in the form of a reported dialogue between the vizier and the representatives of the legatees; it is the sole texteme using interrogative forms. The disponor does not participate in this segment constructed as a cross-examination in a litigation context followed by the measures taken by the authority; it aims to corroborate facts and verify the understanding of the terms of the will by the legatees as well as their position towards these provisions in order to reinforce a warranty against claims by the legatees, with administrative *fiat*, record order, and copy. The texteme is highly interactive, dialogic (allocutive, questions-answers aimed at collecting facts, imperative), and argumentative (modals, questions for corroboration, and rhetorical questions; use of 'but even if' imaginary scenario in order to make a point). It is probably the product of a careful reworking of the original speeches (no personal stance, highly formal dialogue using archaisms, isotopy, explicitness, agentless impersonal form for generalization, degree 2 Neo-Egyptian), although it uses prothetic *yod* forms in addition to more classical ones embedded in actualized patterns.

The deeds are sometimes concluded by a *meta-comment* texteme, the technical-legal colophon focussing on the procedural context, detached and integrated; it may be extremely laconic, limited to a prepositional phrase mentioning witnesses without naming them (on ostraca), or more specific and limited to a mere mention of the recording scribe (where the document itself is referred to as the object of the commentary) or adding a list of witnesses' names (on papyrus). It usually does not comprise a nexus and the dialect is of a degree 1 Neo-Egyptian.

A unique case of an epistolary document including a testamentary or gift disposition, *oGardiner/Ashmolean* 90, exhibits in its dispositive texteme features observed in the wills and gift deeds: blending of delocutive mode and locutive reference (but with epistolary allocutive notification formulae already in use during the Old and Middle Kingdom), use of retributive principle as grounding, impersonal/agentless passive forms, high frequency of nouns in topicalized structure, implicit performative forms, filiation binomial, reasonably referentially explicit but with context-dependent expressions, formulaic style, relatively high dialect (degree 1 Neo-Egyptian), partly due to its legal topic and partly to its early date.

On the lexical level, consistency in the use of specific terms and combinations is also remarkable throughout the entire corpus; the terms are usually different from the ones used in the normative Ramesside royal decrees as they relate to other topics, but there are examples of common lexemic usage (*i̓myt-pr, ẖt, smn, ḳnbt, i̓ṯi̓, mtr, i̓ri̓ m-mi̓tt, hp, sr, sšw, di̓ m ḥr, m-di̓.f*). The categorization system revealed by the classifiers used with terms of special relevance in the legal register again exhibits a reduced range of categories, and the classifiers are mainly metaphorically related to the lexemes they categorize. The papyrus roll classifier 𓏛 of the superordinate [ABSTRACT/WRITTEN] category is dominant (26 lexemes are classified with 𓏛, of which 18 lexemes are exclusively classified by this classifier in our corpus). Main other categories involved are the following: the categories of [MOTION] (10 lexemes), [MOUTH LINKED ACTIVITIES] (8 lexemes), [MALE-HUMAN], [FEMALE], [CHILDHOOD] (globally 7 lexemes), [COERCION] in remarkably fewer instances than in the Ramesside royal decrees (with only 6 lexemes), [BINDING] (5 lexemes), [UNION/DIVISION] (3 lexemes, often in combination with other classifiers). The 𓅪 metaphoric classifier of the superordinate [INFERIORITY/PERTURBATION] category is used with only one lexeme (*šw*) in the penalty of warranty clauses which are not part of the will or gift deed but of related (contentious) procedures. There are numerous cases of zero-classification in our deeds. It is interesting that most of the terms of special relevance in the legal register are categorized in superordinate categories, as these lexemes usually represent legal abstractions. The opposition oral *vs.* written practice is expressed in the categorization system: some legal activities are categorized as oral with the 𓀁 classifier in the [MOUTH LINKED ACTIVITIES] category (*mtr, th3mw, (iri) md(w)t (m)*), whereas others are typically written and classified by the 𓏛 [ABSTRACT/WRITTEN] or 𓍼 [BINDING] classifiers (*iri m-mitt, iri sḫrw, mn, mdn, wsfy, iri spḫr m, p(s)š, iris š n, iri h3rwy, rdyt, dni*). The combination of orality and script is noted for *ʿrḳ ḥr*𓍼𓏛𓀁 'to swear about' and *sḏm*𓀁𓏛 *r3* 'to hear a deposition'.

Diachronic continuity is observable in the corpus (for instance in the fixed sequence of textemes and in the textemic and lexemic composition), as well as between earlier private deeds and our Ramesside documents (but with an evolution towards a more developed argumentation on the basic retributive principle). Regional variations are not seriously observable based on a unique instance of a non-Theban deed representative of the 'Spermeru dialect' for Groll (1984).

A specific Ramesside private deeds register distinct from the normative register of the Ramesside royal decrees is thus observable: it presents a specific mixture of high and low dialects, parallel but distinct textemic structure, and lexical choices adapted to its legal topic. Thus the subtle blend of classical Middle Egyptian and actualized Neo-Egyptian forms throughout the deeds, in various proportions relative to each texteme, is different from the one observed in the Ramesside royal normative decrees, although nowhere in our corpus or in the normative royal decrees is a degree 3 Neo-Egyptian achieved. The most important difference consists in the integration in the private deeds of prothetic *yod* forms alongside archaic Middle Egyptian ones. Although the *normative* royal decrees (protection/criminal law decrees) of the same period are also composed in a degree 2 Neo-Egyptian register, they never use prothetic *yod* forms. Apart from this important distinction, we observe the same extensive use of phoric determinators and relatively few non-phoric grammaticalized articles (indicative of the relatively high register used). An important common pattern is the topicalization of a nominal segment and its ritualizing repetition; cohesion marks are important in both legal registers, as well as binomials specific to the textual genre (e.g. *ḫwi-mki* in protection/criminal law decrees and *šri*𓀔 *šri*𓁐 binomials in wills and gift deeds). Private bodies' unilateral expressions of will are recorded and thus reconstructed, authenticated and endowed with authority in an appropriate format. Vernacular speeches are censored and the resulting grapholect creates a compromise between the original low dialect of the disponor and its authoritative reception and sanction effected by the use of the script and of high dialect forms.

The communicative purpose of these documents is thus both to objectify and stabilize personal will and to endow them with the legal authority they need to function. In these mixtures of linguistic varieties we have again evidence of a 'cultural diglossia' (Loprieno 1996: 522-3), a tool for discriminating between written genres and registers already observed in the context of our study of the Ramesside royal decrees. In spite of the existence of a specific register associated with our corpus, no *register markers*[942] have been found in the consentient genre; but *register features*[943] have been distinguished. As Jackson (1988: 30-1) notes, 'When one collects together all such features [e.g. nominalisation, binomials] of legal language (I would prefer to say, of legal languages) one approaches an account of the specificity of law, despite the fact that many of these features, taken individually, are features which are also found in other types of discourse.' Biber (1995: 31) remarked that 'Some registers (e.g., legal documents) have well-defined norms so that there is relatively little variation among the texts within the register', and this assertion has been verified in our corpus, although it is less homogenous than the one constituted by the Ramesside normative royal decrees, since private law instruments are less 'crystalized' than public norms emanating from the highest authority.

Most of the records are from the village of Deir el-Medina and its surroundings, whereas the royal decrees were probably composed in Memphis, the administrative capital of Egypt. Meaningful changes have been noted in our corpus: the documents belonging to the later part of the 20th dynasty (*pAdoptions* and *pTurin* 2021) comprise elements previously unnoticed in earlier Ramesside deeds, such as the use of explicit performative forms in the operative part, of a curse to strengthen this performativity (*pAdoptions*), of general principles stated by an unnamed king to conclude the *recital* and the operative part (*pTurin* 2021). Furthermore, the process of authentication of the act is recorded in *pTurin* 2021, thus visible for the first time. All these are indications of an increasing performativity and autonomy of the written text.

Documents associated with wills and gift deeds were also included in our analysis in order to complete the picture and establish distinctions with our material that are not always clear in egyptological researches.

Partition records do not belong to the consentient genre; but they can be associated with accounting documents when they establish a preliminary *allotment* of assets, or to reports relating to the material execution of wills and gifts by actual, physical repartition of the assets. Some may represent administrative records, others notes for private use. The documents are highly informational (with high noun and proper noun frequency, relational expansions, agentless passives, prepositional phrases, quantifiers); they are well organized with isotopic listing layout denoting structural elaboration and use lexemic/graphic dividers, but often lack contextual precision and thus are not completely detached. Usually non narrative, they use a relatively high bureaucratic register of degree 1 or 2 Neo-Egyptian. The textemic structure is composed of a rather brief pre-material (title and/or date, rarely with beneficiaries of the partition or executors, archaic anaphora) followed by the main informative texteme (partition list of assets, sometimes with PN topicalization format, *rdyt/nty n* PN syntagm, or notification formula, accounting features). Additions may follow (renunciation of a beneficiary, *exemption from hotchpot* or mention of debt, warranty of the beneficiaries) using narrative sequential past or perfect report forms.

The so-called *social gifts records* are also not part of the consentient genre and represent a mixed bag of documentary genres (epistolary documents, administrative duty rosters and distribution records, contract-related records, records of regular allowances, etc.). These are

942 Biber (1995: 28): 'distinctive linguistic features found only in particular registers' such as ''count' (balls and strikes) (...) found only in broadcasts of baseball games'; these are 'relatively rare'.

943 *Ibid.*

usually brief records on ostraca, context-dependent, written in a formulaic style and a relatively high bureaucratic register.

No true enforceable written *contract* comprising the *essentialia* of the transaction, functioning as memorial and evidence of the agreement, as an operative fact with legal consequences, is to be found in our corpus: Ramesside agreements were mostly verbal. Contract-related records do exist from the Ramesside Period but they belong to various genres such as epistolary, contentious (with or without oaths), private memos and accounts, administrative or workshop records. These documents are generally recorded on ostraca, brief, formulaic, impersonal, detached and informative, and they use a relatively high bureaucratic register; this register is peculiar to people trained to write in a certain way, drawing on a repertoire of formulae with a certain measure of variation. It is not a case of idiosyncratic register reflecting the personality and style of their writers. Some of the records are so cursory they could not even serve an evidenciary purpose. Brief records of oaths relating to transactions were probably concerned with litigation procedures. Westbrook (2003: 13) also concluded his *tour d'horizon* of Ancient Near East legal systems by admitting that the 'thousands of "contractual" documents preserved are not contracts as such; they are protocols of oral transactions made usually before witnesses' that could be used as evidence but 'rebutted by the testimony of the witnesses to the transaction'. Most of the Deir el-Medina records are not even protocols of oral transactions but only laconic mentions of transfers of assets that may belong to private individuals or to the State.

The *autonomy* of the written private deed has been assessed during our research.

It appears that a will or gift deed is necessary only in cases in which some derogation is made to the customary *descent and distribution* mode; a statement is made verbally by the disponor in public, with a consecutive record. The speech is thus the constitutive act, of which the recording is an authoritative adaptation, not a *verbatim* record. The written format is probably more abstract than the speech; it is a summary, the fruit of a process of selection aimed at clarifying legally relevant facts and expressions and endowing the provisions with authority, but important information may be lost in the process.

In the event of a discrepancy after the disponor's death between the record and the witnesses' recollection of the verbal act, the written deed may be used to justify a contestation of the deed; the intention of the disponor appears to be interpreted with the help of witnesses to the act who also knew the disponor (*Naunakhte*).

The record assumes major importance when the witnesses to the oral speech have disappeared, the written record remaining the sole evidence of the deed; thus there might be a temptation to falsify the record (*Mes*). Epistolary documents containing testamentary or gift dispositions could probably be used directly as quasi-olograph deeds, no witness being available in this case; but there is no example of a claim in court based on epistolary evidence. Documentary evidence in legal context is also provided by official records, such as official registers, court and administrative proceedings, notarial wills and gift deeds. Title deeds, often dated, are not exact copies of original wills or contentious proceedings, although they may be based on such records; they are excerpts or summaries of deeds and procedures grounding a right, recorded before the main deed and by the same hand. Title deeds are used since the Middle Kingdom, perhaps even before.

Dated normative texts such as royal decrees (mandatory sources of obligation) are not referred to in our deeds, although a general principle may be quoted in the form of a laconic 'Pharaoh's word'. The text is not held to be sacrosanct, but that does not mean it had only marginal value.

To return to the criteria proposed by Danet & Bogoch (1994: 107-27) in order to evaluate the autonomy of the legal texts, the instruments presented in our corpus do not comment on writing as an exceptional operation, rather writing seems to represent a customary procedure; they use performative forms, locutive expressions of will, and narratives usually limited to the *recital*; a curse (*terrorem* clause) may enhance a will's performativity (*pAdoptions*); their textemic structure is well-ordered, with cohesion marks, standard expressions, and linguistic stylizations devices; decontextualization is achieved at least in the pre-material. The written wills and gift deeds of the Ramesside Period are in this respect quite similar to the ancient Anglo-Saxon testamentary provisions of the 5th to the 11th centuries A.D presented by Danet and Bogoch. The text (*sš*) becomes an object when its compliance to the disponor's intentions is tested (*Naunakhte*) or when the legatee refers to it as the will (*pAdoptions*, lines 3-4). There are indications of an increasing performativity and autonomy of the written text in the later part of the 20th dynasty (explicit performative, curse, and addition of general principles to substantiate the document).

There is a long tradition of categorization of abstract legal concepts in the script, a fact that demonstrates a complex writing tradition. *Authentic* wills and gift deeds written on papyrus are more than memorization and evidence of the verbal act: they are authoritative objects legitimizing personal expressions of will, crystalizing them in the temporal flow, embedding the voice of the individual in the impersonal formality of the legal dimension, and endowing it with permanence (to record is to fix: *mn*), dignity, authority, and importance. The notary procedure before the court is conceived as a spoken () and written () procedure, not as an exclusively verbal ceremony in which symbolic gestures and words are the main issue and witnesses and oaths the unique way of bringing evidence. No reference is made to the legal event as a multi-sensorial experience, as is to be expected in a 'performance' culture.

Finegan[944] distinguishes in the language of modern wills several features that we observed in our corpus: use of locutive pronouns, absence of the imperative 'despite the nature of wills as basically directive proclamations'[945], absence of interrogative but presence of conditional sentences, complex sentences, agentless passives downplaying background information, use of performative forms involving a delayed performance 'not only in the canonical first-person active (…) but also in the passive, the third-person, and future tenses–as in "The Trustees shall be authorized…"'[946]. Tiersma[947] adds wordiness and redundancy (e.g. binomials), formal and ritualistic qualities to the list[948].

Wills are emotionally laden documents that strive to find a balance between imponderable fate and control, between information, motivation, and authority, endeavoring to provide for certainty and order in a world full of confusion, where ignorance of death's consequences upon the living world left behind goes hand in hand with the superstitious fear of acknowledging mortality. Since ancient times the linguistic features of the will have attempted to deal with both the inevitable and the improbable in incontrovertible assertions and with formal assurance, in order to arrange an orderly transfer of assets to preserve family heirloom, to provide a sense of continuity, and to ensure control from the grave[949]. Ultimately, analogous

944 (1982: 115-9).
945 *Ibid.*, p.116.
946 *Ibid.*, p. 119.
947 (1999: 59, 101).
948 Compare with the language of Roman private law *tabulae* written in the '*carmen*-style' (Meyer 2004: 44-72).
949 See Roth (1987) concerning the 'psychiatry of writing a will'.

linguistic means serve the same communicative ends today as they did in the distant Ramesside past or in 1456, when François Villon wrote in his mock will *Le Lais* (The Legacy, VIII):

And since I have to go
And I can't be sure of coming back
I'm a man not without weaknesses
No more than the next made of steel or tin
Life is uncertain for humans
And there's no way-station after you die
And I go into a distant land
So I draw up this present legacy.

(Translation: Kinnell, G.,1982.
The Poems of François Villon.
Hanover/London: UPNE).

Bibliography (including abbreviations); critical devices

[ ] are used for textual lacuna

( ) are used for textual omission (scribal choice)

(...) are used for textual omission (our choice)

< > are used for textual omission (scribal error)

{ } are used for textual superfluity (dittography, etc.)

are used for delimitating a syntagm

Periodicals, series, and collections are referred to as in *LÄ* VII, XIV-XIX

Ahmose's Karnak stela = Harari (1959)

Albright, W.F., 1934. *The Vocalization of the Egyptian Syllabic Orthography*. American Oriental Series 5. New Haven: American Oriental Society.

Allam, S., 1967. Zwei Schlussklauseln zur Übertragung eines Rechts im Alten Ägypten. *BiOr* 24: 14-20.

— 1967b. Eine Abstandsurkunde aus der Zeit des Neuen Reiches. *JEA* 53: 47-50.

— 1968. Sind die nichtliterarischen Schriftostraka Brouillons? *JEA* 54: 121-8.

— 1972. De l'adoption en Egypte pharaonique. *Oriens Antiquus* 11: 277-95.

— 1973. *Hieratische Ostraka und Papyri aus der Ramessidenzeit*. URAÄ 1. Tübingen: S. Allam.

— 1973b. *Das Verfahrensrecht in der altägyptischen Arbeitersiedlung von Deir el-Medineh*. URAÄ 1. Tübingen: S. Allam.

— 1974. An Allusion to an Egyptian Wedding Ceremony? *GM* 13: 9-11.

— 1975. Ehe. *LÄ* I: 1162-81.

— 1977. Les obligations et la famille dans la société égyptienne ancienne. *OA* 16: 89-97.

— 1981. Quelques aspects du mariage dans l'Egypte ancienne. *JEA* 67: 116-35.

— 1982. Einige hieratische Ostraka der Papyrussammlung der Staatlichen Museen zu Berlin. *Forschungen und Berichte* 22: 51-61.

— 1982b. La vente dans l'Egypte ancienne. *RHDFE* 60 : 377-93.

— 1983. Familie und Besitzverhältnisse in der altägyptischen Arbeitersiedlung von Deir-el-Medineh. *RIDA* 30: 17-39.

— 1985. Bemerkungen zur Abstandsschrift. *Enchoria* 13: 1-5.

— 1990. A new look at the Adoption Papyrus (reconsidered). *JEA* 76: 189-91.

— 1992. Review of McDowell, A.G., Jurisdiction in the Workmen's Community of Deir el-Medîna. *BiOr* 49: 379-86.

— 1993. Papyrus Turin 2021: Another Adoption Extraordinary. In *Individu, société et spiritualité dans l'Egypte pharaonique et copte: Mélanges égyptologiques offerts au Professeur Aristide Théodoridès*, eds. C. Cannuyer & J.-M. Kruchten, 23-8. Ath, Brussels, Mons: Association Montoise d'Egyptologie.

— 1994. The Agreement after Judgement. *Egitto e Vicino Oriente* 17: 19-28.

— 1996. Aspects de la vie sociale, juridique et municipale à Deir-el-Médineh. *Méditerranées* 6/7: 195-232.

Amarah stela (*Stela Brooklyn* 38.544) = Fairman (1938: pl. XI)

Andreu, G. (ed), 2002. *Les artistes de Pharaon: Deir el-Médineh et la Vallée des Rois*. Paris: Réunion des musées nationaux.

Anthes, R., 1928. *Die Felseninschriften von Hatnub*. UGAÄ 9. Leipzig: J.C. Hinrichs'sche Buchhandlung.

Architrave Cairo CG 1634 = Goedicke (1970 : pl. 7)

Austin, J.L., 1962. *How to Do Things with Words*. Oxford: Clarendon Press.

ÄW = Hannig (2003-6)

Baer, K., 1965. Temporal *wnn* in Late Egyptian. *JEA* 51: 137-43.

— 1966. A deed of endowment in a letter of the time of *Ppjj* I? *ZÄS* 93: 1-9.

Baines, J., 1983. Literacy and Ancient Egyptian Society. *Man* 18: 572-99.

— 1999. On Wenamun as a Literary Text. In *Literatur und Politik im pharaonischen und ptolemäischen Ägypten: Vorträge der Tagung zum Gedenken an G. Posener 5.-10. September 1996 in Leipzig*, eds J. Assmann & E. Blumenthal, 209-233. BdE 127. Cairo: IFAO.

Baines, J. & Eyre, C.J., 1983. Four notes on literacy. *GM* 61: 65-96.

Bakhtin, M., 1981. *The Dialogic Imagination: Four Essays* (ed. M. Holquist). Austin: University of Texas Press.

Bakir, A.M., 1952. *Slavery in Pharaonic Egypt*. SASAE 18. Cairo: IFAO.

— 1970. *Egyptian Epistolography from the Eighteenth to the Twenty-First Dynasty*. BdE 48. Le Caire: IFAO.

Balat tablet 5955 = Philip-Stéphan (2008: 260)

Balat tablet 3689-7, 8 & 11 = Philip-Stéphan (2008: 260)

Bbi Leiden stela V 88 = Gardiner (1957: 309)

BD = Naville (1971)

Bedell, E.D., 1973. *Criminal Law in the Egyptian Ramesside Period*. Dissertation Brandeis University.

Bhatia, V.K., 1993. *Analysing Genre: Language Use in Professional Settings*. London: Longman.

— 1994. Cognitive structuring in legislative provisions. In *Language and the Law*, ed. J. Gibbons, 136-155. London: Longman.

Biber, D., 1994. An Analytic Framework for Register Studies. In *Sociolinguistic Perspectives on Register*, eds. D. Biber & E. Finegan, 31-56. New York/Oxford: Oxford University Press.

— 1995. *Dimensions of register variation: A cross-linguistic comparison*. Cambridge: Cambridge University Press.

Bierbrier, M.L., 1975. *The Late New Kingdom in Egypt (c. 1300 ~ 664 B.C.): A Genealogical and Chronological Investigation*. Warminster: Aris & Phillips.

Blackman, A.M., 1926. Oracles in Ancient Egypt. *JEA* 12: 176-85.

— 1932. *Middle-Egyptian Stories*. BAe 2. Brussels: Fondation Egyptologique Reine Elisabeth.

— 1935. The Stela of Nebipusenwosret: British Museum no. 101. *JEA* 21: 1-9 and pl. 1.

Bleiberg, E., 1996. *The Official Gift in Ancient Egypt*. Oklahoma: University of Oklahoma Press & Norman and London.

Block Saqqara RM 22-11-1956 = Goedicke (1970: table 17a)

Boochs, W., 1982. *Siegel und Siegeln im Alten Ägypten*. KFKA 4. Sankt Augustin: Hans Richarz.

Borghouts, J.F., 1972. A Special Use of the Emphatic *sḏm.f* in Late Egyptian. *BiOr* 29: 271-6.

Bottéro, J., 1987. *Mésopotamie: L'écriture, la raison et les dieux*. Paris: Gallimard.

Brunner-Traut, E., 1956. *Die altägyptischen Scherbenbilder (Bildostraka) der deutschen Museen und Sammlungen*. Wiesbaden: Franz Steiner.

Burkard, G., 2006. Das *ḫtm n pꜣ ḫr* von Deir el-Medine: Seine Funktion und die Frage seiner Lokalisierung. In *Living and Writing in Deir el-Medine: Socio-historic Embodiment of Deir el-Medine Texts*, eds. A. Dorn & T. Hofmann. AH 19, 31-42. Basel: Schwabe Verlag.

Bruyère, B., 1930. *Rapport sur les fouilles de Deir el Médineh (1929)*. FIFAO 7/2. Le Caire: IFAO.

— 1937. *Rapport sur les fouilles de Deir el Médineh (1933 - 1934)*. FIFAO 14. Le Caire: IFAO.

— 1952. *Rapport sur les fouilles de Deir el Médineh (1935 - 1940)*. FIFAO 20.II. Le Caire: IFAO.

— 1953. *Rapport sur les fouilles de Deir el Médineh (années 1948 à 1951)*. FIFAO 26. Le Caire: IFAO.

Bryce tablet = Griffith (1908 : 272)

Cairo letter to the dead JE 25975 = Keller (1989: 29-33)

Cairo statue CG 42208 = Legrain (1914: pl. 15-16)

Calamari, J.D. & Perillo, J.M., 1998 (4th ed.). *The Law of Contracts*. St. Paul: Thomson West.

Caminos, R.A., 1954. *Late-Egyptian Miscellanies*. Brown Egyptological Studies 1. London: Oxford University Press.

Carawan, E., 2007. Oath and Contract. In *Horkos: The Oath in Greek Society*, eds. A.H. Sommerstein & J. Fletcher, 73-80. Exeter: Bristol Phoenix Press.

Carr, D.M., 2005. *Writing on the Tablet of the Heart: Origins of Scripture and Literature*. Oxford: Oxford University Press.

Černý, J., 1931. Une expression désignant la réponse négative d'un oracle. *BIFAO* 30: 491-6.

— 1931b. Les ostraca hiératiques, leur intérêt et la nécessité de leur étude. *CdE* 6: 212-24.

— 1945. The Will of Naunakhte and the Related Documents. *JEA* 31: 29-53.

— 1935. Questions adressées aux oracles. *BIFAO* 35: 41-58.

— 1935b. *Catalogue général des antiquités égyptiennes du Musée du Caire (25501-25832): Ostraca hiératiques.*2 vols. Cairo: IFAO.

— 1935-70. *Catalogue des ostraca hiératiques non littéraires de Deir el Médineh*. DFIFAO 3/7, 14. Cairo: IFAO.

— 1937-38. La constitution d'un avoir conjugal en Egypte. *BIFAO* 37 : 41-8.

— 1941. *Ꞽnn* in Late Egyptian. *JEA* 27: 106-12.

— 1939. *Late Ramesside Letters*. BAe 9. Bruxelles: Fondation Egyptologique Reine Elisabeth.

— 1949. On the Origin of the Egyptian Conjunctive. *JEA* 35 : 25-30.

— 1952. *Paper & Books in Ancient Egypt*. London: H.K. Lewis.

— 1972. Troisième série de questions adressées aux oracles. *BIFAO* 72: 49-69.

— 1976. *Coptic Etymological Dictionary*. Cambridge: Cambridge University Press.

— 2001 (2nd ed.). *A Community of Workmen at Thebes in the Ramesside Period*. BdE 50. Cairo: IFAO.

Černý, J. & Koenig, Y, 1986. *Papyrus hiératiques de Deir el-Médineh*. II. DFIFO 22. Cairo: IFAO.

Černý, J. & Gardiner, A.H., 1957. *Hieratic Ostraca*. I. Oxford: Griffith Institute, University Press and C. Batey.

Černý, J. & Israelit-Groll, S., 1993 (4th ed.). *A Late Egyptian Grammar*. StudPohl 4. Roma: Editrice Pontificio Istituto Biblico.

Černý, J. & Peet, T.E., 1927. A Marriage Settlement of the Twentieth Dynasty: An Unpublished Document from Turin. *JEA* 13: 30-39.

Černý, J. & Posener, G., 1978. *Papyrus hiératiques de Deir el-Médineh*. I. Documents de fouilles 8. Cairo: IFAO.

Chafe, W.L., 1982. Integration and Involvement in Speaking, Writing, and Oral Literature. In *Spoken and Written Language: Exploring Orality and Literacy*, ed. D. Tannen. Advances in Discourse Processes 9, 35-53. Norwood: Ablex.

Charrow, V.R., Crandall, J.A. & Charrow, R.P., 1982. Characteristics and Functions of Legal Language. In *Sublanguage: Studies of Language in Restricted Semantic Domains*, eds R. Kittredge & J. Lehrberger, 175-190. Berlin: W. de Gruyter.

Charpin, D., 2008. *"Garde ma lettre en témoignage"*. Communication presented at the first meeting of the 'Legal Documents in Ancient Societies' workshop concerning 'The Letter' (The American Academy in Rome, 28-30.9.2009).

Chauveau, M., 1991. P. Carlsberg 301: Le manuel juridique de Tebtynis. In *The Carlsberg Papyri I: Demotic Texts from the Collection*, ed. P.J. Frandsen. CNI Publications 15, 103-23. Copenhagen: Museum Tusculanum Press, University of Copenhagen.

Clanchy, M.T., 1993 (2nd ed.). *From Memory to Written Record: England 1066-1307*. Oxford & Cambridge: Blackwell.

Clarysse, W., 1995. Ptolemaic Wills. In *Legal Documents of the Hellenistic World: Papers from a Seminar Arranged by the Institute of Classical Studies, the Institute of Jewish Studies and the Warburg Institute, University of London, February to May 1986*, eds. M.J. Geller, H. Maehler & A.D.E. Lewis, 88-105. London: Warburg Institute, University of London.

Clère, J.J., 1968. Un mot pour « mariage » en égyptien de l'époque ramesside. *RdE* 20: 171-5.

Collier, M. & Quirke, S., 2002. *The UCL Lahun Papyri: Letters*. BAR International Series 1083. Oxford: BAR.

— 2004. *The UCL Lahun Papyri: Religious, Literary, Legal, Mathematical and Medical*. BAR International Series 1209. Oxford: BAR.

— 2006. *The UCL Lahun Papyri: Accounts*. BAR International Series 1471. Oxford: BAR.

Cooney, K.M., 2006. An Informal Workshop: Textual Evidence for Private Funerary Art Production in the Ramesside Period. In *Living and Writing in Deir el-Medine: Socio-historic Embodiment of Deir el-Medine Texts*, eds. A. Dorn & T. Hofmann. AH 19, 43-55. Basel: Schwabe Verlag.

— 2007. *The Cost of Death: The Social and Economic Value of Ancient Egyptian Funerary Art in the Ramesside Period*. Egyptologische Uitgaven 22. Leiden: NINO.

Cornu, G., 1990. *Linguistique juridique*. Paris: Montchrestien.

— 2003. *Vocabulaire juridique*. Association Henri Capitant. Paris: Quadrige/PUF.

Crum, W.E. & Steindorff, G., 1912. *Koptische Rechtsurkunden des achten Jahrhunderts aus Djême (Theben)*. Leipzig: Zentralantiquariat der Deutschen Demokratischen Republik.

Cruz-Uribe, E., 1982. Slavery in Egypt during the Saite and Persian Periods. *RIDA* 29: 47-71.

— 1985. *Saite and Persian Demotic Cattle Documents: A Study in Legal Forms and Principles in Ancient Egypt*. ASP 26. Chico: Scholars Press.

— 1988. A new look at the Adoption Papyrus. *JEA* 74: 220-3.

Crystal, D. & Davy, D., 1969. *Investigating English Style*. London: Longman.

CT (*Coffin Texts*) = de Buck (1935-61)

Dahl, H.S., 2001. *Dahl's Law Dictionary French to English/English to French: An Annoted Legal Dictionary, Including Definitions from Codes, Case Law, Statutes, and Legal Writing*. Buffalo/Paris: Hein/Dalloz.

Dakhla royal decree of Pepy II = Pantalacci (1985)

Dakhla stela Ashmolean Museum 1894.107b = Janssen (1968)

Danet, B., 1980. Language in the Legal Process. *Law & Society Review* 14 (3): 445-564.

— 1984. (Ed.) Studies of legal discourse. *Text* (special issue) 4-1/3.

— 1985. Legal Discourse. In *Handbook of Discourse Analysis: Disciplines of Discourse*, ed. T.A. Van Dijk, I, 273-291. London: Academic Press.

— 1990. Language and Law: An Overview of 15 Years of Research. In *Handbook of Language and Social Psychology*, eds H. Giles & P. Robinson, 537-559. Chichester: John Wiley & Sons.

— 1997. Speech, writing and performativity: an evolutionary view of the history of constitutive ritual. In *The construction of professional discourse*, eds. B.-L. Gunnarsson, P. Linell & B. Nordberg, 13-41. Harlow/New York: Addison Wesley Longman.

Danet, B. & Bogoch, B., 1992. From Oral Ceremony to Written Document: The Transitional Language of Anglo-Saxon Wills. *Language & Communication* 12: 95-122.

— 1992b. "Whoever Alters This, May God Turn His Face from Him on the Day of Judgment": Curses in Anglo-Saxon Legal Documents. *Journal of American Folklore* 105: 132-65.

— 1994. Orality, literacy, and performativity in Anglo-Saxon wills. In *Language and the law*, ed. J. Gibbons, 100-35. Harlow: Longman.

Das digitalisierte Zettelarchiv des Wörterbuches der ägyptischen Sprache: http://aaew.bbaw.de/tla

David, A., 2000. *De l'infériorité à la perturbation: L'oiseau du "mal" et la catégorisation en Egypte ancienne.* GOF IV. Reihe Ägypten 38. Classification and Categorization in Ancient Egypt 1. Wiesbaden: Harrassowitz.

— 2000b. *m.k* + forme nominale au coeur de la controverse. *LingAeg* 7: 113-123.

— 2003. Review of Borchers, D., Kammerzell, F. & Weninger, S., Hieroglyphen Alphabete Schriftreformen. *BiOr* 60: 569-579.

— 2004. Analyse du discours juridique dans les décrets royaux ramessides. *GM* 199: 31-44.

— 2006. *Syntactic and Lexico-Semantic Aspects of the Legal Register in Ramesside Royal Decrees.* GOF IV. Reihe Ägypten 38/5. Wiesbaden: Harrassowitz.

— 2007. Ancient Egyptian Forensic Metaphors and Categories. *ZÄS* 134: 1-14.

Davies, B.G., 1999. *Who's Who at Deir el-Medina: A Prosopographic Study of the Royal Workmen's Community.* Egyptologische Uitgaven 13. Leiden: Nederlands Instituut voor het Nabije Oosten.

Dawson, W.R., 1925. An Oracle Papyrus. BM. 10335. *JEA* 11: 247-8.

de Buck, A., 1935-61. (Ed.) *The Egyptian Coffin Texts,* 7 vols. Chicago: Oriental Institute Publications.

de Cenival, F., 1967. Deux serments démotiques concernant des comptes de bétail. *Recherches de Papyrologie* 4: 99-106.

De Linage, 1939. L'acte d'établissement et le contrat de mariage d'un esclave sous Thoutmès III. *BIFAO* 38: 217-34.

Demarée, R.J., 2002. *Ramesside Ostraca.* London: British Museum Press.

— 2006. A House is not a Home – What exactly is a Hut ? In *Living and Writing in Deir el-Medine: Socio-historic Embodiment of Deir el-Medine Texts*, eds. A. Dorn & T. Hofmann. AH 19, 57-66. Basel: Schwabe Verlag.

— 2006b. *The Bankes Late Ramesside Papyri.* London: British Museum Press.

— 2008. Two "New" Donkey Texts from Deir el-Medina: O. Hildesheim PM 5160, O. Leiden F.2002/10.1. In *Mélanges offerts à François Neveu par ses amis, élèves et collègues à l'occasion de son soixante-quinzième anniversaire*, eds. C. Gallois, P. Grandet & L. Pantalacci. BdE 145, 83-98. Cairo: IFAO.

Denderah = Petrie (1900)

Depauw, M., 1997. *A Companion to Demotic Studies.* Papyrologica Bruxellensia 28. Brussels: Fondation égyptologique Reine Elisabeth.

Der Manuelian, P., 1986. An Essay in Document Transmission: *Nj-kꜣ-ꜥnḫ* and the Earliest *ḥrjw rnpt*. *JNES* 45: 1-18.

Dmḏibtꜣwy Coptos R decree (Cairo JE 41894) = Goedicke (1967: Abb. 28)

Dominicus, B., 1994. *Gesten und Gebärden in Darstellungen des Alten und Mittleren Reiches.* SAGA 10. Heidelberg: Heidelberger Orientverlag.

Donker van Heel, K., 1990. *The Legal Manual of Hermopolis [P.Mattha]*. Stichting Het Leids Papyrologisch Instituut 11. Leiden: Papyrologisch Instituut.

Donker van Heel, K. & Haring, B.J.J., 2003. *Writing in a Workmen's Village: Scribal Practice in Ramesside Deir el-Medina*. Leiden: Nederlands Instituut voor het Nabije Oosten.

Edel, E., 1955. Inschriften des Alten Reiches. V. Die Reiseberichte des *Ḥrw-ḫwjf* (Herchuf). In *Ägyptologische Studien*, ed. O. Firchow. DAWB 29, 51-75. Berlin: Akademie Verlag.

— 1955-64. *Altägyptische Grammatik*. 2 vols. AnOr 34/39. Roma: Pontificium Institutum Biblicum.

Edfu stela Cairo JE 52456 = Vernus (1986)

EG = Gardiner (1957)

Eichler, E., 1991. Zwei Bemerkungen zu den hieratischen Briefen des Alten Reiches. *GM* 123: 21-6.

Eichler, S., 1991. Untersuchungen zu den Wasserträgern von Deir-el-Medineh II. *SAK* 18: 173-205. (part I in *SAK* 17 (1990) 135-75)

Eloquent Peasant (*Berlin* 3023, 3025, 10499 r°, *BM* 10274 r°) = Parkinson (1991)

Erichsen, W., 1933. *Papyrus Harris I: Hieroglyphische Transkription*. BAe 5. Bruxelles: Fondation Egyptologique Reine Elisabeth.

Erman, A., 1905. Aus dem Volksleben des neuen Reiches. *ZÄS* 42: 100-6.

— 1911 (ed.). *Hieratische Papyrus aus den königlichen Museen zu Berlin III: Schriftstücke der VI. Dynastie aus Elephantine, Zaubersprüche für Mutter und Kind, Ostraka*. Leipzig: J.C. Hinrichs'sche Buchhandlung.

— 1933. *Neuägyptische Grammatik*. Leipzig: J.C. Hinrichs.

Erman, A. & Grapow, H., 1955. (Eds) *Wörterbuch der ägyptischen Sprache*, 6 vols. Berlin: Akademie Verlag.

Even-Zohar, I., 1990. Polysystem Studies. *Poetics Today* 11: 1-268.

Eyre, C.J., 1980. *Employment and Labour Relations in the Theban Necropolis in the Ramesside Period*. Unpublished Ph.D. dissertation. Oxford.

— 1984. A Draughtsman's Letter from Thebes. *SAK* 11: 195-207.

— 1984b. Crime and Adultery in Ancient Egypt. *JEA* 70: 92-105.

— 1987. The Use of Data from Deir el-Medina (review of Gutgesell, 1983, Die Datierung der Ostraka und Papyri aus Deir el-Medineh und ihre ökonomische Interpretation). *BiOr* 44: 21-36.

— 1992. The Adoption Papyrus in Social Context. *JEA* 78: 207-21.

— 1994. Feudal Tenure and Absentee Landlords. In *Grund und Boden in Altägypten (rechtliche und sozio-ökonomische Verhältnisse): Akten des internationalen Symposions Tübingen 18.-20. Juni 1990*, ed. S. Allam. URAÄ 2, 107-33. Tübingen: Allam.

— 2007. The Evil Stepmother and the Rights of a Second Wife. *JEA* 93: 223-43.

Eyre, C.J. & Baines, J., 1989. Interactions between Orality and Literacy in Ancient Egypt. In *Literacy and Society*, eds. K. Schousboe & M.T. Larsen, 91-118. Copenhagen: Akademisk Forlag.

Fairman, H.W., 1938. Preliminary Report on the Excavation at Sesebi (Sudla) and 'Amārah West, Anglo-Egyptian Sudan, 1937-8. *JEA* 24: 151-9.

Faulkner, R.O., 1935. The Verb *i* 'to Say' and its Developments. *JEA* 21: 177-90.

— 1962. *A Concise Dictionary of Middle Egyptian*. Oxford: Griffith Institute.

Ferguson, C.A., 1964. Diglossia. In *Language in culture and society: A Reader in Linguistics and Anthropology*, ed. D. Hymes, 429-439. New York: Harper & Row.

— 1994. Dialect, Register, and Genre: Working Assumptions About Conventionalization. In *Sociolinguistic Perspectives on Register*, eds. D. Biber & E. Finegan, 15-30. New York/Oxford: Oxford University Press.

Feucht, E., 1980. Kind. *LÄ* III: 424-37.

Finegan, E., 1982. Form and Function in Testament Language. In *Linguistics and the Professions: Proceedings of the Second Annual Delaware Symposium on Language Studies*, ed. J. di Pietro, 113-120. Norwood: Ablex.

Fischer, H.G., 1961. The Nubian Mercenaries of Gebelein during the First Intermediate Period. *Kush* 9: 44-80.

— 1973. Further Evidence for the Logic of Ancient Egyptian: Diminishing Progression. *JARCE* 10: 5-9.

Fitzpatrick, M.E., 1983. *Sḫꜣ* or *Ḫrw*? *JEA* 69: 163-5.

Frandsen, P.J., 1974. *An Outline of the Late Egyptian Verbal System*. Copenhagen: Akademisk Forlag.

— 1990. Editing Reality: The Turin Strike Papyrus. In *Studies in Egyptology Presented to Miriam Lichtheim*, ed. S. Israelit-Groll, I, 166-99. Jerusalem: Magnes Press, Hebrew University.

Funk, W.-P., 1985. On a Semantic Typology of Conditional Sentences. *Folia Linguistica* 19: 365-413.

Gagarin, M., 2008. *Writing Greek Law*. Cambridge: Cambridge University Press.

Ganley, A.H., 2002. Equity in Antiquity. *DE* 54: 71-80.

— 2003a. The Legal Deeds of Transfer from 'Kahun' (Part Two). *DE* 56: 37-44.

— 2003b. The Legal Deeds of Transfer from 'Kahun' (Part One). *DE* 55: 15-27.

Gardiner, A.H., 1906. Four Papyri of the 18th Dynasty from Kahun. *ZÄS* 43: 27-47.

— 1911. *Egyptian Hieratic Texts: I. Literary Texts of the New Kingdom*. Leipzig: J.C. Hinrichs'sche Buchhandlung.

— 1932. *Late Egyptian Stories*. BAe 1. Brussels: Fondation égyptologique Reine Elisabeth.

— 1935. A Lawsuit Arising from the Purchase of Two Slaves. *JEA* 21: 140-6.

— 1937. *Late-Egyptian Miscellanies*. BAe 7. Bruxelles: Fondation Egyptologique Reine Elisabeth.

— 1940. Adoption Extraordinary. *JEA* 26: 23-9.

— 1940b. The word *mꜥḏꜣ* and its various uses. *JEA* 26: 157-8.

— 1948. *Ramesside Administrative Documents*. Oxford: Oxford University Press.

— 1956. A Pharaonic Encomium. *JEA* 42: 8-20.

— 1957. *Egyptian Grammar: Being an Introduction to the Study of Hieroglyphs*. Oxford: Griffith Institute.

— 1964. *The Inscription of Mes: A Contribution to the Study of Egyptian Judicial Procedure*. Hildesheim: Georg Olms.

Garner, B.A., 1987. *A Dictionary of Modern Legal Usage*. New York/Oxford: Oxford University Press.

— 2004 (ed.). *Black's Law Dictionary* (8th ed.). St. Paul: Thomson West.

Gasse, A., 1992. Les ostraca hiératiques littéraires de Deir el-Medina: Nouvelles orientations de la publication. In *Village Voices: Proceedings of the Symposium "Texts from Deir el-Medîna and their Interpretation » Leiden, May 31-June 1, 1991*, eds. R.J. Demarée & A. Egberts. CNWS 13, 51-70. Leiden: CNWS.

Gauthier, H., 1936. Une foundation pieuse en Nubie. *ASAE* 36: 49-71.

Gee, J., 2001. Notes on Egyptian Marriage: P.BM 10416 Reconsidered. *BES* 15: 17-25.

Gebelein pCairo JE 66844-1/6 = Posener-Kriéger (1979: 320)

Gewirtz, P., 1996. Narrative and Rhetoric in the Law. In *Law's Stories: Narrative and Rhetoric in the Law*, eds. P. Brooks & P. Gewirtz, 2-13. New Haven & London: Yale University Press.

Gilula, M., 1970. Review of Die negativen Konstruktionen im Alt- und Mittelägyptischen by H. Satzinger. *JEA* 56: 205-214.

Gitton, M., 1975. Ahmose Nofretere. *LÄ* I: 102-9.

— 1976. La résiliation d'une fonction religieuse: Nouvelle interprétation de la stèle de donation d'Ahmès Néfertary. *BIFAO* 76: 65-89.

Giza boundary stone Cairo JE 42787 = Goedicke (1970: table XVI)

Giza coffin Cairo 1787 = *Urk*. I, 22

Glanville, S.R.K., 1928. The Letters of Aaḥmōse of Peniati. *JEA* 14: 294-312.

Goddeeris, A., 2002. *Economy and Society in Northern Babylonia in the Early Old Babylonian Period (ca. 2000-1800 BC)*. OLA 109. Leuven: Peeters.

Goedicke, H., 1967. *Königliche Dokumente aus dem alten Reich*. ÄA 14. Wiesbaden : Harrassowitz.

— 1967b. Ein Brief aus dem Alten Reich (Pap. Boulaq 8). *MDAIK* 22: 1-8.

— 1970. *Die privaten Rechtsinschriften aus dem Alten Reich*. BWZKM 5. Wien: Notring.

— 1986. Bilateral Business in the Old Kingdom. *DE* 5: 73-101.

Gödecken, K.B., 1980. Imet-per. *LÄ* III: 141-5.

Goelet, O., 2007. Writing Ramesside Hieratic: What the *Late-Egyptian Miscellanies* Tell us about Scribal Education. In *Servant of Mut: Studies in Honor of R.A. Fazzini*, ed. S.H. D'Auria. PÄ 28, 106-14. Leiden: E.J. Brill.

Goldwasser, O., 1990. On the Choice of Registers – Studies on the Grammar of Papyrus Anastasi I. In *Studies in Egyptology Presented to Miriam Lichtheim*, ed. S. Israelit-Groll, I, 200-240. Jerusalem: The Magnes Press, The Hebrew University.

— 1991. On Dynamic Canonicity in Late-Egyptian: The Literary Letter and the Personal Prayer. *LingAeg* 1: 129-141.

— 1995. *From Icon to Metaphor*. OBO 142. Fribourg & Göttingen: University Press Fribourg, Vandenhoeck & Ruprecht.

— 1999. "Low" and "High" Dialects in Ramesside Egyptian. In *Textcorpus und Wörterbuch: Aspekte zur ägyptischen Lexikographie*, eds S. Grunert & I. Hafemann. PÄ 14, 311-328. Leiden: E.J. Brill.

— 1999b. The Determinative System as a Mirror of World Organization. *GM* 170: 49-68.

— 2001. Poetic License in Nineteenth Dynasty Non-Literary Late-Egyptian? *LingAeg* 9:123-38.

— 2002. *Lovers, Prophets and Giraffes: Wor(L)d Categorization in Ancient Egypt*. GOF IV. Reihe Ägypten 38. Classification and Categorization in Ancient Egypt 3. Wiesbaden: Harrassowitz.

— 2005. Where is Metaphor? Conceptual Metaphor and Alternative Classification in the Hieroglyphic Script. *Metaphor and Symbol* 20: 95-113.

— 2006. A Comparison between Classifier Languages and Classifier Script: The Case of Ancient Egyptian. In *Egyptian, Semitic and General Grammar: Workshop in Memory of H.J. Polotsky (8-12 July 2001)*, ed. G. Goldenberg & A. Shisha-Halevy, 16-39. Jerusalem: The Israel Academy of Sciences and Humanities.

Goodrich, P., 1994. Legal Language: History. In *The Encyclopedia of Language and Linguistics*, eds R.E. Asher & J.M.Y. Simpson, IV, 2080-6. Oxford/New York/Seoul/Tokyo: Pergamon Press.

Goody, J., 1986. *The Logic of Writing and the Organization of Society*. Cambridge: Cambridge University Press.

Grandet, M., 2000. *Catalogue des ostraca hiératiques non littéraires de Deîr el-Médînéh: VIII – N°s 706-830*. DFIFAO 39. Le Caire: IFAO.

— 2003. *Catalogue des ostraca hiératiques non littéraires de Deîr el-Médînéh: IX – N°s 831-1000*. DFIFAO 41. Le Caire: IFAO.

Grdseloff, B., 1949. A New Middle Kingdom Letter from El-Lāhūn. *JEA* 35 : 59-62.

— 1951. Le "bois" cachet officiel des gouverneurs. *ASAE* 51 : 153-7.

Greengus, S., 1969. The Old Babylonian Marriage Contract. *JAOS* 89: 505-32.

Gregory, M., 1967. Aspects of varieties differentiation. *Journal of Linguistics* 3: 177-198.

Griffith, F.LL., 1889. The Inscriptions of Siût and Dêr Rîfeh. London: Trübner.

— 1908. A Contract of the Fifth Year of Amenhotp IV. *PSBA* 30: 272-5.

Grimal, N., 1988. *Histoire de l'Egypte ancienne*. Paris: Fayard/Le Livre de Poche.

Groll, S., 1967. *Non-Verbal Sentence Patterns in Late Egyptian*. London: Griffith Institute & Oxford University Press.

— 1969. *Ἰw.f* [*ḥr*] *tm sḏm* in Late Egyptian. *JEA* 55: 89-97.

— 1970. *The Negative Verbal System of Late Egyptian*. London: Oxford University Press.

— 1973. Late Egyptian of Non-Literary Texts of the 19th Dynasty. In *Orient and Occident: Essays Presented to C.H. Gordon on the Occasion of his Sixty-fifth Birthday*, ed. H.A. Heffner. AOAT 22, 67-70. Kevelaer: Verlag Butzon & Bercker / Neukirchen-Vluyn: Neukirchener Verlag.

— 1975. The Literary and the Non-literary Verbal Systems in Late Egyptian. *OLP* 6-7: 237-246.

— 1984. A Short Grammar of the Spermeru Dialect. In *Studien zu Sprache und Religion Ägyptens: Zu Ehren von W. Westendorf*, ed. F. Junge. I, 41-61. Göttingen: Hubert & Co.

— 1993. Various Criteria for Measuring Syntactic Units: Measuring P.Bulaq 10 = P.Cairo 58092. In *Individu, société et spiritualité dans l'Egypte pharaonique et copte: Mélanges offerts au Pr. A. Théodoridès*, ed. C. Cannuyer & J.-M. Kruchten, 123-34. Ath/Brussels/Mons: Illustra.

Gunn, B., 1916. The Religion of the Poor in Ancient Egypt. *JEA* 3: 81-94.

— 1924. *Studies in Egyptian Syntax*. Paris: Librairie Orientaliste Paul Geuthner.

Gunnarsson, B.L., 1984. Functional comprehensibility of legislative texts: Experiment with a Swedish act of parliament. In *Studies of legal discourse*, ed. B. Danet, 71-105. *Text* (special issue) 4-1/3.

Gustafsson, M., 1984. The syntactic features of binomial expressions in legal English. In *Studies of legal discourse*, ed. B. Danet, 123-141. *Text* (special issue) 4-1/3.

Haiman, J., 1978. Conditionals Are Topics. *Language* 54: 564-589

Halliday, M.A.K., 1989 (2nd ed.). *Spoken and written language*. Oxford: Oxford University Press.

Halliday, M.A.K., McIntosh, A. & Strevens, P., 1964. *The Linguistic Sciences and Language Teaching*. London: Longmans.

Hannig, R., 2003-6. *Ägyptisches Wörterbuch*. 3 vols. KAW 98 & 112. Mainz: Philipp von Zabern.

Ḥꜥpydf3 tomb = Montet (1930)

Harari, I., 1959. Nature de la stèle de donation de fonction du roi Ahmôsis à la reine Ahmès-Nefertari. *ASAE* 56: 139-201.

Haring, B.J.J., 2003. Pratique écrite et pratique orale à Deir el-Médineh. In *Deir el-Médineh et la Vallée des Rois : La vie en Egypte au temps des pharaons du Nouvel Empire, Actes du colloque organisé par le musée du Louvre les 3 et 4 mai 2002*, ed. G. Andreu, 141-56. Paris: Khéops & Musée du Louvre.

— 2003b. From Oral Practice to Written Record in Ramesside Deir el-Medina. *JESHO* 46: 249-72.

— 2006. Scribes and Scribal Activities at Deir el-Medina. In *Living and Writing in Deir el-Medine: Socio-historic Embodiment of Deir el-Medine Texts*, eds. A. Dorn & T. Hofmann. AH 19, 107-12. Basel: Schwabe Verlag.

Hasan, R., 1973. Code, register and social dialect. In *Class, Codes and Control: Applied Studies towards a Sociology of Language*, ed. B. Bernstein, II, 253-292. London: Routledge & Kegan Paul.

Hatnub graffiti = Anthes (1928)

Hayes, W.C., 1955. *A Papyrus of the Late Middle Kingdom in the Brooklyn Museum*. WM 5. Brooklyn: The Brooklyn Museum.

Heckel, U., 1957. Studien zum Eigenschaftsverbum und zum prädikativen Adjektivum im Altägyptischen. *ZÄS* 82: 19-47.

Helck, W., 1961-70. *Materialien zur Wirtschaftsgeschichte des Neuen Reiches*. 5 vols. AMAW. Wiesbaden: Akademie der Wissenschaften und der Literatur in Mainz & Franz Steiner.

— 1963. Der Papyrus Berlin P 3047. *JARCE* 2: 65-73.

— 1969. *Der Text der 'Lehre Amenemhets I. für seinen Sohn'*. Kleine ägyptische Texte. Wiesbaden: Harrassowitz.

— 1975. Akten I. *LÄ* I: 118-26.

— 1975b. *Historisch-biographische Texte der 2. Zwischenzeit und neue Texte der 18. Dynastie*. Wiesbaden: Harrassowitz.

— 1977. Fremde in Ägypten. *LÄ* II: 306-10.

— 1980. Kauf. *LÄ* III: 370.

— 1986. Werkverträge und andere Privatverträge. *LÄ* VI: 1225-7.

— 2002. *Die datierten und datierbaren Ostraka, Papyri und Graffiti von Deir el-Medineh*. ÄA 63. Wiesbaden: Harrassowitz.

Helck, W. & Westendorf, W., 1975-89. (Eds) *Lexicon der Ägyptologie*. Wiesbaden: Harrassowitz.

Hermopolis Code (*pCairo* JE 89127-30 & 89137-43 r°, *pMattha*) = Donker van Heel (1990)

Hibbitts, B.J., 1992. Coming to Our Senses: Communication and Legal Expression in Performance Cultures. *Emory Law Journal* 41: 873-960.

Hintze, F., 1950-52. *Untersuchungen zu Stil und Sprache neuägyptischer Erzählungen*. VIO 2 & 6. Berlin: Akademie Verlag.

Hoch, J.E., 1994. *Semitic Words in Egyptian Texts of the New Kingdom and the Third Intermediate Period*. Princeton: Princeton University Press.

Hodge, R.I.V. & Kress, G.R., 1988. *Social Semiotics*. Ithaca: Cornell University Press.

Hofmann, T., 2006. Arbeitseinsätze und Löhne der sogenannten Sklavinnen von Deir el-Medine. In *Living and Writing in Deir el-Medine: Socio-historic Embodiment of Deir el-Medine Texts*, eds. A. Dorn & T. Hofmann. AH 19, 113-8. Basel: Schwabe Verlag.

Horus and Seth = *LES*, 37-60

Ḥrḫwf tomb = *Urk*. I, 120-31

ỉdw tomb = Goedicke (1970: table XVIII)

Instruction of Ptahhotep = Žába (1956)

Jackson, B.S., 1988. *Law, Fact and Narrative Coherence*. Merseyside: Deborah Charles Publications.

— 1995. *Making Sense in Law: Linguistic, Psychological and Semiotic Perspectives*. Liverpool: Deborah Charles Publications.

Jansen-Winkeln, K., 1995. Diglossie und Zweisprachigkeit im alten Ägypten. *WZKM* 85: 85-115.

Janssen, J.J., 1961. *Two Ancient Egyptian Ship's Logs: Papyrus Leiden I 350 verso and Papyrus Turin 2008 + 2016*. Leiden: E.J. Brill.

— 1966. A Twentieth-Dynasty Account Papyrus. *JEA* 52: 81-94.

— 1968. The Smaller Dâkhla Stela (Ashmolean Museum no. 1894.107b). *JEA* 54: 165-72.

— 1974. An Allusion to an Egyptian Wedding Ceremony? *GM* 10: 25-8.

— 1975. *Commodity Prices from the Ramessid Period: An Economic Study of the Village of Necropolis Workmen at Thebes*. Leiden: E.J. Brill.

— 1975b. The Rules of Legal Proceeding in the Community of Necropolis Workmen at Deir el-Medîna (review of Allam, S., 1973. Hieratische Ostraka und Papyri aus der Ramessidenzeit). *BiOr* 32: 291-6.

— 1982. Gift-Giving in Ancient Egypt as an Economic Feature. *JEA* 68: 253-8.

— 1988. Marriage Problems and Public Reactions (P.BM 10416). In *Pyramid Studies and Other Essays Presented to I.E.S. Edwards*, eds. J. Baines, T.G.H. James, A. Leahy, A.F. Shore, 134-7. London: E.E.S.

— 1988b. Two Egyptian Commandments. In *Essays dedicated to Professor M.S.H.G. Heerma van Voss on the occasion of his retirement from the Chair of the History of Ancient Religions at the University of Amsterdam*, eds. J.H. Kamstra, H. Milde, K. Wagtendonk, 52-57. Kampen: J.H. Kok.

— 1993. *B3kw*: from Work to Product. *SAK* 20: 81-94.

— 1994. Debts and Credit in the New Kingdom. *JEA* 80: 129-36.

— 1997. *Village Varia: Ten Studies on the History and Administration of Deir el-Medina*. Egyptologische Uitgaven 11. Leiden: Nederlands Instituut voor het Nabije Oosten.

— 1999. A Marital Title from the New Kingdom. In *Gold of Praise: Studies on Ancient Egypt in Honor of Edward F. Wente*, eds. E. Teeter & J.A. Larson. SAOC 58, 185-92. Chicago: Oriental Institute of the University of Chicago.

— 2005. *Donkeys at Deir el-Medîna*. Egyptologische Uitgaven 19. Leiden: NINO.

Janssen, J.J. , Frood, E. & Goecke-Bauer, M., 2003. *Woodcutters, Potters and Doorkeepers: Service Personnel of the Deir el-Medina Workmen*. Egyptologische Uitgaven 17. Leiden: NINO.

Janssen, J.J. & Pestman, P.W., 1968. Burial and Inheritance in the Community of the Necropolis Workmen at Thebes (Pap. Bulaq X and O. Petrie 16). *JESHO* 11: 137-70.

Jasnow, R., 2003. Egypt: Old Kingdom and First Intermediate Period. In *A History of Ancient Near Eastern Law*, ed. R. Westbrook. Handbook of Oriental Studies I Near and Middle East 72/1, 93-140. Leiden/Boston: Brill.

— 2003b. Egypt: Middle Kingdom and Second Intermediate Period. In *A History of Ancient Near Eastern Law*, ed. R. Westbrook. Handbook of Oriental Studies I Near and Middle East 72/1, 255-88. Leiden/Boston: Brill.

— 2003c. Egypt: New Kingdom. In *A History of Ancient Near Eastern Law*, ed. R. Westbrook. Handbook of Oriental Studies I Near and Middle East 72/1, 289-359. Leiden/Boston: Brill.

— 2003d. Egypt: Third Intermediate Period. In *A History of Ancient Near Eastern Law*, ed. R. Westbrook. Handbook of Oriental Studies I Near and Middle East 72/2, 777-818. Leiden/Boston: Brill.

Jin, S., 2001. Ein Gottesurteil im pBoulaq X: Ein Fall von "Balance of Power" bei dem Gottesorakel? *JESHO* 44: 95-102.

Jori, M., 1994. Legal Performatives. In *The Encyclopedia of Language and Linguistics*, eds R.E. Asher & J.M.Y. Simpson, IV, 2092-2097. Oxford: Pergamon Press.

Junge, F., 2005 (2nd English ed.). *Late Egyptian Grammar: An Introduction*. Oxford: Griffith Institute.

K3mnfrt? *Cairo block* CG 1432 = Goedicke (1970: table V)

Kamose stela Luxor J 43 = Helck (1975b)

Kanais (Wadi Abbad or Mia/Redesieh) decree = *KRI* I, 67-70 n.32C

Kaplony, P., 1975. Eid. *LÄ* I: 1188-200. Wiesbaden: Harrassowitz.

Keller, S.R., 1989. *Egyptian Letters to the Dead in relation to the Old Testament and other Near Eastern sources*. Ann Arbor: UMI.

Kitchen, K.A., 1968-90. *Ramesside Inscriptions, Historical and Biographical*, 8 vols. Oxford: B.H. Blackwell.

— 1993-2001. *Ramesside Inscriptions Translated and Annoted*. 3 vols. Oxford: B.H. Blackwell.

— 1993-99. *Ramesside Inscriptions Translated and Annoted: Notes and Comments*. 2 vols. Oxford: B.H. Blackwell.

Koenig, Y., 1997. *Les ostraca hiératiques inédits de la Bibliothèque nationale et universitaire de Strasbourg*. DFIFAO 33. Cairo: IFAO.

KRI = Kitchen (1968-90)

Kruchten, J.-M., 1981. *Le Décret d'Horemheb. Traduction, commentaire épigraphique, philologique et institutionnel*. Bruxelles: Editions de l'Université de Bruxelles.

— 2004. Derechef l'ostracon DM 764. *GM* 198: 39-42.

Kurzon, D., 1984. Themes, hyperthemes and the discourse structure of British legal texts. In *Studies of legal discourse*, ed. B. Danet, 31-55. *Text* (special issue) 4-1/3.

— 1986. *It is hereby performed...: Explorations in Legal Speech Acts*. Pragmatics & Beyond VII: 6. Amsterdam: John Benjamins.

— 1997. 'Legal language': varieties, genres, registers, discourses. *International Journal of Applied Linguistics* 7: 119-39.

LÄ = Helck & Westendorf (1975-1989)

Lacau, P., 1949. *Une stèle juridique de Karnak*. CASAE 13. Cairo: IFAO.

Lakoff, G., 1986. Classifiers as a Reflection of Mind. In *Noun Classes and Categorization: Proceedings of a Symposium on Categorization and Noun Classification, Eugene, Oregon, October 1983*, ed. C. Craig, 13-51. Amsterdam: J. Benjamins.

Lakoff, G. & Johnson, M., 1980. *Metaphors We Live By*. Chicago: University of Chicago Press.

LEG = Černý & Israelit-Groll (1993)

Legrain, G., 1914. *Catalogue général des antiquités égyptiennes du Musée du Caire (42192-42250): Statues et statuettes de rois et de particuliers*. III. Cairo: IFAO.

Leiden Deir el-Medina database: http://www.leidenuniv.nl/nino/dmd/dmd.html

LEM = Gardiner (1937) and Caminos (1954)

LES = Gardiner (1932)

Lisht tomb = Goedicke (1970: table 12)

Löfstedt, L., 1981. A propos des articles et des articloïdes. In *Logos Semantikos: Studia linguistica in honorem Eugenio Coseriu IV*, eds H. Geckeler, B. Schlieben-Lange, J. Trabant & H. Weydt, 269-279. Berlin: De Gruyter.

Logan, T., 2000. The *Jmyt-pr* Document: Form, Function, and Significance. *JARCE* 37: 49-73.

López, J., 1978-84. *Ostraca Ieratici: Catalogo del museo egizio di Torino*. Serie II. Collezioni 3, 1-4. Milano: Istituto editoriale Cisalpino – La Goliardica.

Loprieno, A., 1996. Linguistic Variety and Egyptian Literature. In *Ancient Egyptian Literature: History and Forms*, ed. A. Loprieno. PÄ 10, 515-529. Leiden: E.J. Brill.

— 1997. Slaves. In *The Egyptians*, ed. S. Donadoni, 185-219. Chicago: University of Chicago Press.

Lord, A.B., 1987. Characteristics of Orality. *Oral Tradition* 2: 54-72.

Louvre stela C 34 = Sethe (1924: 96 (31))

LRL = Černý (1939)

Luft, U., 1984. *dj.j rḫ.k*. In *Studien zu Sprache und Religion Ägyptens: Zu Ehren von W. Westendorf*, ed. F. Junge. I, 103-11. Göttingen: Hubert & Co.

Malek, J., 1986. *In the Shadow of the Pyramids: Egypt during the Old Kingdom*. Echoes of the Ancient World. London: Orbis.

Maley, Y., 1994. The language of the law. In *Language and the law*, ed. J. Gibbons, 11-50. London: Longman.

Malinine, M., 1947. Notes juridiques (à propos de l'ouvrage de E. Seidl). *BIFAO* 46: 93-123.

— 1953. *Choix de textes juridiques en hiératique « anormal » et en démotique (XXVe-XXVIIe dynasties)*. BEHE fasc. 300. Paris: Librairie ancienne Honoré Champion.

— 1967. Partage testamentaire d'une propriété familiale. *RdE* 19: 67-85.

— 1983. *Choix de textes juridiques en hiératique anormal et en démotique (deuxième partie)*. RAPH 18. Cairo: IFAO.

Malkiel, Y., 1959. Studies in Irreversible Binomials. *Lingua* 8: 113-160.

Manning, J.G., 2003. Egypt: Demotic Law. In *A History of Ancient Near Eastern Law*, ed. R. Westbrook. Handbook of Oriental Studies I Near and Middle East 72/2, 819-62. Leiden/Boston: Brill.

Martin, C.J., 1995. Marriages, Wills and Leases of Land: Some Notes on the Formulae of Demotic Contracts. In *Legal Documents of the Hellenistic World: Papers from a Seminar arranged by the Institute of Classical Studies, the Institute of Jewish Studies and the Warburg Institute, University of London, February to May 1986*, eds. M.J. Geller & H. Maehler, 58-78. London: Warburg Institute.

Maspero, G., 1881. Notes sur quelques points de Grammaire et d'Histoire. *ZÄS* 19: 116-31.

Massart, A., 1957. The Egyptian Geneva Papyrus MAH 15274. *MDAIK* 15: 172-85.

Mattila, H.E.S., 2006. *Comparative Legal Linguistics*. Aldershot/Burlington: Ashgate.

McDowell, A. G., 1990. *Jurisdiction in the Workmen's Community of Deir el-Medîna*. Leiden: Nederlands Instituut voor het Nabije Oosten.

— 1992. Agricultural Activity by the Workmen of Deir el-Medina. *JEA* 78: 195-206.

— 1993. *Hieratic Ostraca in the Hunterian Museum Glasgow (The Colin Campbell Ostraca)*. Oxford: Griffith Institute, Ashmolean Museum.

— 1995. An incised hieratic ostracon (Ashmolean HO 655). *JEA* 81: 220-5.

— 1998. Legal Aspects of Care of the Elderly in Egypt to the End of the New Kingdom. In *The Care of the Elderly in the Ancient Near East*, eds. M. Stole & S.P. Vleeming. SHCANE 14, 199-221. Leiden, Boston, Köln: Brill.

— 1999. *Village Life in Ancient Egypt: Laundry Lists and Love Songs*. Oxford: Oxford University Press.

— 2000. Teachers and Students at Deir el-Medina. In *Deir el-Medina in the Third Millenium AD: A Tribute to Jac. J. Janssen*, eds. R.J. Demarée & A. Egberts, 217-33. Leiden: Nederlands Instituut voor het Nabije Oosten.

Megally, M., 1977. *Notions de comptabilité à propos du papyrus E. 3226 du musée du Louvre*. BdE 72. Cairo: IFAO.

Mellinkoff, D., 1963. *The Language of the Law*. Boston: Little, Brown.

Menu, B., 1971. Quelques remarques à propos de l'étude de la stèle juridique de Karnak et de la « stèle » d'Ahmès-Nefertari. *RdE* 23: 155-63.

— 1982. *Recherches sur l'histoire juridique, économique et sociale de l'ancienne Egypte (I)*. Versailles: B. Menu.

— 1985. Ventes de maisons sous l'Ancien Empire égyptien. In *Mélanges offerts à Jean Vercoutter*, eds. F. Geus & F. Thill, 249-62. Paris: Editions Recherche sur les Civilisations.

— 1985b. Cessions de services et engagements pour dette sous les rois kouchites et saïtes. *RdE* 36 : 73-87.

— 1988. Les actes de vente en Egypte ancienne, particulièrement sous les rois kouchites et saïtes. *JEA* 74 : 165-81.

— 1998. *Recherches sur l'histoire juridique, économique et sociale de l'ancienne Egypte (II)*. Le Caire: IFAO.

— 2004. *Egypte pharaonique: Nouvelles recherches sur l'histoire juridique, économique et sociale de l'ancienne Egypte(III)*. Paris: L'Harmattan.

Mes = Gardiner (1964)

Meyer, E.A., 2004. *Legitimacy and Law in the Roman World: Tabulae in Roman Belief and Practice*. Cambridge: University Press.

Montet, P., 1930. Les tombeaux de Siout et de Deir Rifeh (2). *Kêmi* 3 : 45-111.

Morison, J. & Leith, P., 1992. *The Barrister's World and the Nature of Law*. Philadelphia: Open University Press, Milton Keynes.

Mrsich, T., 1968. *Untersuchungen zur Hausurkunde des Alten Reich: Ein Beitrag zum altägyptischen Stiftungsrecht*. MÄS 13. Berlin: Bruno Hessling.

— 1975. Erbe. *LÄ* I: 1235-60.

— 1995. Erenofres Verteidigung. In *Gedenkschrift für Winfried Barta*, eds. D. Kessler & R. Schulz. MÄU 4, 291-310. Frankfurt: Peter Lang.

— 2005. *Fragen zum altägyptischen Recht der Isolationsperiode vor dem Neuen Reich: Ein Forschungsbericht aus dem Arbeitskreis Historiogenese von Rechtsnormen*. München: Herbert Utz.

Mṯn tomb Berlin 1105 = Goedicke (1970: table Ib)

Müller-Wollermann, R., 1985. Warenaustausch im Ägypten des Alten Reiches. *JESHO* 28: 121-68.

Munich Deir el-Medine online: http://obelix.arf.fak12.uni-muenchen.de/cgi-bin/mmcgi2mmhob/mho-1/hobmain/

Muñoz, J.E., 2006. Performance as a Doing in and for Futurity. *Performance Studies International* website: psi-web.org/texts/polemics.html

Muszynski, M., 1977. P.Turin Cat. 2070/154. *OA* 16: 183-200.

Naunakhte (pAshmolean Museum 1945.97 and related documents) = *KRI* VI, 236-43 n.20

Nauri decree = *KRI* I, 45-58 n.24 & 416 n.180

Navailles, R. & Neveu, F., 1989. Qu'entendait-on par "journées d'esclave" au Nouvel Empire ? (*hrw m ḥm(t), hrw n bꜣk*). *RdE* 40 : 113-23.

Naville, E., 1971. (Ed.) *Das ägyptische Totenbuch der XVIII. bis XX. Dynastie,* 2 vols. Graz: Akademische Druck.

Nbkꜣwḥr tomb = Goedicke (1970: tables IX-X)

Nbḫprwrꜥ Ỉntf Coptos decree (CG 30770) = Petrie (1896: pl. VIII)

Neveu, F., 1986. Le tarif de location des ânes à Deir el-Médineh. *RdE* 37: 151-5.

— 1988. La particule *Ḫr* en néo-égyptien. In *Akten des vierten internationalen Ägyptologen Kongresses München 1985*, ed. S. Schoske. BSAK 3, 99-110. Hamburg: Helmut Buske.

Nfrirkꜣrꜥ Abydos decree (*Boston* 03.1896) = Goedicke (1967: Abb. 2)

Nfrprt stelaphorous statue Cairo CG 42121 = *Urk*. IV, 1019-21

Nfrḥrnptḥ's lintel = Petrie (1907: pl. 7A, 1-2)

Nḫtfmwti statue Cairo CG 42208 = Legrain (1914: 20-3)

Nkꜣwrꜥ tomb = Goedicke (1970: table IIb)

Nkꜥnḫ tomb = Goedicke (1970: tables XI and XIIIa)

Nordh, K., 1996. *Aspects of Ancient Egyptian Curses and Blessings: Conceptual Background and Transmission.* USAMNEC 26. Uppsala: Uppsala University Press.

oAberdeen 1317 v° = *KRI* V, 586-7 n.233 A 260

oAG 55 = Černý *Notebook,* 31.54 & 112.32

oAG 77 = Černý *Notebook,*112.42

oAshmolean 655 = McDowell (1995)

oAshmolean 1933.810 = *KRI* V, 525-6 n.223 A 135/136

oAshmolean 1945.39 = *KRI* V, 587-8 n.233 A 261

oBerlin P 1268 r° = *KRI* VII, 284-5 n.268 A 358

oBerlin P 10626 = Munich Deir el-Medine online

oBerlin P 10627 = *KRI* VI, 155-6 n.88 A 105

oBerlin P 10629 = *KRI* V, 574 n.231 A 237

oBerlin P 10631 = Erman (1911: pl. 36)

oBerlin P 10637 = *KRI* V, 455 n.216 A 20

oBerlin P 10655 = *KRI* V, 573-4 n.231 A 236

oBerlin P 10665 = *KRI* VI, 244 n.21 A 6

oBerlin P 11260 = Munich Deir el-Medine online
oBerlin P 12343 = *KRI* VI, 164-5 n.91 A 126
oBerlin P 12405 = Munich Deir el-Medine online
oBerlin P 12406 (+ *oGlasgow* D 1925.71) = Munich Deir el-Medine online and *KRI* VII, 361-2 n.61 A 31
oBerlin P 12635 = Munich Deir el-Medine online
oBerlin P 12636 v° = *KRI* VII, 288 n.269 A 364
oBerlin P 14262 = *KRI* VII, 343 n.A 202
oBerlin P 14328 = Munich Deir el-Medine online
oBerlin P 14357 ('C') = *KRI* VII, 343 n.A 203
oBerlin P 14365 = *KRI* VII, 343 n.A 204
oBM EA 5624 = *KRI* V, 475-6 n.218 A 60
oBM EA 5633 = *KRI* V, 588-9 n.233 A 262
oBM EA 5637 = *KRI* V, 577 n.231 A 241
oBM EA 5649 = *KRI* V, 589 n.233 A 263
oBM EA 50729 = *KRI* VII, 351 n.142 B VIII.13
oBM EA 50736 = Demarée (2002: 136-7)
oBM EA 50737 = Demarée (2002: 138)
oBM EA 65941 (*oNash* 4) = Demarée (2002: 191-2)
oBodleian Library 253 = *KRI* V, 485 n.218 A 70
oBorchardt = Allam (1973: pl. 23)
oBrooklyn 37.1880 & *oBM* EA 5644 = *KRI* VII, 310 n.278 A 402 & *KRI* V, 589-90 n.233 A 264
oBrussels E 6311 = *KRI* IV, 230-1 n.28 A 14
oCairo CG 25553 = *KRI* V, 454 n.216 A 18
oCairo CG 25555 = *KRI* V, 456-7 n.216 A 22
oCairo CG 25557 = *KRI* V, 569 n.231 A 228
oCairo CG 25583 = *KRI* IV, 329-30 n.59 A 21
oCairo CG 25590 = *KRI* VI, 165 n.91 A 127
oCairo CG 25604 = *KRI* V, 526 n.223 A 137
oCairo CG 25612 = Černý (1935-70: pl. 61)
oCairo CG 25624 & 25365 = *KRI* V, 516-7 n.222 A 123
oCairo CG 25650 = *KRI* VI, 172 n.94 A 140
oCairo CG 25660 & JE 37649 = *KRI* VI, 168-9 n.93 A 134 and Černý *Notebook*, 106.98
oCairo CG 25667 = Černý (1935-70: pl. 71)
oCairo CG 25722 = Černý (1935: pl. 88)
oDeM 31 = *KRI* III, 823-4 n.303:1
oDeM 49 = *KRI* VII, 195 n.A 67bis
oDeM 56 = *KRI* V, 502 n.220 A 102
oDeM 57 = *KRI* V, 554 n.227 A 192
oDeM 58 = *KRI* III, 546 n.232 A 53
oDeM 59 = Černý (1935-70: I, pl. 46)
oDeM 61 = *KRI* III, 546 n.232 A 54
oDeM 62 = *KRI* V, 527 n.223 A 141
oDeM 63 = Černý (1935-70: I, pl. 48)
oDeM 64 = *KRI* V, 536 n.224 A 161

oDeM 66 = *KRI* VI, 128 n.80 A 26
oDeM 67 = *KRI* V, 536 n.224 A 160
oDeM 68 = *KRI* V, 460 n. 216 A 34
oDeM 69 = *KRI* VI, 374 n.53 A 21
oDeM 71 = *KRI* VI, 159 n.89 A 114
oDeM 72 = *KRI* V, 468 n.217 A 45
oDeM 73 = *KRI* V, 472-3 n.217 A 55
oDeM 108 = *KRI* I, 409 n.172:8
oDeM 112 = *KRI* III, 546 n.232 A55
oDeM 113 = *KRI* VI, 102-3 n.77 A 2
oDeM 116 = *KRI* III, 540 n.229 A39
oDeM 125 = *KRI* III, 543 n.231 A47
oDeM 133 = *KRI* VI, 425-6 n.22 A 3
oDeM 134 = *KRI* VI, 172 n.94 A142
oDeM 146 = *KRI* VI, 664 n. 67 A 39
oDeM 185 = Černý (1935-70: II, pl. 51)
oDeM 195 + *oBerlin [D]*, = *KRI* VI, 166 n.91 A 130
oDeM 222 = *KRI* V, 480-2 n.218 A 63
oDeM 225 = *KRI* VI, 157-8 n.89 A 111
oDeM 231 =*KRI* V, 579-80 n.232 A 245
oDeM 239 =*KRI* III, 684 n.257:8
oDeM 242 = Černý (1935-70: VI, pl.1)
oDeM 244 = Černý (1935-70: VI, pl.1)
oDeM 245 = Černý (1935-70: IV, pl. 1)
oDeM 255 = *KRI* VI, 250 n.23 A 16
oDeM 261 = *KRI* V, 580 n.232 A 246
oDeM 282 = *KRI* VI, 172 n.94 A 141
oDeM 305 = *KRI* V, 556 n.227 A 199
oDeM 319 = *KRI* IV, 334-5 n.63 A 30
oDeM 399 = *KRI* VI, 256 n.28 A 31
oDeM 400 = *KRI* V, 554 n.227 A 191
oDeM 402 = *KRI* VI, 140 n.82 A 58
oDeM 407 = *KRI* VI, 160 n.89 A 117
oDeM 410 = *KRI* V, 507 n.221 A 109
oDeM 411 = Černý (1935-70: V, pl. 18)
oDeM 423 = *KRI* V, 591-2 n.233 A 269
oDeM 424 = *KRI* V, 470-1 n.217 A 50
oDeM 425 = *KRI* V, 569 n.231 A 229
oDeM 428 = *KRI* V, 580 n.232 A 247
oDeM 432 = *KRI* V, 455-6 n.216 A 21
oDeM 433 = *KRI* VI, 130-1 n.80 A 35
oDeM 435 = Černý (1935-70: V, pl. 25)
oDeM 451 = *KRI* V, 495 n.219 A 91
oDeM 553 = *KRI* V, 658-9 n.247:2

oDeM 556 = *KRI* V, 592 n.233 A 271
oDeM 557 = *KRI* V, 570 n.231 A 231
oDeM 564 = *KRI* V, 451 n.215 A 14
oDeM 579 = *KRI* V, 581 n.232 A 249
oDeM 586 = *KRI* V, 583 n.232 A 253
oDeM 593 = *KRI* VI, 374 n.54 A 23
oDeM 619 = Sauneron (1959: pl. 30)
oDeM 624 = Černý (1935-70: VII, pl.1)
oDeM 627 = Černý (1935-70: VII, pl.3)
oDeM 632 = Černý (1935-70: VII, pl.4)
oDeM 643 = *KRI* V, 602-3 n.235 A 293
oDeM 648 = *KRI* V, 569-70 n.231 A 230
oDeM 666 = *KRI* V, 617 n.235 A 333
oDeM 671 & 765 = Grandet (2000: 169)
oDeM 702 = *KRI* VI, 149 n.85 A 87
oDeM 764 = Grandet (2000: 166)
oDeM 767 = Grandet (2000: 171)
oDeM 772 = Grandet (2000: 177)
oDeM 774 = Grandet (2000: 179)
oDeM 775 = Grandet (2000: 180)
oDeM 779 = Grandet (2000: 182-3)
oDeM 780 = Grandet (2000: 183)
oDeM 781 = Grandet (2000: 184)
oDeM 782 = Grandet (2000: 184)
oDeM 928 = Grandet (2003: 364)
oDeM 930 = Grandet (2003: 367)
oDeM 933 = Grandet (2003: 370)
oDeM 934 = Grandet (2003: 371)
oDeM 935 = Grandet (2003: 372)
oDeM 936 = Grandet (2003: 373)
oDeM 937 = Grandet (2003: 374)
oDeM 938 = Grandet (2003: 375)
oDeM 939 = Grandet (2003: 376)
oDeM 940 = Grandet (2003: 377)
oDeM 941 = Grandet (2003: 378)
oDeM 942 = Grandet (2003: 379-80)
oDeM 943 = Grandet (2003: 381)
oDeM 944 = Grandet (2003: 384)
oDeM 945 = Grandet (2003: 385)
oDeM 946 r° = Grandet (2003: 387)
oDeM 947 = Grandet (2003: 388)
oDeM 948 = Grandet (2003: 389-90)
oDeM 952 (*oIFAO* 1069) = Grandet (2003: 396-8)
oDeM 958 = Grandet (2003: 408)

oDeM 959 = Grandet (2003: 409-11)
oDeM 960 = Grandet (2003: 412)
oDeM 962 = Grandet (2003: 413)
oDeM 963 = Grandet (2003: 414)
oDeM 964 = Grandet (2003: 415, 417)
oDeM 1068 r° = *KRI* VI, 250 n.23 A 17
oDeM 2928 = Vandier d'Abbadie (1959: pl. 133)
oEdgerton 1 = Černý *Notebook,* 107.69
oFaulkner 1 = Černý, *Notebook* 31.79a
oFlorence 2620 = *KRI* V, 467 n.217 A 40
oFlorence 2625 = *KRI* V, 501 n.220 A 99
oGardiner/Ashmolean 9 = Černý & Gardiner (1957: pl. 24, 4)
oGardiner/Ashmolean 33 v° = *KRI* VI, 257 n.28 A 32
oGardiner/Ashmolean 36 = *KRI* VI, 429-30 n.23 A 7
oGardiner/Ashmolean 51 = Černý (1972: 67)
oGardiner/Ashmolean 53 = *KRI* V, 484 n.218 A 67
oGardiner/Ashmolean 55 = Černý & Peet (1927: 38-9)
oGardiner/Ashmolean 63 = *KRI* VI, 664 n.67 A 38
oGardiner/Ashmolean 66 = *KRI* VI, 256 n.28 A 30
oGardiner/Ashmolean 68 = *KRI* V, 555-6 n.227 A 195
oGardiner/Ashmolean 89 = *KRI* III, 724 n.271:9
oGardiner/Ashmolean 90 = *KRI* III, 683 n.257:7
oGardiner/Ashmolean 103 = *KRI* V, 571-2, n.231 A 234 (Text A) and 585-6, n.233 A 257 (Text B)
oGardiner/Ashmolean 104 = *KRI* V, 555 n.227 A 194
oGardiner/Ashmolean 105 = Černý & Gardiner (1957: pl. 53, 1)
oGardiner/Ashmolean 106 = *KRI* V, 515 n.222 A 120
oGardiner/Ashmolean 112 = *KRI* IV, 330 n.59 A 22
oGardiner/Ashmolean 119 = *KRI* VI, 161 n.91 A 121
oGardiner/Ashmolean 121 = *KRI* VI, 159 n.89 A 115
oGardiner/Ashmolean 123 = *KRI* IV, 219-20 n.23 A 5
oGardiner/Ashmolean 126 = *KRI* V, 586 n.233 A 258
oGardiner/Ashmolean 128 = *KRI* VI, 159 n.89 A 116
oGardiner/Ashmolean 135 = *KRI* VII, 344-5 n.A 207
oGardiner/Ashmolean 136 = *KRI* V, 586 n.233 A 259
oGardiner/Ashmolean 137 = *KRI* VI, 251 n.23 A 18
oGardiner/Ashmolean 140 = *KRI* V, 490-1 n.219 A 81
oGardiner/Ashmolean 152 = *KRI* V, 487 n. 218 A 75
oGardiner/Ashmolean 154 = *KRI* VII, 298-9 n.273 A 385
oGardiner/Ashmolean 157 = *KRI* VII, 369-70 n.36 A 15
oGardiner/Ashmolean 163 = *KRI* VI, 255-6 n. 28 A 29
oGardiner/Ashmolean 164 v° = *KRI* VII, 380-1 n.93 A 54
oGardiner/Ashmolean 178 = Černý *Notebook,* 45.81
oGardiner/Ashmolean 185 = *KRI* VII, 297-8 n.273 A 382
oGardiner/Ashmolean 196 = *KRI* V, 502 n.220 A 101

oGardiner/Ashmolean 204 = *KRI* VI, 258 n.28 A 35
oGardiner/Ashmolean 254 v° = Černý *Notebook,* 31.56
oGardiner/Ashmolean 260 = Černý *Notebook*, 31.64
oGardiner/Ashmolean 261 = Černý *Notebook,* 31.64
oGardiner/Ashmolean 272 = *KRI* VII, 283-4 n.268 A 356
oGlasgow D 1925.66 (*oColin Campbell* 1) = McDowell (1993: pl. 1)
oGlasgow D 1925.70 (*oColin Campbell* 5) = *KRI* VI, 162-3 n.A 123
oGlasgow D 1925.71 (*oColin Campbell* 6) = *KRI* VII, 361-2 n.61 A 31
oGlasgow D 1925.76 (*oColin Campbell* 11) & *oGardiner/Ashmolean*52 = *KRI* VII, 293-5 n.272 A 376
oIFAO 290 = Černý *Notebook,*103.120
oIFAO 388 = Černý & Gardiner (1957: pl. 69)
oIFAO 389 = *KRI* V, 595 n.233 A 278
oIFAO 424 + *oPetrie* 9 = *KRI* V, 525-6 n.223 A 135/6
oIFAO 556 = Černý (1935-70: 52)
oIFAO 765 = Černý *Notebook,*105.31
oIFAO 1069 (*oDeM* 952) = Grandet (2003: 396-8)
oIFAO 1305 = Černý *Notebook,* 61.79
oIFAO 1322 + *oVarille* 38 + *oCairo* 25705 = Černý *Notebooks,* 2.23 & 62.24
oIFAO 1403 = Černý *Notebook,* 116.8
oIFAO 1425 = *KRI* VI, 372 n.51 A 16
oLeiden F 2002/10.1 = Demarée (2008: fig. 4-5)
oLeipzig 5 = Černý & Gardiner (1957: pl. 36)
oLouvre E 3262b,f,g = *KRI* VII, 314 n.280 A 409
oLouvre E 3263 = *KRI* III, 555-6 n.233 A 69
oLouvre E 13156 (*oLouvre* E 2425, *oAnastasi*) = *KRI* III, 547 n.232 A 56
oMichaelides 1 = *KRI* V, 451-2 n.215 A 15
oMichaelides 2 = *KRI* V, 461 n.217 A 37
oMichaelides 3 = *KRI* VI, 373 n.53 A 20
oMichaelides 5 = *KRI* V, 509 n.221 A 113
oMichaelides 6 = *KRI* VI, 137-8 n.82 A 55
oMichaelides 13 = *KRI* IV, 152-3 n.92 A 6)
oMichaelides 14 = *KRI* IV, 328-9 n.59 A 20
oMichaelides 47 = *KRI* III, 514-5 n.229 A 14
oMichaelides 48 r° = *KRI* III, 556-7 n.234 A 70
oMichaelides 84 = *KRI* V, 487 n.218 A 74
oMunich 1547 v° = Brunner-Traut (1956: pl. 43)
oNash 1 (*oBM* EA 65930) = *KRI* IV, 315-7 n.55 A 12
Ong, W.J., 1982. *Orality and Literacy: The Technologizing of the Word*. London/New York: Routledge.
oOIC 12073 = *KRI* VI, 138-9 n.82 A 57
oOIC 16994 = Černý *Notebook*, 107.30
oOIC 17005 (*oNelson* 14) = Černý, *Notebook* 107.32-4
oOIC 19123 = Černý *Notebook*, 65.37 & 107.72
oOIC 19154 (*oEdgerton* 10) = *KRI* VII, 297 n.272 A 380
oPetrie 2 = *KRI* VI, 369-70 n.51 A 12

oPetrie 3 (*oUC* 39606) = Černý & Gardiner (1957: pl. 16.3)
oPetrie 5 (*oUC* 39608) = *KRI* V, 537 n.224 A 164
oPetrie 14 = *KRI* V, 524 n.223 A 133
oPetrie 16 = Černý & Gardiner (1957: pl. 21)
oPetrie 17 (*oUC* 39618) = *KRI* VI, 247 n.22 A 11
oPetrie 18 = *KRI* VI, 430 n.23 A 8
oPetrie 31 (*oUC* 39630) = *KRI* VI, 169-70 n.93 A 135
oPetrie 34 = Černý & Gardiner (1957: pl. 29 n.1)
oPetrie 51 (*oUC* 39649) = *KRI* VI, 869-70 n.48 A 10
oPetrie 67 (*oUC* 32054) = *KRI* VI, 143 n.83 A 66
oPetrie 78 = *KRI* V, 540 n.225 A 169
oPrague H 12 = *KRI* III, 548 n.232 A 57
oPrague H 24 = Černý, *Notebook* 26.31
oQueen's College Oxford 1115 = *KRI* VI, 167-8 n.92 A 133
oStrasbourg H 84 = *KRI* VI, 428-9 n. 23 A 6
oStrasbourg H 182 = Koenig (1997: pl. 93)
oTurin 57010 = *KRI* V, 517 n.224 A 124
oTurin 57150 = *KRI* V, 471 n.217 A 52
oTurin 57151 = López (1978-84: II, pl. 67)
oTurin 57159 = López (1978-84: II, pl. 71)
oTurin 57173 = *KRI* V, 457-8 n.216 A 24
oTurin 57362 = *KRI* VII, 287-8 n.269 A 363
oTurin 57368 = *KRI* VII, 322 n.285 B III.5:4
oTurin 57389 = Allam (1973: pl. 67)
oTurin 57456 = López (1978-84: IV, pl. 155)
oTurin 57457 = López (1978-84: IV, pl. 155)
oVienna H 2 = *KRI* VI, 132-3 n.81 A 43
pAbbott (*pBM* 10221) = *KRI* VI, 468-81 n.18
pAdoptions (*pAshmolean Museum* 1945.96) = *KRI* VI, 735-8 n.19
pAnastasi I 21, 6 (*pBM* 10247) = *Gardiner* (1911: 33)
pAnastasi II v° 4-5 (*pBM* 10243) = *LEM*, 19
pAnastasi V 13,2-14,6 (*pBM* 10244) = *LEM*, 62-3
Pantalacci, L., 1985. Un décret royal de Pépi II en faveur des gouverneurs de l'oasis de Dakhla. *BIFAO* 85: 245-54.
Parkinson, R.B., 1991. *The Tale of the Eloquent Peasant*. Oxford: Griffith Institute, Ashmolean Museum & Parkinson.
pAshmolean Museum 1945.95 (*Naunakhte* Doc. IV) = *KRI* VI, 242-3 n.20 A 4
pAshmolean Museum 1945.96 cf. *pAdoptions*
pAshmolean Museum 1945.97 (*Naunakhte*) = *KRI* VI, 236-43 n.20
pBankes I (*pBM* EA 75015) = Demarée (2006b: 7-9, 34-7)
pBeatty I v° D (*pBM* 10681) = Gardiner (1931: pl. 27)
pBerlin P 3047 = *KRI* II, 803-6 n.285
pBerlin P 8523 = Allam (1973: pl. 76-7)
pBerlin P 9010 = Sethe (1926)

pBerlin P 9784-5 and *pGurob* II,1-2 = Gardiner (1906)

pBerlin P 10470 = Smither (1948)

pBerlin P 10496 = *KRI* V, 476-8 n. 218 A 61

pBM EA 10052 (= *Great Tomb Robberies*) = *KRI* VI, 767-803 n.25

pBM EA 10053 v° = *KRI* VI, 755-63 n.23

pBM EA 10100 = *LRL*, 50-1

pBM EA 10335 = Dawson (1925)

pBM EA 10373 = Janssen (1991: pl. 29-30)

pBM EA 10403 = *KRI* VI, 828-33 n.27

pBM EA 10416 = Janssen (1988)

pBM EA 10425 = Pestman (1968)

pBM EA 10591 = Thompson (1934: text B)

pBN 198 II = *LRL*, 67-8

pBN 198 III = *LRL*, 68-70

pBN 199 I = *LRL*, 53

pBN 237 carton 1 = *KRI* VI, 339-40 n.33

pBoulaq 8 (*pCairo* CG 58043) = Baer (1966) and Goedicke (1967b)

pBoulaq 10 (*pCairo* CG 58092) = *KRI* V, 449 n.215 A 13

pBrooklyn 35.1446 B = Hayes (1955)

pCairo CG 58057 = *KRI* I, 238 n.108

pCairo ESP (B) = *KRI* VI, 518-9 n.17B

pCairo JE 65739 = Gardiner (1935)

pCairo JE 66844-1/6 = Posener-Kriéger (1979)

pCairo JE 89127-30 & 89137-43 r° (*pMattha, Hermopolis Code*) = Donker van Heel (1990)

pCarlsberg 301 = Chauveau (1991)

pDeM 11 = *KRI* VI, 268-9 n.36 B IV.2:1

pDeM 23 (*Naunakhte* Doc. II) = *KRI* VI, 240-2 n.20 A 2

pDeM 25 (*Naunakhte* Doc. III) = *KRI* VI, 240-2 n.20 A 3

pDeM 26 = *KRI* V, 461-6 n.217 A 38

pDeM 27 = *KRI* V, 578-9 n.231 A 244

pDeM 30 = Černý (1986: pl. 21)

Peet, T.E., 1923. *The Rhind mathematical papyrus British Museum 10057 and 10058: Introduction, transcription, translation and commentary*. London: Univ. Pr. of Liverpool/Hodder & Stoughton.

— 1930. *The Great Tomb-Robberies of the Twentieth Egyptian Dynasty*. Oxford: Clarendon Press.

— 1932. The Egyptian Words for 'Money', 'Buy', and 'Sell'. In *Studies Presented to F. Ll. Griffith*, 122-7. London: EES, Humphrey Milford, Oxford University Press.

Pestman, P.W., 1961. *Marriage and Matrimonial Property in Ancient Egypt: A Contribution to Establishing the Legal Position of the Woman*. Papyrologica Lugduno-Batava 9. Leiden: E.J. Brill.

— 1968. Eine Demotische Doppelurkunde. In *Antidoron Martino David oblatum Miscellanea Papyrologica*, eds. E. Boswinkel, B.A. Van Groningen & P.W. Pestman. Papyrologica Lugduno-Batava 17, 99-111. Leiden: E.J. Brill.

— 1969. The Law of Succession in Ancient Egypt. In *Essays on Oriental Laws of Succession*, eds. J. Brugman, M. David, F.R. Kraus, P.W. Pestman & M.H. van der Valk. Studia et Doc. 9, 58-77. Leiden: E.J. Brill.

— 1982. Who were the Owners, in the 'Community of Workmen', of the Chester Beatty Papyri. In *Gleanings from Deir el-Medîna*, eds. R.J. Demarée & J.J. Janssen, 155-72. Leiden: Instituut voor het Nabije Oosten.

— 1982b. The 'Last Will of Naunakhte' and the Accession Date of Ramesses V. In *Gleanings from Deir el-Medîna*, eds. R.J. Demarée & J.J. Janssen, 173-81. Leiden: Instituut voor het Nabije Oosten.

— 1985. Le démotique comme langue juridique. In *Textes et etudes de papyrologie grecque, démotique et copte*, ed. P.W. Pestman. P.L.Bat 23, 198-203. Leiden: E.J. Brill.

— 1987. "Inheriting" in the Archive of the Theban Choachytes (2nd cent. B.C.). In *Aspects of Demotic Lexicography: Acts of the Second International Conference for Demotic Studies. Leiden, 19-21 September 1984*, ed. S.P. Vleeming. SD 1, 59-73. Leuven: Peeters.

— 1994. *Les papyrus démotiques de Tsenhor (P. Tsenhor): Les archives privées d'une femme égyptienne du temps de Darius Ier*. I. Leuven: Peeters.

— 1995. Appearance and Reality in Written Contracts: Evidence from Bilingual Family Archives. In *Legal Documents of the Hellenistic World: Papers from a Seminar Arranged by the Institute of Classical Studies, the Institute of Jewish Studies and the Warburg Institute, University of London, February to May 1986*, eds. M.J. Geller, H. Maehler & A.D.E. Lewis, 79-87. London: Warburg Institute, University of London.

Petrie, W.M.F., 1896. *Koptos*. London: B. Quaritch.

— 1900. *Dendereh: 1898*. EEF 17. London: Egypt Exploration Fund.

— 1907. *Gizeh and Rifeh*. BSAE / ERA 13. London: British School of Archaeology in Egypt; Quaritch.

pGeneva D 409 = *KRI* VI, 738-42 n.20

pGurob II,1-2 = Gardiner (1906)

pHarris I (*pBM* 9999) = Erichsen (1933)

Philip-Stéphan, A., 2008. *Dire le droit en Egypte pharaonique: Contribution à l'étude des structures et mécanismes juridictionnels jusqu'au Nouvel Empire*. Brussels: Safran.

Pierce, R.H., 1972. *Three Demotic Papyri in the Brooklyn Museum: A Contribution to the Study of Contracts and their Instruments in Ptolemaic Egypt*. SOFS 24. Oslo: Universitetsforlaget.

Pirenne, J., 1934. *Histoire des institutions et du droit privé de l'ancienne Egypte: La Ve Dynastie (2750-2625).* II. Bruxelles: Fondation Egyptologique Reine Elisabeth.

pKahun I.1 (*pUC* 32058) = Collier & Quirke (2004: end plates)

pKahun I.2 (*pUC* 32167) = Collier & Quirke (2004: 118)

pKahun I.3 (*pUC* 32163) = Collier & Quirke (2004: 110)

pKahun II.1 (*pUC* 32055) = Collier & Quirke (2004: 102)

pKahun VI.10 r° (*pUC* 32179) = Collier & Quirke (2006: end plates)

pKahun VII.1 (*pUC* 32037) = Collier & Quirke (2004: 100)

pKraeling 9 = Porten & Szubin (1987)

pKRU = Crum & Steindorff (1912)

pLansing = *LEM*, 99-116

pLouvre E 3228e = Malinine (1983: 14-7)

pMallet (*pLouvre* E 11006) = *KRI* VI, 65-8 n.53

pMattha (*pCairo* JE 89127-30 & 89137-43 r°) = Donker van Heel (1990)

pMayer B1 (*pLiverpool* M 11186) = *KRI* VI, 515-6 n.23

pMoscow 123 = Malinine (1967)

pMunich ÄS 809 (*pMook*) = Spiegelberg (1928)

Polotsky, H.J., 1930. The Stela of Heka-Yeb. *JEA* 16 : 194-9.

— 1944. *Etudes de syntaxe copte*. Le Caire: Société d'archéologie copte (= *Collected Papers* 102-107).

— 1960. The Coptic Conjugation System. *Orientalia* 29: 392-422.

— 1971. *Collected Papers*. Jerusalem: The Magnes Press, The Hebrew University.

— 1976. Les transpositions du verbe en égyptien classique. *Israel Oriental Studies* 6: 1-50.

pOrbiney = *LES*, 9-29 (= *The Tale of Two Brothers*)

Porten, B., 1993. Elephantine Aramaic Contracts and the Priestly Literature. In *Minhah le-Nahum: Biblical and Other Studies Presented to Nahum M. Sarna in Honour of his 70th Birthday*, eds. M. Brettler & M. A. Fishbane. JSOT Suppl. Series 154, 257-71. Sheffield: Sheffield Academic Press.

Porten, B. & Szubin, H.Z., 1987. An Aramaic Deed of Bequest (Kraeling 9). In *Community and Culture: Essays in Jewish Studies in Honor of the Ninetieth Anniversary of the Founding of Gratz College*, ed. N.M. Waldman, 179-92. Philadelphia: Gratz College, Seth Press.

Posener, G., 1938. *Catalogue des ostaraca hiératiques de Deir el-Medineh (Nos 1001 à 1108)*. v. 1. DFIFAO 1. Cairo: IFAO.

— 1951. Sur l'emploi de l'encre rouge dans les manuscrits égyptiens. *JEA* 37: 75-80.

— 1971. Amon juge du pauvre. In *Beiträge zur ägyptischen Bauforschung und Altertumskunde zum 70. Geburtstag von Herbert Ricke*, ed. Schweizerischen Institut für ägyptische Bauforschung und Altertumskunde in Kairo. ÄBA 12, 59-63. Wiesbaden: Franz Steiner.

Posener-Kriéger, P., 1979. Le prix des étoffes. In *Festschrift Elmar Edel 12. März 1979*, eds. M. Görg & E. Pusch, 318-31. ÄUAT 1. Hamburg: Bamberg.

pPrisse = Žába (1956)

Pepy II *Giza decree* = Goedicke (1967: Abb. 12)

papyrus Rhind (*pBM* 10057-8) = Peet (1923)

Prince, G., 1987. *A Dictionary of Narratology*. Lincoln: University of Nebraska Press.

pSallier I (*pBM* 10185) = *LEM*, 79-88

pSalt 124 (*pBM* 10055) = *KRI* IV, 408-14 n.54 A 26

PT (Pyramid Texts) = Sethe (1908-22)

pTsenhor = Pestman (1994)

pTurin 1880 (Strike) = *RAD*, 45-58

pTurin 1881 = *KRI* VI, 609-19 n.48 A 6

pTurin 1882 r° = *KRI* VI, 70-6 n.55

pTurin 1885 v° = *KRI* VI, 371 n.A 15 & 424 n.20 A1

pTurin 1887 (Indictment) = *RAD*, 73-82

pTurin 1894 = *KRI* VI, 656-7 n.62 A 20

pTurin 2021 and *pGeneva* D 409 = *KRI* VI, 738-42 n.20

pTurin 2024, 2052 & 2077 = Černý *Notebook*, 15.21-2

pTurin 2070 = *KRI* VI, 426-8 n.23 A 5

pTurin 2082 (Giornale 17B) v° 8-9 = *KRI* VI, 590-4

pUC 32109B = Collier & Quirke (2002: 20-1)

pUC 32109E = Collier & Quirke (2002: 20-1)

pValençay I = *RAD* 72-3

Rabinowitz, J.J., 1958. Semitic Elements in the Egyptian Adoption Papyrus Published by Gardiner. *JNES* 17: 145-6.

RAD = Gardiner (1948)

Redford, D.B., 1986. *Pharaonic King-Lists, Annals and Day-Books: A Contribution to the Study of the Egyptian Sense of History*. SSEA Publications 4. Mississauga: Benben Publications.

Rekhmire = Sethe (1927-30: 1071-1172)

Richter, T.S., 2002. *Rechtssemantik und forensische Rhetorik: Untersuchungen zu Wortschatz, Stil und Grammatik der Sprache koptischer Rechtsurkunden*. Kanobos 3. Leipzig: Helmar Wodtke & Katharina Stegbauer.

— 2005. What's in a Story?: Cultural Narratology and Coptic Child Donation Documents. *Journal of Juristic Papyrology* 35: 237-64.

RITA = Kitchen (1993-2001)

RITANC = Kitchen (1993-99)

Robb, K., 1994. *Literacy and Paideia in Ancient Greece*. Oxford/New York: Oxford University Press.

Robichon, C. & Varille, A., 1936. *Le temple du scribe royal Amenhotep fils de Hapou*. I. FIFAO 11. Cairo: IFAO.

Rosch, E., 1978. Principles of Categorization. In *Cognition and Categorization*, eds E. Rosch & B. Loyd, 28-49. Hillsdale: Erlbaum.

Roth, N., 1987. The Psychiatry of Writing a Will. *American Journal of Psychotherapy* 41: 245-51.

Russo, B., 2007. Some Notes on the Funerary Cult in the Early Middle Kingdom: Stela BM EA 1164. *JEA* 93: 195-209.

S3b3stt stelaphorous statue Louvre E 11673 = De Linage (1939: 219)

S3mwt tomb (lower inscription) = Vernus (1978: 133)

Sass, B., 2002. Wenamun and his Levant – 1075 BC or 925 BC? *Aegypten und Levante* 12: 247-55.

Satzinger, H., 1976. *Neuägyptische Studien*. Beihefte zur WZKM 6. Wien: VWGÖ.

— 1997. How Good was Tjeker-Baʿl's Egyptian? *LingAeg* 5: 171-176.

Sauneron, S., 1959. *Catalogue des ostraca hiératiques non littéraires de Deir el Médineh*. DFIFAO 13. Le Caire: IFAO.

Scheepers, A., 1992. Le voyage d'Ounamon: Un texte "littéraire" ou "non-littéraire"? In *Amosiadès: Mélanges offerts au Prof. C. Vandersleyen*, eds C. Obsomer & A.-L. Oosthoek, 355-365. Louvain-la-Neuve: UCL.

Schipper, B.U., 2005. *Die Erzählung des Wanamun: Ein Literaturwerk im Spannungsfeld von Politik, Geschichte und Religion*. OBO 209. Fribourg/ Göttingen: Academic Press Fribourg/Vandenhoeck & Ruprecht.

Searle, J.R., 1976. A classification of illocutionary acts. *Language in Society* 5: 1-23.

Searle, J.R. & Vanderveken, D., 1985. *Foundations of Illocutionary Logic*. Cambridge: Cambridge University Press.

Seidl, E., 1957. *Einführung in die ägyptische Rechtsgeschichte bis zum Ende des neuen Reiches*. ÄF 10. Glückstadt: J.J. Augustin.

— 1957b. Vom Erbrecht der alten Ägypter. *ZDMG* 107: 270-81.

Sethe, K., 1903. *Urkunden des alten Reichs*. Leipzig: J.C. Hinrichs.

— 1908-22. *Die Altägyptischen Pyramidentexte*. 4 vols. Leipzig: J.C. Hinrichs.

— 1924. *Aegyptische Lesestücke zum Gebrauch im akademischen Unterricht: Texte des Mittleren Reiches*. Leipzig: J.C. Hinrichs'sche Buchhandlung.

— 1926. Ein Prozessurteil aus dem alten Reich. *ZÄS* 61: 67-79.

— 1927-30. *Urkunden der 18 Dynastie: Historisch-biographische Urkunden*, 4 vols. Leipzig: J.C. Hinrichs.

Shalomi-Hen, R., 2000. *Classifying the Divine: Determinatives and Categorization in CT 335 and BD 17*. GOF IV. Reihe Ägypten 38. Classification and Categorization in Ancient Egypt 2. Wiesbaden: Harrassowitz.

— 2006. *The Writings of Gods: The Evolution of Divine Classifiers in the Old Kingdom*. GOF IV. Reihe Ägypten 38. Classification and Categorization in Ancient Egypt 4. Wiesbaden: Harrassowitz.

Shisha-Halevy, A., 1978. Quelques thématisations marginales du verbe en Néo-Egyptien. *OLP* 9: 51-67.

— 1981. Bohairic-Late Egyptian Diaglosses: A Contribution to the Typology of Egyptian. In *Studies Presented to H.J. Polotsky*, ed. D.W. Young, 314-338. Massachusetts: Pirtle & Polson.

— 1984. Notes on Some Coptic Nominal Sentence Patterns. In *Studien zu Sprache und Religion Ägyptens: Zu Ehren von W. Westendorf*, ed. F. Junge. I, 175-89. Göttingen: Hubert & Co.

— 1988. *Coptic Grammatical Chrestomathy: A Course for Academic and Private Study*. OLA 30. Leuven: Peeters.

— 1989. Work-Notes on Demotic Syntax, I. *Or* 58: 28-60.

— 1998. *Structural Studies in Modern Welsh Syntax: Aspects of the Grammar of Kate Roberts*. Münster: Nodus.

— 2000. Stability in Clausal/Phrasal Pattern Constituent Sequencing: 4000 Years of Egyptian (with Some Theoretical Reflections, also on Celtic). In *Stability, Variation and Change of Word-Order Patterns over Time*, eds R. Sornicola, E. Poppe & A. Shisha-Halevy, 71-100. Amsterdam: John Benjamins.

— 2007. Rhetorical Narratives: Notes on Narrative Poetics in Shenoutean Sahidic Coptic. In *Literary-Linguisitc Approaches to Narrative: The Ancient Near East (including Egypt), and Neighbouring Regions*. OLA. Leuven: Peeters, *forthcoming*.

— 2007b. Determination-Signalling Environment in Old and Middle Egyptian: Work-Notes and Reflections. In *Studies in Semitic and General Linguistics in Honor of Gideon Goldenberg*, eds. T. Bar & E. Cohen, 223-54. AOAT 334. Münster: Ugarit Verlag.

Shupak, N., 1992. A New Source for the Study of the Judiciary and Law of Ancient Egypt: "The Tale of the Eloquent Peasant". *JNES* 51: 1-18.

Simpson, R.S., 1996. *Demotic Grammar in the Ptolemaic Sacerdotal Decrees*. Oxford: Griffith Institute.

Sinuhe (*pBerlin* 3022) = Blackman (1932)

Smither, P.C., 1948. The Report Concerning the Slave-Girl Senebet. *JEA* 34: 31-4.

Snims Cairo stela CG 34016 = *Urk*. IV, 1065-70

Snnwꜥnḫ tomb = Goedicke (1970: table VIII)

Snḏmib tomb = *Urk*. I, 59-67

Sottas, H., 1913. *La préservation de la propriété funéraire dans l'ancienne Egypte avec le recueil des formules d'imprécation*. Paris: Librairie ancienne Honoré Champion.

Spalinger, A.J., 1984. The Will of Senimose. In *Studien zu Sprache und Religion Ägyptens: Zu Ehren von W. Westendorf*, ed. F. Junge. I, 631-51. Göttingen: Hubert & Co.

— 1985. A Redistributive Pattern at Assiut. *JAOS* 105: 7-20.

Spiegleberg, W., 1892. *Studien und Materialien zum Rechtswesen des Pharaonenreiches der Dynast. XVIII-XXI (C. 1500-1000 v. Chr.): Inaugural-Dissertation*. Hannover: Hahn'schen Buchhandlung.

— 1896. *Rechnungen aus der Zeit Seti I. (circa 1350 v. Chr.) mit anderen Rechnungen des Neuen Reiches*. Strassburg: Trübner.

— 1903. Die Tefnachthosstele des Museums von Athen. *Rec. Trav*. 25: 190-8.

— 1928. Ein Gerichtsprotokoll aus der Zeit Thutmosis' IV. *ZÄS* 63: 105-115.

Stela Berlin 23077 = Gunn (1916)

Stela BM 101 = Blackman (1935)

Stela BM 138 = Robichon & Varille (1936)

Stela Cairo 27.6.24.3 = Bakir (1952: pl. II-IV)

Stèle juridique de Karnak JE 52453 = Lacau (1949)

Stricker, B.H., 1938. Etudes de grammaire égyptienne. *AcOr* 16: 81-4.

Strudwick, N.C., 2005. *Texts from the Pyramid Age*. SBL - Writings from the Ancient World 16. Leiden/Boston: Brill.

Sweeney, D., 2001. *Correspondence and Dialogue: Pragmatic Factors in Late Ramesside Letter-Writing*. ÄUAT 49. Wiesbaden: Harrassowitz.

Taylor, J.R., 1989. *Linguistic Categorization: Prototypes in Linguistic Theory*. Oxford: Clarendon Press.

Teaching of Amenemhat = Helck (1969)

Te Velde, H., 1967. *Seth, God of Confusion: A Study of his Role in Egyptian Mythology and Religion*. PÄ 6. Leiden: E.J. Brill.

Tfḫ3i's false door Cairo JE 56994 = Goedicke (1970: table XVIIb)

Théodoridès, A., 1957. Le 'Procès' dans la *Stèle Juridique de Karnak*. *RIDA* 4: 33-52.

— 1958. A propos de *Pap. Lansing*, 4,8-5,2 et 6,8-7,5. *RIDA* 5: 65-119.

— 1960. Du rapport entre le parties du Pap. Brooklyn 35.1446. *RIDA* 7: 55-145.

— 1961. La vente à crédit du *Pap. Kahoun I, 2* et ses conséquences. *RIDA* 8: 41-76.

— 1962. Le rôle du Vizir dans la *Stèle Juridique de Karnak*. *RIDA* 9: 45-135.

— 1962b. Considérations sur la cohérence des documents de droit égyptien. *BSFE* 34-5 : 23-9.

— 1963. Propriété, gérance et mandat dans le *Papyrus Berlin 8523*. *RIDA* 10: 91-113.

— 1964. La stèle juridique d'Amarah. *RIDA* 11: 45-80.

— 1965. Le Papyrus des Adoptions. *RIDA* 12: 79-142.

— 1966. Le « testament » de Naunakhte. *RIDA* 13: 31-70.

— 1966b. La répudiation de la femme en Egypte et dans les droits orientaux anciens. *BSFE* 47: 6-19.

— 1967. De la prétendue expression juridique *pnꜥ r mdt*. *RdE* 19: 111-21.

— 1967b. A propos de la loi dans l'Egypte pharaonique. *RIDA* 14: 107-52.

— 1968. Procès relatif à une vente qui devait être acquittée par la livraison d'un travail servile (*Papyrus Berlin 9785*). *RIDA* 15: 39-104.

— 1968b. Le testament d'Imenkhâou. *JEA* 54: 149-54.

— 1969. Les ouvriers-« magistrats » en Egypte à l'époque ramesside. *RIDA* 16: 103-88.

— 1970. Le testament dans l'Egypte ancienne. *RIDA* 17: 117-216.

— 1970b. La notion égyptienne de possession exprimée par la locution prépositive *m-di*. *RdE* 22: 139-154.

— 1971. Les contrats d'Hâpidjefa (XII e dynastie, 20e s. av. J.-C.). *RIDA* 18: 109-251.

— 1976. Le droit matrimonial dans l'Egypte pharaonique. *RIDA* 23: 15-55.

— 1977. Review of Allam, S., Hieratische Ostraka und Papyri aus Ramessidenzeit. *CdE* 52: 67-76.

— 1979. L'acte (?) de vente d'Ancien Empire (26e s. av. J.-C.). *RIDA* 26: 31-83.

— 1993. Du rapport entre un contrat et un acte de disposition appelé « imyt-per » en égyptien. *RIDA* 39: 77-105.

Thomas, R., 1996. Written in Stone? Liberty, Equality, Orality and the Codification of Law. In *Greek Law in its Political Setting: Justifications not Justice*, eds. L. Foxhall & A.D.E. Lewis, 9-31. Oxford: Clarendon Press.

Thompson, H., 1934. *A Family Archive from Siut from Papyri in the British Museum, including an Account of a Trial before the Laocritae in the Year B.C. 170*. Oxford: Oxfeord University Press.

Tiersma, P.M., 1999. *Legal Language*. Chicago: University of Chicago Press.

— 2007. Writing, Text, and the Law. In *Handbook of Research on Writing: History, Society, School, Individual, Text,* ed. C. Bazerman, 129-42. Lawrence Erlbaum, available at SSRN (http://ssrn.com/abstract=850305) as *Loyola Law School LA Legal Studies* Paper No. 2005-31.

Ṯnti tomb provisions Cairo JE 57139 = Goedicke (1970: table XIII)

Toivari-Viitala, J., 1998. Marriage at Deir el-Medina. In *Proceedings of the Seventh International Congress of Egyptologists, Cambridge, 3-9 September 1995*, ed. C.J. Eyre. OLA 82, 1157-63. Leuven: Peeters.

— 2001. *Women at Deir el-Medina: A Study of the Status and Roles of the Female Inhabitants in the Workmen's Community during the Ramesside Period*. Leiden: Nederlands Instituut voor het Nabije Oosten.

— 2003. O.DeM 764: A Note Concerning Property Rights. *GM* 195: 87-96.

Tomb Robberies = Peet (1930)

Trosborg, A., 1997. Contracts as social action. In *The construction of professional discourse*, eds. B.-L. Gunnarsson, P. Linell & B. Nordberg. Harlow: Addison Wesley Longman.

Urk. I = Sethe (1903)

*Urk.*IV = Sethe (1927-30)

Valbelle, D., 1985. *« Les ouvriers de la Tombe » : Deir el-Médineh à l'époque ramesside*. BdE 96. Cairo: IFAO.

— 2003. Les archives de la Tombe, aujourd'hui. In *Deir el-Médineh et la Vallée des Rois : La vie en Egypte au temps des pharaons du Nouvel Empire, Actes du colloque organisé par le musée du Louvre les 3 et 4 mai 2002*, ed. G. Andreu, 159-71. Paris: Khéops & Musée du Louvre.

van den Boorn, G.P.F., 1988. *The Duties of the Vizier: Civil Administration in the Early New Kingdom*. London/New York: Kegan Paul Int.

Vandier d'Abbadie, J., 1959. *Catalogue des ostraca figurés de Deir el Médineh (Nos 2734 à 3053)*.DFIFAO 2. Cairo: IFAO.

Ventura, R., 1986. *Living in a City of the Dead: A Selection of Topographical and Administrative Terms in the Documents of the Theban Necropolis*. O.B.O. 69. Freiburg/Göttingen: Universitätsverlag Freiburg/Vandenhoeck & Ruprecht.

Vernus, P., 1978. Littérature et autobiographie: Les inscriptions de *Sꜣ-Mwt* surnommé *Kyky*. *RdE* 30: 115-46.

— 1982. Deux particularités de l'égyptien de tradition: *nty iw* + présent 1; *wnn.f ḥr sḏm* narratif. In *L'égyptologie en 1979: Axes prioritaires de recherches* I. Colloques internationaux du Centre National de la Recherche Scientifique 595, 81-89. Paris: CNRS.

— 1985. « Ritual » *sḏm.n.f* and Some Values of the "Accompli" in the Bible and in the Koran. In *Pharaonic Egypt: The Bible and Christianity*, ed. S. Israelit-Groll, 307-16. Jerusalem: Magnes Press & Hebrew University of Jerusalem.

— 1986. Allusion au partage des acquêts dans une autobiographie de la Deuxième Période Intermédiaire. *DinE* 6 : 79-86.

— 1990. Les espaces de l'écrit dans l'Egypte pharaonique. *BSFE* 119: 35-56.

— 2005. L'écriture du pouvoir dans l'Egypte pharaonique: Du normatif au performatif. In *L'écriture publique du pouvoir*, eds. A. Bresson, A.-M. Cocula & C. Pébarthe. Etudes 10, 123-42. Paris: Ausonius.

VerSteeg, R., 2000. *Early Mesopotamian Law*. Durham: Carolina Academic Press.

Vleeming, S.P., 1991. *The Gooseherds of Hou (Pap. Hou): A Dossier Relating to Various Agricultural Affairs from Provincial Egypt of the Early Fifth Century B.C.* Leuven: Peeters.

Von Beckerath, J., 2000. Bemerkungen zu Papyrus Turin 1885 Verso II-III. In *Deir el-Medina in the Third Millennium AD : A Tribute to Jac. J. Janssen*, eds. R.J. Demarée & A. Egberts, 1-7. Leiden: Nederlands Instituut voor het Nabije Oosten.

Warburton, D.A., 2007. Work and compensation in Ancient Egypt. *JEA* 93 : 175-94.

Wb = Erman & Grapow (1955)

Weinrich, H., 1973. *Le temps: Le récit et le commentaire*. Paris: Seuil.

Wenamun (pMoscow 120*)* = *LES*, 61-76

Wente, E.F., 1961. IWIW.F SDM in Late Egyptian. *JNES* 20: 120-3.

— 1967. *Late Ramesside Letters*. SAOC 33. Chicago: University of Chicago Press.

Wente, E.F. & Van Siclen III, C.C., 1976. A Chronology of the New Kingdom. In *Studies in Honor of G.H. Hughes*. SAOC 39, 217-61. Chicago: Oriental Institute.

Westbrook, R., 2003. The Character of Ancient Near Eastern Law. In *A History of Ancient Near Eastern Law*, ed. R. Westbrook. Handbook of Oriental Studies I Near and Middle East 72/1, 1-90. Leiden/Boston: Brill.

Wilkinson, R.H., 1992. *Reading Egyptian Art: A Hieroglyphic Guide to Ancient Egyptian Painting and Sculpture*. London: Thames & Hudson.

Wilson, J.A., 1948. The Oath in Ancient Egypt. *JNES* 7: 129-56.

Wimmer, S., 1995. *Hieratische Paläographie der nicht-literarischen Ostraka der 19. und 20. Dynastie*. I. Wiesbaden : Harrassowitz.

— 2004. Review of Grandet, 2003. Catalogue des ostraca hiératiques non littéraires de Deîr el-Médînéh. *BiOr* 61 : 515-8.

— 2006. « Ihr, die ihr so weit entfernt seid » (O. Berlin P 14257): Neue Erkenntnisse über alte Bekannte aus der Bearbeitung der Berliner Ostraka in *Deir el Medine online*. In *Living and Writing in Deir el-Medine: Socio-historic Embodiment of Deir el-Medine Texts*, eds. A. Dorn & T. Hofmann. AH 19, 161-4. Basel: Schwabe Verlag.

Winand, J., 1992. *Etudes de néo-égyptien: La morphologie verbale*. Aegyptiaca Leodiensia 2. Liège: C.I.P.L.

— 1996. Les constructions analogiques du futur III en néo-égyptien. *RdE* 47: 117-45.

— 2004. L'ironie dans Ounamon : Les emplois de *mk* et de *ptr*. *GM* 200: 105-10.

Winter, S.L., 1988. The Metaphor of Standing and the Problem of Self-Governance. *Stanford Law Review* 40: 1371.

— 1989. Transcendental Nonsense, Metaphoric Reasoning, and the Cognitive Stakes for Law. *University of Pennsylvania Law Review* 137: 1105-1237.

— 2001. *A Clearing in the Forest: Law, Life and Mind*. Chicago: University of Chicago Press.

Wpmnfrt tomb = Goedicke (1970: table IV)

Žába, Z., 1956. *Les maximes de Ptahhotep*. Prague: Académie tchécoslovaque des Sciences.

Zauzich, K.-T., 1980. Kaufurkunden, demotische. *LÄ* III: 370-1.

Index of syntactic forms and technical terms

Index of Egyptian texts

Index of main Egyptian lexemes discussed